ONE
WORLD

In Memory of
My Dear Brother Su-Tien
Who Took Me Adventurously
To the City Far Away from Our Rural Home
To Start My School Life When I Was Eleven Years Old.

—The Author

ONE WORLD
The Approach
to Permanent Peace on Earth
and the General Happiness of Mankind

A Popular Manifesto
with Scholarly Annotations

by John Kiang

天下一家，獲致世界永久和平
與人類普遍福利之道

姜逸樵著

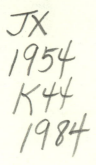

JX
1954
K44
1984

Library of Congress Catalog Card No. 83-63090
ISBN—Hard: 0-916301-00-1 $24.95

Published by:

ONE WORLD PUBLISHING CO.
P.O. Box 423
Notre Dame, Indiana
U.S.A. 46556

Printed by Harlo Press/50 Victor/Detroit, Michigan 48203

Contents

Contents

Preface

"As we look back on what has happened, we see what can happen."

When I learned in my early years from history that China was formed through merging of a great number of groups: from thousands to hundreds, from hundreds to tens, and from tens to one nation; and that all the other nations of the world were formed in more or less this same manner, I started to believe that the merging process which has converted enormous groups into a small number of nations will eventually bring all nations into One World. This prospect is so important to the future of mankind that I decided to study it thoroughly with utmost efforts, beginning with my A.B. thesis, "An Introduction to One World," at the University of Hunan.

Soon after my graduation from the University of Hunan, China was caught up in a war with Japan, and I was obliged to take some public administration jobs which kept me too busy to do any academic study. When Japan was defeated by the Allies, a bitter civil war was still raging in China. I left it for the United States to pursue my study. To my disappointment, the subject of One World was considered too broad and too unrealistic by the academic establishment. I had to follow a program which was related to my own subject, but would also meet regular academic requirements. This was a compromise arrangement, ending up with a M.A. Thesis, "The Christian Conceptions of War," and a doctoral thesis, "Conditions for Federation," at the University of Nebraska.

Meanwhile, I studied at the University of Michigan for a Master's degree in library science which helped me technically to open the door wide for my study. The trouble now was that there was no job which would provide a living and at the same time give me some free

ix

time to do my own study. Under these circumstances, I ventured to invent a marketable library card duplicator and ran the business myself in the hope that someday I could make enough money to free myself for the study. This hope was not realized until 1975, when I quit the profitable business completely to devote all my time and energy to the study. This work is the result of such devotion of more than seven years.

This work is faithfully done for mankind and hereby humbly presented to the whole world. My position is more or less reflected in the following prelude. The only note I would like to make here is about the unique style developed in the work: I began by trying to make the text as terse as possible and render supporting materials as annotations, but these materials turned out to be the flesh, blood and muscle of the text, which stands as the skeleton. Each of the annotations is worth reading.

I want to take this opportunity to thank with my whole heart all the authors who provide the text with flesh, blood and muscle. As I alone am responsible for the selection, adoption and judgment of all the references, any correction or excuse for any error will be very deeply appreciated. I was much touched by the missionary spirit of Rev. Edward G. Nelson who made a special trip from hundreds of miles away to take a quick look at a part of this work and suggest several changes in English usage. More suggestions on English usage, as well as on other aspects of the work, from Professor Robert T.L. Lee, a serious scholar in history and sinology, and from Dr. Catherine Bicknell, an English teacher and oral historian, were most helpful. I owe a major debt to Mrs. Beverly Squint for her invaluable assistance through the years in typing and checking my manuscript. And, finally, I want to express my gratitude to my wife, Susan, for her patient help in my work, besides taking care of all our social obligations.

—John Kiang
March 4, 1984
South Bend, Indiana

Prelude

"I write as a citizen of the world who serves no prince. I lost my Fatherland, to exchange it for the great world. What is the greatest of nations but a fragment?" Friedrich von Shiller (1759-1805). (Quoted by Frank M. Russell, *Theories of International Relations,* New York, 1936, p. 187.)

* * *

"I appeal as a human being to human beings: remember your humanity, and forget the rest. If you can do so, the way lies open to a new paradise; if you cannot, nothing lies before you but universal death." (Bertrand Russell, quoted by Edgar M. Bottome, *The Balance of Terror,* Boston, 1971, p iiix.)

* * *

" . . . To be men, members of the great and universal family of mankind, who know their interest and that of all the human race to be the same." (Friedrich Engels, reprinted in *Marx-Engels Gesamtausgabe,* Vol. IV, p. 6.)

* * *

"We feel we are making our own the voice of the dead and of the living; of the dead who fell in the terrible wars of the past; of the living who survived those wars, bearing in their hearts a condemnation of those who would try to renew wars, and also of those living who rise up fresh and confident, the youth of the present generation, who legitimately dream of a better human race. And we also make our own the voice of the poor, the disinherited, the suffering, of those who hunger and thirst for justice, for the dignity of life, for freedom, for well-being and progress." (Pope Paul's address to the United Nations, *The Evening Star,* Washington D.C., Oct. 5, 1965, p. A-4)

* * *

"Either we have to make a world by deliberate plan, or we court disaster. It is a grim alternative. It makes men feel how near their feet lie to the abyss. But it is also an alternative that may prove the pathway to their salvation." (Harold J. Laski, *A Grammar of Politics,* London, 1925, p. 666)

* * *

"A world authority and an eventual world state are not just desirable in the name of brotherhood; they are necessary for survival." (*Einstein on Peace,* edited by Otto Nathan and Heinz Norden, New York, 1960, p. 384)

* * *

"Facts alone are meaningless, no matter how many you accumulate, without a ruling idea behind them; which is why Pasteur once observed that a man cannot go on without a theory to guide him." (Sydney Harris, *South Bend Tribune,* Oct. 21, 1976, p. 14)

* * *

"In starting our great fight for a better world, we must be guided by the wisdom of Sun Yat-Sen: The difficulty is to know, to understand; with understanding, action is easy." (Emery Reves, *The Anatomy of Peace,* New York, 1946, p. 295)

* * *

"I'd like to build the world a home
and furnish it with love;
Grow apple trees and honey bees
and snow white turtle doves.
I'd like to teach the world to sing
in perfect harmony...
A song of peace that echoes on
and never goes away.
Put your hand in my hand,
let's begin today.

xii

Prelude

And put your hand in my hand,
help me find the way."
(Popular song lyrics quoted from a pamphlet of One Earth Week,
April 14-19, 1975, with slight modifications.)

*   *   *

Introduction

John Kiang has written a plea to the people of all countries on earth to work together to achieve the goal of permanent peace on earth and the achievement of a society in which every person has the opportunity to lead a good life. His argument is presented in detail, and it is supported by many references and footnotes. He points out that the nature of the world has been changed through scientific discoveries and technological developments. The full impact of this change has, however, not yet been appreciated.

The principal message is that war has now ruled itself out—a war in which the existing nuclear weapons were used would with little doubt mean the end of our civilization, and possibly the end of the human race. To contemplate such a war is irrational, and for the human race to destroy itself in such a war would be the height of insanity.

The author points out that the major block remaining in achieving the goal of sanity in the world is national sovereignty and its agitator, nationalism. The time has come now for the people of the world to join together in eliminating the evil of war and in building the world of the future.

Everyone should read this book and heed its message.

—Linus Pauling
March 20, 1984

ONE
WORLD

I
Group Expansion

a.
The Law

MANKIND HAS, IN THE COURSE OF SOCIAL EVOLUTION,[1] experienced a series of group life. The groups in this series, generally speaking,[2] run from the early single family through a primitive community, clan and tribe, to the nation.[3]

---

1. There are two major theories concerning the course of social evolution, one unilinear and the other multilinear. The unilinear theory holds that peoples the world over have traversed the same stages of development. The multilinear theory maintains that social evolution has been traveling by different routes in diverse areas. Robert H. Lowie, in his *Social Organization,* New York, 1948, p. 35, remarks that "theories of multilinear evolution, in prescribing a fixed order, assume a law of sequence just as much as do the unilinear systems. In both theories specific causes bring about the alleged modifications."

2. This is the general line along which most peoples of the world have advanced in the course of social evolution, but not always at the same pace. Some started early, and some made leaps. Others still lag behind in various stages of development under various conditions. Indeed, throughout the world today it is possible to find examples of all these groups. This offers us a unique opportunity to review the actual situation of their evolution along with historical records, anthropological studies, and archeological remains. L.T. Hobhouse, G.C. Wheeler and M. Ginsburg, in their *The Material Culture and Social Institutions of the Simpler Peoples,* London, 1915, p. 30-45, list 650 distinctive primitive peoples, and each of these peoples is divided into many groups. Thus, there may be 50,000 to 60,000 primitive groups in the world. Clark Wissler said in *Man and Culture,* New York, 1923, p. 14, that there were seven cultural provinces and six hundred distinctive Indian cultures in the United States.

3. It should be noted that, although these groups have been outstanding in the course of social evolution, no clear and exact demarcation can be made in their

There is an important common nature in these groups: their independence,[4] which has been symbolized with sovereignty in modern times;[5] and the significant physical differences between them lies in their normal size in both population and territory.[6]

---

succession. Intermediate groups may exist between them, such as moiety or phratry between the clan and tribe. (Cf. William H.R. Rivers, *Social Organization,* New York, 1924, p. 33.)

It should also be noted that "state" and "empire" are different in status from these groups. The state is a political machinery, or simply stated, the government of a group, whether it is run by a family, a class, a party, or a certain circle, in the form of autocracy or democracy. Thus, there are national state, tribal state, clan state, etc. There have been groups without a state, but there has been no state without a group. The existence of a state depends on a group. While the state may represent a group or act as its agent, as it always does, it is nevertheless not the group itself. Neither is an empire, which is virtually a state, but extends its control over more than one group. There have been national empires, such as the French Empire under Napoleon I, and the British Empire in the last centuries. There also were clannish or tribal empires, such as the Empires of Sumer, Babylonia, Egypt, Mycenae, Phoenicia, Assyria, Persia, Crete, Macedonia and Rome in the ancient Western world; the Inca Empire in South America before the Spanish conquest; and the dynasties of Shang and Chou in ancient China. The rise and fall of an empire does not necessarily mean the expansion or the end of a group. An empire may be transformed into a group, but it remains as an empire until a long process of transformation is completed. (Cf. Harold J. Laski, *The State in History and Practice,* New York, 1935, p. 11-12; and Samuel N. Eisenstadt, *The Political System of Empires,* New York, 1963.)

4. There are various groups formed with a major element: sex, blood, kinship, language, religion, economics, politics, custom and habit, way of life, etc. The early single family, primitive community, clan, tribe, and nation are different from these various groups by the fact that they usually contain most, if not all, of the preceding elements, although the significance and importance of these elements attached to them vary from period to period and from area to area. Culturally, nevertheless, they are overall groups in their respective stages. This overall character is usually signified by an independent nature by which a group normally recognizes no other group as superior to itself, and is not willing to be regulated, interfered with, or controlled by any other group. If a group has lost this nature and has become a local or social unit of a greater group, it no longer remains as a group distinguished in the series of social evolution. The present-day family, for example, is a basic unit of greater groups, and is quite different from the early single family, which is independent in nature.

5. "Sovereignty as supreme authority, which is independent of any other earthly authority, may be said to have different aspects. As excluding dependence upon any other authority, and in particular from the authority of another State, sovereignty is independence. It is external independence with regard to the liberty of action outside its borders in the intercourse with other States which a State enjoys. It is internal independence with regard to the liberty of action of a State inside its borders." (Lassa F.L. Oppenheim, *International Law; A Treatise,* London, 1935, Vol. I, p. 233)

The early single family[7] usually consists of an adult couple with a few young children.[8] Their territory is usually confined to the area within walking distance[9] of their temporary dwelling place.[10]

---

6. Territory, in a legal sense, is the domain over which a sovereign state exercises jurisdiction. For groups which have not grown up with a proper sovereign state, or are not able to have a proper sovereign state, territory means a living area in which subsistence is procured and upon which trespass is resented. Robert M. MacIver says that in primitive societies "the territorial basis is not sharply defined" and "when the tribe is nomadic we have the extreme case of the detachment of political government from a clearly delimited territory." (*The Web of Government,* New York, 1947, p. 158)

7. "The earliest unit of social and political organization was not a horde, or even a clan or tribe, but a small group corresponding in a general way to the present day family in the narrower sense of the word, i.e., father, mother, children." (William M. McGovern, "The Growth of Institutions," in *Making Mankind,* New York, 1929, p. 78)

There are some early families found in modern times. For example, "The Indians of the Rocky Mountains existed in small detached bodies and single families," according to the *Information Respecting the History, Conditions and Prospects of the Indian Tribes of the United States,* Philadelphia, 1855, by H.R. Schoolcraft, pt. I, p. 224.

8. Lives of extreme privation and hardship in this stage made it very difficult for the early single family to become big. Women, like men, wandered here and there day by day in the quest for food. It was hard for them to be fertile, to carry and feed the babies. Hence, children were always limited to a very small number, and wandered away when they grew up. "The nomadic life exhausted women early. Plants that had to be gathered daily, with the limited amount of stored food, made but poor substitutes when the babies were weaned. Consequently the children were usually suckled for as long as was biologically possible, and this was another factor in keeping the birth-rate low." (Fritz Heichelheim, *An Ancient Economic History,* rev. and complete English ed., Leiden, 1958, v. 1, p. 11-12) There also have been some artificial means used by primitive peoples to keep the family size small. In South Australia, for example, no mother would bring up more than two children (R.B. Smyth, *The Aborigines of Victoria,* Melbourne, 1878, v. 1, p. 46) In Madagascar, the superstition of the people caused them to put their children to death if born on certain unlucky days. (J. Sibree, *The Great African Island,* London, 1880, p. 139) The West Australians ate every tenth child born. (H.P. Whitmarsh, *The World's Rough Hand,* New York, 1898, p. 178)

9. E.M. Curr, in *The Australian Race,* Melbourne and Leipzig, 1887, p. 242, described the march of a native Australian family spreading over a front of half a mile to a mile and a half, for the purpose of collecting food.

10. A few very primitive peoples have still retained the simple life of the earliest times. An African Bushman in certain isolated areas as late as the last century, for instance, "has no settled dwelling-place, but spends the night in a cleft in the rocks, bends down a bush as shelter and protection, or hollows out a trench in the ground into which perhaps two adults and several children squeeze." (H. Lichtenstein, *Travels in Southern Africa,* trans., London, 1815, vol. 2, p. 46)

11. "We have used the term community to signify a group of people camping

The primitive community[11] usually consists of a few scores of people[12] with a territory up to a few hundred square miles.[13]

---

together, or living in one locality, regarding themselves as a unit and operating as such." "Such a primitive community may be composed of several married pairs and their dependents, and in that sense it is a camp of cooperating families." (Clark Wissler, *An Introduction to Social Anthropology,* New York, 1929, p. 14, 15) The primitive community has also been called "camp" because the group camped together and moved together from place to place when it became necessary in the food quest. Other terms, such as "band" (Cf. Elman R. Service, *A Profile of Primitive Culture,* New York, 1958, pt. 1.) and "horde" (Cf. *Journal of the Anthropological Institute of Great Britain and Ireland,* XLVIII, p. 222-, and XIV, p. 143.) are also widely used for the primitive community.

12. For example, "among the Bushmen ... each band, containing on the average from fifty to one hundred persons, is self-governing and independent." "[Among] the Bergdama ... the largest political aggregate is also the band, consisting of from ten to thirty persons who live together habitually in a separate area of their own. There are said to be 'hundreds' of such bands, all independent of one another." (Isaac Schapera, *Government and Politics in Tribal Societies,* London, 1956, p.9)

"The Eskimo ... [lives in] camps of twenty to sixty persons each, and this is about the range for the Chukchee peoples of Siberia." (Clark Wissler, *An Introduction to Social Anthropology,* New York, 1929, p. 35)

A.R. Brown estimated that the average number of persons in the Australian hordes was about sixty; it could hardly have been over 100 or less than 25. (Cf. his "Notes on the Social Organization of Australian Tribes," in the *Journal of the Anthropological Institute of Great Britain and Ireland,* XLVIII, p. 230-231.)

13. For example, "the average Bushman band is said to have an area of 200 sq. miles or more; for Bergdama no figures are available, though other evidence suggests that their territories are much smaller." (Isaac Schapera, *Government and Politics in Tribal Societies,* London, 1956, p. 11)

"The largest local group (of Australian natives) in one district consisted of forty souls upon one hundred sq. miles." (B. Spencer and F.J. Gillen, *Native Tribes of Central Australia,* New York, 1904, p. 9)

"Professor Radcliffe Brown recognizes ten tribes in the Great Andaman, and three in the Little Andaman.... Every tribe consisted of approximately ten autonomous land-owning bands with distinctive hunting territories on which trespass was resented. Each of these minor groups embraced on the average from forty to fifty persons of all ages, the mean area being about 16 sq. miles." (Robert H. Lowie, *The Origin of the State,* New York, 1962, p. 4)

14. The clan is an exogamous group "the members of which are held to be related to one another by some tie; it may be belief in descent from a common ancestor, common possession of a totem, or habitation of a common territory." (A committee-definition cited by William H.R. Rivers, *Social Organization,* New York, 1924, p. 19)

Early in America the term "clan" was used only for the matrilineal family group which traces its descent through the mother. The patrilineal family group, which traces its descent through the father, was called "gens." Nowadays, however, the term "clan" has been generally used to include not only both the matrilineal and patrilineal family groups, as well as the good old Anglo-Saxon term "sib" (Cf. Robert H. Lowie, *Primitive Society,* New York, 1925, p. 111), but

The clan[14] usually consists of hundreds of people[15] with a territory of hundreds of square miles.[16]

---

also other similar groups, as the above cited definition implies. "In the 19th century it was almost universally believed that not only did all peoples pass through
the sib type of organization, but also that all peoples passed through both
matrilineal and patrilineal types of sib (i.e. through both the clan and the gens
stage), the generally accepted theory being that at a very early period all men were
grouped in matrilineal clans, and that later the clans gave way in favor of
patrilineal gens. This theory of the matrilineal system always preceding the
patrilineal system has now lost most of its support ... [and] nearly all of the
American authorities deny any validity to the theory.... The majority of scholars
would therefore claim that the patrilineal and the matrilineal sibs are equally early
and equally primitive. Some peoples have evolved the one, others the other...."
(William M. McGovern, "The Growth of Institutions," in *Making Mankind,* New
York, 1929, p. 88-9)

"One of the most frequent, almost certainly the most frequent, form of the
clan is one in which all its members believe in their relationship to a species of objects, animal, plant, or inanimate, called totems, of which animal totems are by far
the most frequent." (William H.R. Rivers, *Social Organization,* New York, 1924,
p. 21-22)

15. For example (note that the general terms "tribe," "village" and "community" are used for the Indian clan group in the following statements): "The
prime factor of uncertainty is size of the tribe. Two hundred and fifty souls seems
an over-conservative estimate. There may have been tribes that surpassed 500....
Three to four hundred persons is perhaps the soundest estimate that can be made.
(A.L. Kroeber, *Handbook of the Indians of California, Bulletin* 78, Bureau of
American Ethnology, Washington, 1925, p. 488)

"A review of the data for Vancouver Island and the Puget Sound Area, in
general, gives an average of two to four hundred for the group, and the old French
estimates for the Indians of Louisiana range around three hundred for village
group. The distinctively aboriginal village dwellers of the United States are the
Pueblo Indians of New Mexico and Arizona. The Spanish estimates around the
year 1680 give a range of five hundred to one thousand per village, the average being about eight hundred. This is about twice that of the other Indians.... In
general, then, a tribe of Indians in the United States and Canada, operating as a
social unit, living in neighboring camps, would rarely exceed fifteen hundred individuals, the actual communities being much smaller on the average." (Clark
Wissler, *An Introduction to Social Anthropology,* New York, 1929, p. 34-35)

16. For instance, Clark Wissler, *Ibid,* p. 30-34, estimated that at the time
when the white men began to come, there were approximately 25,000 aboriginal
Indians in the New England region of approximately 66,424 sq. miles; 30,600
aboriginal Indians in the Middle Atlantic region of approximately 99,574 sq.
miles; 52,200 in the South Atlantic region of approximately 140,739 sq. miles;
75,300 in the Central states region of approximately 283,394 sq. miles, and 114,400
in the Gulf States region of approximately 307,322 sq. miles. The five regions
together had approximately 297,500 Indians, with an area of approximately
902,453 sq. miles. All of these Indians lived in independent clan groups of an
average of 300 persons. Accordingly, therefore, each group had a territory of an
average of 900 sq. miles. This is close to the territory size of the clan group in an-

The tribe [17] usually consists of thousands of people[18] with a territory of thousands of square miles.[19]

---

cient China. According to Mencius, "King Wen of Chou (1027-256 B.C.) was with a hundred lis. and King Tang of Shang (1523-1028 B.C.) only seventy lis." ("文王以百里，湯方七十里。" 孟子公孫丑章) If the ancient li is about the same as the modern li, which is equal to about one third of a mile, Mencius' statement may be interpreted as that at the beginning, the Chou clan had a territory of approximately 1,000 sq. miles and the Shang, approximately 700 sq. miles.

17. The term "tribe" has been widely used for any kind of group of primitive peoples, their subdivisions, or their federations. But in a better defined sense, it is "a group of simple kind, nomadic, or settled in a more or less definite locality, speaking a common dialect, with a rude form of government, and capable of uniting for common action as in warfare." (*Notes and Queries on Anthropology,* ed. Barbara Freire-Marreco and John L. Myers, 4th ed., London, 1912, p. 156) It differs from the clan by the characteristic that it is "an inbreeding or intermarrying group," (listed as one of its four characteristics by Clark Wissler, *An Introduction to Social Anthropology,* New York, 1929, p. 15) while the clan is normally exogamous. The small groups it contains are more or less politically federated, unlike the small primitive communities which usually lack any political cohesion.

18. For example, "among the Bantu ... in South Africa. Altogether there are probably well over a thousand separate tribes. They vary greatly in size. Some have only a few hundred members each, others several thousand, and others as many as twenty thousand or more. In Bechuanaland, for example, the principal tribes are the Tlokwa (pop. 2,300), Khurutshe (3,000), Malete (9,500), Kgatla (20,000), Ngwaketse (39,000), Tawana (39,000), Kwena (40,000), and Ngwato (101,000). By far the largest tribe, at present, are the Sotho of Basutoland (682,000) and then come the Eastern Mpondo (260,000) and the Swazi of Swaziland (204,000)." (Isaac Schapera, *Government and Politics in Tribal Societies,* London, 1956, p. 10)

"Lacking more recent data, the map and the population estimates will serve as a point of departure for an analysis of social structure. ... The largest and most stable of the Hazara tribes are the Dai Kundi (population 52,000), Dai Zangi (60,000), Besud (100,000), Polada (45,000), Jaghuri (117,000) and Uruzgani (65,000)." (Elizabeth E. Bacon, Obok, *A Study of Social Structure in Eurasia,* New York, 1958, p. 6)

The names of the twelve Hebrew tribes, with their numbers of males twenty years and over, are listed in Chapter 1, "Book of Numbers," of the *Bible:*

Reuben	46,500	Zebulun	57,400	Dan	72,700
Simeon	59,300	Ephraim	45,000	Asher	41,500
Judah	74,600	Manasseh	32,200	Gad	45,650
Issachar	54,400	Benjamin	35,400	Naphtali	53,400

"To appreciate the intensity of Greek urban civilization, one must always remember the smallness, both in territory and in population, of the city-states.... Athens, with 43,000 adult male citizens at its peak in the 5th century B.C., had the largest population and was in a class by itself. The majority of the city-states, including Sparta, had less than 5,000 citizens." (Professor Norman O. Brown, in

The nation[20] usually consists of millions of people[21] with a territory of from thousands to millions of square miles.[22]

Encyclopedia Americana, 1973, v. 13, p. 392-393, under "History of Greece to 330 A.D.")

19. "Elsewhere (in Africa) compact tribal territories still exist. They vary greatly in size. In Bechuanaland, for example, where there has been relatively little disturbance, the Kgatla occupy some 3,600 sq. miles, the Ngwaketse 9,000, the Kwena 15,000, the Tawana 34,000, and the Ngwato 42,000; similarly, the Sotho of Basutoland have about 11,700 sq. miles." (Isaac Schapera, *Government and Politics in Tribal Societies,* London, 1956, p. 14)

"To appreciate the intensity of Greek urban civilization, one must always remember the smallness, both in territory and in population, of the city-states. Sparta (3,360 sq. miles) and Athens (1,060 sq. miles) were the largest. Some idea of the average size may be had from the fact that in Boeotia, a prosperous agricultural area, there were, apart from Thebes, 12 cities, each averaging about 52 sq. miles." (Professor Norman O. Brown, in *Encyclopedia Americana,* 1973, v. 13, p. 392, under "History of Greece to 330 A.D."

20. The word "nation" stems from the Latin verb *nasci,* "to be born," and originally meant a group of people born in the same place. In prevailing usage, a "nation" is either synonymous with a state or its inhabitants, or else denotes a human group whose members place loyalty to the group as a whole over any conflicting loyalties. This definition was first proposed by John Stuart Mill. (Cf. his *Consideration on Representative Government,* New York, 1958, originally 1861, Chapter 16.)

It is "something quite new in history. Antiquity was not acquainted with [it]. [Ancient] Egypt, China and Chaldea were in no degree nations." (Cyclopaedia of Political Science, Political Economy and Political History of the United States, ed. by John Lalor, New York, 1904, Vol. 2, p. 924) It is "the largest society of people united by a common culture and consciousness." (*A Dictionary of the Social Sciences,* ed. by Julius Gould and William L. Kolb, New York, 1964, p. 451) The two features of "new in history" and "largest society" distinguished the nation from the tribe.

"The exclusive possession of a dialect and of a territory has led to the application of the term nation to many Indian tribes, notwithstanding the fewness of the people in each. Tribe and nation, however, are not strict equivalents. A nation does not arise, . . . until the tribes united under the same government have coalesced into one people." (Clark Wissler, *An Introduction to Social Anthropology,* New York, 1929, p. 115)

21. The average population of the 135 nations in the United Nations in the early 1970s was approximately 24,000,000, ranging from the smallest nations such as Tonga, 90,000 (1971); Maldives, 110,000 (1971); Iceland, 210,000 (1971); Bahrain, 216,078 (1971); and Barbados, 238,141 (1970), to the most populous nations such as China, 800,000,000 (mainland China 787,180,000 [1971]; Taiwan 14,350,000 [1971]); India, 547,367,926 (1971); U.S.S.R., 241,720,134 (1970); U.S.A., 208,232,000 (1972); and Indonesia, 124,890,000 (1971). (Cf. *United Nations Statistical Yearbook,* 1974, Table 18.)

22. The average territory of the 135 nations in the United Nations at the present time is approximately 300,000 sq. miles, with some extremely small nations

It is obvious, then, that the size of our independent groups has been expanding all the way from the tiny early single family to the great nation, and that in the long run, this expansion clearly represents an unchangeable course of social evolution.[23]

Group expansion, therefore, is a social evolutionary law.

It is an historical law, too, since it has been at work for thousands of years.[24]

---

such as Maldives 115 sq. miles; Malta, 122 sq. miles; Barbados, 166 sq. miles; Bahrain, 231 sq. miles; Tonga, 270 sq. miles; and some exceptionally large nations such as the U.S.S.R., 8,649,489 sq. miles; Canada, 3,851,787 sq. miles; China, 3,705,387 (Mainland 3,691,502; Taiwan, 13,885) sq. miles; U.S.A. 3,540,939 sq. miles; and Brazil, 3,286,470 sq. miles. (Cf. *The Time's Atlas of the World,* Comprehensive ed., New York, 1975, p. xi-xv.)

23. The group expansion, as a course of social evolution, has been widely but roughly envisaged by scholars. Says William M. McGovern in his article, "The Growth of Institutions," in *Making Mankind,* New York, 1929, p. 78-79: "Present-day scholars are, to be sure, very far from agreement as to details, but I believe that the vast majority of them would accept in a general way the following points: The earliest unit of social and political organization was not a horde, or even a clan or tribe, but a small group corresponding in a way to the present family in the narrower sense of the word, i.e. father, mother, children.... From this early unit there gradually evolved at different times and at different places different types of social and political organization. Sometimes these units were small groups of persons living together generally but not necessarily related; at other times the units consisted of sibs or families in the larger sense of the word.... Some peoples have never passed beyond the community, or the sibs, type of organization, but in most cases force of circumstances has caused the federation of communities and sibs into tribal units.... from the tribe has developed by confederation and coalescence the Horde, the Nation, and the State."

William G. Sumner and Albert G. Keller, in *The Science of Society,* New Haven, 1927, v. 1, p. 415, put it in this way: "Evidently the degree of association attained is indicated in all cases by the size of the in-group or peace group, and the quality by the intensity of the in-group organization. In size the in-group runs all the way from the smallest aggregation ... to the greatest nation, and in organization from the loosest and vaguest of integration to the strictest and most definite."

24. The figure of thousands of years is a rough, and very conservative, estimate, since the existence of our remote ancestors has been traced back as early as 1,750,000 years ago, based on the findings of human remains up to the 1960s. Richard Leakey, a famous scientist from Kenya, estimated man's existence on earth to have covered 2.6 million years in an important announcement made on Nov. 9, 1972, simultaneously by the National Geographic Society, in Washington. Lately, the time has been extended to 4 million years by Donald C. Johanson of the Cleveland Museum of Natural History and T.D. White of the University of California at Berkeley, based on the fossil skulls, jaws and other bones uncovered in Tanzania and the Afar region of Ethiopa. They also asserted that human ancestors were walking on two feet millions of years before they made stone tools, according to an AP report, *South Bend Tribune,* Jan. 18, 1979, p.4.

· And it is also a universal law, since it prevails everywhere.[25] In the whole world today, most of the peoples have expanded their groups to nations, with only a small portion still left behind as tribes, clans, primitive communities, or even as the early single families.[26]

How does this powerful law operate?

Generally speaking, it expands groups not by growth,[27] but

---

25. Says Lewis H. Morgan: "Throughout the latter part of the period of savagery, and the entire period of barbarism, mankind in general were organized in gentes, phratrics and tribes. These organizations prevailed throughout the entire ancient world upon all the continents.... Since mankind were one in origin, their career has been essentially one, running, in different but uniform channels upon all continents, and very similarly in all the tribes and nations of mankind down to the same status of advancement. It follows that the history and experience of the American Indian tribes represent, more or less nearly, the history and experience of our own remote ancestors when in corresponding conditions." (In his *Ancient Society,* New York, 1877, p. vi-vii).

Sir Edward B. Tylor once said: "The institutions of man are as distinctly stratified as the earth on which he lives. They succeed each other in series substantially uniform over the globe, independent of what seem the comparatively superficial differences of race and language, but shaped by similar human nature acting through successfully changed conditions in savage, barbaric and civilized life." (Quoted in Robert H. Lowie, *Social Organization,* New York, 1948, p. 33) It is important to note that the above statements implicate not only the universal law, but also the historical law and the social evolutionary law.

Speaking of clan, for instance, "in the literature of historic peoples there is evidence which indicates that the clan was a very widespread institution in ancient times. The clan existed among the Greeks.... The clan or gens existed among the Romans in the early historical period; those related to each other through males were known as agnati, those related to each other through females were known as cognati. Among the Hindoos the clan is called the Gotra and among the Arabs the Hayy. Among the ancient Irish the clan was variously called the Thath, Cinel, or Clann." (Francis S. Chapin, *An Introduction to the Study of Social Evolution: The Pre-Historic Period,* New York, 1913, p. 238-239)

26. Among those who have remained far behind in terms of social evolution are some Australian natives, Asiatic Negritos, American Eskimos, African Twides, Pygmies and Bushmen. Literature about these peoples are numerous. For instance: Adolphus P. Elkin, *The Australian Aborigines,* Garden City, N.Y., 1964; Paul Schebesta, *Die Negrito Asiens,* Wien-Modling, 1952; Kaj Birket-Smith, *The Eskimos,* rev. ed. by Cyril Forde, London, 1959; Martin Gusinde, "Pygmies and Pygmoids, Twides of the Tropical Africa," in *Anthropological Quarterly,* v. 28, 1955, p. 3-61; and Isaac Schapera, *The Khoisan Peoples of South Africa, Bushmen and Hottentots,* London, 1930.

27. It is hardly possible to find a case in history anywhere in which a group expands its population and territory to a very great size by its own growth alone, and not through merging with other groups. "There has never been any great race, but a continual integration, dispersal, and even reintegration of active peoples drawn from the most diverse sources, and there is hardly a people which has not contrib-

through merging: A number of early single families merge as a primitive community, a number of primitive communities merge as a clan, a number of clans merge as a tribe, and a number of tribes merge as a nation.

There are many ways leading to merging:
The most natural way is inter-marriage.[28]

---

uted some important release or achievement to the common progress." (Herbert G. Wells, *The World of William Clissold,* New York, 1926, Vol. II, p. 615)

28. The famous Chou rule (established by the Chou Dynasty (1027-256 B.C.) that no marriage is allowed between members of the same family (禮記大傳云：「繫之以姓 …… 雖百世而婚姻不通者，周道然也。」) has been regarded by some scholars as one of the main reasons for the development of the Chinese nation. For instance, Chi-Chao Liang, 梁啓超 , remarked in his *History of Pre-Chin Political Thought* (in Chinese) 6th ed., Taipei, 1972, p. 38, that "this rule has played a great role in developing our nation, because the more the blood-mixing, the easier the group-merging.... This rule has been in effect for almost 3000 years and has had no change up to date. It is the main reason that our nation has grown up rapidly and healthily."

As a matter of fact, this kind of rule has been a common practice, or even a strict taboo, of almost all the clan organizations throughout the world. "The provision of exogamy, whereby the totem must be crossed, is characteristic of the clan." (William G. Sumner and Albert G. Keller, *The Science of Society,* New Haven, 1927, vol. 1, p. 431-2)

It has even been extended to groups larger than clan. "Among certain peoples a further complication has been developed. All the gens constituting a tribe are divided into two groups usually called moities or phratries. Where this is done, all of the gens which form a phratry are considered so closely related that a man is not only prohibited from marrying within his own gens, he is also prohibited from marrying within his own phratry." (William M. McGovern, "The Growth of Institutions," in *Making Mankind,* New York, 1929, p. 96)

"Trade and the practice of exogamy were the main factors in breaking down the barriers that separated one community from another. It is not by chance that the Latin terms "commercium" and "connubium" came to be linked together in a formula; interchange of goods and of wives went along side by side. The reader will recall that civilization is a function not alone of numbers, but of the contact of numbers as well. Endogamy provided for no contacts, while exogamy secured them in regular, frequent, and peaceable form, then followed the contagion of ideas or what has been called the cross-fertilization of culture." (William G. Sumner and Albert G. Keller, op. cit., vol. 3, p. 1618)

29. "Adam Smith regarded a 'propensity to truck, barter, and exchange one thing for another' as one of the basic ingredients of human nature.... The exchange of gifts between leading members of different tribes (often mentioned both in Homer and in the Old Testament) played an important part in social and economic life. Besides their social and political role such gifts enabled one group to share in the products of another and so provided a forerunner of more organized forms of exchange." (E. Victor Morgan, *A History of Money,* Baltimore, 1965, p. 9-10)

E.F. Im Thurn in his *Among the Indians of Guiana,* London, 1883, p. 270,

Inter-group trade is also a natural way.[29] Language[30] and religion[31] may provide natural ways, too.

---

said that there existed among the Guiana Indians a rough system of division of labor between the tribes, and that this served not only the purpose of supplying all of them with better made articles, but also brought the different tribes together and spread among them ideas and news of general interest. Each tribe had some manufacture peculiar to itself, and its members constantly visited other tribes, often hostile ones, for the purpose of exchanging the products of their own labor for such as were produced by the other tribes. These trading Indians were allowed to pass unmolested through an enemy's country.

"It can be seen from the evidence now before us that trade, as a special development in the organization for societal self-maintenance, takes its origin in group-specialization, and represents certainly one of the factors that brought into peaceful inter-group relations. In this respect 'commercium' and 'connubium' support each other, justifying the Romans in their yoking together of the terms; and there is a widespread custom whereby markets are put under both civil and religious sanction, as places of peace." (William G. Sumner and Albert G. Keller, *The Science of Society,* New Haven, 1927, vol. 1, p. 159)

"In the development of civilization the exchange of materials and of ideas has been of an importance second only to their origination. For by exchange all the new departures that have turned out well for their originators have been transmitted to other peoples, back and forth; and each of several communicating groups has been able to profit by a set of adjustments which include the best that any and all of them have succeeded in hitting upon. Intercommunication is a prime essential. Men must not only know what is going on in the minds of other men, so as to compare and mutually adopt ideas, but, still more important, especially among backward tribes which can most readily deal with ideas when embodied in things, they must be able to see and handle those things—in this case, other people's products.... The exchange of products precedes that of ideas or processes, at least on the primitive stage. It should not be understood, however, that hard and fast lines of distinction can be drawn between these two forms of exchange; the transfer of products is hardly possible without a simultaneous transmission of ideas, for the products are themselves ideas expressed in material form." (*Ibid,* vol. 1, p. 159-160)

"The principle of exchange of commodities in its most elementary forms seems universal. It was the experience of European explorers that natives at first contact were ready to barter and understood the principles involved. Whether among such natives trade was limited to persons outside of their own community, is not clear, but in some instances one gets the impression that formal trade was wholly a matter of intertribal relations. However this may be, it is certain that intertribal trade was of considerable importance in remote times. Archeologists have frequently called attention to the wide distribution of localized products, implying trade." (Clark Wissler, *An Introduction to Social Anthropology,* New York, 1929, p. 78)

30. As soon as human language appeared, dialects developed. But contact between dialects was inevitable, and when two or more dialects came into contact, they were bound to react upon one another. This mutual influence always resulted

The most unnatural ways are conquest, occupation, and annexation.[32]

---

in a common language in a wider area; and this common language served as one of the most important factors which have widened the group life of mankind.

"Allied with language is writing, as a means for the preservation and transmission of ideas and culture across time and space. Literature discharges an important function in acquainting people with one another's characteristics; the novel has been highly effective in that way." (William G. Sumner and Albert G. Keller, *The Science of Society,* New Haven, 1927, v. 1, p. 161)

It is well known, for instance, that written Chinese has played a great role in merging the various peoples of that vast land into a nation.

It is also well known that, together with Buddhism, Chinese script has played an important role in merging the Japanese clans into greater groups and eventually a nation since it was adopted from China about 400-550 A.D.

31. Speaking of the ancient city-state, for instance, "it is of little account to seek the cause which determined several neighboring tribes to unite. Sometimes it was voluntary. Sometimes it was imposed by the superior force of a tribe, or by the powerful will of a man. What is certain is, that the bond of the new association was still a religion. The tribes that united to form a city never failed to light a sacred fire, and to adopt a common religion." "As soon as the families, the phratries, and the tribes had agreed to unite and have the same worship, they immediately founded the city as a sanctuary for this common worship, and thus the foundation of a city was always a religious act." (Numa D. Fustel de Coulanges, *The Ancient City,* tr. by Willard Small, 11th ed., Boston, 1873, p. 167 and 177)

"How then can a relation between hostile and mutually suspicious tribes be founded? Only, is the answer, by a rite appealing to what was to be an even higher unity than that of blood, which was the only unity conceived of by the most primitive people. This rite was religious and resulted in the various taboos on places and times just alluded to: the temple-peace, peace of God, house-peace, market-peace, church-peace, holiday-peace." (Statement of Julius Lippert, quoted in *The Science of Society,* by William G. Sumner and Albert G. Keller, New Haven, 1927, vol. 1, p. 393)

32. "Take the case of conquest, where two groups fall into conflict and one overcomes the other; then the ensuing relation is one of dominion. Conquest extends the peace-group while producing inequality with it; but the classes thus differentiated as dominant and subject tend to amalgamate by inter-marriage and to regard themselves as kin, if not in demonstrable fact, at least through some eponymous ancestor." "... once the masters and their subjects come into proximity the process of amalgamation goes on very 'slyly' through political adjustments. By 'slyly' ... means ... 'automatically.' " (William G. Sumner and Albert G. Keller, *The Science of Society,* New Haven, 1927, vol. 1, p. 450, 584)

For instance, in ancient Rome, starting with patricians and plebeians, the process of amalgamation was carried out. "Thanks to the tribunes ... the people went forward to more and more equality; they obtained successively the abolition of the prohibition relative to marriage between the orders, the right to occupy offices called curule, i.e. the quaestorship and censorship, then half of the consulship, and finally the dictatorship." "Thus the linguistic and religious barriers fell first and

Adoption,[33] blood-drawing,[34] migration[35] and colonization[36] are ways which are between natural and unnatural.

---

they gained more rights, culminating in that of intermarriages.'' (Ch. Letourneau, *L'évolution Politique dans les Diverses races Humaines,* Paris, 1890, p. 378)

''But as we know the situation in the Old World to have been, conquerors subjugated peoples of diverse biological types, and when such diverse peoples are brought under one political system and inter-marriage facilitated, a general mixture results, which may, in due course, become stabilized and so constitute a new type. The Japanese people, for example, are believed to be a resultant of an original Ainu population crossed with Mongoloid conquerors.... The languages and customs of the conquered tribes may be displaced in a generation or two, if the ruling power so decrees, but if a subject people are permitted to survive, their blood will enter into the population and under certain conditions dominate.'' (Clark Wissler, *An Introduction to Social Anthropology,* New York, 1929, p. 52)

For example, the Mongols, Manchus and some other peoples had conquered China for from tens to hundreds of years, but finally were mixed with and even absorbed by the majority Chinese.

33. The adoption of strangers into the group is a practice so common in the primitive societies that it has been listed by scholars as one of the most important privileges of the members of the ancient Grecian clan, the Roman clan, and the North American Indian Iroquois clan. (Cf. Lewis H. Morgan, *Ancient Society,* New York, 1877, p. 71, 221-3, 285. Cf. also Mary K. Benet, *The Politics of Adoption,* New York, 1976)

34. ''An application of the common-blood idea in relation to the out-group remains to be noted. So deeply ingrained in the mores is the conviction that close human relationship means blood-relationship that the exchange of blood between those who are establishing friendship is a relatively common ceremony (in the primitive societies). If two men draw and mix their blood, by drinking it, or otherwise, what they are doing is establishing a peace-relation between them such as existed traditionally between people of the same blood.'' (William G. Sumner and Albert G. Keller, *The Science of Society,* New Haven, 1927, vol. 1, p. 440. For examples, cf. *Ibid.,* p. 441-)

''An analysis of the descent of the population of every part of Europe proves that intermingling has been going on for long periods. The movements of tribes in prehistoric times and during antiquity also illustrate the ways in which different strains became mixed: the Doric migration into Greece, the movements of the Kelts into Spain, Italy and eastward as far as Asia Minor; the Teutonic migrations which swept through Europe from the Black Sea into Italy, France, Spain and on into Africa; the invasion of the Balkan Peninsula by Slavs, and their extension over eastern Russia and into Siberia; Phoenician, Greek and Roman colonization; the roving Normans; the expansion of the Arabs; the Crusades, are a few of the important events that have contributed to the intermingling of the European population.'' (Franz Boas, *Anthropology and Modern Life,* rev. ed., New York, 1932, p. 88. Cf. also V. Gordon Childe, *Prehistoric Migration in Europe,* Cambridge, Mass., 1950.)

The Carib Indian constantly moved about the coast of South America from the Amazon to the Orinoco and Magdalena, and even over to the Antilles; ''often it was impossible for him to find his own people again and since women took part

Alliance, confederation, and federation are politically conventional ways.[37]

---

only in small numbers in these wandering and thieving expeditions, the . . . savage
formed new unions where he could." The result was "a mass of human beings,
flowing together from the most diverse hordes and tribes, was regarded as a
genetically homogeneous community, as a tribe or a people, because they were
concordant in their manner of life." (K.F.P. von Martius, *Beiträge zur
Ethnographie und Sprachenkunde Amerikas, zumal Brasiliens,* Leipzig, 1867, vol.
1, p. 377-378, 263)

"The Australians are prone to blood-letting, which they perform by cutting
with a stone or, if procurable, a glassflake. Every adult native has a series of little
lumps marking the course of the veins on the forearm which indicate the places
where he has cut himself for the purpose of drawing blood. . . . The drawing and
also the drinking of blood on certain special occasions is associated with the idea
that those who take part in the ceremony are thereby bound together in friendship
and obliged to assist one another. At the same time it renders treachery
impossible." (B. Spencer and F.J. Gillen, *The Northern Tribes of Central
Australia,* New York, 1904, p. 596)

"Blood-drinking is associated with special meetings of reconciliation which
sometimes take place between two groups who have been on bad terms with one
another without actually coming to a fight. . . . If the offending group be willing,
which they are almost sure to be, then the meeting is held, and at the beginning
each party drinks the blood of its own members, and a more or less sham fight
takes place with boomerangs, no one being hurt." (B. Spencer and F.J. Gillen,
Native Tribes of Central Australia, New York, 1899, p. 462) This was a very common and serious practice in politics in ancient China, such as "to unite into a
blood-ally" "訂血盟 "and "to ally under blood-oath." "歃血爲盟 " 。

35. For example, "in Holland the immigrants from the region of Antwerp in
the second generation married Dutch women and took up Dutch mores. They
came thus to feel at home. The antagonism between natives and immigrants was
almost gone in the course of one generation, and the latter regarded Holland not as
a refuge but as a fatherland. Such assimilation has been marked in America."
(William G. Sumner and Albert G. Keller, *The Science of Society,* New Haven,
1927, vol. 1, p. 450)

"The Angoni, a section of the Zulus that migrated toward the north, all
become gradually assimilated to the surrounding populations." (R. Codrington,
"The Central Angoniland District of the British Central Africa Protectorate," in
The Geographical Journal, London, vol. XI, p. 512)

36. For instance, the colonization of hundreds of southern countries by the
Chou dynasty (1027-256 B.C.), and the settling of the royal family and their
relatives among these countries as supervisors led to the founding of the Chinese
nation two thousand years ago (周室分封同姓諸侯，化被南國 。 The coloniza-
tion of a great number of Indian tribes by the British Empire resulted in the federation of modern India.

37. "Even before the formation of tribes, many of the communities speak the
same or similar language. They are frequently allied by ties of blood. . . . It is quite
natural therefore that a group of such communities especially in times of unusual
stress such as invasion of their territory by aliens, or of forced wholesale migra-

By so many ways, natural, unnatural and conventional, merging has been persistently working for the group expansion throughout mankind's existence.[38] As a result, the number of independent

---

tions due to change of climate, etc., should recognize and give expression of their underlying unity of interests by formation of either formal or informal alliances.... These alliances tend to disintegrate in times of peace, but continued stress annihilates the constituent communities or forces the alliances to become more permanent in their nature. In the latter case the alliance soon develops into what we term a tribe." "At various times and at various places we have the spectacle of tribes gathering into federations, and federations developing into nations." (William M. McGovern, "The Growth of Institutions," in *Making Mankind,* New York, 1929, p. 94, 97)

For example: In the United States the germ of union is to be found in the United Colonies of New England (1643-1684) whose Articles declared that "as in Nation and Religion, so in other respects we be and continue one." During the period between 1690 and 1754, there were numerous so-called "Congresses" of governors or representatives of the colonies to make joint treaties with the Indians and to arrange for common military operations. The last Congress of such kind was called in 1754 at Albany. The Albany Congress also took up a plan of union drafted by Benjamin Franklin.

The First Continental Congress, which met in June, 1774, was called in much the same spirit. Twelve colonies were represented. It spoke boldly and adopted an agreement not to import British goods. When the Second Continental Congress met on May 10, 1775, war between the colonies and their mother country had already broken out. The Congress therefore took upon itself the management of the military, financial, and foreign affairs of the thirteen colonies. In 1781, these powers were transferred to a newly organized confederation which lasted until the federal constitution was put into operation in 1789. The Articles of Confederation were framed in 1777, but it was not until 1781 that they were ratified by all thirteen states. The Articles brought these states into a "firm league of friendship" with each other, offensive and defensive, and created for them a common name, "the United States of America." (Cf. Merrill Jensen, *The New Nation: A History of the United States during the Confederation 1781-1789,* New York, 1950.)

Switzerland's political development as a confederation and then a federation stretches over five and a half centuries. The first important date in the history of this process was 1291, when the three cantons of Uri, Schwyz, and Unterwalden entered what was known as the first Perpetual League. Then came the Confederation of eight cantons (1353), the Confederation of thirteen cantons (1513), the Helvetic Republic (1798), the Act of Mediation, with nineteen cantons (1803), and the Federal Pact, with twenty-two cantons (1815). It was not until 1848 that Switzerland transformed itself from a confederation into a federation. (Cf. Francis O. Adams and C.D. Cunningham, *The Swiss Confederation,* 1889, London, p. 1-2.)

38. "This process of enlargement of political units and the reduction of the number of those that were naturally at war with one another began in the earliest times, and has continued without interruption, almost always in the same direction. Even though hostilities have broken out frequently between parts of what had come to be a large political unit, the tendency for unification has in the long run been more powerful than that of disintegration. We see the powers at work in

groups has been reduced from thousands[39] to less than two hundred,[40] while the size of the groups has expanded from the tiny early single family to the great nation.

Thus, merging is the key to group expansion, as a social evolutionary, historical, and universal law.

b.
Testimonials

IN THE PROCESS OF MERGING, USUALLY THE SMALLER groups give up their independence first and become some kind of autonomous units, which are then transformed into local or custom units, and finally lose all their traces in the larger group.[41] It is a pro-

---

antiquity, when the urban states of Greece and of Italy were gradually welded into larger wholes; we see it again at work after the breaking up of ancient society in the development of new states from the old ones; and later on in the disappearance of the small feudal states." (Franz Boas, *Anthropology and Modern Life,* rev. ed., New York, 1932, p. 100)

"Mankind is proceeding toward greater and greater homogeneity, racially, culturally, and linguistically. In this process the world's primitive cultures are disappearing. Some are simply dying out or being exterminated; some are undergoing radical changes as they become involved in various kinds of functional relationships with the expanding industrial civilizations; others are being ethnically assimilated." (Elman R. Service, *A Profile of Primitive Culture,* New York, 1958, p. ix)

39. Based on the estimates of population in early times—approximately 500,000 in 30,000 B.C., 1,000,000 in 10,000 B.C., 15,000,000 in 5,000 B.C., 150,000,000 in 1,000 B.C., and 1,550,000,000 in 1900 A.D. (Cf. Julian Huxley, "Population and Human Destiny, *Harper's* Magazine, v. 201, no. 1204, Sept., 1950, p. 38-46; Palmer C. Putnam, *Energy in the Future,* New York, 1953, p. 16-17; and M. King Hubbert, *Energy Resources,* Washington, 1962, p. 15-20)—and the estimates of average population: early family, 5; primitive community, 50; clan, 1,500; and tribe, 75,000 (Cf. Clark Wissler, *An Introduction to Social Anthropology,* New York, 1929, p. 28-41, and Ia notes on the sizes of the groups.), the numbers of the independent groups in their culminating time are calculated as follows: early family, 100,000; primitive community, 20,000; clan, 10,000; and tribe, 2,000.

40. At the beginning of the 20th century, when the world population increased to approximately 1,550,000,000, as noted above, there were about 200 nations with an average of approximately 8,000,000 people each. By 1973, the number of nations had dwindled to about 180, of which 135 were members of the United Nations. (Cf. *Yearbook of the United Nations,* 1973, p. 975.)

cess of amalgamation[42] and is usually a long and common process: too long to be remembered and too common to be noticed. There are, however, some historical accounts which serve well as testimonies for the operation always and everywhere of the merging process as the key to the law of group expansion.

The first Egyptian kingdom was formed about 3,000 B.C. by some groups which were made up of a great number of villages or clans during a long period of time.[43]

41. "Usually as the larger units came into being, the intermediate units tended to become of less importance. The gens, the phratry, even the tribe tended to become obscured once a federation of tribes had been formed." "In this case the old gens or clan organization is gradually weakened and eventually disappears, leaving only the tribe as a whole, with only the family, and perhaps the community as subunits." (William M. McGovern, "The Growth of Institutions," in *Making Mankind,* New York, 1929, p. 97, 95)

42. L. Gumplowicz catalogued the factors which bring about unification and amalgamation in his *Sociologie und Politik,* Leipzig, 1892, p. 145-146. The material factors are contiguity, familiarity, and blood-kinship, the last being the most powerful. Then come what he called the economic factors: class (noble, burgher, peasant, clergy, etc.), possessions (rural, urban, etc), and vocation (landowners, manufacturers, merchants, artisans, etc.). The larger moral factors are language, religion, art, science, etc. It is understood that their effectiveness depends upon the length of time they have been in operation. Language differences fall first as a sacrifice to the process of unification and amalgamation. Later, the much more stubborn barriers of religion are surmounted, together with other distinguishing usages and customs. When these are gone, the major hurdles have been cleared. Last of all comes intermarriage, which means the end of the blood barrier. This is often long delayed through caste-exclusiveness.

43. "Gerontocracy, therefore, begins very far back in Egyptian traditions; it dates back, very likely, to the time of the chalcolithic villages. Grouped thus in villages, perhaps forming clans, lived those who devoted themselves to the rough task of improving the oasis of Egypt. . . . From the end of the fourth millennium Egypt was marching towards the decisive transformation; the chalcolithic industries gave birth to a true civilization; the groupings of men in villages or clans were united to form first States or kingdoms, and then one single kingdom." (Alexandre Moret, *From Tribe to Empire,* New York, 1926, p. 124, 125)

44. "Several families formed the phratry, several phratries the tribe, several tribes the city. Family, phratry, tribe, city, were, moreover, societies exactly similar to each other, which were formed one after the other by a series of federations." "Thus the city was not an assemblage of individuals; it was a confederation of several groups, which were established before it, and which it permitted to remain." (Numa D. Fustel de Coulanges, *The Ancient City,* tr. by Willard Small, 11th ed., Boston, 1873, p. 168, 167)

45. Down to about 500 B.C., it was possible for Greek civilization to develop hundreds of small city-states and to cultivate in each of these the ideals of economic self-sufficiency and political autonomy. They formed a series of confederations. Then Athens became the head of a maritime confederation organized

About 500 B.C., there existed in Greece a large number of cities with economic self-sufficiency and political autonomy. Each of them was formed step by step out of a series of smaller groups similar to one another.[44] Later, some 200 of these cities joined in a confederation led by Athens, while others joined in another league led by Sparta.[45]

---

in 478 B.C., on a voluntary basis, as the Delian League, which grew to include some 200 city-states in the Aegean Islands and along the coasts of Asia Minor, the Thracian Chersonese, and the rest of Thrace. Sparta had also placed itself at the head of a military alliance known as the Peloponnesian League, which embraced all the city-states of the Peloponnesus with the exception of Argos and Achaea. (Cf. Victor Ehrenberg, *The Greek State,* New York, 1961.)

46. "It will be sufficient to remind the reader of the general facts that Romulus united upon and around the Palatine Hill a hundred Latin gentes, organized as a tribe, the Ramnes; that by a fortunate concurrence of circumstances a large body of Sabines were added to the new community whose gentes, afterwards increased to one hundred, were organized as a second tribe, the Tities; and that in the time of Tarquinius Priscus a third tribe, the Luceres, had been formed, composed of a hundred gentes drawn from surrounding tribes, including the Etruscans. Three hundred gentes, in about the space of a hundred years, were thus gathered at Rome, and completely organized under a council of chiefs now called the Roman Senate, an assembly of the people now called the comitia curiata, and one military commander, the rex; and with one purpose, that of gaining a military ascendency in Italy." (Lewis H. Morgan, *Ancient Society,* New York, 1877, p. 280)

47. (Cf. The *Bible,* "Book of Numbers," Chapter 1.) The names of these groups are: Reuben, Simeon, Judah, Issachar, Zebulun, Ephraim, Manasseh, Benjamin, Dan, Asher, Gad, and Naphtali.

"The twelve tribes of the Hebrews, as they appear in the Book of Numbers, represent a reconstruction of Hebrew society by legislative procurement. The condition of barbarism had then passed away, and that of civilization had commenced. The principle on which the tribes were organized, as bodies of consanguinei, presuppose an anterior gentile system, which had remained in existence and was now systematized." (Lewis H. Morgan, *Ancient Society,* New York, 1877, p. 366)

48. The Celts or Gauls existed, in a set of clan organization. It would seem that no one clan ever rose to a complete hegemony over the rest. The victory of Caesar over the Gauls (57-52 B.C.) was, above all, the result of the fact that he never had to face a united Gaul except when, after six years of spasmodic effort, it united for a day round Vercingetorix, only to die heroically at Alesia. (Cf. Gustave Bloch, *Les Origines de la Gaule indépendante et la Gaul romaine,* Paris, 1900.)

49. "The Celtic branch of the Aryan family retained, in the Scottish clan and Irish sept, the organization into gentes to a later period of time than any other branch of the family, unless the Aryans of India are an exception. The Scottish clan in particular was existing in remarkable vitality in the Highlands of Scotland in the middle of the last century. It was an excellent type of gens in organization and in spirit, and an extraordinary illustration of the power of the gentile life over its members." (Lewis H. Morgan, *Ancient Society, New York, 1877, p. 357)*

50. England in the Middle Ages was occupied by a number of separate

Rome was founded by Romulus in about 753 B.C. from a community formed out of a hundred small Latin groups around the Palatine Hill. It was later joined by the united people of a hundred small Sabine groups, and later by an alliance of a hundred other surrounding small groups.[46]

According to the Bible, Moses organized twelve tribes of the Hebrews as one group called the Children of Israel, with the tribe of Levi as a special unit.[47]

The Celts or Gauls, ancestors of the French people, were a set of loosely organized clans before the Christian Era.[48]

Some other Celts retained the clan system in Scotland and Ireland until a much later time. The clans in the Highlands of Scotland, in particular, did not lose their vitality until the middle of the 18th century.[49]

Up until the Middle Ages, England was still occupied by a number of groups,[50] as were Scotland[51] and Wales.[52] The union of

---

kingdoms, each with a royal family of its own. The districts north of the Humber contained two kingdoms, Bernica and Deira, which were eventually united in Northumbria. South of the Humber, Lindsey seems to have had a dynasty of its own. The upper basin of the Trent formed the nucleus of the kingdom of Mercia, while farther down the east coast was the kingdom of East Anglia. Between these two lay a territory called Middle Anglia. Essex, Kent, and Sussex preserve the names of ancient kingdoms, while the old diocese of Worcester grew out of the kingdom of the Hwicce. The south of England, between Sussex and "West Wales" (eventually reduced to Cornwall), was occupied by the Wessex, who originally also possessed some territory to the north of the Thames. Lastly, even the Isle of Wight appears to have had a dynasty of its own. (Cf. Frank M. Stenton, *Anglo-Saxon England,* 2nd ed., Oxford, 1947.)

51. By about 600 A.D. four peoples were living on the Scottish mainland. The Picts occupied most of the Highlands, except for the Scots colony in Dalriada (Argyll), while the western Lowlands (Strathclyde) were held by partially Romanized Britons, and the southeastern Lowlands (Lothian) by the Angles. Caithness and Sutherland had been invaded by the Norsemen. These peoples did not actually unite until nine hundred years later. (Cf. Eric Linklater, *Survival of Scotland,* New York, 1968.)

52. In the 7th century, Wales was divided into a number of small units, constantly at war among themselves. After 1066, the Normans quickly overran most of south Wales, individual Norman lords conquering the small states one by one and taking over the semiregal powers of the Welsh rulers whom they displaced. The lordships of the March (borderland) of Wales thereby came into existence. In the lowlands of these lordships, the Normans introduced a manorial system. In north Wales, on the other hand, a strong line of princes withstood the Anglo-Norman kings. Wales was united by the conquest of Edward I of England in 1282. (Cf. Sir John E. Lloyd, *A History of Wales from the Earliest Time to the Edwardian Conquest,* 3rd ed., New York, 1939, v. 1, chap. VIII to v. 2, chap. XX.)

England, Scotland and Wales as Great Britain has only been in effect for about 400 years.[53]

In China, it was said that Emperor Huang divided the land into 10,000 states of 100 lis[54] each 4,600 years ago.[55] Some 600 years later, when the Holy King Yu held a convention at Tu Shan, 10,000 states were presented with jade and silk.[56] The number of states was reduced to less than 2,000 when King Wu of the Chou Dynasty took over the hegemony from the Shang Dynasty 3,000 years ago,[57] to less than 200 in the period of the Eastern Chou,[58] to seven in the later period of

---

53. Great Britain is the official title of the political unity of England, Scotland, and Wales. The name was used in 1604 after James VI of Scotland had succeeded to the English throne, and it was formally adopted in 1707 at the date of the union of the crowns of England and Scotland. (Cf. Christopher Hill, *The Century of Revolution, 1603-1714,* London, 1961.)

54. This is cited in *Tzu-Hai,* a Chinese encyclopedia. A Chinese li at the present time is equal to approximately one third of a mile. This legend indicates that in very early times, China was a composite of thousands of primitive communities along the Yellow River. ("黃帝畫野分州，分成一百里的諸侯國一萬區。" 辭海，中華版，釋封建條，未註明出處。)

55. Emperor Huang was said to be the inventor of the oldest Chinese Calendar commencing with the year 2698 B.C. It was called the Calendar of Emperor Huang. The U.S. bicentennial of 1976 took place in the year of 4,674, according to the oldest Chinese calendar.

56. "The achievement of the Holy Yu of Hsia Dynasty (1994-1523 B.C.), besides establishing an irrigation system, was the conquest of Miau. . . . Then he held a convention at Tu Shan [and] there presented 10,000 states with jade and silk. The chief of Fang-Fung was sentenced to death because of arriving at the convention too late." ("神禹功德，治水而外，厥惟征苗⋯⋯其後禹遂會諸侯於塗山，執玉帛者萬國。防風氏後至。戮之以徇。") (Cited by Chi-Chao Liang in an essay on "The Achievements of the Hsia and Shang Dynasties," in his *Six Essays on the Study of Chinese History,* (in Chinese), 3rd ed., Taipei, 1971, p. 19-20)

The Miau were a people spreading widely along the Yangtze River. It seems that the exploration of Yu extended China much southward. Therefore, the "state" in this time might be somewhat larger than in the time of Emperor Huang.

57. When Chou, the last king of the Shang Dynasty (1523-1028 B.C.), was defeated by Wu, the second king of the Chou Dynasty, in 1027 B.C., there remained less than 2,000 states, as recorded in several ancient books. For instance, *The Lu's Review,* a great work of about 2200 years ago by Lu Pu-wei and associates, stated that "Chou established a feudal system to control more than 400 states, and in addition, extended a hegemony over more than 800 states." (呂不韋氏所輯呂氏春秋中呂覽觀世篇稱周所封四百餘，服國八百餘.) The "state" of this stage probably was clan and exogamous as evidenced by the famous Chou rule that no marriage was allowed between members of the same family. (Cf. I, 14, 28.)

58. At the beginning of the Eastern Chou period (770-256 B.C.), there still existed about 200 states; Chi-Chao Liang listed 164 of their names as an appendix to the essay on "Wars in the Period of Spring and Autumn" (772-481 B.C.), p.

the Warring States,[59] and finally to a single nation 2,200 years ago, when the first emperor of the Chin Dynasty eliminated all the remaining states.[60] Yet, in China today, the ancient clan system can still be traced back clearly.[61]

84-85, in his *Six Essays on the Study of Chinese History* (in Chinese), 3rd ed., Taipei, 1971. It seems that the "state" in this period had been transformed from clan to tribe.

Joseph Needham in his *Science and Civilization in China,* London, 1954, v. 1, p. 94, made a chart showing the gradual merging process of the various states from the middle period to the end of the Chou Dynasty. It seems, however, that the chart includes only the well-known states, and not all of them.

59. In the late stage of the Warring States Period (403-222 B.C., a subperiod of the Eastern Chou Period), there remained only seven states: Wei, Chu, Yen, Chao, Chi, Han, and Chin. (魏 ， 楚 ， 燕 ， 趙 ， 齊 ， 韓 ， 秦 .) Each of them was formed through the merging of a number of states. For example, Chu merged with 67 states as listed by name in an appendix to the essay on "Wars in the Period of Spring and Autumn (722-481 B.C.)," p. 84-85 in the *Six Essays on the Study of Chinese History,* (in Chinese), by Chi-Chao Liang, 3rd ed., Taipei, 1971. Undoubtedly the seven "states" were great tribes.

60. Chin snuffed out the hapless Chou in 256 B.C., and in lightning campaigns from 230-221 B.C., destroyed all the remaining rival states. For the first time in its history, China became a nation under the First Emperor, Shih Huang Ti of the Chin Dynasty (221-206 B.C.).

61. "The Chinese expression for the people is Pih-sing, which means the Hundred Family Names; but whether this is mere word-painting, or had its origin at a time when the Chinese general family consisted of one hundred subfamilies or tribes (gentes?) I am unable to determine. At present there are about four hundred family names in this country, among which I find some that have reference to animals, fruits, metals, natural objects, etc., and which may be translated as Horse, Sheep, Ox, Fish, Bird, Phoenix, Plum, Flower, Leaf, Rice, Forest, River, Hill, Water, Cloud, Gold, Hide, Bristles, etc., etc. In some parts of the country large villages are met with, in each of which there exists but one family name; thus in one district will be found, say, three villages, each containing two or three thousand people, the one of the Horse, the second of the Sheep, and the third of the Ox family name. . . . Just as among the North American Indians husbands and wives are of different tribes [gentes], so in China husband and wife are always of different families, i.e., of different surnames." The above is a letter to Lewis H. Morgan from his friend Robert Hart of Canton. Rightly, Morgan remarked "a peculiar family system prevails among the Chinese which seems to embody the remains of an ancient gentile organization," This remark, together with Hart's letter, may be found in Morgan's *Ancient Society,* New York, 1877, p. 364-365. I would like to point out that among the present-day family names there are a good many which are ancient family, clan, or "state" names. For instance, both family names: Chiang and Mao 蔣， 毛 of the Chinese Nationalist leader Chiang Kai-shek and the Communist leader Mao Tse tung, are ancient "state" names: "蔣，姓，周公子伯齡封於蔣，其後子孫以國為氏。河南固始縣東有蔣鄉，即古蔣國也"。 "毛，姓，周武王母弟毛叔鄭後，一云文王子毛伯明後，世為周卿士，食采於毛，其後因以為氏"。上二註皆見辭源。

Fifteen hundred years ago, Japan was an area in which many groups competed with one another. Despite the imperial rule begun in the 5th century by a leader of a clan of the Yamato people, the other clans claimed independence[62] until national unity was established in the last century.[63]

Some of the old family names, such as Yao, Szu, Chi, Chiang, Ying, Huan, Chi, and Jen 姚，姒，姬，姜，嬴，嬛，姞，妊 may even be traced back to a matrilineal family system, because the characters of these family names are significantly composed with a female symbol "女"

According to the study of Chen Jen-te 陳仁德, Chairman of the Institute for the Study of Chinese Genealogy, there are at the present 9177 family names in China. Among them, 6668 belong to Han or Chinese proper, and the rest originated from various other races. This unique study reveals that the ethnic composition of the Chinese people is much more complex than was ever envisaged. (Cf. *China Voice Daily,* April 20, 1979, p. 4.)

62. In pre-historic times, the country was peopled by immigrants from several parts of eastern Asia, mostly of Tungusic origin. Neolithic remains show that prior to these migrations Japan was sparsely inhabited by ancestors of the people now known as the Ainu. In the first four or five centuries of our era, Japan consisted of a number of tribal communities competing with one another for influence or military strength. Those native chieftains who made the best use of new techniques acquired from Korean teachers were able in the course of time to outstrip their rivals; and before long certain tribes or clans had achieved a measure of dominance which by the beginning of the 5th century had brought a group known as the Yamato people to a position of supremacy in central Japan. In the eventual recognition of the leader of one clan as the sovereign of the Yamato people, we see the beginnings of the tradition of imperial rule in Japan. But despite the obedience nominally due to the head of the imperial clan, the other clans claimed independence and the history of Japan for many succeeding centuries is a record, on the one hand, of attempts by powerful clan leaders to supersede or dominate the imperial clan and, on the other, of efforts by the imperial clan to form a centralized, monarchical state. (Cf. Sir George B. Sansom, *A History of Japan to 1334,* Stanford, Calif., 1958.)

The "Geographical Notes" in the *Han Book* (historical records of the Chinese Han Dynasty, 202 B.C.-220 A.D.) states that the Ainu people had more than 100 states, and among them the strongest was Yamato, ruled by Queen Birfu. This is probably the earliest account about Japan, written long before any of Japan's own records. 漢書地理誌記載，蝦夷有一百餘國，其中最強大者是卑爾呼女王所領導之耶馬 台。耶馬台復轉稱太和。蝦夷在漢書中又稱倭奴，本於)音，不必有賤視之意。

63. In 1868, a new era opened in the history of Japan. The feudal rule of the islands, upheld for almost 700 years, came to a close. With the easy overthrow of the Tokugawa, Japan took a major step in uniting into a modern nation. (Cf. William G. Beasley, *The Modern History of Japan,* 2nd ed., New York, 1974, p. 98-116.)

"In the West the territorial theory of government now holds universal sway, but in the Orient traces of the old popular organization can still be seen. In Japan

The above historical accounts merely provide some examples. Similar records may be found in the history of any country, and a clearer picture can be seen in the formation of modern federations:

The Germans were impacted into a federation of 25 states[64] by the Franco-Prussian War in 1871. Before that, they had experienced a number of confederations[65] and early had lived for a long time under a common spiritual crown in hundreds of small groups.[66]

---

until 1868 the political unit was not a territorial parish but the Kumiai, a group of five families." (William M. McGovern, "The Growth of Institutions," in *Making Mankind,* New York, 1929, p. 100)

64. They are: Prussia, Bavaria, Wurtemberg, Saxony, Baden, Mecklenburg-Schwerin, Hesse, Oldenburg, Brunswick, Saxe-Weimar, Mecklenburg-Strelitz, Saxe-Meiningen, Anhalt, Saxe-Coburg, Saxe-Altenburg, Waldeck, Lippe-Detmold, Schwarzburg-Rudolstadt, Schwarzburg-Sondershausen, Reuss-Schleiz, Schaumburg-Lippe, Reuss-Greiz, Hamburg, Lubeck, and Bremen. (Cf. William H. Dawson, *The German Empire, 1867-1914,* New York, 1919, vol. 1, chap. X.)

65. The first was the Confederation of the Rhine. When the Roman Empire was finally dissolved in 1806, Napoleon set up the Kingdoms of Saxony, Bavaria, and Wurtemberg. The two latter states, with Baden and thirteen others, constituted themselves into a Confederation of the Rhine by a treaty negotiated at Paris. Eventually, thirty-nine members in all were admitted. This confederation existed until 1813 when Napoleon was driven across the Rhine. The next one was the German Confederation (1815-1866). Upon the overthrow of Napoleon, the Allies attempted to re-establish as far as possible the conditions which had existed prior to 1789, and a German Confederation was formed. The Constitution of the Confederation was drafted by a committee of the Vienna Congress during the presidency of Metternich. Germany was reorganized into thirty-eight states of widely varying sizes. By authorization of the Congress, these states were now brought together into a Confederation. The number of member states was increased to thirty-nine in 1817. Through successive changes the number was reduced to thirty-three before the dissolution of the Confederation in 1866. The third union was the North German Confederation set up by Prussia after the defeat of Austria in the War of 1866. It was essentially a federation, and included twenty-two states to the north of the river Main. Its principal political organs were: the President, the Federal Council, and the Diet. With the incorporation of the south German states, the North German Confederation was transformed into the German Imperial Federation in 1871. (Cf. Otto Planze, *Bismarck and the Development of Germany: The Period of Unification, 1815-1871,* Princeton, N.J., 1963.)

66. The historical connection of the German people may be traced back to the ninth century when the leadership of the powerful Frankish kings succeeded in welding most of the Germanic tribes together into the Christian universal monarchy of the Franco-Roman Empire, the nucleus and framework of the Holy Roman Empire, which was to follow. That strange political entity, later called the First Reich, was destined to last down to the age of Napoleon I. Throughout its existence, however, it was hardly more than a loose association of scattered Germanic tribes governed by their own dynasties, joined together at most by the spiritual idea of a common Imperial Crown. In the later period of the Holy Roman

After the Second World War, while East Germany adopted a unitary form of government, West Germany was reorganized into a federation of 9 states.[67]

To the south of Germany lies the Swiss federation of 22

Empire, there were in Germany more than seventeen hundred territorial possessions. After the Peace of Westphalia in 1648, these were consolidated into 355 states. The number shrank rapidly as various unions were formed. Only thirty-nine were left when the Congress of Vienna united them into the German Confederation, in 1815. (Cf. Arnold Brecht, *Federalism and Regionalism in Germany,* New York, 1945, p. 146-147; and Ivo D. Duchacek, *Nations and Men, International Politics Today,* New York, 1966, p. 41.)

67. They are: Bavaria, Bremen, Hesse, Wuerttemberg-Baden, Hamburg, Lower Saxony, North Rhine Westphalia, Schleswig-Holstein, and Rhineland-Palatinate. (Office of the U.S. High Commissioner for Germany, *Report on Germany, September 21, 1949-July 31, 1952,* the last page)

68. Switzerland is composed of twenty-two cantons, and three of them are divided into "half-cantons," as they are called, so that there are twenty-five units altogether. (Henry D. Lloyd, *A Sovereign People,* New York, 1907, p. 4)

69. The following table shows the Swiss cantons as distinct governmental entities before they came into the federation of 1848, and lists the dates of their entry into earlier confederations in which they retained their independent and sovereign status.

Dates of the entry of the Swiss Cantons into the Confederations:

Date	Canton	Date	Canton
1291	Uri	1501	Schaffhausen
1291	Schwyz	1573	Appenzell
1291	Unterwalden	1803	St. Gall
1332	Lucerne	1803	Graubunden
1351	Zurich	1803	Aragau
1352	Glarus	1803	Thurgau
1352	Zug	1803	Ticino
1353	Berne	1803	Vaud
1481	Freiburg	1814	Valais
1481	Solothurn	1814	Neuchatel
1501	Bale	1814	Geneva

(Francis O. Adams and C.D. Cunningham, *The Swiss Confederation,* London, 1889, p. xiii)

cantons.[68] It took more than 500 years to merge together the 22 small groups with their various languages and religions.[70]

---

70. Religious and linguistic divisions in Switzerland at about the beginning of the 20th Century:

Canton	Religion		Language			
	Protestant	Catholic	German	French	Italian	Romansch
Aragau	55%	44%	99%			
Appensell						
Outer	91%		99%			
Inner		94%	99%			
Bale						
City	78%	21%	99%			
Rural	67%	30%	96%			
Berne	86%	12%	83%	15%		
Freiburg	15%	84%	31%	68%		
St. Gall	40%	59%	98%			
Geneva	48%	49%	11%	84%		
Glarus	76%	23%	99%			
Graubunden	55%	45%	46%		14%	38%
Lucerne	5%	94%	99%			
Neufchatel	87%	11%	20%	77%		
Schaffhausen	87%		99%			
Schwyz		98%	99%			
Solothurn	25%	74%	98%			
Ticino		99%			98%	
Thurgau	70%	28%	99%			
Unterwalden						
Le haut		97%	97%			
Le bas		99%	96%			
Uri		98%	99%			
Vaud	84%	8%	9%	81%		
Valais		99%	31%	67%		
Zug		93%	99%			
Zurich	87%	12%	99%			

(Cf. Henry D. Lloyd, *A Sovereign People,* New York, 1907, p.4.)

71. Population of South Africa (1970 Census of South Africa):

Population		Percent of total population	
		1970	1960
Blacks	15,057,952	70.2	68.3
Whites	3,751,328	17.5	19.3
Coloureds	2,018,453	9.4	9.4
Asians	620,436	2.9	3.0
Total	21,448,169	100.0	100.0

The federation of South Africa is composed of the Cape of Good Hope, Natal, the Transvaal, the Orange Free State, with a combination of black, white, and various other peoples.[71] Among the blacks, there are 9 major ethnic groups,[72] and among the whites, there are two major racial origins,[73] with more than 10 religions.[74]

Nigeria is a new federation in West Africa. It has a central government which shares power with 12 regional units—6 in the north, 3 in the east, 2 in the west, and one in the midwest.[75] Its

72. Black ethnic groups of South Africa (1970 Census of South Africa):

Zulu	4,026,058	Shangaan-Tsonga	737,169
Xhosa	3,930,087	Swazi	498,716
West Sotho (Tswana)	1,719,567	Ndebele	414,769
North Sotho (Pedi)	1,603,854	Venda	357,919
South Sotho	1,451,790	Other ethnic groups	318,223

73. Distribution of English and Dutch descent in the Union of South Africa in 1936:

	English	**Afrikaans**	**Both Languages**
Cape Colony	297,077	461,356	10,692
Natal	141,550	38,301	3,727
Transvaal	318,090	452,252	23,192
Orange Free State	26,534	168,861	3,794
Total	783,251	1,120,770	50,411

(*Encyclopedia Britannica,* 1952 ed., Vol. 21, p.47)

74. Religions of the European population of the Union of South Africa in 1926:

Religion	**Number of Persons**	**Percent**
Nederduits-Gereformeerde-Kerk	831,713	49.61
Gereformeerde Kerk van Suid-Afrika	45,722	2.73
Hervormde Kerk	44,526	2.66
Anglican Communion	311,281	18.57
Presbyterian	79,516	4.74
Methodist	105,217	6.28
Lutheran	23,371	1.39
Roman Catholic	71,227	4.25
Baptist	17,316	1.03
Jewish	71,816	4.28
Others	77,478	4.46
Total	1,676,660	100.00

(*Official Year Book of the Union of South Africa, 1927-1928,* p. 888)

75. Nigeria, a former British colony and protectorate, achieved in-

population is made up of a wide variety of language and culture groups, the three principle linguistic groups corresponding to its major ethnic groups: the Ibo,[76] Yoruba,[77] and Hausa.[78]

---

dependence on October 1, 1960, and was joined by the northern part of the British Cameroons in July, 1961. Nigeria's extremely heterogeneous population of over 57,000,000 is made up of a wide variety of language and culture groups. Nearly 250 different languages have been identified. In addition to a distinct language, each group has its own customs, religion, and political organization. A federal system of government was established on May 27, 1967. (Cf. *Area Handbook for Nigeria,* by Foreign Area Studies of the American University, Washington, 1972, p. 1-11, 103-128, 239-248.)

76. Over 8 million Ibo inhabit the southeastern part of Nigeria between the Niger and Cross rivers. The population density in this area is very high, averaging approximately 300 persons per square mile, and in some places over 800 per square mile. The Ibo are a combination of linguistically and culturally related village groups. Before the British conquered the area, there had never been large states or even strong chiefs in Iboland. Their politics were a viable form of village-oriented democracy. Ibo traditional religion is a composite of ancestor worship and the belief in natural forces. Most Ibo, however, have become Christians. (Cf. *Area Handbook for Nigeria,* by Foreign Area Studies of the American University, Washington, 1972, p. 108-110.)

77. Southwestern Nigeria is the homeland of some 10 million Yoruba. Living predominantly in large towns, they have inhabited the territory west of the Nigeria River for over seven centuries. In contrast to the Ibo, the Yoruba at an early stage in their history developed powerful states, each with a king and bureaucracy. Although British and later Nigerian administration minimized the rulers' power, they are still an important part of Yoruba life. Before the British conquest, the Yoruba were more urban than any other people of Nigeria. Yoruba traditional religion is a complex form of animism, which in modern times has been deeply eroded by Christianity. (Cf. *Area Handbook for Nigeria,* by Foreign Area Studies of the American University, Washington, 1972, p. 110-111.)

78. The 7,500,000 Hausa and 4 million Fulani are the dominant ethnic groups in northern Nigeria. As early as the 13th century, the Hausa had established major city-states such as Kano, Zaria, and Katsina. Each separate Hausa state was govered by an emir and known as an emirate. Fulani pastoralists settled in Hausaland and overthrew their Hausa overlords in the 19th century, creating powerful kingdoms which owed allegiance to the sultan of Kokoto. Both the Hausa and Fulani are Muslims. Other major ethnic groups in the north include 2 million Kanuri and 1 million Tiv. (Cf. *Area Handbook for Nigeria,* by Foreign Area Studies of the American University, Washington, 1972, p. 106-108.)

79. India divided its territory into twenty-eight states and territories, and the states were again classified into three groups. The unit names are: (Part "A" States) Assam, Bihar, Bombay, Madhya Pradesh, Madras, Orissa, Punjab, Uttar Bradesh, and West Bengal; (Part "B" States) Hyderabad, Madhya Bharat, Mysore, PEPSU, Rajasthan, Saurashtra, and Travoncare-Cochin; (Part "C" States) Ajmer, Bhopal, Bilaspur, Coorg, Delhi, Himachal Pradesh, Kutch, Manipur, Tripura, Vindhya Pradesh; (Part "D" Territories) Andaman and Nicobar Isles, and Sikkim. (*India and Pakistan Yearbook,* 1951, p. 15)

In Asia, an Indian federation of 28 political units[79] was formed shortly after the Second World War with jurisdiction over an immense population[80] speaking no fewer than 800 languages.[81]

Stretching across Europe and Asia is the huge Soviet federation of 15 major units called Union Republics,[82] and within each of these

---

80. According to its 1971 census, India has an area of 1,261,811 square miles, including Jammu and Kashmir, and a population of 546,955,945.

81. India's census of 1961 lists 826 different languages, with the language of Pakistan omitted. The following table enumerates the languages of more than 3 million speakers. Major languages of India:

Language	Major area of usage	Number of speakers (in millions) 1961
Indo-Arayan		
Assamese	Assam	6.8
Bengali	West Bengal	33.9
Bihari	Bihar	16.8
Gujarati	Gujarat	20.3
Hindi	Uttar Pradesh	133.4
Kashmiri (a Dardic language	Kashmir	9
Marathi	Maharashtra	33.2
Oriya	Orissa	15.7
Pahari	Himalayan slopes	3
Panjabi	Punjab (Panjab)	10.9
Rajasthani	Rajasthan	14.9
Urdu	(Literary language of educated Muslims)	23.3
Dravidian		
Kannada	Mysore	17.4
Malayalam	Kerala	17
Tamil	Tamil Nadu	30.5
Telugu	Andhra Pradesh	37.6
Munda		
Santali	Bihar and West Bengal	3.2

82. As a result of territorial annexations effected in 1939-1940, the number of Union republics was increased from 11 to 16, but in 1956 the Karelo-Finnish SSR

are a great number of smaller units with various statuses.[83] Basically, all the units represent different ethnic groups which, taken together

lost its status as a Union republic and became an autonomous unit (the Karelian Autonomous SSR) within the Russian Soviet Federated Socialist Republic (RSFSR), reducing the number to 15, as shown in the following table—Area and population of the USSR:

Union Republic	Area (sq. mi.)	Population (1959 census)
RSFSR	6,593,000	117,534,315
Ukrainian SSR	232,000	41,869,046
Belorussian SSR	80,000	8,054,648
Uzbek SSR	158,000	8,105,572
Kazakh SSR	1,064,000	9,309,847
Georgian SSR	27,000	4,044,045
Azerbaidzhan SSR	33,000	3,697,717
Lithuanian SSR	25,000	2,711,445
Moldavian SSR	13,000	2,884,477
Latvian SSR	25,000	2,093,458
Kirghiz SSR	77,000	2,065,837
Tadzhik SSR	55,000	1,980,029
Armenian SSR	12,000	1,763,048
Turkmen SSR	188,000	1,516,375
Estonian SSR	17,000	1,196,791
	8,599,000	208,826,650

(Central Statistical Administration of the USSR, *National Economy of the USSR in 1960,* Eng. Tr. by U.S. Joint Publications Research Service, Washington, 1962.)

83. Each of the 15 Union Republics is inhabited by a predominant ethnic group. Further recognition is accorded the principle of nationality by the organization, within these main ethnic divisions, of smaller ethnic units described as autonomous Soviet Socialist republics, autonomous oblasts, and national okrugs. As of 1975, there were 20 autonomous republics, 8 autonomous oblasts, and 10 national okrugs. (*Stateman's Year-Book,* 1975-1976, p. 1388. Cf. *Handbook of Major Soviet Nationalities,* ed. by Zev Katz, Rosemarie Rogers, and Frederic Harned, New York, 1976.)

with these groups not recognized as political entities, exceed one hundred in number.[84]

In the course of 200 years, the well-known federation of the United States of America, which began with 13 colonies, has incor-

---

84. Ethnic composition of the population of the USSR in 1939:

Group	Percent	Group	Percent
Russians	58.41	Moldavians	0.15
Ukrainians	16.58	Karelians	0.15
White Russians	3.11	Karakalpaks	0.11
Uzbeks	2.86	Koreans	0.11
Tartars	2.54	Kabardinians	0.10
Kakakhs	1.83	Finns	0.08
Jews	1.78	Estonians	0.08
Azerbaidjanians	1.34	Kalmyks	0.08
Georgians	1.33	Latvians and Latgols	0.07
Armenians	1.27	Bolgars	0.07
Mordvians	0.86	Ingush	0.05
Germans	0.84	Adygeitsy	0.05
Chuvash	0.81	Karachayevtsy	0.04
Tajiks	0.72	Abkhasians	0.03
Krighis	0.52	Khakasy	0.03
Peoples of Daghestan	0.50	Oriots	0.03
Bashkir	0.50	Kurds	0.03
Turkmenians	0.48	Balkartsy	0.03
Poles	0.37	Iranians	0.02
Udmurts	0.36	Lithuanians	0.02
Maritsy	0.28	Chinese	0.02
Komy	0.24	Czechs and Slovaks	0.02
Chechentsy	0.24	Arabs	0.01
Osetians	0.21	Assyrians	0.01
Greek	0.17	Other groups	0.48

(Cf. Bernard Pares, *A History of Russia,* New York, 1953, p. 580-581.)

porated 50 states,[85] and its population has increased from about 4 million whites and negros, including a great number of slaves[86] to

---

85. The official admission dates in chronological order of the 50 states are as follows:

State	Date of admission	State	Date of admission
Delaware	December 7, 1787	Michigan	January 26, 1837
Pennsylvania	December 12, 1787	Florida	March 3, 1845
New Jersey	December 18, 1787	Texas	December 29, 1845
Georgia	January 2, 1788	Iowa	December 28, 1846
Connecticut	January 9, 1788	Wisconsin	May 29, 1848
Massachusetts	February 6, 1788	California	September 9, 1850
Maryland	April 28, 1788	Minnesota	May 11, 1858
South Carolina	May 23, 1788	Oregon	February 14, 1859
New Hampshire	June 21, 1788	Kansas	January 21, 1861
Virginia	June 25, 1788	West Virginia	June 20, 1863
New York	July 26, 1788	Nevada	October 31, 1864
North Carolina	November 21, 1789	Nebraska	March 1, 1867
Rhode Island	May 29, 1780	Colorado	August 1, 1876
Vermont	March 4, 1791	North Dakota	November 2, 1889
Kentucky	June 1, 1792	South Dakota	November 2, 1889
Tennessee	June 1, 1796	Montana	November 8, 1889
Ohio	March 1, 1803	Washington	November 11, 1889
Louisiana	April 30, 1812	Idaho	July 3, 1890
Indiana	December 11, 1816	Wyoming	July 10, 1890
Mississippi	December 10, 1817	Utah	January 4, 1896
Illinois	December 3, 1818	Oklahoma	November 16, 1907
Alabama	December 14, 1819	New Mexico	January 6, 1912
Maine	March 15, 1820	Arizona	February 14, 1912
Missouri	August 10, 1821	Alaska	January 3, 1959
Arkansas	June 15, 1836	Hawaii	August 21, 1959

The admissions dates for the first 13 states represents the dates on which the individual states ratified the Constitution. The date for Ohio was finally determined in 1953 by an enactment of the United States Congress. The rest are actual recorded dates.

more than 200 million[87] from almost everywhere and with almost
every kind of ethnic background.[88]

---

86. Composition of the United States population in 1790:

Total Population	3,929,214		
The North	1,968,040		
White		1,900,616	
Negro		67,424	
Free			27,070
Slave			40,305
The South	1,961,174		
White		1,271,390	
Negro		698,784	
Free			32,457
Slave			657,327

(U.S. Bureau of the Census, *Historical Statistics, 1790-1945,* 1949, Chap. B, 13,
48-50, 52-53, 60-62, 64-65)

87. Population of the United States, 1790-1970:

Census year	Population	Per square mile of land area
1790	3,929,214	4.5
1800	5,308,483	6.1
1810	7,239,881	4.3
1820	9,638,453	5.5
1830	12,866,020	7.3
1840	17,069,453	9.8
1850	23,191,876	7.9
1860	31,443,321	10.6
1870	39,818,449	13.4
1880	50,155,783	16.9
1890	62,947,714	21.2
1900	75,994,575	25.6
1910	91,972,266	31.0
1920	105,710,620	35.6
1930	122,775,046	41.2
1940	131,669,275	44.2
1950	151,325,798	42.6
1960	179,323,175	50.5
1970	203,184,772	57.3

(Based on *Statistical Abstract of the United States,* 1974, p. 5)

In addition to the seven modern federations listed above, there are nine others, all of them formed by a number of units.[89] These 16

---

88. The ethnic origins of the U.S. population, in addition to the native Indians, are reflected in the following immigration statistics:

Countries	1820-1965	Countries	1820-1965
All countries	43,291,273		
Europe	35,105,902	Poland	465,200
Albania	2,232	Portugal	297,363
Austria	3,761,145	Rumania	160,218
Belgium	194,432	Russia (USSR)	3,345,351
Bulgaria	66,732	Spain	196,972
Czechoslovakia	130,283	Switzerland	333,823
Denmark	356,389	Turkey in Europe	161,833
Estonia	997	Yugoslavia	71,983
Finland	29,185	Other Europe	49,747
France	709,359	Asia	1,202,077
Germany	6,845,239	China	416,695
Great Britain		India	16,209
England	2,998,344	Japan	345,155
Scotland	802,248	Turkey in Asia	208,050
Wales	93,359	Other Asia	215,968
Not Specified	798,321	America	6,548,294
Greece	506,479	Canada	3,798,798
Hungary	523,931	Mexico	1,367,056
Irish Free State)		West Indies	739,383
Northern Ireland)	4,704,251	Central America	167,752
Italy	5,041,268	South America	372,813
Latvia	2,166	Other America	102,492
Lithuania	3,470	Other areas	435,000
Luxembourg	2,372	Africa	57,150
Netherlands, the	343,114	Australia-New Zealand	88,038
Norway	848,191	Pacific Islands	22,128
Sweden	1,259,905	Not specified	267,684

(Based on *Statistical Abstract of the United States,* 1966, p. 94)

federations at the present time represent about 40 percent of the
world's population and cover more than half of the world's land.[90]

The above historical accounts, together with the figures, clearly
and strongly demonstrate how effectively the process of merging has
been working throughout the history and over the world for the law
of group expansion.

---

89. The number of their original units and the date of the adoption of federal
constitution are as follows:

Federation	Units	Year
Argentina	14	1853
Australia	6	1900
Burma	4	1947
Brazil	21	1891
Canada	4	1867
Malaysia	13	1963
Mexico	28	1824
Venezuela	21	1830
Yugoslavia	6	1946

(Based on the author's thesis, *Conditions for Federation,* 1956, tables no. 2, 8, 11,
12, 13, 17, 19, 20, 20. For Malaysia, cf. *The World Almanac,* 1964.)

90. Area and population of modern federations in 1971:

Federation	Area (sq.m.)	Population
Argentina	1,072,157	23,362,204
Australia	2,967,877	12,728,461
Brazil	3,286,470	93,215,301
Burma	261,789	27,584,000
Canada	3,851,787	21,569,000
India	1,261,810	547,367,926
Malaysia	128,430	10,434,034
Mexico	761,600	48,381,547
Nigeria	356,667	56,570,000
South Africa	471,442	21,448,169
Switzerland	15,941	6,269,783
USSR	8,649,489	241,720,134
United States	3,540,939	208,232,000
Venezuela	352,143	10,399,000
West Germany	95,742	59,378,500
Yugoslavia	98,766	20,504,216
Total	26,820,906	1,410,104,275
World	51,230,000	3,634,400,000
% in the world	52%	40%

(Based on *Information Please Almanac,* 1973, p. 308-309)

c.
For Our Existence

THE LAW OF GROUP EXPANSION IS NOT MADE BY HU-man beings,[91] yet it is an iron rule for our existence.

Existence is a struggle for all creatures. For the lesser creatures, it means avoiding instant dangers and procuring subsistence for immediate needs. For mankind, however, it means more. It requires the extension of peace[92] and the promotion of happiness.[93]

---

91. "Human beings never make laws; it is the accidents and catastrophes of all kinds, happening in every conceivable way, that make the laws for us." —Plato (Quoted by Emery Reves, *The Anatomy of Peace,* New York, 1946, p. 251)

92. History shows that the preference for peace is in any time universal. (For ancient society in this regard, cf. William G. Sumner and Albert G. Keller, *The Science of Society,* New Haven, 1927, Vol. 1, p. 392-397) Whether this preference is rooted in human nature, as some philosophers hold, or as Thomas Hobbs says, "The passions that incline men to peace are fear of death, desire of such things as are necessary to commodious living, and a hope by their industry to obtain them." (*Leviathan,* Part I, ch. 13), the conclusions of these philosophers are somewhat in accord: "All men agree on this, that peace is good." (*Leviathan,* Part I, ch. 15); "The object of war must be the establishment of peace." (Aristotle, *Politics,* VII, 14) "Peace is the first law of nature." (Charles L. de Secondat Montesquieu, *Spirit of the Law,* Book I, sect. 2) "Every society aims at peace." (Aurelius Augustius, *City of God, XIX)*

93. The pursuit of happiness has been essential to existence to meet man's growing wants and needs since the beginning of civilization, but was not fully understood and clearly recognized until the unanimous Declaration of Independence of the thirteen United States of America, July 4, 1776, in which it was asserted as one of the most important inalienable rights, next only to life and liberty. The part of the Declaration referred to reads as follows: "We hold these truths to be self-evident: that all men are created equal, that they are endowed by their Creator with certain unalienable rights, that among these are life, liberty, and the pursuit of happiness."

94. The perceived glamor of war comes out of the inexperience of those who have not known its deadly furies. The agonies of war do not touch, in any practical way, those who direct its operations, or those who sit down at their leisure and under a comfortable atmosphere write about the art of war. For a few, of course, war offers the occasion for chivalrous exploit; but for the others it means the organized and deliberate destruction of all that makes life good, as well as fear, starvation, maimed lives, disease, and death; in short, it creates a threat to man's very existence. "War is forceful enough. The trouble with it is that it gets promptly out of hand and runs its own course. To start a war is like throwing society upon the mercies of some ruthless natural process concerning the nature of which men

We have to extend peace, because war has been a serious threat to our existence[94] since very early times.[95] We have to promote happi-

---

know very little. It is a sort of abdication of reason.... The trouble with war is that while it may cure the disease, it is likely to kill the patient." (William G. Sumner and Albert G. Keller, *The Science of Society,* New Haven, 1927, Vol. I, p. 409-410. Cf. Albert G. Keller, *Through War to Peace,* New York, 1921, chaps. III and IV; William G. Sumner, "Purposes and Consequences," in his collected *Essays,* New Haven, 1934, Vol. I, p. 11-19.)

In Australia, "strangers invariably look on each other as deadly enemies. Now-a-days, when accidentally brought together, they usually feign friendship; but, before the Whites interfered with native manners, no Black ever neglected to assassinate a stranger at the moment that he could do so without risk to himself.... The Australian Black, without exception, nurtures, one might almost say from the cradle to the grave, an intense hatred of every male at least of his race who is a stranger to him. The reason they themselves assign for what I must term this diabolical feeling is, that all strangers are in league to take their lives by sorcery. The result of this belief is that, whenever they can, the Blacks in their wild state never neglect to massacre all male strangers who fall into their power. Females are ravished and often slain afterwards if they cannot be conveniently carried off." (E.M. Curr, *The Australian Race,* Melbourne and Leipzig, 1887, v. 1, p. 64, 85-86)

"I have heard Akamba say that they dislike all foreigners, but they hate each other.... it is that natives living quite close to each other remain perfect strangers, not necessarily because they have an old account to settle, but because from old habit the Mkamba has nothing to do with 'strangers.' I have known this to be the case with villages not half an hour apart. And being now unable to settle his old grievances, the Mkamba turns to litigation and perseveringly adheres to some old claim to foster his hostile inclinations. Thus despite Government and order the Akamba of Kitui continue to live as isolated as they can, caring nothing for the fate and fortune of most of their neighbours and utterly opposed to undertaking anything in common." (C. Dundas, "History of Kitui" in the *Journal of the Anthropological Institute of Great Britain and Ireland,* XLII, p. 485-486)

In New Guinea, "for the most part every village has been at bitter hostility with its neighbor since ancient times." (H. Blum, *Neu-Guinea und der Bismarck-archipel,* Berlin, 1900, p. 23)

"There are people in Madagascar who are said to live in such constant suspicion and dread of an enemy that they never bathe in their houses but only in the open air; and even then they wash only one side of the face at a time, leaving one eye open and one hand grasping gun or spear." (Albert G. Keller, *Man's Rough Road,* New York, 1932, p. 16)

95. "In the eighteenth century it was assumed that the primitive state of mankind was one of Arcadian peace, joy, and contentment. In the nineteenth the assumption went over to the other extreme—that the primitive state was one of universal warfare.... The proper course, if one is looking for the truth and not defending a thesis, is to go to the facts instead of inferring or meditating. So doing, one finds that there are very few peoples who do not quarrel and use violence and that these few are generally, if primitive, in such isolation that there is no one to fight or so poverty-stricken that they have nothing to tempt aggression." (William G.

ness to meet our growing wants which, with the advance of civiliza-tion[96] have become increasingly inseparable from our existence.

War is a conflict between groups, particularly between indepen-

---

Sumner and Albert G. Keller, *The Science of Society,* New Haven, 1927, vol. 1, p. 368-369. Also cf. William G. Sumner, Collected Essays, Vol., chap. 1 and 2. For "Or-igin of War," cf. Quincy Wright, *A Study of War,* 2nd ed., Chicago, 1965, p. 29-41)

"Back in the Palaeolithic Age an even more certain indication of cannibalism is that human bones, including the skull, were often made into tools. So that in the earliest period of his existence, man seems to have been, as he still is, the biggest enemy of man. If a tribe of the Old Stone Age met a strange tribe who was trespass-ing without permission on their hunting grounds or their special magic rites, the encounter was often far more dangerous for both sides than any between a hunter and an unexpected, huge wild beast." (Fritz Heichelheim, *An Ancient Economic History,* rev. and complete English ed., Leiden, 1958, v. 1, p. 14)

In New Guinea, a cause of strife among the natives is the custom that a youth, before he can chew sirih, that is, be counted as an adult, must have 'fetched a head.' (M. Krieger, *Neu-Guinea,* Berlin, 1899, p. 416)

Guise enumerates twelve badges of distinction for warriors, the standard be-ing the number of lives taken. (Cf. R.E. Guise, "On the Tribes Inhabiting the Mouth of the Wanigela River" in the *Journal of Anthropological Institute of Great Britain and Ireland,* XXVIII, p. 213.)

"Among the nomadic or unsettled Indian tribes, especially the Algonkins and Sioux, the young men are expected to display their bravery by taking scalps; and a race of farmers, hunters, and fishermen, like the Iroquois, would be tempting vic-tims." (H. Hale, *The Iroquois Book of Rites,* Philadelphia, 1883, p. 92)

96. "Human wants and desires are countless in number and very various in kind. . . . The uncivilized man indeed has not many more than the brute animal; but every step in his prograss upwards increases the variety of his needs together with the variety in his methods of satisfying them. He desires not merely larger quantities of the things he has been accustomed to consume, but better qualities of those things: he desires a greater choice of things, and things that will satisfy new wants growing up in him. Thus though the brute and the savage alike have their preferences for choice morsels, neither of them cares much for variety for its own sake. As, however, man rises in civilization, as his mind becomes developed, and even his animal passions begin to associate themselves with mental activities, his wants become rapidly more subtle and more various; and in the minor details of life he begins to desire change for the sake of change, long before he has conscious-ly escaped from the yoke of custom." (Alfred Marshall, *Principles of Economics,* 8th ed., New York, 1920, p. 86)

"In developed nations of the world today, where energy is abundant and available, it is often hard for people to realize that for most of man's stay on earth he has had to struggle to obtain enough food energy to remain alive. The average citizen of the United States uses at least 200 times as much energy as had one of his food-gathering ancestors, and this rate continues to rise alarmingly even as the world's population soars." (Professor David M. Evans, in *Encyclopedia Americana,* 1973 ed., v. 10, p. 342, under "Energy")

dent groups.⁹⁷ It is independent groups by whom most wars are fought,⁹⁸ and it is independent groups for whom most wars are fought.⁹⁹ So, whenever and wherever there are many independent

---

97. The term war is generally applied to armed conflict between groups. Armed conflict between groups that legally enjoy complete and unlimited sovereignty is typically treated as war in modern thought. Within such a group conflict between provinces, sections, religious units, political parties, or economic classes, is defined as insurrection or rebellion. Professor Quincy Wright's definition, as given in his famous *A Study of War*, 2nd ed., Chicago, 1965, p. 698, is: "War is a legal condition which equally permits two or more hostile groups to carry on a conflict by armed force."

War, as a social phenomenon, has been defined as "a fight between human societies, in primitive conditions between savage tribes, in the civilized world between states." (Quoted by Joachim V. Elbe, *The Evolution of the Concept of the Just War in International Law*, 1939, p. 665)

The term war is generally applied to "armed conflict between population groups conceived of as organic unities." (G.L. Dickinson, *Causes of International War*, London, 1920, p. 7)

According to the Greek idea, war did not merit the name unless it was between Greeks and strangers. (J.C. Burckhardt, *Griechische Kulturgeschichte*, Stuttgart, 1898, v. 1, p. 327-328)

As we know, mankind has lived in a series of groups: the early single family, primitive community, clan, tribe and nation. While within each of these groups there is peace, yet between these groups "there exist, as a rule, uncontrolled and unreconciled antagonisms; and the regular way of settling them, though not the only one, is the primal mode of violence." (William G. Sumner and Albert G. Keller, *The Science of Society*, New Haven, 1927, vol. 1, p. 355)

98. Since very early times, war has been fought by independent groups: the early single family, primitive community, clan, tribe, and nation. These groups have successively been the fighting body with traditional and legitimate rights to wage war, with the power to get money and men, organized and equipped to fight, and always on the alert and in a position for armed struggle. There were wars in history initiated by church or class, but neither church nor class has been a fighting body. There were also wars waged by fractional forces within a group, such as the so-called "civil war," but most major wars in history were fought by independent groups, appearing as inter-clannish war, inter-tribal war, and international war.

99. It is because most important objects of war have been generally regarded as either belonging to, or as inalienable rights of independent groups as a whole. These objects include: in primitive times, hunting ground and pasture, and later, territory and resources, commonly security and defense, and not unusually, aggression and conquest. Indeed, women, thrones and personal power have often been objects of war, but mostly of "civil war." Wars between independent groups for these objects are usually claimed or interpreted as fighting primarily for the group, not merely for any particular person.

100. The natives of New Caledonia believed they had increased in number from early times. "They accounted for it by there being less war now than formerly. Still, it was war, war, war, incessant war! They said that formerly they did not stop a fight until one party was killed right out to the verge of extinction, but that

groups, there will be more wars.[100] It follows, therefore, that the best way to eliminate war is to reduce independent groups.

---

now they are more merciful.'' Raid and foray, massacre and pillage, were the order of the day in New Zealand and did not cease until the whites came. (J. Cowan, *The Maoris of New Zealand,* Christchurch, 1910, p. 3-5)

W. Junker reported that ''the history of the African peoples has been, in the course of the millennia, undoubtedly a frightfully bloody one. Among savage communities that live in the darkness of superstition and in slavery, acknowledge only the might of the stronger, and without cessation war upon, subject, or oppress one another, it is indeed hardly thinkable that it was anything else. Even in the most recent history and in the present it is not otherwise.'' (*Reisen in Afrika,* Wien, 1875-1886, v. 3, p. 292; cf. also v. 2, p. 271.) The Berbers, too, in an arid habitat, show a ''state of eternal warfare existing among themselves.'' (W.B. Harris, ''The Berbers of Morocco'' in the *Journal of the Anthropological Institute of Great Britain and Ireland,* XXVII, p. 64)

The dominant and aggressive Sea Dyak are a ''ruthless destroyer of tribes, which, owing to an inherent and fatal weakness, are already tottering to the verge of extinction.'' (C. Hose and R. Shelford, ''Materials for a Study of Tatu in Borneo'' in the *Journal of the Anthropological Institute of Great Britain and Ireland,* XXXVI, p. 60)

The Aru Islanders ''are rarely without fighting somewhere.'' (A.R. Wallace, *The Malay Archipelago: The Land of Orangutan and the Bird of Paradise,* London, 1872, p. 471)

In Timorlaut, there are incessant intertribal fights and no one dares go beyond the palisades without spear and bow. (H.O. Forbes, ''Ethnology of the Timorlaut'' in the *Journal of the Anthropological Institute of Great Britain and Ireland,* XIII, p. 21)

''All of Nauru is a scene of war,'' even boys carrying weapons. Feuds arising out of trade are common. (A. Bastian, *Die Mikronesischen Colonien aus Ethnologischen, Gesichtspunkten,* Berlin, 1899, p. 5-6)

When Turner first visited the Loyalty Islands, in 1845, ''a chronic state of war prevailed, and each island was divided into two parties.... Kidnapping from one another was common. These and others who fell in battle were dressed for the oven. They were inveterate cannibals.'' The Tannese lived in a state of perpetual war. They were fighting during five out of the seven months that Turner lived among them. ''There is ample proof there,'' he states, ''that war is the enemy of civilisation and the element of savage life. We were never able to extend our journeys above four miles from our dwelling at Port Resolution.'' (G. Turner, *Samoa: A Hundred Years Ago and Long Before,* London, 1884, p. 337, 312-313)

Between the different tribes in the regions inhabited by the Jibaros of Ecuador, there exists almost perpetual enmity and destructive wars are often carried out, especially between neighboring tribes. (R. Karsten, ''Blood Revenge, War, and Victory Feasts among the Jibaro Indians of Eastern Ecuador'' in *Bureau of American Ethnology Bulletin,* LXXIX, 1923, p. 14-16)

''One South American tribe believes that their deity has bidden them live by making war on others, taking their property and wives and killing their men.'' ''A certain Brazilian tribe regards it as a natural duty to kill the members of a neighboring weak people, preserving the victims' heads as trophies. Almost every

This is just what the law of group expansion has been doing, merging small independent groups together as a larger one, step by step. As soon as the smaller groups lose their independence in the large group, the chances for war between them diminish, and peace is normally extended over the whole large group.

By pursuing the merging process step by step, the law of group has been successful in extending peace from normally inside of the early single family to nation-wide,[101] while reducing warfare from the

---

tribe has its open tribal enemy.'' ''The Botocudos are in constant war with neighboring peoples.'' ''Of the Fuegians: The different tribes have no government or chief, yet each is surrounded by other hostile tribes, speaking different dialects, and separated from each other only by a deserted border or neutral territory.'' ''Among the Araucanians armed raids were constantly made on the neighboring villages, and thus a continual state of warfare was kept up.'' (William G. Sumner and Albert G. Keller, *The Science of Society,* New Haven, 1927, vol. 4, p. 130-131)

101. ''If we put together what we have learned about the mitigation of war and the measures to prevent and limit it, we see that there has been a persistent drift toward peace. This becomes the clearer when one considers the progressive increase in the size of the peace-group. The degree to which war could be excluded at any time has always been a question of how large a body of people could become an in-group. Far back in the evolutionary series the family seems to have been the largest peace-group; then as civilization increased kin-association took on greater scope. The clan or gens, composed of a number of families, and at length the tribe, composed of several clans or gentes, appear as peace-groups of a wider comprehensiveness. At length comes the nation, which might be figured as a super peace-group including all the rest.'' (William G. Sumner and Albert G. Keller, *The Science of Society,* New Haven, 1927, vol. 1, p. 395-396)

Quincy Wright makes a somewhat similar observation when he says, ''Political groups have increased in size from the clan, village and tribe to the kingdom, nation and federation; and peace has been striven for within these enlarging areas with varying degrees of success.'' (His *A Study of War,* 2nd ed., Chicago, 1965, p. 6)

''If human history can be said to have a pattern, the basic trend has been toward the abolition of armed conflict over larger and larger areas of the earth. First, fighting was ended within tribal areas; next, within nations; and, finally, between nations in such large regions as Scandinavia and North America. As war has been abolished in ever-widening communities, so civilization has been developed. Law has grown. Justice has prevailed. Knowledge has advanced. And the arts have flourished.'' (Philip Noel-Baker, in *Encyclopedia Americana,* 1973 ed., v. 21, p. 439a, under ''Peace.'' Mr. Noel-Baker was the 1959 recipient of the Nobel Peace Prize and the author of *Arms Race: A Program for World Disarmament,* New York, 1958.)

102. Among primitive peoples, there is little or no fixed differentiation between the fighters and the rest except upon the basis of sex and age. Even among the Aztecs, ''with the exception of children, old people, infirm or crippled persons, and sometimes priests, everyone had to go to war. . . . There was no standing

early times when every man had to be a fighter as well as a hunter for a lifetime[102] to a situation in which only a limited number of people are recruited to be soldiers for a limited time.[103]

In the same way, the law of expansion has been successful in promoting happiness by meeting our growing needs.

Basically, our growing wants can be met only by increasing our productive power, and our productive power can be increased only by applying useful tools and effective methods.

The most effective method ever applied to increase productive power is the division of labor, the advantages of which have been recognized since the time of Plato.[104] But it was Adam Smith who exploited the principle of the division of labor as the foundation of his

---

army, the available force being composed of all the able-bodied men of the tribe of Mexico." (O.T. Mason, *The Origin of Invention,* New York, 1895, p. 370)

Speaking of the Ismailia: "Every man is a warrior from his childhood, as the Baris are always at war." (S.W. Baker, *Ismailia,* New York, 1875, p. 135.)

In Northeast Africa, "the sole field that they cultivate is the field of the dead." The whole life of the Somali and others is a permanent campaign; only he remains victor who can use his weapons promptly and skillfully. "Neither the development of spiritual nor that of physical strength guarantees life; he only possesses it to whom his lance has become staff, and his dagger mattock and spade." "The picture of armed children and women, which the traveller encounters everywhere, impresses upon the landscapes of Africa's eastern horn a characteristic stamp. Even the construction of the weapons, the majority of which are designed for close fighting, indicates the never-ceasing feuds among the tribes themselves and a world in arms. To be unarmed (hubla) is regarded as the same thing as being naked." (P. Paulitschke, *Ethnographie Nordost Afrikas,* Berlin, 1896, v. 1, p. 109)

103. Adam Smith's penetrating discussion of the "Expense of defense," in *An Inquiry into the Nature and Causes of the Wealth of Nations,* Book V, Ch. I, suggests a diminution of the proportion of the population engaged in war from practical unanimity in hunting and pastoral societies, to 20-25 per cent (all able-bodied men between seed time and harvest) among simple agriculturalists, to only 1 per cent in the industrial society of the time in which he wrote (1776).

104. The farmer produces more food than he needs, while the shoemaker produces more shoes than he can wear. Hence it is advantageous to both that each should produce for the other, since both will be better fed and better clothed by working together than by each dividing his work to make all the various things he needs. This rests, according to Plato, upon two fundamental facts of human psychology; first, that different men have different aptitudes and so do some kinds of work better than others, and second, that skill is gained only where men apply themselves steadily to the work for which they are naturally fitted. "We must infer that all things are produced more plentifully and easily and of a better quality when one does one thing which is natural to him and does it at the right time, and leaves other things." (*Republic,* 370c. Cf. George H. Sabine, *A History of Political Theory,* New York, 1938, p. 48-50.)

famous economic theory,[105] attaching its importance to the progress of history.[106] There are two major forms in the division of labor, intensive specialization [107] and extensive regionalization.[108] Both forms

---

105. "The author of the *Wealth of Nations*—a work whose fame has not been dimmed by time—explained the influence of the division of labour on a society's productivity. Soon the idea was widespread that the further the lengths to which the individuals in a community push the specialization of their particular activities, the greater will be the production of that community—or, as Bentham put it, the more means of happiness will they create." (Bertrand de Jouvenel, *On Power, Its Nature and the History of Its Growth,* trans. by J.F. Huntington, New York, 1949, p. 52)

106. The principle of the division of labor had been expounded by several of the mercantilist writers before Adam Smith. Smith, however, surpassed their treatment of the subject not only in the thoroughness of his analysis, but even more in the importance he attributed to the phenomenon in his theory of economic progress: "The greatest improvement in the productive powers of labour, and the greater part of the skill, dexterity, and judgment with which it is anywhere directed, or applied, seem to have been the effects of the division of labour." (Adam Smith, *An Inquiry Into the Nature and Causes of the Wealth of Nations,* Book I, Ch. 1)

The development of the division of labor may have been, as Adam Smith believed, not the result of any human wisdom, which foresaw and intended the general opulence to which it would give occasion, but the necessary, though very slow and gradual, consequence of a certain propensity in human nature. (*Ibid,* Book I, Ch. 2) Or it may be, according to Emile Durkheim, a result of the struggle for existence. (Cf. his *The Division of Labor in Society,* trans. by George Simpson, New York, 1933, Book II, Ch. 2) Whatever the arguments, however, their conclusions are the same: the division of labor brings mankind the greatest advantage by increasing and improving products. For this reason, the division of labor has been extended as far as possible at any time. The history of mankind may be viewed as simply the ever-widening application of the principle of the division of labor. Some historians even use it as a standard to measure progress, on the grounds that only through it could mankind have progressed.

107. The specialization began when mankind first tried to use his forefeet to hold his prey. By dint of practice he developed a hand-like claw, and after innumerable attempts, he balanced the whole of his body upon the hind legs. A primitive social application was the division of labor between the two sexes, according to which the men went to war, hunted, fished, and made the tools necessary for these pursuits, while the women cared for the shelter and prepared food. The next application was the separation of different trades and employments. A further application was the division of a specialized craft into separated processes, and the specialization of "detail" workers for each of these processes. The classic illustration is that of pin-making as given by Smith: "One man draws out the wire, another straightens it, a third cuts it, a fourth points it, a fifth grinds it at the top for receiving the head; to make the head requires two or three distinct operations; to put it on is a peculiar business; to whiten the pin is another; it is even a trade by itself to put them into a paper; and the important business of making a pin is in this manner divided into above 18 distinct operations, which in some manufactories

are actuated by exchange,[109] and consequently the extension of exchange is the key to the development of the division of labor.[110]

---

are all performed by distinct hands. In this way 10 men could make about 48,000 pins in a day, whereas, if they worked separately and independently, they certainly could not each of them have made 20, perhaps not one pin a day." "This is," enumerates Smith, "owing to three different circumstances: first to the increase of dexterity in every particular workman; second, to the saving of time which is commonly lost in passing from one species of work to another; and lastly, to the invention of a great number of machines which facilitate and abridge labor, and enable one man to do the work of many." (Adam Smith, *An Inquiry Into the Nature and Causes of the Wealth of Nations,* Book I, Ch. 1)

108. Regionalization is the division of labor by areas, affected by resources, raw materials, communication, soil, climate, traditional crafts, etc. It is the twin of specialization. When the two sexes began to specialize in their work, regionalization began by the fact that the men worked in the forest, while the women worked in the house; each sex was master of its own field of activity. Later, when handicrafts separated from agriculture, the artists congregated in the cities, while the farmers remained in the country. The advanced form of regionalization is the division of labor between districts, and even between countries. Adam Smith says, for example, that the silks of France are better and cheaper than those of England, because silk manufacturing is not so well suited to the climate of England as that of France. But the hardware and coarse woolens of England are superior beyond all comparison to those of France, and are also much cheaper. (Adam Smith, *An Inquiry Into the Nature and Causes of the Wealth of the Nations,* Book 1, Ch. 1)

The chief advantages of regionalization come from the opportunities for greater specialization which concentration affords. Where many factories engaged in the same industry are grouped together, the worker has a better chance to use his specialized skill and is encouraged to specialize still further. The industry, moreover, can command a large number of varied services which no single factory could afford and no scattered industry could maintain. Among the most important of such services are the special transport facilities and the subsidiary industries, supplying the major industry with its machinery and the incidental requirements of manufacture, and utilizing its by-products.

109. Exchange originates in the mutual dependence which arises from the limited capacity of an individual to supply his own wants, and the natural diversity in the capacities of individual men, which makes individuals able to supply each other's wants. The art of exchange is possessed by mankind alone. We have seen some other animals, such as the ant and bee, live under a system utilizing division of labor. But we have never seen any other animals make a fair and deliberate exchange with one another. This is why the division of labor can be carried much further by mankind than by the other animals. And this is also why mankind can be superior to all other animals. Through exchange, people are satisfied by giving and receiving the different products of their respective talents. The gains of both sides in exchange are mutual and reciprocal and the division of labor is in this, as in other cases, advantageous to the different persons employed in the various occupations into which it is subdivided. And through exchange, people are able to utilize mutually and to enjoy reciprocally the various resources of different areas. Exchange is not only a method of transmitting the advantage of the division of

To extend exchange, it is necessary to overcome the various social, political and economic barriers, which have always existed as hindrances to exchange between independent groups since very early times.[111] Where there are more independent groups, there are more hindrances to exchange; therefore, the best way to eliminate such hindrances is to reduce the number of independent groups. This is just what the law of group expansion has been doing, merging small independent groups together as a larger one, step by step.

As soon as the smaller groups lose their independence in the large group, hindrances to exchange between them are normally eliminated, exchange can be extended, and the division of labor can be developed.

With the development of the division of labor, along with the im-

---

labor to all, but also a condition for the advance of the division of labor itself. Without exchange, every man must have procured to himself every necessity and convenience of life which he wants. All must perform the same duties, and do the same work, and there could be no such difference in employment as could alone give occasion to a great difference in talents. (Cf. Adam Smith, *An Inquiry Into the Nature and Causes of the Wealth of the Nations,* Book 1, Ch. 2.)

110. "As it is the power of exchanging that gives occasion to the division of labour, so the extent of this division must always be limited by the extent of that power, or, in other words, by the extent of the market. When the market is small, no person can have any encouragement to dedicate himself entirely to one employment, for want of the power to exchange all that surplus part of the produce of his own labour, which is over and above his own consumption, and for such parts of the produce of other men's labour as he has occasion for." (Adam Smith, *An Inquiry Into the Nature and Causes of the Wealth of the Nations,* Book 1, Ch. 3; cf. the whole chapter. Also cf. George Stigler, "The Division of Labor Is Limited by the Extent of the Market," *Journal of Political Economy,* 1951, v. 59, p. 185-193.)

111. Even highly civilized ancient Greece, for instance, was handicapped by the barriers existing between its city-states. "Greece was badgered by serious political problems that ate away its strength. For one thing, Greece never achieved political integration, but remained divided into city-states, which reduced the size of its domestic market, mitigated against an extension of the division of labor, and led to rivalries which resulted in intermittent wars." (Shepard B. Clough, *The Economic Development of Western Civilization,* New York, 1959, p. 41)

As a result of the situation described in the above note, "in ancient Greece, specialization of craft or trade is found only on the broadest lines; a man could turn his hand to almost any task. The first specialization approaching distinctness was that of the smith, who did almost all the work in metals. He derives his name and the names of his tools from the metal copper, but his operations were not confined to it. He worked in gold, silver, tin, and iron, and his function did not stop even there, for he sewed the leathern parts of shields and otherwise supplemented his main work. There is in Homer no clearly marked case of division of labor in the manufacture of any single product." (Albert G. Keller, *Homeric Society,* New York, 1902, p. 80, and cf. to p. 84 for full references to the typical case portrayed by Homer.)

provement of tools, comes an increase in productive power, and with the increase in productive power comes the promotion of happiness to meet our growing needs. It is not difficult to appreciate how far we have advanced in happiness if we just look back over our "original destitution"[112] and compare our life in general with that of some of the peoples who still lag behind in the primitive situation.[113]

---

112. The point that man began in destitution, and not, as the fairytale of old times would have us believe, in a "state of nature" in which there was a free abundance of food, as well as peace, brotherly love, justice, liberty and equality, has been made clearly in the section entitled "Original Destitution" in *The Science of Society* by William G. Sumner and Albert G. Keller, New Haven, 1927, Vol. 1, p. 95-97 and Vol. 4, p. 20-26.

Man started from an unfavorable position, for he originally lived within a limited habitat, probably a tropical jungle. He satisfied his appetite with a narrow and definite range of foodstuffs. He had no natural weapons, such as fangs, claws, or horns; nor was he protected by a thick skin or great speed of movement. He was thus vulnerable in his own body and exposed to many dangers because of the long maturation of the young. In short, he was the very poor captive of his physical environment when he began his struggle. Albert G. Keller in his *Man's Rough Road,* New York, 1932, p. 83, pointed out that "it is a basic fact that men start with nothing. What needs explanation is not poverty but wealth. Poverty is not 'caused' by others' oppression; it is there, as a zero-line from which all departure toward wealth is reckoned."

113. There is no evidence whatsoever of the conditions of equality and abundance which the utopians have pictured as the state of natural peoples. The only purpose of life for the natives in Southwest Africa, writes C.G. Büttner in *Das Hinterland von Walfischbai und Angra Pequena,* Heidelberg, 1884, p. 229, "is to fill their bellies with something that looks edible; they eat gum arabic, the pounded roots of trees, steal grass seed from ants, and regard a swarm of locusts as a blessing."

Of certain natives of Borneo we learn: "Like the animals of the bush they pass a rambling life, caring only for the satisfaction of their subsistence-needs.... They remain where nature affords them for a time sufficient sustenance, later to seek out new sources of existence. With tillage of any sort whatsoever they are wholly unacquainted; for food they use all sorts of animals, even the most loathesome, together with sago and wild fruits. They do not want salt and believe that fatal sicknesses rise from the use of it." (C.A.L.M. Schwaner, *Borneo,* Amsterdam, 1853, I, p. 229-230)

"The natives of New Zealand, by no means the lowest of mankind, were pinched for food in the 'grumbling months' of winter. They had no other name for them, being a blank in their calendar, as they could do nothing but sit in their smoky huts, with eyes always filled with tears. Among the American Indians known to the Jesuit fathers, starvation was common, and after eating their skin clothing, and even the lacings of their shoes, the natives ate one another." (Albert G. Keller, *Man's Rough Road,* New York, 1932, p. 83)

114. "The world has progressed to its present high position—a position in which the average man leads a more comfortable and prosperous life than has ever before been the case in the world's history—by the integration of small political

Since the law of group expansion can extend peace, and promote happiness,[114] no wonder it is an iron rule for our existence.

---

units into ever larger states, and the consequent abolition of the innumerable wars that formerly raged between every neighboring little principality.'' (Oscar Newfang, *The Road to World Peace,* New York, 1924, p. 62)

115. "The notion that primitive populations are directly limited by the food supply is prevalent, and, further, that the type of community life in itself determines how many individuals can be fed in a given locality. We have then, in theory, a kind of vicious circle in which primitive man is caught and his numbers held approximately at one level. This circle is supposed to function thus: a hunting people depends upon the game within walking distance of its camp. They may increase this radius by occasionally shifting their base, provided they are not opposed by other camps. Yet, in any case, if they kill an excess of game, the number of animals will decrease, and the penalty will be direct or indirect starvation. So automatically, without thought on the part of the community, a balance would be preserved between the number of game animals and the human population.'' "This is what was meant by the statement that the type of life followed in a community determined its food supply and this in turn, the population. That this is generally true, is indicated by taking certain specific areas for comparison. For example, New England seems to have supported about 25,000 Indians in aboriginal days, but the population of English colonies displacing them soon rose to several times that number, whereas the population of present-day New England is counted in millions. Changes in mode of life and the mechanisms for feeding go hand in hand with such increase.'' (Clark Wissler, *An Introduction to Social Anthropology,* New York, 1929, p. 28-29)

"First, we find societies at widely varying levels of economic productivity with consequent differences in population size and in social complexity. Some are lowly hunters and gatherers with a simple band type of social organization. Others are hunters in a rich environment, or horticulturalists and pastoralists with a larger society, compounded of several segments, forming a tribe. A few primitive societies reached a productivity which permitted large populations and a complex state organization. Finally, some are peasant or "folk" communities, local rural subcultures within contemporary national states.'' (Elman R. Service, *A Profile of Primitive Culture,* New York, 1958, p. x)

"The kin-based communities of Bushmen and Bergdama are very small, seldom exceeding twenty elementary families and often, especially among Bergdama, consisting of less than half a dozen; the heterogeneous communities of Hottentots and Bantu are very much larger, many Bantu tribes especially having 20,000 members or more. These differences in size are related partly to mode of subsistence, since the nature of the food supply necessarily determines how many people can live together continuously. Bushmen and most Bergdama, as hunters and collectors, depend entirely upon the natural resources of their environment. Both Hottentots and Bantu also hunt game and gather wild foods. But Hottentots, further, keep cattle and sheep, which are available at all times and normally tend to increase by reproduction. Bantu have a still more regular and abundant source of food, since they not only keep livestock but grow various crops that can be stored for future use. They are consequently able to provide for much larger populations

d.
Mode of Life

OUR EXISTENCE HAS ALWAYS BEEN A MATTER OF UR-
gency. Why has the law of group expansion worked so slowly for it?
It has taken thousands of years to expand step by step from the early
single family to the nation. Why did it not go all the way without interruption?

The answer to these questions may be found in the physical conditions to which the law of group expansion is subject, and the most
important physical condition may be found in the mode of life,
which represents the basic ways of procuring subsistence from nature
for our existence.

The importance of the mode of life to group expansion lies in the
fact that the size of the group in both population and territory is virtually controlled by the mode of life: the population is always determined by the subsistence the mode of life can provide,[115] and the territory is always limited to the range suitable for the mode of life to
operate.[116] This fact gives rise to the most important physical condi-

---

than Bushmen, Bergdama, or even Hottentots.'' (Isaac Schapera, *Government
and Politics in Tribal Societies,* London, 1956, p. 34)

"Biologically speaking, the term *overpopulation* is somewhat misleading. All
species normally produce more young than can survive to adulthood. The number
that does survive is limited by the available requirements for living, principally
food and space. Thus, all populations normally expand to the limits permitted by
the resources available to that population." (Clement L. Markert, "Biological
Limits on Population Growth," in *Population Crisis: An Interdisciplinary
Perspective,* ed. Sue T. Reid and David L. Lyon, Glenview, Ill., 1972, p. 40. Also
cf. in this book the article "Population Density and the Style of Social Life,"
Nathan Keyfitz, p. 112-117.)

116. "We have noted that the size of the primitive community will vary according to the environment and the form of life, but it is conceivable that there are
limits to the range in size. It is clear that three or four adults cannot support a series
of social institutions; hence, there must be an approximate average minimum for
each region and for each type of life. On the other hand, there will also be an upper
limit in size, because too great a concentration will prevent adequate feeding, fueling, etc. When all the necessities of life must be carried on the backs of men and
women, the area from which subsistence is drawn will be reduced to walking
radius. We should expect, then, to find primitive peoples living in small groups."
"That there is also a lower limit to the size of a hunting community is shown by the
necessity for reserve hunters and for defenders of the community. A single hunter

tion: group expansion can go only as far as the mode of life allows, and any further expansion depends on a change in the mode of life.

There have been five significant consecutive changes in the mode of life in the course of economic evolution up to modern times: food-gathering, hunting-fishing, hoe-cultivation, animal-raising, and agriculture.[117] They have generally corresponded by group expansion with five group sizes: the early single family, primitive community, clan, tribe and nation.

The food-gathering people had to live from day to day and from place to place.[118] Their food-supply from the wild land was generally

---

and his dependents presents too great a hazard, even in a country rich in game." (Clark Wissler, *An Introduction to Social Anthropology,* New York, 1929, p. 33, 39)

"Mode of subsistence also affects patterns of settlement. Bushmen and Bergdama must wander about intermittently, following the movements of game and the growth of wild plants. The Hottentots, owing to the grazing and water needs of their livestock, are also essentially nomadic. The Bantu in contrast tend to be sedentary, since cultivation ties them to the soil, nor need they ever go far for new land when their fields are exhausted." (Isaac Schapera, *Government and Politics in Tribal Societies,* London, 1956, p. 34. Cf. Melville J. Herskovits, *The Economic Life of Primitive Peoples,* New York, 1952, p. 331-370.)

117. This is a general ordering of the five significant modes of life in our economic history. There are bound to be some exceptions because of long periods of time and various environments. It seems that some peoples never had a proper hoe-cultivating life before entering a life of animal-raising, and some others never had a proper animal-raising life before entering an agricultural life. Again, as of today, there are peoples who have jumped from an agricultural life to a new life—industrial, while some others are still maintaining a life of food-gathering.

It should be noted that in some regions and under certain circumstances, the domestication of animals appeared to precede or parallel hoe-cultivation, making a jump or by-pass in group life for some peoples from the primitive community directly to tribe. (Cf. Lewis H. Morgan, *Ancient Society,* New York, 1877, p. 22-26.)

118. ". . . in the course of the Old Paleolithic Age. Man had to gather his daily food from Nature with great trouble and adapt the means it offered him without being particularly fastidious about the food which presented itself. Modern research terms such a primitive way of living 'The Stage of the Foodgatherers.' Men and women gathered everything for their use which grew in a given area, and then went on to another locality. . . . There are such wandering tribes today whose existence may be taken as a parallel for the way of life of the Paleolithic peoples: Australian natives, Papuans, some Saharan and Red Indian races." (Fritz Heichelheim, *An Ancient Economic History,* rev. and complete English ed., Leiden, 1958, v. 1, p. 10-11)

Certain Orinoco peoples always travelled from river to river collecting wild fruits, never built houses, and had no shelter from sun or rain. (W.E. Roth, "An Introductory Study of the Arts, Crafts, and Customs of the Guiana Indians," in *Bureau of American Ethnology,* XXXVIII, p. 214-215)

Certain peoples of the Malay States are said to have "subsisted entirely on the

meager and irregular.[119] They had to grasp everything available to satisfy their immediate needs.[120] Nature was not under any kind of control. Their life was highly hazardous and subject to the element of chance or luck and to changes in weather and the seasons.[121] It is no wonder, under these circumstances, that a group larger than the early single family could hardly exist.

---

root of the tapioca plant, wild herbs gathered by the women, and animals trapped or killed with the aid of the blow-pipe by men. . . . They changed camping ground at least three or four times in the course of a year. They had no system of chieftain-ship, nor did they look up to any single person as their head." (F. W. Knocker, "Notes on the Wild Tribes of the Ulu Plus, Perak," in *Journal of the Anthropological Institute of Great Britain and Ireland,* XXXIX, p. 146)

119. It is estimated, based on observations of the Australians, American Indians, and other aboriginals of very low status, that the amount of land required to support an individual food-gathering life runs from several to tens of square miles, except under favorable or unfavorable environmental conditions. (Cf. William G. Sumner and Albert G. Keller, *The Science of Society,* New Haven, 1927, v. 4, p. 17-19; and A.R. Brown, "Three Tribes of Western Australia," in *Journal of the Anthropological Institute of Great Britain and Ireland,* XLIII, p. 146-147.)

120. In the food-gathering stage, men "picked berries, harvested nuts, and foraged for tubers, the eggs of birds and reptiles and the seeds of plants, which came to be called grains. They did some hunting, clothed themselves, if at all, in skins, and sought shelter in caves, thickets, or trees. They had no surplus to allow leisure for pursuits other than the satisfying of bodily needs. Indeed, it is probable that, much like hibernating animals, they had to rely on their own fat rather than on stores of food to get them through the unproductive seasons of the year." (Shepard B. Clough, *The Economic Development of Western Civilization,* New York, 1959, p. 20)

The conditions of life during this stage have been reconstructed in story form by several authors, such as: *Before Adam,* by J. London, in his *Works;* and *The Story of Ab,* by S. Waterloo, New York, 1901.

There are also a number of actual cases which may be found in William G. Sumner and Albert G. Keller, *The Science of Society,* New Haven, 1927, v. 4, p. 8-9.

121. ". . . man is dependent upon what he can gain as a naked animal, the amount and quality of his sustenance are limited. For physically he is, as the savages well realize, inferior in power, speed, and other qualities to most of his fellow-animals. . . . And so, when forced to exist by the collection of available plant and animal food, his successes cannot be conspicuous. In order to get enough to support life, he must have recourse to an extended range of land. The supporting power of any given area is necessarily small, since it can be worked only in the most superficial and extensive manner. Hence an artless population, at the limit of this available supporting power of land, must remain sparse. Population, thus quantitively limited, was also kept down in quality. For the food-supply, besides being meager, was both irregular and of low quality. . . . Inevitably, the whole matter of living is highly hazardous and subject to the element of chance or luck." (William G. Sumner and Albert G. Keller, *The Science of Society,* New Haven, 1927, v. 1, p. 51-52)

The hunting-fishing people[122] still had to wander about here and there, but their fishing ability began to be a great resource for subsistence.[123] They were also able to gain more and better subsistence by aggressive hunting,[124] especially of big game.[125] Because of the exten-

---

122. In this stage, some peoples in certain areas adjacent to water courses, lakes, or the sea, depended mainly on fishing for a living; others in mountain, steppe, or plain regions, relied mainly upon hunting game, while still gathering anything else available for subsistence. The success of the mesolithic hunter was his ability to use a wide range of food sources, both animal and vegetable. A good example is the early Maglemosian settlement of Star Carr in Yorkshire. It covered some two hundred square meters and was probably seasonally occupied from October to April, for 12 to 15 years, by some 16 to 25 individuals, of whom five were adult males able to hunt large game. The community fished and collected food on the coast in the summer and hunted game and wildfowl in the winter. (Cf. J.G.D. Clark, *Excavations at Star Carr: An Early Mesolithic Site at Seamer Near Scarborough, Yorkshire,* Cambridge, England, 1954.)

123. "In fish must be recognized the first kind of artificial food, because it was not fully available without cooking. Fire was first utilized, not unlikely, for this purpose. Fish were universal in distribution, unlimited in supply, and the only kind of food at all times attainable. . . . Upon this species of food mankind became independent of climate and of locality; and by following the shores of the seas and lakes, and the courses of the rivers could, while in the savage state, spread themselves over the greater portion of the earth's surface. Of the fact of these migrations there is abundant evidence in the remains of flint and stone implements of the Status of Savagery found upon all the continents." (Lewis H. Morgan, *Ancient Society,* New York, 1877, p. 21)

124. In the hunting-fishing stage, "a given range is worked more intensively through their use than it can be by mere collection. Hence more people can live on and form a unit area. Not only is there more food, together with more adequate clothing and shelter, but it is of better quality and diet is more diversified. This makes for an increase of quality as well as of quantity in population." (William G. Sumner and Albert G. Keller, *The Science of Society,* New Haven, 1927, v. 1, p. 53)

There have been some estimates regarding the supporting power of land upon the hunting-fishing stage. Whereas under difficult environmental conditions, one person may need several square miles for his support, relatively favorable circumstances allow for a population of as high as one per square mile. (Cf. William G. Sumner and Albert G. Keller, *The Science of Society,* New Haven, 1927, v. 4, p. 179-199; and Clark Wissler, *An Introduction to Social Anthropology,* New York, 1929, p. 30-36.)

125. "From the bones found by excavations and the contemporary paintings and sculptures, we know that the animals which were mainly hunted were hippopotamus, elephant, mammoth, rhinoceros, wild horses, ox, deer, reindeer, elk, bison, ibex, chamois, boar, hare, and rabbit. Small animals were hunted also, but apparently more occasionally and mainly in the later periods. Probably man preferred to gain large portions of meat with one stroke." (Fritz Heichelheim, *An Ancient Economic History,* rev. and complete English ed., Leiden, 1958, v. 1, p. 13. Also cf. John E. Pfeiffer, *The Emergence of Man,* New York and London, 1969, Chapter VI, "The Rise of Big-Game Hunting and the Psychology of the Hunt.")

sion of fishing and hunting, more people were apt to live and work together,[126] thus forming the primitive community.

In the hoe-cultivation stage,[127] people still more or less depended on hunting and fishing for a living. But they started to invest labor in cultivating the land to produce food, thus opening up a relatively

---

In the Young Paleolithic Age, when big game was successfully hunted, hundreds of people might live close together in rock shelters or open encampments, as indicated by the spectacular paintings and engravings at cave sites such as Lascaux in France and Altamira in Spain. Normally, however, they lived in small groups, the primitive community roving here and there. "Larger groups could not find sufficient food for any length of time and might only meet in large numbers for a short time of festivity." (Fritz Heichelheim, *An Ancient Economic History,* rev. and complete English ed., Leiden, 1958, v. 1, p. 11)

The fact that aggressive hunting requires more people to work together may be illustrated by the following hunting method: "As artificial means of frightening hunted animals into traps, lanes were formed through which the animals were driven towards rocks and down steep cliffs, where the hunters fell on them. In France the remains of tens of thousands of wild horses show how efficient these methods were." (*Ibid,* v. 1, p. 13)

127. "... Here we see a significant transition taking place: the shift from a food-gathering to a food-producing economy, which we associate with the Neolithic Age. Paleolithic and Mesolithic men were hunters and fishermen; our Neolithic ancestors were also farmers and herdsmen. The overall result comprised what has been described as the first economic revolution in the history of man—and in the view of some scholars, perhaps the most far-reaching breakthrough in the dynamite relationship of man to his external environment." (Alastair M. Taylor, Nels M. Bailkey, Mark Mancall, and T. Walter Wallbank, *Civilization Past and Present,* 6th ed., Glenview, 1970, v. 1, p. 20-21)

Hoe-cultivation may have been developed by women. "Woman always had the chance of finding a modest supply of the different plants needed for food. While hunting and fishing vary in their success, both require courage and cunning, and only are carried out at great risk. Preferably woman sought to find some plants that grow quickly, to char them from the ground with tools or by hand. Later on she even may have planted seeds or cuttings. In this way she arrived finally at the correct method of setting plants and at the cultivation of gardens." (Fritz Heichelheim, *An Ancient Economic History,* rev. and complete English ed., Leiden, 1958, v. 1, p. 11)

128. With hoe cultivation, man started to invest his labor for a later return rather than for immediate gain; to produce something rather than merely to gather, hunt and fish; and to utilize the land positively rather than to merely rely upon what it offered.

"Undoubtedly the most important of the cultivated grains were related to our wheat and barley and were selected from the seeds which food gatherers had been gleaning from mountains and marshes. In certain places Neolithic man had rice, millet, Indian corn, yams, manioc, and squash. Besides the dog, he numbered goats, sheep, cattle and pigs among his animals." (Shepard B. Clough, *The Economic Development of Western Civilization,* New York, 1959, p. 24-25)

reliable source of subsistence.[128] They also started to domesticate animals for meat.[129] These adventures not only tended to increase the size of the group, but also made life more tied to the land, resulting in less wandering.[130] For these reasons, the clan gained ground.

From the archaeological evidence, southwestern Asia—including most of what is now called the Middle East—seems to have been the focus of hoe-cultivation. This region was the homeland of wheat and barley. In addition, it furnished rye, peas, lentils, broad-beans, onions, garlic, carrots, grapes, olives, dates, apples, pears, cherries, flax, and a great many other plants. At the lowest level excavated at Jericho in Jordan, artifacts of hoe-cultivation have been found dating from 9500 B.C.; at this time hunting and gathering were still important. By around 8000 B.C., emmer wheat and barley were being grown by villages in a wide zone extending from Asia Minor to Western Iran and south into Israel and Jordan. Neolithic sites, with evidence of hoe-cultivation, have been discovered in Iraq, Jordan, Turkey, and Cyprus. About 2500 B.C., the Neolithic North Chinese grew two kinds of millet, kaoliang sorghum, dry rice, hemp, wheat, and probably mulberry. Irrigation was present by about 1500-1050 B.C., but wet rice was not cultivated until a later date. (Cf. Eliot C. Cumen and Gudmune Hatt, *Plough and Pasture,* London, 1946, p. 10-25. Also cf. Carl O. Sauer, *Agricultural Origins and Dispersals,* New York, 1969, and Karl J. Narr, "Early Food-Producing Populations" in *Man's Role in Changing the Face of the Earth,* ed. by William L. Thomas and others, Chicago, 1955, p. 134-151.)

129. It is widely held that the dog was the first domesticated animal. Archaeological evidence indicates that the next animals to be domesticated were sheep and goats. At Zawi Chemi in Iraq, archaeologists have found bones of sheep dating from around 9200 B.C. The initial motive in domesticating sheep and goats was to have a source of meat when game was scarce. Wool was not yet gathered from sheep, and goats were presumably not yet regularly milked. The third major animal to be domesticated was the pig. Archaeologists have found some evidence of domestic pigs by 5500 B.C. in southern Turkey. Pigs do not congregate in large herds and are far less mobile than sheep, goats, or cattle; they thus fit well into sedentary village economies. Like dogs, pigs may have been self-domesticated, attracted by opportunities for scavenging. Cattle also are believed to have been domesticated very early, but there is no definite proof of this before 4000 B.C. In the New World, the Indians of Mexico and some other regions domesticated duck, stingless bees, and turkeys, along with their hoe-cultivation. The Indians of the Andean regions in South America also domesticated the llama and alpaca and even used the llama as a pack animal. (Cf. Friedrich E. Zeuner, *A History of Domesticated Animals,* London, 1963, p. 129-198, 256-271, 437-438; and C.A. Reed, "Animal Domestication in the Prehistoric Near East" in *Science,* no. 130, 1959, p. 1629-1639)

130. "The transition to hoe cultivation was far-reaching in its consequences, and its effect can be seen most easily in the increase of the size of the tribes. The number of children who reached adult age was greater. Large tribes and small groups increased in size. Definite camping sites were founded and inhabited. Cultivation of the plants in each of these new tribal areas followed a planned traditional cycle of events so that a change in the place of settlement was only made after the harvest once a year or so, and in particularly favourable climates no

There were two kinds of pastoral animal-raising lives: nomadic and settled. The nomadic pastoral people moved from place to place, but usually according to a seasonal mass-migration, reappearing in the same regions at regular intervals.[132] The settled pastoral people

---

change at all was necessary." (Fritz Heichelheim, *An Ancient Economic History,* rev. and complete English ed., Leiden, 1958, v. 1, p. 33)

"While Paleolithic and Mesolithic peoples could not develop any permanent settlements or accumulate an excess of food, a food-producing economy was radically different. By cultivating plants or by stock breeding, men could now add to the food acquired by hunting. As a consequence, they greatly increased their control over the external environment. A food-producing way of life required permanent settlements and also enabled larger populations to be sustained. Any food surplus could be put aside for planting the following year's crops or, alternatively, was available as barter to obtain various commodities not locally produced." (Alistair M. Taylor, Nels M. Bailkey, Mark Mancall, and T. Walter Wallbank, *Civilization Past and Present,* 6th ed., Glenview, 1970, v. 1, p. 22)

A French-Syrian archeological expedition discovered an 8,500-year-old village revealing much about the critical period when man changed from a nomadic hunter to a settled farmer. The village, the best preserved settlement of its time uncovered in the Middle East, was found beneath a deserted hill called Tel Ramad, 15 minutes southwest of Damascus. It was the outcome of annual excavations begun in 1963. According to Henri De Contenson, French expert on prehistoric archeology and head of the joint expedition, houses in the village were huts built of dried mud and straw and roughly circular in shape. Wheat, barley, lentils, beans and almonds were found in the barns of the houses, he said. Tests by botanical laboratories have proved the grains were cultivated by man and did not grow wild. (AP, Farouk Nassar reported from Damascus, Syria, *South Bend Tribune,* date and p. to be added.)

131. "The Animal-Raising or Pastoral Stage has all the arts of the hunting stage, out of which it develops, plus one of exceeding importance: the domestication of animals. . . . domestication means breeding in captivity; it is therefore considerably more than taming, and normally includes that." (William G. Sumner and Albert G. Keller, *The Science of Society,* New Haven, 1927, v. 1, p. 56)

The domestication of animals began much earlier than the pastoral stage. What is the difference between domestication in earlier times and that during the pastoral stage? Generally speaking it is the difference between primitive and advanced, between amateur and professional. Techniques in taming, breeding, etc., were much improved in the pastoral stage. Some of the larger animals, such as cattle and horses, were not domesticated until the pastoral stage. Furthermore, in the pastoral stage, animals were domesticated in the herds rather than a few at a time, and for longer term gains of milk, wool, etc., rather than merely for meat, as in earlier times. (Cf. Douglas English, *Friends of Mankind,* New York, 1924, p. 42-95.)

132. "The Pastoral stage has been called also the nomadic stage. . . . The wanderings of genuinely and typically pastoral peoples are indeed spectacular. They practice a seasonal mass-migration, reappearing, however, in the same regions at regular intervals. This migration is imposed upon them by the distribution of the water-supply and the exhaustion of pasture-areas. It is no wonder that they came by the distinctive title of nomads, yet their movements were of different

led a sedentary life,[133] but they wanted a tighter and larger organization to protect themselves and their herds, just as the nomadic pastoral people did.[134] Both utilized the land extensively, assuring more subsistence.[135] Thus, the tribe developed.

---

type from that of the hunters, being migratory and less desultory. They moved about as a body, as a society, not as individuals or segregated small family-groups. They populated a shifting emplacement rather copiously.... They had their greater numbers, and these remained in proximity and contact. Their nomadism, though striking in its manifestations, did not have as a consequence the negation of organization." (William G. Sumner and Albert G. Keller, *The Science of Society,* New Haven, 1927, v. 1, p. 57)

The pastoral people could still remain nomads, to be sure, but their wanderings were not restricted to where food could be found for themselves anymore. They could go anywhere food could be found for their herds.

133. The life of those who settled down in some areas to raise animals has much in common with the nomadics, but is more stable. The population of the two kinds of pastoral people "can become more dense and remain in closer contact.... The herds are capital and form insurance against the ills of life.... Hence a heightening of confidence and of other qualities leading to continued success; hence also a further freeing of energies from the animal-routine of food-getting and assimilation.... There is a further development of foresight, of the arts, and of civilization in general, and a higher potency is lent to the mutual action and reaction between numbers and civilization." (William G. Sumner and Albert G. Keller, *The Science of Society,* New Haven, 1927, v. 1, p. 57)

134. "Moreover, economic features of vast importance were introduced in the fact that the herds of a people became a natural prey of less civilized peoples of the same region. It became necessary, therefore, to make provision for the protection of the herds, and in so doing an increased feeling of communal unity was necessarily engendered.... It is curious to reflect on these two opposite results that must have grown almost directly from the introduction of the custom of domesticating food animals. On the one hand, the growth of the spirit of war between tribes; on the other, the development of the spirit of tribal unity, the germs of nationality." (*The Historians' History of the World,* 1907, v. 1, p. 48)

135. The pastoral life "very materially extends the supporting power of the land and so allows of a great increase of number over the figure for the hunting stage. Sustenance is more copious, better in quality, more regular. The land is utilized more intensely—in fact, it may be cleared of vegetation altogether by the grazing and close cropping of cattle and sheep." (William G. Sumner and Albert G. Keller, *The Science of Society,* New Haven, 1927, v. 1, p. 56)

"The domestication of animals provided a permanent meat and milk subsistence which tended to differentiate the tribes which possessed them from the mass of other barbarians." (Lewis H. Morgan, *Ancient Society,* New York, 1877, p. 25)

"The domestication of food-producing animals not only brought man a more dependable source of animal protein than the produce of the hunt, but also further expanded the number of people the earth could support, since those animals provided a means of converting into human food many plants that are not edible by man." (Ralph W. Phillips, "The Livestock Industry: Its Scope and Potential" in

The agricultural mode of life[136] has been relatively peaceful and stable, depending primarily on longer-term gains. It has naturally led to a much larger group for more security.[137] After all, agriculture can extend the supporting power of the land several times over the capabilities of animal-raising,[138] and produce much more subsistence for

---

the *Introduction to Livestock Production including Dairy and Poultry,* ed. by H.H. Cole, San Francisco, 1966, p. 2)

136. The Agricultural Stage was initiated by the domestication of plants, but tillage has advanced far beyond mere hoe cultivation. Utilization of the land has expanded not only to wider coverage, such as was encouraged by Shang-yang, the famous statesman of the early Chin Dynasty in China, 商鞅開阡陌 , but also in intensity, to actual penetration beneath the surface, tapping into the earth's resources in a way which went beyond the superficial skimmings of preceding stages.

137. "Hunters and pastoral nomads have been typically warlike throughout their course. The agriculturist has no such characteristics fostered in him by contact with plant-life. He becomes, in a word, industrial. His qualities are those of patience and perseverance in labor rather than of aggressiveness and violence against animal and human competitors.... For agriculture, as it advances in efficiency, demands a progressive renunciation of movement from place to place. The tiller stays by one piece of improved land, investing in it more and more of his labor and capital and seeing it gain steadily in value. From short-season crops he advances at length to the planting of vines and trees whose bearing-period will outlast his own life-time. He wants title in perpetuity and has no idea at all of abandoning his holdings and moving on. He thus automatically develops a degree of foresight clear beyond that of any previous stage.... except on the basis of agriculture no high culture has ever developed. By staying in one place and holding, without loss or diffusion, the gains of successive generations, a real civilization can be built up and retained." (William G. Sumner and Albert G. Keller, *The Science of Society,* New Haven, 1927, v. 1, p. 59-60)

138. It was estimated that the supporting power of the land from agriculture was from 4 to 25 times as much as from pasture. (Cf. E.C. Semple, *Influence of Geographic Environment on the Basis of Ratzel's System of Anthropo-Geography,* New York, 1911, p. 65. The referred F. Ratzel's work was translated as *The History of Mankind,* 3 vols., New York, 1896-1898. Also cf. J.H. Dudgeon, *The Land Question, with Lessons to be Drawn from Peasant Proprietorship in China,* Glasgow, 1886, p. 9.)

One acre of the midwestern American corn belt, if used to grow maize, will produce three million calories of food. If it is used to produce milk, it will provide only 700,000 calories, and for raising beef, only 100,000 calories ... Meat, worldover, needs twenty times the land cereals do. (Cf. C.L. Walker, *Man and Food: Headline series* no. 73, 1949, p. 21.)

139. "Agriculture represents a momentous advance in the art of life, with a corresponding effect upon numbers, for it immensely extends the supporting power of land. The food-supply is more copious, of better quality, and more variegated.... Further, when methods of brand-tillage and the use of manure have been discovered, the land is not merely exploited but its productivity is restored and maintained. Population may increase to limits hitherto unimagined

dense populations.[139] So, with the development of agriculture, the nation began to emerge.

The correspondence of the five sizes of group to the five modes of life confirms how the most important physical condition for group expansion has actually worked: group expansion can only go as far as the mode of life allows, and any further expansion depends on a change in the mode of life.

---

and may remain in closer contact than ever before." (William G. Sumner and Albert G. Keller, *The Science of Society,* New Haven, 1927, v. 1, p. 58)

"Moreover, dense population in limited areas now became possible. Prior to field agriculture it is not probable that half a million people were developed and held together under one government in any part of the earth. If exceptions occurred, they must have resulted from pastoral life on the plains, or from horticulture improved by irrigation, under peculiar and exceptional conditions." (Lewis H. Morgan, *Ancient Society,* New York, 1877, p. 26-27)

Of the agricultural development in Europe, for instance, "by the early ninth century all the major interlocking elements of this revolution had been developed: the heavy plough, the open fields, the modern harness, the triennial rotation. . . . the northern plains where the heavy plough was appropriate to the rich soils, where the summer rains permitted a large spring planting, and where the oats of the summer crop supported the horses to pull the heavy plough. It was on those plains that the distinctive features both of the late medieval and of the modern worlds developed. The increased returns from the labour of the northern peasant raised his standard of living and consequently his ability to buy manufactured goods. It provided surplus food which, from the ninth century on, permitted rapid urbanization. . . . And in this new environment germinated the dominant feature of the modern world: power technology." (Charles Singer, "East and West in Retrospect" in *A History of Technology,* Oxford, 1956, v. II, p. 774)

140. Tools may be regarded as extensions or projections of the body's physical endowments. The hammer, for example, is the lengthened arm with a harder and heavier fist at the end; the mill represents more powerful 'molars.' Without tools, we would not be able to survive, because physically we are inferior to many of the other creatures in strength, speed, and other qualities, and we could not compete with them in the struggle for existence. The use of tools is not an exclusively human trait, naturally shaped tools being used by insects, birds, and certain mammals. However, tool-using is most characteristic of man, and tool-making is almost by definition human. (Cf. Kenneth P. Oakley, *Man the Tool-Maker,* 3d ed., Chicago, 1957.)

"The most important contribution of the preliterary period to human material culture lay in the origins of tools, thus making possible a more efficient conquest of nature by man than would have been possible by his unaided hands. The importance of the tool in human history becomes startlingly clear when we realize that to a considerable degree the measure of human progress lies in the progressive development of tools, and that tools are the instruments of control with which man attained whatever mastery over nature he possessed down to the rise of modern machinery." (Harry E. Barnes, *An Economic History of the Western World,* New York, 1937, p. 5. Cf. Franz C. Muller-Lyer, *History of Social*

e.
Tools and Energies

WHAT, THEN, CAN CHANGE THE MODE OF LIFE? IT IS the development of tools[140] and energies.[141] The reason for this is simple but fundamental: the mode of life represents the basic ways of procuring subsistence, and procuring subsistence depends primarily

---

Development, New York, 1921, Book II, chap. 2, for the rise of tools and their significance.)

141. The ultimate source of energy available to man is the sun, the huge thermonuclear furnace that supplies the earth with the heat and light essential to life. The solar energy that reaches the earth's surface is used by green plants to convert carbon dioxide and water into various energy-storing compounds. When such plants are eaten, the energy stored in their tissues is transferred to and used by animal bodies, spreading throughout the food chain. In addition, the remains of plants and animals buried in the sands and muds of swamps and seas millions of years ago were transformed into the fossil fuels—coal, liquid petroleum, and natural gas—that provide a large percentage of the energy consumed by man today. The sun's heat also evaporates water from the oceans, which is carried by winds which are themselves driven by the thermal energy of the sun.

Some of this water falls on land as rain or snow and eventually returns to the sea in streams and rivers. Thus the wind that fills the sails of ships and turns the vanes of windmills and the water that spills over waterwheels and spins turbines are also forms of solar energy. The story of man can be told in the ways he has learned to convert these various sources of energy to his own uses. At first he knew of only one basic source: the food he needed simply to remain alive. He then learned to use fire, the energy of rapid combustion, animals' energies, and other natural energies.

The forms of natural or raw energy upon which man has drawn to transform them into what is useful for the preservation of his life and the furthering of his projects, have been classified by an eminent chemist, W. Ostwald, into the following five categories: mechanical energies; heat; light; electric and magnetic energies; and chemical energies. Ostwald, whose theory is that the relation of society to the energies in nature is its fundamental relation, goes on to show that human systems and economies are directed toward the maximum use, or the minimum waste and neutration, of these several nature-given resources. (Cf. W. Ostwald, *Energetische Grundlagen der Kuturwissenschaft,* Leipzig, 1909, p. 13-14.)

"Man appropriates, in the domesticated animal, a sort of living tool or weapon which, within limits, can be shaped to his hand as are other implements. There are certain works of man whose accomplishment is dependent upon his disposal over animal forces much surpassing his own.... Concentration of animal energy under his control has meant more for man's advancement than this age is wont to recognize." (William G. Sumner and Albert G. Keller, *The Science of Society,* New Haven, 1927, v. 1, p. 211)

on tools and energies.[142] When there is a great development in tools
and energies, there is necessarily a great change in the mode of life.
This is why the five typical modes of life: food-gathering, hunting-
fishing, hoe-cultivation, animal-raising, and agriculture have
generally gone along with the five important ages in the development

---

142. Is the mode of life determined by environment as geographical determinism holds? "The study of the cultural history of any particular area shows
clearly that geographical conditions by themselves have no creative force and are
certainly no absolute determinants of culture. Before the introduction of the horse
the western American prairies were hardly inhabited, because the food supply was
uncertain. When the Indians were supplied with horses their whole mode of life
changed, because buffalo hunting became much more productive and the people
were able to follow the migrating herds of buffalo.... Another example will not
be amiss. The Arctic Indians and Eskimos and those of the tribes of Siberia are not
the same. The Americans are exclusively hunters and fishermen. The Asiatics have
domesticated reindeer.... The environment can only act upon a culture and the
result of environment influences is dependent upon the culture upon which it acts.
Fertility of the soil has nowhere created agriculture, but when agriculture exists it is
adapted to geographical conditions. Presence of iron ore and coal does not create
industries, but when the knowledge of the use of these materials is known,
geographical conditions exert a powerful influence upon local development."
(Franz Boas, *Anthropology and Modern Life,* rev. ed., New York, 1932, p.
240-242. Cf. also: Julius Lippert, *The Evolution of Culture,* translated and edited
by George P. Murdock, New York, 1931, p. 160-186.)

143. There has been no generally accepting chronological division of our appropriation of energies from fire, wind, water, and animals such as the dog, horse,
and ox. But the development of different forms of energy can be appropriately
discussed in terms of the tool ages, since development in converting energies
always keeps pace with that of making tools. Tools and energies virtually are inseparable. They are interdependent and interwoven.

"It was the combination of the use of tools and the use of inanimate energy
which caused the decisive step in the evolution of mankind. The application of fire
and its heat led to the transition from the Stone Age to the Bronze Age, and subsequently to the Iron Age, and in addition it rendered greater, by the provision of
warmth, the world's habitable area. For thousands and thousands of years,
through all the prehistoric ages, heat was the only form of inanimate energy used
by men. To do the work necessary to supply food, clothing, and shelter man had to
use his own muscles or those of his slaves or animals. It was only in historic ages,
many millennia after the invention of fire, that a small part of human and animal
labour began to be replaced by machines using the natural forces of water and
wind. The Chinese were probably the first to use windmills, and waterwheels,
originally devised by the Babylonians for irrigation, were used in the Roman Empire for driving mills—saw mills and hammer-mills." (Hans Thirring, *Energy for
Man, Windmills to Nuclear Power,* Bloomington, Ind., 1958, p. 31)

144. Since tools are so essential to the development of civilization, to the
most important materials used for tools has gone the honor of furnishing names
for the ages of history. Thus, archaeologists, anthropologists, historians, and

of tools and energies:[143] Old Stone Age, Young Stone Age, New Stone Age, Copper Age and Iron Age.[144]

In the Old Stone Age,[145] which may be traced back some million years,[146] we first appeared as naked animals,[147] and had practically

---

economists generally agree that we have the Stone Age, subdivided into the Old Stone Age (Paleolithic), the Young Stone Age (Young Paleolithic), and the New Stone Age (Neolithic), and the Metal Age subdivided into the Copper Age and the Iron Age. But the dates for these ages cannot be fixed with finality for the whole world, because peoples in different places have advanced at different rates, and even today it is possible to find man in nearly every historical stage. (Cf. Harry E. Barnes, *The History of Western Civilization,* New York, 1935, Vol. 1, p. 14-36.)

The use of the principal materials of tools to identify ages in a scientific sense was initiated in 1819 by Christian Jürgensen Thomsen, then director of the Danish National Museum. Thomsen divided the museum's collection into three chronological ages, which he called Stone, Bronze, and Iron.

It should be noted that there is a significant exception to the correspondence of the mode of life to tool age in sub-Saharan Africa, where hoe-cultivation appears not to have held firm ground until iron had been in use ("It is now generally held that there was no independent invention of agriculture in sub-Saharan Africa. The people of the savanna region of the Sudan, directly south of the Sahara and north of the forest, probably did not begin to cultivate crops until after 2000 B.C. In fact, the earliest important Neolithic farm culture yet identified dates from 800 B.C. to 200 A.D. Known as the Nok culture, it originated in northern Nigeria. Its people had begun to work iron and tin, and their most distinctive accomplishment was the production of strikingly beautiful terra-cotta sculpture." (Alastair M. Taylor, Nels M. Bailkey, Mark Mancall, and T. Walter Wallbank, *Civilization Past and Present,* 6th ed., Glenview, 1970, v. 1, p. 183) Yet even with the use of iron, the people did not develop a proper agricultural life either. This is probably because iron had been used to produce decorative articles, but had not been applied for making agricultural tools.

145. "Australopithecine sites in South Africa would indicate that while man's early Pleistocene ancestors perhaps did not fashion tools, they at least occasionally made use of objects as improvised tools and weapons. Improvisation probably continued to play an important part among the first men—even as today some Australian aborigines carve wooden implements with naturally fractured stone pieces. Progressively, however, men developed the ability to fashion tools by striking pieces of rocks with other stones. Since this method of making implements was the most distinctive feature of man's earliest culture, the first stage in his cultural development is known as the Paleolithic, or Old Stone, Age.... From an economic standpoint, the Paleolithic is also a food-*collecting* stage." (Alistair M. Taylor, Nels M. Bailkey, Mark Mancall, T. Walter Wallbank, *Civilization Past and Present,* 6th ed., Glenview, 1970, v. 1, p. 18)

146. Cf. I, 24.

147. It is said, for instance, of the Shoshones of the Salt Lake Desert, that they were more improvident than birds and more brutal than beasts. Some tribes, it is stated, had neither arms nor utensils and but rarely ate cooked food. (S.

nothing except rough stones and perhaps a wood stick as tools.[148]. The ability to make fire was not yet under control,[149] and no animals had been tamed for working.[150] Under these circumstances, it was, of course, difficult for men to go beyond the food-gathering stage of life.

By the beginning of the Young Stone Age, probably 30,000 years ago,[151] better methods for using fire had been discovered,[152] rough

---

Cognetti de Martiis, *Le Forme Primitive nella Evoluzione Economica,* Torino, 1881, p. 156)

148. Besides improvised stones, "the only tool in early use in this sphere of economic activity was a pointed stick made of wood or bone. We can conjecture as much by analogy with staffs used by primitive races today. This tool consisted simply of a wooden stick hardened in the fire and strengthened occasionally by a pointed stone or a piece of bone. In the course of development the second tool, which has often been found, was a kind of pike, of antlers or similar horny material." (Fritz Heichelheim, *An Ancient Economic History,* rev. and complete English ed., Leiden, 1958, v. 1, p. 12)

149. "Although archaeologists, who specialize in the study of primitive man and his cultures, have relatively little evidence on the subject, they believe that remains which have been unearthed and that the behavior of the most primitive people now extant indicate that the first men on earth had practically no tools, could not control fire well enough to have it always available, followed animal traits in their relations with their fellowmen, and were primarily food gatherers rather than food producers." (Shepard B. Clough, *The Economic Development of Western Civilization,* New York, 1959, p. 20)

150. For instance, "the Bushmen never cultivate the soil or rear any domestic animal, save wretched dogs. The chief subsistence of the Bushmen is the flesh of game, but this is eked out by what the women collect of roots and beans, and fruits of the desert." (D. Livingstone, *Missionary Travels and Researches in South Africa,* London and New York, 1858, p. 49)

151. "Our own physical ancestor, Homo sapiens, who looked like modern man, only appeared, or at least developed a progressive civilization, as late as the so-called Young Paleolithic Age after 30,000 B.C. or so." (Fritz Heichelheim, *An Ancient Economic History,* rev. and complete English ed., Leiden, 1958, v. 1, p. 9)

The above statement was based on radiocarbon research developed by Willard F. Libby (*Radiocarbon Dating,* 2nd ed., Chicago, 1955) and others. Libby's Radiocarbon Dating has greatly modified the chronology for the Young Paleolithic Age developed earlier by Gerard J. De Geer with his *Geochronologia Suecica Principles* (Stockholm, 1940) and by other scholars. (For a general review on the development of tools and energies in this age, cf. V. Gordon Childe, "The Prehistory of Science: Archaeological Documents" in *The Evolution of Science,* ed. by Guys Metraux and Francois Crouzet, New York, 1963, p. 45-58.)

152. "The older methods of kindling fire must have been very difficult. But we have found good hearths with flint and tinder in the Young Paleolithic Age of homo sapiens that show that the flint fire was already known." (Fritz Heichelheim, *An Ancient Economic History,* rev. and complete English ed., Leiden, 1958, v. 1, p. 13)

hooks and lines had been devised for catching fish,[153] and more and better hunting weapons had been developed,[154] culminating in the invention of the bow and arrow.[155] Equipped with these tools, and assisted by the domesticated dog for the chase,[156] we entered the hunting-fishing era proper.

It should be noted that the discovery of the flint fire, which made fire always available, was very important to early men. It enabled them to extend the use of fish and meat when men could not eat them raw, by roasting, and to preserve them for some time by roasting, burying, baking or drying. Fire was also used as a hunting weapon. (Cf. *op. cit.,* v. 1, p. 14.)

153. "Still later he devised hooks and lines for catching fish, domesticated the dog so that he would have some help in the chase . . . and invented the bow and arrow, the first composite mechanism of which we know." (Shepard B. Clough, *The Economic Development of Western Civilization,* New York, 1959, p. 21-22)

154. "Horse, cattle, deer, reindeer, elk were caught with the help of beaters . . . . Pits which are still archaelogically identifiable today were constructed for the capture of the large wild beasts. They were sunk with the help of the hand axes or of horn pikes . . . . Slings were used also, but are not preserved because the material perishes too quickly, but they are represented in drawings and paintings . . . . Excellent spears, harpoons, slings, stones, bows and arrows, and probably boomerangs enabled man to kill from a distance. Hunting and tracking are portrayed in the cave drawings of Southern Europe, and the search for honey is also documented there." (Fritz Heichelheim, *An Ancient Economic History,* rev. and complete English ed., Leiden, 1958, v. 1, p. 13-14)

(For some pictures of tools of the New Stone Age, cf. the typology in M.C. Burkitt, *Our Early Ancestors,* Cambridge, England, 1929, p. 102-130.)

155. ". . . and in the permanent addition of game through improved weapons, and especially through the bow and arrow. This remarkable invention, which came in after the spear and war club, and gave the first deadly weapon for the hunt, appeared late in savagery. It has been used to mark the commencement of its Upper Status. It must have given a powerful upward influence to ancient society, standing in the same relation to the period of savagery, as the iron sword to the period of barbarism, and fire-arms to the period of civilization." (Lewis H. Morgan, *Ancient Society,* New York, 1877, p. 21-22)

In this period we find man "taking to the air" by applying mechanical principles to the movement of tools and weapons. "Spears were launched with throwers which, working on the lever principle, increase the effective propelling power of a man's arm. The bow was invented late in this period, probably in north Africa. It was the first means of concentrating muscular energy for the propulsion of an arrow, but it was soon discovered that it also provided a means of twirling a stick, and this led to the invention of the rotary drill." (Kenneth P. Oakley, "Skill as a Human Possession," in *A History of Technology,* Oxford, 1958, v. 1, p. 33)

156. It is widely held that the dog was the first animal to become truly domesticated. "That the dog was already domesticated in the late Palaeolithic is possible, though not established with any degree of probability. According to Narr (1959), Russian workers have found coprolites (fossilised faeces) in the Crimea, as well as in Siberia. At Timonovka on the Desna River, coprolites and fragments of

By the beginning of the New Stone Age, about 12,000 years ago,[157] stone tools had been notably improved,[158] and of special importance was the appearance of the hoe and sickle sharpened from stone or bone,[159] and the earthen pot.[160] These made possible the

---

jaws of a *Canis* occur in a 'Gravettian' context. Another of the late Palaeolithic sites where the presence of dogs is suspected is Afantova Gora on the Yenisei. Narr holds that the presence of canine coprolites in a human occupation level would carry some weight if their occurrence in an undisturbed condition could be established. Even then, however, the site may have been temporarily abandoned by man, when wolves would have entered it for scavenging purposes. These are precisely the conditions under which domestication of the dog must have begun, but they do not amount to proof that it was achieved in the palaeolithic and under glacial conditions. The earliest archaeologically dated evidence for the presence of domesticated dogs comes from various Mesolithic sites, ranging from north Europe to Palestine." (Frederich E. Zeuner, *A History of Domesticated Animals,* London, 1963, p. 31, 84-85)

When man "has a good hunting-dog, he is virtually as well off as if he himself possessed the sense of smell, the keenness of sight, the speed, swimming capacity, and so on, of his animal." (William G. Sumner and Albert G. Keller, *The Science of Society,* New Haven, 1927, v. 1, p. 211)

In the hunting-fishing stage, hunting dogs had been specially bred and trained, and were so valuable that they were one of the few objects of exchange. "The Tarumas and Woyowais have a complete monopoly of the manufacture of the graters on which Indians of all tribes grate their cassava. They are also breeders and trainers of hunting-dogs.... The Wapianas visit the Tarumas and Woyowais, carrying canoes.... Leaving the canoes they walk back, carrying a supply of cassava-graters and leading hunting-dogs. The Macusis visit the Wapianas to obtain graters and dogs." (E.F. Im Thurn, *Among the Indians of Guiana,* London, 1883, p. 270)

157. Man entered the Neolithic Age with the development of hoe-cultivation. "The practice of investing human labor in cultivating plants with the help of seeds or cuttings which yielded a permanent revenue began about 10,000 B.C. Very little further output of labor was required to tend and harvest them in subtropical and tropical climates." (Fritz Heichelheim, *An Ancient Economic History,* rev. and complete English ed., Leiden, 1958, v. 1, p. 29)

158. "... man entered the Neolithic or New Stone Age. Tools were now improved by polishing, were given finer edges, and were further differentiated." (Shepard B. Clough, *The Economic Development of Western Civilization,* New York, 1959, p. 22. Cf. V. Gordon Childe, "The Prehistory of Science: Archaeological Documents," in *The Evolution of Science,* ed. Guys Metreaux and Francois Crouzet, New York, 1963, p. 58-75.)

159. The hoe and the sickle appeared, to be used in the cultivation and harvesting of grain. They brought about hoe-cultivation, and the so-called "Old Planter Civilization." It was a very rudimentary practice of planting. At its early stage, the important tools—hoe and sickle—were shaped out of stone, bone, or shell, and were not made of metal until several thousand years later when copper came into use. (Cf. Shepard B. Clough, *The Economic Development of Western*

development of hoe-cultivation, and the domestication of some animals. However, there still appeared no plow,[161] nor any animal domesticated for wide and deep tilling.[162] This is the main difference

---

Civilization, New York, 1959, p. 22, and Fritz Heichelheim, *An Ancient Economic History,* rev. and complete English ed., Leiden, 1958, v. 1, p. 29.)

"We must not imagine that the use of the plough is as ancient as agriculture itself. On the contrary, it was a comparatively late invention, as we shall see presently. Before its appearance the ground was broken up with the aid of digging-sticks or hoes—a fact which limited the amount of ground cultivated. A digging-stick was a strong, straight, pointed stick, possibly weighted with a stone.... The hoe was an instrument consisting of a blade, made of hard wood, stone.... Both of these implements—the digging-stick and the hoe—have survived among primitive tribes down to the present day where ploughing is not practised.... Hoe-blades, made of flint or chert, have been found in the remains of the predynastic cultures of both Egypt and Mesopotamia.... The earliest European farmers used hoes for breaking up the ground before they had any knowledge of the plough. The people of the Danube valley during the third millenium B.C. practised nomad agriculture, cultivating small plots with stone-bladed hoes. The same was probably true of Britain down to about 1000 B.C., and the practice of using hoes appears to have survived among some European mountain tribes as late as the beginning of our era. It even survives today in large parts of Africa, where, for one reason or another, the plough has not been introduced." (Elliot C. Curwen and Gudmund Hatt, *Plough and Pasture,* London, 1946, p. 50-51)

160. "The earthen pot was shaped by hand for storing grain; other pots were developed because grains, unlike meat, could not be cooked over an open fire on a spit but had to be contained in some sort of vessel." (Shepard B. Clough, *The Economic Development of Western Civilization,* New York, 1959, p. 22-23)

161. Plows, unambiguous evidence of farming, appeared no earlier than about 3000 B.C. in the Middle East. They were an invention of Iraq or Egypt, and probably coincided with the discovery that the castration of bulls produces a more docile work animal, the ox. Ox-drawn carts appeared about the same time in Iraq. But the early plow was made of bronze and was too expensive for common farming use. The heavy plow did not appear until the harder and cheaper iron was available for making it. In Europe, a record shows that about the 6th century A.D. the invading Anglo-Saxons introduced heavy plows to England along with the method of farming in long, narrow strips. Plowing in China did not begin until sometime before the Han dynasty (202 B.C.-220 A.D.). Horses began to be used for plowing around 100 B.C., after the invention of the horse collar by the Chinese. Over several centuries, the use of horses for plowing spread westward. (Cf. Eliot Curwen and Gudmund Hatt, *Plough and Pasture,* London, 1946, p. 50-76.)

James H. Breasted, in "The Origin of Civilization—II," *Scientific Monthly,* v. 9, 1919, p. 424-425, held that sometime before 2000 B.C., the ancient Egyptians first took the step of putting onto their hoe the attachments needed to turn it into a horse-drawn plow.

162. "On the other hand, Central African agriculture is hardly more than gardening because there is rarely power available to handle a tool more efficient

between hoe-cultivation and agriculture, which did not develop until several thousand years later.

The Age of Copper began about 7,000 years ago,[163] bringing in for the first time the use of a metal from which handy and efficient tools[164] could be made for the domestication of animals in taming, hiding, and shearing, as well as for wool-works. Its quality was im-

---

than the hoe." (William G. Sumner and Albert G. Keller, *The Science of Society,* New Haven, 1927, v. 1, p. 211)

Some of the American Indians were hoe-cultivators, especially those in the east and south, who combined tillage with fishing and hunting and resided for the greater part of the year in villages. Their agricultural development was checked by the lack of domesticated animals. When the American aborigines first saw oxen plowing, they pitied them, and blamed the Spaniards for laziness in putting their work onto animals. (Cf. L. Bourdeau, *Les forces de L'industrie: Progrès de la Puissance Humaine,* Paris, 1884, p. 99.)

"Up to the present time the Araucano only takes to agriculture in a desultory fashion, and to provide the mere necessities of life. Their methods are of the most primitive. Probably the principal reason why the barbarian tribes take to agricultural life with such distaste is the difficulty of inadequate implements, and the consequent amount of labor entailed by such work, especially before the introduction of domestic animals." (R.E. Latcham, "Ethnology of the Araucanos," in *Journal of the Anthropological Institute of Great Britain and Ireland,* XXIX, p. 343)

163. It is believed that copper was used by man at least as early as 6000 B.C. and perhaps even earlier. Evidence of hammered copper exists among the Chaldean remains dating back to 4500 B.C. There is evidence of more ancient native copper in the Badarian graves of Fayoum in Egypt. Because copper was found in a native state and could be easily hammered into tools and utensils having sharp and durable edges, it was the first important metal to be widely used by man. Copper and gold are the only metals having distinct colors other than shades of gray. Although gold was used earlier than copper, its practical uses are limited. Early man worked copper by the same processes used in working stone or fiber. It was discovered that heat made copper more malleable, and tempering was used as early as 5000 B.C., probably in southwestern Asia and North Africa. The casting and smelting of copper occurred around 4000 to 3500 B.C. and reduction around 1580 B.C. (Cf. J. Newton Friend, *Iron in Antiquity,* London, 1926, p. 15-26; and Thomas S. Lovering, *Minerals in World Affairs,* New York, 1943, p. 36-37.)

164. "... man of the Age of Copper ... thus had a metal for tools and weapons which was far superior to stone, for it was lighter and less fragile, took a sharper edge, and could be more easily shaped to produce a greater variety of products." (Shepard B. Clough, *The Economic Development of Western Civilization,* New York, 1959, p. 26)

(For some pictures of copper or bronze tools, cf. the typology in V. Gordon Childe, *The Bronze Age,* Cambridge, Mass., 1930, p. 60-138. Cf. also: Thomas A. Rickard, *Man and Metals, A History of Mining in Relation to the Development of Civilization,* New York, 1932, v. 1, p. 91-176.)

proved and application extended when it was developed into bronze.[165] Durable vessels and containers[166] could be made with bronze, as well as pottery,[167] to store meat and dairy products in

---

165. Bronze is a mixture of copper and tin. "Because ores from a given locality were likely to be fairly similar in composition, the smelted ore, although unlikely to be pure metal, would also be fairly uniform and would possess certain properties. Certain alloys were thus characteristic of certain localities. Tin and copper are closely associated in many ores, and as they are the constituents of the alloy, bronze, it is not surprising that bronze was produced at an early date in what is now Cornwall, Bohemia, and western China where such ores occur. Similarly, the primitive smelting of zinc-copper ores, such as those containing calamine and native copper, may have yielded brass. It was a long time before ores were deliberately mixed to obtain a desired product, and still longer before metals were separated and refined or intentionally mixed to obtain an alloy. Although bronze was used in Europe before 2000 B.C., the intentional manufacture of this alloy began about five hundred years later in Egypt." (Thomas S. Lovering, *Minerals in World Affairs,* New York, 1943, p. 37)

It should be noted that some scholars have named bronze, which appeared much later in history than copper, to designate the age, instead of copper. Some have tried to separate the Age of Bronze from that of Copper, while others treated the Age of Bronze as a substage of the Age of Copper. We do not associate bronze with an age or stage because bronze, to be sure, "provided a harder and more durable metal for tools and weapons, but it was not so much better than copper that it could do more than accelerate developments already initiated." (Shepard B. Clough, *The Economic Development of Western Civilization,* New York, 1959, p. 30)

166. Numerous copper or bronze and pottery vessels, containers, and other tools have been unearthed from the sites of ancient countries and exhibited in museums the world over. In China, for instance, in the 14th Century B.C., at the time of the founding of the capital of the Shang dynasty (1523-1027 B.C.) at Anyang, on a tributary of the Yellow River in Northern China, a bronze-casting industry was already in existence, which produced elaborate vessels. These appear to have had their prototypes in the pottery of the same culture. Similar bronzes have been unearthed at an early site of the same Shang dynasty, which must have been made between 1700 and 1500 B.C., while copper arrowheads dating from perhaps 500 years earlier were found on sites of the North Chinese Yang-shao culture, a culture otherwise strictly Neolithic. Prehistoric Chinese pottery includes a type of painted pottery executed in bold brush strokes in black upon simple forms. The ware of the dynasties Shang and Chou (1027-256 B.C.) includes several types of soft, porous, unglazed pieces that were fired at relatively low temperatures. The Han Dynasty (202 B.C.-220 A.D.) saw the beginning of glazed pottery in China. Many pottery forms of this period were derived from bronzes. (Cf. William Watson, *Ancient Chinese Bronzes,* Rutland, Vt., 1962, p. 23-38; Albert J. Koop, *Early Chinese Bronzes,* New York, 1971, p. 10-37; and Seizo Hayashiya and G. Hasebe, *Chinese Ceramics,* trans. by C.A. Pomeroy, Rutland, Vt., 1966, p. 24-29.)

167. "The Age of Copper witnessed the development of other techniques of the greatest moment. Pottery, which had previously been shaped by hand and fired for greater durability began to be made on the potter's wheel and to be baked

larger quantities for longer times. With these tools, together with the use of the dog for watching sheep,[168] and the help of the horse[169] for guarding cattle,[170] the pastoral life grew into full bloom.

Finally came the Iron Age, about 3,000 years ago.[171] Iron is a

---

in special kilns.... (The kiln) seems to have appeared first in Hither Asia before 3000 B.C., to have reached Egypt by 2700 B.C., and the Indus River valley by about 2500 B.C." (Shepard B. Clough, *The Economic Development of Western Civilization,* New York, 1959, p. 26. Cf. R.J. Forbes, *Man, the Maker: A History of Technology and Engineering,* New York, 1950, p. 25.)

168. "Herders ... For many centuries man has used these dogs to guard sheep, cattle, goats and pigs, and he has trained many of them to actually guide, or herd, groups of these animals. In Europe, when herds of cattle had to be driven over relatively great distances to grazing grounds or slaughterhouses, tough, robust droving dogs were used to sustain the ponderous forward progress of the cattle. Today the able herding dogs, such as the German shepherd, have been singled out and trained to do a variety of tasks." (Erich Schneider-Leyer, author of *Dogs of the World* [translated by E. Fitch Daglish, London, 1964], in the *Encyclopedia Americana,* under "Dog," 1973 ed., v. 9, p. 236)

169. "Of these the horse was probably the last to be domesticated, since we find that the Egyptians did not employ this animal until a relatively late stage of the historic period, namely, about the twentieth century B.C. This does not mean that the horse was unknown to the Asiatic nations until so late a period, but it suggests a relatively recent use of this animal...." (*The Historians' History of the World,* 1907, v. 1, p. 48. Cf. Friedrich E. Zeuner, *A History of Domesticated Animals,* London, 1963, p. 313-337.)

"There are certain works of man whose accomplishment is dependent upon his disposal over animal forces much surpassing his own; the highest development of the nomadic stage is impossible in the absence of the horse, for without him the widely grazing herds cannot be held together and supervised." (William G. Sumner and Albert G. Keller, *The Science of Society,* New Haven, 1927, v. 1, p. 211)

170. Among domesticated large animals, the most important were cattle. They were derived from widespread Eurasian and North African wild bovines, with which they were later frequently recrossed to yield new breeds. The advent of cattle herding added a new dimension to animal husbandry. Kept in large numbers, cattle could provide subsistence for an entire human community. There is no definite proof of cattle domestication before about 4000 B.C., and the actual date may be later. Numerous finds of bones in ancient Middle Eastern sites may be those of domestic livestock or wild bovines that were still being hunted. Clear traces of dairying, in the form of pictures of milking scenes, go back only to about 3000 B.C., in Iraq and Egypt. Regular milking of cattle and goats probably came before, however. Zebu or humped cattle were domesticated around 3000 B.C. in Baluchistan and the Indus Valley. (Cf. Friedrich E. Zeuner, *A History of Domesticated Animals,* London, 1963, p. 201-244.)

171. The earliest use of iron is still shrouded in mystery, but there is evidence that a tribe in the Armenian Mountains was employing iron even before 2000 B.C. At all events, iron tools and weapons began to be used in Palestine, Syria, and Greece by 1100 B.C. and thence spread to other lands. (Cf. J. Newton Friend, *Iron*

metal which is not only harder and more durable, but also more economical[172] than copper or bronze, enabling farmers to have more and better tools.[173] Furthermore, iron made the production of heavy-duty implements possible to utilize animal[174] and natural energies,[175]

---

in Antiquity, London, 1926, p. 27-34, and R.J. Forbes, *Man, the Maker: A History of Technology and Engineering,* New York, 1950, p. 53-55.)

"The smelting of iron was beyond the technical skill of man for thousands of years after he was able to reduce the ores of copper, silver, lead, mercury, and tin. Metallic iron was obtained from meteorites and wrought into swords for the early emperors and kings. Attila, Timur, and various Caliphs are known to have carried these "swords from Heaven" as one of their most valued possessions. One of the earliest records of iron weapons is that which refers to the iron knives used in Palestine about 1350 B.C. Such iron was not smelted in the true sense of the word, which implies melting of the metal; rather it was hammered out at a forge with great labor from a hot, somewhat plastic mass of slowly reducing ore, slag, charcoal, and metal. Actual smelting was not accomplished in Europe until about the fourteenth century." (Thomas S. Lovering, *Minerals in World Affairs,* New York, 1943, p. 37-38)

172. "The development of iron metallurgy and the use of iron products constituted in itself an economic revolution. Unlike copper and tin, iron ore is quite abundant in nature and weapons were relatively cheap in terms of human input and came within the reach of nearly everyone. At last even rather poor people could avail themselves of equipment that was in most respects as good as that of the well-to-do. Iron was in ancient times, as it is today, a plebian metal and it had a democratizing effect, at least from an economic point of view." (Shepard B. Clough, *The Economic Development of Western Civilization,* New York, 1959, p. 36)

173. "A long list of old tools, including shovels, spades, forks, mattocks, axes and scythes, were now made of iron, and new tools made their appearance, such as pickaxes for road work.... In general, therefore, agricultural workers were able to increase their production." (Shepard B. Clough, *The Economic Development of Western Civilization,* New York, 1959, p. 36-37)

174. "When man began to use animals for packing and some agricultural works, probably 4000 calories were added to his energy consumption per capita per day." "Even at this low level of energy consumption (a little less than is used in an average home today in daily electrical energy alone) mankind produced impressive results. The massed energy of man and animals built Egypt's Pyramids and the awesomely scaled temples and palaces of Assyria." (John M. Fowler, *Energy and the Environment,* New York, 1975, p. 67)

175. Sometime around 1000 B.C., however, man made his next great energy breakthrough and began to harness the kinetic energy of wind, first to drive his ships and later to turn windmills. The Romans, at about the time of Christ, developed the waterwheel. The sailing ships speeded up exploration of the planet man was beginning to master; the machines that water turned began to amplify the productivity of a single man, thus leaving others free to take on the inward exploration of self." (John M. Fowler, *Energy and the Environment,* New York, 1975, p. 67)

such as the plow and harrow drawn by the ox for field work,[176] the rotary quern driven by the ass,[177] the mill turned by water[178] or wind[179] for grinding grain, and the water-raising wheel[180] for irrigation and drainage. Also appropriated into use were various other

176. "The domestic animals supplementing human muscle with animal power, contributed a new factor of the highest value. In the course of time, the production of iron gave the plow with an iron point, and a better spade and axe. Out of these, and the previous horticulture, came field agriculture; and with it, for the first time, unlimited subsistence. The plow drawn by animal power may be regarded as inaugurating a new art. Now, for the first time, came the thought of reducing the forest, and bringing wide fields under cultivation. Moreover, dense populations in limited areas now became possible." (Lewis H. Morgan, *Ancient Society,* New York, 1877, p. 26-27)

The use of oxen for plowing was one of many ways in which agriculture and animal husbandry became interdependent. Special crops such as alfalfa and sweet clover were grown for forage. Animal dung was used to fertilize fields, and stock were grazed on stubble. Oxen sometimes were used to tread out grain on threshing floors or to drag flint-studded sledges over harvested grain ears. With the invention of the wheel, animal labor could be used in irrigation and in milling or to haul farm produce into market towns. (Cf. W.C. Lowdermilk, "Conquest of the Land Through Seven Thousand Years," in *U.S. Department of Agriculture Information Bulletin,* No. 99, Washington, 1953.)

177. "Indeed, one of the most notable mechanical devices of the Iron Age was the rotary quern for grinding grain into flour. It consisted of two circular stones, the upper one of which turned on an iron pivot protruding from the center of the lower, which crushed the grain between them. By the fifth century B.C. this mechanism was being turned by animals hitched to a lever attached to the upper stone, which was the first use of animal power save for draft purposes." (Shepard B. Clough, *The Economic Development of Western Civilization,* New York, 1959, p. 39)

178. "Once the principle of using nonhuman energy in industry became established, it is possible to conceive of employing inorganic sources of energy for power. It is not strange, indeed, that the water wheel, developed sometime after 100 B.C. was first applied to the grinding of grain and continued to be used almost exclusively for this purpose well into the Middle Ages." (Shepard B. Clough, *The Economic Development of Western Civilization,* New York, 1959, p. 39. Cf. Abbott P. Usher, *A History of Mechanical Inventions,* Cambridge, Mass., 1955, p. 161-186.)

179. "In addition, our medieval forebears increased the number of prime movers beyond sheer human and animal muscle power. They developed watermills, both horizontal and vertical, as well as windmills with rotating turrets to catch the variable winds in the higher latitudes. Useful not only for grinding grains, these water- and windmills provided power for draining marshlands, for reclaiming areas from the sea (as in the Low Countries), for lumbering, and for new woolen mills, such as those in Flanders." (Alastair M. Taylor, Nels M. Bailkey, Mark Mancall, T. Walter Wallbank, *Civilization Past and Present,* 6th ed., Glenview, v. 1, p. 368)

Windmills, well-known in the Netherlands, were built as early as the 13th century in Europe and were later adopted in North America for grinding grain and pumping water. In the West Indies, they were put to the task of grinding sugar-

sources of energy,[181] including coal and some other fossil fuels.[182] Since then, agricultural life has developed remarkably.

So, changes in the mode of life have invariably followed the development of tools and energies.[183]

---

cane. (Cf. Joseph J. DiCerto, *"The Electric Wishing Well; The Solution to the Energy Crisis,* New York, 1976, p. 158-162.)

180. "Furthermore, iron made possible improvement in various types of machines that did not stand up well when made of wood or the more fragile copper. Among these mechanisms was the water-raising wheel for irrigation and drainage; this consisted of a wheel fitted with pots or with chains holding pots that, as it turned, dipped water at the bottom of its arc and dumped it at the top." (Shepard B. Clough, *The Economic Development of Western Civilization,* New York, 1959, p. 39. Cf. R.J. Forbes, *Man, the Maker: A History of Technology and Engineering,* New York, 1950, p. 111-113.)

181. "By the time of the Babylonian, Greek and Roman civilizations, man had also learned to produce light from various types of fats and vegetable oils, and from pitch, a black oily substance from the earth." (Joseph J. DiCerto, *The Electric Wishing Well; The Solution to the Energy Crisis,* New York, 1976, p. 14)

182. Ancient civilizations knew of fossil fuels. The Chinese employed coal for domestic heating and cooking long before 1000 B.C. They also drilled for natural gas, which was then transported considerable distances from the wells in bamboo pipelines so that the palaces of the emperors would have illumination and heat. Even earlier than that—perhaps 2500 B.C.—the Babylonians had used asphalt and crude petroleum for fuel, illumination, mortar, waterproofing, and the laying of roads. However, the heavy use of fossil fuels is a more recent development. (Cf. John Holland, *The History and Description of Fossil Fuel, the Collieries, and Coal Trade of Great Britain,* New York, 1968, p. 15-16.)

"Lost in the mist of unrecorded history is man's first encounter with a black rocklike substance that could burn with a very hot flame. There is archaeological evidence that coal was used by inhabitants of Glamorgan, Wales, during the Bronze Age, 3000 to 4000 years ago, and that Roman soldiers in Britain burned coal to heat their quarters as early as the fourth century A.D. This fossil material provided a rich source of energy, but one that would not be used extensively until the seventeenth century. The energy wishing well was beginning to give man a wider variety of choices." (Joseph J. DiCerto, *The Electric Wishing Well; The Solution to the Energy Crisis,* New York, 1976, p. 14)

183. Fifty years ago, in a striking article on "The Empire of Machines," John M. Clark warned of the dominion of modern machines over our lives, and stated that humanity was in the grip of a force beyond its control and of purposes not its own. Although this force did not threaten our physical life, it was threatening our supremacy, our freedom of will, and our control over our own destiny, and was driving us, lashing us onward at a racking pace towards some goal which we could not even foresee, let alone choose for ourselves. (*Yale Review,* Oct. 1922, p. 132-133) The influence of tools and energies upon our lives becomes startlingly clear only after we realize the tremendous force of modern machines, which have significantly crowded mankind out of the place of prominence. In fact, however, it is nothing new, but goes back hundreds of thousands of years to a time when

Since group expansion depends primarily on a change in the mode of life, and a change in the mode of life invariably follows the development of tools and energies, it is beyond any doubt that the development of tools and energies is the major factor determining the validity and extent of group expansion.

f.
Transportation
and Communication

THE PHENOMENON THAT THE DEVELOPMENT OF TOOLS and energies is the major factor for group expansion can be seen not only in the mode of life, but also in transportation and communication.

Transportation is important to the expansion of the group, because for expansion, it is necessary to conquer long distances and to overcome other physical obstacles, such as high mountains, great deserts, wide rivers, big lakes, and immense oceans.[184] But transportation necessitates tools and energy as means.

Before the end of the Stone Age, no means of transportation appeared except some crude rafts, canoes, or kayaks on the water,[185]

---

mankind learned how to use fire and crude tools, and human life began to depend on them instead of on nature. It is true that tools and energies are the servants of mankind, but they are servants so indispensable to the survival of their master that man had to adjust himself to conform to their development. So, on the whole and in the long run, tools and energies have become the pilots of history, and have become forces which determine the mode of life and, consequently, the size of groups since time immemorial. The more we learn the true significance of events, the more we understand the dominion of tools and energies over our lives.

184. Because we cannot run like a horse, cannot swim like a fish, and cannot fly like a bird, it is obviously very difficult for us to conquer long distances and to overcome the obstacles of wild forests, high mountains, great deserts, wide rivers, big lakes, vast seas and immense oceans. If there were no means of transportation to channel us, we would have to live separately in numerous small groups forever.

185. There is little doubt that primitive man found the waterways the best means of conveyance, and he therefore tended to live in the vicinity of waterways, unless security considerations directed retreat to less accessible locations. Floating logs were found to be more buoyant if rotted out in the center, and this led to the dugout, a vehicle carved from a log. The raft also became an important vehicle for

and some sledges or drags on the land.[186] In general, travel was by walking, and everything was carried by hand, or on the head or back.[187] Contacts between peoples were very feeble.[188] This is one of the main reasons why the group could not expand larger than the clan.

By the Copper Age, tools and energies were beginning to be used for transportation. The most important was the invention of the wheeled vehicle pulled by an animal. This kind of vehicle first appeared around 3500 B.C. and was seen in different places later.[189]

---

prehistoric man. Some primitive peoples, like the American Indians and the Eskimos, developed very refined canoes. The Indians made their canoes out of birch bark, whereas the Eskimos stretched skin over a skillfully constructed framework. The canoe of the American Indian was often a true work of art. (Cf. Marvin L. Fair and Ernest W. Williams, *Economics of Transportation,* New York, 1959, p. 4-5; John G.D. Clark, *Prehistoric Europe; the Economic Basis,* London, 1952, p. 282-284; and Lionel Casson, *Ships and Seamanship in the Ancient World,* Princeton, New Jersey, 1971, p. 3-5.)

186. "Whether pulled by man or beast, the earliest land vehicle seems to have been the sledge. The remains of one of the oldest known, perhaps 7,000 years old, was found in a peat bog. Very possibly the sledge had its origin in a simple branch drawn behind a man or beast. Certain primitive peoples still use a Y-shaped, forked branch pulled by oxen. The Indian travois, a fixed, V-shaped framework of two poles fastened to a horse was much the same kind of device." (Maurice Fabre, *A History of Land Transportation,* London, 1967, p. 10)

187. "Paleolithic man ... did not have yet, however, the principle of the wheel and when he moved by land, as he frequently did in search of food because of droughts or 'overpopulation,' he carried his few belongings on his back, dragged them on poles, or pulled them on sledges." (Shepard B. Clough, *The Economic Development of Western Civilization,* New York, 1959, p. 22)

188. "It is evident that agencies promoting intercourse are of high import. Where there were no suitable domestic animals, communication and trade have always remained rudimentary over stretches of country without navigable waters; thus in Australia, much of Africa, and the Americas, there existed among the aborigines but the feeblest of contacts." (William G. Sumner and Albert G. Keller, *The Science of Society,* New Haven, 1927, v. 1, p. 211-212)

189. "The wheel, which is essential for transmission of mechanical power and for the reduction of friction in land transportation, began to be used on the cart.... Wheeled vehicles appeared in Sumer about 3500 B.C., in Egypt by 1600 B.C., and in China and Sweden by 1000 B.C. Incidentally, the Mayan, Incan, and Aztec cultures never made economic use of the wheel." (Shepard B. Clough, *The Economic Development of Western Civilization,* New York, 1959, p. 27)

It is interesting to note that the invention of the wheeled vehicle in China was attributed to Emperor Huang (or Yellow) about 4000 years ago, and because the invention was so important, his name and the name of his birthplace were honored with the symbols of the wheeled vehicle: "軒轅"

The donkey and white ass were probably used as beasts of burden[190] before the horse started to play a great role in civilization,[191] and not much later, the mule was also used.[192] On the water, wind power was first applied to the sail of the boat around 3000 B.C.[193] All these developments led to the growth of the tribe.[194]

---

190. The donkey is a domesticated member of the horse family. It is generally agreed that the donkey, now found throughout the world, is a descendant of the African wild ass. Related to the donkey is the domesticated white ass, a descendant of Asian ancestors. Domestication of both occurred in Neolithic times, some 5000 years ago, and both played important roles in the development of early civilizations in Africa and Asia. In rough, undeveloped areas they are unequaled as beasts of burden. (Cf. Friedrich E. Zeuner, *A History of Domesticated Animals*, London, 1963, p. 374-382.)

Man began to domesticate the burro (a small donkey) for packing and agricultural work in the highlands of Iran around 5000 B.C., according to John M. Fowler, *Energy and the Environment*, New York, 1975, p. 67.

191. John Trotwood Moore, in a tribute to the horse, wrote "wherever man has left his footprint in the long ascent from barbarism to civilization we will find the footprint of the horse beside it." According to Western European mythology and folklore, all the great early civilizations arose among horse-owning, horse-breeding, and horse-using nations; those in which the horse was either unknown or untamed, were backward states, and no great forward movement of mankind was made without the assistance of the horse. So consistently was this the case that the glorified figure of "the man on horseback" became the symbol of power. The image of the horse was stamped upon man's coinage, sculptured on his temples, and even elevated to his pantheon and worshipped as divine. (Cf. M. Oldfield Howey, *The Horse in Magic and Myth*, New York, 1958, p. 161-171, 180-195.)

"The domestication of the horse put a source of speed and power at man's disposal—a source that was not excelled until the invention of steam and internal-combustion engines." (Ralph W. Phillips, "The Livestock Industry: Its Scope and Potential," in the *Introduction to Livestock Production including Dairy and Poultry*, ed. by H.H. Cole, San Francisco, 1966, p. 2)

192. A side effect of the spread of the horse from Central Asia beginning about 4000 years ago was its encounter with the African ass, which resulted in the creation of a new animal type, the very useful but infertile mule. (Cf. Friedrich E. Zeuner, *A History of Domesticated Animals*, London, 1963, p. 382-383.)

193. "Carrying by water became more efficient because of the use of the sail (circa 3000 B.C.) which was one of the first instances of the employment of inorganic power for economic purposes, the construction of larger boats, and improvements in methods of steering. . . . At this time the oar or oars used for steering were fixed on one or both sides of the stern of the ship. The hinged rudder, installed directly astern, was to come much later." (Shepard B. Clough, *The Economic Development of Western Civilization*, New York, 1959, p. 28)

In Shepard B. Clough, *op. cit.,* p. 29, there is a picture of an Egyptian vessel from Thebes of circa 2000 B.C. Its mast for the sail is short, and its steering apparatus is not a hinged rudder, but consists of two steering oars lashed to posts.

194. A reason for the peoples in the New World to remain in the clan stage

In the Iron Age, more and more tools and energies were used for transportation. The sailing vessel was greatly improved;[195] the wheeled vehicle was widely used[196] on better roads;[197] the camel appeared

---

before the coming of the white man is that they had not had the right means of transportation for expansion. They had canoes or kayaks on the water, but had no wheeled vehicle for economic use. They had no animal for transportation except the llama, which was used for packing by the Indians of the Andean region in South America.

Although there were some small horses in South America about 12,000 years ago, probably as food animals, they disappeared for reasons which are still unclear. The modern horse was introduced into the New World by Columbus and other white men. Lost, traded, and stolen horses soon found their way into Indian hands. The result was a rapid transformation in Indian life. The new mobility brought the hunting of the bison more easily within the capabilities of the Indian archer and lancer, and thus a new, more dependable food source to the Plains Indians. By use of the travois, the horse became an Indian draft animal. After the acquisition of guns, the Indians became extremely adept at rapid raids and mobile warfare. (Cf. Friedrich E. Zeuner, *A History of Domesticated Animals,* London, 1963, p. 437-438; Bernard Mishkin, *Rank and Warfare Among the Plains Indians,* Seattle, 1966, p. 5-23; and Basil Toger, *The Horse in History,* London, 1908, p. 168-172.)

195. The sailing vessels of the Babylonians, Phoenicians, Egyptians, and Chinese were great improvements over the crude craft of prehistoric man. The hull, as well as the sails, received important development: frames were constructed about which the hull could be built, and improved materials for sails, including woven textiles, were produced. Better hull design, sails, and rigging led to larger and better ships. During the Greek and Roman periods, the sailing vessel developed still further in efficiency and size. The larger Roman vessels, which brought grain from the Nile Valley in Egypt to Rome, attained some 400 tons and more in size, not exceeded until the 19th century. The Romans also built canals at the mouth of the Nile and installed a lighthouse at Alexandria as an aid to navigation. (Cf. Edward K. Chatterton, *Sailing Ships; the Story of Their Development from the Earliest Times to the Present Day,* London, 1915, p. 20-88.)

196. Before 1000 B.C., the people of north China were making use of two-wheeled carts and war chariots on land and crude sailboats on the rivers and along the coast. Carts pulled by man or beast were the dominant form of local transportation, except for extensive use of wheelbarrows for carriage of both goods and passengers. Large carts using three or four animals—horses, mules, or camels—came to be well-known throughout China. For more distant transportation, caravans of pack animals came into general use in the 1st and 2nd centuries A.D. The first long-distance caravans, carrying silk and other precious products from China to Iran, were in 106 A.D.; trade with the Roman Empire by this means was established by 138 A.D. (Cf. H.G. Creel, "The Role of the Horse in Chinese History," *American Historical Review,* v. 70, p. 647-672. Also: Joseph Needham, *Science and Civilization in China,* London, 1954, v. 1, Section 7.)

It is interesting to note, for instance, that in the Periods of Spring and Autumn and Warring States (722-222 B.C.), which were transitional times between the tribes and a nation in Chinese history, the horse and wheeled vehicle

as the "ship of the desert";[198] the elephant[199] and reindeer[200] were
used in some areas for riding, packing, or carrying vehicles; and the
horse became bigger[201] and was better equipped.[202] Later, the

---

were so widely used and were considered so important that the status of a state and
its head was often identified with the number of horses and vehicles, such as "a
thousand-chariot state" 千乘之國, and "your majesty with ten thousand
chariots," 萬乘之尊 (an honor exclusively for the Emperor or Empress). The size
and especially the strength of a state was sometimes measured by how many horses
and how many chariots, not by how many people and how much territory, it had.
Examples of this kind of identification and measurement reoccur frequently in the
Four Books 四書 and the *Policies of the Warring States,* 戰國策.

197. The great roman military roads, for instance, built between the 4th century B.C. and 400 A.D., had an aggregate length of over 50,000 miles, extending to
all parts of Italy and to France, Spain, England, western Asia Minor, and northern
Africa. Via Appia, or the Appian Way, a portion of which remains today, was
built by order of the censor Appius Claudius (312 B.C.). It extended 366 miles
from Rome to Brundisium (modern Brindisi), at the heel of the Italian peninsula,
where ships from eastern Mediterranean ports docked. Over it flowed the commerce of all of Italy south of Rome. (Cf. Geoffrey M. Boumphrey, *Along the
Roman Roads,* 2nd ed., New York, 1964.)

198. Camels were late in being domesticated. They were used as mounts by
the Assyrians and by others in southwest and central Asia, but were not brought to
North Africa until Roman times. The two-humped Bactrian breed was used in central Asia, notably as a pack animal on the great trans-Asian silk caravan route. The
one-humped dromedary is a general-purpose animal in southwestern Asia and
North Africa, especially among nomadic groups, who ride, pack, milk, and eat
their camels. (Cf. Friedrich E. Zeuner, *A History of Domesticated Animals,* London, 1963, p. 338-365.)

199. From probably 2500-1500 B.C., elephants have been used as beasts of
burden in India and Burma. Trained elephants carry human cargo in a howdah or
miniature hunting structure on their backs. More particularly, they were employed
for moving and stacking timber or other heavy materials, using both tusks and
trunks in the operation. In the teak industry, huge logs are floated down rivers and
then hauled out with chains by elephants. (Cf. Friedrich E. Zeuner, *A History of
Domesticated Animals,* London, 1963, p. 275-298.)

200. Reindeer occur wild in a wide zone of northern forest and tundra from
Scandinavia to northern (where they are known as caribou). They were domesticated relatively late—not much more than 2000 years ago—and possibly in several
different regions independently. The peoples of northern Eurasia, from the Lapps
to the Chukchi, use reindeer in varied ways, from dairying and sled pulling to
riding, or for meat and skins. Neither the Eskimo nor the northern Indians domesticated the American caribou. (Cf. Friedrich E. Zeuner, *A History of Domesticated Animals,* London, 1963, p. 46-48.)

201. When the barbarians invaded the Roman Empire, the vast number of
horses that they possessed helped them to overthrow the Romans. The ages following witnessed the diffusion of Oriental horses throughout the countries of northern Europe and the breeding of improved types. The most important of these was
the "great horse" which originated in the Low Countries; its size and strength

mariner's compass was invented[203] and ships were built for open-sea navigation.[204] All these developments led to the growth of the nation.

Communication is important to the expansion of the group because, for expansion, it is necessary to overcome obstacles to understanding, to the dissemination of information and to trade.

---

were required to carry the heavy load of the medieval knight in heavy armour. These horses, the ancestors of modern draft breeds, were bred from the largest and most powerful of the northern European horses, but there was apparently an admixture of the Oriental blood that the Romans brought in. The early horses were probably around 12 hands (48 in.) at the withers, and 14 hands was exceptional. Some modern horses reach 17 hands and occasionally 20 hands (80 in.). (Cf. Walter Gilbey, *The Great Horse; or The War Horse from the Time of the Roman Invasion Till its Development into the Shire,* 2nd ed., London, 1899.)

202. "Our medieval ancestors succeeded to an unprecedented degree in maximizing the muscle power of draft animals by three major developments. First, for the traditional horse collar which fastened around the animal's neck and choked him when pulling a heavy load, they substituted a harness fitted so that the shoulders bore the weight. Second, they developed a tandem harness in order to utilize the strength of several horses; and finally, they improved traction with a new type of horseshoe. These inventions are said to have done for the eleventh and twelfth centuries what the steam engine did for the nineteenth." (Alastair M. Taylor, Nels Bailkey, Mark Mancall, T. Walter Wallbank, *Civilization Past and Present,* 6th ed., Glenview, v. 1, p. 386.)

A picture of harnesses for four horses of the sixth century B.C. is shown in Shepard B. Clough, *The Economic Development of Western Civilization,* New York, 1959, p. 27, with a note: "The ancient harness was quite inefficient, being so designed that when the horse pulled a heavy load the breastplate would slip up on the animal's throat and might cut off his breath. Horses were used to pull only light loads, and were in general much smaller than our modern draft animals." There is also a picture of an Egyptian wooden chariot from the period of 1800-1354 B.C. shown in the same book, p. 28.

203. By far the most important invention in aid of transportation during the medieval period was the compass, which emancipated sea transportation from coastal to open-sea navigation. In ancient times, the sailing boats of the Chinese, Phoenicians, Egyptians, Greeks, and Romans were compelled to hug the coastline to determine position and direction. There was some use of celestial navigation, but this was not dependable in certain seasons of the year when the sky was often clouded. The era of ocean transportation, really began, therefore, with the invention of the compass early in the Middle Ages. (Cf. G.A.A. Grant and J. Klinkert, *The Ship's Compass,* London, 1952.)

204. Between about 1100 and 1460, several important changes occurred. Most significant of all, some unknown northern shipwright, possibly in the region of the Netherlands, developed the stern rudder around 1200. This was firmly attached to the stern post, in place of the old steering oar. It would help greatly in enabling vessels to sail to windward, a process that would be further aided by building deeper hulls. By 1400, the changes began to occur with rapidity. Until then, most ships still had just one mast and one sail. A half century later, some had

But communication must have tools and energies to carry it over distance and for the process of multiplication and recording.[205]

Unquestionably, the most important medium of communication is language. It is one of the greatest inventions[206] and one of the most useful tools of mankind.[207] It distinguishes us from other animals,[208]

---

three masts—which would become the fore, main, and mizzen—and three sails. After that, sails became further subdivided—it was much easier to handle several small ones than a single great one. By 1500, the new types of vessels were sufficiently seaworthy to be able to go anywhere. (Cf. Edward K. Chatterton, *Sailing Ships: The Story of Their Development from the Earliest Times to the Present Day,* London, 1915, p. 128-169.)

205. "There are many different aspects of communication. First there is the matter of distance. Two people can communicate with each other by speech over a short distance, but as the distance increases, speech is no longer sufficient—so the problem is one of overcoming distance or of making speech carry. Second, there is the multiplication aspect. For instance, by the use of radio or TV one man can communicate with millions of others at the same time. Third, there is the recording aspect. Until the invention of wireless and telegraphy, all long-distance communication involved recording the message and then physically carrying this record over the distance (by horse or ship). Recording can also help multiplication, as when a newspaper or book repeats a message and delivers it to thousands of different people. Recording has yet another advantage in that it can conquer time. The recorded message can be kept for an almost indefinite period." (*Eureka, An Illustrated History of Inventions from the Wheel to the Computer; A London Sunday Times Encyclopedia,* ed. by Edward De Bono, New York, 1974, p. 15)

206. In the Foreword to Jacques Jean Marie de Morgan's *Prehistoric Man,* London, 1924, Henry Berr remarked that in the hand and language is comprised humanity: "We feel that these things should be given the premier place in this work—the things that mark the close of zoological, and the beginning of human history; one, if we may so put it, is the invention of the hand, and the other is the invention of language. In these two lies the decisive progress in practical logic and in mental logic that characterizes mankind."

207. "The first and prime instrumentality for the exchange of anything between human beings is language. It might be called a tool without stretching that term out of all recognition; it is, at any rate, no organic product, but a societal one.... It developed gradually, through variations, selection, and transmission, in adjustment to needs. It furnishes one of the best cases of evolution in the societal field. Nobody made it; everybody made it. The various languages have grown by gradual and almost imperceptible changes; they are evidently the handiwork of whole peoples—as are the rest of human institutions as well, though we are sometimes deceived into thinking otherwise." (William G. Sumner and Albert G. Keller, *The Science of Society,* New Haven, 1927, v. 1, p. 160-161)

208. The distinction of man from the animal, through his ability to convey objective ideas by speech, dating from about a million years ago, is recognized by Robert M. Yerkes in *The Great Apes,* New Haven, 1929, p. 303.

209. "Perhaps the greatest single step ever made in the history of man's upward progress was taken when the practice of articulate speech began.... Without

and sets the first important step toward civilization.[209] It started with simple speech,[210] leading us to expand our group life up to the clan stage. Then writing[211] boosted the growth of the tribe,[212] and advanc-

---

language of an explicit kind not even the rudiments of civilization would be possible. No one perhaps ever epitomised the value of articulate speech in a single phrase more tellingly than does Herder when he says: 'The lyre of Amphion has not built cities. No magic wand has transformed deserts into gardens. Language has done it—that great source of sociality.' '' (*The Historians' History of the World,* 1907, v. 1, p. 45-46)

210. "Human speech seems to have been developed from the rudest and simplest forms of expression. Gesture or sign language, as intimated by Lucretius, must have preceded articulate language, as thought preceded speech. The monosyllabical preceded the syllabical, as the latter did that of concrete words. Human intelligence, unconscious of design, evolved articulate language by utilizing the vocal sounds." (Lewis H. Morgan, *Ancient Society,* New York, 1877, p. 5)

211. Written language brought the progress of language to another phase by enlarging its use in time and space. This advance so impressed mankind that, originally, written language was attributed to divine inspiration. The Hebrews believed that Moses had received it direct from God; the Egyptians attributed it to their god Thoth; the Greeks considered the invention of writing as important as the practice of agriculture or the discovery of fire, and raised Cadmus to the rank of Triptolemus and Prometheus, just as the Chinese ranked Tsang-chien, 倉頡 , the inventor of letters about equal to Shen-nung, 神農 , the god of agriculture, and Sui-jen, 燧人 , the originator of fire. In this phase of the development of language, mankind progressed into tribal life.

"The earliest forms of writing were pictograms. Then came in turn hieroglyphs, which are conventional signs for things; ideograms, which are symbols for ideas; phonograms, which gave sound values to ideas and things; and finally in the nineteenth century B.C. the alphabet." (Shepard B. Clough, *The Economic Development of Western Civilization,* New York, 1959, p. 31. Cf. *The Historians' History of the World,* 1907, v. 1, p. 50-52.)

212. "As the intelligence of man increased, and his consequent need for better means of expressing himself in writing increased, the idea occurred to someone to use conventional drawings to represent vocal sounds, instead of pictures of visible objects. The first writing of this kind, called phonetic writing, used characters that represented spoken words, and therefore required many characters and necessitated long and tedious study to master it. It was gradually replaced among most peoples by an improved phonetic system, in which each character represented a syllable instead of a word; though the Chinese have never wholly abandoned it. The syllabic system needed, of course, fewer characters, and was much more easily learned, much more flexible and generally satisfactorily. The syllabic system was finally replaced among the more progressive peoples by the alphabetical system, in which each character represents a separate vocal sound. As the number of separate vocal sounds is few, only a few characters are needed. In most alphabets, the number of characters varies between twenty-two and thirty-six." (Bradley A. Fiske, *Invention, the Master-Key to Progress,* New York, 1921, p. 22)

Around 1000 B.C., there arose four main branches of the original Semitic alphabet: South Semitic, Canaanite, Aramaic, and Greek. The South Semitic

ed writing systems, along with the use of papyrus and parchment,[213] made communication more reliable over the limits of time and space,[214] thus assisting the expansion of the tribe to the nation. The

---

Branch later developed a number of scripts in the Arabian peninsula. The Canaanite Branch was subdivided into the Early Hebrew and the Phoenician alphabets. The Aramaic Branch was the most widespread script in western Asia, and various local offshoots became distinctive entities between the late third century B.C. and about 100 B.C. The Greek Branch emerged from the troubled darkness that shrouded the transition from the Bronze Age and Mycenaean civilization to the Iron Age and early Greek geometric art of the 800s B.C. Through its direct and indirect descendants, the Etruscan and the Latin alphabets on the one hand and the Cyrillic on the other, it became the progenitor of all the European alphabets, and in the course of its history, had offshoots in Asia Minor and Africa. In addition, there are Indian and Korean Branches. The early styles of Indian scripts were used in various parts of India from about the 6th century B.C. to the 4th century A.D. The Korean Branch seems to be a late development of the Indian Branch. (Cf. David Diringer, *The Alphabet, a Key to the History of Mankind*, New York, 1968, v. 1, p. 145-432. For the various stages of the development of writing, cf. *op. cit.* p. 4-13.)

213. Papyrus, which was extensively used as a writing material in the ancient world, was made by the Egyptians in the third millennium B.C. and continued in use in the Mediterranean region until about the 10th century A.D., after which it was gradually displaced by parchment. Of all the early writing materials, papyrus most closely resembled paper. Parchment, made from animal skins (usually those of sheep and goats), was probably known in the second millennium B.C. It continued in use even after the beginning of paper manufacture. (Cf. Dard Hunter, *Papermaking, the History and Technique of an Ancient Craft,* 2nd ed., New York, 1947, p. 17-23, 12-17.)

214. Lewis H. Morgan attributed the commencement of the "Status of Civilization" to the "invention of a phonetic alphabet with the use of writing." (Cf. his *Ancient Society,* New York, 1877, p. 12-13.)

"How many people try to realize what writing has meant to mankind? How could there be accumulation of wisdom without its being recorded in written characters? If culture is, as many scholars think, 'a communicable intelligence,' and if writing is, as it is, one of the most important means of communication—the only one indeed which can defy time and space—it is not an exaggeration to say that writing is the main currency of man's civilization. Wherever there has been civilization there have been writing and reading, in the remote past as in the present day. Written language has become the vehicle of civilization, and so of learning and education. Writing is thus one of the main aspects of culture which clearly distinguish mankind from the animal. . . . No wonder that in the past writing was held in much esteem. The ancient Egyptians attributed its creation either to Thoth, the god who invented nearly all the cultural elements, or to Isis. The Babylonian god of writing, Nebo, Marduk's son, was also the god of man's destiny. An ancient Jewish tradition considered Moses as the inventor of script. Greek myths attributed writing to Hermes or to other gods. The ancient Chinese, Indians and many other peoples also believed in the divine origin of script. Writing had always an enormous importance in learning and a magic power over the unlearned, in

invention of paper,[215] and the application of movable type in print-ing[216] sped up this expansion greatly.

Another very important medium of communication is money, which has been called "the universal language."[217] Various

---

such a way that even today 'illiterate' is almost synonymous with 'ignorant.' " (David Diringer, *The Alphabet, a Key to the History of Mankind,* New York, 1968, v. 1, p. 1)

215. Ts'ai Lun, 蔡倫, a Chinese court official, reported his invention of papermaking to the Emperor Ho-ti in 105 A.D. He is said to have used fibrous material from the bark of trees, hemp waste, old rags, and fish nets. By 610 A.D. the craft of papermaking had spread to Japan. Finally, by the 12th century, over a thousand years after its invention in China, the art of papermaking reached Europe by way of Baghdad, Damascus, Egypt, and Morocco. The first paper to be made in Europe was manufactured in Játiva in the Spanish province of Valencia, by 1150. (Cf. Dard Hunter, *Papermaking; the History and Technique of an Ancient Craft,* 2nd ed., New York, 1947, p. 48-63. Cf. also Joseph Needham, *Science and Civilization in China,* London, 1954, v. 4, section 32.)

Paper is so important to the advancement of our civilization that a popular book by John H. Ainsworth, Kaukauna, Wis., 1958, is entitled *Paper, the Fifth Wonder.*

216. The exact origin of the printing press, like the origin of printing from movable types, is debated by historians. It is generally acknowledged that Chinese craftsmen produced prints from hand-carved wooden blocks hundreds of years before the art was practiced in Europe, possibly as early as 400 A.D. In making these prints, they placed dampened paper over the inked block and rubbed or brushed the sheet until all parts of the printing surface made firm contact. There is no record of their having developed a device to produce an over-all impression at one stroke. About 1450, Johann Gutenberg of Mainz, Germany, originated a practical method of printing by bringing together his movable type, the paper and ink of European block printers, and a wooden bed-and-platen press. None of the elements he used—type, paper, ink, or press—was entirely new, but he adapted them in a unique manner to produce books in quantity. His genius did away with laborious hand copying, increased the circulation of books and knowledge, and contributed to a new era, the Renaissance. Until the middle of the 15th century, the only books available to Europeans were handwritten manuscripts, which were costly and often inaccurate copies. The development of printing brought books within the reach of the common people and contributed to the popularization of learning that was an element of the Renaissance. (Cf. Cyril Davenport, *The Book, Its History and Development,* New York, 1930, p. 85-99; Joseph Needham, *Science and Civilization in China,* London, 1954, v. 4, section 32; and R.J. Forbes, *Man, the Maker: A History of Technology and Engineering,* New York, 1950, p. 134-135.)

217. " . . . the invention of money, which, I am prepared to argue, was one of the most important inventions of all time in that it greatly facilitated the exchange of goods and thus a division of labor. . . . Economists usually define money as a medium of exchange, a measure of value, and a store of wealth. With the growth of trade it was essential to have some such instrument, for when one produces for unknown buyers, one cannot be certain that the purchasers will have goods to exchange which

objects,[218] notably the cowrie shell,[219] were used as money from very early times, and their development was associated with group expansion from the early family to the clan.[220] Metallic money began to appear about 1000 B.C., first in the form of tools,[221] then of coins.[222]

---

are really wanted in the market. Money is acceptable, however, in any market, because it is exchangeable for anything that is for sale." (Shepard B. Clough, *The Economic Development of Western Civilization,* New York, 1959, p. 30)

218. Anthropologists, archaeologists, and historians have reported thousands of decorative and useful objects—from sharks' teeth to cows—serving as a kind of "money" in primitive and archaic societies on all the continents. It has not been easy to fully understand the functions such monetary objects perform nor to assess their importance. (Cf. G. Dalton, "Primitive Money," *American Anthropologist,* v. 67, February, 1965. Also cf. Paul Einzig, *Primitive Money in its Ethnological, Historical and Economic Aspects,* 2nd ed., Oxford, 1966.)

"Metals were first used by man as ornaments. Gold was probably the metal discovered earliest, as it occurs in nuggets of native metal in many streams and its color and luster would arrest the attention of the most primitive man. So soft and malleable that it can be easily worked, it lends itself naturally to the first use to which primitive man put it." (Thomas S. Lovering, *Minerals in World Affairs,* New York, 1943, p. 36)

219. "The best known and most widespread of the ornamental currencies is, however, the cowrie shell. It was used as a means of payment in India, the Middle East, and China, probably for several thousand years before Christ, and it continued to circulate in historical times over large parts of Asia, Africa, and the Pacific Islands, from Nigeria to Siam, and from the Sudan to the New Hebrides. Even now its use is not quite extinct." (E. Victor Morgan, *A History of Money,* Baltimore, 1965, p. 12)

It is interesting to note that the cowrie shell's use as money was so important in ancient China that most of the Chinese characters relating to money were composed with the symbol of shell, "貝", such as 貨 (money, goods), 財 (money, wealth), 寶 (treasure), 賺 (to earn), 賒 (to charge), 貴 (high-priced), 貧 (poor), and 賤 (cheap).

220. In the early development of money in tropical regions, the articles chosen for monetary purposes were chiefly those that could be used in fishing and hunting and in ornamenting the person. Such articles included fishhooks; flints for arrows; beads made of cowrie shells, porcelain, and turquoise; the teeth of sharks and whales; elephant tusks; and tiger claws. In colder climates, articles of clothing, such as skins and furs, were widely used as money. As the art of domesticating animals progressed, cattle and sheep were commonly selected as standards of value; indeed, the ox remained the standard of value in many early civilizations long after the coining of metals had been introduced. The growth of agriculture led to the adoption of such commodities as sugar, corn, wheat, tobacco, tea, and coconuts as money. (Cf. Rupert J. Ederer, *The Evolution of Money,* Washington, 1964, p. 19-48.)

221. "Meanwhile the metal 'tool money' of northern Europe was working its way towards the Mediterranean, and spits, tripods, basins, axes, and rings, served as money for small payments in Homeric Greece. These articles were originally of

The silver and gold coins, especially, inspired confidence because of their durable and precious qualities, and universal demand for them, and facilitated exchange tremendously,[223] thus stimulating the expansion of the clan to the tribe. The rise of the banking system to extend the use of money[224] had a great impact on the expansion of the tribe to the nation.

The above reviews of the means of transportation and the media of communication reaffirm that the development of tools and energies is a major factor for group expansion.

---

bronze but in post-Homeric times iron spits were used." (E. Victor Morgan, *A History of Money,* Baltimore, 1965, p. 12-13. Cf. Rupert J. Ederer, *The Evolution of Money,* Washington, 1964, p. 50-72.)

222. "The earliest European coins of a recognizably modern type came from Lydia, in Asia Minor, and were probably struck during the ninth or eighth century B.C., though some scholars put the date even later. The earliest coins were probably made by merchants, but the function of coinage was soon taken over by governments, and between the eighth and sixth centuries B.C. the various states and cities of the Aegean and Asia Minor each came to issue coins bearing their own emblem—the lion's head of Lydia, the turtle of Aegina, the winged horse of Corinth, and the owl of Athens. The early coins of Asia Minor were of electrum, an alloy of gold and silver.... Silver was coined in Aegina about 750 B.C., and the first coinage of gold on its own is attributed to Croesus, king of Lydia, in the sixth century. The coinage of China goes back to the Chou dynasty, which held power from the twelfth to the third century B.C. Some of the earliest coins had the shape of cowrie shells, others of swords, knives, and spades. Several centuries before Christ, however, round discs of copper with square holes in the middle were being made, the 'cash' which survived until modern times." (E. Victor Morgan, *A History of Money,* Baltimore, 1965, p. 13)

223. "The use of coins has revolutionized the commerce of all subsequent time, and it is at the very basis of the organization of large modern cooperative communities. In its own time it enormously facilitated buying and selling for profit and speculation. It was equally momentous in its social and political effects. It vastly increased freedom of movement." (Arthur R. Burns, *Money and Monetary Policy in Early Times,* New York, 1927, p. 52)

224. "With the increasing use of money, banking came into being, and with it the practice of charging interest. The former innovation meant that there were businessmen who specialized in the safekeeping of funds, in the accumulation of moneys from diverse savers, and in the lending of sums to those who would engage in business enterprise. Interest taking meant the creation of an incentive to hold savings in money and this practice made mobile wealth available for those who would pay to use others' savings in the hope of making a profit. Here were added features of the monetary system which were almost as important to economic growth as money itself." (Shepard B. Clough, *The Economic Development of Western Civilization,* New York, 1959, p. 31. Cf. Abbott P. Usher, *The Early History of Deposit Banking in Mediterranean Europe,* Cambridge, Mass. 1943, p. 3-192.)

g.
Weapons

IN WARFARE, TOOLS AND ENERGIES ARE CALLED
weapons.

Since their first appearance in history, weapons have played an important role in group expansion: directly, through military conquests, occupations and annexations achieved by their force; and indirectly through alliances, leagues, confederations and federations united under their pressure. The force and pressure which weapons can exert over groups have grown steadily as their striking power, reaching distance, speed and mobility have continually increased.

Our early ancestors probably first used hand-held stones as weapons, then learned to use clubs[226] before starting to use stone-bladed spears and stone axes.[227] The striking power of the club and stone weapons was apparently awkward and their reaching distance limited to several yards; their speed depended on man's hands, and their mobility on man's feet. Notwithstanding, it would be very diffi-

---

225. Man's bodily equipment for combating or preying on other animals is inadequate; he has no great strength, and neither fangs nor claws. Among the tools extending his ability to cope with his environment are weapons for securing food, and for self-defense, as well as offence. "Inasmuch as the most important employment of man from his first breath until his last has always been the struggle to preserve his life; inasmuch as the endeavor of primeval man to defend himself against wild beasts must have been extremely bitter (for many were larger and stronger than he), and inasmuch as man eventually achieved the mastery over them, one seems forced to conclude that man overcame wild beasts by employing some means to assist his bodily strength, and that probably his first invention was a weapon." (Bradley A. Fiske, *Invention, the Master-Key to Progress,* New York, 1921, p. 2)

226. The club is a cudgel or heavy, blunt weapon made of any of a variety of materials and used to deliver a crushing blow. The club is probably the most primitive of all weapons, and hunters through the ages have used it in various forms to kill small animals caught in snares or large ones wounded by spears or arrows. It is also used for throwing and in close-combat fighting. (Cf. B.E. Sargeaunt, *Weapons,* London, 1908, p. 13-14, and the pictures of clubs in the following plate.)

227. Early man of the Middle Pleistocene period first used hand-held stones, to which he gave cutting edges, and also clubs; and later, the throwing of weapons extended the power of attack, with stone-bladed spears and stone axes. (Cf. Charles Boutell, *Arms and Armour in Antiquity and the Middle Ages,* New York, 1870, p. 1-8; and Peter Young, *The Machinery of War,* London, 1973, p. 14-28.)

cult for group expansion to have started through the primitive community without their help.[228]

The transition from throwing a stone as a missile to blowing a blowgun,[229] releasing a sling,[230] or projecting a javelin,[231] was a slow journey. But a great leap forward was made with the invention of the bow and arrow.[232] This invention reduced to seconds the time needed to reach a target tens of yards away, and increased striking power,

---

228. In the early stage, weapons and tools were inseparable. They were used to fight against human competitors, and animals, as well as for hunting and fishing. They promoted group expansion in both ways.

229. The blowgun is a primitive weapon in the form of a tube through which a projectile is propelled by a puff of breath from the mouth. The tube is often made of bamboo. The projectile is most commonly a slender arrow, sometimes a bamboo splinter, with a cuplike base. The blowgun is native to tropical South America and to Southeast Asia, Indonesia, and the Philippines. (Cf. Edwin Funis, *Weapons, a Pictorial History,* Cleveland, 1954, p. 18.)

230. The sling is a primitive weapon used to propel rocks and other missiles. The simple sling consisted of a pocket, usually of leather, with a string tied to each end. One string was looped over the fourth finger, and the other was held between the thumb and forefinger. A missile was placed in the pocket. The weapon was operated by whirling it over the head and letting go of the unlooped string, thereby releasing the projectile. The centrifugal force gained in the whirling action gave power and range to the shot. The biblical David used a sling to kill Goliath. (Cf. Peter Young, *The Machinery of War,* London, 1973, p. 14, 19; and Yigael Yadin, *The Art of Warfare in Biblical Lands,* New York, 1963, p. 9.)

231. The javelin is a throwing spear. Except for the stone, the spear is probably man's earliest missile weapon. Levers called spear-throwers, which were used in order to give spears a longer range, have been found on Upper Paleolithic sites, and are similar to those used by Eskimos and Australasians in modern times. The Greeks, among others, used a loop of cord on the middle of a spear shaft for the same purpose. Used by Greek hoplites (heavily armed infantrymen) in the 7th century B.C., the javelin was later used only by the light infantry. The Roman legionary of the period 200 B.C. to 200 A.D. carried the pilum, a javelin of which the head and forward section of the shaft were made of a single piece of iron. A similar weapon, the angon, was used by the early Franks. (Cf. Peter Young, *The Machinery of War,* London, 1973, p. 14, 18-19; and Yigael Yadin, *The Art of Warfare in Biblical Lands,* New York, 1963, p. 10.)

232. "The invention of the bow and arrow was one of the first order of brilliancy, and would be so even now. It is not easy to think of any simple accident as accounting for the invention; because the bow and arrow consists of three entirely independent parts—the straight bar of wood, the string, and the arrow; for the bow was not a bow until the string had been fastened to each end, and drawn so tight that the bar of wood was forced into a bent shape, and held there at great tension. When one realizes this, and realizes in addition the countless centuries during which the bow and arrow held its sway, the millions of men who have used it, and the important effect it has had in the overcoming of wild beasts, and the deciding of many of the critical battles of the world, he can hardly escape the conclusion

especially with poison and fire arrows. With the advantage of the bow and arrow, the clan grew rapidly.[233]

The substitution of metal weapons for stone ones started about 6000 years ago.[234] It was a long process,[235] but greatly increased the power of weapons, because weapons made of metal are much sharper, much more durable and maneuverable, and much more conve-

---

that the invention of the bow and arrow was one of the most important occurrences in the history of mankind." (Bradley A. Fiske, *Invention, the Master-Key to Progress,* New York, 1921, p. 5. Cf. Bridget Allchin, *The Stone-Tipped Arrow,* New York, 1966; Peter Young, *The Machinery of War,* London, 1973, p. 14, 19-20; and Edwin Funis, *Weapons, a Pictorial History,* Cleveland, 1954, p. 17-20.)

233. "As a combination of forces it is so abstruse that it not unlikely owed its origin to accident. The elasticity and toughness of certain kinds of wood, the tension of a cord of sinew or vegetable fibre by means of a bent bow, and finally their combination to propel an arrow by human muscle, are not very obvious suggestions to the mind of a savage. As elsewhere noticed, the bow and arrow are unknown to the Polynesians in general, and to the Australians. From this fact alone it is shown that mankind were well advanced in the savage state when the bow and arrow made their first appearance." This invention "[which] came in after the spear and war club, and gave the first deadly weapon for the hunt, appeared late in savagery. It has been used to mark the commencement of its Upper Status. It must have given a powerful upward influence to ancient society, standing in the same relation to the period of savagery, as the iron sword to the period of barbarism, and firearms to the period of civilization." (Lewis H. Morgan, *Ancient Society,* New York, 1877, p. 21-22)

234. Cast copper axes found at Kish, also in Mesopotamia, are about the same age (from 5500 years ago). At Luristan, Persia, a series of beautiful and elaborately decorated weapons, implements, and ornaments of bronze, probably 4000 years old, have recently been discovered in cemeteries scattered over a considerable area. These include axes of several forms, and daggers. Recent excavations in China, in the district of Hsiao Tun Tsun, near An Yang, in the province of Honan, illustrate the eastward extension of the use of bronze. This locality was a capital of the Shang Dynasty, about 1500 B.C. Here many bronze weapons and ornaments were found, including socketed spear heads, knives, socketed axes and arrowheads. Montelius divides the Bronze Age in Sweden into five periods: 1900-1600 B.C. with flat bronze axes, daggers, and armlets; 1600-1400 B.C. with more developed axes, and swords; 1400-1050 B.C., with swords with decorated hilts. (Cf. Vesey Norman, *Arms and Armor,* New York, 1964, p. 95-128; Charles Boutell, *Arms and Armour in Antiquity and the Middle Ages,* New York, 1870, p. 10-152; Harold L. Peterson, *Daggers and Fighting Knives of the Western World,* New York, 1968, p. 1-7; and Rutherford J. Gettens, Roy S. Clarke, Jr., and W.T. Chase, *Two Early Chinese Bronze Weapons with Meteoritic Iron Blades,* Washington, 1971, p. 1-2.)

235. "Native copper, like gold, was used as an ornament by Stone Age man; but because of its greater hardness, copper was soon used for more practical purposes. Copper weapons were much superior to those made of stone, so it was not surprising that, in man's perennial desire for increased security, he fashioned

nient for developing and training a professional skill, such as the use of the sword.[236] The striking power also increased when the battering-ram was used.[237] Meanwhile, the mobility, speed, and reaching distance of weapons were greatly extended by using the horse and chariot in warfare,[238] other animals for moving and fighting,[239] the

---

native copper into knives, arrowheads, and spear points. The art of hardening copper by hammering was known to the Chaldeans about 4500 B.C." "For a long time metal weapons were only for the rich and powerful. Many soldiers of Xerxes' army were still equipped with stone weapons. The use of metal for peaceful occupations slowly followed its introduction as a material for improving armaments." (Thomas S. Lovering, *Minerals in World Affairs,* New York, 1943, p. 36-37, 38)

236. The short-handled, long-bladed weapon akin to a dagger but larger, the sword, has numerous types of blades, which can be broken down into four main groups: (1) straight cutting blades sharp on one or both edges; (2) straight, stiff blades solely for thrusting; (3) curved cutting blades usually sharp on the convex edge; (4) recurved, or S-shaped, blades, in which the cutting edge curves on the forward edge from the hilt and then on the backward edge toward the point. This type usually widens near the point to place maximum weight at the point of percussion. (Cf. R. Ewart Oakeshott, *The Sword in the Age of Chivalry,* New York, 1965, p. 25-143. Also Charles Boutell, *Arms and Armour in Antiquity and the Middle Ages,* New York, 1870, p. 10-55, 65-69, 83-152.)

237. The earliest, simplest, and, until the development of heavy artillery in the 1300s, most effective device for destroying stone walls and the ordinary defenses of fortified towns was the battering ram. Ancient armies used two different kinds of battering ram: one type was suspended and swinging, like a pendulum, and the other moved on rollers. The rolling ram seems to have been used first at the siege of Byzantium in 196 A.D. These rams were often extremely heavy. In Roman literature, Appian writes that at the siege of Carthage he saw two rams so colossal that 100 men worked each of them. Vitruvius affirms that the beam was often from 100 to 120 feet in length; and Justus Lipsius describes some as 180 feet long and 2 feet 4 inches in diameter, with an iron head weighing at least a ton and a half, and a total weight of more than 45,000 pounds. (Cf. Peter Young, *The Machinery of War,* London, 1973, p. 25; and Edwin Funis, *Weapons, a Pictorial History,* Cleveland, 1954, p. 31.)

238. Sometime before 2000 B.C., tribes north of the Caucasus or in the Ukraine were domesticating horses. A light two-wheeled vehicle, the chariot, was developed some hundred years later, and this military vehicle was taken by raiders westward into Europe and southward into the old centers of Bronze Age civilization. Chariot-using armies of the Hyksos invaded Egypt around 1700 B.C. and northwestern India about 1500 B.C. War chariots also appear about this time in North China. The regular use of cavalry dates from 900-800 B.C. in southern Russia. (Cf. William H. McNeill, *The Rise of the West,* Chicago, 1964, p. 104-109, 234-239, 322-323; Yigael Yadin, *The Art of Warfare in Biblical Lands,* New York, 1963, p. 4, 37, 74, 86, 113; and Courtlandt Canby, *A History of Weaponry,* New York, 1963, p. 23-38.)

crossbow,[240] the catapult,[241] and the ballistae[242] on land; and the battleship[243] on water. Amid these developments, the tribe reached its heyday.

The most significant development in weapons, however, was yet

239. For instance, African elephants may have been domesticated by the ancient Carthaginians and used in war against the Romans. Elephants were depicted on medals of Faustina and of Lucius Septimius Severus, with heads and bodies of the Asiatic, but ears of the African species. In 218 B.C., Hannibal and his army crossed the Alps with elephants. In later times, they were used in Roman amphitheatres and for military pageants, a practice that continues to this day in the form of exhibitions at circuses, carnivals, and zoological parks. In warfare, elephants were used for dragging heavy equipment through mud and up steep slopes. As late as World War II, elephants were of considerable value in southeast Asia. (Cf. Sir Gavin de Beer, *Alps and Elephants: Hannibal's March,* London, 1955.)

There are some stories in Chinese history about the use of buffalos in warfare. It was said, for instance, that King Kou-chien of Yueh (越王勾踐), used buffalos with fire attached to their tails to attack the army of King Fu-tsai of Wu (吳王夫差), in a decisive war 2500 years ago.

240. Improvements of the bow were made in antiquity, producing the composite (reinforced) bow and crossbow, both with very powerful spring action, which threw a heavier missile a greater distance and with greater penetration. The huge crossbows and slings developed as siege engines (corresponding to artillery) by the ancients, early Chinese, and medieval Europeans were magnified forms of primitive weapons. (Cf. Peter Young, *The Machinery of War,* London, 1973, p. 32-34; and Ralph Payne-Gallwey, *The Crossbow,* London, 1958, p. 3-53.)

241. The catapult was the lightest and most flexible Roman siege engine, used from about 200 B.C. to 400 A.D. It threw 6-pound javelins about 500 yards, to which were often attached flaming materials. Siege engines confused with the catapult are the ballista, which was 10 times larger and threw 60-pound stones, and the onager, whose single spar moved in a vertical arc to hurl head-sized stones. (Cf. Peter Young, *The Machinery of War,* London, 1973, p. 27; Edwin Funis, *Weapons, a Pictorial History,* Cleveland, 1954, p. 34.)

242. "Ballistae ... [were] shot stones, beams, or balls up to 162 lbs. weight, at an angle of 50°. The average range of the ballistae was from about 293 yards to about 503 yards." Power for tossing the missiles was acquired by "twisting strong elastic cords, the sinews of animals, or the long hair of animals or of women." (James M. Gavin, *War and Peace in the Space Age,* New York, 1958, p. 215)

243. For more than 2,000 years, the principal warships of the world were slender Mediterranean galleys which were propelled by oars, at least when they went into action. They dominated naval battles from Salamis in 480 B.C., and even earlier, down to Lepanto in 1571 A.D. Long before the galley proper had been developed by the Greeks, there were scattered recorded examples of Mediterranean fighting vessels. Around 1400 B.C., pirate raiders in fast, slender vessels threatened Egypt's commercial communications with Phoenicia and other parts of the eastern Mediterranean. Some two centuries later, the Greeks captured Troy with a major expedition. Homer, the Greek poet, gave a detailed description of the Greek galleys in his *Illiad* (C. 850 B.C.), but he was writing long after the event.

to be introduced by the invention of black powder,[244] and its application to artillery,[245] rockets,[246] firearms,[247] and naval fleets.[248] It strengthened weapons with a striking power so formidable as to eliminate almost all the defensive value of feudal castles, heavy city

---

(Cf. Lionel Casson, *The Ancient Mariners: Seafarers and Seafighters of the Mediterranean in Ancient Times,* New York, 1959, p. 66-246.)

244. The powerful black powder was the sole explosive material available for almost 600 years, from the time of its discovery to the mid-19th century when nitroglycerin and nitrocellulose were discovered. There is no certainty as to the actual date of the invention of black powder, but early experiments with such materials as oil, pitch, sulfur, and other ingredients were all steps on the road to its discovery. These predecessors were of a sticky nature; they not only adhered to the objects they hit, but their fire was difficult to extinguish, especially with water. The most famous of these mixtures was known as Greek fire, long a terror to the enemies of the ancient Byzantine empire. Among the many claimants of the honor of discovering black powder are the Chinese, Hindus, Greeks, Arabs, English, and Germans. Black powder attained greater prominence when the first guns were invented to utilize it as a propellant, early in the 14th century. (Cf. Dudley Pope, *Guns,* London, 1969, p. 16-23.)

245. In ancient times, man increased the range of his weapons by using various types of catapults. These were great slings used to hurl stones and other large heavy objects over large distances. The history of artillery as we know it today dates roughly from the first use of gunpowder in Europe, about 1250 A.D., which brought into use the first smoothbore cannon. The development of the cannon preceded that of small arms by about 50 years. The tube of a cannon was made like the barrel of those days, straight-sided out of wooden staves bound together with hoops of iron; it has been known ever since as the barrel of the weapon. The earliest artillery was used chiefly against the walls and gates of besieged towns, forts, and castles. (Cf. William Y. Carman, *History of Firearms from the Early Times to 1914,* New York, 1956, p. 1-54; and Peter Young, *The Machinery of War,* London, 1973, p. 24-31, 39-40, 45.)

"It was a very long time before fire-arms reached the shape they assumed in the middle of the nineteenth century. Although the military reforms of Gustavus Adolphus early in the seventeenth century, had foreshadowed the importance of artillery in the field, instead of merely in sieges, it was not until the Napoleonic wars that this heavier kind of weapon began to play a preponderant part in deciding the issues of battles." (F.O. Miksche, *Atomic Weapons and Armies,* New York, 1955, p. 25)

246. The simplest substance which can be packed into a rocket chamber to deliver large quantities of combustion gases when burned is ordinary black powder. The early histories of powder and rockets coincide, therefore, especially since the rocket was invented almost a century earlier than the gun. The invention must have been made around the year 1200 A.D., in China, for the earliest recorded use of rockets was at the siege of Kaifeng in 1232. It was probably the battle in which the Chinese shot rockets called "fire arrows" against the invading Mongols. (Cf. Willy Ley, *Rockets, Missiles, and Men in Space,* New York, 1968, p. 3-24; also Peter Young, *The Machinery of War,* London, 1973, p. 65.)

247. Small arms are firearms whose caliber is not greater than 20 mm, or .79

walls, and other fortifications. It also enlarged the reaching distance, speed and mobility of weapons tremendously. Up to the turn of this century, for example, improved guns had been able to hit targets tens of miles away;[249] magazine rifles to fire 15 rounds a minute at 1000 yards,[250] and naval fleets to carry the far-reaching and high-speed weapons to attack a country across the ocean.[251] This significant de-

---

inch, such as the arquebus, carbine, machinegun, musket, pistol, revolver, and rifle. There is no record of the use of firearms before 1247, and it was not until a century later that the first small arms came into use. (Cf. Charles Boutell, *Arms and Armour in Antiquity and the Middle Ages,* New York, 1870, p. 242-260; Frederick Wilkinson, *Small Arms,* New York, 1966, p. 11-31; and Robert Held, *The Age of Firearms,* New York, 1957, p. 45-187.)

248. For example, "the slender Mediterranean galleys, dominated naval battles from Salamis in 480 B.C., and even earlier, down to Lepanto in 1571 A.D. ... The ancient fleets contained far more numerous capital ships than those of later days. Whereas there were only 27 British and 33 French and Spanish ships of the line at Trafalgar in 1805, and similar small numbers in the later great battles of Jutland (1916) and Leyte Gulf (1944), there seem to have been at least 1,000 triremes, and possibly 1,800, in the decisive Battle of Salamis in 480 B.C. At Aegospotami, in 405 B.C., the Spartans captured 171 of the 180 Athenian triremes, whose crews had gone ashore to forage for food." (Robert G. Albion, "Warships" in the *Encyclopedia Americana,* 1973 ed., Vol. 28, p. 363)

249. The reaching distance of weapons has increased rapidly since the powerful black powder was applied to artillery in the 14th century. It has been asserted that cannons with a range of a mile were used in 1453. Field guns at the time of the American Civil War had effective ranges of 1.6 miles. Siege guns in the Boer War had ranges of five miles. In 1918, the Germans shelled Paris by means of a gun with a range of 75 miles. And a gun designed to shoot 200 miles has already been experimented with by the French government. Such artillery is not developed, however, because bombing planes are so much more effective and economical as weapons for slaughter and destruction at long distances. (Cf. Hornell N. Hart, *The Technique of Social Progress,* New York, 1931, p. 80-81.)

250. "On the other hand, the second half of the nineteenth century witnessed a rapid progress during which the infantry equipment changed from the muzzle-loading rifles firing two shots a minute with a range of 200 yards to the magazine rifle firing fifteen rounds a minute at 1,000 yards, not to mention the first automatic weapons, such as the Maxim gun. Muzzle-loading guns were replaced by modern field artillery, hitting targets at distances of several miles with high-explosive shells, imcomparably greater in effect than simple round-shot." (F.O. Miksche, *Atomic Weapons and Armies,* New York, 1955, p. 25-26)

251. This was the case in July, 1853, when an American naval squadron dropped anchor in Tokyo Bay. The squadron headed by Commodore Matthew C. Perry threatened to attack and refused to depart until a message from the President of the United States, requesting the conclusion of a treaty, had been properly delivered. Negotiations between Japanese and American representatives culminated in the Treaty of Kanagawa, signed on March 31, 1854. The Japanese

velopment introduced by the invention and application of black powder accelerated the growth of the nation to the peak of its history.

Thus, in weapons, we see clearly too that the development of tools and energies is the major factor in group expansion.

h.
From Wonderful Fire
to Useful Knowledge

THE INQUIRY INTO THE RELATIONSHIP BETWEEN group expansion and the development of tools and energies has proceeded through a wide range from mode of life, transportation and communication to weapons. In order to shed more light on the picture, a unique case of wonderful fire is presented here as a retrospective episode.

Fire is a tool as well as an energy, with many splendid faces.[252] It

---

policy of national isolation had begun to crumble. (Cf. The story in *Japan Since Perry,* by Chitoshi Yanaga, New York, 1949.)

252. Fire is the agent of purification, one of the so-called four elements which burns, inflames, warms, or heats; the igneous principle, heat and light emanating visibly, perceptibly and simultaneously from any body, caloric, the effect of combustion. The terrific energy of fire, the most important agent of civilization, the similarity of its effects with that of the sun, its intimate connection with light, its terrible and yet genial power, and the beauty of its changeful flame, easily account for the reverence in which it was held in ancient times. At a period when cause and effect, and form and essence, were not distinctly separated, fire became an object of religious veneration, a distinguished element in mythology, an expressive symbol in poetry, and an important agent in the systems of cosmogony. It gained a place among the elements, and for a long time was believed to be a constituent part in the composition of all bodies. At a later period, fire, under the name of phlogiston, was considered to be the source of all chemical action. (Cf. Gaston Bachelard, *The Psychoanalysis of Fire,* translated by Alan C.M. Ross, Boston, 1964, p. vi-viii, 59-98, 109-112.)

"Fire is thus a privileged phenomenon which can explain anything. If all that changes slowly may be explained by life, all that changes quickly is explained by fire. Fire is the ultra-living element. It is intimate and it is universal. It lives in our

was probably the first and greatest discovery we ever made,[253] and it has been used everywhere[254] and during all times.[255]

---

heart. It lives in the sky. It rises from the depths of the substance and offers itself with the warmth of love. Or it can go back down into the substance and hide there, latent and pent-up, like hate and vengeance. Among all phenomena, it is really the only one to which there can be so definitely attributed the opposing values of good and evil. It shines in Paradise. It burns in Hell. It is gentleness and torture. It is cookery and it is apocalypse. It is a pleasure for the good child sitting prudently by the hearth; yet it punishes any disobedience when the child wishes to play too close to its flames. It is well-being and it is respect. It is a tutelary and a terrible divinity, both good and bad. It can contradict itself; thus it is one of the principles of universal explanation." (*Ibid*, p. 1)

In Chinese philosophy fire is one of the five elements: metal, plant, water, fire and earth (五行：金，木，水，火，土).

253. "Man, it is well to remember, is the discoverer but not the inventor of fire.... but he did make it one of the giant powers on the earth. He began this experiment long ago in the red morning of the human mind. Today he continues it in the midst of coruscating heat that is capable of rending the very fabric of his universe. Man's long adventure with knowledge has, to a very marked degree, been a climb up the heat ladder, for heat alone enables man to mold metals and glassware, to create his great chemical industries, to drive his swift machines." "Today the flames grow hotter in the furnaces. Man has come far up the heat ladder. The creature that crept furred through the glitter of blue glacial nights lives surrounded by the hiss of steam, the roar of engines and the bubbling of vats. Like a long-armed crab, he manipulates the tongs in dangerous atomic furnaces. In asbestos suits he plunges into the flaming debris of hideous accidents. With intricate heat-measuring instruments he investigates the secrets of the stars, and he is already searching for heat-resistant alloys that will enable him to hurl himself into space." (Loren C. Eiseley, "Man the Fire-Maker," in *Scientific American*, v. 191, 1954, p. 52 and 57. Cf. Omer C. Stewart, "Fire as the First Great Force Employed by Man," in the *International Symposium on Man's Role in Changing the Face of the Earth*, ed. William L. Thomas, Jr., Chicago, 1956, p. 116-118.)

254. "The use of fire is very ancient and, so far as direct evidence goes, universal ... it is certain that over the whole earth no fireless tribe of men has been found. The diluvial man had it, and even knew how to generate it, and the lowest of historic or contemporary tribes possess it, even though they do not own any fire-making apparatus." (William G. Sumner and Albert G. Keller, *The Science of Society*, New Haven, 1927, v. 1, p. 187-188)

"Of all human inventions the discovery of the method of kindling fire has probably been the most momentous and far-reaching. It must date from an extreme antiquity, since there appears to be no well-attested case of a savage tribe ignorant of the use of fire and of the mode of producing it." (James G. Frazer, *Myths of the Origin of Fire*, London, 1930, p. 1. Cf. Edward B. Tylor, *Researches into the Early History of Mankind*, London, 1878, p. 229-274.)

255. Archaeological investigations indicate that the control of fire is an extremely old technical attainment, though the time, place, and mode of its origin will probably never be learned. The earliest evidence derives from a living site near Nice, France, that may have been occupied as early as a million years ago. By the

It was probably the use of fire which differentiated us from other animals, and led to group expansion.[256]

Middle Pleistocene period, about 500,000 years ago, in European and Chinese sites, evidence for fire has been found in abundance. Man's movement into these northern areas was probably a direct consequence of his control of fire, since the climate at that time was influenced by glacial activity, and some source of heat would have been necessary for survival. By the last ice age, fire is universally attested in the Old World by the abundance of hearths within the living sites. (Cf. Omer C. Stewart, "Fire as the First Great Force Employed by Man," in the *International Symposium on Man's Role in Changing the Face of the Earth,* ed. by William L. Thomas, Jr., Chicago, 1956, p. 115. Also: Chester Chard, *Man in Prehistory,* New York, 1969.)

256. "Man is scarcely man till he is in possession of fire; or, to put it in another way, when man got control of fire, a chasm was opened between him and all other creatures which was never closed again." (William G. Sumner and Albert G. Keller, *The Science of Society,* New Haven, 1927, v. 1, p. 188)

"Among the expedients by which man irrevocably widened the gap between himself and all his fellow creatures, the most appropriate for bringing to a natural conclusion the first epoch of human history is fire." (Julius Lippert, *The Evolution of Culture,* trans. and ed. by George P. Murdock, New York, 1931, p. 130)

It is interesting to note that the Chinese word 伙 (company, community, or group) is composed of man and fire. It suggests that, originally, fire was as essential as men to form a group.

"Some wish to go still farther back on the evolutionary trail and to refer the physical development of Homo, and in particular the differentiation of function between hand and foot, the importance of which has been so often emphasized, in good part to the use of fire. Certainly one of the prime needs of man, living amidst a hostile and physically better endowed animal environment, was protection in the inevitable struggle for existence. It seems that such protection was to be attained in good part, as it is still attained by most primates, through an arboreal life. . . . But there was only one element in nature, mastery over which enabled men to spend the night as well as the day upon the earth-surface, and that was fire; for it is universally feared by animals and dazes them. Hence with the possession of fire there came to man, or to his precursor, that possibility of a terrestrial existence which drew after it significant structural changes, extending by way of the hand and its power of manipulation even to the brain, which are now recognized as specifically human." (Julius Lippert, *The Evolution of Culture,* trans. and ed. by George P. Murdock, quoted from Murdock's thesis, v. 1, p. 69)

257. "Surprisingly enough, the use of fire seems to be as early as, if not earlier than the earliest certain tools. Perhaps it had been used by Pithecanthropus in the second Ice Age, to keep him alive during that terrible time. Its use at the beginnings of the Old Palaeolithic Age distinguished human food gathering from that of the animals." "The invention of fire may even have produced that increase in the numbers of early man which make his remains conspicuous to archaeology for the first time." (Fritz Heichelheim, *An Ancient Economic History,* rev. and complete English ed., Leiden, 1958, v. 1, p. 10)

"Clothed, housed, and provided with fire, man was able to undertake the conquest of all regions, but without fire he dare not have braved the winters even

It was fire which kept us surviving through the terrible Ice Age and enabled us to conquer the vast cold regions for group expansion.[257]

It was fire which helped us to eat fish and dry grains by cooking them, making it possible to exploit many more food resources for group expansion.[258]

---

of the middle latitudes, to say nothing of Arctic regions." (*The Historians' History of the World,* 1907, v. 1, p. 45)

"There are many climates in which man could not possibly have come to dwell without this element (fire); in its absence his habitat could include only tropical regions, and not all of these. Hence the wideness of man's dispersal, unparalleled in the geographical distribution of organisms, must be regarded as one of the results of the discovery and appropriation of fire." (William G. Sumner and Albert G. Keller, *The Science of Society,* New Haven, 1927, v. 1, p. 188)

258. "In fish must be recognized the first kind of artificial food, because it was not fully available without cooking. Fire was first utilized, not unlikely, for this purpose. Fish were universal in distribution, unlimited in supply, and the only kind of food at all times attainable. The cereals in the primitive period were still unknown, if in fact they existed, and the hunt for game was too precarious ever to have formed an exclusive means of human support. Upon this species of food mankind became independent of climate and of locality; and by following the shores of the seas and lakes, and the courses of the rivers could, while in the savage state, spread themselves over the greater portion of the earth's surface." (Lewis H. Morgan, *Ancient Society,* New York, 1877, p. 21)

Man's first chemical experiment involving the use of heat was to make certain foods digestible. He had cooked his meat; now he used fire to cook his grain. To cook grain was more necessary than to cook meat, because grain had to be dried for storing for a longer time, and dry grain could hardly be eaten unless cooked. Cooking softened the tough material to conform to the needs of the human stomach and to shorten the digestive process. Thus, fire allowed man to exploit a great source of subsistence and enabled him to expand his numbers rapidly and to press on from hunting to more advanced cultures. Yet we take fire so much for granted that this first great upswing in human numbers, and its relation to this first real gain in the seizure of vast quantities of free energy, have to a remarkable degree eluded our attention. (Cf. Loren C. Eiseley, "Man the Fire-Maker," in *Scientific American,* v. 191, 1954, p. 55-56; and Walter Hough, *Fire as an Agent in Human Culture,* U.S. National Museum *Bulletin* 139, Washington, 1926, p. 30-45.)

259. "Among the rude aids of primitive hunters fire became one of the most important. The advancing forest or prairie fire brought out the terrified game better and more quickly than a line of beaters. To this day the Navahos burn over large areas of the forests in the White Mountains of Arizona in their annual hunts. The fascination of fire by night is potent to the destruction of fish, bird, or beast, and thick smoke drives any unwilling animal whatever from his impregnable lair. At some time animals acquired an instinctive fear of fire. This is shown by the use of hot irons in controlling animals in menageries. In the work of circus men lions and tigers will cringe before a heated poker, and no matter how restless and fretful they may have been, the sight of the glowing iron immediately brings them to their

It was fire which helped us to fight, hunt, and control many strong animals,[259] thus providing more subsistence for group expansion.

It was fire which helped us to develop agriculture, by burning bushes, jungle, and clearing fields,[260] to provide more subsistence for group expansion.

---

best of animal senses. A number of methods have been developed, based on a knowledge of the habits and other characteristics of animals. Chief of these are the lures of light, remarked on in another section, and probably later than capture by smoke and heat.... The use of the smudge (to repulse insects) is almost universal." (Walter Hough, *Fire as an Agent in Human Culture,* U.S. National Museum *Bulletin* 139, Washington, 1926, p. 61)

260. Certainly long before history, fire was employed to burn forest and field to improve the environment for human use. With the achievement of hoe-cultivation in Neolithic times in the Near East, about 7000 B.C., there came a new urgency to clear brush and trees. The early farmers made use of fire to clear fields and to produce ash to serve as fertilizer. This practice, called slash-and-burn, or milpa, cultivation, persists in many tropical areas and some temperate zones to-day. The record of the antiquity and widespread use of fire for this purpose is seen in the windy steppes of Russia, the Great Plains and pampas of the New World, and the Sudan and velds of Africa. There are also examples on record in Chinese history. For instance, Mencius said that "the Emperor Shun (sometime before 2000 B.C.) told Yi to burn the forests over the mountains and along the rivers." (孟子：〝舜使益掌火，烈山川而焚之〞。) (Cf. Omer C. Stewart, "Fire as the First Great Force Employed by Man" in the *International Symposium on Man's Role in Changing the Face of the Earth,* ed. William L. Thomas, Jr., Chicago, 1956, p. 119-129.)

Anthropologist Omer Stewart says: "The number of tribes reported using fire leads one to the conclusion that burning of vegetation was a universal culture pattern among the Indians of the U.S. Furthermore, the amount of burning leads to the deduction that nearly all vegetation in America at the time of discovery and exploration was what ecologists would call fire vegetation. That is to say, fire was a major factor, along with soil, moisture, temperature, wind, animals, etc., in determining the types of plants occurring in any region. It follows then, that the vegetation of the Great Plains was a fire vegetation." (Quoted in "Man the Fire-Maker," by Loren C. Eiseley in *Scientific American,* v. 191, 1954, p. 55)

261. "Of these innovations the development of copper metallurgy was exceptionally significant. It set off a chain of technological changes in the fifteen hundred years before 3000 B.C. which may be considered to have had more far-reaching consequences than any subsequently arrived at up to the seventeenth century A.D. ... He thus had a metal for tools and weapons which was far superior to stone, for it was lighter and less fragile, took a sharper edge, and could be more easily shaped to produce a greater variety of products. Of special importance was the fact that men were acquiring knowledge about and skill in metallurgy which were applicable with minor variations to a great number of metals. Thus they were laying an essential foundation for the use of materials which were more efficient and more durable than anything known hitherto, and tapping large sources of sup-

It was fire which helped us to develop metallurgy;[261] thus giving us more and better tools to produce more and better subsistence for group expansion.

It was fire which helped us to develop pottery,[262] glass,[263] and steam and other powers to speed up group expansion directly or indirectly.[264]

---

plies—those which had been stored up over eons of time in the earth's crust. Without these advances neither the high machine speeds of today nor the large amount of energy from inorganic materials, which we now take for granted, would be possible." (Shepard B. Clough, *The Economic Development of Western Civilization,* New York, 1959, p. 26)

In the *Proceedings of the National Academy of Sciences,* vol. 2, March 1916, Walter Hough concludes in an article, "Man and Metals," that the progress of metallurgy up to this age of great progress was dependent on the increase of heat by various devices. In this way, man was gradually able to work the great pentad of metals familiar to him in nature, namely, copper, tin, gold, silver, and iron, forming the substantial basis upon which modern metallurgy rests.

262. To produce true pottery one must destroy the elasticity of clay through a chemical process which can only be induced by subjecting the clay to intense baking at a temperature of at least 400 or 500 degrees centigrade. The baking drives out the so-called water of constitution from the aluminum silicate in the clay. Thereafter, the clay will no longer dissolve in water; a truly fired vessel will survive in the ground for centuries. Pottery can be hardened in an open campfire, but the results can never be as excellent as those produced in a kiln. At some point, the early potter must have learned that he could concentrate and conserve heat by covering his fire—perhaps making it in a hole or trench. From this, it was only a step to the true closed kiln, in which there was a lower chamber for the fire and an upper one for the pottery. Most of the earthenware of simple cultures was fired at temperatures around 500 degrees centigrade, but really thorough firing demands temperatures in the neighborhood of 900 degrees. (Cf. Loren C. Eiseley, "Man the Fire-Maker," in *Scientific American,* v. 191, 1954, p. 56-57; and Walter Hough, *Fire as an Agent in Human Culture,* U.S. National Museum *Bulletin* 139, Washington, 1926, p. 75-76.)

263. "One of the by-products of more intensified experiments with heat was glass—the strange, impassive substance which, in the form of the chemist's flask, the astronomer's telescope, the biologist's microscope and the mirror, has contributed so vastly to our knowledge of ourselves and the universe." (Loren C. Eiseley, "Man the Fire-Maker," in *Scientific American,* v. 191, 1954, p. 57. Cf. R.J. Forbes, *Man, the Maker: A History of Technology and Engineering,* New York, 1950, p. 11-12.)

264. Just as the initial control of fire was essential to the development of man from the Old Stone Age hunters of the tropical forests into the first village-dwelling farmers of the Neolithic Age, so fire has been essential at every stage of the growth of civilization during the succeeding 10,000 years. It has been applied to vessels of clay to make pottery, to pieces of coloured stone to draw out copper and tin, and to combine these to make bronze, and to obtain iron. The modern history of technology and science might be characterized as a continual increase in the

Fire has also been credited with placing the early family in a firm position to begin group expansion,[265] and with inducing primitive peoples to extend their kinship and political affiliations for group expansion.[266]

In addition, fire had been regarded as a civil force, socializing primitive peoples for group expansion,[267] and as a religious influence

---

amount of energy made available to mankind by bringing fire under human control. Most of the increased available energy has come from ever greater amounts and kinds of heat, such as that produced from coal, blackpowder, steampower, gas, and electricity. The control of atomic energy is merely the most recent step in the use of fire for the benefit of mankind. (Cf. Loren C. Eiseley, "Man the Fire-Maker," in *Scientific American*, v. 191, 1954, p. 52-57.)

265. "The fire constituted the headquarters of the primitive family, and the hearth has remained the center of the domestic economy through the ages. Fire was of great efficacy, then, in defining the most primitive form of specialization and cooperation, that is, of organization. It follows from the above that the fire and hearth, coming to be the center of the family, were almost synonymous with family-organization." (William G. Sumner and Albert G. Keller, *The Science of Society*, New Haven, 1927, v. 1, p. 195)

"Tending the fire, however, is woman's affair. It formed the center of the sphere of life which woman dominated. It made the woman's domestic establishment more stable and to some extent more onerous than it had formerly been, but it likewise made it much more permanently attractive to the men than when her intermittent sexual charm had been the sole allurement. Those who had previously sought the company of woman only for limited periods were now bound permanently to her hearth, and soon no longer as mere guests but by ties of reciprocal duties and obligations. About the hearth there arose the home in every sense of the word. The old society based on community of blood, the primitive or consanguine family, began to recede into the background before a new type of domestic association." (Julius Lippert, *The Evolution of Culture*, trans. and ed. by George P. Murdock, New York, 1931, p. 131)

266. "Many tribes of North America maintained an eternal fire before the Europeans came. The general council of the Five Nations was held at Onondaga, where there has, from the beginning, been kept a fire continually burning, made of two great logs, whose flames were never extinguished. The council-fire was a symbol of political unity, and was employed by the Indians when they called the Thirteen Colonies the 'Thirteen Fires.' " (William G. Sumner and Albert G. Keller, *The Science of Society*, New Haven, 1927, v. 1, p. 198)

"Just as the vanishing Maoris of today believe that they still possess the cherished and sacred fire of their unknown ancestral home, so the historical peoples of Europe, the Greeks at their head, preserved a similar bond between original home and colony. Whenever the Greeks left home to found a new colony, they took with them fire from the common hearth of the mother community." (Julius Lippert, *The Evolution of Culture*, trans. and ed. by George P. Murdock, New York, 1931, p. 131)

267. "There is a respect in which fire differs from all other human possessions. . . . It can be given to another without depletion of the giver's store; it can be

which encourages, inspires, attracts and forces primitive peoples to think and act somewhat in common, leading to group expansion.[268]

As a summary, it is fair to say that if there had been no "taming

---

conferred and kept, at one and the same time. Precisely this exceptional quality of fire renders it of an especial educative value, upon the primitive stage, in the direction of socialization.... Something could be given which, though costing nothing, might assure a return in kind in case of need. In other terms, here was a species of insurance cheaply taken and yet capable of breaking down the barriers to a wider socialization." (William G. Sumner and Albert G. Keller, *The Science of Society,* New Haven, 1927, v. 1, p. 198-199)

"At Athens it was a duty recognized by the state to give fire to a person seeking it. So important was this matter held in that civilized state that one who could not himself comply with the request felt obliged to accompany the seeker to a place where his wish could be gratified.... Cicero in his moral philosophy urges that fire be shared with the stranger, and Plautus includes even the enemy in this obligation. It is certainly not accidental nor without significance that the very same obligation which was the first to extend beyond the range of consanguinity was also the first to shake the conception of the spatial limitation of morality and was the first tenet of the budding idea of humanism." (Julius Lippert, *The Evolution of Culture,* trans. and ed. by George P. Murdock, New York, 1931, p. 147. Also cf. Walter Hough, *Fire as an Agent in Human Culture,* U.S. National Museum *Bulletin* 139, Washington, 1926, p. 165-166.)

268. "What seems to [the primitive man] of surpassing importance is the service of fire in its relation to the imaginary environment.... The light and, to some extent, the heat of fire are regarded as most efficacious agencies in dealing with the ghosts and spirits; the flame is thought to be effective where the most perfect of weapons are of no avail. Within the circle of fire-light there is a semblance of day, while without are night and its shapes and voices.... The foregoing cases demonstrate the magical or fetishistic quality of fire. That it became, farther along the path of evolution, an object of actual worship, forming the characteristic spirit of certain developed religions, is well known.... It should be recognized, finally, that in systematic fire-worship there is formed yet another societal bond; and the fire-myths could not but unite, to some degree, fellow-believers." (William G. Sumner and Albert G. Keller, *The Science of Society,* New Haven, 1927, v. 1, p. 189, 202-203. Also cf. H. Spencer, *Principles of Sociology,* New York, 1904-1907, section 622 ff.)

Fire has been a center of religious ritual since earliest times. The primitive peoples danced and sang around it and bowed before it on almost all public religious occasions. These rites are survived in modern time by the common use of candle and incense for worship by almost all religions. Zoroastrianism and many other religions have looked upon fire as either a sun-deity or an earthly representative of one. The myth of Prometheus in Greece and the cult of Vesta in Rome, as well as countless other legends and beliefs, exhibit a common tendency to link the idea of fire with the concept of immortality. (Cf. Walter Hough, *Fire as an Agent in Human Culture,* U.S. National Museum *Bulletin* 139, Washington, 1926, p. 126-144, 198-216; and Gaston Bachelard, *The Psychoanalysis of Fire,* trans. by Alan C.M. Ross, Boston, 1964, p. 1-42, 99-108.)

of fire,''[269] we would have no group expansion, even no civilization at all.[270]

The case of wonderful fire has indeed further verified that the development of tools and energies is the major factor for group expansion.

Now we have the crucial question: how to develop tools and energies?

Basically, there is only one answer to this question: to increase useful knowledge which is the key to the making and use of tools, and to the conversion of energies for our service.[271]

How, then, to increase useful knowledge?

Generally speaking, there are three important ways to increase useful knowledge: invention, which is the original resource of useful knowledge;[272] accumulation, which makes useful knowledge richer

---

269. For the "Taming of Fire" see: Julius Lippert, *The Evolution of Culture*, trans. and ed. by George P. Murdock, New York, 1931, chap. III.

270. "To gain an adequate idea of the importance of fire to the races of the present day and to our civilization, one needs only imagine its absence, with the consequent cessation of most forms of industry and the lowering of efficiency in the struggle for existence to such a degree that, at least in the cooler climates, mankind must disappear." "There are many climates in which man could not possibly have come to dwell without this element (fire); in its absence his habitat could include only tropical regions, and not all of these . . . Since it is in the cooler regions only that the necessary conditions for the development and accumulation of civilization have been found to exist, it is fair to say that the use of fire has been a precondition to the rise of culture. That is, the feat of adaptation represented by this basic invention has drawn in its train a sequence of feats whose possibility lay in the initial conquest." (William G. Sumner and Albert G. Keller, *The Science of Society,* New Haven, 1927, v. 1, p. 203, 188)

271. Is the development of tools and different kinds of energies determined by environment, as geographical determinism holds, rather than by technical knowledge? An answer may be found by comparing the sequence of events in two areas in which different developments have taken place. "For instance, though Africa has deposits of copper, the stone age of the Dark Continent was not followed by a copper age, but directly by a period of iron. Southern Scandinavia, however, had no copper deposits. But this region not only had a bronze age, but the people even excelled in certain kinds of bronze work." (Albert S.J. Muntsch, *Introductory Sociology,* Boston, 1928, p. 14) The above facts can only be explained by the possession in Sweden of technical knowledge in using copper and iron.

272. Invention is the term employed to describe that human activity which results in the production of some contrivance which will make new things, perform labor in a new and more efficient way, and in general, lessen the burden of mankind in its economic and cultural tasks. As such, the term invention stands opposed to discovery, by which is generally meant the detection of things or relations already existing in nature. This distinction is probably no longer sharp enough to be entirely justifiable, however, as invention nearly always implies a certain

and richer;[273] and diffusion, which renders useful knowledge for more and wider services.[274]

In early times, we, like other animals, were largely occupied with procurement of the most basic necessities of life, and had little time

---

amount of discovery. In a broader sense, invention includes discovery and development. (Cf. Roland B. Dixon, *The Building of Culture,* New York, 1928, p. 34; R.J. Forbes, *Man, the Maker: A History of Technology and Engineering,* New York, 1950, p. 4-9; and H.S. Harrison, "Opportunism and the Factors of Invention," in *American Anthropologist,* v. 32, 1930, p. 108.)

"The mind of man cannot even conceive what wonders of beneficence inventors may accomplish: for the resources of invention are infinite." (Bradley A. Fiske in the Preface to his book *Invention, the Master Key to Progress,* New York, 1921)

273. The importance of the accumulation of knowledge is next, if not equal, to that of invention. "The latest investigations respecting the early condition of the human race, are tending to the conclusion that mankind commenced their career at the bottom of the scale and worked their way up from savagery to civilization through the slow accumulations of experimental knowledge." (Lewis H. Morgan, *Ancient Society,* New York, 1877, p. 3)

"In any case, Western man would do well to realize that knowledge both of the physical world and of society has been an accumulative process from which he is the chief beneficiary; and that all of his wonderful achievements would not be possible if it were not for this rich legacy." (Shepard B. Clough, *The Economic Development of Western Civilization,* New York, 1959, p. 19)

We may feel a certain pride in contemporary inventions, but let us remember that we owe to savage hunters and illiterate neolithic farmers the accumulation of knowledge and skill without which none of our modern experimentation would be possible. Where would we be without fire, speech, clothing, and bread? (Cf. Bradley A. Fiske, *Invention, the Master-Key to Progress,* New York, 1921, p. 22-23.)

"Emergent novelty becomes truly significant only through cumulation. Although the higher animals show some power of insight in their behavior, their behavior is restricted by the narrowness of the time span in which they live. The accumulation of experience in the individual and the group becomes important as soon as organized communication has been achieved." (Abbott P. Usher, *A History of Mechanical Inventions,* Cambridge, Mass., 1954, p. 67)

274. Since its introduction by E.B. Tylor, diffusion in its broad sense has generally been used by anthropologists and sociologists to mean the spread of culture through the factors of borrowing, suggestion, or migration, alone or in combination. The word has met the need for a term to refer to all the orderly processes which produce cultural similarities other than independent invention of similar traits to meet similar needs. Although most anthropologists have employed diffusion in conjunction with invention in the explanation of cultural similarities there have been schools of thought which emphasized diffusion over invention. For example, the English diffusionists, G.E. Smith and W.J. Perry, made Egypt the center of cultural origins, and argued that borrowing explained almost all cultural similarities throughout the world. (Cf. R.J. Forbes, *Man, the Maker: A History of Technology and Engineering,* New York, 1950, p. 9-11; and William J. Perry, *The Children of the Sun,* London, 1923, p. 1-4.)

to think and act for anything else. Invention depended on accident; accumulation depended on memory; and diffusion depended on imitation. Since accident was unpredictable and unlikely to result in anything elaborate or complex,[275] memory was usually gone with time and death and imitation was limited by the little contact between the sparsely scattered[276] and always hostile peoples,[277] it was obviously very difficult to increase useful knowledge, and consequently very difficult to develop tools and energies. For this reason, it took some million years for us to get through the Old Stone Age, and more than 20,000 years to get through the Young Stone Age.

At last came the time when our life was gradually improved as tools and energies were gradually developed, we were able to gain some time and save some capital to stimulate invention through specialization and competition.[278], [279] At the same time, progress was

---

275. For instance, we learned to produce fire more than a million years ago probably by an accidental striking together of stones. Since then we have had long experience with fire and have always tried to discover surer and easier ways to generate it. But not too much knowledge was obtained until 1827, when an English chemist named John Walker invented a friction match containing phosphorous sulphate, essentially the same match we use today. (Cf. Walter Hough, *Fire as an Agent in Human Culture,* U.S. National Museum *Bulletin* 139, Washington, 1926, p. 123-125.)

276. Archaeologists and demographers estimate that in the millions of years from the Old Stone Age to the New Stone Age, the world's human population may not have reached the one million mark, and that from about 10,000 B.C. to the beginning of the Christian era, the number increased from about 1 million to 275 million. (Cf. Palmer C. Putnam, *Energy in the Future,* New York, 1953, p. 16-17.)

277. (Cf. I, 100.)

278. Specialization and competition between trades always require better tools and better ways of using energy. For this reason, they bring about inventions more frequently than other circumstances. (Cf. S. Colum Gilfillan, *The Sociology of Invention,* Cambridge, Mass., 1970, p. 49-54.)

279. "Every basic invention (such as fire-making, iron smelting, domestication of plants and animals, generation of electricity, printing, representative government. . . .) opens the way to a large number of other inventions. The invention of human control of fire, for example, opened the way to cooking, metallurgy, chemistry, house warming, fire-worship, and so forth. Among the inventions thus released in metallurgy was iron smelting. This opened the way to improved tools, weapons and armor, to structural iron bridges and buildings, to engines, and to a series of other developments. . . . This produces a fan-like growth in the number of culture elements offered to the public. Every inventive combination of factors produces a new unit which may in turn be combined with previously existing units. The number of possible combinations, and hence the number of culture choices which may be offered, tends therefore to increase in geometrical ratio." (Hornell N. Hart, *The Technique of Social Progress,* New York, 1931, p.

made in the accumulation of useful knowledge by the use of writing
to keep data and records,[280] by the development of numerical notations[281] to advance measurement,[282] and by the formulation of

---

668. Cf. the table showing an accelerating increase in the number of inventions
from 3000 B.C. to 1900 A.D. The table was prepared by Boris Weinberg in *The
Revue Générale des Sciences Pures et Appliquées,* Vol. 37, 1926, p. 44. Cf. also
*Eureka, An Illustrated History of Inventions from the Wheel to the Computer; A
London Sunday Times Encyclopedia,* ed. by Edward de Bono, New York, 1974.)

280. "Some order in empirical knowledge appears in the records of ancient
Egypt and Babylon—units and rules of measurement, simple arithmetic, a calen-
dar of the year, the recognition of the periodicity of astronomic events, even of
eclipses." (William C. Dampier, *A History of Science and Its Relations with
Philosophy and Religion,* 3rd ed., Cambridge, 1943, Introduction. Cf. Henry
Hodges, *Technology in the Ancient World,* New York, 1970.)

"The work of the Aristotelian school is scattered through a large portion of
the general Aristotelian corpus. The concepts of dynamics appear only as features
of the general theory of physics, and thus involve large portions of the primary
treatises: the eight books on physics, the four books on the heavens, the two books
of the treatise on generation and destruction, the four books on meteors, the thirteen books on metaphysics. The concepts of dynamics are clearly an integral part
of the general philosophy." (Abbott P. Usher, *A History of Mechanical Inventions,* Cambridge, Mass., 1954, p. 87)

281. The idea of numeration (counting) is almost as old as civilization itself.
Marks on sand tables, pebbles in marked slots, beads on wires, or even knots in
strings have been used to tally the numbers of things counted. More than five thousand years ago, the Sumerians and the Chaldeans had developed a system of
counting with 60 as a base. About a thousand years later, among the Egyptians,
there existed a set of numerals defined by pictures: the symbol for 100 was a chain;
for 1,000, a lotus flower; for 10,000, a pointed finger; for 100,000, a tadpole; and
for a million, a man with his hands outstretched as if in astonishment at such a
large number. The Egyptian system was based on 10 as a unit. Then came the
Greek numerals, Hebrew numerals, Roman numerals, Chinese numerals, and
Arabic numerals. Arabic numerals, developed from many sources, particularly
from the Hindus and the Arabians, came to be the base of our present system of
numbers. They were developed in Europe into the system now in almost universal
use. (Cf. David E. Smith and Jekuthiel Ginsburg, "From Numbers to Numerals
and From Numerals to Computation," quoted by James R. Newman in *The
World Mathematics,* New York, 1956, Vol. 1, p. 442-464. Cf. also David E. Smith,
Number Stories of Long Ago, Boston, 1919.)

282. "The 'Greek miracle' occurred not only because of the application of deductive reasoning but also because of the importance the Greeks attached to the
concept of metric, namely, the use of precise techniques of measurement (such as
those developed by Euclid or employed by Eratosthenes and Ptolemy). Reliance
upon objective, impersonal forms of measurement is basic both to any truly scientific method and to a scientific attitude of mind. The Eotechnic phase in turn placed
a new emphasis on measurement—which is essential both to the construction and
the functioning of a machine." (Alastair M. Taylor, Nels Bailkey, Mark Mancall,
T. Walter Wallbank, *Civilization Past and Present,* 6th ed., Glenview, v. 1, p. 369)

theories for application.[283] This progress made it possible not only to maintain useful knowledge on a permanent basis, but also to diffuse

---

"Evidence of the advances made can be illustrated from arithmetic, where the multiplication table was developed and from geometry where proofs were sought to explain why given conditions always gave the same answers. From such beginnings it eventually became possible to construct large buildings with accuracy. The Great Pyramid of Cheóps (2420-2270 B.C.), for instance, contains 2,300 blocks of stone, some of which weigh 350 tons, has a base of 777 and three quarters feet on each side, and has less than an inch of error in either length or level. Also celestial observation led to a development of astronomy, which permitted the accurate measuring of time, the seasons, and points of the compass. Accordingly sundials for regularizing human activity were invented and a calendar of 365 days was created." (Shepard B. Clough, *The Economic Development of Western Civilization,* New York, 1959, p. 32)

283. "Lastly, in the Iron Age, more attention was given by the educated in society to economic matters and one begins to get written descriptions of various kinds of mechanical devices. Archimedes (287-212 B.C.), one of the greatest mathematicians of all time, described the theory of the lever and thereby laid the foundation for theoretical mechanics, albeit that building on his work was slight until the end of the Middle Ages. He also wrote about the screw pump, which he may have invented, and he developed many military devices, especially the launching of stones by the elastic power of twisted ropes. Hero of Alexandria (circa 50 B.C.) described a number of gadgets, many of which were mere toys, such as pumps, the syringe, a fire engine, devices for adjusting the wick on a lamp, a windmill arranged to drive a bellows of an organ, and a contraption moved by the expansive power of steam. The Roman Vitruvius in about 1 A.D. wrote a famous book on architecture and mechanics, nearly all of which had been borrowed from the Greeks, which discloses that Rome had knowledge of all the principles thus far mentioned, as well as a solution to the problem of the transmission of power by gears. Then in the allied field of mathematics Euclid published his *Elements* of geometry in about 300 B.C. Apollonius of Perga (247-205 B.C.) prepared his geometry of cones and Hipparchus (160-125 B.C.) invented plane and spherical trigonometry." (Shepard B. Clough, *The Economic Development of Western Civilization,* New York, 1959, p. 38)

This excerpt from the first book of Hero's *Mechanics* (Book 1, 34) may serve as a sample: "Suppose we have a wheel or mobile pulley set upon an axle whose center is A: the diameter of the wheel will be the line parallel to the horizon. At the points B and G two cords are attached to which are suspended equal weights. It is evident that the pulley will not move in either direction, because the weights are equal and the distances from the center are equal. Suppose, however, that the weight C is heavier than the weight E; it is evident that the pulley will be drawn down on that side, and the point B will descend with its weight. We must discover at what position the heavier weight will come to rest after its descent. Let us then lower the point B and bring it to F; the cord BC will come to the position FD and the weight will stop. It is clear that the cord GE will be rolled up in the throat of the pulley and that the weight will still be suspended at the point G. The line DF, if prolonged, comes to H. Since the two weights are in equilibrium, the ratio of their weights is the inverse of the ratio of the distances of the points of suspension from

it to more peoples and wider areas.[284] Under these circumstances, it is no wonder that there was a remarkable success in the development of tools and energies, which shortened the New Stone Age to approximately 5,000 years, the Copper Age to 4,000 years, and finally launched the Iron Age.[285]

However, great speed in the increase of useful knowledge had yet to wait until modern times.

i.
Modern Science
and Technology

IN MODERN TIMES, THE INCREASE OF USEFUL KNOWLedge signifies the advance of science and technology,[286] and the fast pace of the advance of science and technology is determined primari-

---

A. Thus HA/AG is equal to the ratio of the weight E to the weight D. We may apply the same reasoning to any other weight. It is thus possible to balance any given weight with a smaller weight." (Quoted in Abbott P. Usher, *A History of Mechanical Inventions,* Cambridge, Mass., 1954, p. 89-90.)

284. Take ancient Greece as an example: "Its superior agricultural and industrial techniques were diffused to other lands in the process of trade and colonization, particularly to the eastern Aegean and Mediterranean Seas, to Sicily, to Magna Graecia in southern Italy, and to the Black Sea area." (Shepard B. Clough, *The Economic Development of Western Civilization,* New York, 1959, p. 41)

285. The Old Stone Age lasted roughly to 30,000 B.C.; the Young Stone Age, from 30,000 to 10,000 B.C.; the New Stone Age, from 10,000 to 5,000 B.C.; and the Copper Age, from 5,000 to 1,000 B.C., when the Iron Age got started. (Cf. Harry E. Barnes, *The History of Western Civilization,* New York, 1935, Vol. 1, p. 14-36.)

286. "Sometimes technology is defined as applied science. Science itself is viewed as an attempt by man to understand the physical world; technology is the attempt by man to control the physical world. This distinction may be briefly put as the difference between the "know-why" and the "know-how." But technology for much of its history had little relation with science, for men could and did make machines and devices without understanding why they worked and why they turned out as they did." (*Technology in Western Civilization,* ed. by Melvin Kranzberg and Carroll W. Pursell, Jr., New York, 1967, Vol. 1, p. 5-6. Cf. Abbott P. Usher, *A History of Mechanical Inventions,* Cambridge, Mass., 1954, p. 8; and Norman Campell, *What is Science,* London, 1921, p. 37-157.)

"It is only in the 19th century that science came to be commonly regarded as affording a means of improving the general level of human life, not by moral

ly by significant changes in the process of invention, which are characterized as follows:

It is not a hazardous enterprise anymore. It is generally protected by a patent system.[287]

---

regeneration, and not by political reform, but by increasing men's command over the forces of nature. This point of view was, of course, due to the Industrial Revolution, and to various inventions, such as steamship, railways and telegraphs. This view of science as the handmaid of industry has now become a commonplace." (Bertrand Russell, quoted by Harry E. Barnes, *An Economic History of the Western World,* New York, 1937, p. 448)

287. Not until the Renaissance did the idea gain currency that a new technological discovery was a valuable contribution to society, for which the discoverer should be rewarded. In 1474, the Republic of Venice enacted the first formal patent law and the idea of protection of invention by patents spread throughout Europe. Article I, section 8 of the United States Constitution gives Congress the power "to promote the progress of science and useful arts by securing for limited times to authors and inventors the exclusive right to their respective writings and discoveries." The first federal patent act was signed by President George Washington in 1790. While there is no international patent law, there is an international agreement relating to patent rights. This agreement is generally known as the International Convention for the Protection of Industrial Property and includes trademarks as well as patents. It was first executed in 1883 in Paris, and revised in Brussels on December 14, 1900, in Washington on June 2, 1911, in The Hague on November 6, 1925, and in London on May 1, 1934. The treaty is a multilateral one, open to participation by any country. An international office, known as the International Bureau for the Protection of Industrial Property, was established under a treaty at Berne, Switzerland. This office collects information relating to patents and related matters and publishes a periodical dealing with international patent laws. (Cf. William R. Ballard, *There Is No Mystery About Patents,* New York, 1946, p. 90-95; and Stephan P. Ladas, *Patents, Trademarks and Related Rights: National and International Protections,* Cambridge, Mass., 1975, v. 1, p. 59-95.)

"The Patent System added the fuel of interest to the fire of genius." (Abraham Lincoln, quoted by Ramon A. Klitzke in his "History of Patents—U.S." in the *Encyclopedia of Patent Practice and Invention Management,* ed. by Robert Calvert, New York, 1964, p. 394.)

288. Such agencies in the United States are: the National Science Foundation, the National Research Council, the Department of Defense, the Department of Health, Education, and Welfare, the National Aeronautics and Space Administration, and the Atomic Energy Commission. The National Science Foundation has responsibility for developing and encouraging the pursuit of a national policy for the promotion of basic research in the mathematical, physical, medical, biological, engineering, and other sciences, and for appraising the impact of research upon industrial development and upon the national welfare. In view of the magnitude of the overall federal research and development program, an especially important function of the foundation is the study of the federal program in support of scientific research, the role of the federal government in support of

It is not just a personal enterprise anymore. It is usually supported by official agencies[288] with public funds.[289]

---

science, and the correlation of the foundation's scientific research program with
those of other groups, both private and public. The National Research Council
was organized at the request of President Wilson in 1916 "for the purposes of promoting research in the natural sciences and encouraging the application and
dissemination of scientific knowledge." Its membership is composed of representatives of nearly 100 scientific and technical societies, research institutes, and
government agencies; and of members-at-large appointed by the council. There
are about 225 members. In addition to its general committees, the council has eight
divisions: international relations; mathematical and physical sciences, including
astronomy; engineering and industrial research; chemistry and chemical
technology; geology and geography; medical sciences; biology and agriculture;
and anthropology and psychology. The work of the council is carried on largely
through its approximately 400 committees, boards, and panels, which have as
members more than 2,000 distinguished scientists. The council does not maintain
its own scientific laboratories; its chief concern is the cooperation between and integration of research activities. (Cf. U.S. Congress, *National Science Foundation
Act,* Washington, 1946; *The Mighty Force of Research,* by the editors of *Fortune,*
New York, 1956, p. 7-12; *Historical Statistics of the United States, Colonial Times
to 1970,* p. 965-966.)

289. For example, in the United States, the great bulk of the sum spent for
research and development—and hence, supposedly, for discoveries and inventions—has come from the federal government. Since World War II, it has been
estimated that this country is spending more for R & D in any single year than was
spent in the whole of its national history from the American Revolution to the end
of World War II. In the decade from 1951 to 1960, such expenditures totaled
roughly $80 billion, four times as much as in the preceding 10 years, a period which
covered a world war. This $80 billion was about the size of the total federal budget
for the 1961 fiscal year. Approximately 9 percent of this sum ($7 billion) went for
basic research. There has been a continual rise in funds for both R & D and basic
research. The United States is by no means unique in its emphasis upon research
and development and in the large-scale support accorded science and technology.
Throughout the world, discovery and invention have become major tools for
achieving national objectives. In the Soviet Union, recognition of the importance
of science and technology has resulted in priority being given to technical education and the granting of preferential treatment to scientists and engineers. The
growth in the number of scientific workers in the Soviet Union has been similar to
that in the United States, and the prestigious Academy of Sciences, which runs the
great research institutes, has been credited with the extraordinary success of the
Soviet Union in rocketry, space exploration, and related fields. (Cf. Alan T.
Waterman, President, American Association for the Advancement of Science,
"Basic Research: Key to Scientific Progress," *Congressional Record,* Sept. 22,
1961. For a comprehensive review of the situation in Soviet Russia, cf. Alexander
G. Korel, *Soviet Research and Development, Its Organization, Personnel and
Funds,* Cambridge, Mass., 1965.)

"Spending for research and development in the United States is expected to
reach $38.1 billion in 1976, an eight per cent increase over last year.... [account-

It is not just an amateur enterprise anymore. It is usually worked out by a group of various specialists[290] with efficient instruments.[291]

---

ing] for 2.2 per cent of the estimated 1976 gross national product.... Federal R & D expenditures are estimated at \$20.1 billion; industry, \$16.6 billion; universities and colleges, \$800 million; and other nonprofit institutions, \$600 million." (*South Bend Tribune,* August 1976, p. 8; based on a recently released report of the National Science Foundation.)

Trends in expenditures for research and experimental development as represented by typical countries are shown in the following table:

Country	Canada	Italy	Japan	Poland
Currency	Dollar	Lira	Yen	Zloty
1967	888,000	344,300,000	702,484,000	10,825,480
1968	944,000	399,827,000	877,487,000	13,700,000
1969	1,046,000	464,214,000	1,064,653,000	15,900,000
1970	1,066,000	554,671,000	1,355,505,000	16,900,000
1971	1,160,000	622,834,000	1,532,372,000	20,600,000

(Cf. *UNESCO Statistical Yearbook,* 1973, New York, 1974, p. 556-560.)

290. During the 19th century, inventors came from every milieu of society and ranged in education from university graduates to men with little or no formal schooling. By the second half of the 20th century, technical knowledge had increased to the point where people were required to specialize to a much greater extent and it was almost impossible for any individual to master all the knowledge even in a specialized field. This increasing complexity and specialization of science and technology have necessitated higher education for potential scientists and inventors, resulting in the growth of postgraduate education in science and technology and in science-oriented industry's surrounding the great centers of advanced education. Recently, the role of the individual inventor in the development of technology has been considerably diminished, as the derivation and working out of new ideas has increasingly become the responsibility of research and development teams. Hence, "the inventor" as a peculiarly gifted personality with a special insight or inspiration for seeing further into engineering problems than other men becomes an anonymous member of a group of engineers. (For some personnel samples in the industrial laboratories of the United States, cf. Harley H. Bixler, *The Manufacturing Research Function,* New York, 1963, p. 38. Also cf. David B. Hertz, ed., *Research Operations in Industry,* New York, 1953, p. 142-211; and *Historical Statistics of the United States, Colonial Times to 1970,* p. 967.)

"It would be highly misleading to consider the change from the individual inventor in his garret, who took his little knowledge out of old textbooks of physics and chemistry, to the modern super-team, with all grades of men, from the mathematician to the mechanic, and the compression of time from a generation or two to a few years, merely as a change in quantity. A change on such a scale means a change in quality, a change in the intrinsic nature aims, and consequences of the process of invention and innovation." (Dennis Gabor, *Innovations: Scientific, Technological and Social,* Oxford, 1970, p. 6)

A great number of scientists, engineers, and technicians the world over have

It is not just an individual enterprise anymore. It is usually done in a well-equipped industrial[292] or academic research laboratory.[293]

---

engaged in research and experimental development. For instance, there were 328,665 in Finland in 1971; 1,702,260 in France in 1970, 35,126 in Nigeria in 1970/71; 11,205 in Papua New Guinea in 1972; 2,725,000 in the United States of America in 1971; 50,346 in Uruguay in 1970; and 21,500 in Zambia in 1970. (Cf. *UNESCO Statistical Yearbook,* 1973, p. 504-508.)

291. Inventions of scientific instruments and apparatus have had a profound effect on discoveries. The invention of the microscope and the telescope led to many discoveries that would have been impossible without these aids to the human eye. In more recent times, radio and radar have contributed to astronomy, and the electron microscope to microscopy. Discoveries in high-energy nuclear physics have been largely dependent upon the invention of the cyclotron and other atom-smashing devices. A number of inventive improvements have enabled these devices to achieve the ever-higher energies demanded by physicists in order to probe more deeply into the heart of the nucleus. Furthermore, associated inventions of detectors, counters, scalers, and control devices have made possible the identification and characterization of nuclear interactions that result from the operations of the atom smashers. (Cf. Carl T. Chase, *Frontiers of Science,* New York, 1936, p. 27-55, 324-358; Frank C. Jean, *Man and His Physical Universe,* Boston, 1943, p. 22-36; and René Taton, *Reason and Chance in Scientific Discovery,* trans. by A.J. Pomerans, New York, 1957, p. 57-73. For a general review on scientific instruments, cf. A. Elliott and J. Home Dickson, *Laboratory Instruments: Their Design and Application,* 2nd ed., New York, 1960.)

292. The industrial research laboratory had its beginnings in the 1880s in the chemical industry in Germany, and as late as 1895, only one industrial laboratory—Thomas Edison's—existed in the United States. By the second half of the 20th century, the industrial research laboratory had become the major employer of scientists and inventors. As employees of large corporations or of the U.S. government, inventors assigned all their patents to the firm or the government and received only a salary. (Cf. William S. Calcott, "Industrial Research," *Nieuwland Lectures,* no. 1, Notre Dame, In., 1946; Harley H. Bixler, *The Manufacturing Research Function,* New York, 1963, p. 15-16. The *Industrial Research Laboratories of the United States,* 10th ed., compiled by James F. Mauk, Washington, 1956, lists 4060 such laboratories; and *Historical Statistics of the United States from Colonial Times to 1970,* p. 966.)

293. "The basic difference between industrial research and academic research is only that industrial research, in the long run, must produce results that are pleasing to and accepted by a considerable portion of the non-scientific public, and that this approval must be expressed by their willingness to purchase this result. Academic research, broadly speaking, is a success if the results are accepted and approved by other workers in the same field. The result may be, at the time, of no conceivable practical interest or value, but if the work is well done and the findings are of interest to other workers in the field, the investigation is a success. It is necessary to qualify the statement of the practical value as it is impossibly difficult to say what may be the case in the future. Obviously unimportant scraps of knowledge of this year may be of very great importance a short time later."

It is not just a casual enterprise anymore. It is usually well-planned and systematically executed to produce the expected result.[294]

It is no longer an enterprise motivated just by curiosity. It is usually stimulated by high incentives and pressing demands.[295]

(William S. Calcott, "Industrial Research," *Nieuwland Lectures,* no. 1, Notre Dame, In., 1946, p. 5)

After World War II, academic research in the United States was greatly expanded, sponsored by both government and industry. By government alone, "between 1963 and 1966, the number of institutions performing some research supported by one or more Federal agencies increased by over one hundred, to approximately 600. . . . In 1962 there were 100 institutions receiving at least $1 million annually for research activities; in 1966 more than 140 institutions received Federal research support of that magnitude." (In the Preface to the *Sponsored Research in American Universities and Colleges,* ed. Stephen Strickland, Washington, 1967. Cf. also *Federal Support of Basic Research in Institutions of Higher Learning,* National Academy of Science — National Research Council, Washington, 1964.)

294. A distinguishing feature of the 20th century industrial research laboratory is the fact that it represents systematized invention; it is largely devoted to technological research, discovery, and innovation. In order to accomplish these goals, it brings together men from a wide array of disciplines, each contributing his specialized knowledge, to form a research team. At the same time, it embodies a new methodology of technological work, being based on the systematic application of science to technology. (Cf. "The Design of an Integrated Research Program," James A. Stewart, in *Research Operations in Industry,* ed., David B. Hertz, New York, 1953.)

"When the *Polaris* submarine was conceived, four major inventions were needed for its success: the nuclear drive, accurate location under water, the solid-fuel rocket, and intertial guidance. As a fifth, one can add 'PERT,' a planning scheme that made it possible for millions of parts supplied by 11,000 manufacturers to arrive in time and to fit together." (Dennis Gabor, *Innovations: Scientific, Technological and Social,* Oxford, 1970, p. 6)

295. In addition to economic incentive, military requirement is a factor contributing to vigorous competition. It is well known that the growth of aeronautics in modern times has owed much to military needs. In World War II, radar and the atomic bomb are two outstanding examples of scientific and technological innovations fostered by military demand. (Cf. Donald L. Brown, "Incentives for Inventors and Stimulation of Invention and Disclosure," in the *Encyclopedia of Patent Practice and Invention Management,* ed. by Robert Calvert, New York, 1964, p. 412-424; and "Incentive Contracting" by W. Austin Davis, in the *Research and Development Contracting,* by the Law Center of George Washington University, Washington, D.C., 1963.)

296. An invention or discovery or the rectification of an ancient error does not become a part of civilization until it has been accepted by society and added to its habits of action and thought. Plenty of shocking tales could be recalled of professional and popular opposition to innovations on grounds which now seem grotesque. We owe discoveries to individual men and women, but new information and skills can only be propagated and disseminated in a favorable culture medium. Many instances could be cited of promising knowledge which failed to

It is no longer an enterprise which is often ignored, suspected, and ridiculed by the public.[296] It is usually encouraged by various grants[297] and awards.[298]

For these reasons, the spirit of invention has been carried higher and higher.[299] Hundreds of inventions a day now come out,[300] in con-

---

get a footing in civilization. (Cf. Bernard Barber, *Science and the Social Order,* Glencoe, Ill., 1952, chap. 9; "Resistance by Scientists to Scientific Discovery," in *Science,* v. 134, Sept., 1961, p. 596-602; René Taton, *Reason and Chance in Scientific Discovery,* trans. by A.J. Pomerans, New York, 1957, p. 147-154.)

297. Many grants are received from foundations. "A foundation is an instrument for the contribution of private wealth to public purposes." There were in the United States in the late 1960s some 22,000 foundations, with assets approximating $20 billion, making grants of about $1.5 billion annually. The foundation idea has also grown in other parts of the world. A famous early foundation in the United States is the Smithsonian Institution. Its purpose is "to found ... an establishment for the increase and diffusion of knowledge among men." Other major foundations include: the Carnegie Corporation, the Ford Foundation, the Rockefeller Foundation, etc. (Cf. Marrianna O. Lewis, ed., *The Foundation Directory,* 3rd ed., New York, 1967; and *The Mighty Force of Research,* by the editors of *Fortune,* New York, 1956, p. 17-18.)

298. Perhaps the most famous awards are the Nobel Prizes, a series of annual awards provided for by a fund of $9,200,000 in the will of Alfred Bernhard Nobel. There are five classifications to reward men and women who have worked for the benefit of mankind and have made outstanding contributions in: (1) physics, (2) chemistry, (3) physiology or medicine, (4) peace, and (5) literature. A prize in economic science in Nobel's memory was established by the Central Bank of Sweden, in 1969. (Cf. *Nobel, the Man and His Prizes,* edited by the Nobel Foundation, Stockholm, 1951, p. 13-24, 80-84.)

299. "As Gabriel Tarde pointed out, inventions are the chief source of innovation in modern culture. Only by inventions can culture be changed in any very fundamental way, except through the mere borrowing of the inventions that another group has earlier produced. Above all, the spirit of invention is a denial of the philosophy of repetition and stability, so characteristic of the old regime." (Harry E. Barnes, *An Economic History of the Western World,* New York, 1937, p. 490)

"A really new thing has come into the world. That thing is the invention of invention. Men have not merely invented the modern machines. There have been machines invented since the earliest days, incalculably important, like the wheel, like sailing ships, like the windmill and the watermill. But in modern times men have invented a method of inventing, they have discovered a method of discovery. Mechanical progress has ceased to be casual and accidental and has become systematic and cumulative. We know, as no other people ever knew before, that we shall make more and more perfect machines." (Walter Lippman, *Preface to Morals,* New York, 1929, p. 235)

"In the early 1940s, two of the West's finest intellects, Michael Polanyi, the scientist, and Bertrand Russell, the mathematician, appeared on a British radio panel called the 'Brains Trust.' They were asked if they could imagine any practical use to which Einstein's relativity theory might be put—and both answered in the

trast to one in hundreds of years in earlier times;[301] and we have been able to accomplish very complex tasks at miraculously accelerating rates.[302]

---

negative. Just a few months later, the first atomic fission experiment was successfully performed under the grandstand of the University of Chicago stadium. It owed its genesis, of course, to Einstein's famous equation on the conversion of matter and energy. Scarcely a half-dozen years later an eminent biologist stated publicly that because heredity was obviously very complicated, it was useless to hope that a single type of molecule would be 'the' genetic material. Less than 18 months after this, Watson and Crick announced the structure of DNA, probably the most important biological discovery of the last few centuries. The great Victorian physicist, Lord Kelvin, having made numerous important inventions, from the Atlantic cable to the mariner's compass, made the pronouncement in the 1880s that all the discoveries in physics had already been found and only a few accurate measurements remained to be learned. Within a decade of his statement, the Second Scientific Revolution was upon us—and every decade since then has seen more basic activity, both in theory and in application, than in the two centuries between Newton and Kelvin." (Sydney Harris, "Man Can Conquer Nature, But Fails to Rule Himself," *South Bend Tribune,* Nov. 12, 1979, p. 6)

300. No certain measure of the rate of invention is possible. Historical study yields qualitative impressions. For some modern states, patents issued can be counted year by year. While history records major steps only, patent offices know no distinctions by importance. However, since major inventions serve as nuclei about which subsidiary developments and improvements cluster, patent statistics measure not only the importance society attaches to technical innovation, but also its rate of change. For instance, the number of British patent applications per year increased rapidly from about 1770 onward; there were about 10 per year in 1770, about 100 per year in 1800, and about 26,000 per year in 1900. After World War II, the number rose to about 35,000 annually, and in 1965 it was 55,507. In the United States, the first federal patent act was signed by President George Washington in 1790. Between 1790 and 1799, only 268 patents were granted, but between then and the 1960s, the Patent Office issued about 3,000,000 patents. The following table gives the number of patents issued by a number of different countries during the decade 1930 to 1939:

Argentina	17,674	France	190,365	New Zealand	7,938
Australia	25,796	Germany	196,558	Norway	14,489
Austria	35,800	Great Britain	187,349	Poland	15,991
(8 years)		Hungary	24,012	(9 years)	
Belgium	70,525	Italy	107,337	Sweden	29,281
Canada	89,725	Japan	49,288	Switzerland	70,736
Denmark	15,746	Netherlands	26,352	United States	485,203

(For U.S. patent statistics, cf. *Historical Statistics of the United States, Colonial Times to 1970,* p. 957-959. British patent statistics are cited in *Encyclopedia Americana,* 1973 ed., v. 15, p. 334, and the other countries' are cited in v. 21, p. 385-386.)

For a comprehensive review, cf. James G. Crowther, *Discoveries and Inventions of the Twentieth Century,* rev. ed., New York, 1966. "The book is written

At the same time, modern library services,[303] educational audio-visual media,[304] scientific and technical training,[305] conferences[306]

---

for those, young and old, who wish to have a non-technical account of the great scientific and material triumphs which man has achieved and is achieving in their own day; and it seemed desirable to give the first place to those theories, facts, and accomplishments, which are now exercising the greatest influence upon human life. For science exists not so much to tickle the intelligences of the few as to brighten the lot of the many." (Preface)

301. "Inventions were few and relatively infrequent down to the middle of the eighteenth century. In fact, the state of technology was generally static for thousands of years prior to 1750. Relatively slight material progress was achieved between the close of the Stone Age and the Industrial Revolution. At the present time, inventions come in great numbers. Even such inventions as the airplane or the radio, which would have been regarded as nothing short of miraculous a century ago, are now complacently accepted. We have become so accustomed to the everyday occurrence of notable scientific and mechanical achievements that only the most striking inventions attract our full attention." (Harry E. Barnes, *An Economic History of the Western World,* New York, 1937, p. 490)

302. For instance, between the first idea of the power of steam, known to the Hellenistic Alexandrians, and the wide application of steam power during the Industrial Revolution, approximately 1,700 years went by and the time lag between the discovery of gunpowder and its use as a propellant for projectiles was about 400 years. Between the discovery of the thermionic effect and its use in the manufacture of triodes for radios, some 35 years elapsed; between the discovery of neutrons and the first atomic pile, ten years; between the discovery of microwaves and their use in radar, ten years; between the discovery of nuclear fission and the first atomic bomb, six years; between the discovery of the properties of semiconductors and the manufacture of the first germanium transistor radio, only three years; and between the discovery of the method of turning opaque plastic products into transparent ones and its industrial application, only two years. (Cf. Bradley A. Fiske, *Invention, the Master-Key to Progress,* New York, 1921; James G. Crowther, *Discoveries and Inventions of the Twentieth Century,* rev. ed., New York, 1966; and David C. Cooke, *Inventions that Make History,* New York, 1968.)

"Heinrich Hertz produced, in 1887, the electro-magnetic waves that had been implicit in Maxwell's equations since 1868, but it was left to Marconi in 1896 to utilize the antenna, whose complete theory was contained in Hertz's equations. This gap of twenty to forty years between scientific discovery and technological exploitation remained typical for most of the nineteenth and early twentieth century. It was dramatically shortened only in our own times. It took only six years from Otto Hahn's discovery of nuclear fission to the first atomic bomb in 1945, and the men who led the enormous team of the first crash programme in history were themselves scientists, moreover mostly theoretical physicists." (Dennis Gabor, *Innovations: Scientific, Technological and Social,* Oxford, 1970, p. 5)

303. Modern library service has greatly improved with the aid of many efficient tools, especially indexes which indicate the place in a book or collection in which particular information is to be found, classification schemes, and subject headings which arrange books and other materials into a systematic order for easy access. Book indexing began at least as early as the 16th century. The first famous

and publications[307] have made the accumulation and diffusion of science and technology easy, safe and quick. Above all, the appear-

---

index book, *What Is an Index,* written by Henry B. Wheatley, was published in 1878. The idea of classifying reading material was pioneered by the Swiss, Konrad Gesner, when he published a classified list of 20,000 scholarly books, the *Pandectarum sive partitionum universalium,* in 1548. In the United States, the famous Dewey Decimal system, worked out by Melvil Dewey, and first published in 1876 with 12 pages, has been developed into 1150 pages in its 17th edition, published in 1965. The other famous system is the Library of Congress classification, first published in 1904, and since then continuously expanded and revised. Many other systems are in use throughout the world's libraries; a Universal Decimal Classification was first published in French in 1899, and has since been developed in great detail by the Fédération de Documentation and published in many languages. Much money has been used for the library service. The United States, for instance, spent $1,381,000,000 in 1972 for library services in higher educational institutions alone (*Statistical Abstract of the United States,* 1975, p. 140. Cf. Henry E. Bliss, *The Organization of Knowledge in Libraries,* New York, 1937; Robert C. Collison, *Indexes and Indexing,* New York, 1959, p. 16-21; and *Rutgers Series on Systems for the Intellectual Organization of Information,* v. 1, "The Universal Decimal Classification," by J. Mills.)

304. Audiovisual media, such as slides, tape recordings, motion pictures and television, have been widely used for education. In the United States, for instance, by the mid-1960s, in addition to 250 AM and 32 educationally-owned and operated FM radio stations, there were 109 educational television stations on the air. These media are especially effective in instruction for science and technology. (Cf. Paul Saettler, *A History of Instructional Technology,* New York, 1968, Part 2; and Fritz Machlup, *The Production and Distribution of Knowledge in the United States,* Princeton, N.J., 1962, p. 250-265.)

ance of the computer,[308] and its rapid progress[309] and wide development,[310] have facilitated inventive activities[311] and their accumula-

---

305. A great number of students complete their scientific and technical training at higher educational institutions every year. The following table shows the
number of such graduates in 1970 in representative countries:

Country	Natural Sciences	Engineering	Medical Sciences	Agriculture
Australia	3,863	3,129	2,177	889
Brazil	4,357	7,487	8,225	1,924
Canada	9,941	5,262	4,236	991
Egypt	1,205	5,071	4,263	3,917
Greece	1,266	758	1,648	559
Hungary	808	5,841	1,279	1,844
Iran	2,164	3,129	1,724	766
Italy	7,562	5,249	5,935	786
Japan	8,980	65,803	14,104	11,443
Norway	682	627	384	180
Poland	4,078	23,395	10,564	5,736
Romania	2,016	8,121	1,566	2,035
Sweden	2,406	2,185	2,911	272
United Kingdom	17,865	12,075	6,589	1,347
United States	107,582	70,127	45,348	17,467
Yugoslavia	1,492	6,076	3,022	1,530

(Cf. *UNESCO Statistical Yearbook,* 1973, New York, 1974, p. 334-357.)

306. There were, for instance, approximately 1300 international meetings on
science, technology, agriculture, and medicine in 1969, as listed in the *World List
of Future International Meetings,* by the Library of Congress, Washington, 1969,
part 1, p. 1-45.

307. Consider the case of periodicals, for instance: "Estimates of the total
number of scientific and technical journals published throughout the world have
run as high as 100,000. However, a very thorough and accurate worldwide journal
inventory currently being performed by the Science and Technology Division of
the Library of Congress for the National Science Foundation has given
preliminary indications that there are about 30,000 to 35,000 journals.... Using
30,000 journals as a starting point, and using empirical factors of 30 to 70 articles
per journal per year, we can estimate that a total of one to two million scientific articles are published annually throughout the world. However, more realistic
estimates seem to point to a world-wide publication of about 15,000 significant
journals, and 1 million significant papers per year." (Charles P. Bourne,
"World's Technical Journal Literature, Estimate of Volume, Origin, Language,
Indexing, and Abstracting," *American Documentation,* v. 13, April, 1962, p. 160)

308. Computers go back to the ancient finger-operated abacus of the
Chinese. In 1823, Englishman Charles Babbage invented a steam-powered computer that supposedly would have done almost all the figuring a basic modern computer could do if anybody then had known how to build it. Electronic computers

tion and diffusion[312] to an extent beyond the limits of our imagination.[313]

With the tremendous increase in the number of inventions and facilities for their accumulation and diffusion, rapid advances in

---

came along during World War II in time to revolutionize artillery calculations with ENIAC, short for Electronic Numerical Integrator and Calculator. This secret machine went civilian in 1946. A successor, UNIVAC I, helped the Census Bureau speed up nose-counting and now spends its old age as a museum piece in the Smithsonian Institution. (Cf. Edmund C. Berkeley, *The Computer Evolution,* Garden City, N.Y., 1962, p. 3-41; T.E. Ivall, *Electronic Computers, Principles and Applications,* London, 1960, p. 1-13.)

309. In the *Scientific American,* v. 214, Sept. 1966, p. 67, John McCarthy comments on the rapid progress of computer capability: "A scientific problem that took an hour on a big 1950 machine at 1000 operations per second can be run on the fastest contemporary computers in less than half a second." Along with the increase in numbers has come an increase in the speed capabilities of individual computers. Computers of the late 1960s operated at internal speeds about 20 to 100 times the speeds of their counterparts of 10 years earlier. In addition, the storage capabilities increased eightfold, yet occupied half the former volume. (Cf. Herman H. Goldstine, *The Computer from Pascal to Von Neumann,* Princeton, N.J., 1972, p. 239-347; and Elias M. Awad, *Business Data Processing,* 3rd ed., Englewood Cliffs, N.J., 1972, p. 21-23, 42-47.)

"In 1951 there were only 10 computer systems in the United States. Today there are 325,000 computers with 700,000 people making, selling, repairing and attending them. That is not even counting that mutation of miniaturization, the pocket calculator, expected to increase another 16 million this year. The miniaturizing breakthrough of the computer came with the invention of the microprocessor. Half the size of a stick of chewing gum, it contains up to 3,000 transistors, equivalent to a room-sized computer of 10 years ago. With microprocessors, electronic hobbyists can build a computer for $1,000 that outworks the best that was available in the early 1960s." (*South Bend Tribune,* August 12, 1976, p. 27; based on recently released reports of the National Geographic Society)

310. "The number of digital computers in worldwide use increased from less than 15 in 1950 to over 10,000 in the late 1960s with over 100,000 predicted for the 1970s," according to Louis Robinson, Manager of Systems Research, IBM, in the *Encyclopedia Americana,* 1973 ed., v. 7, p. 473, under "Computers." (Cf. Herman H. Goldstine, "World-Wide Developments," in his book *The Computer from Pascal to Von Neumann,* Princeton, N.J., 1972, p. 349-362.)

311. Before the development of electronic analog computers and electronic digital computers in the 1940s, industry and engineering personnel were severely restricted by the vast amount of data manipulation and calculation time that were required to analyze and solve problems. With the computer, the engineer can seek a solution in depth, at great time savings, in such areas as automatic control, critical path scheduling, simulation techniques, design, and complex mathematical problems. For the scientist, the computer has led to the restructuring of investigative techniques in the laboratory, to comprehensive data organization and

modern science and technology have made two fundamental changes
in tools and energies. One is the transformation of simple tools into

---

data analysis for experimental and theoretical work, and to construction of new
scientific theories. In each of these areas, the role of the computer has grown until
it now plays an indispensable part in scientific discovery. (Cf. Edmund C.
Berkeley, *The Computer Evolution,* Garden City, N.Y., 1962, p. 3-53; and
William H. Desmonde, *Computers and Their Uses,* 2nd ed., Englewood Cliffs,
N.J., 1971.)

A photo of an electronic computer, IBM 7094, appears on p. 41 of the *History
of Science: Science in the Twentieth Century,* ed. by René Taton, trans. by A.J.
Pomerans, New York, 1964, with the following note in the illustrations table:
"With this fully transistorized assembly, many scientific, technical, economic and
management problems can be solved at a rate of 250,000 additions a second. There
is a central ferrite core memory containing 1,179,800 binary positions."

312. "The computer is also becoming an increasingly familiar feature on college and university campuses. It is estimated that in 1969 more than 1,200 institutions had computer facilities of some type in use. And the rate of increasing use has
been impressive, averaging 42 percent a year between 1963 and 1968 and 22 percent
between 1968 and 1969. Itself a creature of university-based research, the electronic computer is now most intensively used as a research instrument. Such activity accounted for about 40 percent of computer use in 1966-67. Administrative uses
—for accounting, personnel, scheduling, and planning operations—accounted
for an additional 28 percent. Instructional use accounted for 30 percent."
(Foreword by Clark Kerr, Chairman of Carnegie Commission on Higher Education, to *The Emerging Technology: Instructional Uses of the Computer in Higher
Education,* by Roger E. Levin, New York, 1972; cf. the book's parts one and two.
Cf. also: Karl L. Zinn, "A Computer-Based Technology for Learning and
Research on Instruction," *Review of Educational Research,* v. 37, 1967.)

"The family room TV set could become a home learning center for free, pulling in all kinds of teaching courses and information from huge electronic
memories fed and updated in storehouses at the far end of a transmission line."
(*South Bend Tribune,* August 12, 1976, p. 27, based on a recently released report
of the National Geographic Society.)

313. Digital and analog computers now make feasible the answer to the problem of data storage, and the solution to scientific and engineering problems virtually impossible to solve before. The electronic computer is thus an example of an
invention which facilitates further discoveries and inventions. (Cf. Vannevar
Bush, "As We May Think" in the *Atlantic Monthly,* v. 176, 1945, p. 101-108; and
D.S. Halacy, Jr., *Computers, the Machines We Think With,* rev. ed., New York,
1969, p. 1-17, 251-268.)

314. Machines may be distinguished from tools in that the latter are relatively
undifferentiated and may be used for more than one kind of operation, always
under the control of the worker, whereas machines are designed to perform one
particular function, with an accuracy, speed, or regularity not readily attained by
the individual worker. Machines have been in use since the potter's wheel, but it remained for man in modern times not only to invent machines in unprecedented
numbers, but also to develop them into a very complex structure. By their command
of power and by their facility for mass production, they tend to drive out more in-

complex machines,[314] and the other is the conversion of more and more energies[315] from water,[316] coal,[317] petroleum,[318] and nuclear

---

dividualistic methods of production, and the order they achieve not only prevails in the factory but spreads into the office, the market, and even the home. The final step in this process, already reached in certain industries, is complete automation. (Cf. Lewis Mumford, *Technics and Civilization,* New York, 1934, p. 9-12.)

315. World energy production:

(million metric tons of coal equivalent):

1929	1,778	1956	3,499	1965	5,318
1937	1,910	1957	3,668	1966	5,623
1949	2,365	1958	3,815	1967	5,759
1950	2,607	1959	4,050	1968	6,144
1951	2,808	1960	4,297	1969	6,512
1952	2,876	1961	4,274	1970	6,989
1953	2,953	1962	4,514	1971	7,257
1954	3,009	1963	4,795	1972	7,566
1955	3,295	1964	5,093	1973	8,027

(Based on the *United Nation's Statistical Yearbook,* 1960, p. 270; 1965, p. 70; and 1974, p. 48.)

The following table gives a rough idea of how in the evolution of human civilization new sources and new contrivances of inanimate energy have been added step by step to the already existing means in the major fields of energy demand—namely, for domestic and industrial heat, and industrial and transport power. It should be noted that the table only gives the means of energy newly added at each stage of development, while actually the whole stock of previously known means is generally being used along with the new ones. (The table appears in Hans Thirring, *Energy for Man, Windmills to Nuclear Power,* Bloomington, Ind., 1958, p. 31.)

Stage of Development	Domestic Heat	Industrial Heat	Industrial Power	Transport Power
Animal stage	—	—	—	—
Primitive caveman	Wood fire	—	—	—
Prehistoric civilization	″	Wood fire	—	—
Antiquity	″	″	Wind, water	Wind
Since about 1250	″	Coal	″	″
″ ″ 1400	Coal	″	″	″
″ ″ 1710	″	″	Steam	″
″ ″ 1820	″	″	″	Steam
″ ″ 1890	″	″	Electricity	Electricity
″ ″ 1900	Oil prods.	Electricity	″	Petrol motors
″ ″ 1955	″	″	Atomic power	Atomic power

materials[319] to actuate the complex machines besides for domestic uses. Thus, the complex machines become a combination of tools and energies, and the development of tools and energies in modern times is actually a process of mechanization.

"In 1850 work animals and human beings accounted for over 94 percent of the energy in the United States. Mineral fuels and water power accounted for the remaining 5.8 percent. In that year wood accounted for more than 90 percent of inanimate energy and coal for the remainder. The petroleum industry had not come into being. Wood largely disappeared as a source of energy during the latter half of the nineteenth century and is no longer considered a significant energy fuel. Coal became the most important source of mechanical energy and continued in that lofty position until it was replaced by petroleum and natural gas about 1950. The work animal has ceased to be a significant source of energy, and human beings account for less than one percent of the energy used in industry. The shift from muscular energy derived from food and feed to mechanical energy derived from mineral fuels and falling water is almost complete." (*Zimmermann's World Resources and Industries,* 3d ed., ed. by W.N. Peach and James A. Constantin, New York, 1972, p. 334)

316. The increase in world production of hydro electricity from 1929 to 1959 is shown in the following table

(quantity: million metric tons of coal equivalent)

1929	14	1951	47	1955	59
1937	22	1952	50	1956	64
1949	38	1953	52	1957	68
1950	41	1954	54	1958	76
				1959	79

(Based on the *United Nation's Statistical Yearbook,* 1960, p. 270.)

317. The increase in world production of coal and lignite from 1929 to 1973 is shown in the following table

(million metric tons of coal equivalent)

1929	1,412	1956	1,909	1965	2,268
1937	1,404	1957	1,976	1966	2,310
1949	1,476	1958	2,071	1967	2,207
1950	1,605	1959	2,147	1968	2,274
1951	1,651	1960	2,191	1969	2,326
1952	1,648	1961	2,023	1970	2,394
1953	1,656	1962	2,072	1971	2,392
1954	1,650	1963	2,162	1972	2,430
1955	1,807	1964	2,241	1973	2,486

(Based on the *United Nation's Statistical Yearbook,* 1960, p. 270; 1965, p. 70; and 1974, p. 48.)

Coal was mined in Europe from the 12th century A.D., beginning in England. It was soon discovered that the burning of coal was a serious cause of pollution.

For production whose original purpose was to procure subsistence, as in earlier times, mechanization began in factories where it

---

Early in the 14th century, the smog problem became so bad in London as the result of the use of coal in home fireplaces that King Edward I decreed coal burning a capital offense. At least one man was executed for violating the law. However, the use of coal continued, and with the development of the steam engine during the Industrial Revolution, its production increased rapidly. By 1850, the world output of coal was 130 million tons per year, and by the early 20th century, this amount had increased tenfold. (Cf. Edward A. Martin, *The Story of a Piece of Coal,* New York, 1911, p. 101-111.)

318. The increase in world production of petroleum and gas from 1929 to 1973 is shown in the following table:

(quantity: million metric tons of coal equivalent)

Year	Crude petroleum	Natural gas	Year	Crude petroleum	Natural gas
1929	276	76	1961	1486	674
1937	381	104	1962	1610	737
1949	627	225	1963	1727	805
1950	701	261	1964	1867	880
1951	806	304	1965	2001	931
1952	850	329	1966	2172	1014
1953	898	348	1967	2329	1092
1954	940	365	1968	2543	1189
1955	1029	400	1969	2736	1302
1956	1118	434	1970	3002	1436
1957	1176	473	1971	3169	1529
1958	1206	508	1972	3340	1616
1959	1299	567	1973	3657	1695
1960	1395	625			

(Based on the *United Nations Statistical Yearbook,* 1960, p. 270; 1965, p. 70; and 1974, p. 48.)

319. The growth of the world installed capacity of nuclear electricity is shown in the following table:

(quantity: thousand KW)

Year	Capacity	Year	Capacity
1964	4,160	1969	15,390
1965	6,440	1970	18,920
1966	8,480	1971	25,020
1967	10,810	1972	36,710
1968	12,210	1973	46,200

(Based on the *United Nations Statistical Yearbook,* 1974, p. 371.)

320. In automated production lines or the so-called assembly lines, parts are automatically transferred to, into, and out of a series of machines which perform

has gone as far as to assembly line,[320] automation[321] and robots.[322] It then proceeded to operate in the agricultural field with a number of power equipments.

---

successive operations on them. The only limiting factor on the productivity of the machine is the speed of the machine itself, since loading and unloading mechanisms are geared to the machine cycle. Thus the full productivity of the machine is realized, and the heavy manual effort formerly associated with many metal-working operations is reduced to a minimum. (Cf. S.E. Rubinoff, *Automation in Practice,* Chicago, 1957, p. 1-18.)

321. Automation may be defined as any continuous integrated operation of a production system that uses electronic computers or related equipment to regulate and coordinate the quantity and quality of what is produced. Automatic control of production is achieved in factories by transfer machines, which move a product from place to place for successive operations. Computers, transfer machines, and related equipment use the principle of "feedback," a concept of control in which the input of machines is regulated by the machines' own output. Although the use of machines dates back to the steam engine of the 18th century and to the assembly line of the early 20th century, feedback is a new development truly unique to automation. (Cf. Walter Buckingham, *Automation: Its Impact on Business and People,* New York, 1961.)

322. Robot, a mechanical device that can perform a task of manipulation or locomotion under automatic control. The name robot derives from the Czech word for "worker," and was first popularized by the play, "R.U.R." (Rossum's Universal Robots), written by Karel Capek in 1921. Industrial robots already are beginning to make a significant contribution to several manufacturing processes such as loading and unloading punch presses, tending die-casting machines, spot-welding automobile bodies, handling materials, and arc welding. Robot technology is crucial to the performance of modern missile guidance systems, particularly in the cruise missile, and will undoubtedly soon be incorporated into many other weapons systems as well. Robots will surely play a major role in planetary exploration and in the exploitation of the ocean floor. Eventually, robots will appear in the household, although the cost of early general-purpose mechanical servants will probably limit their widespread use. (Cf. James S. Albus and John M. Evans, Jr., "Robot Systems," *Scientific American,* Feb. 1976.)

323. "Specialization in one or two major crops makes possible the most efficient use of machinery and seasonal labour. Giant gasoline tractors, large gang plows, pulverizing harrows, and grain drills enable farmers to plow, harrow, and sow grain in one process. Likewise, at harvest time a combined header, thresher, cleaner, and bagger permits the execution of the harvesting process in a single act." (Harry E. Barnes, *An Economic History of the Western World,* New York, 1937, p. 483)

324. The steam engine, improved by James Watt in 1765, was applied to both water and rail transportation early in the 19th century, ushering in the Machine Age in transportation. The steamboat, which represented the first practical application of the steam engine to transportation, was invented independently by several Americans, among them John Fitch, James Runsey, Oliver Evans, Robert Fulton, and John Stevens. Fulton's *Clermont* demonstrated on the Hudson River in 1807 a practical type of steamboat that could be used on tidewater and inland

Mechanization began in transportation with the boat[324] and train[325] moved forward by steam, followed by the automobile[326] and

---

waters. The first steamship to cross the Atlantic entirely under steam was the *Canadian Royal William,* in 1833. (Cf. Courtlandt Canby, *A History of Ships and Seafaring,* New York, 1963, p. 80-96; James T. Flexner, *Steamboats Come True,* New York, 1944, p. 364-378.)

325. Steam railroad transport began in England and the United States between 1825 and 1830. In the United States, the first railroads were short and often merely supplemented to water transportation. The first connecting link between the two coasts was completed at Promontory Point, Utah, amidst a colorful celebration in 1869. By 1890, the United States was ribbed with steel from east to west and from north to south. The steam locomotive went through great technical development in power and efficiency until it was replaced by diesel power after World War II. (Cf. Michael Robbins, *The Railway Age,* London, 1962, p. 10-37, 160-168, 189-198.)

326. In 1887, the German engineer Gottlieb Daimler first applied the gasoline engine to a highway vehicle. The development of the automobile in the United States began about 1895. Today, all the developed nations are provided with large systems of improved highways, including many superhighways; large quantities of freight are conveyed by truck and tractor-trailer units: and millions of persons travel daily in buses and cars all over the world. (Cf. Eugen Diesel, *From Engines to Autos,* Chicago, 1960, p. 284-297 and R.J. Forbes, *Man, the Maker: A History of Technology and Engineering,* New York, 1950, p. 258-261.)

327. The first air navigation took place on June 5, 1783, when a balloon filled with heated air was floated over Annonay, France, by Joseph Michel Montgolfier and his brother Jacques. Airplane transportation began with the successful flight of the Wright brothers at Kitty Hawk, N.C., in 1903. The gas engine, first used successfully by the Wright brothers, led the industry to expand rapidly after World War I. In the 1950s the airlines began to abandon gas engines in favor of jets, which offered new possibilities in speed, and economy of maintenance and operation. (Hendrick de Leeuw, *Conquest of the Air, the History and Future of Aviation,* New York, 1960, p. 7-20)

328. It was on April 25, 1955, that the President of the United States, Dwight D. Eisenhower, first suggested construction of a nuclear-powered merchant ship: "The new ship, powered with an atomic reactor, will not require refueling for scores of thousands of miles of operation. Visiting the ports of the world, it will demonstrate to people everywhere this peacetime use of atomic energy, harnessed for the improvement of human living. In part, the ship will be an atomic exhibit; carrying to all people practical knowledge of the usefulness of this new science in medicine, agriculture, and power production." The ship was named *Savannah* after the first steam-powered S.S. *Savannah* of the early 19th century. Compare this new vessel to the old one in terms of fuel-carrying capacity: the old vessel could carry fuel for only about 80 hours of steaming; the new nuclear-powered ship expects to run under normal operation for at least three years, or some 300,000 miles, on her initial fuel charge, possibly longer. (Cf. A.W. Kramer, *Nuclear Propulsion for Merchant Ships,* Washington, 1962, p. 128-131.)

329. "Since 1812 the evolution of printing presses has been one of the most notable features of the progress of modern mechanical ingenuity.... One of the

airplane[327] driven by petroleum, and lately by huge ships propelled by nuclear power.[328]

In the media of communication, mechanization has, in addition to various new printing devices,[329] brought forth many miracles such as the telegraph,[330] telephone,[331] radio[332] and television.[333] These are

---

latest printing presses can print, fold, cut, and count no less than 1,000 thirty-two-page newspapers per minute.... A remarkable new invention, the teletypesetting machine, has been worked out in recent years." (Harry E. Barnes, *An Economic History of the Western World,* New York, 1937, p. 467)

330. Experimenters from the early Greeks to Benjamin Franklin knew how to store and discharge electricity, but not how to control or use it. The work of Volta, Galvani, Ampere, Joseph Henry, Faraday, Clerk Maxwell, Heinrich Hertz, and others led to the basic understandings on which the electric age rests. Several people tried the voltaic battery as a source of current for transmitting signals. But Samuel F.B. Morse, a professional painter, scholar of literature and design, and inventor, first hit upon the idea of sending long and short impulses, coded to represent letters, through 10 miles of wire strung around and around in his workshop, and patented his invention in 1837. The first telegraph, which was built in 1844 with a government grant, tapped out Morse's historic message: "What hath God wrought?" (Alvin F. Haslow, *Old Wires and New Waves,* New York, 1936, p. 13-99)

331. Alexander Graham Bell invented the telephone in 1876 while working toward a harmonic telegraph designed to send several distinct signals over the same wires. The American Telephone and Telegraph Company was founded in 1885 to build long-distance lines, and service between New York and Chicago opened in 1892. Telephone systems are now very large and almost incredibly complex. A caller in the United States, for instance, can dial a few numbers and reach any one of the 110 million telephones in the country. He can also reach more than 209 other countries and more than 96% of the telephones in the world, according to Herbert S. Feder of the Bell Telephone Laboratories. (Cf. John E. Kingsbury, *The Telephone and Telephone Exchanges, Their Invention and Development,* New York, 1972, p. 42-76.)

332. Radio waves were the subject of intense interest and speculation after Heinrich Hertz demonstrated that they could pass through solid objects. Guglielmo Marconi used his understanding of both Hertzian waves and the Morse code to send the first wireless message in 1895, and Aleksandr Popov of Russia reported a similar experiment in the same year. In 1906, Reginald Fessenden, a Canadian who had worked for Edison, first transmitted the human voice by radio. Lee De Forest invented an improved vacuum tube that made "wireless telephony" an instant sensation, and in 1910 a Caruso performance was broadcast from the Metropolitan Opera House to the astonishment of radio "hams" and ship operators. De Forest delivered the first newscast when he announced the presidential election returns of 1916. Since then, radio waves have conquered space over the world for mass communication. (Cf. Alvin F. Harlow, *Old Wires and New Waves,* New York, 1936, p. 435-476; and Edwin Emery, Philip H. Ault and Warren K. Agee, *Introduction to Mass Communication,* p. 235-242.)

333. This medium of communication primarily used for broadcasting visual impressions of reality through space, is the most effective means of mass com-

powered by electricity, have quickly expanded,[334] and today are even hooked up with satellite transmitters.[335]

In the development of weapons, mechanization has led to the ap-

---

munication known to mankind. After about 80 years of development, first by Paul Nipkow, a German scientist, then by the American inventor Charles F. Jenkins, the Scottish inventor John Logie Baird, and others, television made it possible for millions of people to share a single experience. (Cf. *A Technological History of Motion Pictures and Television,* ed. by Raymond Fielding, Berkeley, California, 1967, p. 227-254.)

334. The world had approximately 23,000 radio broadcasting transmitters in 1971, according to the *UNESCO Statistical Yearbook,* 1973, p. 725, and had approximately 760,000,000 radio receivers, 282,000,000 televisions, and 336,000,000 telephones in use in 1973, according to the *United Nations Statistical Yearbook,* 1974, p. 6. (For the development of radio and television in the United States, cf. Richard E. Chapin, *Mass Communications, A Statistical Analysis,* East Lansing, Michigan, 1957, p. 78-87.)

335. In 1946, Arthur C. Clarke of Great Britain first suggested the concept of a global communications system consisting of three active communications satellites properly spaced at the same altitude. In 1955, John R. Pierce of Bell Telephone Laboratories analyzed two methods of communicating via satellites. Since this beginning, both kinds of communications satellites have been built. Echo I, the first passive communications satellite, was launched on August 12, 1960. Courier IB, launched on October 10, 1960, was the first successful active satellite. Communications satellites permit the beaming of programs to any one or all of the thousands of television stations broadcasting in over 100 countries to millions of sets. By means of satellites, continental networks can exchange programs anytime they find it commercially or politically feasible to do so. Communications satellites hold out the prospect of stations broadcasting directly to communities and even to individual homes anywhere in the world. (Cf. Leonard Jaffe, *Communication in Space,* New York, 1966, p. 5-47, 161-167.)

"In April 1965 the successful launching from Cape Kennedy of Early Bird set the stage for a new era of worldwide communications. Placed in 'stationary' orbit 22,300 miles above the Atlantic, this 85-pound cylinder began receiving and transmitting all types of communications, including telephone calls, television, photographs, teletype, and similar data. Since then the International Telecommunications Satellite Consortium (Intelsat) has been developing a global communications satellite system, including coverage of both the Atlantic and Pacific areas. The four satellites to be constructed in 1970 were to have a combined capacity for handling 84,000 simultaneous telephone calls or 48 full-time color television channels, while each of the four satellites envisioned for the 1978 model would possess a capacity at least five times as great." (Alastair M. Taylor, Nels M. Bailkey, Mark Mancall, T. Walter Wallbank, *Civilization Past & Present,* 6th ed., Glenview, Illinois, 1970, Book I, p. 503)

336. Tanks evolved from war chariots and first appeared in World War I. They are the principal assault weapons of armored infantry troops, and, because they combine fire-power, mobility, and armor protection, they are the most formidable non-nuclear ground weapons of modern armies. Main battle tanks range from 52 to 37 tons. Their primary armament consists of guns of 120-mm to

pearance of tanks on the land,[336] warplanes in the air,[337] fighting
ships on the sea[338] and submarines under the water,[339] with a great

---

90-mm. Light tanks of 25 tons to 9 tons have main guns of 90-mm to 76-mm.
Tanks also carry machine guns. They attack swiftly, using all guns, acting either as
independent units or with infantry. (Cf. Mildred H. Gillie, *Forging the Thunder-
bolt, A History of the Development of the Armed Forces,* Harrisburg, Pa., 1947;
John Milsom, *Russian Tanks, 1900-1970,* Harrisburg, Pa., 1971, p. 82-158; and
Alton H. Quanbeck and Archie L. Wood, *Modernizing the Strategic Bomber
Force,* Washington, 1976, p. 29-30, 55-57.)

337. Before the introduction of nuclear bombs, the most important change in
weapons had been the invention of the gun in the 15th century and of the airplane
in the 20th century. Modern warfare began with the utilization of the former invention and has witnessed steady improvement in its utilization through the
developments of greater accuracy and speed of fire; penetrability and ex-
plosiveness of the projectile; steadiness, speed, and security of the vehicle which
conveys it over land or sea toward the enemy; and adaptation of military organizations to such utilization. The airplane has continued this development by providing an even swifter vehicle for carrying the gun. It has also introduced the third
dimension into warfare, making possible the use of gravitation to propel explosives, more extensive and accurate scouting, and military action behind the
front, over vast areas, and across all barriers of terrain. The improvement in naval
equipment—the armored vessel and heavy ordnance, and the use of submarines;
the utilization of railroads and motor trucks for mobilization, and the use of
tanks; and the invention of radar and rockets; have all marked a great development in the technique of war, and have led to the possibility of total and absolute
war. (Cf. Bradley A. Fiske, *The Art of Fighting,* New York, 1920, p. 361; Jean de
Bloch, *The Future of War,* trans. by Robert C. Long, Boston, 1914, Preface, xvii-
xxxi; and Laurence Martin, *Arms and Strategy,* London, 1973.)

338. Fighting ships include the battleship, carrier, cruiser, destroyer, and
submarine. Well-known battleships are the German 52,600-ton *Bismarck* and *Tir-
pitz,* and the Japanese 69,100-ton *Yamato* and *Mushashi,* used in World War II.
Samples of carriers are the British 54,000-ton *Ark Royal* and *Eagle* and the U.S.
76,000-80,700-ton *Forrestal* class carriers and the 87,000-ton *Enterprise,* built
after World War II. An example of a new cruiser is the U.S. guided missile cruiser
Long Beach, commissioned in 1961, which is estimated to have a cruising radius of
140,000 miles without having to replenish fuel or stores, and to have a top speed of
around 45 knots. A high speed of 30 to 40 knots is required of destroyers. Their
size varies greatly, from about 250 to 600 feet in length, and from about 1,000 to
over 9,000 tons displacement. Most are around 3,000 tons and 300 to 400 feet long.
The world's first nuclear-powered destroyer was the frigate U.S.S. *Bainbridge,*
commissioned in 1962; it was able to cruise around the world 16 times without refueling. (Cf. Arch Whitehouse, *Fighting Ships,* Garden City, N.Y., 1967, 45-235;
and the latest edition of *Jane's Fighting Ships,* London and New York, annually.)

339. Before the advent of nuclear propulsion, all but a few experimental submarines were essentially surface craft that could submerge completely for only a
relatively limited time. The nuclear submarine, which dates from the launching of
the USS *Nautilus* in 1954, is a true submarine in the sense that it normally operates
below the surface, where it is faster and more maneuverable and where it can remain

number of long-range, high-speed and deadly devices, such as guided missiles[340] and atomic bombs.[341]

---

indefinitely. There are roughly two types, ballistic missile and attack. Both are nuclear-powered and therefore have virtually unlimited range, restricted only by the endurance of their crews and the amount of provisions they can carry. They are capable of operations well below 400 feet at speeds of well over 20 knots. (Cf. *The Future of the Sea-Based Deterrent,* ed. by Kosta Tsipis, Anne H. Cahn, and Bernard T. Feld, Cambridge, Mass., 1973, p. 3-76; and Alton H. Quanbeck and Archie L. Wood, *Modernizing the Strategic Bomber Force,* Washington, 1976, p. 57-58.)

340. The guided missile is the most recent development in weapons designed to hit a target from a safe distance. It is a logical sequel to the thrown stone, the cast spear, and the bullet fired from a gun. It is an unmanned space-traversing vehicle that carries a warhead and has within itself the means for controlling its flight path. By contrast, artillery shells and free-flight rockets, once fired, are unguided in flight. The advent of nuclear fission and fusion warheads have brought guided missiles to the forefront of strategic significance. Rocket engines enable missiles to deliver megaton warheads accurately across intercontinental distances in minutes, thereby vitally enhancing the possessor's power to attack or to deter others from attacking. This capability makes it possible for a nation to destroy any of its enemies by a preemptive attack. A "Pearl Harbor" of the future would kill millions rather than thousands. There have been various kinds of guided missiles: surface-to-surface, surface-to-air, surface-to-undersea, air-to-surface, air-to-air, undersea-to-surface, undersea-to-undersea, and so on. (Cf. Wernher von Braun, Frederick I. Ordway III, and Harry H. K. Lange, *History of Rocketry and Space Travel,* New York, 1966, p. 120-149; Edgar M. Bottome, *The Balance of Terror,* Boston, 1971, p. IV, 39-58; and the International Institute for Strategic Studies, *The Military Balance, 1978-1979,* London, 1978, p. 92-97.)

341. As early as 1914, Herbert G. Wells in his book *The World Set Free* recounted the story of the bomb long before its development was even thought of in military circles. He discussed atomic problems which are now commonplace: the fission of uranium; the effects of blast, fire, residual radio activity, the towering column of flame and smoke arising from the first flash—each destroyed city "a flaming center of radiant destruction that only time could quench"—the possibilities of underwater explosions. (Cf. *The World Set Free,* New York, 1914, p. 152-154.)

This invention is indeed far more terrible than George Bernard Shaw could have imagined when he has the Devil say, in *Man and Superman:* "Have you walked up and down upon the earth lately? I have; and I have examined Man's wonderful inventions. And I tell you that in the arts of life man invents nothing, but in the arts of death he outdoes Nature herself . . . when he goes out to slay, he carries a marvel of mechanism that lets loose at the touch of his finger all the hidden molecular energies, and leaves the javelin, the arrow, the blowpipe of his fathers far behind." (Quoted by Ralph E. Lapp, *Arms Beyond Doubt, The Tyranny of Weapons Technology,* New York, 1970, p. 2)

342. Under the subtitle "The Social Impact of the Machine Age," Harry E. Barnes wrote that "Every generation during the last century has imagined itself to have attained approximate finality in the development of mechanical technique. Our generation, owing to the remarkable introduction of mechanical devices into

j.
Harvesting Time

CONSEQUENTLY, MECHANIZATION HAS OPENED A NEW age for our civilization: the Machine Age, to replace the Iron Age, since simple tools made of iron were no longer adequate to characterize a time which had been brought under the domination of complex machines actuated by enormous energies.

Following the opening of the Machine Age, our mode of life progressed from agricultural to industrial. The fundamental reason for this change was that agriculture had been yielding its prominent position in the economy to a cluster of industries[343] developed by modern

---

every phase of life, might perhaps be forgiven for special assurance on this point. Yet it is quite possible that we are today only in the beginning of the mechanical age, provided man is able to show sufficient inventiveness in the institutional field to allow him to operate successfully the revolutionized type of life that his machines inevitably create." (In *An Economic History of the Western World,* New York, 1937, p. 489)

343. The following table shows (1) the trend of decline in significance of agricultural products in general, and (2) the decreasing significance of agricultural products in the more industrial countries, such as the second group:

Group I				Group II			
Country	Percentage of Agricultural Product in Total Gross Domestic Product			Country	Percentage of Agricultural Product in Total Gross Domestic Product		
	1960	1970	1972		1960	1970	1972
Bulgaria	32	23	23	Australia	12	6	...
Colombia	32	27	27	Belgium	6	4	4
Ecuador	33	24	22	Canada	6	4	4
Ethiopia	61	52	48	France	9	6	6
Guyana	33	20	22	Israel	9	5	5
Honduras	34	31	32	Italy	13	9	8
Indonesia	54	47	40	Japan	13	7	6
Ivory Coast	43	31	29	Norway	9	7	6
Nigeria	59	45	40	Sweden	7	4	4
Romania	33	19	22	United Kingdom	4	3	3
Turkey	38	28	27	United States	4	3	3

(Based on the *United Nations Statistical Yearbook,* 1974, Table 184, p. 622-633.)

machinery in conjunction with the expansion of the division of labor,[344] the application of mass production,[345] and the utilization of

---

344. The advance of the division of labor in modern times results in the growth of large-scale enterprises, and the growth of large-scale enterprises in turn speeds a further advance of the division of labor. As a matter of fact, systems of economic organization such as so-called "scientific management," or the "planned economy," and "cooperative economy" are but conscious applications of the principles of the division of labor. (Cf. Charles Babbage, *On the Economy of Machinery and Manufactures,* 4th ed., New York, 1963, p. 173-175; Alfred Marshall, *Principles of Economics,* 9th ed., New York, 1961, v. 1, p. 255-266; also v. 1, Book 4, Chapters 9-11; and Allyn A. Young, "Increasing Returns and Economic Progress," *Economic Journal,* 1928, v. 38, p. 527-542.)

The International Labor Office lists approximately 6,000 occupational titles in its *Standard Classification of Occupations,* rev. ed., Geneva, 1969. The list does not go into the subdivisions of each occupation, or attempt to define specializations in the processing or operation of any job.

345. Although the best-known characteristic of mass production is the manufacture of great quantities of goods, it is more than mere quantity output. It is distinguished from all previous types of manufacture by scientific planning and management, which coordinate all available methods for obtaining the maximum number of identical products of uniform quality at the lowest unit cost. The essential elements of mass production are: (1) simplification of product; (2) standardization of parts; (3) use of production and machine tools; (4) careful arrangement of workers, machines, and materials in sequence, combined with the continuous motion of work; (5) high volume; (6) planning and coordination of all activities relative to production and distribution. (Cf. William Butterworth and Pierre Gounod, "Mass Production," in *Europe-United States of America,* v. iii, Paris, 1931, p. 71-109, 110-143; and John A. Shubin, *Managerial and Industrial Economics,* New York, 1961, p. 23-26.)

346. "With the advance of science and technology, combined with the tremendous population growth and improving standards of living, there have been vast changes in man's appraisal of natural resources. Today, more than 75 minerals are used in significant quantities by modern industry; less than a century ago the figure was no more than 25." (Richard M. Highsmith, Jr., "Conservation" in the *Encyclopedia Americana,* 1973 ed. Vol. 7, p. 619)

347. "Chemistry, in particular, has to its credit remarkable accomplishments in the industrial field in recent years. Indeed, it is probable that no other department of science has had so large an influence in transforming our material culture.... We are familiar enough with the fact of the remarkable achievements of contemporary synthetic chemistry in producing, from various by-products, perfumes, flavoring extracts, and a vast variety of other commercial products. We are also acquainted with the like achievements in creating cellulose, sugar, and other similar substances. We have also heard of the striking accomplishments of modern chemistry in revolutionizing the dye industry. We are not, however, always so conscious that the iron and steel industries, the petroleum industry, the rubber industry, and many of the modes of contemporary illumination rest just as decisively upon the contributions of applied chemistry." (Harry E. Barnes, *An Economic History of the Western World,* New York, 1937, p. 448. Cf. Floyd Darrow, *The*

new materials,[346] especially those produced by chemistry,[347] such as clothing fibers,[348] plastics,[349] and synthetic rubber.[350]

Story of Chemistry, New York, 1930; and E.E. Slosson, *Creative Chemistry,* New York, 1930.)

"... more than 50,000 different man-made chemicals are currently in commercial and industrial use, and between 500 and 1,000 new chemicals are put on the market every year." (Sydney Harris, "Of Chemicals, Energy and Magnificent Feast," *South Bend Tribune,* Nov. 20, 1979, p. 10)

An interesting and illustrative example of the remarkable contributions of organic chemistry to modern economic life can be seen in the following table, which lists the diverse products that are extracted from ordinary maize or Indian corn. About twenty more products could be added today. (See E.E. Slosson, *Creative Chemistry,* New York, 1930, p. 184.)

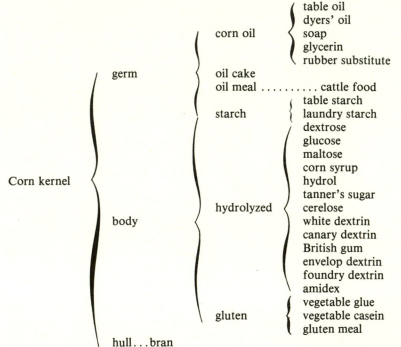

348. In the thousands of years before the last century, we developed only three basic fibers: silk, wool, and cotton. Now man-made fibers have become so numerous that it has been necessary for the United States government to classify them with a law: the Textile Fiber Products Identification Act (1960). Under its requirements, man-made fibers must be labelled as belonging to one of 17 different classes, determined by their chemical base: acetate or triacetate, acrylic, anidex, azlon, glass, metallic, modacrylic, nylon, nytril, olefin, polyester, rayon, rubber,

Although still in its early stages,[351] our industrial life has been developing successfully,[352] and has proved itself able to produce

---

saran, spandex, vinal, and vinyon. (Cf. Douglas C. Hague, *The Economics of Man-Made Fibers,* London, 1957, p. 15-20.)

349. Besides man-made plastic fibers, there are many other kinds of plastics for many other kinds of uses: from toy-making to house-building. The chemist has been able to produce resinous materials having the hardness of stone, the transparency of glass, the elasticity of rubber, or the insulating ability of mica. In combination with suitable fillers, these materials are readily molded into products characterized by strength, lightness, dimensional stability, and resistance to moisture, moderate heat, sunlight, and other deteriorating factors. (Cf. "Plastics Yesterday, Plastics Today, Plastics Tomorrow," in *Modern Plastics Encyclopedia,* 1968, p. 14-23, by the editor of the magazine.)

350. A most widely produced and used plastic is synthetic rubber. In 1966, the world output of synthetic rubber totaled nearly 3.6 million metric tons. The leading producer was the United States, with an output of 2.0 million metric tons. Japan, West Germany, and Canada each produced between 200,000 and 250,000 metric tons, while Britain, France, Italy, and the Netherlands each produced more than 100,000 metric tons. Synthetic rubber accounted for 57 per cent of the total world output of rubber. The United States is also the leading consumer of synthetic rubber. About three fourths of the rubber used in the United States is synthetic, and about five eighths of the synthetic rubber consumed is of the GBR type, which is used primarily in tires. Other important consumers of synthetic rubber are Japan, West Germany, Britain, France, Italy, and Canada. (Cf. H.J. Stern, *Rubber: Natural and Synthetic,* 2nd ed., London, 1967, p. 68.)

Production of synthetic rubber in the 22 leading countries (Argentina, Australia, Belgium, Brazil, Bulgaria, Canada, Czechoslovakia, Denmark, East Germany, France, India, Italy, Japan, Mexico, the Netherlands, Poland, Romania, South Africa, Spain, United Kingdom, United States, and West Germany) in the 10 years from 1964 to 1973 is shown in the following table:

Year	Total (Metric Tons)	Year	Total (Metric Tons)
1964	3,003,092	1969	4,743,810
1965	3,232,245	1970	5,049,133
1966	3,586,586	1971	5,240,840
1967	3,702,686	1972	5,619,003
1968	4,227,966	1973	6,251,295

(Based on *The Growth of World Industry,* 1973 ed., v. 2, New York, 1975, by the Department of Economic and Social Affairs, Statistical Office of the United Nations, p. 323.)

351. Our industrial life began with the Industrial Revolution, the name applied to the dramatic period of economic and technical change in Britain during the late 18th and early 19th centuries, usually arbitrarily designated as between 1760 and 1840, when the steam engine first came into widespread use and provided power for other newly developed machines that did the work previously performed by human hands. Today, two hundred years later, most of us still remain far

more goods, commodities,[353] and incomes,[354] and support more people.[355] This mode of life is superior to previous ones because it can re-

---

behind the progress of the Industrial Revolution; thus, modern industrial life is
certainly just in its infancy. (Cf. Thomas S. Ashton, *The Industrial Revolution,
1760-1830*, New York, 1962; and Phyllis Deane, *The First Industrial Revolution*,
Cambridge, Mass., 1965.)

352. The growth of world industry, excluding Albania, China, Mongolia,
North Korea, and Vietnam, from 1961 to 1973 is shown in the following table:
(Index: 1970 = 100)

Year	%	Year	%	Year	%
1961	62	1965	77	1969	94
1962	66	1966	81	1971	104
1963	69	1967	85	1972	107
1964	74	1968	90	1973	115

1961-1973 annual growth rate: 5.3%

(Based on Statistical Office of the United Nations, Department of Economic and Social Affairs, *The Growth of World Industry*, 1973 ed., New York, 1975, v. 1, p. 620.)

353. The increase of world production, excluding China, Mongolia, North
Korea and Vietnam, from 1958 to 1973 is shown in the following table:
(Index: 1970 = 100)

Year	Primary Commodities	Manufactured Goods
1958	70	44
1960	75	52
1963	81	62
1965	85	73
1966	89	79
1967	92	83
1968	95	89
1969	97	96
1971	102	104
1972	103	112
1973	108	123

(Based on the *United Nations Statistical Yearbook*, 1974, p. 25.)

World trends in population and production from 1876 to 1957 are shown in
the following table excerpted from Alfred Maizels, *Industrial Growth and World
Trade*, Cambridge, England, 1963, p. 80:

ly on much less land for our living[356] and can utilize much more power from tools and energies to work for us;[357] and it has enabled us

| | | Production | |
	Population	Manu- factures	Primary produce
1876-80	79	25	. . .
1896-1900	90	54	76
1911-13	99	95	93
1926-30	111	141	123
1931-33	117	110	120
1934-35	120	133	125
1936-38	124	158	135
1948-50	145	238	156
1951-53	151	297	176
1954-56	158	341	191

The above statistics show that manufactured goods have increased faster than primary commodities? This comes as no surprise. What about food production, which is included in the primary commodities? It has also done well, as shown in the following table:

Year	Volume Index	Per Capita Index	Year	Volume Index	Per Capita Index
1963	100	100	1969	118	105
1965	105	101	1970	122	106
1966	110	104	1971	126	108
1967	114	106	1972	125	105
1968	117	107	1973	131	108

(Based on the *United Nations Statistical Yearbook,* 1974, p. 23-24.)

through mechanization to increase our productive ability up to hundreds of times,[358] thus making it possible to provide adequate subsis-

---

Farm production of the United States from 1940 to 1973 gives an even clearer picture:
(Index 1967 = 100)

Year	Farm Output per man-hour	Crop Production per acre
1940	21	63
1950	35	69
1955	47	74
1960	67	88
1965	91	100
1969	112	107
1970	113	102
1971	125	112
1972	131	115
1973	133	114

(Based on the *Statistical Abstract of the United States,* 1974, p. 614.)

354. According to economists, no large pre-industrial society produced more than the equivalent of some $200 per capita per year. With industrialization, the situation altered radically, so that societies such as the United States and some European countries were producing between $600 and $1,500 per capita before World War II. Since then, per capita income has increased in the United States, Canada, Japan, and much of western Europe to between $1,500 and $6,000. Observers suggest that by the year 2000, these countries will have attained a per capita income of about 50 times that of the pre-industrial stage. (Cf. Herman Kahn and Anthony J. Wiener, *The Year 2000: A Framework for Speculation on the Next Thirty Years,* New York, 1967, Ch. 4, "Postindustrial Society in the Standard World.")

According to the *United Nations Statistical Yearbook,* 1974, p. 650-652, in 1973, there were six countries with average per capita incomes exceeding $5,000 and with populations in excess of one million: the United States, $6,167; Switzerland, $5,130; Sweden, $6,185; Canada, $5,412; West Germany, $5,671; and Denmark, $5,481. 17 per cent of the world population lived in countries with per capita incomes of from $2,000 to $5,000; and 14 per cent, from $500 to $2,000.

The relationship between industrialization and increased productivity can be viewed in many ways. For example, Alfred Maizels, in his *Industrial Growth and World Trade,* Cambridge, England, 1963, p. 8-9, summarizes his opinion as follows: "The main causal connection ... is that industrialization tends to raise physical output per head in the economy. There are several ways in which this comes about, and these tend to operate simultaneously. First, with industrialization the share of manufacturing in national output increases. Since the average product per worker is higher in manufacturing than in agriculture in low-income countries, this shift in the pattern of output will raise total commodity output per head in the economy. Second, with the progress of industrialization, productivity in the manufacturing sector itself tends to increase relatively rapidly, compared

tence for all the peoples of the world to live together as one group, assuming a reasonable limitation on population.

with progress in other sectors. Increasing manufacturing output will often be accompanied by economies of scale (within plants and in industry generally), by increases in capital assets employed, and by the development of new skills and attitudes to work. Finally, the level of productivity in the rest of the economy may be raised as a result of industrialization (by increasing the supplies of farm equipment and fertilizers to agriculture, for example; or, more indirectly, by improving transport facilities, educational levels, and so on)."

355. The above world food production statistics show that in the Machine Age we can produce more for more people even in the area of food, as indicated by the per capita indexes. During this period, although the world population increased by approximately 700,000,000 (from approximately 3,160,000,000 in 1963 to 3,860,000,000 in 1973) we were still able to produce more food per capita. Back at the beginning of the Industrial Revolution about 200 years ago, there were only approximately 700,000,000 people on earth. Since then, the world population has increased almost fivefold. This fact tells us clearly that industrial life and the gradual industrialization of agriculture have been able to support more and more people so far. (Cf. the *United Nations Statistical Yearbook,* 1974, p. 8; and M. King Hubbert, *Energy Resources,* Washington, 1962, p. 20.)

The fact that industrial life can support more people is well demonstrated by the rapid growth of modern cities. At the beginning of the 16th century, there were only six European cities—Constantinople, Paris, Naples, Venice, Milan, and Lisbon—with populations of more than 100,000. Ghent at that time boasted 50,000 people; London and Bruges 40,000 each; and Brussels, Louvain, and Liege 20,000 to 30,000. The number of capitol cities and cities with populations of 100,000 and more have increased to more than 1500 in the world. At least 40 cities had populations exceeding 2,000,000 in the 1960s. Especially in the United States and western Europe, city life has become the characteristic mode of existence for the majority of the people. In the United States 1960 census, almost 70 percent of the population was classified as urban, and this figure was exceeded in the more densely populated western European countries. About 63 per cent of the U.S. population lived in 212 metropolitan areas in the 1960s, and half the U.S. population lived in just 13 megalopoli. (Cf. Wolf Schneider, *Babylon Is Everywhere: The City as Man's Fate,* New York, 1963, p. 228-231, 225; Lewis Mumford, *The City in History,* New York, 1961, p. 355; and *United Nations Demographic Yearbook,* 1966, table 6.)

Actually, the industrial life not only makes it possible for us to live together as one group, but ties us together as one group by estab-

---

In our time, there have been peoples who were able to supply not only many more industrial commodities, but also more agricultural products to the world. The following table shows the agricultural products and exports of the United States in 1973 as an example:

		Production			Exports		
		U.S.	World		U.S.	World	
Commodity	Unit		Total	% U.S.		Total	% U.S.
Wheat	Mil. metric tons	46.6	367.0	12.7	31.7	72.2	43.9
Corn for grain	Mil. metric tons	143.3	312.6	45.8	32.0	42.2	75.8
Soybeans	Mil. metric tons	42.6	57.7	73.8	13.2	15.5	85.2
Rice, rough	Mil. metric tons	4.2	308.8	1.4	1.8	6.5	27.7
Tallow and greases	Mil. pounds	5,628	10,116	55.6	2,296	3,555	64.6
Edible vegetable oils	1,000 metric tons	7.1	26.9	26.4	3.3	9.3	35.5
Cotton	1,000 bales	13,786	59,367	23.2	5,311	20,453	26.0
Sorghum for grain	1,000 metric tons	20,556	41,403	49.6	5,389	8,739	61.7

(Based on the *Statistical Abstract of the United States,* 1974, p. 616.)

356. The amounts of land required by the various modes of life to support one person are roughly estimated as follows: food-gathering, 15 square miles; hunting-fishing, 10 square miles; hoe-cultivating, 1 square mile; animal raising, ⅕ square mile; agricultural, ⅟₅₀ square mile, and industrial, ⅟₁₅₀ square mile. (Cf. William G. Sumner and Albert G. Keller, *The Science of Society,* New Haven, 1927, v. 4, p. 17-19; and Clark Wissler, *An Introduction to Social Anthropology,* New York, 1929, p. 28-41.)

357. The previous modes of life: food-gathering, hunting-fishing, hoe-cultivation, animal-raising, and agriculture, gradually learned to utilize the energy power of fire, wind, water, dog, horse, ox and other animals, and the mechanical power of tools made of stone, copper, iron, and other materials. But such additional powers did not increase to much more than several times that of the user himself until the Industrial Revolution. Industrialization has now increased these powers with the horse-power of machines to up to hundreds of times the power of the user himself. In the United States, for example, the total horsepower of all prime movers in 1850 was 8,495,000, or approximately .35 per capita. This total increased to 20,408,000,000 in 1970, or about 100 per capita. (Cf. *Historical Statistics of the United States from Colonial Times to 1970,* p. 818, Series S 1-14.)

358. Take the increase in farming ability as an illustration. Although generally lower than the increase of productive ability in most other industries, the increase in farming ability in the United States has been high as indicated by a comparison of Chinese and American agricultural laborers in their acreages. According to the *Statistical Year-Book for Asia and the Pacific,* 1974, by a UN commis-

lishing a world-wide economic interdependence.[359] This is because industries do not depend, like agriculture, on soil which can be found everywhere. They require various resources which are unevenly

---

šion, China in 1971 had a population of 784,970,000 (p. 87) and a total agricultural area of 327,000,000 hectares (arable land and land under permanent crops, 127,000,000 hectares, and permanent meadows and pastures, 200,000,000 hectares, p. 88). This translates into a total of 808,017,000 acres (1 hectare is equal to 2,471 acres). In the same year—1971—according to the *Statistical Abstract of the United States,* 1973, the United States had a total farm population of 9,426,000, or 4.6% of the total population (p. 584), and a total of 1,097,000,000 acres of farm land (p. 585), with a labor force of 2,292,000 employed in agriculture. (This is about 24% of the total farm population. The others are: 2,395,000 under 14 years of age; 1,864,000 employed in non-agricultural industries; 108,000 not employed, and 2,767,000 not in the labor force, p. 584.) No Chinese farm population statistics are available. If the Chinese farm population is more than 80% of its total population, as is generally claimed, and more than 50% of the farm population are employed in agriculture (under the present regime, every man and woman is required to work), then in 1971 China would have had over 300,000,000 agricultural laborers to work 808,017,000 acres, while the United States had 2,292,000 agricultural laborers to work 1,097,000,000 acres. That is to say, each Chinese agricultural laborer worked approximately 2.70 acres, and each American agricultural laborer worked approximately 478.62 acres. In other words, one American agricultural laborer is equal to about 177 Chinese agricultural laborers. What a difference that is! And why? Because American agricultural laborers are equipped with power tractors and other power tools (cf. the cited statistical abstract, p. 598), while Chinese agricultural laborers generally only work with the help of some animal, old-fashioned ploughs, and other hand tools. They do not have many power tools. (Cf. the cited statistical yearbook, p. 89.)

359. More than a hundred years ago, Karl Marx described this change in his *Manifesto of the Communist Party,* Part I, as follows: "The industry no longer works up indigenous raw materials, but raw materials drawn from the remotest zones: and its products are consumed, not only at home, but in every quarter of the globe." "The need of a constantly expanding market for its products chases the bourgeoisie over the whole surface of the globe. It must nestle everywhere, settle everywhere, establish connections everywhere." As a result, "the bourgeoisie has through its exploitation of the world-market given a cosmopolitan character to production and consumption in every country," and "in place of the old wants satisfied by products of the country, we find new wants, requiring for their satisfaction the products of distant lands and climes. In place of the old local and national seclusion and self-sufficiency, we have intercourse in every direction, universal interdependence of nation." (*Manifesto of the Communist Party,* by Karl Marx and Friedrich Engels, authorized English trans. ed. and annotated by Friedrich Engels, Chicago, 1947)

"International trade reflects international interdependence. The improvement of transport facilities during the last hundred years rendered it possible gradually to extend the range of products which could be exchanged not only in local trade between neighboring countries but over the whole world. More and

distributed over the earth[360] and no country has them all in sufficient amounts at all times.[361] This uneven distribution, together with local differences in climate, the availability of technical skills, equipment,

---

more countries were thus drawn into the orbit of 'world economy'; and more and more the economic effects of local events have tended to spread over wide areas." (League of Nations, Economic Intelligence Service, *The Network of World Trade,* Geneva, 1942, p. 73)

360. First of all, nature did not distribute her minerals equally over the earth. Iron, coal, petroleum, copper, lead, and zinc do not exist in equal abundance, or with the same qualities, even in the regions where they are found. Some countries are either entirely devoid of these substances, or possess them in inadequate quantities. With respect to rare metals and precious stones, distribution is even more unequal. The most important known sources of nickel are in Canada; of manganese, mainly in Russia, Brazil, India, and the Gold Coast of Africa. The chief exporter of tungsten since 1917 has been China; and of antimony, mainly China, Mexico, and Bolivia. These are only illustrations, but they could be multiplied to cover practically all the minerals. This uneven distribution has, of course, existed for a long time, but it has become more significant as the minerals have come into important and extensive use, one after another, in modern industry. A recent example of this phenomenon is the intense search for uranium, which is essential to the development of atomic power. Uranium is believed to be so unequally distributed that large deposits exist only in Canada and the Belgian Congo. Some has been found in the Soviet Union, the United States, Czechoslovakia, and Brazil, but these locations are of less importance. (Cf. George T. Renner, *World Economic Geography,* New York, 1951, p. 355-497.)

Equally significant are statistics resulting from differences in climate and topographical figuration. For example, more than 90 per cent of the world's natural rubber is produced in Southeastern Asia, mainly because most other parts of the world, especially in the northern hemisphere, do not have the right climate for growing rubber. Europe, with 500,000,000 people, has no good cotton growing climate while the United States could produce enough cotton for the whole world. The Belgian Congo contains waterpower resources, due to its topographical configuration, twice as great as those possessed by the whole European continent. (Cf. George T. Renner, *Global Geography,* New York, 1947, p. 598-599.)

361. We are now in a world where no country is self-sufficient, and this may be expressed by imports as a percentage of national consumption 30 years ago. These were between 40% and 50% for such countries as Belgium, Norway, and Denmark; between 30% and 40% for countries like New Zealand and Ireland; and between 20% and 30% for Sweden, Switzerland, United Kingdom, and several other countries. (Cf. Stephen Enke & Virgil Salera, *International Economics,* New York, 1947, p. 12.) Before World War II, the percentages for the United States

capital and labor,[362] necessarily intensifies the division of labor between countries and regions. The result is an expansion of the world economy,[363] which inevitably makes all the peoples of the world

---

were low, but important to American life, as shown in the table—U.S. imports as a percentage of consumption for selected commodities before World War II:

Commodity	Percentage Quantity	Commodity	Percentage Quantity
1 Crude rubber	100	15 Cocoa	100
2 Tin	100	16 Bananas	100
3 Coffee	100	17 Tea	100
4 Raw silk	100	18 Tung oil	90
5 Newsprint	75	19 Manganese ore	98
6 Sugar cane & beets	50	20 Flaxseed	63
7 Carpet wool	100	21 Spices	100
8 Apparel wool	23	22 Asbestos	95
9 Furs	50	23 Chromite	99
10 Wood pulp	25	24 Tungsten	50
11 Raw hides & skins	25	25 Manila fiber	100
12 Jute fiber & burlap	100	26 Bauxite	50
13 Diamonds	100	27 Crude chicle	100
14 Nickel	99	28 Quebracho	100
		29 Cobalt	100

(Cf. U.S. Chamber of Commerce, *Our 100 Leading Imports,* 1945. The commodities are listed in the order of their total imported value. Most of the figures are from the 1938-40 period.)

362. "The geographical concentration of trade in individual products is due in part to differences in the natural conditions, the uneven distribution of available mineral deposits throughout the world, differences in climate, differences in accessibility. But even more important perhaps are the disparities in the relative supply of labour, capital, equipment and productive land." (League of Nations, Economic Intelligence Service, *The Network of World Trade,* Geneva, 1942, p. 7, Summary nos. 3 and 4)

363. "Developments in science and technology are thus closely linked with important economic factors affecting the international community. As societies have become increasingly complex technologically, the points of contact among national economies have multiplied. During the last three decades we have witnessed a tremendous expansion of the world economy, characterized by removal of barriers to trade and increased international division of labor. Abrupt changes in one nation's trade, fiscal, or monetary policies, in its level of economic activity, or in its production or consumption patterns may now have a discernible impact throughout the global economy—and a brutal effect on particular trading partners. Recent gyrations in world agricultural markets, generating dislocations in developed as well as developing nations, illustrate the extent of world economic interdependence." (*Science and Technology in an Era of Interdependence,* by UNA-USA National Policy Panel, New York, 1975, p. 17)

dependent upon each other[364] through exchange for mutual benefits.[365]

---

364. "But the need for a world pattern of multilateral trade will remain as long as climates and geological deposits continue to vary from one area to another, as long as the factors of production are unevenly distributed over the face of the globe." (League of Nations, Economic Intelligence Service, *The Network of World Trade*, Geneva, 1942, Summary no. 19)

In a table on page 45 of *World Minerals and World Peace*, by Charles K. Leith, James W. Furness, and Cleona Lewis (Washington, D.C., 1943), 11 nations were rated according to their potential self-sufficiency with regard to each of 26 important industrial minerals. This table has been outdated by the change of positions of the nations involved as a result of World War II. It may, however, still serve to give us a general idea. The table indicates the number of minerals for which the nation depends almost entirely upon foreign sources: the United States, 9; British Empire, 7; Soviet Union, 8; Germany, 17; France and colonies, 18; Belgium and colonies, 21; Netherlands and colonies, 21; Spain and colonies, 18; Italy, 18; China, 19; and Japanese Empire and Manchukuo, 10.

Economic protectionism has employed various methods to restrict international exchange. An examination of the situation discloses that all the restrictions, however sharply effective they may be in given instances, are insufficient in their total effect to substantially check the general tendency of economic interdependence. Furthermore, protectionist methods always induce considerable costs which cannot be long sustained by any country. One calculation which illustrates how much this cost may be is given in the following table:

	Total Cost of Domestic Production	Total Cost if Obtained from Foreign Sources	Cost of Self-Sufficiency
Germany			
Barley	$ 232,000,000	$ 94,000,000	$ 138,000,000
Wheat	366,000,000	186,000,000	180,000,000
Pork	1,139,000,000	566,000,000	583,000,000
France			
Wheat	628,000,000	290,000,000	338,000,000
Italy			
Wheat	533,000,000	255,000,000	278,000,000
Total	$2,898,000,000	$1,381,000,000	$1,517,000,000

(Cf. Ernest M. Patterson, *An Introduction to World Economics*, New York, 1947, p. 631-34.)

"Scientific and technological advances have also facilitated the growth of profound and widespread interdependencies among nations. Certain technologies, such as the automobile, have created large external resource dependencies. Oil pipelines and supertankers, which make vast supplies of fuel accessible over long distances, have encouraged the use of petroleum rather than coal or other widely-distributed energy sources. The tremendous expansion of multinational

Economic interdependence through exchange has been clearly demonstrated in terms of world trade. Since the Industrial Revolu-

---

manufacture, which brings together widely separated technology, management, material and labor, has made the resources and the markets of one country essential elements in the production process and consumption patterns of other countries—even those separated by great distances." (*Science and Technology in an Era of Interdependence,* by UNA-USA National Policy Panel, New York, 1975, p. 16. Cf. *The World Makes an Automobile* by the Automobile Manufacturers Association, Detroit, 1956, which shows that the manufacture of an automobile requires various materials from all parts of the world.)

As a result of these varied supply patterns, national economies have come to depend on other countries' products and this dependence is growing. The United States, for example, which is one of the world's richest countries with respect to its mineral resources, imported $6 billion worth of non-fuel minerals in 1971 and at current prices is expected to pay more than three times that amount by 1985. The U.S. is almost completely dependent on foreign sources for its entire supply of a few minerals, including chromium and platinum, and imports more than 80 percent of its supply of a number of other minerals, such as cobalt, manganese and bauxite. The Committee on Materials Policy of the National Academy of Sciences estimates that the U.S. is "now almost completely dependent on foreign sources for 22 of the 74 non-energy mineral commodities considered essential for a modern industrial society." (*Elements of a National Materials Policy,* A Report of the National Materials Advisory Board, NAS/NAE, 1972, p. 1. Cf. *Science and Technology in an Era of Interdependence,* by UNA-USA National Policy Panel, New York, 1975, p. 36-37.)

365. Exchange as expanded by the international division of labor is "instrumental in increasing the economic efficiency of both production and scientific and technical progress, which, in turn, results in accelerated growth. This means first of all that with developing national production the individual countries will increasingly tend to export the goods they can produce under comparatively advantageous conditions, and to reduce or gradually stop domestic production of such ones as can be produced at a loss only, meeting home demand for the latter more reasonably by import. This makes it possible to combine and utilize more efficiently the various factors of production available to a country: natural resources, scientific standards and, above all, the capacity of live labour depending on the technological attainment and skill of the working people. Relying on exports, even small or medium-size countries with relatively narrow domestic markets can develop up-to-date mass production and benefit from the economies of scale. At the same time, their imports help them to introduce modern technology. Moreover, under conditions of developed market relations, international competition—forcing a country to compete with strong rivals on export markets and fight competitive imports even at home—exercises a stimulating effect on domestic production. Finally, foreign trade contributes to economic development also by facilitating and accelerating the elimination of temporary *bottlenecks and disproportions* which almost inevitably arise in the course of development." (Tibor Kiss, *International Division of Labor in Open Economies, with Special Regard to the CMEA,* trans. by J. Racz and rev. by I. Gombos and P.M., Budapest, 1971, p. 14-15; cf. p. 13-42. Cf. also Bertil Ohlin, *Interregional*

tion, world trade has increased rapidly in volume,[366] has expanded
from luxury items to goods for common consumption and essential

---

and International Trade [Harvard Economic Studies, v. 39], Cambridge, Mass.,
1933, Ch. 2.)

The essential reason for the interdependence of people brought about by the
division of labor through exchange was noted by Plato two thousand years ago. In
the *Republic* (II), he regarded the city-state as having come into being because of
the mutual needs and the resulting interdependence of individuals. Out of this interdependence arises the division of labor, the specialization of individuals in different occupations in accordance with their natural gifts, and the mutual exchange
of their products for those of others out of self-interest. A further consequence of
exchange is the development of markets and the use of a currency to facilitate
transactions. All goods produced are in greater quantities and are of better quality
than they would be otherwise.

366. The development of the economic interdependence of the world is evident from the enormous increase of commodity exchange between countries in recent centuries. It was estimated that the trade of commercial countries in 1700 was
about $125,000,000, which doubled in 1750. (Clive Day, *A History of Commerce,*
New York, 1919, p. 270) The increase has accelerated since the beginning of the
19th century, as shown in the following table. (Cf. Clive Day, *op. cit.,* p. 271;
Harry E. Barnes, *An Economic History of the Western World,* New York, 1937,
p. 496; and The League of Nations, *Review of World Trade,* 1939, p. 60.)
World trade from 1800 to World War II (Gross in millions of old U.S. dollars):

Year	Gross Commerce	Per Capita
1800	1,400	$ 2.31
1820	1,600	$ 2.13
1830	1,900	2.34
1840	2,700	2.93
1850	4,000	3.76
1860	7,200	6.01
1870	10,600	8.14
1880	14,700	10.26
1890	17,500	11.80
1900	20,100	13.02
1910	33,600	20.81
1913	40,598	24.59
1929	68,619	34.98
1934	23,314	11.65
1937	31,796	14.94
1938	27,736	13.04

The above table shows that world trade increased steadily through the whole
19th century without fluctuation. This increase reached its climax in the prosperous times of 1929; then a decline occurred with the Depression, and this decline approached its lowest point in 1934. In 1937, world trade had a considerable rise, but
dropped again in 1938 when war became imminent. The fluctuations of world
trade after 1929, as shown in values, however, was chiefly due to the fact that

uses,[367] and has developed into a network[368] covering all countries, at every level of economic development[370] and under every economic

---

prices, in terms of dollars, had fallen by about a fourth. The actual volume of goods traded during this period fluctuated only slightly. The quantum index of world trade, which takes 100 for 1929 as a base, is 78.2 for 1934, 96.5 for 1937, and 88.8 for 1938. (The League of Nations, *Review of World Trade,* 1939, p. 60)

A more scientific way to measure the increase of world trade is to compare it, as measured in values, with the increase of world population by per capita value. The share of the average human being in world trade grew about sixfold from 1800 to World War II, as shown in the above table. The increase of world exports since 1938 (excluding Albania, Bulgaria, China, Czechoslovakia, East Germany, Hungary, Mongolia, North Korea, Poland, Romania, U.S.S.R., and Vietnam) is shown in the following table:

Year	At Current Prices U.S. $ 000,000	At 1963 Prices U.S. $ 000,000	Quantum Index 1963 = 100	Population Index 1963 = 100
1938	21,100	54,000	40	68
1948	53,900	53,200	39	75
1958	96,000	95,710	71	90
1963	135,400	135,400	100	100
1967	189,300	181,700	134	109
1968	212,200	205,200	152	111
1969	242,700	227,600	169	114
1970	280,000	250,000	185	116
1971	314,100	263,000	194	119
1972	373,900	288,000	213	122
1973	516,500	325,500	240	124

(Based on the *United Nations Statistical Yearbook,* 1974, p. 55.)

367. In the earlier stage of modern times, the most important wares of commece were "colonial products," textiles, and some light metallic manufactures. The so-called "colonial products" included tea, coffee, sugar, spices, etc. Most of these commercial wares were articles of luxury rather than goods for common consumption. The important position of these wares in commerce may be exemplified by the imports and exports of England at the end of the 18th century. In millions of pounds the imports were, in the order of their values: sugar 7.1, tea 3.1, grain 2.7, linen 2.6, cotton 2.3, coffee 2.2, wood 1.5, butter 1.0, tobacco 1.0, hemp 1.0. These wares amounted to more than half the total import of 42.6. (Cf. Clive Day, *A History of Commerce,* New York, 1919, p. 219) The total export amounted to 29.0: manufactures of wool 7.7, manufactures of cotton 4.1, manufactures of iron and steel 2.0, haberdashery 1.5, linens 1.0. These five items include over one-half of the total (*Ibid.,* p. 209-210)

Through the 19th century, many goods more necessary to common consumption and more essential to economic life were added to the list of commercial wares. The most important among them were foodstuffs, such as the great bulk of wheat and rice, stock and meat; and mineral products, such as coal, iron and steel, and petroleum. The composition of world trade before World War II is shown in

system.[371] It has also been facilitated by the establishment of a General Agreement on Tariffs and Trade.[372]

the following table adapted from *The Network of World Trade,* by the League of Nations, Economic Intelligence Service, Geneva, 1942, p. 22 (in millions of new U.S. dollars):

	Values			Percentage		
Imports	**1928**	**1935**	**1937**	**1928**	**1935**	**1937**
Foodstuffs and live animals	15,450	5,120	6,430	25.7	24.3	22.8
Materials, raw or partly manufactured	21,735	8,100	11,550	36.2	38.5	41.0
Manufactured articles	22,900	7,820	10,190	38.1	37.2	36.2
Total	60,080	21,040	28,170	100	100	100
Exports						
Foodstuffs and live animals	14,080	4,480	5,610	25.5	23.5	22.1
Materials, raw or partly manufactured	19,280	7,150	9,920	34.9	37.6	39.0
Manufactured articles	21,860	7,400	9,880	39.6	38.9	38.9
Total	55,220	19,030	25,410	100	100	100

368. The network of world trade, as reflected by the orientation of the balances of merchandise trade in 1928, is illustrated in the following diagram. (League of Nations, Economic Intelligence Service, *The Network of World Trade,* Geneva, 1942, p. 78) Both import and export balances are shown in millions of dollars. The smaller of the two figures in each circle represents the export balance of the group from which the arrows emerge, and the larger figure the import balance of the group to which the arrows point. The difference between the

However, it would be very difficult, if not impossible, for world trade to increase, develop and expand so dramatically, if modern

amounts in question is largely due to the inclusion in import costs of transportation between the frontiers of the exporting and importing countries:

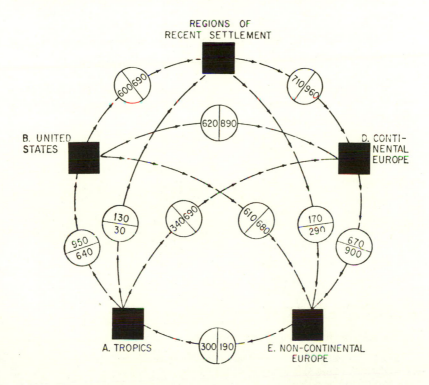

machines, had not increased the speed and carrying ability of transportation up to thousands of times,[373] and had not made global communication a matter of hours, minutes and even seconds.[374]

---

369. (Cf. League of Nations, Economic Intelligence Service, *The Network of World Trade,* Geneva, 1942, Annex III, p. 106-171 for details before World War II; and the *United Nations Statistical Yearbook,* 1974, Table 148, "World Trade by Region, Country or Area," for recent information.)

370. The growth of exports from developed and developing market economies in recent years is shown in the following table by unit value index (in U.S. dollars) 1963 = 100:

Regions	1962	1964	1965	1966	1967	1968	1969	1970	1971	1972	1973
World	99	102	103	105	105	104	107	113	119	128	154
Developed Market Economies	99	102	103	105	105	104	108	114	119	130	156
Developing Market Economies	98	103	102	104	103	103	106	109	116	121	146

(Based on the *United Nations Statistical Yearbook,* 1974, table 13, p. 52.)

371. The growth of exports from market economies and centrally planned economies in the last 40 years is shown in the following table (value in million U.S. dollars):

	World	Developed Market Economies	Developing Market Economies	Centrally Planned Economies
1938	25,400	17,900	5,800	1,700
1948	63,500	41,200	18,600	3,700
1958	114,500	74,100	27,600	12,800
1963	162,900	111,100	32,700	19,100
1966	216,600	151,800	40,700	24,100
1967	227,100	159,700	41,800	25,600
1968	252,300	179,300	45,300	27,700
1969	286,500	206,200	49,900	30,400
1970	328,500	237,600	56,200	34,700
1971	365,300	264,500	63,300	37,500
1972	429,300	312,100	71,300	45,900
1973	587,400	429,700	95,800	61,900

(Abstracted from the *United Nations Statistical Yearbook,* 1974, table 148, p. 406.)

The following table may serve as a good example of foreign trade originating in the centrally planned economies of the Communist countries. It appears in the *Area Handbook for Romania,* by Foreign Area Studies, American University, Washington, D.C., 1972, p. 250. COMECON stands for Council for Mutual Economic Assistance, consisting of the U.S.S.R., Czechoslovakia, Poland, Hungary,

Furthermore, in space as well as in time, modern medicines have enabled transportation to shrink[375] our world into a small country,[376]

Romania, Bulgaria, East Germany and Mongolia which was established in 1949, partly in response to the organization of Western Europe's Recovery Plan (Marshall Plan). The title of the table is Foreign trade of Romania, by groups of countries, 1960 and 1969 (in millions of lei):

Country Group	1960			1969		
	Exports	Imports	Total	Exports	Imports	Total
Western industrial states	918	913	1,831	2,980	4,432	7,412
COMECON	2,821	2,636	5,458	5.042	4,819	9,862
Other communist states	318	206	524	781	506	1,286
Developing countries	245	131	376	996	686	1,682
Total	4,302	3,887	8,189	9,799	10,443	20,242

Imports of grain in recent years by the People's Republic of China from Canada, Australia, Argentina, and the United States, serve as a good example of trade between different economic systems, different economic levels, and different regions, as well as of goods which are necessary for common consumption. According to *Foreign Agriculture,* published by the Foreign Agricultural Service of the U.S. Department of Agriculture, v. XV, no. 8, Feb. 21, 1977, p. 7, China's grain imports in 1976-77 were expected to total at least 3.5 million metric tons, up 52 per cent from the record low of 2.3 million tons in 1975-1976. The previous ebb in purchases was in 1971-72, when they dropped to three million tons. But after that China bought heavily on the world grain market for three consecutive years: 6.3 million tons in 1972-73, including 1.5 million of U.S. wheat and corn; 7.9 million tons in 1973-74, including five million from the U.S.; and six million in 1974-75, including 1.5 million tons of U.S. grain. Traditionally, China has bought wheat regularly from Canada, Australia and Argentina, with the United States being a "residual" supplier of last resort.

372. "The General Agreement on Tariffs and Trade, signed initially by representatives of 23 countries in Geneva in 1947, has contributed materially to the reduction of tariff and nontariff restrictions on world trade. The agreement incorporated a code of international-trade rules, made provisions for multilateral trade negotiations, established a procedure for adjusting trade grievances among members, and provided for the continuing review of actions by member countries. The recurring deliberations of the GATT have germinated ideas for resolving world trade problems. The membership of the GATT increased from 23 original signatories in 1947 to 77 at the start of the 1970s. A permanent staff of about 100, under a director general, serves the GATT. Its offices are in Geneva. Most of the work in negotiations, consultations, complaints, and reviews is carried on either by the Council of Representatives or by selected groups composed of representatives of member countries." (Glenn W. Sutton, "General Agreement on Tariffs and Trade," in the *Encyclopedia Americana,* 1973 ed. Vol. 26, p. 296)

373. The increase in modern transportation facilities may be illustrated by the

and have enabled communication to connect all peoples as nearby neighbors.[377] Thus, it is possible to manage the public affairs of the

---

growth of ship and railway building. From the beginning to the end of the 19th century, the carrying power of world sailing and steamships grew from 4 million tons to 63.2 million tons. From 1890 on, steamships began to grow faster than sailing vessels. By 1913, they had far exceeded sailing ships even in number, 23,897 as against 6,694, omitting those of 100 tons or less. Their larger size made their gross tonnage more than ten-fold that of sailing ships, and their effective power was proportionately even greater. (Cf. Clive Day, *A History of Commerce,* New York, 1919, p. 291; 581-82.)

The growth of ships continued in the period between the two World Wars and has greatly accelerated since 1950. Seaborne shipping tonnage increased from 550 million metric tons in 1950 to 3,190 million metric tons in 1973. (Cf. the *United Nations Statistical Yearbook,* 1974, p. 63.)

Railroad building is primarily of domestic importance, but the effect is also felt in world trade. Vast quantities of crude materials and manufactured goods are moved by railroad to the ports for foreign sale, or from the ports to inland markets. Furthermore, many countries are directly linked at their borders with railroads. The practical use of railroads began in 1829 when the Liverpool and Manchester railroad was opened. A hundred years later, the world had 772,130 miles of railroads. (Cf. Isaac Lippincott, *The Development of Modern World Trade,* New York, 1936, p. 458-459.) After 1930, the railway mileage of the world continued to grow, but the most striking feature has been the enormous increase of freight. Taking 100 for 1948 as a base, the index for the total freight of the world railroads for 1931 was 50; for 1938, 62; for 1946, 86; and for 1950, 102. (The *United Nations Statistical Yearbook,* 1951, table 134) Furthermore, taking 100 for 1970 as a base, the index for 1950 was 40; 1955, 52; 1960, 67; 1965, 80; and 1973, 115. (The *United Nations Statistical Yearbook,* 1974, Table 16) In addition, the completion of the Suez Canal in 1869, the Panama Canal in 1914, as well as other important canals, has increased shipping power greatly. (Cf. Isaac Lippincott, *op. cit.,* p. 447-450.)

374. A new communications satellite can carry data at a rate of 6.3 million bits per second—fast enough to transmit the entire text of *War and Peace* in under 10 seconds, according to Sydney Harris, *South Bend Tribune,* July 28, 1981, p. 18.

375. The shrinkage of the world during recent times is well exemplified by the number of days required to circle the globe at various dates (Cf. Hornell N. Hart, *The Technique of Social Progress,* New York, 1931, p. 80):

Year	Record Holder	Days Required
1522	Magellan's crew	1090
1889	Nellie Bly	72
1903	Henry Frederick	54
1913	John Henry Mears	36
1926	Evans and Wells	29
1928	Collyer and Mears	23
1929	Graf Zeppelin	21
1931	W. Post and H. Gatty	9
1970	Supersonic jet	1½

world for all peoples today as conveniently as it was to run a little kingdom a hundred years ago.

Indeed, our world has become as small as a little kingdom in the sense of modern transportation and communication, it has also become as small as a tactical theater[378] in the sense that modern weapons are able to reach targets thousands of miles away in minutes,[379] and to kill millions of people and destroy hundreds of

---

376. As is well-known, the circumference of the world is approximately 25,000 miles. (The equatorial circumference is 24,902 miles and the polar circumference, 24,860 miles.) It would take about 8,300 hours for a man to walk around the earth at 3 miles per hour, but an airplane flying at a speed of 500 miles per hour would need only 50 hours to cover the distance. In terms of this comparison the world would shrink about 166 times, and have a circumference of only 150 miles and a surface area of only 7,160 square miles, less than one 29th of France (211,209 sq.m.), one 19th of Japan (142,811 sq.m.), and one 35th of the state of Texas (262,134 sq.m.).

377. "The new devices for transmitting information have tended to shrink our planet enormously through rapid communication between its most distant points. It is possible today to transmit news from central Siberia to New York City with greater ease and speed than it was to send information across the Hudson River in 1750." (Harry E. Barnes, *An Economic History of the Western World,* New York, 1937, p. 466)

"Modern technology has made the world of today smaller in communication time than was or is the House of Commons or Independence Hall." (Quincy Wright, *A Study of War,* 2nd ed., Chicago, 1965, p. 3)

378. "It should be apparent from the foregoing that the world has shrunk to the area of a tactical theater. The world that was beyond man's comprehension in the time of Alexander the Great, that was considered the theater of grand strategy in World War II, will have shrunk to a tactical theater by 1965. Men will be able to launch weapons from any point within the United States and to strike any point within the USSR and vice versa." (James M. Gavin, *War and Peace in the Space Age,* New York, 1958, p. 218)

379. When Soviet Russia first launched a multi-stage ballistic missile, Nikita Khrushchev announced on August 26, 1957: "The missile flew at a very high, unprecedented altitude. Covering a huge distance in a brief time, the missile landed in the target area. The results obtained show that it is possible to direct missiles into any part of the world." (*New York Times,* August 27, 1957)

"Now we can foresee that by the end of the Decade of Decision, 1965, manned space flight will be here. We will then be ready to undertake manned exploration of the planetary system. The earth will have shrunk, in a military sense, to a rather small tactical theatre. It will be entirely possible to launch weapons from any point on the earth to impact at any other point on the earth, exactly as in past combat it has been possible in a tactical engagement to engage directly any opponent with the weapons at hand." (James M. Gavin, *War and Peace in the Space Age,* New York, 1958, p. 19)

380. Herman Kahn, the famous American writer on war, has investigated with scientific detachment the results of the hypothetical destruction of 53 of the

cities by a strike.[380] It is a tactical theater so small that there is no place in it which is safe and not covered by terror.[381] The shrinkage of the world into a mere tactical theater by the devastating power of modern weapons is certainly the greatest threat to all peoples today. It is a danger so intimate and imminent that if we do not unite and live together as one group in peace, in order to eliminate it, it will soon eliminate us.[382]

We have now been driven to the point where rapid advances in modern science and technology have led us into a Machine Age which, through mechanization, has changed our mode of life, accelerated the progress of transportation and communication, and produced weapons to threaten us with a total destruction. Clearly the Machine Age has made it not only possible, but also necessary and

---

greatest cities or metropolitan areas of the United States. This could quite possibly occur in a nuclear war with Russia. He estimates that the American people could suffer casualties amounting to 90,000,000. (Cf. His book *On Thermonuclear War,* 2nd edition, New York, 1969. Cf. also William L. Laurence, *The Hell Bomb,* New York, 1951, p. 3-28.)

A nuclear physician, Joseph Rotblat, Polish-born emeritus professor at London University, told a gathering of 160 doctors and medical researchers from 30 countries that a nuclear holocaust would so contaminate the atmosphere, it would be dark in the daytime. According to Dr. Rotblat, a nuclear war in Europe would kill at least 150 million people and most of the survivors would probably die from injuries or starvation. Dr. Rotblat was addressing the Second Congress of International Physicians for Prevention of Nuclear War at Newnham College, Cambridge University. The first congress was held at Airlie House near Washington, D.C., in March, 1981. Soviet academician M.A. Leonid Ilyin backed up Dr. Rotblat's statement by claiming that a nuclear war in Europe would leave 168 million dead and 146 million injured. (AP report, *South Bend Tribune,* April 4, 1982, p. 5)

381. "In World War II, for example, a tactical theater was usually thought of as a continent, or a major segment of a continent. By 1965 missiles and satellites will have shrunk the world to such small size that the earth itself will be a tactical theater. We will truly live a hair-triggered existence in a 'balance of terror.' Everyone will be faced with the threat of immediate death and destruction, if means of guaranteeing peace are not found." (James M. Gavin, *War and Peace in the Space Age,* New York, 1958, p. 19)

382. "We now have before us the clear choice between adjusting the pattern of our society on a world basis so that wars cannot come again, or of following the outworn tradition of national self defence, which if carried through to its logical conclusion must result in catastrophic conflict." (Arthur H. Compton in his introduction to *One World or None, A Report to the Public on the Full Meaning of the Atomic Bomb,* ed. by Dexter Masters and Katharine Way, forwarded by Niels Bohr, with articles by H.H. Arnold, Hans Bethe, E.U. Condon, Albert Einstein, Irving Langmuir, Walter Lipmann, Philip Morrison, J.R. Oppenheimer, Louis Ridenour, Frederick Seitz, Harlow Shapley, Leo Szilard, Harold Urey, Eugene P. Wigner, Gale Young, and the Federation of American Scientists, New York, 1946)

383. The law of group expansion is summarized in the following table for a comprehensive review:

Age	Culminating time	Mode of life	Land needed per person[1] (sq.mi.)	Population[2]	Series	Independent group Size expansion Average		Number reduction
						Population	Territory (sq.mi.)	
Old Stone	30,000 B.C.	Food-gathering	15	500,000	Early single family	5	75	100,000
Young Stone	10,000 B.C.	Hunting-fishing	10	1,000,000	Primitive community	50	500	20,000
New Stone	5,000 B.C.	Hoe-cultivating	1	15,000,000	Clan	1,500	1,500	10,000
Copper	1,000 B.C.	Animal-raising	$\frac{1}{5}$	155,000,000	Tribe	75,000	10,000	2,000
Iron	1,900 A.D.	Agricultural	$\frac{1}{50}$	1,550,000,000	Nation	8,000,000	150,000	200
Machine	Near future	Industrial	$\frac{1}{150}$	7,500,000,000	One World	All peoples	All lands	1

1. Cf. in general, William G. Sumner and Albert G. Keller, *The Science of Society*, New Haven, 1927, v. 4, p. 17-19, and Clark Wissler, *An Introduction to Social Anthropology*, New York, 1929, p. 28-41.

2. Based on estimates in *Energy Resources*, a report on the Committee on National Resources of the National Academy of Sciences–National Research Council, by M. King Hubbert, Chairman of the Energy Resources Study, Washington, 1962, p. 15-20; and United Nations, *The Future Growth of World Population*, New York, 1958, p. 17.

imperative for all the peoples of the world to live together as one group. In other words, modern science and technology have prepared the necessary physical conditions for group expansion to go forward to merge all nations into One World.

To merge all nations into One World is the last step in the long process of group expansion, as an historical, universal and social evolutionary law. It is not only desirable but logical, not only expected but inevitable.[383]

---

384. In the opinion of Alighieri Dante, for example, the whole human race should form one community under a single ruler, whose rule he compared to the government of God over nature. He held that the largest number of humanity had the greatest unity and that unity among men was a positive good. (Cf. George H. Sabine, *A History of Political Theory,* New York, 1938, p. 259.)

385. "The ideal of a universal federation of states to preserve peace and to promote progress has been perennial in the modern world. This ideal, however, did not enter the realm of practical statesmanship until the late nineteenth century, when communication and transportation inventions had created a high degree of economic interdependence throughout the world, a general awareness among the elite everywhere of important developments in any part of the world, and a possibility of a universal centralization of current information and of administration." (Quincy Wright, *A Study of War,* 2nd ed., Chicago, 1965, p. 1044)

386. The Atlantic Union Committee was organized in March, 1949, as the newest federalist group to seek public support. It was, in fact, an up-to-date continuation of the oldest organized effort, the Federal Union, formed in 1939 as a membership organization to further the basic proposal set forth in Clarence K. Streit's book, *Union Now.* To be included in the union were the United States, Britain, Canada, Australia, New Zealand, South Africa, Ireland, France, Belgium, Holland, Luxembourg, Denmark, Norway, Sweden and Finland, or a total of some 280 million people. The union was to confer a second, common citizenship upon the peoples of the constituent nations and was to govern only in matters relating to tariff, currency, communications, immigration and foreign affairs, the nation-states exercising sovereignty over the remaining matters. (Cf. Alfred M. Lilienthal, *Which Way to World Government, Headline Series* no. 83, New York, 1950, p. 7-11.)

387. European federalism, "Union Now," and similar halfway measures are, at best, merely other versions of the League of Nations, and at worst, naive and ineffective. They would never be able to perform the chief functions of an adequate world control. All such compromises are not only useless, but harmful, since they frustrate the desirable and postpone the inevitable. Edward M. Earle summarized Herbert G. Wells' views on regional federation, and other halfway measures in the *Nationalism and Internationalism,* New York, 1959, p. 115-116. (Cf. Wells' works: *The New World Order,* New York, 1939, Chap. VII; *The Common Sense of War and Peace; World Revolution or War Unending,* London, 1940, Chap IX; and *The Anatomy of Frustration,* New York, 1936, Chap. XII.)

388. "Regional adventures in federalism fare scarcely better, and may even prove antithetical to the larger purpose." (Frederick L. Schuman, *The Com-*

The idea of One World is not quite new. At least since Confucius in the East and the Stoic philosophers in the West, various writings about world unity, a world state or world government have appeared here and there.[384] But these were nothing more than dreams or utopias for the simple reason that nobody even knew what the world was actually like until recent centuries.[385]

---

monwealth of Man; An Inquiry into Power Politics and World Government,* New York, 1952, p. 492)

"Universality of membership is of crucial importance if the world government is to be a non-military federation. For only if membership is all-inclusive will world government be able to supervise the simultaneous demobilization and disarmament of its member nations without at the same time perpetuating the military system at the world federal level. Anything less than a universal federation, however huge, would be merely another sovereign federation in a world of other potentially hostile sovereign federations and nations." (*The Worried Woman's Guide to Peace Through World Law,* ed. by Lucile Green and Esther Yudell, Piedmont, Calif., 1965, p. 57-58)

389. "Nor must we fail to realize the urgency of the issue. The day of the Laodicean passed when scientific discovery made possible the steel ship and the aeroplane. There are no longer lotus-fields where men may linger careless of the life about them. The world is one and indivisible in a sense so compelling that the only question before us is the method by which we represent its unity." (Harold J. Laski, *A Grammar of Politics,* London, 1925, p. 238)

"Those who can find no argument against the logical and urgent necessity of transforming the institutions of national sovereignty into institutions capable of creating and maintaining law, ... and yet are reluctant or unwilling to accept responsibility, seek escape in the argument that the time is not yet ripe for such reforms.... The truth is that ever since the beginning of the 20th century these reforms have been overdue. If we used our brains for the purpose for which they are created—for thinking—and if we let our actions be guided by principles arrived at by rational thinking these changes in our society would have been carried out before the events of 1914." (Emery Reves, *The Anatomy of Peace,* New York, 1946, p. 248)

390. "No single age can show the true end of man and meaning of civilization. History must reap the harvest of all the ages." (Lynn Thorndike, from the title page of his *A Short History of Civilization,* New York, 1937)

391. It is interesting to note that Albert G. Keller entitled his book describing the basic reasons behind and general process of man's group expansion as *Man's Rough Road.* The book was published in 1932, in New York.

392. "The growing awareness that we are faced with an unimaginable and utterly incomprehensible fate may drive man towards the unifying of all peoples on this bruised planet. Compelled by the fear of extinction we may be facing the most dramatic evolutionary leap in the story of man: a propulsion in which, as Teilhard said of the geophysical year, 'For the first time in many billions of years, a unanimous deed, unanimously oriented, shall occur throughout the dimensions of the earth.' " (Justus G. Lawler, *Nuclear War,* Westminster, Md., 1965, p. 3-4)

393. The first moon landing was made by Neil A. Armstrong, Edwin E. Aldrin, Jr., and Michael Collins, aboard the U.S. spacecraft Apollo 11, in July,

The world is well-known to us now. It is one, not just because it is one physically and morally should be one, but because it has actually been driven into one by a tremendous force led by the advance of modern science and technology, along with historical development and social evolution. This force is irresistible. It has overcome obstacles and overrun limits, and has left no room for the last step of group expansion to stop short with halfway measures, such as the Atlantic Union,[386] European Federation,[387] or other regional plans.[388] Nor is there any time left for delay.[389]

1969. Since then, four more landings have been made: Apollo 12 in November, 1969; Apollo 14 in February, 1971; Apollo 15 in July-August, 1971; and Apollo 16 in April, 1972. It is interesting to recall the vivid picture of the first moon landing. On July 16, the Apollo 11, with the lunar module Eagle, began its 8-day journey. Four days later, it approached the moon. "Tranquility Base here. The Eagle has landed," said Armstrong. The time was 4:17:41 P.M. (EDT), July 20. "That's one small step for a man, one giant leap for mankind." With these words Armstrong stepped down from the ladder of Eagle. The astronauts showed television viewers the plaque on the Eagle's descent stage, which read:

HERE MEN FROM THE PLANET EARTH
FIRST SET FOOT UPON THE MOON
JULY 1969, A.D.
WE CAME IN PEACE FOR ALL MANKIND

The plaque was signed by the astronauts and President Richard M. Nixon, who later made a telephone call from the White House through facilities in Houston. Nixon observed, "Because of what you have done, the heavens have become a part of man's world." In reporting the details of the first moon landing (*South Bend Tribune,* July 27, 1969, p. 1 and 5), Howard Benedict, the Associated Press correspondent, remarked that the astronauts "may have accomplished more than opening the gateway to space. For, as much of the world reflected on the incredible events taking place 250,000 miles away, it also reflected on what is happening on earth. It seemed it was on the threshold of a new era in which the globe and the universe suddenly are shrinking."

394. For instance, the Russian spacecraft Venera IV made a soft landing on Venus on October 17, 1967; the Mars 2 made a hard landing with a capsule on Mars on November 27, 1971; the Mars 3 made a soft landing with a capsule on Mars on December 2, 1971; and Venera VIII landed on Venus on July 22, 1972. The U.S. spacecraft Mariner 9 began to orbit Mars on November 13, 1971, and sent back hundreds of photographs and thousands of feet of data about that planet; the Pioneer 10 soared past Jupiter on December 3, 1973, and beamed back valuable pictures and data about Jupiter; Mariner 10 flew by Venus on February 5, 1974, arriving at Mercury on March 29, 1974. It had a second encounter with Mercury on September 21, 1974, and a third on March 16, 1975. Viking 1 and 2, carrying life detection laboratories, landed on Mars on July 20, 1976, and September 3, 1976, respectively. (Cf. *United States and Soviet Union Progress in Space: Sum-*

Our harvest is quite ripe.[390] What are we waiting for?

We started the group expansion thousands of years ago, along a rough road[391] toward One World. Has the journey not been long enough, and are we still not anxious to take the last step?[392]

---

mary Data through 1976 and a Forward Look, by the Congressional Research Service of the U.S. Library of Congress, Washington, 1977 (CRS 77-99 SP), p. 62-65.)

395. "Modern communication is perhaps man's most astonishing achievement. It is amazing enough to know that man has gone to the moon, landed there, and come back; but what seems to me even more incredible is that we can actually see the spacemen as they walk on the surface of the moon and hear what they say at the time they are saying it, 250,000 miles away. Millions of people on earth sitting in front of their TV sets can all watch and listen at the same time. To a man born one hundred years ago this would have been completely beyond belief. Yet the moon is not the limit. The same thing could have been done at a distance a hundred times greater than that." (*Eureka, An Illustrated History of Inventions from the Wheel to the Computer; A London Sunday Times Encyclopedia,* ed. by Edward de Bono, New York, 1974, p. 15)

396. "Adlai Stevenson and Buckminster Fuller have been variously credited with coining the term Spaceship Earth. The authors of *Blueprint* clearly understand the profound implications of the term:

In an expanding universe, the galaxies and stars grow farther apart each moment.

The void of empty blackness through which they fly becomes ever larger, ever lonelier.

Our little Spaceship Earth whirls on through the fleeing stars of night. Except for sunlight, her fuel and supplies are all on board.

There's no going back for more.

And there's no getting off to go to some better place.

Spaceship Earth is off the pad.

And we're the crew.

The only crew she's got."

(R. Thomas Tanner, *Ecology, Environment, and Education,* Lincoln, Nebraska, 1974, p. 14-15)

We have been able to land on the moon[393] and contact Mars, Jupiter, Venus, and other planets millions of miles away[394] through the miraculous media of communication.[395] Is the Spaceship Earth[396] in the ever expanding universe still not too small for us to remain apart?[397]

---

397. Here is a song for us to remember:

> "It's a world of laughter, a world of fears;
> It's a world of hopes and a world of tears.
> There is so much that we share, it is time we are aware:
> It's a small world after all. Let us join together,
> For peace forever and happiness everywhere."

I add, "Let us join together for peace forever and happiness everywhere," to the popular song, "It's a Small World," and translate it into Chinese as follows:

> 我們的世界，有歡笑，也有泣哭，
> 我們的世界，有希望，也有憂慮。
> 我們須同舟共濟，及時覺悟：
> 這是一個小小的世界呵，讓大家緊緊的結合，
> 求永久的和平，與普遍的幸福。

II

One World in the Making[1]

ALONG WITH THE ADVANCE OF MODERN SCIENCE AND technology in getting all the necessary physical conditions ready for the last step of group expansion, the building of One World has actually been underway in various important works. These works are not quite new. They had slow beginnings and deep roots in the past, but have grown very fast and with new vigor in modern times. Their achievements are not quite unknown, but their contributions to the building of One World are not fully recognized. They are led by geographical exploration.

a.

Geographical Exploration

GEOGRAPHICAL EXPLORATION HAS HAD A LONG HIStory. As early as 600 B.C., the Phoenicians may have ventured around Africa.[2] Alexander the Great of Greece reached northern India about 330 B.C.[3] The initiative in opening the long Silk Route

---

1. *One World in the Making* is the title of a book written by Ralph B. Perry, Professor at Harvard University, published in New York, 1945. It may be read as a general introduction to this chapter.

2. One of the most intriguing episodes in the history of exploration was the alleged circumnavigation of Africa undertaken by a force of Phoenicians for King Necho of Egypt around 600 B.C. The name of the leader of the expedition has not been preserved. According to the Phoenicians' story, they made a three-year east-

153

came from both its European and Far East ends about the first century.[4] A thousand years later, Ericsson probably reached North
America.[5] But it was not until the 1400s that the great explorations
fanned out over the oceans. Henry the Navigator started the drive in

---

to-west voyage, keeping Africa on the starboard side. To provide food, they put
ashore, sowed seed, and waited until they could gather a harvest. Nothing was
mentioned about rounding the stormy Cape of Good Hope, but they said they
finally returned by way of Gibraltar and North Africa. The story rests on the
authority of the Phoenicians, who were said to be among the greatest explorers—and liars—in history. Historians, ancient and modern, are divided on the
story, conceding that the voyage was possible, but not proven. (Cf. Samuel E.
Morrison, *The European Discovery of America: the Northern Voyages, A.D.
500-1600,* New York, 1971, p. 5; and Percy Sykes, *A History of Exploration, from
Early Times to the Present Day,* London, 1935, p. 5-6.)

3. The primary objective of the campaigning of Alexander the Great from
334 to 323 B.C. was the defeat of Darius III and his Persians. After achieving that
end, and moved perhaps by geographical curiosity as well as a desire for further
conquests, he advanced into the rugged heart of Asia, thereby greatly increasing
the geographic knowledge of the Greeks. He penetrated through what is now
Afghanistan and Turkestan, and then moved down into northern India. He might
have gone further if his army, which had undergone constant hardship, had not
mutinied. Alexander, when he died sick and exhausted in 323—not yet 33 years
old—was planning to explore Arabia and possibly circumnavigate Africa. (Cf.
John W. McCrindle, *The Invasion of India by Alexander the Great,* Westminster,
2 ed., 1896, especially the preface to the second edition.)

4. The Silk Route led through several thousand miles of the most dreary and
forbidding regions on earth. Crossing parts of Mongolia and Turkestan, the
passage included the huge Gobi Desert and the icy Pamir Plateau, "The Roof of
the World." The whole area was sparsely populated by fierce nomadic horsemen
who terrorized the outside world as marauding Huns, Mongols, Tartars, or Turks.
The initiative in opening the Silk Route came from both its east and west ends
about the 1st century of the Christian era. One of China's greatest explorers,
Chang Ch'ien (張騫), spent years on the western frontier and helped to open the
eastern end of the Silk Route. (Cf. Joseph Needham, *Science and Civilization in
China,* Cambridge, England, 1954, V. 1, p. 170-176, 181-185; and Luce Boulnois,
The Silk Road, tr. by Dennis Chamberlain, New York, 1966, p. 23-60.)

5. The Ericsson episode goes as follows: one Eric the Red, charged with
manslaughter, left Norway for Iceland. Then, after becoming involved in a feud,
he decided to move farther west. In 984, he located a great island that he named
Greenland and brought some settlers to colonize its west coast. In 986, one Bjarne
Herjulfson, seeking to visit his father in Eric's new colony, missed Greenland and
sighted two flat wooded areas, "parts of North America—Labrador and Baffin
Island." In 1001, Eric's son Leif (Leif Ericsson) purchased Bjarne's vessel and set
out to get some of that wood, as "Greenland had no timber bigger than a willow
bush." After touching on some Labrador beaches, he decided to settle near the
northwest tip of Newfoundland at a site called by later French settlers L'Anse-aux-
Meadows. By 1013, three groups led by relatives of Leif's, had settled there briefly.

1415,[6] and within little more than a century, Columbus reached North and Central America;[7] Vespucci attained South America;[8] Da

---

In 1964, Helge Ingstad, a Norwegian archaeologist, reported finding and excavating the foundations of two great houses and several smaller ones at L'Anse-aux-Meadows, apparently occupied by Leif or some of the later settlers from Greenland. (Cf. William B. Goodwin, *The Truth About Leif Ericsson and the Greenland Voyages,* Boston, 1941, especially p. 13-17; and Samuel E. Morrison, *The European Discovery of America: the Northern Voyages,* A.D. 500-1600, New York, 1971, p. 32-62.)

6. In 1415, young Prince Henry, third in succession to the Portuguese throne, decided to develop exploration down the west coast of Africa. That decision made 1415 one of the most significant dates in the whole history of exploration. In that year, he participated with distinction in the capture of the Moroccan port of Ceuta, across the straits from Gibraltar. Ceuta was a northern terminal of a desert caravan route which brought gold and slaves from the Guinea coast, and may have given him the idea of bringing treasure north by ship instead of by camel. The idea of going all the way to the Indies by sea seems to have developed later. By 1418, Henry was well set up to make his great contributions to exploration and discovery. To finance his ambitious plans, the Portuguese king made Henry head of the wealthy military-crusading Order of Christ. Henry took this seriously, observing his monastic vows, and marking the sails of his caravels with the cross of the order. He established his headquarters on Cape Sagres in southwest Portugal, and gathered about him mariners, maps, and records. Then Henry ordered his captains to start down the west coast of Africa and keep going. He died in 1460, after his explorers had rounded the bulge and reached the Guinea coast as far as Sierra Leone. (Cf. Kingsley G. Jayne, *Vasco da Gama and His Successors,* London, 1910, p. 7-14; and John H. Parry, *The Age of Reconnaissance,* London, 1963, p. 131-145.)

7. Christopher Columbus' little squadron sailed from Palos, Spain, on August 3, 1492. Considering the crude instruments available, his navigation was excellent. As an expert sailor, he took advantage of the wind both ways. He made his momentous landfall on October 12 in the Bahamas—probably the present Watling Island—where he went ashore in full pomp. That was the high-water mark of his career—the rest of his 14 years were to be a series of anticlimaxes. He made three more voyages to America—1493-1496, 1498, and 1502-1504. On the second voyage, he sailed up through the Caribbean, bestowing names on many of the islands. He later visited Cuba, Jamaica, and his sorry colony on Hispaniola. On the third voyage, he reached Trinidad and saw the mainland of South America. Later, by order of the Spanish court, he was returned from Hispaniola in disgrace and in chains. On the fourth voyage, he visited the coast of Central America. He died in Spain on May 20, 1506, still apparently believing he had reached the Indies. (Cf. J. Franklin Jamesson, *Original Narratives of Early American History: The Northmen, Columbus and Cabot,* 985-1503, New York, 1906, p. 77-418; and Samuel E. Morrison, *The European Discovery of America: The Southern Voyages A.D. 1492-1616,* New York, 1974, p. 3-270.)

8. The most conspicuous and perhaps most controversial voyages were those of the man for whom America was named—Amerigo Vespucci or Americus Vespucius, a Florentine aristocrat who had been associated with the Medici financial interests. Although claimed to have made four voyages between 1497 and

Gama voyaged to India;[9] Balboa discovered the Pacific;[10] and Magellan's ship sailed around the globe.[11]

1503, scholars are inclined to credit him with only the second and third. In 1499, sailing for Spain, Vespucci may have discovered Brazil. In 1501, sailing for Portugal, he may have discovered a considerable stretch of the South American coast. Vespucci's reputation stems from the fact that a German geographer and cartographer, Martin Waldseemüller, gave the impression that Vespucci was responsible for discovering much of the region that became known as America. (Cf. Charles H.L. Johnston, *Famous Discoverers and Explorers of America,* Boston, 1941, p. 45-62; and Samuel E. Morrison, *The European Discovery of America: the Southern Voyages, A.D. 1492-1616,* New York, 1974, p. 272-312.)

9. In 1488, Bartholmeu Dias had discovered the Cape of Good Hope (the Stormy Cape, as he first called it). Nine years later, the Portuguese king appointed Vasco da Gama to follow Dias' course. Da Gama was a man of the lesser nobility with scant seagoing experience, but with a reputation for having a forceful character. His four vessels sailed from Lisbon on July 8, 1497. Somehow he hit upon a novel and effective course down through the South Atlantic. Instead of hugging the African coast as others had done, he took advantage of the prevailing winds to run almost over to Brazil before turning southeast for the Cape of Good Hope. That was to remain the standard South Atlantic route all through the age of sail. Da Gama rounded the Cape of Good Hope late in November, suppressed a mutiny, and continued up the coast of East Africa, finding most of the ports in inhospitable Muslim hands. At Malindi, in the present Kenya, the sultan generously lent him the services of an able Muslim pilot. Riding with the monsoon winds, the expedition arrived on May 22, 1498, at Calicut, India, busiest of the malabar trading centers. He returned to Lisbon in mid-1499 with a modest cargo of spices. (Cf. Kingsley G. Jayne, *Vasco da Gama and His Successors,* London, 1910, p. 33-66; and Henry H. Hart, "Vasco da Gama, Around Africa to India," in *Exploration and Discovery,* ed. by Robert G. Albion, New York, 1965, p. 39-49.)

10. Seven years after Columbus died it was demonstrated that he had not found the Indies. Vasco Núñnez de Balboa in 1513 crossed the Isthmus of Panama, looked out upon a great ocean, waded into it, and took possession of it in the name of the king of Spain. He called it the 'Great South Sea,' but seven years later, Ferdinand Magellan was to give it its lasting name, the Pacific. (Cf. Samuel E. Morrison, *The European Discovery of America: the Southern Voyages, A.D. 1492-1616,* New York, 1974, p. 380-437; and Vilhjalmur Stefansson, *Great Adventures and Explorations, from the Earliest Times to the Present as Told by the Explorers Themselves,* New York, 1947, p. 223-233.)

11. Ferdinand Magellan was a Portuguese who had fought with Portuguese forces in India and the East Indies until he fell out of favor with his king. Thereupon, he persuaded Charles V. of Spain to give him command of an expedition to look into Balboa's "Great South Sea." He discovered and traversed the strait at the tip of South America that still bears his name and set out upon the ocean that he named "Pacific." It proved very much larger than he had imagined. The crew suffered agonies as by some mischance they missed scores of small islands and sighted only two where they could replenish their supplies. They finally reached Guam in the Marianas and then continued on to the Philippines, where Magellan was killed in a scuffle with the islanders. One of his captains, Juan Sebas-

In succeeding years, intrepid men explored some of the New World's mightiest rivers: the St. Lawrence,[12] the Mississippi,[13] and the Amazon.[14] Later, Tasman explored Australia and New Zealand.[15]

Then came the age of Scientific Discovery opened by Captain Cook.[16] In quest of knowledge, he made three great voyages at the time of the American Revolution.[17]

---

tian del Cano, managed to bring the *Victoria* back through hostile waters to Sanlúcar, Spain, on September 6, 1522, thus completing the first circumnavigation of the world. (Cf. Samuel E. Morrison, *The European Discovery of America: the Southern Voyages, A.D. 1492-1616,* New York, 1974, p. 313-472; and C.E. Newell, "Magellan—the First Circumnavigation," in *Exploration and Discovery,* ed. Robert G. Albion, New York, 1965, p. 64-68.)

12. Jacques Cartier of St.-Mâle explored the St. Lawrence River and made it the center of France's colonial efforts. In his first voyage, in 1534, he reached the lower part of the river. During his second voyage, in 1535, he went on up the river to the great rock of Quebec that was later to be the capital of French Canada. Then, by small sailing vessel, he went up to Hochelaga, as Montreal was then called. (Cf. Samuel E. Morrison, *The European Discovery of America: the Northern Voyages, A.D. 500-1600,* New York, 1971, p. 339-463.)

13. The Mississippi exploration was rounded out by the Sieur de La Salle, the most spectacular of the French explorers, who had already explored the Great Lakes. He followed the Mississippi to its mouth where, in 1682, he dramatically took possession of the whole area that the river drained as "Louisiana." He had great hopes for its development. Returning from France to establish a colony, La Salle missed the mouth of the Mississippi and landed on the Texas coast, where he was murdered by some of his associates in 1687. (Cf. Charles H.L. Johnston, *Famous Discoveries and Explorers of America,* Boston, 1941, p. 385-410.)

14. There were heroic and colorful attempts to cross from west to east in the region of the Amazon River. One of the few who succeeded was Francisco de Orellana, the first man to sail and navigate the whole length of the Amazon River in the period around 1540. (Cf. Gerald R. Crone, *The Explorers, Great Adventurers Tell Their Own Stories of Discovery,* New York, 1962, p. 228-231.)

15. Abel Tasman's voyaging in 1642 gave him first place among Dutch navigators. There had been some minor landfalls on what is now called Australia, but the Dutch East India Company's settlement wanted more definite information. They sent Tasman to find out if Australia was really an island. He discovered the big island south of Australia, which was later named for him—Tasmania. He also discovered New Zealand and various lesser islands. (Cf. Hendrik W. van Loon, *The Golden Book of the Dutch Navigators,* New York, 1916, p. 303-321.)

16. With the Age of Enlightenment producing an appreciation of things scientific and exotic, explorations for scientific discovery were carried out by naval vessels. In addition, naturalists and other scientists were also interested and involved during this period. This was a pattern that was to go beyond the Cook period. In the 1830s, H.M.S. *Beagle,* under Comdr. Robert FitzRoy, carried Charles Darwin, who was then developing his theory of evolution. The U.S. Exploring Expedition under Lt. Charles Wilkes in 1828-1842 produced charts that the U.S. Navy us-

In the 19th century, exploration by land received more attention. Lewis and Clark opened the American West,[18] Livingstone penetrated Africa,[19] Stuart crossed Australia,[20] and Przhevalsky investigated

---

ed a century later. Investigations made during the cruises of H.M.S. *Challenger,* 1872-1876, laid the foundations of oceanography. (Cf. Robert FitzRoy, *Narrative of the Surveying Voyages of His Majesty's Ships,* Adventure *and* Beagle, *Between the Years 1826 and 1836,* London, 1839, 3 vols.; Charles Wilkes, *Narrative of the United States Exploring Expedition During the Years 1838, 1839, 1840, 1841, 1842,* Philadelphia, 1845, 5 vols; and Margaret Deacon, *Scientists and the Sea,* 1650-1900, London, p. 333-358.)

17. Capt. James Cook was a specialist in hydrography. He had charted the St. Lawrence River for Gen. James Wolfe's approach to Quebec in 1759 and then made a detailed charting of Newfoundland. He had a combination of excellent qualities—imagination, meticulous accuracy in professional matters, and a natural gift of leadership. He made three voyages that contributed greatly to the map of the Pacific Ocean. In the first (1768-1771), he observed the astronomical transit of Venus at Tahiti, rediscovered New Zealand, which had been sighted by Tasman, and then moved on to the previously neglected southern "fertile crescent" of Australia, where Joseph Banks was particularly enthusiastic about Botany Bay. Cook's second expedition (1772-1775) produced important negative results. He crossed and recrossed the Pacific, down to the Antarctic Circle, and could finally report definitely that there was no Terra Australis Incognita. On his third voyage, starting in 1776, Cook discovered the Hawaiian Islands and then moved over to the American coast, sailing north from the present Oregon to the Aleutian Islands and Bering Strait. Following instructions to look for a Pacific outlet to the Northwest Passage, Cook reported that he found no trace of one. Early in 1779, he returned to Hawaii and, like Magellan, was killed in a chance scuffle with islanders. His ships returned home by way of China and the Cape of Good Hope. (Cf. J. Holland Rose, "Captain Cook and the South Seas," in *Exploration and Discovery,* ed. by Robert G. Albion, New York, 1965, p. 79-102; and Andrew Kippis, *Captain Cook's Voyages,* New York, 1925.

18. When the United States purchased the extensive "Louisiana" territory from France in 1803, President Jefferson sent two Army captains, Meriwether Lewis and William Clark, to explore it. In two years, between 1804 and 1806, going by way of the Missouri River, the Rocky Mountains, and the Columbia River, they reached the Pacific and returned safely. There were later explorations in the West, but none as important. (Cf. Gerald R. Crone, *The Explorers, Great Adventurers Tell Their Own Stories of Discovery,* New York, 1962, p. 194-199.)

19. Even as late as the mid-19th century, Africa was still the "Dark Continent." The extreme north and south were known, but the vast central portion was still pretty much of a blank on the maps. David Livingstone, a Scottish medical missionary, began his long African exploring activity—from 1840 to 1872—centered on the Zambezi River and the thriving slave trade. His writings aroused popular interest in Africa. From that time on there was a steady filling in of the map of Africa. (Cf. Paul Herrmann, *The World Unveiled,* London, 1956, p. 443-486; Percy Sykes, *A History of Exploration, from Early Times to the Present Day,* London, 1935, p. 220-227; and Henry M. Stanley's Report on Livingstone in the *New York Herald,* August 20, 1872.)

Central Asia.[21] The long-sought Northeast and Northwest Passages through the Arctic Seas were found at last.[22]

Finally, Peary reached the North Pole,[23] Amundsen the South Pole,[24] and during the International Geophysical Year of 1957-1958,

---

20. In 1861-1862, John M. Stuart, on his third try, made a south-to-north crossing of the entire continent, from Adelaide up to the site of Darwin, traversing the huge semiarid interior region. By 1875, further explorations had brought most of the interior onto the map. (Cf. Gerald R. Crone, *The Explorers, Great Adventurers Tell Their Own Stories of Discovery,* New York, 1962, p. 279-283.)

21. Referring to Central Asia, the historian Baker remarks that "during the 19th century, its characteristic feature is to be found in the large number of expeditions rather than in the outstanding importance of any one. Yet an important exception must be made. One name, that of the Russian Nikolai M. Przhevalsky, stands out conspicuously. From the beginning of his work in 1871 to his death in 1888, great changes were made in the map of Central Asia." (John N.L. Baker, *A History of Geographical Discovery and Exploration,* new ed. rev., New York, 1967, p. 280. Cf. p. 280-289; also Percy Sykes, *A History of Exploration, from the Earliest Times to the Present Day,* London, 1935, p. 247-248.)

22. The searches for a Northeast Passage over Europe and Asia, and a Northwest Passage over or through America were the original motives for Arctic exploration in the 16th century. In the northeast quest, efforts by the Englishman Richard Chancellor and Stephen Borough and the Dutchmen Barents and Hudson between 1553 and 1609 reached only as far as Spitsbergen and Novaya Zemlya. Ice prevented further progress. Arctic exploration revived after 1815, when the British Admiralty sent out almost annual expeditions to the Atlantic Northwest Passage approaches. The most celebrated of these, headed by Sir John Franklin in 1845, failed when the ships were lost in the ice, and the men disappeared. The Northeast Passage finally materialized in 1878-1879, when a Swede, Baron Nils A.E. Nordenskjöld, sailed east along the northern coast of Asia and out through the Bering Strait. Eventually, Russian icebreakers were able to use this passage during the summer months. The Northwest Passage was first traversed in 1903-1905 by the Norwegian Roald Amundsen in his sloop Gjøa. In 1970, the huge tanker *Manhattan* used the passage both ways to find whether it was practicable to bring out Arctic oil that way. (Cf. Ernest S. Dodge, *Northwest by Sea,* New York, 1961, p. 294-318; Vilhjalmur Stefansson, *Great Adventures and Explorations, from the Earliest Times to the Present as Told by the Explorers Themselves,* New York, 1947, p. 385-544; and Terence Armstrong, *The Northern Sea Route: Russian Exploration of the North East Passage,* Cambridge, England, 1952.)

23. In 1909, it was claimed that Robert E. Peary, an American naval officer, had reached the North Pole after a series of expeditions made over more than 11 years. It was said that he made his laborious approach over the ice with dogsleds. The American nuclear submarine *Skate* surfaced at the North Pole on March 17, 1959. (Cf. Vilhjalmur Stefansson, *Great Adventures and Explorations, from the Earliest Times to the Present as Told by the Explorers Themselves,* New York, 1947, p. 565-622; and Robert E. Peary, *Northward Over the "Great Ice,"* New York, 1898, 2 vols.)

24. On December 4, 1911, Roald Amundsen was the first to reach the South

many countries cooperated in advancing the frontiers of knowledge in the Antarctic.[25]

The era of great geographical explorations is now about closed. The accomplishments of these explorations have been miraculous. They have unveiled the world, completed its map, and transformed it from numerous scattered, isolated and unknown parts into an integral body. It is this accomplishment that has cleared the ground for the building of One World.

b.
Migration
and Tourism

LIKE GEOGRAPHICAL EXPLORATION, MIGRATION[26] HAS existed since time immemorial.[27] In modern times, however, following the great explorations and the accelerating development of transportation and communication, it has become much more active than

---

Pole, traveling by dogsled. In November, 1929, Richard E. Byrd made the first flight over the South Pole. He had made the first flight over the North Pole in 1926. (Cf. Roald Amundsen, *The South Pole,* translated by A.B. Chater, London, 1913, v. 2, p. 1-134; and Richard E. Byrd, *Little America, Aerial Exploration in the Antarctic, the Flight to the South Pole,* New York, 1930, p. 117-138, 326-345.)

25. After World War II, many countries set up bases and made scientific explorations in Antarctica, notably during the International Geophysical Year (1957-1958). During this time, the British scientist Sir Vivian Fuchs crossed the continent by land, using sno-cats, weasels, and dog teams. (Cf. Hugh Odishaw and Stanley Ruttenberg, *Geophysics and the I G Y,* Washington, 1958, p. 203-206; and Walker Chapman, *Antarctic Conquest, The Great Explorers in Their Own Words,* New York, 1965, p. 330-355.)

26. International agencies have endeavoured to provide a definition in order to make possible the preparation of comparable statistics for emigration and immigration. Thus the International Labour Office suggested that "Statistics of permanent migration should cover every person passing from one country to another for more than a year, whatever the reason for their removal ... The statistics of temporary migration should cover every person who passes from one country to another for more than a month and not more than a year, for the purpose of carrying on an occupation." (International Labor Office, *Studies and Reports, Series N, no. 18, Statistics of Migration,* Geneva, 1932, p. 28.)

27. (Cf. Donald R. Taft and Richard Robbins, *International Migrations,*

ever before. Meanwhile, it has assumed new forms—tending to be less predominantly movements of groups, like the Huns in the past,[28] and more movements of individuals seeking land to settle on, work, religious freedom, or other special conditions in other lands. Migrations have, consequently, made great contributions to the building of One World, including: complete possession of the globe, redistribution of the population, racial intermarriage, and cultural assimilation.[29]

The most significant migration in modern times has been of an intercontinental type. Mass emigration from Europe to America began in the 16th century. Until the end of the 19th century, emigrants from the British Isles were the largest group, while the United States was the largest country of immigration.[30] After 1880, immigration to the American countries increased to immense proportions

---

New York, 1955, p. 23-31; Thomas S. Foster, *Travels and Settlements of Early Man,* New York, 1929; and Alfred C. Haddon, *The Wanderings of Peoples,* Cambridge, England, 1912.)

28. For at least 3,000 years, the widening deserts of central Asia have witnessed genuine group migrations. Archaeological evidence indicates prehistoric movements to China, Europe, and the Fertile Crescent. Central Asian peoples are usually nomads. When the desert expanded, these tent dwellers were organized to move as units with their herds and beasts of burden. For example, the fierce Hsiung-nu repeatedly invaded China as early as the 3rd century B.C.; their armed incursions stimulated the Chinese to build the Great Wall. Repulsed from China, they turned westward. In the 5th century A.D., the Huna (White Huns or Ephthalites) invaded India via the passes of the Hindu Kush. In the same century, other groups of Hun stock invaded the Germanic countries and drove the Ostrogoths, Visigoths, and Vandals into the crumbling Roman Empire. The successes of the Huns and the Vandals were the result of their social organization; they were organized for war and entered new territory as conquerers. (Cf. Wolfram Eberhard, *Chinas Geschichte,* tr. by E.W. Dickes as *A History of China,* Berkeley, Calif., 1950, p. 68 ff.; and Hugh G. Rawlinson, *India, A Short Cultural History,* London, 1937, p. 110-111, 199-200, 243.)

29. (Cf. *The Positive Contribution by Immigrants,* a Symposium prepared for Unesco by the International Sociological Association and the International Economic Association, General Rapporteur: Oscar Handlin, Unesco, 1955; W.D. Borrie, *The Cultural Integration of Immigrants, A Survey Based Upon the Papers and Proceedings of the Unesco Conference Held in Havana, April 1956,* Paris, UNESCO, 1959, p. 99-115; Donald R. Taft and Richard Robbins, *International Migrations,* New York, 1955, p. 3-10; 126-147; F.S.C. Northrop, *The Meeting of East and West,* New York, 1946; and Conrad Bekker, "Historical Patterns of Culture Contact in Southeast Asia," *The Far Eastern Quarterly,* Nov. 1951, p. 3-16.)

30. It was estimated that emigrants from the British Isles were about 500,000 in the seventeenth century and 1,500,000 in the eighteenth century. Between 1776 and 1840, the United States received approximately 1,000,000 immigrants, and

until World War I. During this time, the annual average was up to over one million.[31] Negro slaves were also an important element in modern intercontinental migration. It is estimated that from the 16th century to the middle of the 19th, about twenty million Negroes were brought from Africa, most of them imported to the tropical and sub-tropical regions.[32]

---

between 1841 and 1880, about 9,500,000, of which 90 per cent came from Europe. (Cf. Donald R. Taft and Richard Robbins, *International Migrations,* New York, 1955, p. 370-374.)

31. The annual average between 1866 and 1870 was 405,324; between 1871 and 1875, 410,442; and between 1876 and 1880, 259,913. During the three subsequent five-year periods it rose to 652,425, 709,036, and 650,057, respectively. It was 1,039,774 between 1901 and 1905; 1,481,844 between 1896 and 1910; 1,403,442 between 1911 and 1915, and 843,983 between 1921 and 1924. (Cf. Walter F. Willcox, *International Migrations,* Publications of the National Bureau of Economic Research, No. 14, New York, 1929, Vol. I, p. 168.)

32. It has been estimated that between 1680 and 1786 about 2,130,000 Negroes were brought to North America and the British West Indies. The total number of Negroes imported annually toward the end of the eighteenth century by England, France, Holland, Denmark and Portugal was about 100,000. The peak of the negro slave trade was reached at the end of the eighteenth century and the beginning of the nineteenth century. It is probable that during the course of the three and a half centuries preceding 1888, about 20,000,000 Negroes were brought from Africa, most of whom were imported for the tobacco, sugar and coffee plantations of the Caribbean and Brazil. Many, perhaps a million, were moved on to the cotton fields of the southern United States. (Cf. *Encyclopedia of the Social Sciences,* New York, 1935, Vol. X, p. 433.)

33. The intercontinental migration of Indian workers reached its peak in 1858, when it totaled approximately 46,000. The recruiting of Chinese coolies for working outside Asia began in the 1850s; before 1883, over 300,000 Chinese were imported by the United States to build railroads. Between 1904 and 1910, 170,000 Chinese were taken to the Transvaal to work in the mines. During the first World War, more than 200,000 Chinese workers were imported by France and England. (Cf. G. Findlay Shirras, "Indian Migration," in Walter F. Willcox's *International Migrations,* New York, Vol. II, 1931, p. 595-598; Ta Chen, *Chinese Migrations,* United States Bureau of Labor Statistics, *Bulletin* No. 340, 1923, p. 128-158; and Alexander McLeod, *Pigtails and Gold Dust,* Caldwell, Idaho, 1948.)

34. "In the 16th century the French established trading posts in Algeria, but large-scale settlement did not begin there until French rule was established in 1830. today about 15 percent of the population of this newly independent nation is of European ancestry. Few Europeans settled in Central Africa before 1880, when diamond deposits were discovered in Rhodesia. Since then the British (nearly 300,000) have settled in Rhodesia and the Belgians in the Congo in large numbers. In East Africa, which received settlers from 1906 on, nearly 100,000 Europeans have made permanent residence, principally in Kenya, Uganda and Tanganyika. In South Africa the first Europeans to settle were the Dutch in 1652. By the end of the 18th century emigrants from the British Isles began arriving in great numbers,

After the abolition of Negro slavery in the British colonies, the great demand for labor was met, to a large extent, by the importation of contracted Indian and Chinese laborers.[33] Meanwhile, more Europeans started to settle in Africa,[34] Australia and New Zealand.[35]

The most active period of modern migration was the 19th century

---

and in the 19th century the establishment of British rule in Cape Colony was followed by the revolt of the Dutch farmers (Boers) and their Great Trek to the Transvaal. In this century there have been mass movements of South Africans into mining and industrial areas.'' (Reader's Digest, *Great World Atlas,* New York, 1963, p. 150)

35. ''The first Europeans settled in Australia in 1788, but immigration was slow until the Gold Rush period between 1850 and 1860. After 1860 it slowed down again until the turn of the century. Between 1901 and 1920 about 400,000 emigrated to Australia, principally from the United Kingdom, but since 1945 more than a million people from many European countries have settled in Australia. Emigration to New Zealand has followed much the same pattern but on a smaller scale.'' (Reader's Digest, *Great World Atlas,* New York, 1963, p. 150. Cf. Walter F. Willcox, *International Migrations,* New York, Vol. II, 1931, p. 169-200.)

36. ''Information regarding the volume of international migration prior to 1820 is very limited. That year the United States and Brazil both began to keep count of immigrant arrivals; Canada had begun to do so a few years earlier. From 1820 to 1930, the latest date for which comparable information is available, immigration statistics for the most important immigrant-receiving countries show a total of nearly sixty-two million immigrant arrivals.'' (*International Migration and One World,* by National Committee on Immigration Policy, New York, 194?, p. 7)

The countries which received large numbers of intercontinental immigrants were: (in 1,000)

Country	Period	Immigrants
United States	1821-1924	33,188
Argentina	1857-1924	5,486
Canada	1821-1924	4,520
Brazil	1821-1924	3,855
British West Indies	1836-1924	1,477
Cuba	1901-1924	766

The countries which between 1846 and 1924 supplied over 1,000,000 intercontinental migrants were: (in 1,000)

Country	Emigrants	Country	Emigrants
United Kingdom	16,974	Spain	4,314
Italy	9,474	Russia	2,253
Austria-Hungary	4,878	Portugal	1,633
Germany	4,533	Sweden	1,145

(Cf. *Encyclopedia of the Social Sciences,* New York, 1935, Vol. X, p. 436; and Maurice R. Davie, *World Immigration,* New York, 1936, p. 11-12.)

and the early decades of the 20th. During this period, intercontinental migration totaled approximately sixty million.[36]

Modern migration within Europe first followed deliberate plans;[37] then it became a common means of adjustment for the labor

---

37. In the seventeenth century, for instance, the Prussian rulers undertook large scale immigration projects to remedy the loss of population caused by the Thirty Years' War. The example of Frederick the Great, who colonized approximately 250,000 settlers, was followed by the Hapsburgs, who tried to colonize the devastated regions in Hungary and Galicia by a systematic importation of settlers from Germany, Alsace, Switzerland, and Italy. Maria Theresa settled 50,000 between 1765 and 1770, and Joseph II colonized 38,000 from 1783 to 1788. Catherine of Russia succeeded in attracting 75,000 German peasants to the Volga regions between 1763 and 1769. A large-scale emigration from Germany also took place between 1783 and 1808 to the southern regions of European Russia. In 1863, there were 260,000 Germans in Russian Poland, and that number was continually increased by immigration throughout the century. (Cf. *Encyclopedia of the Social Sciences,* New York, 1935, Vol. X, p. 436-437; also Walter F. Willcox, *International Migrations,* New York, 1929, Vol. I, p. 89-140.)

38. By 1867, a large number of skilled workers had emigrated from Germany to Hungary, and there were later emigrations to those Balkan states which encouraged industrial development. Emigration of skilled labor from the advanced countries to the backward was followed in the last third of the nineteenth century by the emigration of unskilled labor in the opposite direction. In the 1880s, there began a migration of seasonal workers from Russia and Galicia to meet the increasing labor needs of German agriculture. From 1910 to 1913, such migration totaled yearly from 600,000 to 850,000. Beginning in the 1870s, Italy supplied Germany and France with agricultural and industrial workers until the first World War, totaling 250,000 annually. the most important immigration country in Europe after the first World War was France. Between 1920 and 1930 it received 1,147,000 foreign industrial workers and 760,000 foreign agricultural workers. The number of foreigners in France rose from 1,133,000 in 1911 to 3,300,000 in 1931. After World War II, emigrants from Italy to other European countries became active again, averaging about 300,000 a year in the 1960s. (Cf. *Encyclopedia of the Social Sciences,* New York, 1935, Vol. X, p. 436-437; Walter F. Willcox, *International Migrations,* New York, 1929, Vol. I, p. 89-140; and J.A. Jackson, *Migration,* Cambridge, England, 1969, p. 33.)

39. In Asia, the chief countries of emigration have been China, India, and Japan; and the most important immigration regions have been Southeast Asia and Manchuria. In about 1947, the number of Chinese residing in Indo-China, Burma, the East Indies, Java, Siam, Malaya, and other places in Southeast Asia, amounted to about eight million. In addition to the Chinese, Indians have been the principal immigrants to Southeast Asia, especially Malaya, where the Indian population in 1924 was 470,000. India also emigrated a great number of people to Ceylon where the number of Indian immigrants rose from 208,000 in 1926 to 238,000 in 1929. While an ever-increasing number of agricultural workers, reaching over 1,000,000 in the 1920s, had been moving into Manchuria from overpopulated North China, especially from Hopeh and Shantung, about 200,000 Japanese and 800,000 Koreans also immigrated to that area between 1908 and

situation.[38] From the middle of the 19th to the early 20th century, migration within Asia,[39] Africa,[40] and America[41] was also extensive.

After World War I, world migration in general tended to decline. This slowdown was disrupted, however, by World War II when millions of refugees, displaced people, war prisoners, and armed forces moved across oceans and borders.[42]

1923. Of the more than 1,000,000 Korean laborers who entered Japan between 1917 and 1929, approximately 800,000 returned to Korea. (Cf. Ta Chen, *Chinese Migrations,* United States Bureau of Statistics, *Bulletin,* No. 340, 1923, p. 51-110; Idei, Seishi, "Japan's Migration Problem," *International Labor Review,* Vol. XXII, 1930, p. 773-789; and Victor Purcell, *The Chinese in Southeast Asia,* New York, 1951, p. 2-9.)

40. In Africa, continental migration was also extensive. For a number of years, the Witwatersrand Association annually obtained approximately 80,000 temporary laborers from Mozambique and the British colonies for the mines of the Transvaal. The Native Labor Corporation in South Africa imported laborers from Basutoland, whose annual emigration averaged 70,000 between 1920 and 1924, and from other places. (Cf. *Encyclopedia of the Social Sciences,* New York, 1935, Vol. X, p. 439.)

41. After the first World War, continental movements of population in the Americas became unusually active. For example, the recorded immigration from Canada and Mexico to the United States, which averaged 59,305 annually from 1908 to 1910, rose to 290,000 by 1924. During the same time period, illegal immigration also rose to a large scale. (Cf. Walter F. Willcox, *International Migrations,* New York, 1929, Vol. I, p. 390-393.)

42. For instance, "the heaviest political migration movements of the post-war period have taken place in Germany, which has had to find room within its shrunken frontiers for more than 12.5 million refugees from the lost eastern provinces or from abroad. This immense westward shift of the German people, which has revolutionised the ethnic map of Central Europe, has been not only one of the most important demographic results of the Second World War but a landmark in German history as well. The resulting problems of adjustment have literally dominated the country's economic and social life during the 12 years following the end of the war, and only now is the final solution within sight." (International Labor Office, *International Migration, 1945-1957, Studies and Reports New Series,* no. 54, Geneva, 1959, p. 7, cf. p. 7-129; Cf. also Donald R. Taft and Richard Robbins, *International Migrations,* New York, 1955, p. 236-300; and Anthony T. Bouscaren, *International Migrations Since 1945,* New York, 1963, p. 3-31.)

43. According to the *United Nations Guidelines for Tourism Statistics,* New York, 1971, p. 8, a "visitor" who is the subject of international tourism statistics, is "any person visiting a country other than that in which he has his usual place of residence, for any reason other than following an occupation remunerated from within the country visited." This definition includes both tourists and excursionists. "Tourists" are temporary visitors staying at least 24 hours in the country visited and the purpose of whose journey can be classified as leisure or business. "Excursionists" are temporary visitors staying less than 24 hours in the country visited.

In addition to migration, international tourism[43] contributes to
the building of One World, not only in promoting cultural assimilation,[44] but in economic development.[45] After World War I, the number of international travellers increased steadily.[46] Recently, between

---

44. For instance, "Americans who traveled abroad also began to appreciate
the varied delights of foreign cuisine—French, Italian, German, Spanish, and on
to Oriental. The sale of specialty foods zoomed in the United States. European and
Japanese restaurants became almost as common a sight as European and Japanese
cars. Cross-pollination of taste around the world was furthered by heavily attended world's fairs in Brussels, New York, Montreal, and Osaka. Americans acquired
a taste for foreign artifacts, foreign crafts, and foreign dress. Indian and Oriental
influences appeared in both interior design and apparel. The internationalization
of American tastes created enthusiasm for traveling performers from other countries, and in turn American theater, orchestras, and performers received wide ac-
claim in many countries. Many returned to their own countries enlightened by
their stay in other lands and equipped with a better perspective on their homeland
and its relation to the rest of the world. Domestic difficulties could be assayed in
relation to similar problems in other nations. Moreover, there was the opportunity
to view at first hand the chief examples of other forms of government, both of the
right and of the left." (Horace Sutton, "Tourism," in *Americana*, 1973 ed., Vol.
26, p. 878. Cf. Robert W. McIntosh, *Tourism Principles, Practices and
Philosophies*, Columbus, Ohio, 1972, p. 26-27; and Charles E. Gearing, William
W. Swart and Turgut Var, *Planning for Tourism Development, Quantitative Approaches*, New York, 1976, p. 30-32.)

45. Tourism is often called an invisible export because many countries accumulate large sums in foreign currency by successfully encouraging foreign
visitors to travel inside their borders. Tourism accounts for 6% of all the
"exports" in the world. From 1960 to 1968, its average growth was almost double
that of other world "exports." Visitors to the United States from other countries
totaled more than 14 million in 1973, and spent about $3.9 billion. In 1968-1969,
tourism was the primary source of foreign revenue in Israel, Portugal, and Spain.
It was second in Egypt, Greece, and Italy, and third in Britain, France, South
Africa, and Switzerland. Foreign travel earning, viewed as a product, has
represented good percentages in the Gross National Products of most countries.
(Cf. Charles E. Gearing, William W. Swart, and Turgut Var, *Planning for
Tourism Development, Quantitative Approaches*, New York, 1976, p. 29-30,
32-41; George J. Anderia, *International Travel Payments*, doctoral thesis at Co-
lumbia University, New York, 1965, p. 172-175; C. Langhorne Washburn, *1973:
Tourism Action Year*, Washington, 1974, first page; and United Nations,
*Elements of Tourism Policy in Developing Countries, Report by the Secretariat of
UNCTAD*, New York, 1973, p. 8.)

46. In 1920, for instance, 137,601 citizens of the United States departed from
Atlantic ports, while in 1930 the number was 404,390. In recent years, international tourist travel has become more vigorous. In 1948, for instance, Australia
had 26,171; Austria, 149,041; France, 2,028,000; Italy, 1,590,033; Kenya, 10,953;
Peru, 6,623; Thailand, 656; Turkey, 11,071; the United States, 2,166,859; and
Uruguay, 204,101. In 1973, the numbers for these countries, respectively, were:
472,100; 10,215,000; 10,158,300; 101,607,700; 397,700; 228,100; 1,037,000;

1958 and 1973, tourism throughout the world increased 5 times.[47]
This increase is expected to continue[48] as transportation and accom-

---

1,341,500; 14,000,000, and 551,900. (Cf. *Encyclopedia of the Social Sciences,*
New York, 1935, Vol. XIV, p. 663; *United Nations Statistical Yearbook,* 1974, p.
517-518.)

47. International tourist statistics:

Year	Number in Millions	Increase over Previous Year (%)
1958	55.3	—
1959	63.0	13.9
1960	71.2	13.0
1961	75.3	5.8
1962	81.4	8.1
1963	93.0	14.3
1964	108.0	16.2
1965	115.5	6.9
1966	130.8	13.2
1967	139.5	6.6
1968	139.7	0.1
1969	154.9	9.4
1970	168.0	8.4
1971	181.0	7.0
1972	198.0	9.0
1973	215.0	9.0

(Cf. Charles E. Gearing, William W. Swart and Turgut Var, *Planning of Tourism
Development, Quantitative Approaches,* New York, 1976, p. 28.)

48. Forecasts of tourist arrivals and dollar receipts, region, 1970-80 (million
visits and million dollars, at current prices)

	1970		1975		1980	
	Visits	Revenue	Visits	Revenue	Visits	Revenue
Central America and the Caribbean	7.04	1,408	10.40	2,132	13.30	2,793
South America	1.00	270	1.25	410	1.60	592
Africa	1.20	180	1.80	350	2.60	494
Asia and Oceania	4.20	630	5.70	1,040	7.50	1,575
Western Europe	64.20	5,457	78.00	7,870	94.00	10,810
Communist countries	16.90	406	23.40	690	30.90	1,236
Mediterranean	51.00	4,080	69.00	6,210	90.00	9,450
North America	57.00	2,850	70.00	4,600	85.00	6,800
Totals (rounded)	203.00	14,281	260.00	23,302	325.00	33,750

(Cf. John G. Hamilton, Robert Cleverdon, and Quentin Clough, "International
Tourism," *Quarterly Economic Review,* Special no. 7, 1971, p. 23-24.)

modations become more and more convenient, and as the travel trade is promoted, through various efforts of private enterprise as well as by governments.[49]

c.
Intellectual Dissemination

INTELLECTUAL DISSEMINATION IS LARGELY ACHIEVED through the migrations of students and scholars, learning and the applications of foreign languages, exchange and translation of foreign publications, screenings of foreign movies, the gathering and spreading of international news, and transmission of information by mail, telegraph, telephone, radio and television to other lands. All of the above serve to generalize modern civilization and encourage the sharing of various cultural attainments. All are essential for the building of One World.

Student migration is a phenomenon of ancient origin, and to it the university as an institution owes its existence.[50] It was not, however, until modern times that the migratory student became notably numerous. At first, Germany occupied a pre-eminent place in the attraction of migratory students.[51] Then, the United States,

---

49. Government travel offices in many countries have not only served their own populations, but sought bookings from travel agents who could send them foreign tourists. Old national grudges and conflicting ideologies have been temporarily forgotten, and the combinations are often unusual. The Spanish government operates a travel office in Sweden; the Danes try to attract the Germans, their oppressors during World War II. The state of Hawaii opened a travel office in Tokyo; Bulgaria, Czechoslovakia, the USSR, Poland, and Yugoslavia have all opened bureaus in the West. (Cf. Herbert M. Bratter, *The Promotion of Tourist Travel by Foreign Countries, Trade Promotion Series no. 113,* Washington, 1931, p. 2-8, 11-64; Organization for Economic Co-operation and Development, *Tourism Development and Economic Growth,* Paris, 1967, p. 15-42; and United Nations Economic Commission for Europe, *Planning and Development of the Tourist Industry in the ECE Region,* New York, 1976.)

50. (Cf. William R. Wheeler, and others, *The Foreign Student in America,* ed. by William R. Wheeler for the Commission on Survey of Foreign Students in the United States of America, New York, 1925, p. 3-6.)

51. As early as 1835-36, there were in attendance in Germany universities 475

France, and Great Britain became active in this respect,[52] and special roles were played by Switzerland,[53] Austria,[54] Belgium,[55] Japan[56]

---

foreign students, representing 4.02 per cent of the entire enrollment. By 1870-71, this number had increased to 735; and by 1899, to 6,284. (Cf. William R. Wheeler, and others, *The Foreign Student in America,* New York, 1925, p. 9.)

52. In 1904, when the number of foreign students in Germany was approximately 8,786, it was 2,673 in the United States, and 2,047 in France. The numbers in the United States and France, however, increased rapidly just before and after World War I. Figures for 1911-12 show 5,227 foreigners enrolled in the universities and colleges of the United States, and for 1920-21, 8,357. By January, 1914, the number of foreign students in France was 6,132, and by July, 1921, 6,477. In modern times, the enrollment of foreign students in the United Kingdom is less impressive than in Germany, France, and the United States. Before the first World War, the annual number of foreign students in Great Britain was not much more than 2,000, but in the 1920s this number increased to more than 4,000. (Cf. William R. Wheeler, and others, *The Foreign Student in America,* New York, 1925, p. 11-12, 23-26.)

53. Switzerland doubtless enjoys the distinction of having been the nation which enrolls among its students the largest proportion of foreigners to be found in any modern land. In 1895-96, there were among the 3,908 students of Switzerland 1,667 of foreign nationality. During the winter term of 1913-14, 4,538 of the 9,475 students in the Swiss universities were foreigners. (Cf. William R. Wheeler, and others, *The Foreign Student in America,* New York, 1925, p. 27-28.)

54. Describing Vienna as a foreign student center, Mr. Robert P. Wilder wrote in 1914: "There are in Vienna about 15,000 students, of whom 6,000 are foreigners. Practically every nationality of Southeastern Europe is found in this university; also Italians, Greeks, and Turks. Here the Orient and Occident meet." (*The Student World,* July, 1914)

55. Liege in Belgium seems to have been especially attractive to foreign students. In 1913, the total number of students enrolled there was 2,793, of which 1,448 were foreigners. In 1921-22, foreign student enrollment in the universities of Belgium decreased to 868, but they represented 54 nationalities. A most interesting foreign student center is the Université Internationale at Brussels. This institution was created by the International University Conference of 1920, and has as its object to unite the universities and international associations into a movement of advanced educational and universal culture. In 1921, it was composed of 15 universities, 346 professors representing 23 countries, and international associations of an unspecified number, by which 23 chairs were organized. (Cf. "Students in Belgium," *Student World,* April, 1914; and William R. Wheeler, and others, *The Foreign Student in America,* New York, 1925, p. 32-33.)

56. The most remarkable student migration to Japan was that of Chinese students during the 1900s. "It was only ten years ago," Dr. John R. Mott wrote in 1908, "that two young men went from Shanghai as the first officially commissioned students of China to study in Japan." "As recently as six years ago, ... on inquiring the number of Chinese students then in Japan, I was told that it probably did not exceed a score. Two years later the number had grown to five hundred; the next year it exceeded two thousand. In the following year the Chinese students came over to Japan at the rate of about five hundred each month so that by the end

and Russia.[57] The total number of migratory students throughout
the world in the middle of the 1920s reached 50,000[58] and increased
more than ten times in fifty years.[59] The great increase is partially attributable to the support of various private and public agencies.[60]

---

of 1905 there were over eight thousand of them in Japan. In the autumn of 1906,
The Japan Mail stated that there were then fully thirteen thousand. Last spring . . .
there were in Tokyo, according to the estimate of the Chinese Ambassador, not
less than fifteen thousand." (*The Student World,* Jan., 1908)

57. Before World War I, Russian students had long occupied a very prominent place numerically in every foreign student center of Western Europe. In the
early 1920s, it was estimated that the number of Russian students residing in
foreign lands was greatly in excess of 12,000. There were also a limited number of
foreign students in the Russian Empire. After the Bolshevik Revolution, a great
number of students from China as well as from other lands came to Russia to be
trained, especially in Communist theory. (Cf. William R. Wheeler, and others,
The Foreign Student in America, New York, 1925, p. 7-38.)

58. A general impression of the foreign student situation throughout the
world in the middle of the 1920s may be obtained from the following statistics:
there were in Austria 3,000 foreign students; Belgium, 868; Bulgaria, 2,000;
Czechoslovakia, 3,000; Denmark, 15; Egypt, 661; Esthonia, 250; France, 6,477;
Germany, 6,334; Italy, 304; Japan, 2,000; Poland, 1,700; Switzerland, 1,200;
Turkey, 1,000; United Kingdom, 4,171; United States, 8,357; Yugoslavia, 2,500.
The total was 43,837. But the same authority stated that in view of unavoidable
omissions and of the very restricted scope of some of the statistical data presented,
it seemed entirely safe to estimate the total number as considerably in excess of
50,000. (Cf. William R. Wheeler, and others, *The Foreign Student in America,*
New York, 1925, p. 38, 322.)

59. Estimated foreign student enrollment at the third level of education
(*UNESCO Statistical Yearbook,* 1973, p. 115):

	1960	1965	1970	1971
World Total	238,671	354,950	500,805	528,774
Africa	18,238	27,059	27,303	27,999
America	72,892	112,766	192,321	200,153
Asia	22,294	42,313	70,136	73,565
Europe	105,742	148,513	184,136	199,591
Oceania	5,505	8,108	9,507	10,066
U.S.S.R.	14,000	16,200	17,400	17,400

60. Cf. the 21st edition, for 1977-79, of UNESCO's *Study Abroad,* which
was first published in 1948, with the subtitle, "International Handbook of
Fellowships, Scholarships, International Exchange." The 21st edition states that
its purpose continues to be "to provide details of all available opportunities for
transnational study. . . . What really distinguishes the more recent editions from
their predecessors is the enormous increase in the volume of the opportunities
available. From the 280 governmental agencies, universities, foundations and
other sponsoring agencies contributing to the first edition, the list of contributors

Running parallel to the student migration has been the migration of professors. In this century, in most of the famous universities of the world, there have been migratory professors,[61] and some of them has been highly distinguished scholars.[62]

Although students in the western world were encouraged to study

---

has grown to reach over 2,200 in the twenty-first edition. Together they account for several hundred thousand individual scholarships, assistantships, travel grants, course and seminar places in all academic and professional fields in over 100 countries of the world for the period 1977 to 1979. This total, it may be noted, no longer covers some of the very largest international training programs and a number of direct exchange arrangements which operate their own internal selection systems and need not, for that reason, be advertised in *Study Abroad.*" (p. 10-12) The cover page of this edition claims to have "more than 200,000 scholarships, fellowships, assistantships, travel grants, plus hundreds of international courses throughout the world." (Cf. also John A. Garraty, Lily von Klemperer, and Cyril J. H. Taylor, *The New Guide to Study Abroad,* 1974-1975 ed., New York, 1974.)

61. For example, in the period of 1949-1973, there were 8,282 grants made to United States lecturers teaching in foreign countries, and 2,959 grants to foreign lecturers teaching in the United States. In the same period, there were 4,112 grants made to United States scholars doing research in foreign countries, and 10,500 grants to foreign scholars doing research in the United States, according to the *Report on Exchanges,* by the U.S. Board of Foreign Scholarship, 11th annual report, Dec. 1973, Washington, p. 14-15. Cf. UNESCO's *Teaching Abroad,* which, according to its 10th edition, Paris, 1958, p. 8, "summarizes the information so far assembled and describes how exchanges of teachers are related to the over-all programme of the Organization.... The exchange of teachers has proved to be one of the most effective methods of developing international understanding and co-operation. Teachers of languages, or of subjects connected with the history and civilization of a particular country, derive the most immediate benefit from such programmes. A visit to the countries about which they will subsequently teach is of inestimable value to them.... Although such travel may not equip a teacher with special knowledge of direct value in his professional activities, it cannot fail to give him an exceptional opportunity of making the acquaintance of foreign peoples; there is also the additional benefit which pupils may derive from studying under a foreign teacher.... Every effort is being made to help East and West towards a greater knowledge, understanding and appreciation of each other's cultures, by enabling the greatest possible number of teachers to gain direct experience of another region. Unesco also contributes to the international dissemination of knowledge and techniques. In this sphere, the most urgent task is to provide countries whose industry is underdeveloped with the technical knowledge required for the improvement of their living standards."

62. A special migration of professors occurred when many famous professors were driven out by the Nazi forces after Hitler came into power. Most of these migrant professors were offered posts by American universities; among them were at least eight Nobel prize winners: A. Einstein, T. Mann, S. Undset, M. Maeterlinck, J. Franck, V.F. Hess, O. Loewi, and O. Meyerhoff. (Cf. *They Can Aid*

Latin and Greek, the schools offered little opportunity for the study of modern foreign languages until the 19th century. However, after about 1850, modern foreign languages were studied in most countries.[63] As a result, a great many people have used a foreign language as a secondary or even official language;[64] and there has also been a tendency to incorporate into one language terms and forms from another.[65]

The international exchange of publications has long been promoted by official conventions and agreements,[66] and publications have been vigorously exchanged[67] directly between libraries,[68]

America; Survey of Alien Specialized Personnel, published by the U.S. National Refugee Service in 1943, New York, p. 2.)

63. In the schools of some countries, one or two modern languages then became compulsory, such as English in most Chinese schools from about 1910 to 1950. For many decades, it has also been commonly accepted that one cannot qualify for the degree of doctor of philosophy without a reading knowledge of one or more foreign languages. For the history of the study of modern languages in England, as a case study, cf. *Modern Studies,* a report of the Committee on the Position of Modern Languages in the Educational System of Great Britain, 1918, p. 1-16.

64. Examples are English in India, Ceylon, Palestine, Malaya, Burma, Egypt, Hongkong, the Philippines, and Cyprus; German in the Netherlands, Denmark, Norway, Sweden, Czechoslovakia, Hungary, and Yugoslavia; French in Italy, Portugal, Spain, Indochina, and Egypt. (Cf. Marie A. Pei, *The World's Chief Languages,* London, 1949, p. 81-82, 123, 183-184, and 227.)

65. This process of amalgamation tends to make the different languages more alike and leads in the direction of a world language. (For illustrations, cf. Marie A. Pei, *The World's Chief Languages,* London, 1949, p. 83-87.)

66. As early as March, 1886, two conventions were contracted at Brussels, one for the exchange of official documents and scientific and literary publications, and the other for the exchange of "Journaux Officiels" and Parliamentary Records and Documents. Clauses on the exchange of publications may also be found in other general cultural agreements between various countries. (Cf. *British and Foreign State Papers,* Vol. 77, p. 886, 888; also *Handbook on the International Exchange of Publications,* Published by UNESCO, 1950, p. 118-127.)

67. For instance, in 1931, Argentina dispatched 5,466 publications in 146 batches; South Australia, in 1937, received 1,546 consignments and dispatched 3,075, and, in 1947, received 1,246 and dispatched 2,192; China received 375 consignments, in 1947, weighing 2,236 kilos and dispatched 274 consignments weighing 6,123 kilos; Finland, in 1947, sent off 1,228 parcels and 6,949 postal packages of publications, and in 1948, 1,528 parcels, 5,513 postal packages and 95 cases of publications; and Switzerland, in 1947, dispatched 15,086 parcels and received 20,500. (Cf. *Handbook on the International Exchange of Publications,* published by UNESCO, 1950, p. 108-109; 111-112, 116.)

68. The international exchange of publications directly between libraries has long been carried on smoothly. For instance, the number of institutions with which the University of Upsala had exchange relations grew from 63 in 1884 to 761 in

through special agencies, and, lately, with assistance from the Clearing House of UNESCO.[69] In addition, the international book trade has also played an important role in supplying foreign publications.[70]

Since the last century, the translation of foreign publications has begun to command wide interest, and lately the volume of translation has increased enormously, including most categories of literature.[71]

In addition to foreign literature, there have been a great number

---

1897, 2,000 in 1913, and 2,200 in 1929. More than 300 of these were German and nearly that many American, with French, British, Italian and Swiss institutions following. The library had all the dissertations of the University at its disposal, plus 120 serials; by 1929, it was receiving 2,828 serials on exchange and purchasing only 785. In the United States, Yale was reported in 1944 to have exchanges with 114 Latin American libraries, and a survey made by a California library in 1932-33 showed that it was currently receiving 4,025 serials by exchange, among which 2,806 were foreign, including 169 from Latin America. (Cf. *Conference on International Cultural, Educational, and Scientific Exchanges,* published by the American Library Association, 1947, p. 84-85.)

69. Since the UNESCO Clearing House for Publications was set up to promote contracts for the exchange of publications between the various countries, "the volume of publication exchanged is increasing. These exchanges are no longer confined to scientific, printed or micro-filmed publications and technical works, but are extended to popular works or even to literature for the general public. Moreover, they are now no longer arranged only between official institutions, but also between scientific establishments, popular libraries, educational groups, etc." (*Handbook on the International Exchange of Publications,* published by UNESCO, 1950, p. 13.)

70. For instance, British exports of books in 1940 totaled about $14,000,000, or about 20 per cent of the total volume of the British book trade, and the German Börsenverein is said to have had a book export trade of $15,000,000 per year. (Cf. *Conference on International Cultural, Educational, and Scientific Exchanges,* published by the American Library Association, 1947, p. 103.)

71. According to the *United Nations Statistical Yearbook,* 1973, p. 800, the number of translations and their classifications for the years 1970 and 1971 are as follows:

	1970	1971		1970	1971
World Total	33,709	42,984	Pure Sciences	2,166	2,553
Generalities	141	220	Applied Science	3.029	3,603
Philosophy	1,700	2,186	Literature	15,422	20,858
Religion	2,253	2,447	Arts	1,608	2,025
Social Sciences	4,466	5,601	Geography, History	2,924	3,491

(Cf. UNESCO's *Index Translationum.* No. 1 to No. 26 of its old series is for 1932 to 1939. Its new series began in 1948 with one volume for each year. Thus, no. 26, published in 1976, is for 1973.)

of films sent out of the producing countries[72] and displayed in foreign lands[73] since the early days of this century.

With regard to international news gathering and dissemination, the rise of the universal postal service[74] had a great effect at first. It remained, however, for the telegraph and telephone to remove physical hindrances,[75] and the establishment of specialized news agencies to overcome personnel and financial difficulties.[76]

---

72. Before World War I, there were approximately 27,000 miles of film going out of the producing countries each day, a band of film which could encircle the earth and leave 2,000 miles to spare. (Cf. John E. Harley, *World-Wide Influences of the Cinema,* Los Angeles, 1940, p. 21. Cf. also UNESCO's *World Communications, Press, Radio, Television, Film,* Paris, 1964, p. 60-61.)

73. The United States alone exported about 600 pictures with an average of 200 prints each, every year from the later 1920s on, while it imported a great number of foreign pictures. In 1937, for instance, there were released in the United States 1,009 films, of which 231 were foreign-made. Among the foreign films, 78 were French, 29 German, 25 Russian, 24 Hungarian, 17 Mexican, 12 Yiddish, 12 Viennese, 9 Italian, 8 Irish, 5 Polish, 4 Czech, 3 Chinese, 2 Swedish, 1 Balinese, 1 Greenland, and 1 Ukrainian. (Cf. John E. Harley, *World-Wide Influences of the Cinema,* Los Angeles, 1940, p. 3, 21-22, 254. Cf. also UNESCO's *World Communications, Press, Radio, Television, Film,* Paris, 1964, p. 41-50.)

74. For some time after the establishment of fairly satisfactory national postal systems, there still remained many annoying and inconvenient obstacles in the path of efficient transit and delivery of international mails. To remedy these evils, the United States suggested in 1862 the calling of an international conference of postal systems, and in 1863 such a congress was held in Paris. The gathering drew up a code of 31 articles which was to serve as the basis for a series of international postal conventions, but the vicissitudes of the American Civil War and the various European wars between 1864 and 1871 prevented, or at least postponed, further progress. Interest in the reform movement, however, remained alive, particularly in view of the successful functioning in the 1860s of a postal union between Austria, Prussia, and some twenty other German states. Upon the invitation of the Swiss Government, therefore, another meeting was held at Berne, in September, 1874. The Berne congress drew up the first International Postal Convention which, with modifications and amendments, still remains in force. By the terms of this agreement, the members of the International or Universal Postal Union contracted to consider themselves, for the purpose of mail delivery, as one large postal territory, and each member bound itself to dispatch as efficiently as possible the mails coming from and going to every other member. (Cf. George A. Codding, Jr., *The Universal Postal Union, Co-ordinator of the International Mails,* New York, 1964, p. 25-72.)

75. Telegraph wire mileage throughout the world in 1934 was about 7,119,000 miles; it had only been 100,000 in 1860. No telephone service at all was in existence in 1860, but its wire mileage in 1934 was estimated at 140,000,000. Ocean cables were expanded rapidly from about 1,500 miles in 1860 to over 330,000 miles in 1913. (Cf. Isaac Lippincott, *The Development of Modern World Trade,* New York, 1936, p. 60.)

Great changes have occurred in international information systems since radio[77] and television[78] came into use, because the two newcomers recognize no national boundaries, and go everywhere

---

76. If every newspaper were compelled to support its own correspondents in all parts of the world and to maintain its own communication connections, the expense would be such as only a few great newspapers could meet. Instead of this, there has developed a specialized news gathering and supplying agency, through which significant information from all parts of the world is put at the disposal of newspapers that are willing to pay for the service. They are thus able, for a relatively small expenditure, to obtain a variety and volume of news that would otherwise be denied to them. Among the important international news agencies, the first established was Havas, which started its business in 1835. Reuter first set up its business in Aix-la-Chapelle in 1848 and transferred its headquarters to London in 1851. At about the same time, Wolff began its enterprises. In the twentieth century, a lot of new international news agencies have come into competition with the older ones, and among them the most important are the Associated Press, United Press, and Tass. All of these agencies have made a great contribution to the peoples of the world in the exchange of information. (Cf. Ralph O. Nafziger, *International News and the Press,* New York, 1940, p. xviii to xxvii; and UNESCO's *World Communications, Press, Radio, Television, Film,* Paris, 1964, p. 373-377.)

77. Estimated numbers of radio broadcasting transmitters and receivers, excluding the China mainland, in 1971:

	Number of radio broadcasting transmitters	Number of radio receivers	
		Total (millions)	Per 1,000 inhabitants
World Total	23,000	796	215
Africa	700	17	48
America, North	8,640	372	1,137
America, South	2,650	27	138
Asia	2,400	135	64
Europe	5,300	141	303
Oceania	320	3.8	193
U.S.S.R.	3,030	100	408

(Based on *UNESCO Statistical Yearbook,* 1973, p. 725-726. Cf. UNESCO's *World Radio and Television,* Paris, 1965, p. 13, 26.)

without much difficulty. However, the postal service and telegraph[79] still remain important channels in the international exchange of information.

d.
Agricultural Dispersal

THE DISPERSAL OF DOMESTIC PLANTS HAS HAD A LONG history which may be traced back to as early as 8,000 B.C. in the Old

---

78. Estimated numbers of television transmitters and receivers, excluding the China mainland, in 1971:

	Numbers of regular television transmitters		Numbers of television receivers	
	Total	Auxiliary transmitters	Total (millions)	Per 1,000 inhabitants
World Total	18,210	13,720	288	78
Africa	140	45	1.4	4
America, North	3,440	2,225	105	321
America, South	290	100	13	67
Asia	4,460	4,170	29	14
Europe	8,190	6,950	96	206
Oceania	350	230	3.7	188
U.S.S.R.	1,340	. . .	39	160

(Based on *Unesco Statistical Yearbook,* 1973, p. 753-754. Cf. UNESCO's *Television, A World Survey,* Paris, 1972, p. 11-13.)

79. This fact is demonstrated by the great annual number of international letters and telegrams. For instance, Switzerland in 1938 received 68,700,000 letters from and sent 74,200,000 letters to foreign countries, and in 1973, received 171,100,000 and sent 214,883,000; Argentina in 1938 received 46,000,000, sent 22,000,000, and in 1973 received 88,000,000 and sent 54,000,000; Australia in 1938 received 49,000,000, sent 41,000,000, and in 1973 received 182,634,000, and sent 112,028,000; and Turkey in 1938 received 8,173,000, sent 10,573,000, and in 1973 received 50,450,000 and sent 68,500,000. Egypt in 1937 received 183,000 telegrams from and sent 164,000 telegrams to foreign countries, and in 1947, received 267,000 and sent 215,000; New Zealand in 1937 received 327,000, sent 348,000, and in 1947 received 427,000, and sent 414,000; Bulgaria in 1937 received 127,000,

World, when some domestic plants began to spread from the Middle East,[80] and to as early as 5,000 B.C. in the New World, when some plants began to spread from southern Mexico.[81] But it was not until modern times that the dispersal became fast and wide,[82] as difficulties were overcome in circumventing the restrictions which had previously been in effect.[83]

---

sent 115,000, and in 1947 received 122,000, and sent 143,000; and Canada in 1937 received 692,000, sent 797,000, and in 1947 received 803,000 and sent 811,000. (Cf. *United Nations Statistical Yearbook 1951,* Table, 144, 145; and the same *Statistical Yearbook, 1974,* Table 161.)

80. From the archaeological evidence, southwestern Asia—including most of what is now the Middle East—seems to have been the site of the earliest agricultural focus. This region was the homeland of wheat and barley and of the chief Old World domestic animals and the site of the invention of the plow. Influences from this ancient center spread into Europe, Africa, across the rest of Asia to Malaysia and Indonesia, and after 1500 A.D., to almost all inhabited parts of the world. In addition to wheat and barley, the Middle Eastern area furnished rye, peas, lentils, broad-beans, onions, garlic, carrots, grapes, olives, dates, apples, pears, cherries, flax, and a great many other plants. At the lowest level excavated at Jericho in Jordan, hoe-cultivation artifacts have been found dating from 9500 B.C. At this time hunting and gathering were still important. By around 8000 B.C., emmer wheat and barley were being grown by villagers in a wide zone, extending from Asia Minor to Western Iran and south into Israel and Jordan. Neolithic sites with evidences of hoe-cultivation beginnings have been discovered in Iraq, Jordan, Turkey, and Cyprus. (Cf. James Mellaart, *Earliest Civilizations in the Near East,* London, 1965, p. 11-38; Erich Isaac, *Geography of Domestication,* New York, 1970, p. 57-64; and Charles B. Heiser, Jr., *Seed to Civilization, A Story of Man's Food,* San Francisco, 1973, p. 5-6.)

81. Southern Mexico is considered to have been the first center of New World agriculture. Hoe-cultivation began there about 6000 B.C., although hunting and gathering persisted as the backbone of the economy long after. The first crops were chile peppers and avocados. Findings in the caves of northeastern Mexico show bottle gourds, peppers, and pumpkins to be the earliest plants cultivated there. Maize (Indian corn) first appeared as a cultigen around 5000 B.C. in Coxcaltan Cave in the Tehuacan Valley. Squash appeared in the same valley about the same time, and beans about 3000 B.C. It is believed that maize and some other plants spread from southern Mexico to both North America and South America. (Cf. Charles B. Heiser, Jr., *Seed to Civilization, A Story of Man's Food,* San Francisco, 1973, p. 6-10.)

82. "In the Age of Reconnaissance, Europeans first leapt the barrier of the Atlantic, completed the circle, and initiated a much more rapid movement of men, plants, and animals which, in a few centuries, drastically altered the physical aspect of many regions, both of the Old World and the New." (John H. Parry, *The Age of Reconnaissance,* London, 1963, p. 288)

83. For example, silk was invented probably 4500 years ago in China. Traditional Chinese accounts ascribe the cultivation of silkworms and the weaving of silk to the wife of the legendary emperor Huang-Ti 黃帝, who began his reign in

Wheat, for example, was first brought to the New World by the great explorer Columbus,[84] although it had existed in the Old World for many thousands of years.[85] Today, wheat has spread over the

---

2698 B.C. In any event, silk culture flourished by the time of the Shang Dynasty, 1523-1027 B.C. Chinese silk was for a long-time well-known and envied by people in the western world, who thought it was grown on trees or spun by spiders. They could not get the secret of silk until 552 A.D. when two Nestorian monks, who had lived in China, concealed a small quantity of silkworm eggs and brought them to Constantinople. From there, it still took some hundred years for sericulture to spread through the Balkan Peninsula to western Europe and northern Africa. (Cf. Luce Boulnois, *The Silk Road,* tr. by Dennis Chamberlain, New York, 1966, p. 17-22; and William F. Leggett, *The Story of Silk,* New York, 1949, p. 83-85, 185-191.)

Another account is that around 140 B.C. a Chinese princess who went to Khotan in the northern Kwen-Lun mountains took silkworm eggs with her which she hid in her hair. After all, one could hardly blame her for doing so, for ever since the days of Lady Hsi-ling-shi, royal ladies had specialized in silk-raising. The princess evidently did not see why she should give up her hobby just because she was to be married to a prince in a faraway land. From Khotan, silk-raising spread to Turkestan, from Turkestan to Persia, and from Persia to Syria. But Justinian, the emperor of Syria, realized the commercial value of the new industry and monopolized it forthwith. This action prevented the spread of sericulture westwards for some centuries. In 536 A.D., however, Syrian monks succeeded in bringing silkworm eggs to Constantinople, hidden in a cane. (Cf. Frederick E. Zeuner, *A History of Domesticated Animals,* London, 1963, p. 484-492.)

84. It is believed that wheat did not exist in America before Christopher Columbus discovered the continent. Columbus brought wheat to the West Indies in 1493; the grain was taken to Mexico by Hernando Cortes in 1519; and Jesuit and Franciscan missionaries carried it into what is now Arizona and California. Colonists in Massachusetts and Virginia began cultivation of the grain early in the 17th century. Colonists also grew wheat in Canada, South America and Australia. (Cf. R.F. Peterson, *Wheat: Botany, Cultivation, and Utilization,* London, 1965, p. 100-102.)

85. Archaeologists have found carbonized grains of wheat in prehistoric lake dwellings in Switzerland, in remains from the Stone Age in England, in the tombs of the pharaohs in Egypt, and in the excavations of ruins in Turkey, some of which date back to 4000 B.C. There is evidence that wheat was cultivated in China in 3000 B.C. Some scientists believe that cultivated wheat originated in Mesopotamia (Iraq), although many others hold the view that the plant once grew wild in the valleys of the Euphrates and Tigris rivers, and spread from these regions to the rest of the old world. (Cf. Peter T. Dondlinger, *The Book of Wheat, An Economic History and Practical Manual of the Wheat Industry,* New York, 1916, p. 1-2; and Nikolai I. Valilov, "Scientific Basis of Wheat Breeding," tr. by K. Starr Chester, in the *Chronica Botanica,* Vol. 13, 1945/50, p. 170-175.)

The first wheat grown was emmer, little different from its wild ancestor, which was probably native to the Syria-Palestine area. Einkorn wheat was also cultivated. Emmer predominated in Iraq and Egypt until Graeco-Roman times. Einkorn spread from Asia Minor into southeastern Europe. Today's bread wheats

whole world and has become the most widely grown of all cereal grains.[86]

In return, Indian corn was first brought by modern explorers[87] to Europe from the New World where it had been propagated for some

---

are hybrids of emmer and einkorn. (Cf. Herbert G. Baker, *Plants and Civilizations,* Belmont, Calif., 1965, p. 67-72.)

86. Today wheat is the most widely grown of all cereal grains; it is raised at elevations of 8,000 to 10,000 feet in the tropics of Mexico, northwestern South America, and Abyssinia, and below sea level in the Imperial Valley of California. It grows within the Arctic Circle in Europe, Asia, and North America, and in such warm countries as Brazil and the tropics of the Philippines. Several thousand varieties are grown. Except in the rice-eating regions of Asia, wheat products are the principal cereal foods of the overwhelming majority of the world's inhabitants. The following table summarizes world wheat acreage and production data prior to World War II and during the year 1960:

Continent or Country (Estimated)	Acreage (1,000 acres)		Production (1,000 bushels)	
	1935-39 average	1960	1935-39 average	1960
North America	84,170	77,780	1,086,000	1,900,000
Europe	74,850	71,640	1,600,000	1,905,000
Russia	104,000	148,500	1,240,000	1,700,000
Asia	114,190	143,880	1,558,000	1,950,000
Africa	13,850	18,760	143,000	210,000
South America	20,490	15,260	281,000	245,000
Oceania	13,349	13,022	176,873	268,250
World	424,900	488,840	6,085,000	8,180,000

(Cf. William C. Edgar, *The Story of a Grain of Wheat,* New York, 1915, p. 44-57; *Wheat and Wheat Improvement,* ed, by K.S. Quisenberry, Madison, Wis., 1967, p. 7-17; and R.F. Peterson, *Wheat: Botany, Cultivation, and Utilization,* London, 1965, p. 384-394.)

87. The earliest recorded contact of Europeans with corn occurred on November 5, 1492, when a Spanish scouting party returning from the interior of Cuba reported that a grain called mahiz tasted good and could be baked, dried, and made into flour. Since then, corn has been brought to and grown in Europe, Asia, Africa, from latitude 58 °N in Canada and Siberia, to 42 °S in New Zealand. Within this broad belt, corn is an important crop only where temperature and moisture conditions are favorable. (Cf. Melville L. Bowman, *Corn Growing, Judging, Breeding, Feeding, Marketing,* Waterloo, Iowa, 1915, p. 1-3, 24-34; Organization for European Economic Co-operation, *Hybrid Maize (corn) in European Countries,* Paris, 1950, p. 9-11, 21-23; and Marvin P. Miracle, *Maize in Tropical Africa,* Madison, Wisconsin, 1966, p. 87-100.)

88. Maize (Indian corn) first appeared as a cultigen around 5000 B.C. in Coxcaltan Cave in the Tehuacán Valley, Mexico. Conversion of maize into a dietary staple was slow. Later, maize was scattered with beans and squash, which were often planted together. Maize came into the area that is now the United States

thousand years.[88] Now this corn is grown wherever the temperature is favorable, and ranks third among the world's cereals.[89]

The potato is another food brought from its traditional home-land of South America[90] to grow first in Europe and then in other

---

from northwestern Mexico about 2000 B.C. Bat Cave, New Mexico, is the earliest known site of maize in the United States. About 1500 B.C., maize entered South America from Central America and seems to have encouraged population growth and cultural advancement. It seems that China has had a native corn, called 玉蜀、玉米、or 包谷, for a long time, but there are no substantiated written, pictorial, or archaeological records. Experts say it is a peculiar type of endosperm known as "waxy," and different from maize. For this reason, they reject the hypothesis that maize either originated there or was taken there in pre-Columbian times. (Cf. Howard T. Walden, ed., *Native Inheritance, the Story of Corn in America,* New York, 1966, p. 1-18; Herbert G. Baker, *Plants and Civilization,* Belmont, Calif., 1965, p. 57-58; and Paul C. Mangelsdorf, *Corn, Its Origin, Evolution, and Improvement,* Cambridge, Mass., 1974, p. 147-186, 201-204.)

89. World production of corn in 1972 totaled 310,768,000 metric tons. The leading producer was the United States, accounting for 48% of the total. Europe produced 13% and Asia 15%, both exclusive of Russia, which accounts for 4%. The balance of production is accounted for by South America, 8%; Africa, 7%; and North America, 4%, excluding the United States. In the United States, the dollar value of the corn crop is equal to the combined value of wheat, oats, barley, rice, rye, and sorghum. On a world basis, corn is exceeded in value only by wheat and rice. It ranks third among the world's cereals as a human food. In the United States, it is used principally for livestock feed and industrial processing. (Cf. Melville L. Bowman, *Corn Growing, Judging, Breeding, Feeding, Marketing,* Waterloo, Iowa, 1915, p. 4-5, 8-10; *United Nations Statistical Yearbook,* 1974, p. 121-122, 133, 138; and the *Statistical Abstract of the United States,* 1975, p. 634-635.)

90. While the origin of the potato is still not well-known, it is considered to be native to South America. Both the sweet and white potato and various cultigens still confined to western South America were being grown by the early centuries A.D. When indigenous settlements expanded into the high Andean valleys, the people relied chiefly on potatoes and quinoa. By the time of the Spanish conquest of Peru in the 16th century, there were over 100 varieties of potatoes alone. (Cf. Radcliffe N. Salaman, *The History and Social Influence of the Potato,* Eng., 1949 (reprinted in 1970), p. 1-72; and Herbert G. Baker, *Plants and Civilization,* Belmont, Calif., 1965, p. 51-55.)

I wonder, however, if South America is the original and only homeland of the sweet potato. As far as I know, there is a kind of sweet potato in China which also looks like the yam as often seen in the American food market. The Chinese sweet potato grows in all the southern and central provinces during the period from late spring to early autumn. It has several tubers, weighing from a few ounces to a few pounds each. Its vines usually creep more than ten feet, and its heart-shaped leaves are about three inches long and of a dark green color. The Chinese potato can be eaten fresh or dry, steamed, boiled, fried, or baked, and it is a good food, especially important for poor people. It is commonly called hung chu (红薯, literally red potato), but its color is a light brown. There is a pink-skinned sweet potato which is different than the common one not only in the color of the skin but also in the

areas around the world by modern colonists.[91] It has become the most important domestically grown food in Europe.[92]

The coffee tree is believed to be indigenous to Ethiopia and had grown within the Arabic countries for more than a thousand years.[93] In the late 17th century, it began to be planted in the Netherlands,

---

taste. I do not know the origin and history of the Chinese sweet potato, but in view of its wide and traditional usage, it is obviously not a food transplanted from any foreign land in modern times.

91. It is believed that Spanish sailors brought potatoes into Spain and Portugal before 1560. From Spain and Portugal they were probably taken to Italy, and from there, in the early 17th century, to Austria, the Netherlands, Germany, Switzerland, and finally to France. They were grown experimentally in England before 1586, probably introduced from Spain, and soon found their way to Ireland. The English introduced the potato into Bermuda in 1613, and from there it was brought to the Virginia colonies in 1621. Potatoes were cultivated in Sweden in 1725 and Frederick the Great enforced potato growing on a large scale in 1744. Shortly after that, Russia started cultivating them. Captain James Cook introduced the potato into New Zealand in 1733. Cultivation began in 1776 in Lower Guinea, Africa, and in 1880 in Tibet. Potatoes were generally known in the East Indies in 1822 but never became popular there nor with the Chinese and other rice-eating peoples. They were introduced into Assam in 1830 and into Persia in 1844. The early Irish, English, and Scottish colonists carried the potato to the New World, most of them ignorant of its New World origin. The potato's rapid expansion around the world as a valuable food crop was most spectacular. (Cf. Radcliffe N. Salaman, *The History and Social Influence of the Potato,* Cambridge, Eng., 1949, p. 1-13, 142-158; and Eugene H. Grubb, *The Potato,* New York, 1912, p. 3-16, 489-520.)

92. Potatoes are grown in almost every important agricultural country in the world and are the most important domestically cultivated food in Europe. World potato production was almost 300 million metric tons in 1967. The USSR led with almost 96 million tons; Poland was second with over 48 million tons; and West Germany, with almost 20 million tons, was third. The United States and East German production of potatoes in 1967 was approximately equal—somewhat over 14 million tons. French production totaled more than 10 million tons. The above countries accounted for over two-thirds of world potato output in the mid-1960s. Most of the rest was in European countries. Outside of Europe and the United States, the chief producers were Japan, India, Canada, Argentina, Brazil, and Peru. South America, the home of the potato, produced less than 3 percent of the world crop. (Cf. *United Nations Statistical Yearbook,* 1974, p. 131-132.)

93. The coffee tree is believed to be indigenous to Ethiopia. It is not clear whether the coffee tree was brought from Ethiopia to Arabia or whether it was also native to Arabia. The Arabs cultivated the plant as early as 600 A.D., and the first mention of coffee in literature was by the Arab physician Rhazes around 900 A.D. (Cf. William H. Ukers, *All About Coffee,* New York, 1935, p. 1-2; and Costa Neves, *A Story of King Coffee,* tr. by Mary E. Garland, Rio de Janeiro, 2d. ed., 1942, p. 11-19.)

then spread to the Far East, West Indies, and South America[94] where, in about two hundred years, coffee has become the most important export.[95]

The prominent position of coffee as a favorite drink has been challenged in recent years by the increasing production of tea,[96] over

---

94. The Arabs long maintained coffee as a national monopoly. For centuries they exported large quantities of beans, but did not permit a fertile seed or seedling to leave their territories. In 1690, however, the Dutch managed to obtain a few plants and placed them in botanical gardens in the Netherlands. Then they began cultivation in Java and sent plants to other botanical gardens in Europe. In 1723, Gabriel Mathieu de Clieu, a young French officer serving in Martinique, in the French West Indies, stole a coffee plant from the Jardin des Plantes in Paris. De Clieu managed to keep the plant alive during the voyage back to Martinique in spite of an attempted kidnap, an attack by Barbary pirates, violent storms, and a serious water shortage aboard ship. The plant flourished in Martinique and its progeny spread throughout the West Indies and eventually reached the mainland of South America. In 1727, the coffee plant reached Brazil in a different way. That year, Brazil sent one of its army lieutenants, Francisco de Melo Palheta, to arbitrate a boundary dispute between French and Dutch Guiana. Both were cultivating coffee, but neither allowed the export of seeds or seedlings. Palheta handled the arbitration adroitly and so endeared himself to the wife of the governor of French Guiana that on his departure she presented him with a bouquet. Hidden in the bouquet were fertile coffee beans and cuttings, which Palheta brought to Brazil, where they flourished. (Cf. William H. Ukers, *All About Coffee,* New York, 1935, p. 2-5; Heinrich E. Jacob, *Coffee, the Epic of a Commodity,* New York, 1935, p. 225-227.)

95. Brazil exports more coffee than any other country in the world. Other major coffee-exporting countries in the Western Hemisphere are, in order of importance: Colombia, Mexico, El Salvador, Guatemala, Costa Rica, Ecuador, Peru, Nicaragua, Honduras, Haiti, the Dominican Republic, and Venezuela. Coffee is extremely important to the economies of many Latin American countries. Almost 20% of the value of all exports from those countries is represented by coffee. The percentage in some countries is much higher, over 70% for Colombia, 55% for Haiti, 50% for El Salvador, and 40% to 50% each for Guatemala, Brazil, and Costa Rica. The principal coffee-exporting countries of Africa and Asia are the Ivory Coast, Angola, Uganda, Ethiopia, Indonesia, Cameroon, Madagascar, Kenya, Congo, Tanzania, India, and Burundi. (Cf. John W.F. Rowe, *The World Coffee,* London, 1963, p. 21, 171-185.)

96. The average world production of tea during the mid-1960s was 1.26 million tons per year. India was the leading tea producer, followed by Ceylon, China, Japan, and the USSR. Tea production has continued to rise throughout the world with African and South American nations showing the most marked increase. Countries such as New Guinea, Ecuador, and South Africa, which had not previously grown tea on a significant scale, are now seriously involved in tea production. (Cf. Vernon D. Wickizer, *Tea Under International Regulation,* Stanford, Calif., 1944, p. 28-40; *FAO Commodity Review and Outlook,* 1972-1973, p. 172.)

which China had a monopoly from ancient times.[97] The tea-growing business has only spread into new areas for about the last 150 years.[98]

The very nutritious soybean is also a Chinese plant with a long history.[99] It was not known to Europeans until the 18th century and was not planted in America until eighty years ago.[100] It is now grown extensively in every continent except Europe.[101]

---

97. The Chinese provide the earliest written record of tea. There are several references to a shrub supposed to have been tea in a work edited by Confucius (c. 551-479 B.C.), but the first authentic citation occurs in a biography of a Chinese official who died in 273 A.D. Lu Yu, who wrote the *Book of Tea* in about 780 A.D. of the Tang Dynasty (618-906 A.D.), was called "Dr. of Tea" by a prominent official named Lee Chi Ching. (唐上元時，陸羽著茶經，大吏李季卿稱之爲茶博士。見唐書及封氏聞見記。)

Tea was unknown to Europeans until 1559, when Giovanni Battista Ramusio mentioned it in *Delle navigationi et viaggi*. The first English-language reference to tea was by R. Wickman, an agent of the English East India Company, in a letter from Japan in 1615. (Cf. William H. Ukers, *All About Tea*, New York, 1935, p. 1-22; and Percival Griffiths, *The History of the Indian Tea Industry*, London, 1967, p. 1-13.)

"When tea was first introduced into England in the middle of the 17th century, it cost $50 a pound, equal to about $500 in our time. It was so precious that the purveyors weighed it on apothecary scales." (Sydney Harris, *South Bend Tribune*, Jan. 15, 1980, p. 16)

98. In 1826, the Dutch succeeded in establishing tea plantations in Java, and in 1836, the East India Company introduced tea cultivation into India. About fifty years later, Ceylon also became a tea-growing country. Many attempts have been made to cultivate and manufacture tea in the United States, but labor costs have proved too high to meet Asian competition. (Cf. William H. Ukers, *All About Tea*, New York, 1935, p. 109-216; James M. Scott, *The Great Tea Venture*, New York, 1965, p. 65-88; and Vernon D. Wickizer, *Tea Under International Regulations*, Stanford, Calif., 1944, p. 28-33.)

99. Ancient Chinese literature reveals that the soybean (總稱菽，別名大豆，俗叫黃豆。) was extensively cultivated and highly valued as a food centuries before written records were kept. Mentioned in records prior to 2000 B.C., the crop was considered the most important cultivated legume and one of the five sacred grains essential to Chinese civilization, the others being rice, wheat, barley, and millet. (稻，麥，黍，稷) (Cf. Charles V. Piper and William J. Morse, *The Soybean*, New York, 1943, p. 36-37.)

100. The soybean was first made known to Europeans in the 18th century. It was grown as early as 1740 in botanic gardens in France and in 1790 in the Royal Botanic Gardens, Kew, England. The first mention made of the soybean in American literature was by James Mease, a physician, in 1804. For many years afterward, it was regarded more as a botanic curiosity than as a plant of economic importance. After 1890, however, most of the agricultural stations of the United States experimented with soybeans, and in 1898, the U.S. Department of Agriculture began the introduction of a large number of varieties from Asian countries. (Cf. Charles V. Piper and William J. Morse, *The Soybean*, New York, 1943, p. 3-4, 27-32.)

Sweet tasting sugarcane had been widely planted in the Old World for hundreds of years,[102] but it did not appear in the New World until modern times.[103] New sugarcane planting is limited only by cooler climates,[104] which have proved more favorable for growing the newly developed sugar beet.[105]

---

101. In the early 1970s, the United States was the world's largest soybean producer, and the crop was one of the nation's leading cash crops. The rapid increase in soybean production in the mid-20th century was one of the most striking agricultural developments in the United States. Fair results in soybean production have been obtained in Canada, Cuba, Argentina, Brazil, Columbia, Chile, Costa Rica, Haiti, Puerto Rico, the Dominican Republic, and Mexico, and production has been tried on a small scale in almost all the other American countries. In Asia, China is the original great producer of soybeans. Other important growers are Japan, Korea, Indonesia, and Thailand. The legume has been cultivated with some success in various parts of Africa, of which the leading producers are Nigeria, South Africa, and Tanzania. Soybeans have also been grown with some success in parts of Australia and New Zealand. In general, climatic conditions, as well as other factors in the European countries, are not conducive to extensive soybean production. (Cf. Charles V. Piper and William J. Morse, *The Soybean,* New York, 1943, p. 37-54; and *United Nations Statistical Yearbook,* 1974, p. 135-136.)

102. Sugarcane originated either in the rich valleys of northeastern India or in the South Pacific area. Whichever place was the primary source, the growth of cane spread at an early date from one to the other, probably via China, and thence gradually westward and eastward at an ever-increasing pace. The Arabs spread the culture of sugarcane from Persia to the Mediterranean basin, including Egypt, Sicily and Spain, and developed the earliest refining processes and preparation of candies and confections. (Cf. Jack T. Turner, *Marketing of Sugar,* Homewood, Ill., 1955, p. 4.)

103. The planting of sugarcane in the New World was promoted by the earliest explorers. Columbus took it to Santo Domingo (Hispaniola) from the Canary Islands on his second voyage in 1493. The first mill in the Western Hemisphere was established at Yaguate (now in the Dominican Republic), in 1509. By 1511, cane was established in Cuba, and in this same period its culture spread to most of the islands of the East and West Indies, as well as to Mexico, Brazil, Peru, and Hawaii. (Cf. Jack T. Turner, *Marketing of Sugar,* Homewood, Ill., 1955, p. 4.)

104. In 1958, for instance, world production of sugar cane was 373,400,000 metric tons, divided by regions as follows: (in thousands)

Europe	390	Near East	3,800
North America	13,400	Far East	138,600
Latin America	184,900	Africa	20,400
		Oceania	11,900

(Cf. Food and Agriculture Organization of the United Nations, *Production Yearbook,* Rome, Vol. 13, 1959, p. 69.)

105. The commencement of a beet sugar industry may be definitely dated from the work of two German chemists—Andreas Sigismund Marggraf's ex-

As a clothing material, cotton had appeared in both the Old and New World for a long time in limited areas.[106] Since the invention of effective machines for the cotton industry in the 18th century,[107] cotton has grown very widely and has become the world's chief clothing resource.[108]

---

periments in 1747 and Franz Karl Achard's enterprise in 1802. After they found the right means to separate the sugar from the beet root, sugar beet cultivation soon spread in Germany, France, Russia, the northern and western United States, and adjacent Canada. In 1958, the world production of beet sugar was 158,340,000 metric tons, close to half the total cane sugar production, divided by regions as follows: (in thousands)

Europe	83,750	Near East	3,265
North America	14,950	Far East	3,290
Latin America	515	Africa	9

(Cf. Herbert G. Baker, *Plants and Civilization,* Belmont, Calif., 1965, p. 94; and Food and Agriculture Organization of the United Nations, *Production Yearbook,* Rome, Vol. 13, 1959, p. 70.)

106. It is generally believed that one of the first regions to produce cotton was India, where cotton was grown as far back as 3000 B.C. There is also some evidence to indicate that cotton was grown in Peru earlier than in Mexico and was somehow hybridized with an Asian species around 2500 B.C. Cotton was being grown in the Sudan by 300 B.C., but linen remained the standard Egyptian textile. Cotton did not replace flax until the Arab period of the 7th century A.D. (Cf. Matthew B. Hammond, *The Cotton Industry,* Ithaca, New York, 1897, Part I, p. 3-4; also Harry B. Brown, *Cotton,* New York, 1927, p. 1-4; and Herbert G. Baker, *Plants and Civilization,* Belmont, Calif., 1965, p. 58-63.)

It is interesting to note that cotton was first described as wool from a vegetable lamb by the generals of Alexander the Great when their explorations led them into India about 330 B.C. (Cf. James A.B. Scherer, *Cotton as a World Power, A Study of the Economic Interpretation of History,* New York, 1916, p. 6-7.)

107. Before modern times, cotton growing was generally confined to the central belt of the earth, from India to Egypt and Mexico. When new machines, such as Eli Whitney's cotton gin, were invented to reduce the difficulties in manufacturing cotton, cotton-growing quickly spread far and wide, north to the United States and Russia, and south to Brazil. These new areas grow almost two-thirds of the world's cotton. Cotton growing has also expanded in India, Egypt, and China. (Cf. Matthew B. Hammond, *The Cotton Industry,* Ithaca, N.Y., 1897, Part I, p. 327-352; James A.B. Scherer, *Cotton As a World Power, A Study in the Economic Interpretation of History,* New York, 1916, p. 51-88, and 414; James H. Street, *The New Revolution in the Cotton Economy, Mechanization and Its Consequences,* Chapel Hill, N.C., 1957, p. 3-12; and Harry B. Brown, *Cotton,* New York, 1927, p. 4-24.

108. Cotton has overtaken older fibers such as flax and wool to become the world's chief clothing material. It is grown throughout the world, and each year, a total of about 50 million bales, weighing nearly 500 pounds apiece, are produced. According to Cotton World statistics in the *Quarterly Bulletin of the International*

Another plant example is the rubber tree, which was native to South America.[109] In the approximately 30 years since it was smuggled out and planted scientifically,[110] almost all tropical regions have started to produce the useful stuff.[111]

Cotton Advisory Committee, Oct. 1966, the principal cotton growing countries for the year beginning August 1, 1965, were as follows:

Country	Production (1,000 bales)	Country	Production (1,000 bales)
United States	14,920	Sudan	750
USSR	8,800	Iran	645
China	5,800	Peru	575
India	4,600	Argentina	525
Mexico	2,615	Nicaragua	510
Brazil	2,450	Guatemala	400
Egypt	2,398	Spain	375
Pakistan	1,925	Greece	340
Turkey	1,500	Colombia	300
Syria	830	Salvador	240

(Cf. James A.B. Scherer, *Cotton As a World Power, A Study in the Economic Interpretation of History,* New York, 1916, p. 1-5, 383-395, and 423-425; C.F. Lewis and T.R. Richmond, "Cotton As a Crop," in *Cotton, Principles and Practices,* ed. by Fred C. Elliot, Marvin Hood and Walter K. Porter, Jr., Ames, Iowa, 1968, p. 17-20.)

109. The age of the earliest specimens of rubber is unknown, although samples of fossilized rubber discovered in 1924 in the lignite deposits of Germany are believed to date from the Eocene period. An Aztec wall painting showing a priest offering two balls of rubber as a sacrifice has been traced to the 6th century A.D. The first mention of rubber in print appeared in 1530 when Pietro Martire d'Anghiera, an Italian attached to the Spanish court, described "gummi optimum" in his *De Orbe nuovo decades.* But rubber was for a long time well-known to the South American Indians, and before the beginning of the 20th century, practically all of the world's supply of raw rubber was derived from wild, rubber-yielding plants along the Amazon. (Cf. Loren G. Polhamus, *Rubber,* London, 1962, p. 16-24; and Howard and Ralph Wolf, *Rubber, A Story of Glory and Greed,* New York, 1936, p. 15-29.)

110. In 1873, Dr. James Collins, curator of the Physic Gardens of the London Apothecaries Company, went to Brazil to obtain Hevea rubber seeds. His first lot was shipwrecked, but he eventually brought out some 200 seeds. Unfortunately, only a dozen of these seeds germinated in England, and six plants which were forwarded to Calcutta died. In 1876, Dr. Collins wrote to Henry A. Wickham, a young English adventurer who was then operating as a coffee planter in Brazil above the junction of the Tapajos and Amazon rivers, and asked him to collect and ship several thousand of the Hevea seeds. Wickham turned up in England on June 14, 1876, with 70,000 Hevea seeds, which were quickly shipped by special train to Kew. Of the 70,000 seeds planted in nursery beds, 2,800 germinated. The

Regarding domestic animals, it is significant that almost all the important ones which the New World now has came from the Old World.[112] The New World had only a few native domestic animals.[113]

---

following year, some 1,900 young rubber plants were sent to Ceylon. Most of these plants survived and were transplanted in the botanical gardens of Paradenya and Heneratgodo, where some are still alive and yielding rubber today. A few of the plants were subsequently sent to the British resident at Perak, Malaya, who grew several of them in gardens at Kuala Kangsar and, in 1882, sent both seeds and plants to Singapore, Ceylon, India, and Java. Eventually, rubber trees were also planted in the Congo, Liberia, and Nigeria. (Cf. Loren G. Polhamus, *Rubber,* London, 1962, p. 24-29; Klaus E. Knorr, *World Rubber and Its Regulation,* Stanford, Calif., 1945, p. 9-10, 16, 23; and Howard and Ralph Wolf, *Rubber, A Story of Glory and Greed,* New York, 1936, p. 152-168.)

111. Today natural rubber is produced in three major regions of the world, southeast Asia, tropical South America, and tropical Africa, within latitudes of 20° north and 10° south, a belt about 1,400 miles wide encircling the earth at the equator. In 1958, approximately 11,210,000 acres were under rubber cultivation throughout the world, with the acreage divided as follows: Malaya, 3,517,000; Indonesia, 4,429,283; Ceylon, 659,247; Thailand, 839,600; Vietnam and Cambodia, 307,937; Sarawak, 265,000; India, 207,240; British North Borneo, 128,477; Burma, 115,138; Brunei, 30,575; other Asian countries, 8,852; Brazil, 37,125; other American countries, 12,875; Nigeria, 257,000; Belgian Congo, 197,375; Liberia, 155,000; French Cameroons, 21,000; other African countries, 13,625; Papua, 26,197, and other Oceanian countries, 3,803. (Cf. *Rubber Statistical Bulletin,* April, 1958 [*International Rubber Study Group,* 1958].)

112. "The fifth of October, 1493, dawned no differently from any other day at the port of Gomera in the Canary islands. Importance attached itself to the fact that the Genoan admiral, Christopher Columbus, was in command of a fleet of three galleons and fourteen caravels which put into harbor for supplies that day. This undertaking was his second voyage to the Western Hemisphere, and among the fifteen hundred men in the expedition were included settlers for the new countries he had discovered. The squadron took on wood and water, and the crew hauled overside an unspecified number of sheep, goats, cattle, and calves, as well as eight hogs, with which to stock the new colonies. These were the first domestic animals to be trans-shipped from the old World to the New, and to establish themselves in the new environment.... Spanish records as to the actual numbers of livestock in each expedition to the New World are rare. Normally there was carried at the end of each shipping list the mere statement that sheep, cattle, swine, horses, or mares were included. Wherever livestock arrived, steps were taken immediately to facilitate breeding." (Edward N. Wentworth, *America's Sheep Trails: History, Personalities,* Ames, Iowa, 1948, p. 21-22)

113. Before modern times, most of the Indians already had dogs. The Indians of Mexico domesticated a local duck, stingless bees, and turkeys. Turkeys spread to the Indians of what is now the southwestern United States. The Indians of the Andean region in South America had a few more animals, notably the llama and alpaca. Llamas were used as pack animals and for meat, wool, and hides; alpacas were kept for their wool. This region also had a little guinea pig used for food and

Cattle, the most important of all livestock[114] brought into the New World[115] by the colonists, are now raised here as numerously as anywhere else.[116]

The pig[117] is also raised in the New World in numbers as great as anywhere else.[118]

---

also as a sacrifice to the gods. The only animal the aboriginal Australian domesticated was some kind of dog. (Cf. Frederick E. Zeuner, *A History of Domesticated Animals,* London, 1963, p. 436-439, 458-459; and John H. Parry, *The Age of Reconnaissance,* London, 1963, p. 283.)

114. Cattle are the most important of all livestock animals. They supply approximately 50% of the world's meat and 95% of the world's milk, and their hides are used to produce 80% of the leather used for shoes and other products. (Cf. *United Nations Statistical Yearbook,* 1974, p. 217, 123; and Food and Agriculture Organization of the United Nations, *The State of Food and Agriculture,* 1964, Rome, 1964, p. 182.)

115. Christopher Columbus brought cattle to America on his second voyage, in 1493; cattle of Spanish descent were brought from the West Indies to Veracruz, Mexico, in 1525; Portuguese traders brought cattle to Newfoundland and Nova Scotia, in 1553; and a sizeable shipment of British cattle reached Jamestown, Virginia, in 1611. Subsequent importation and breeding led to the establishment of herds of British breeds in all of Britain's North American colonies. (Cf. Wayne Gard, *The Chisholm Trail,* Norman, Oklahoma, 1959, p. 3-6; Alvin H. Sanders, *Short-Horn Cattle,* Chicago, 1918, p. 157-180.)

116. Numbers of cattle by continents in 1973:

Africa	147,082,000
Asia	347,768,000
USSR (European and Asian)	104,006,000
Europe	125,755,000
North America	182,001,000
Oceania	38,739,000
South America	199,107,000
World Total	1,148,458,000

(Cf. *United Nations Statistical Yearbook,* 1974, p. 112.)

117. Pigs are reported to have first been domesticated in China and Turkey nearly 7,000 years ago. It is believed that the domestication of the pig, unlike that of the dog, sheep, or goat, had to await the development of permanent settlements during the Neolithic period, for pigs are not adaptable to a nomadic life. Undoubtedly, pigs were domesticated from different stocks in different areas of the world, resulting in pigs with somewhat different regional characteristics. Present-day American pigs are thought to have originated from two wild stocks, the European wild boar and the East Indian pig, the latter not infrequently considered to be only a species of the former. The European wild boar, still hunted in some European forests, was also introduced to America, notably in Tennessee. A small domesticated pig called a "Guinea pig" is of South American origin, and is a rodent, not a real pig. The New World had no domesticated or wild pig in pre-Columbian times.

Although wild horses existed in America in prehistoric times, they became extinct very early.[119] Modern horses began to spread over the New World soon after they were brought here by European colonists.[120] Since then, there has been no country in the world which is without horses.[121]

The wild pig of today is not native to America. Domesticated pigs were taken to America by Columbus, De Soto, and others. Some of De Soto's pigs were left with Indian tribes, while others apparently escaped or wandered off into the surrounding wilds where they bred and thrived. The "razorback" hogs of the southeastern United States are believed to be the descendants of these animals. Undoubtedly, feral pigs in other parts of the United States and in other parts of the New World, such as Australia and New Zealand, had similar origins. (Cf. Frederick E. Zeuner, *A History of Domesticated Animals,* London, 1963, p. 257-271, 439; U.S. Department of Agriculture, *Farmer's Bulletin,* no. 2166, p. 1-3.)

118. The total number of pigs in the world during the late 1950s was approximately 453,700,000. China, with 150,000,000, was the leading producer, followed by the United States with 50,980,000; the USSR with 44,300,000; and Brazil with 44,190,000. (Cf. Food and Agriculture Organization of the United Nations, *Production Yearbook,* 1959, Rome, p. 169-172.) The yearly per capita consumption of pork in the early 1960s was, for example: Austria, 78 pounds; Denmark, 66 pounds; West Germany, 81 pounds; the United States, 67 pounds; and Yugoslavia, 25 pounds. (Cf. Organization for Economic Co-operation and Development. *Food Consumption Statistics,* 1955-1971, Paris, 1973, p. 7, 49, 91, 271, and 285.)

119. The earliest known association between man and horse in the Americas has been placed at about 12,000 years ago by archaeologists from the National University of San Marcos who recently discovered fossil remains of a small, powerful horse in the Peruvian Andes. During this period, the horse was probably a food animal. For reasons which are still unclear, the horse disappeared from the Americas before 6,000 B.C., possibly hunted to extinction. (Cf. Walker D. Wyman, *The Wild Horse of the West,* Lincoln, Nebraska, 1945, p. 18-22.)

120. The modern horse was introduced into the New World by the Spanish. A few sorry nags survived Columbus' second voyage and found good pasture in Hispaniola, in 1494. Augmented and improved, they and their descendants were transported to Cuba and Central America. Cortez brought 16 horses—all he could obtain—from Cuba to Mexico, in 1519. They were essential to his amazing conquest and "worth their weight in gold" in demoralizing the awe-stricken Indians. The conquest of Peru a few years later was similarly helped by the presence of a few horses. The Spanish missions of the 17th century again brought the Indians into contact with the horse. Lost, traded, and stolen animals soon found their ways into Indian hands. Lost horses also formed feral herds, which multiplied in the ideal environment of the South American pampas and North American plains, and by natural selection developed the very capable, enduring, and intelligent mustang. (Cf. Robert M. Denhardt, "Spanish Horses and the New World," in *The Historian of Phi Alpha Theta,* University of New Mexico, Vol. 1, no. 1, Winter, 1938; and Francis Haines, "Where Did the Plains Indians Get Their Horses," *American Anthropologist,* Vol. 40, no. 1 [Jan.-March, 1938] p. 112-117.)

Sheep have also spread over[122] the New World since they were brought in by European colonists. Before that time, only some native species could be found.[123]

Finally, it is interesting to note that prior to Columbus, the New World was even without the kind of chicken[124] which had been the most widely raised fowl in the Old World for several thousand years.[125]

The reader might note that there is a movie entitled *Conquista* which relates how the Indians got their first horse on a sunshiny morning in the year 1539.

121. The total number of horses in the world is estimated to be about 65,000,000. The leading countries in horses, in descending order, are the USSR, Brazil, China, the United States, Mexico, Argentina, Poland, and France. (Cf. *United Nations Statistical Yearbook,* 1974, p. 112-120.)

122. Sheep are widely distributed over the world, although they are kept mainly in temperate climates, most being found between the latitudes of 20° and 60° in both the Northern and Southern hemispheres. They are particularly adapted to desert and semiarid areas and to mountainous regions. The world's sheep population is roughly about a billion head. The principal sheep-raising countries in order of importance are: Australia, the Soviet Union, New Zealand, Argentina, India, South Africa, Turkey, the United States, Uruguay, the United Kingdom, Brazil, Iran, and Spain. (Cf. *United Nations Statistical Yearbook,* 1974, p. 112-120.)

123. Three species of sheep are natives of western North America, the big horn, the white sheep, and the black sheep. None of these has been domesticated or successfully hybridized with any domestic breed, nor were any of them found by early explorers under Indian domestication. They were hunted by the "Sheep Eater" Indians of the Rockies. (Cf. Edward N. Wentworth, *America's Sheep Trails: History, Personalities,* Ames, Iowa, 1948, p. 20; and *Special Report on the History and Present Condition of the Sheep Industry of the United States,* by the Bureau of Animal Industry, U.S. Department of Agriculture, Washington, 1892, p. 11-17.)

124. Modern explorers and colonists found no domestic fowls in the New World except the turkey and Muscovy duck. Recently, Carl O. Souler noticed that a chicken with black meat and blue eggs is of South American origin and had probably been domesticated by the aborigines for a long time, but was overlooked by modern explorers and colonists. American chickens of today, such as the Plymouth Rocks, Wyandottes, Rhode Island Reds, Buckeyes, Dominiques, and Javas, originated in England, western Europe, southeastern Asia and China, or are stocks resulting from crossbreeding. (Cf. Frederick E. Zeuner, *A History of Domesticated Animals,* London, 1963, p. 458-459; John H. Parry, *The Age of Reconnaissance,* London, 1963, p. 283; Carl O. Sauer, *Agricultural Origins and Dispersals,* Cambridge, Mass., 2d. ed. 1969, p. 57-60; and Frank L. Platt, *The American Breeds of Poultry,* Chicago, 1921, p. 4-5.)

125. Most available evidence points to Asia as the place of origin of the domestic chicken. The chicken was known to the ancient civilization of the Indus Valley and was probably fully domesticated by 2000 B.C. The chicken spread rapidly over the ancient world and appeared in Egypt in the 15th century B.C. The tomb of the pharaoh Tutankhamen (about 1350 B.C.) contained the painting of a readily recognizable rooster. Images of chickens on coins from northwestern India

The above examples represent a great number of domestic plants and animals[126] which have spread over the world in modern times. Their dispersal has made many contributions to the building of One World, such as greatly enriching our subsistence, distributing natural resources more widely, utilizing the land more effectively, and promoting assimilation in our tastes, habits, and interests in living and understanding in general, and in eating and clothing in particular.

e.
Uniformity and Standards

UNIVERSAL UNIFORMITY AND STANDARDS ARE OBviously essential for building One World. Success in their development has been achieved through various endeavors, beginning with the adoption of common symbols.[127]

---

and on Assyrian seals suggest that domesticated chickens spread from India to Iran sometime during the 1st millennium B.C., and subsequently to Greece. References to the cock or hen in Greek literature and images on coins and seals are common in the 4th and 5th centuries B.C. (Cf. Frederick E. Zeuner, *A History of Domesticated Animals,* London, 1963, p. 443-455; and Edward Brown, *Poultry, Breeding, and Production,* New York, 1929, Vol., p. 16-23.)

126. These include chile peppers, vanilla, tomatoes, manioc, cacao, new species of beans, peanuts, tobacco, pumpkins and squashes, and turkeys from the New World; and bananas, okra, oats, barley, alfalfa, olives, apples, grapes, citrus fruits, yams, the tung tree, and goats from the Old World. (Cf. Herbert G. Baker, *Plants and Civilization,* Belmont, Calif., 1965, p. 39-40, 44-45; Edward Brown, *Poultry, Breeding, and Production,* New York, 1929, Vol. 1, p. 12-16; John H. Parry, *The Age of Reconnaissance,* London, 1963, p. 282-289; and Carl O. Sauer, *Agricultural Origins and Dispersals,* Cambridge, Mass., 2d. ed., 1969, p. 147-167.)

127. "Men are the dominant sign-using animals. Animals other than man do, of course, respond to certain things as signs of something else, but such signs do not attain the complexity and elaboration which is found in human speech, writing, art, testing devices, medical diagnosis, and signaling instruments. Science and signs are inseparately interconnected, since science both presents men with more reliable signs and embodies its results in systems of signs. Human civilization is dependent upon signs and systems of signs, and the human mind is inseparable from the functioning of signs—if indeed mentality is not to be identified with such functioning." (Charles W. Morris, "Foundations of the Theory of Signs," in the *International Encyclopedia of Unified Science,* Vol. 1, no. 2, Chicago, 1938, p. 79)

The most important and widely adopted symbols are the Arabic numerals. They have a long history[128] and have distinguished themselves from many crude numerical systems[129] by their intrinsic merit.[130] They are now used and understood almost everywhere. Since everything in our daily lives, as well as in science and philoso-

---

128. The Arabic or Hindu-Arabic numerals may be traced to inscriptions of King Aśoka in India (3d century B.C.), but these numerals lacked the zero. The system with the zero was introduced into Baghdad sometime in the 9th century, or earlier, and reached Christian Europe prior to or during the 10th century. It was not until the 16th century that the system was completed with the invention of the decimal fraction, which made use of place value by indicating tenths and hundredths, as well as tens and hundreds. The most recent addition to the system is the use of an index notation for numbers that are exceedingly large or exceedingly small. Thus, the weight of the earth is stated to be 6.10^{21} tons, where the exponent 21 indicates that 6 is followed by 21 ciphers. This system is ideal for performing all the operations of arithmetic: addition, subtraction, multiplication, division, involution (powers), and evolution (roots), with accuracy and speed. The use of the zero to mark a missing classification revitalizes the system. It is not known who first had the great idea. Peter Barlow (1776-1862), in his *New Mathematical and Philosophical Dictionary,* 1814, says that the discovery of it "was perhaps one of the most important steps that has ever been made in mathematics, and does as much honour to the inventor as any other in the history of the science." (Cf. David E. Smith and Louis C. Karpinski, *The Hindu-Arabic Numerals,* Boston and London, 1911.)

129. "The number of systems of notation employed before the Christian era was about the same as the number of written languages, and in some cases a single language had several systems. The Egyptians, for example, had three systems of writing, with a numerical notation for each; the Greeks had two well-defined sets of numerals, and the roman symbols for number changed more or less from century to century." (David E. Smith and Louis C. Karpinski, *The Hindu-Arabic Numerals,* Boston and London, 1911, p. 1)

In written Chinese, there are also three sets of numerical notations, as follows:

For formal and serious use:	壹	貳	叁	肆	伍	陸	柒	捌	玖	拾	佰	仟	萬
For common use:	一	二	三	四	五	六	七	八	九	十	百	千	万
For accounting or marking use:	丨	丨丨	丨丨丨	Ⅹ	ᘯ	⊥	≟	≟	ㄨ	十	㇋	㇂	万
Arabic equivalent:	1	2	3	4	5	6	7	8	9	10	100	1000	10000

(For further Chinese numerical notations, Cf. Herbert A. Giles, *Chinese-English Dictionary,* London, 1892, appendix VI, B. "The Chinese Decimal System.")

130. It is easy to see the intrinsic merit of the Arabic numerals if we compare them with the Roman numerals now in use, which differ from many of their historic forms. The Roman numerical system has been generally regarded as one of

phy,[131] involves numerals, they have actually provided us with a basic uniformity, and have broken the ground for a world language.

Other important and widely adopted symbols are signals for transportation and communication. Their chief uses include road traffic control, maritime and aviation operations, and telecommunications. Such symbols have increased rapidly not only in importance, but in volume. In some fields, they have accumulated to many thousands.[132]

---

the best in history and was used through almost the whole of Europe for a long time. The present Roman numerals are based on the following:

Units	I II III IIII or IV V VI VII VIII VIIII or IX
Tens	X XX XXX XXXX or XL L LX LXX LXXX LXXXX or XC
Hundreds	C CC CCC CCCC or CD D DC DCC DCCC DCCCC or CM
Thousands	MMM MMM MMMM—(and so forth)

Thus, MCMLXXVIII = 1978. The simplicity of 1978 alone can win the contest.

131. In our modern daily lives, for example, identification cards, drivers licenses, telephone numbers, zip codes, times, temperatures, bills, checks, accounts, ... all exist in terms of numerals.

It is generally recognized that numerals are the foundation of mathematics and mathematics is the foundation of science. It is also generally recognized that science in its very early stages was a part of philosophy. Or, as a time-honored saying has it: "Philosophy is the mother of the sciences." Therefore, numerals are necessarily an important part not only of science, but also of philosophy. (Cf. Alfred N. Whitehead, "Mathematics as an Element in the History of Thought," quoted in *The World of Mathematics,* New York, 1956, Vol. 1, p. 402-416.) In Chinese philosophy, all begins with one (universe), one develops into two (such as male and female, hot and cold, hard and soft, light and dark, and good and evil), two develops into four, four into eight, and so on. (易：太極生兩儀，兩儀成四象，四象變八卦。)

132. Take maritime signals as an example: "The First International Code was drafted in 1855 by a Committee set up by the British Board of Trade. It contained 70,000 signals using eighteen flags and was published by the British Board of Trade in 1857 in two parts; the first containing universal and international signals and the second British signals only. The book was adopted by most seafaring nations." (Preface of the *International Code of Signals,* U.S. ed., 1969, published by the U.S. Naval Oceanographic Office, Washington)

The first International Code was revised and enlarged again and again. The 1931 edition, compiled by the International Radiotelegraph Conference in two volumes, with a total of 785 pages, looked like a big dictionary. The single volume of the latest edition, however, as adopted by the Fourth Assembly of the Inter-Governmental Maritime Consultative Organization in 1965, was greatly reduced by leaving out the vocabulary method and geographical section. (Cf. *Ibid.*)

133. The term "calendar" derives from the Latin word *Kalendae,* which designated the first day of the month in Roman times. The efforts of various civilizations to create calendars have marked the beginnings of their astronomical

The adjustment of time measurements is another important effort for uniformity and standards. The most comprehensive and complex time measurement is the calendar.[133] There were various calendars in history[134] and some antique calendars are still in use, but the Gregorian Calendar[135] has extended its influence over almost the whole world during the last centuries.[136] The Gregorian Calendar, however, is not absolutely correct and convenient. Many reforms

---

studies. Once a calendar is established and is used for a long time in recording events, it comes to be cherished by its users and is an integral part of their history. It is difficult, therefore, to revise a calendar system; even the best suggestions meet with strong resistance. The basic calendar units are the day, the month, and the year, derived from the movements of the earth, the moon and the sun, respectively. (Cf. Philip W. Wilson, *The Romance of the Calendar,* New York, 1937, p. 11-44; and L.S.F. Pinaud, *Perpetual Calendar,* Albany, N.Y., 1898, p. 5-16.)

134. Three basic kinds of calendars have been developed by man. These are the lunar, lunisolar, and solar calendars, based on the phases of the moon or the apparent motion of the sun. More than 10,000 years ago, a crude calendar consisting of 12 months of 30 days each, was developed in Egypt. The calendar year thus contained only 360 days. Around the year 4000 B.C., however, 5 supplementary days were added at the end of each year. The resulting 365-day year, or "vague year," fell behind the solar year 1 day every 4 years. There were a good number of other ancient calendars, including the famous Babylonian, Chinese, Greek and early Roman ones. All of them were lunar or lunisolar in principle. In 46 B.C., Julius Caesar decided to initiate a solar calendar with 365 days as a civil year, and to insert an extra day after February 24th every 4 years. (Cf. Philip W. Wilson, *The Romance of the Calendar,* New York, 1937, p. 45-113.)

135. The Gregorian Calendar was preceded by the Julian Calendar, which was adopted by the Roman Empire in 46 B.C. The Julian Calendar fixed the year with 365 days and six hours. It was 11 minutes and 14 seconds longer than the actual solar year. This was a very small error, but with constant repetition, century after century, the error accumulated, with the effect that the Spring Equinox was steadily moving back into the winter season. By the time Pope Gregory XIII approved the Gregorian reform of 1582, it had fallen back from March 21 to March 11. Ten days were dropped abruptly from the calendar, and the seasons were restored to their proper places. Leap year was corrected so that three leap days were omitted every 400 years. The beginning of the year was again officially set for January 1. (Cf. Elisabeth Achelis, *The World Calendar,* New York, 1937, p. 80-81.)

136. The year 1582 was the initial year of the Gregorian Calendar, which was at once adopted by the various countries which recognized the spiritual authority of Rome. France adopted the new calendar in December, 1582. Switzerland, the Catholic Netherlands, and the Catholic States of the Empire followed in 1583. The Protestant states for a considerable time refused to follow. In 1699, however, chiefly at the instigation of the philosopher Leibniz, the Protestant States of Germany came into line. In Great Britain, the new calendar was not adopted until 1752, and the countries which officially profess allegiance to the Greek or Eastern Church continued to employ the Julian Calendar up to the beginning of the twentieth century, and have only recently adopted the Gregorian. Some non-Christian

have been proposed[137] and the League of Nations once initiated a conference to study the problem.[138]

Accompanying the wide acceptance of the Gregorian Calendar have been the spread of the use of the Christian Era[139] and the seven-day week.[140] The Christian Era was unknown to the non-Christian

---

countries adopted it even earlier. (Cf. Alexander Philip, *The Calendar, Its History, Structure, and Improvement,* Cambridge, 1921, p. 22-23.)

137. The present Gregorian Calendar, despite its accuracy, still has several defects. For example, the number of days in a month varies about 12%. Business and industrial statistics, in order to be comparable from month to month, must therefore be constantly adjusted. Also, the day of the week on a given date changes from year to year. Conversely, the date of a given day, such as the third Tuesday of the month, varies according to the month and the year. A past date or day is difficult to determine without the calendar of the year in question. Many reforms have been proposed to remedy these defects, two of which still have many supporters: the fixed calendar and the universal or world calendar. In both reforms, the calendar year contains 52 weeks and only 364 days. The 365th day is blank and neither named nor counted. It would be a general holiday. Every 4 years a second blank day has to be added. According to the fixed calendar, the year consists of 13 equal months of 28 days. The months are identical, and each contains 4 weeks. In the universal calendar, the month is not an exact multiple of the week. There are 12 months and 4 identical quarterly periods of 13 weeks or 91 days. Each quarterly period includes one month of 31 days. (Cf. Philip W. Wilson, *The Romance of the Calendar,* New York, 1937, p. 247-273; and Elisabeth Achelis, *The Calendar for the Modern Age,* New York, 1959, p. 30-50.)

138. In 1923, the League of Nations began to give serious consideration to calendar reform, and in 1931 an International Conference on Calendar Reform took place in Geneva with representatives from 44 nations. No practical steps have yet been taken and further studies are still needed. We may say, however, that any reform on the calendar in the future will be in the direction of a complete time uniformity of the world achieved by setting up a more accurate and convenient time standard. (Cf. Special Committee of Enquiry into Reform of Calendar's Report, League of Nations' *Publications Series* VIII, No. 6, 1926; and Elisabeth Achelis, *The Calendar for Everybody,* New York, 1943, p. 59-68.)

139. The Christian era was proposed in 532 A.D. by a monk, Denys le petit, who died in Rome in 540. It did not come into general use in the West until 3 or 4 centuries later. The fixed point of this era is the birth of Christ, which from his research, Denys fixed at December 25 of the Roman year 753. Chronologists, however, have moved the beginning of the Christian era up to Saturday, January 1. Moreover, the church now places the birth of Christ several years before the date adopted by Denys, in accordance with texts relating to Herod's death. (Cf. Philip W. Wilson, *The Romance of the Calendar,* New York, 1937, p. 135-136.)

140. The seven-day week was adopted in pre-Christian times in western Asia, and among Egyptians and Hebrews, and was subsequently carried into Christian civilizations. The Biblical significance of this seven-day period originates in Genesis 2:1-3. In Genesis 29:27, the word "week" is first mentioned. The names of the days of the week originate from varied attempts by the ancient peoples to iden-

world until modern times. The seven-day week was also a Christian tradition, although it was carried down from pre-Christian times. These two systems now bear a universal character.[141]

Further divisions of time into hours, minutes and seconds with clocks[142] have also been universally accepted. These divisions,

---

tify the seven subdivisions of the week with the seven heavenly bodies which they saw recurrently in the sky and to each of which they assigned a deity. The Chaldeans were the first to utilize named weekdays in repeating order. Sunday was set as the first day of the week in 321 A.D. by Emperor Constantine, who also established the seven-day week in the Roman calendar and decreed its usage in the Christian world. The Latin names given to the days of the week were subsequently adapted through various Germanic languages until they assumed their present designations in English, as follows:

Sunday—assigned to the sun
Monday—assigned to the moon
Tuesday—assigned to Mars, the Roman god of war
Wednesday—assigned to Mercury, the Roman god of commerce
Thursday—assigned to Jupiter, the supreme Roman god
Friday—assigned to Venus, the Roman goddess of love and beauty
Saturday—assigned to Saturnus, the Roman god of agriculture

(Cf. Francis H. Colson, *The Week; An Essay on the Origin and Development of the Seven-day Cycle,* Cambridge, 1926.)

141. The Christian Era has been widely recognized as an International era, although other special eras continue to be employed in some countries. The seven-day week has also been widely adopted, in spite of the fact that four or five-day weeks are still used in some East African and Scandinavian areas. The renouncing of their Republic Era and the adoption of the Christian Era, together with the use of Gregorian Calendar and the seven-day week by the Chinese Communist regime, marked a significant development in the time uniformity of the world.

142. There is no record of the date and inventor of the first mechanical clock, which was more reliable than the sundial of Ancient Egypt, Greece, and Rome, the sandglass of medieval Europe, and the Chinese water leak (漏). Some writers have credited the Chinese with the development of a mechanical timepiece as early as 2000 B.C.; others give the honor to the Romans of the 10th century, or the Germans of the 11th century. It is certain that they came into use in Europe in the 13th century, a clock having been installed in a tower at Westminster in 1288. One placed in the tower of the palace of Charles of France in 1397 was constructed on the same principle as modern clocks. The earliest inventors of electric clocks were Alexander Bain in Scotland and Sir Charles Wheatstone in England, who worked independently, and in some rivalry, in 1840. The latest and most accurate clocks utilize the oscillations of atoms and molecules for regular motion. These extremely high-frequency oscillations are used to synchronize a lower-frequency quartz clock. Atomic clocks are accurate to one part in 10^{11} or 10^{12} This is equivalent to an error of only one second in 3,000 years or 30,000 years, respectively. (Cf. F.A.B. Ward, *Time Measurement:* part I, Historical Review, a Science Museum Handbook, 4th ed. rev. London, 1961.)

together with the week system, set a pattern of regularity and order for our daily lives.

Still another important effort is the development of the metric system[143] for weights and measures which unifies and standardizes the diverse systems in use in various countries.[144] This system was worked out by the French government before the end of the 18th century and was soon adopted by several neighboring countries.[145]

In 1875, an international metric convention was signed and an International Bureau of Weights and Measures established.[146] Since

---

143. "In Continental Europe, during the period of recorded history, the number of different units of weights and measures that have been used among the various peoples, run into hundreds, as regards names, and into thousands, as regards appreciably different values. In the metric system, there are only three fundamental units—the meter, gram, and liter—with optional prefixes (kilo-, centi-, milli-, etc.) for decimal multiples and submultiples. Indeed many consider that in view of the close connection between liter, gram, and meter, the system has virtually only one fundamental unit—the meter." (Introduction to the *Vestiges of Pre-Metric Weights and Measures,* by Arthur E. Kennelly, New York, 1928)

144. It is estimated that at the end of the eighteenth century when France undertook needed reforms, there still existed in Europe 391 different units of weight corresponding to the term pound, while the word "foot" applied to 282 different units of length. Similar diversity existed in the other continents in the same time. (Cf. *Encyclopedia of the Social Sciences,* New York, 1935, Vol. XV, p. 390.)

145. As early as 1670, Gabriel Mouton had suggested a decimal system of linear measures. It was said that James Watt had also designed and urged the adoption of a universal system of units of weights and measures, decimally divided, and so related that the establishment of any one of its parts would give the correct indication of all the rest. Nothing was accomplished, however, until 1799, when the French National Assembly formally adopted the metric system. Belgium and the Netherlands adopted this system in 1816; Greece in 1836; Spain in 1849, and Portugal in 1852. In 1872, it became compulsory throughout the German Empire. (Cf. *World Metric Standardization,* compiled by Aubrey Drury, published by World Metric Standardization Council, San Francisco, 1922, p. 39-40.)

146. An international conference on weights and measures met at Paris in 1870, and two years later, established a permanent scientific organization to redetermine and construct new prototype standards for the meter and kilogram, and to distribute accurate and authentic copies. The metric convention, which was signed at Paris in 1875, definitely established the metric system on an international basis and founded the International Bureau of Weights and Measures, where the International Prototype Meter and Kilogram, and the test copies of the same are preserved. The International Bureau is located at Sévres, a suburb of Paris, on a plot of ground dedicated by the government of France as international territory. (Cf. Norman F. Harriman, *Standards and Standardization,* New York, 1928, p. 187-189; also: "The Genesis of the Metric System and the Work of the International Bureau of Weights and Measures," trans. from the French by R.E. Oesper, in the *Journal of Chemical Education,* vol. 30, Jan. 1953, p. 3-20.)

early in this century, the Bureau has been empowered to supervise uniformity and standards, not only for length, mass, area, and volume, but also for electric units and the thermometer.[147] The metric system is now used by almost three-fourths of the world's peoples.[148]

As regards the thermometer, three major scales are currently in use: Kelvin, Celsius, and Fahrenheit,[149] which can be easily converted.[150] The Celsius has virtually become the International Temperature Scale.[151] The evolution of thermometers created little

---

147. The metric system, which came to be used universally for scientific research and experiment, made possible the foundation of an international system of units and standards for all electrical measurements. So, in 1921, through amendments to the metric convention, the functions of the International Bureau of Weights and Measures were extended to the supervision of certain electric units and standards. Through the same amendments, the Bureau also has the power to supervise thermometric standards. (Cf. Norman F. Harriman, *Standards and Standardization,* New York, 1928, p. 50-51, 189.)

148. It was estimated in 1921 that in 40 important nations the metric system was the only legal standard of measures and weights; almost three fourths of the world's people were using the metric units. It is true that the rapid spread of the metric system has long since encountered opposition in English-speaking countries. But, in the United States, this system was recognized by law in 1866 and has been exclusively used in science, medicine, the army and navy, and many other fields. Within the British Commonwealth, Australia, New Zealand, the Union of South Africa, India, and Canada have officially urged metric standardization. (Cf. Aubrey Drury, *World Metric Standardization,* San Francisco, 1922, Frontispiece pages; also p. 32-37.)

149. (1) The Kelvin, or absolute, scale ($^\circ$K), with absolute zero as the bottom limit, and 273.15°K and 373.16°K, respectively, as the freezing and boiling points of water, is used for scientific purposes, especially for low temperature physics. (2) The Celsius, or centigrade, scale ($^\circ$C), with O$^\circ$C and 100°C, respectively, the freezing and boiling points of water, has been adopted throughout most of the world for common usages. (3) The Fahrenheit scale ($^\circ$F), with 32°F and 212°F, respectively, the freezing and boiling points of water, is used in English-speaking countries. (Cf. Robert L. Weber, *Heat and Temperature Measurement,* New York, 1950, p. 4-7.)

150. Since a degree Celsius is of the same magnitude as a degree Kelvin, the only difference between them is in their choice of zero, and it is necessary merely to subtract 273.15 units from $^\circ$K to convert to $^\circ$C. Conversely, one adds 273.15 units to $^\circ$C to convert to $^\circ$K. A degree Fahrenheit is not equal to a degree Celsius, and in conversion between the two scales, the following formulas must be used: $^\circ$F = $\frac{9}{5}$ $^\circ$C + 32 and $^\circ$C = $\frac{5}{9}$ ($^\circ$F − 32). (Cf. Robert L. Weber, *Heat and Temperature Measurement,* New York, 1950, p. 5-6.)

151. The first International Temperature Scale was adopted by the Seventh General Conference on Weights and Measures, in 1927, and is now known as the International Temperature Scale of 1927. This scale agreed with the ther-

local interest,[152] but was a great contribution to the measurement of temperature, which concerns everything and everywhere.

The movement towards uniformity and standards of payment began in Germany, spread to the Scandinavian countries, and was promoted by the Latin Monetary Union.[153] The important gold standard[154] was first used by Britain and eventually prevailed throughout most of the world before World War I. Fluctuation of the gold stan-

---

modynamic centigrade scale (Celsius) as closely as possible according to the knowledge then available. In 1948, the Ninth General Conference met and approved some technical changes and supplements for the International Temperature scale. (Cf. Robert L. Weber, *Heat and Temperature Measurement,* New York, 1950, p. 262-264.)

152. It is interesting to note that in the beginning, "no nation makes popular use of the thermometer designed by its own citizen. The instrument constructed by the German Fahrenheit in the Netherlands is used almost exclusively in English-speaking lands; that invented by the Frenchman Réaumer finds no credit in France, but is popular in Germany; and that of Celsius, the Swede, modified by Christin, of Lyons, is used chiefly in France, Belgium, and Switzerland." (Henry C. Bolton, *Evolution of the Thermometer,* Easton, Pa., 1900, p. 86-87)

153. The movement was first reflected in the German Monetary Convention of 1838, which fixed a ratio between the standard silver coins of the northern and southern German states. The Scandinavian Monetary Conventions of 1873 and 1875 established a common gold standard in Denmark, Sweden and Norway. More significant was the so-called Latin Monetary Union of 1865 by which France, Italy, Belgium, and Switzerland, under the lead of France, agreed on the joint institution of a bimetallistic system of gold and silver coins having identical weight, fineness, and diameter. To promote this program, the French government in 1867 convoked an international Monetary Conference. Greece joined the Union in 1868 while Spain, Serbia, Bulgaria, Rumania, Finland, and some Latin American countries adopted the type of coins specified by the Union without submitting to the other arrangements. The fact that the members of the Union were outnumbered by countries independently converting to the coin types of the Union is indicative of the general phenomenon that in monetary matters, standards may be imposed without binding international agreements. (Cf. Arthur Nussbaum, "International Monetary Agreements," *American Journal of International Law,* vol. 38, 1944, p. 242-257.)

154. In 1821, Britain became the first country to use gold as the standard. Other countries gradually turned to the gold standard beginning in the 1870s, but only during the years from the mid-1890s to 1914 did it prevail through most of the world. What may be regarded as the gold standard in its "classic" or "full" form was defined by Edwin W. Kemmerer in his *Gold and the Gold Standard,* New York, 1944, p. 134, 138 in the following terms: "This standard may be briefly defined as a monetary system where the unit of value in terms of which prices, wages, and debts are customarily expressed and paid, consists of the value of a fixed quantity of gold in a large international market which is substantially free ... the supreme test of the existence of the gold standard is the answer to the question whether or not the money of the country is actually kept at a parity with the value

dard in the 1930s and again in the last decade[155] indicates that a new monetary standard for the whole world is urgently needed.

Closely related to uniformity and standards of payment are the international uniform laws for bills of exchange and for checks. These laws have been in effect since they were worked out in the early 1930s.[156]

In connection with uniformity and standards, mass production as a salient feature of industrialization deserves special mention, because uniformity and standards are a prerequisite for mass production, and mass production is a great force of uniformity and standards in modern life.[157]

---

of the gold monetary unit comprising it, in the outside free international gold market, assuming, of course, that such a market of reasonable size actually exists." In its broader connotations, the term is often used, particularly in recent years, to refer to situations in which somewhat different arrangements govern the relation of the unit of value to gold. Although wide variations have occurred in practice, the central features of the recent variants of the gold standard are that the monetary unit is defined in terms of gold, and that gold or its equivalent is used to settle international balances. (Cf. George N. Halm, *The International Monetary Fund and Flexibility of Exchange Rates,* Princeton, N.J., 1971, p. 3-20.)

155. The direct reasons for the fluctuations of the gold standard are that in the 1930s country after country abrogated or suspended the central bank's obligation to meet its note and deposit liabilities in gold, and in the years prior to 1971, too many dollars were chasing too little gold. The latter situation prompted the U.S. government on August 15, 1971, to suspend what remained of the U.S. commitment made in 1934 to convert dollars into gold at the request of foreign monetary authorities. In the wake of this measure, the world monetary gold stock was expected to become frozen at about $40 billion: the U.S. held about 25% as compared with 71% in September, 1949; West Germany, 10%; France 9%; Italy and Switzerland, 6% each. The British stock was historically low, and Japan began to rebuild its gold reserve in the 1970s. (Cf. *Federal Reserve Bulletin,* Vol. 35, no. 11, Nov. 1949, p. 1414, Vol. 57, no. 8, Aug. 1971, Statistics, A 94.)

156. In 1910, 35 states met at The Hague to study such questions as bills of exchange, and continued the work at the Second Conference, in 1912, which agreed upon regulation, a treaty, and a bureau. The first World War broke up this program, which was renewed in 1923 under the aegis of the League of Nations, becoming part of the vast economic activity of the League. Success was finally attained in the two Geneva conventions of 1930 and 1931, which provided a Uniform Law of Bills of Exchange and a Uniform Law of Checks. (Cf. *League of Nations Treaty Series,* Vol. 143, 1934, p. 317, 332, 409 and 424.)

157. Mass production is impossible in any industry without uniform and standard quantity and quality in raw materials and products; and not only in producing procedures, but in transportation and even in distribution, mass production requires a certain uniform and standard process. As a result, uniformity and standards have been the significant characteristics of mass production. As mass production has dominated most of the important industries and has extended its

f.
Social
Progress

IN SOCIAL SYSTEMS, NO UNIFORMITY OR STANDARD has been reached in modern times. However, a significant progress has been made in some areas, and this progress is nevertheless important to the building of one world.

First instance of this progress is the rise of democracy, primarily as a political system.[158] Democracy was rooted in Greek practice of two thousand years ago.[159] In modern times, it was initiated by the theory of the Social Contract[160] and inspired by the revolutions of the

---

control over the international market, it is natural that uniformity and standards are qualities which have gradually infiltrated the life of people everywhere. The development of mass production has, consequently, been one of the main forces contributing to uniformity and standards in life of the modern world. (Cf. *Industrial Standardization,* published by the U.S. National Industrial Conference Board, New York, 1929, p. 7-11.)

158. The conception of democracy has been extended from politics to economics (Cf. "Economic democracy," as popularized by Marxism, and *Industrial Democracy,* as written by Sidney and Beatrice Webb, 1897, London. Cf. also Hugh A. Clegg, *A New Approach to Industrial Democracy,* Oxford, 1960; and Anthony Downs, *An Economic Theory of Democracy,* 1957, New York) to a way of life (including "social democracy," "ethical democracy," etc. Cf. Alexis de Tocqueville, *Democracy in America,* French original published 1835-1840, trans. by Henry Reeve, New York, 1965; Thomas V. Smith, *Democratic Way of Life,* Chicago, 1926). However, all the extensions are derived from or based on the political system.

159. The city-states of ancient Greece functioned with democratic systems soon after 1000 B.C. (Cf. Tarrot R. Glover, *Democracy in the Ancient World,* Cambridge, Eng., 1927, p. 1-73; and the *New Encyclopedia of Social Reform,* New York, 1908, p. 371) At about the same time, another kind of democratic conception was developing in ancient China. (Cf. Chi-Chao Liang, *History of Pre Chin Political Thoughts,* in Chinese, 6th ed., Taipei, 1972, p. 29-36; and Chung-Shu Lo, "Human Rights in the Chinese Tradition," in *Human Rights, Comments and Interpretations,* A Symposium edited by UNESCO, New York, 1949, p. 186-187.)

160. The Social Contract is an original agreement by which a society, state, or government is constituted. It is a hypothesis shared by many philosophers, most notably Thomas Hobbes, John Locke, and Jean-Jacques Rousseau. Hobbes in his famous work, *Leviathan* (1651, Chapter 14), held that the original state of man was that of a solitary being existing in a constant state of warfare and anarchy, and governed by self-interest. In order to secure order, men entered into an agreement

18th century.[161] Since then, it has developed from a term of abuse to a notion of honor.[162] It was the main object of the great wars[163] and its face value is today almost universally accepted.[164]

---

with one another that resulted in the creation of the state. In return for absolute obedience and the surrender of all individual rights, the state provided security, order, and peace. In his *Second Treatise on Civil Government* (1690, Chapter 8), Locke held that the original state of man was neither anarchic nor totally selfish. The state was created by the people as a matter of convenience to protect the rights of the individual and his property. If the state failed to protect these rights or usurped them, the people no longer owed it allegiance and could arrange a new government. Rousseau's work was entitled *Du Contrat social* (1762. Cf. Book one.). For him, the original state of man was unwarlike, and man was naturally good. Laws and moral sense developed concomitantly with the founding of society. Through them, Rousseau believed that greater freedom was achieved for the individual. The authority of government is derived from the people as a whole and is a reflection of the general will, which always seeks the common good. While there are differences between the ideas of Hobbes, Locke and Rousseau in respect to the reason for establishing the state or government, and the way the state or government is to operate, their basic conception is the same: the state or government is created by the people for their own good. This conception is the foundation of modern democracy. However, as Robert R. Palmer pointed out in his *The Age of the Democratic Revolution,* Princeton, N.J., 1959-1964, Vol. 1, p. 119, "If one were to name the one book in which the revolutionary aspirations of the period from 1760 to 1800 were most compactly embodied, it would be the *Social Contract* of Jean-Jacques Rousseau." (Cf. p. 119-127 of Palmer's book.)

161. Most important are the American Revolution and French Revolution. The American Revolution began near Boston, Massachusetts, in 1775, and formally ended in 1783 with a peace treaty signed in Paris. Though the French Revolution is traditionally dated from 1789 to 1799, it opened in 1787 and ended much later. The American Revolution set an example for the French Revolution, and the French Revolution profoundly affected all of Europe. It also left marks on the Middle East, India, North and South America, and other parts of the globe explored, colonized, and exploited by Europeans. (Cf. Robert R. Palmer, *The Age of the Democratic Revolution,* 2 vols., Princeton, N.J., 1959-1964, especially Vol. I, p. 3-24.)

162. Almost sixty years after the American Revolution, democracy was still something "We have to fear or to hope from its progress," as Alexis de Tocqueville confessed in the preface to his famous book, *Democracy in America.* (French original published 1835-1840, trans. by Henry Reeve, New York, 1965, p. XLVII) Today, even dictators, absolute rulers and hereditary monarchs use the democratic idiom to characterize their regimes and their aspirations. "Probably for the first time in history, 'democracy' is claimed as the proper ideal description of all systems of political and social organization advocated by influential proponents." (*Democracy in a World of Tensions,* A Symposium prepared by UNESCO, ed. by Richard McKeon, Chicago, 1951, p. 527)

163. "It has been the common watchword in two world wars. The victory of November, 1918 was said to be the victory of democracy. The common aim of the Allied Powers in World War II, as formulated by Roosevelt, Stalin, and Churchill at

Democracy, however, has been ambiguous[165] in meaning from the beginning[166] and the more it has become popular, the more it has undergone verbal stretching[167] with various interpretations and continuous controversies.[168]

Outstanding among these interpretations and controversies are

---

the Teheran Conference in December, 1943, was the establishment of 'a world family of democratic nations.' The declarations of Yalta in February and of Potsdam in August, 1945, both stressed the same principle: the Great Powers announced their intention of 'meeting the political and economic problems of liberated Europe in accordance with democratic principles;' they made these principles the basis of their joint policy in Germany." (*Democracy in a World of Tensions,* A Symposium prepared by UNESCO, ed. by Richard McKeon, Chicago, 1951, p. 513)

164. "For the first time in the history of the world, no doctrines are advanced as anti-democratic. The accusation of anti-democratic action or attitude is frequently directed against others, but practical politicians and political theorists agree in stressing the democratic element in the institutions they defend and the theories they advocate." (*Democracy in a World of Tensions,* A Symposium prepared by UNESCO, ed. by Richard McKeon, Chicago, 1951, p. 522) It ought to be noted, however, that there have been arguments against democratic systems by honest thinkers since Plato. In modern times, the most sophisticated expressions of this position may be found in such writings as Gaelano Mosca's *The Ruling Class,* New York, 1939; Vilfredo Pareto's *The Mind and Society,* 4 vols., Florence, 1916; and Roberto Michels' *Political Parties,* Glencoe, Ill., 1949.

165. "In the first place, the idea of democracy was considered ambiguous and even those who thought that it was clear or capable of clarity were obliged to admit a certain ambiguity either in the institutions or devices employed to effect the idea or in the cultural or historical circumstances by which word, idea, and practice are conditioned." (*Democracy in a World of Tensions,* A Symposium prepared by UNESCO, ed. by Richard McKeon, Chicago, 1951, p. 527)

166. The word "democracy" is derived from Greek. "Demo" means "people" and "cracy" means "to rule." But, in practice, the Greek demos who had the right to rule were male citizens or freemen. Women and the great class of slaves of the time had no voice in the government. (Cf. Giovanni Sartori, "Democracy," in the *International Encyclopedia of the Social Sciences,* New York, 1968, Vol. 4, p. 115; and the *New Encyclopedia of Social Reform,* New York, 1908, p. 370.)

167. One result has been a proliferation in the brands of "democracy." There are "organic" democracies, as claimed in Spain under General Francisco Franco; "guided," "tutelary," "people's," "progressive," "socialist," and "new" democracies, as claimed in the Communist countries and elsewhere. Democracy has also been modified by such words as "traditional," "classic," "formal," "real," "Western," "Eastern," etc.

168. Most of the interpretations and controversies are involved with abuses of the word "democracy" and "the criteria of abuses of the word were, for the most part, moral in character, such as the intention to deceive or the probability that a given meaning would in given circumstances deceive." (*Democracy in a World of Tensions,* A Symposium prepared by UNESCO, ed. by Richard McKeon, Chicago, 1951, p. 527. Cf. the "Analytical Survey" in the book, p. 447-512.)

the simplest definition: "Government of the people, by the people and for the people," formulated by Lincoln,[169] and the sharpest conflict between Liberals and Communists.[170] Yet, the real difference between Liberals and Communists lies only in the fact that Liberals emphasize "by the people" while Communists emphasize "for the people."[171] Actually, Liberals have had to care "for the people" just as Communists have had to demonstrate "by the people." As regards the proposition "of the people," both Liberals and Communists have had to hold it as a principle.[172]

Hence, in spite of the different practices and opinions on its con-

---

169. This definition appears in Abraham Lincoln's famous Gettysburg address of November 19, 1863. The preposition "of" indicates that the supreme authority is vested in the people, and the power of the government is derived from that authority. In other words, the ultimate power in political affairs rightly belongs to the people. The preposition "by" indicates the active participation of the people in the formation of decisions through the government; and the preposition "for" indicates the value of these decisions for the general welfare of the people.

170. In his classical work on *Modern Democracies,* for instance, the late Lord James Bryce stated his position in the following way: "...Democracy—which is merely a form of government, not a consideration of the purposes to which government may be turned—has nothing to do with economic equality, which might exist under any form of government, and might possibly work more smoothly under some other form, ... Political equality can exist either along with or apart from equality in property." (*Modern Democracies,* London, 1929, Vol. 1, p. 76) Joseph Stalin, on the other hand, argued in his speech on the Draft Constitution of U.S.S.R. in 1936: "They talk of democracy. But what is democracy? Democracy in capitalist countries, where there are antagonistic classes, is, in the last analysis, democracy for the strong, democracy for the propertied minority. In the U.S.S.R., on the contrary, democracy is democracy for the working people, i.e., democracy for all." (*Leninism,* London, 1946, p. 579)

171. It is a widespread opinion that the opposition between the Liberal and Communist conceptions of democracy is largely due to a difference in emphasis on these two prepositions. The British philosopher Bertrand Russell, for example, thinks that the contrast boils down to this: "The Anglo-Saxon definition of 'democracy' is that it consists in the rule of the majority; the Russian view is that it consists in the interests of the majority, these interests being determined in accordance with Marxist political philosophy." (*What is Democracy?* London, 1946, p. 14)

172. "Of the people" is the traditional claim of the Liberals, and the growing amount of social legislation and reforms in the liberal democratic countries in modern times shows that they do care "for the people." On the other hand, the Communists have in recent decades gone so far as to identify their democracies and governments as the "people's," the People's Republic of China, for instance, and its People's government at all levels in the early stages of the Communist regime—in order to show that they are really interested in the principles of "by the people" and "of the people."

ditions, scope, degree, form, value, means and end,[173] Lincoln's three principles provide a common ground for a fundamental agreement on democracy[174] which is shedding light over the world.

Another significant example of social progress is the promotion of Human Rights.

The main assumption underlying the principles of democracy is that people are important and should be duly respected and protected. But how much are they actually respected and how far are they protected? A yardstick of measurement is human rights.

The term "human rights" is of recent origin,[175] but is deeply rooted in natural law.[176]

---

173. (Cf. Appendices I and II of *Democracy in a World of Tensions,* A Symposium prepared by UNESCO, ed. by Richard McKeon, Chicago, 1951.)

174. "For the agreement signifies at least ... that governments must secure or profess to have secured some sign of the approval of the people and some indication that they are governments of the people. In the degree that such minimum agreements are also indications of a shared conviction, that rule by the people is the means—and the good of the people the end." (Richard McKeon in his Foreword to *Democracy in a World of Tensions,* A Symposium prepared by UNESCO, ed. by Richard McKeon, Chicago, 1951, p. ix)

In a way and to a considerable extent, that agreement was reached in the Universal Declaration of Human Rights, approved almost unanimously by the United Nations on December 20, 1948, particularly in Articles 21 and 25 of the Declaration. Article 21 reads: "(1) Everyone has the right to take part in the government of his country, directly or through freely chosen representatives. (2) Everyone has the right of equal access to public service in his country. (3) The will of the people shall be the basis of the authority of government; this will shall be expressed in periodic and genuine elections which shall be by universal and equal suffrage and shall be held by secret vote or by equivalent free voting procedures." This article is obviously based on the principles of by the people and of the people. Article 25 reads: "(1) Everyone has the right to a standard of living adequate for the health and well-being of himself and of his family, including food, clothing, housing and medical care and necessary social services, and the right to security in the event of unemployment, sickness, disability, widowhood, old age or other lack of livelihood in circumstances beyond his control. (2) Motherhood and childhood are entitled to special care and assistance. All children, whether born in or out of wedlock, shall enjoy the same social protection." This article is obviously based on the principle of for the people.

175. It seems that the term first appeared in the French-inspired "rights of man" (droits de l'homme) contained in the Declaration of the Rights of Man and of the Citizen, issued in 1789 by the National Assembly of France at the outset of the French Revolution. (Cf. E.H. Carr, "The Rights of Man" in the *Human Rights, Comments and Interpretation,* A Symposium edited by UNESCO, Chicago, 1949, p. 19-23.)

176. "The concept of natural law has been so much abused, so much pulled about, distorted, or hypertrophied that it is hardly surprising if, in our age, many

The overall principle of human rights is that men are equal and free, as declared by the American and French Revolutions.[177] Since that period, the struggle for human rights has gained more and more momentum. Significant achievements include the suppression of the slave trade[178] and the abolition of slavery[179] which had existed for

---

minds declare themselves weary of the whole idea. Yet they must admit that since Hippias and Alcidamas, the history of human rights and the history of the natural law are one, and that the discredit into which positivism for a period brought the concept of natural law inevitably involved similar discredit for the concept of human rights." (Jacques Maritain, "On the Philosophy of Human Rights," in *Human Rights: Comments and Interpretations,* A Symposium edited by UNESCO, New York, 1949, p. 75. Cf. the whole article.) What is natural law? As early as two thousand years ago, Marcus Tullius Cicero (106-43 B.C.) called it "the supreme law, which was born in all the ages before any law had been written or any state had been established." (*De Legibus,* I.6.19) He claimed that "True law is right reason in agreement with nature; it is universal, unchanging, everlasting; it summons to duty by its commands; it averts from injury by its prohibitions." (*De Republica,* III.22.33)

177. "All men are created equal" is strongly expressed in the Declaration of Independence of the thirteen United States of America, July 4, 1776; and "Men are free and equal in respect of their rights" is strongly expressed in the Declaration of the Rights of Men adopted by the French National Assembly in 1789. The two elements of "free" and "equal" are reemphasized in Article I of the Universal Declaration of Human Rights, made by the United Nations on December 10, 1948: "All human beings are born free and equal in dignity and rights."

178. In 1772, Lord Mansfield, the English Chief Justice, declared that slavery was illegal in England. Antislavery societies were founded in England in 1787, and in France in 1788, and in 1808, the slave trade was forbidden aboard English and American ships. By 1820, all the chief countries of Europe had prohibited the trade, and in 1842, a joint blockade of the African coast was agreed upon between the United States and Great Britain. (Cf. John K. Ingram, *A History of Slavery and Serfdom,* London, 1895, p. 154-173; and Basil Davidson. *Black Mother, The Years of the African Slave Trade,* Boston, 1961, p. 3-75.)

179. The British abolished legal slavery in the West Indies in 1833, set up an apprenticeship system for the slaves, and paid the slaveholders 20 million pounds in compensation. That system proved unmanageable, and in 1838, the slaves in the West Indies and South Africa got their freedom. Those in British India were freed in 1843. The French abolished slavery as part of the reforms of the Revolution of 1848, and the Danes abolished slavery the same year. By the late 1850s, all the mainland Spanish American republics had abolished slavery, and it had virtually disappeared in Mexico, Central America, and Chile. The Dutch emancipated their slaves in 1863, while the Spanish set free those in Puerto Rico in 1873, and those in Cuba in 1886. Brazil was the last American state to abolish slavery, in 1888. (Cf. John K. Ingram, *A History of Slavery and Serfdom,* London, 1895, p. 174-213.)

Originally, the Constitution of the United States of America recognized slavery. The Emancipation Proclamation of 1863 declared all slaves within areas of rebellion free, but only ratification of the 13th Amendment in 1865 made

some thousand years,[180] and the unprecedented adoption of women's suffrage.[181]

---

slavery unconstitutional. The 14th Amendment, ratified three years later, was designed primarily to guarantee the rights of freed slaves. It provides that no state shall "deprive any person of life, liberty, or property, without due process of law; nor deny to any person within its jurisdiction the equal protection of the laws." The 15th Amendment, ratified in 1870, was passed to protect the right of Negroes to vote. (Cf. Alan P. Grimes, *Equality in America, Religion, Race and the Urban Majority,* New York, 1964, p. 55-57.)

180. Archaeological study indicates that slavery existed before 2000 B.C. among the Sumerians of Mesopotamia, a people who later formed the cultural core of the Babylonian empire. Perhaps the oldest formal slave laws date from this period. According to the Code of Hammurabi, King of Babylon around the 18th century B.C., Babylonian slaves had certain legal rights that they may have enjoyed by custom before that period. Slavery also existed in Israel. By the closing years of the classical Greek period, slavery was taken for granted, and the slave trade from the Black Sea region had assumed such economic importance that Polybius, a Greek historian of the 2nd century B.C., claimed that, along with cattle, slaves were "the necessities of life." It is remarkable that most of the Greek slaves were of foreign origin. The Romans expanded slavery with the territorial growth of their Empire. Warfare produced the most slaves. Caesar's western campaigns, for instance, sent back about 500,000 slaves from Gaul between 58 and 50 B.C., and Rome gained large numbers of slaves from Syria, Greece, and Egypt. Muslim slavery derived its sanction from the injunction of the Koran to the faithful to convert the heathen by persuasion, if possible, but by force if necessary. In pre-Columbian times, certain forms of slavery existed among the Mayans, Aztecs and Incas, with warfare providing the best source of slaves. Slavery was introduced into the colonies during the period of colonial expansion and was almost entirely applied to non-European peoples, chiefly Negro. Negro slavery was introduced into Spanish America in the 16th century, then spread into the Portuguese, English and French colonies. (Cf. John K. Ingram, *A History of Slavery and Serfdom,* London, 1895, p. 1-70, 140-153, 214-274; A.H.M. Jones, "Slavery in the Ancient World," *The Economic History Review,* 2nd ser. 7, 1956, p. 185-199; C.W.W. Greenidge, *Slavery,* London, 1958, p. 15-26.)

181. In Britain, the struggle for women's suffrage began as early as the 15th century, but it was not until the Representation of People Act was completed in 1918, that women at the age of 30 got the right to vote in national elections. In 1928, the age was reduced to 21, putting women on an equal basis with men. In the United States, the struggle started in colonial times and succeeded with the ratification of the 19th Amendment, in 1920, which proclaimed that the right of citizens to vote shall not be denied or abridged on account of sex. Although the women's suffrage movement originated in Britain and the United States, the first country to grant women full suffrage was New Zealand (1893), followed by Australia in 1902, Finland in 1906, Norway in 1913, Denmark in 1915, the Netherlands in 1917, Canada and Luxembourg in 1918, Sweden, Germany, Austria, Czechoslovakia in 1919, Hungary in 1920, and Spain in 1931. Following the Russian Revolution of 1917, women were granted equal rights with men in the Soviet Republics. In Latin America, Uruguay and Brazil adopted universal suffrage in 1932, and Cuba in

After World War I, wide concern for human rights found expression in the Covenant of the League of Nations.[182] The experience of World War II resulted in a deep conviction that effective protection of human rights was an essential condition for peace and progress, and that conviction found expression in a number of statements made while the war was still being fought.[183] The United Nations Charter refers to human rights in its Preamble and in six different articles.[184]

1934. In 1932, Thailand became the first Asian country to establish Universal suffrage, followed by Turkey and Ceylon in 1934, Burma in 1935, and the Philippines in 1937. Soon after World War II, most of the remaining countries of the world granted women full rights to vote. (Cf. Ross E. Paulson, *Women's Suffrage and Prohibition: A Comparative Study of Equality and Social Control,* Glenview, Ill., 1973, p. 85-101; United Nations, *The Road to Equality, Political Rights of Women,* New York, 1953, p. 4-20; United Nations, *Convention on the Political Rights of Women, History and Commentary,* New York, 1955, p. 1-15, 39-46.)

182. The Covenant of the League of Nations demanded that members of the League accept the obligation to endeavor to secure and to maintain fair and humane conditions of labor for men, women and children and also to secure the just treatment of the indigenous inhabitants of their colonies. Under the Mandates System, established by the Covenant, certain powers accepted as a sacred trust responsibility for the well-being and development of the peoples were placed under their Mandate.

183. For example, in the Atlantic Charter of August 14, 1941, which was later subscribed to and endorsed by 47 nations, the President of the United States and the Prime Minister of the United Kingdom expressed their hope "to see established a peace which will afford to all nations the means of dwelling in safety within their own boundaries, and which will afford assurance that all the men in all the lands may live out their lives in freedom from fear and want." In the Declaration of the United Nations, signed on January 1, 1942, by 26 nations then at war, and subsequently adhered to by 21 other nations, the signatory governments expressed the conviction "that complete victory over their enemies is essential to defend life, liberty, independence and religious freedom, and to preserve human rights and justice in their own lands as well as in other lands."

184. In the Preamble, the peoples of the United Nations express their determination "to reaffirm faith in fundamental human rights, in the dignity and worth of the human person, in the equal rights of men and women and of nations large and small." The words "promoting and encouraging respect for human rights" and "assisting in the realization of human rights and fundamental freedoms" appear, with certain variations, in Article 1, on the purposes and principles of the United Nations; in Article 13, on the General Assembly; in Article 62, on the Economic and Social Council; and in Article 76, on the International Trusteeship System. In Article 56, read together with Article 55: "all Members pledge themselves to take joint and separate action in co-operation with the Organization for the achievement" of a number of purposes which "the United Nations shall promote," among them "universal respect for, and observance of human rights

At the San Francisco Conference, which drafted the United Nations Charter, a proposal to embody an international bill of rights in the Charter was put forward. The bill was to consist of a declaration, followed by the necessary conventions and measures of implementation. The declaration was promulgated in 1948 as the Universal Declaration of Human Rights,[185] and in 1966, two covenants and an optional protocol were approved to transform the Declaration into conventional law.[186] In addition, a good number of special[187] and regional[188] conventions have been adapted to implement the Declaration.

---

and fundamental freedoms for all without distinction as to race, sex, language or religion.''

185. The Universal Declaration of Human Rights was adopted on December 10, 1948, in the form of a resolution of the General Assembly. Of the 58 states which were then United Nations members, 48 voted their approval, none voted against, eight abstained, and two were absent. The Declaration differs from traditional outlines of human rights contained in the various constitutional and fundamental laws of the 18th, 19th, and beginning of the 20th century, dealing as it does not only with civil and political, but also with economic, social and cultural rights. It contains a Preamble and 30 Articles, with Article 1 as an overall principle, Articles 2 to 21 concerned with civil and political rights, Articles 22 to 29 devoted to economic, social and cultural rights, and Article 30 providing a general and important protection against "any act aimed at the destruction of any of the rights and freedoms set forth herein.''

186. After the Universal Declaration of Human Rights was completed, in 1948, the Commission on Human Rights concentrated on the draft international covenants. In 1954, it finished the preliminary texts of a draft covenant on civil and political rights and a draft covenant on economic, social and cultural rights. These were sent through the Economic and Social Council to the General Assembly and were considered, article by article, at each Assembly Session from 1955 to 1966, primarily by the Assembly's Third Committee. The two Covenants, and the Optional Protocol to the Covenant on Civil and Political Rights, were adopted by the Assembly on December 16, 1966: the Covenant on Economic, Social and Cultural Rights by 105 votes to none; the Covenant on Civil and Political Rights, by 106 votes to none; and the Optional Protocol by 66 votes to 2, with 38 abstentions.

187. The special conventions include the ILO Right to Organise and Collective Bargaining Convention (1949), the Convention for the Suppression of the Traffic in Persons and of the Exploitation of the Prostitution of Others (1949), the Convention relating to the Status of Refugees (1951), the ILO Equal Remuneration Convention (1951), the Convention on the Political Rights of Women (1952), the Convention relating to the Status of Stateless Persons (1954), the Supplementary Convention on the Abolition of Slavery, the Slave Trade and Institution, and Practices Similar to Slavery (1956), the Convention on the Nationality of Married Women (1957), the Convention on the Abolition of Forced Labour (1957), the ILO Discrimination (Employment and Occupation) Convention (1958), the

It is remarkable that the Declaration, with detailed provisions in the covenants and conventions, tries to protect and promote not only civil and political rights,[189] but also economic, social and cultural rights.[190] This is based on two major but different concepts of human rights: one which accepts and the other which rejects government interference.[191] The reconciliation of these two concepts together with

---

UNESCO Convention against Discrimination in Education (1960), the Convention on the Reduction of Statelessness (1961), the Convention on Consent to Marriage, Minimum Age for Marriage and Registration of Marriages (1962), the ILO Employment Policy Convention (1964), the International Convention on the Elimination of All Forms of Racial Discrimination (1965), the Convention on the Non-Applicability of Statutory Limitations to War Crimes and Crimes against Humanity (1968), and the ILO Workers' Representatives Convention (1971).

188. An example of a regional convention is the European Convention for the protection of Human Rights and Fundamental Freedoms, signed at Rome on November 4, 1950. The Convention preamble proclaims that it was agreed to by the States Parties in order "to take the first steps for the collective inforcement of certain of the rights stated in the Universal Declaration," and the Convention contains detailed provisions on most of the civil and political rights set forth in the Declaration. Another regional human rights convention is the American Convention on Human Rights, signed at the Inter American Specialized Convention on Human Rights at San Jose, Costa Rica, on November 22, 1969.

189. Civil and political rights are contained in Articles 2 to 21 of the Universal Declaration of Human Rights, the International Covenant on Civil and Political Rights, and some special conventions. They include, roughly: the rights to life, justice, liberty, security, privacy, marriage, family life, public service, and to take part in government; protection from slavery, servitude, forced labor, cruel treatment, arbitrary arrest, arbitrary deprivation of property, and any kind of discrimination; equality as a person and before the law; and freedom of movement, opinion, expression, thought, conscience, religion, assembly, and association.

190. Economic, social, and cultural rights are contained in Articles 22 to 28 of the Universal Declaration of Human Rights, the International Covenant on Economic, Social and Cultural Rights, and some special conventions. They include, roughly: the rights to work, leisure, opportunity, education, health, medical care, social security, participation in trade unions, equal pay, free choice of employment, a reasonable standard of living, development of personality and cultural life; and protection for motherhood, childhood, widowhood, old age, unemployment, disability, and author's interest.

191. "Thus from one angle the present state of the subject may be regarded as a confrontation of two different working conceptions of human rights, which have arisen from different historical formulations and have developed in relation to different sets of social circumstances. The one started from the premise of inherent individual rights, and with a bias against a strong central authority and against government interference, while the other was based upon Marxist principles and the premise of a powerful central government, and early wedded to total planning (which automatically magnifies the central power) and to one-party Government (which inevitably restricts certain political freedoms). Each has be-

due consideration for other divergent ideas,[192] has made the Declaration "a common standard of achievement for all peoples" to strive for, as proclaimed by its Preamble.

The third significant sign of social progress is the growing similarity of national laws, paving the ground for a world law.

For a long time, there have existed great differences in the laws of different countries. Generally speaking, such differences have originated from different legal systems.[193] Civil Law and Common Law are the two major legal systems[194] in modern times. Growing similarities in domestic laws have taken place mainly due to the expansion and mutual influence of these two outstanding systems, together with the Occidentalization of the Oriental legal systems.

The Civil Law system reached its maturity at the beginning of the 19th century when the Napoleon Code was completed.[195] This Code

---

come modified in the course of its history, and in both cases many of the modifications have been in the direction of the other system." (*Human Rights: Comments and Interpretations,* A Symposium edited by UNESCO, New York, 1949, p. 254)

192. "The world of man is at a critical stage in its political, social and economic evolution. If it is to proceed further on the path towards unity, it must develop a common set of ideas and principles. One of those is a common formulation of the rights of man. This common formulation must by some means reconcile the various divergent or opposing formulations now in existence. It must further be sufficiently definite to have real significance both as an inspiration and as a guide to practice, but also sufficiently general and flexible to apply to all men, and to be capable of modification to suit peoples at different states of social and political development while yet retaining significance for them and their aspirations." (*Human Rights: Comments and Interpretations,* A Symposium edited by UNESCO, New York, 1949, p. 255)

193. According to Professor Wigmore, there are sixteen major legal systems: Egyptian, Mesopotamian, Chinese, Hindu, Hebrew, Greek, Maritime, Roman, Keltic, Germanic, Church, Japanese, Mohammedan, Slavic, Romanesque and Anglican. Some of them no longer exist, and some remain. (Cf. John Wigmore, *A Panorama of the World's Legal System,* St. Paul, 1928, Vol. I., p. 3-6.)

194. The civil law system has a deep root in Roman law, so it is also called the Romanesque law system. The common law system developed originally in England, so it is also called the Anglican law system. One of the striking contrasts between these two leading legal systems is that civil law, being primarily legislative in origin, is codified, while common law, being primarily judicial in origin, is found mostly in court decisions. For this reason, the term 'common law' is frequently used to describe judge-made law as distinguished from statutory law. (Cf. *The Code Napoleon and the Common-Law World,* ed. by Bernard Schwartz, New York, 1956, p. 378-388.)

195. One of the immediate results of the French Revolution was the impetus given to the movement to unify French law in a single modern code. The Constituent Assembly of 1790, the Convention, in 1793 and 1794, and the Directory, in

was the first attempt to unify the law on a national scale. It succeeded in abolishing the various provincial laws in France[196] and set a fashion for other linguistically related countries of Europe to follow.[197] Its influence subsequently extended to the remaining countries of continental Europe and to Latin America and other areas.[198]

The Common Law system spread mainly through English colonization.[199] As the English colonies grew, the Common Law system expanded.[200]

1796, all promised that they would draw up such a code. Finally, in 1800, Napoleon, then First Consul, appointed and led the commissions that drew up the civil code. Adopted in 36 statutes successively enacted, it was formally consolidated as a single *Code Civil,* in 1804. The entire code contains only 2,281 sections and, even in its modern form, can readily be printed in a convenient pocket-size volume. The code itself, after six short preliminary sections, is divided into three parts. The first deals with persons, the second with property, and the third with the different ways whereby property may be acquired. (Cf. John H. Wigmore, *A Panorama of the World's Legal Systems,* St. Paul, 1928, Vol. III, p. 1027-1033; and *The Code Napoleon and the Common-Law World,* ed. by Bernard Schwartz, New York, 1956, p. 19-43.)

196. "Neither was there in France any such body of common ideas, tested in continual application, as the English common law. Before the Napoleonic Code France had some three hundred and sixty systems of local private law, left standing by the merely administrative unification of the monarchy." (George H. Sabine, *A History of Political Theory,* New York, 1938, p. 548)

197. In all of these countries the task was similar: to extinguish the thousand local law codes, "fueros" in Spain, "statuta" in Italy, "keuren" in the Netherlands, "stadtrechte" and "landrechte" in Germany and Austria, "cantonrechte" in Switzerland; and to weld them with the Roman Common Law into a single Romanesque system. The first to complete the task was Austria, in 1811; then followed the Netherlands, in 1833; Italy, in 1865; Spain, in 1888; Germany, in 1896; and Switzerland, in 1907. (Cf. John H. Wigmore, *A Panorama of the World's Legal Systems,* St. Paul, 1928, Vol. III, p. 1027-1041.)

198. The Civil Law system was further extended by its scientific and political influences. By the former, the legal thought of all the remaining continental countries was moulded more or less in Romanesque form. By the latter, the new nations of Latin-America, on achieving independence in the early 1800s, proceeded to codify their law. As no Spanish code then existed, the Code Napoleon was naturally the chief model. This, too, occurred in Dutch South Africa, Quebec, Louisiana, and other colonies of continental European countries. (Cf. John H. Wigmore, *A Panorama of the World's Legal Systems,* St. Paul, 1928, Vol. III, p. 1027-1041.)

199. "The common law of England is the common law of the plantations. . . . let an Englishman go where he will, he carries as much of law and liberty with him as the nature of things will bear." (Delivered by Attorney-General West, in 1720, quoted in John H. Wigmore, *A Panorama of the World's Legal Systems,* St. Paul, 1928, Vol. III, p. 1099.)

200. The common law system has now encircled the globe, dominating the United States, Great Britain, Canada, Australia, and tens of other countries. (A

Japan was the first Oriental country to Occidentalize its legal system voluntarily,[201] followed by Siam[202] and China.[203] The experience of Turkey in Occidentalizing its legal system is remarkable.[204] Persia, Afghanistan and Egypt also took various steps to reform their laws on Occidental models early in this century.[205]

As a result of the legal Occidentalization, a great assimilation of

---

list of names appears in John H. Wigmore, *A Panorama of the World's Legal Systems,* St. Paul, 1928, Vol. III, p. 1104-1106.)

201. Japan undertook to remake the form of its law on Occidental models in the last quarter of the last century: "The most able younger minds were sent abroad to master the Occidental systems of government and law. During the 1880's and 1890's, in Tokyo, thousands of aspirants in Tokyo schools studied the laws of France, Germany, and Anglo-America, at first under imported law teachers, afterwards under the returned Japanese jurists bearing Occidental degrees. Meanwhile, five new codes were prepared, first drafted by jurists imported from France and Germany; then re-cast, in contents better adapted to Japanese institutions, by the new generation of Japanese jurists trained in the Occidental laws. These went into force in the last decade of the century." Not only the law, but even the mode of the courts was Occidentalized. For example, "Criminal trials were conducted in court-rooms furnished on the Occidental model; and the bailiffs and police, though gentry (samurai) by descent, everyone of them, now wore Occidental uniforms." (Cf. John H. Wigmore, *A Panorama of the World's Legal Systems,* St. Paul, 1928, Vol. II, p. 521, 524.)

202. (Cf. John H. Wigmore, *A Panorama of the World's Legal Systems,* St. Paul, 1928, Vol. I, p. 236-242.)

203. "Since 1850 the irritant influence of a half-century's contact with the democratic Occident, and the suffering under mis-government of the Manchu foreign dynasty, had resulted in profound unrest among the educated classes. This came to an issue in 1906, and the Emperor was then compelled to promise immediate radical changes in China's constitution. Events moved rapidly, for China. In 1911 the Throne fell; and in 1912 came the Republic, and a provisional Constitution. In 1923 this was discarded, and a new Constitution was formally adopted. . . . The Supreme Court was reorganized. The building that now forms the seat of supreme judicial authority bears a thoroughly Occidental appearance in architecture." (Cf. John H. Wigmore, *A Panorama of the World's Legal Systems,* St. Paul, 1928, p. 194-195.)

204. Turkey, with its old cosmopolitan capital of Constantinople, had been gradually Occidentalizing its legal system for three generations, by introducing Romanesque principles from the European codes, mainly in commercial law. But the new Turkish Republic took even more radical steps toward Occidentalization. In April, 1924, the Assembly adopted a new constitution, abolished the old courts of Islamic law, declared the separation of law from religion, and replaced the old laws with a new group of codes founded explicitly on Romanesque European models. (Cf. John H. Wigmore, *A Panorama of the World's Legal Systems,* St. Paul, 1928, Vol. II, p. 636-637.)

205. (Cf. John H. Wigmore, *A Panorama of the World's Legal Systems,* St. Paul, 1928, Vol. II, p. 632-636.)

native, Civil and Common Law systems has appeared in the East.[206] At the same time, the gap between the Civil Law and Common Law systems has gradually been closed by their mutual influence in the West.[207]

In socialist countries, many legal innovations have developed based on ideology. Technically, however, the Civil Law system remains as a model for their new codes and statutes.[208] The jury has ap-

---

206. Generally speaking, it is the Civil Law system that has furnished the chief model for the Occidentalization of Oriental systems. This does not suggest, however, that the Common Law system did not make any contribution to this movement. In fact, the British Empire and the United States, the leading countries of the Common Law system, have always played the principal role in urging Oriental countries towards legal Occidentalization, and their legal principles, as well as political doctrines, have deeply infiltrated into the thought of modern Oriental jurists. Consequently, the reorganization of Oriental legal systems in modern times has resulted from an assimilation of the native, Civil Law, and Common Law systems in the East. (Cf. William Seagle, *The History of Law,* New York, 1946, p. 177-180.)

207. While after the French Revolution, continental countries turned to the late Roman tradition of codification, it was not long before the lawyers of Civil Law countries began to worship precedent as much as the Common Law jurists. France today has its Jurisprudence générale of Dalloz, an immense collection of decided cases, and German courts have written argumentative decisions bristling with the citation of precedents. (William Seagle, *The History of Law,* New York, 1946, p. 179, 180. Cf. also, Arthur T. Vanderbilt, "The Reconciliation of the Civil Law and Common Law," in *The Code Napoleon and the Common-Law World,* ed. by Bernard Schwartz, New York, 1956, p. 389-400; and Frederick H. Lawson, *A Common Lawyer Looks at the Civil Law,* Ann Arbor, Michigan, 1955.) Thus, all that is "peculiar" to the Common Law system is its doctrine, of little significance today, which, moreover, is in rapid eclipse in most Common Law jurisdictions. "The future lies rather with the Civil Law doctrine of the authority of a series of decided cases, particularly as expressed in great authoritative treatises that are now a commonplace in Common Law as well as Civil Law countries." "At the beginning of the present century the Common Law claimed dominion over the British Commonwealth of Nations and America, while the Civil Law ruled the rest of the world, at least wherever European culture was imitated, but at the same time there was a group of internationally minded jurists who were not blinded by the cults of the legal systems and who were thus able to perceive that . . . . the competition between the Civil Law and the Common Law had become unreal. They dwelt upon the importance of the science of comparative law and spoke of the tendency towards a marked assimilation of Western law." (Cf. A.L. Goodhart, "Precedent in English and Continental," in *Law Quarterly Review,* Vol. I, 1934, p. 40-65; and F. Deak, "The Place of the Case in the Common and Civil Law," in *Tulane Law Review,* Vol. VIII, 1934, p. 337-357.)

208. (Cf. John N. Hazard, *Communists and Their Law,* Chicago, 1969, p. 519-528; and *The Code Napoleon and the Common-Law World,* ed. by Bernard Schwartz, New York, 1956, p. 224-244.)

peared in the Soviet Union in a different form, but the basic idea of lay participation in the judicial process to counteract the influence of a professional legal class is the same.[209]

g.
International Developments

STILL MORE INSTANCES OF SOCIAL PROGRESS HAVE been achieved through the development of international laws and organizations in recent centuries. These developments have contributed a great deal to the building of One World by increasing international intercourse, expanding international relations, and ultimately strengthening the ties between all peoples.

International laws include the law of conflicts and the law of nations. The law of conflicts comprises the rules for settling conflicts arising from the laws of different countries in private international relations.[210]

In ancient Greece and Rome, there were special legal practices to take care of foreigners and foreign intercourse.[211] The modern law of

---

209. In the Soviet Union, the lowest courts, known as people's courts, consist of a professional people's judge and two nonprofessional assessors, this being the Soviet equivalent of the Western jury system. (Cf. John N. Hazard, *The Soviet System of Government,* 4th ed., Chicago, 1968, p. 175-176.)

210. The law of conflicts is always used as synonymous with private international law. It owes its existence to the fact that different systems of law prevail in the world. It deals primarily with the application of laws in different places. It may be described as the body of rules dealing with the effect of foreign elements on the decision of a civil case. It grows with private international intercourse, and plays an important role in promoting private international relations. (Cf. Joseph H. Beale, *A Treatise on the Conflict of Law,* New York, 1935, Vol. I, p. 1-2; and J.A. Castel, *Conflict of Laws; Cases, Notes and Materials,* 2nd ed., Toronto, 1968, p. 1.)

211. In ancient Greece, it had become evident that foreigners and foreign transactions could not be governed with recourse to the local law alone. In order to maintain useful foreign intercourse, account had to be taken of foreign law, and this was done by inter-municipal treaties granting "justice" to the citizens of different cities. In dealing with foreigners, Rome developed a jus gentium, which was supposed to be based upon principles of equity derived from common foreign

conflicts was born in Italy and Bartolus was the father.[212] It was further developed in the 19th century by Story and Savigny,[213] and began a new epoch after World War I.[214]

Accompanying the theoretical development of the law of conflicts has been the codification of its rules in various countries,[215] its

---

sources, but was in no sense a law of conflicts, as foreign law is not applied as such. (Cf. Martin Wolff, *Private International Law,* Oxford, 1945, p. 19-20.)

212. The modern law of conflicts may be said to have had its origins in Italy, where growing trade and manufacture were protected by the city-states. Roman law was the common law of the peninsula, but each city had its own "statuta" which undermined this imperial law in many aspects, and hence gave rise to conflicts. Into these circumstances came Bartolus, who may rightly be regarded as the founder of the modern law of conflicts. Bartolus held that a statute which affected persons only would not operate against foreigners; that a statute which affected things would operate against both foreigners and citizens; and, finally, that a statute which related to the person would follow him wherever he went. (Cf. Joseph H. Beale, *Bartolus on the Conflict of Laws,* Boston, 1914.)

213. Great progress in the law of conflicts was made by Joseph Story, who merged Dutch doctrine with Anglo-American cases, and by Friedrich Carl von Savigny who, using Story's materials and rational method, established many principles of modern conflicts law. Their international conception of conflicts law, borrowing from writers of the 16th and 17th centuries, was adopted by almost all outstanding authors in this field in the 19th century. (Cf. Ernst Rabel, *The Conflict of Laws: A Comparative Study,* Ann Arbor, Mich., 1945-1958, Vol. I, p. 6-11.)

214. In 1924, an institute was established in Berlin to encourage the study of private international law by the comparative method. In 1926, this institute initiated a yearbook of German decisions and began in its Review to provide surveys of foreign cases. Several handbooks of cases and treatises followed. The effort of the new German school quickly influenced other European countries, and a little later than in Europe, a corollary reform began in the United States and Canada. Consequently, the long-standing scarcity of writings was replaced by a vigorous stream of literature. As deductive considerations have given way to practical studies, and organizational learning has taken the place of separate efforts, many values have been discovered or modified. (Cf. Ernst Rabel, *The Conflict of Laws: A Comparative Study,* Ann Arbor, Mich., 1945-1958, Vol. I, p. 19-26.)

215. Codification took place first in articles 7 to 31, inclusive, of the Introductory Law that accompanied the German Civil Code of 1896. But this body of rules was reduced by Bismarck so as to cover in its final form only a part of the subject matter. Subsequently, this part of the German law served as a model for a slightly more extensive Japanese Law of 1898, and for a similar Chinese Law of 1918. The Swedish statutes of 1904, and of 1912; the Austrian draft of 1913; the Polish Law of 1926; and the Czechoslovak drafts of 1924 and 1931, were based on the same principles. Short codification also appeared in the civil codes of Greece (1940), Rumania (1939), and Peru (1936). (Cf. Ernst Rabel, *The Conflict of Laws: A Comparative Study,* Ann Arbor, Mich., 1945-1958, Vol. I, p. 26-29.)

216. Examples are the convention concluded in Stockholm on February 6, 1931, containing "provisions of private international law in the field of marriage,

international conventions,[216] and its other progress.[217] Consequently, a great many legal obstacles to private international intercourse have been eliminated.

The law of nations comprises the rules which regulate relations between nations.[218] It was founded by Grotius in the 17th century[219]

---

adoption, and guardianship," (Cf. League of Nations Treaty Series, Vol. 126, 1931, p. 141), and the treaties of Montevideo of February 12, 1889, signed by Argentina, Bolivia, Paraguay, Peru, and Uruguay. (Cf. W.A. Berves, "The Treaties of Montevideo, Text of 1889," *Transactions of the Grotius Society,* Vol. 6, 1920, p. 59.) More important is the code of International Private Law, in 295 sections adopted at the Sixth Pan-American Conference in Havana in February, 1928 (Cf. *League of Nations Treaty Series,* Vol. 86, 1929, p. 711); and the six Hague Conventions of 1902 and 1905 covering the law of conflicts in regard to marriage, divorce and separation, guardianship of minors, property of spouses, interdiction and similar measure of protection, and civil procedure. (Cf. Friedrich Meili, *International Civil and Commercial Law,* London, 1905, p. 532, and Ernst Rabel, *The Conflict of Laws: A Comparative Study,* Ann Arbor, Mich., 1945-1958, Vol. I, p. 30-32.) A very important step was taken by the Protocol signed at The Hague, March 27, 1931, recognizing the competence of the Permanent Court of International Justice to interpret the Hague Conventions on private international law. (Cf. *League of Nations Treaty Series,* Vol. 167, 1936, p. 341.)

217. Progress has included numerous bilateral treaties, containing clauses relating to conflicts rules. Besides these, the international community has developed conflicts rules through custom, such as those whereby the law of the situs governs immovable property, a tort is governed by the law of the place where the allegedly tortious act has transpired, and the formalities of legal acts are determinable by the law of the place where they occur. (Cf. Ernst Rabel, *The Conflict of Laws: A Comparative Study,* Ann Arbor, Mich., 1945-1958, Vol. I, p. 36-40.)

218. The law of nations is also called public international law, or simply and more commonly, international law. It is a term usually defined as that body of rules, principles, and standards to which the nations are bound by common consent. This definition assumes that the source of the law of nations is the consent of those bound and that its sanction is basically good faith. The lack of coercive sanctions has led some writers to infer that the law of nations has the character of morality rather than of law. (Cf. Lassa F.L. Oppenheim, *International Law,* 8th ed., London, 1955, Vol. I, p. 4-23.)

219. The law of nations came into existence only half consciously. It grew with custom and usage, and has had a long history. But it was not until recent centuries, when international relations became more extensive, that the law of nations was given serious and scientific study. A milestone was achieved when Hugo Grotius, a Dutch jurist, published his treatise, *The Law of War and Peace,* in 1625. He has deservedly been given the title of the father of international law. He drew from many sources, but primarily from natural law. He also supported his views by precedents, thus relying on positive law, or practice. Born in 1583, he entered the University of Leiden at the age of 11 and graduated at 14. At 15, while on a diplomatic mission to France, he was called "the miracle of Holland" by King Henry IV. He died in 1645. (Cf. William S.M. Knight, *The Life and Works of*

and developed by Vattel and other scholars.²²⁰ Since the middle of the 19th century, further advancement has been achieved along with an increase in professional literature²²¹ and the growth of international legislation.²²²

Hugo Grotius, New York, 1925.) *The Law of War and Peace* has had an amazing vogue. There were 45 Latin editions before 1748, and innumerable translations have been made. (Clyde Eagleton, *International Government,* New York, 1948, p. 32, note 4.)

220. The most popular of the followers of Grotius was Vattel, who is more often quoted than Grotius himself. (A statistic may be found in "Changing Concepts and the Doctrine of Incorporation," by E.D. Dickinson, *American Journal of International Law,* 1932, p. 259.) He did not claim originality, but admitted that he built upon the work of another disciple, Wolff. He divided his field into natural law and voluntary law, but weakened the former by too great an insistence upon the independent personality of the nation. Other famous followers of Grotius included: Zouche, of Oxford, whose work has been called the first treatise on the law of nations, and who is also regarded as one of the founders of the positivist school; Pufendorf, of Holland, the leader of the natural law school; and Bynkershoek, also Dutch, who had an intimate knowledge of questions of maritime and commercial practice, and played an important role in the development of that side of the law of nations. (Cf. Arthur Nussbaum, *A Concise History of the Law of Nations,* New York, 1947, p. 142-162.)

221. In addition to a good number of treatises, periodical literature has been increasing remarkably since the *Revue de droit international et de législation comparée,* the first periodical primarily dedicated to the subject, was founded in Brussels, in 1869. There were more than 35 such periodicals in the early 1950s. (Cf. the list of periodicals in Lassa F.L. Oppenheim, *International Law,* 8th ed., London, 1955, Vol. I, p. 113-114.) This development was partially stimulated by the works of various organizations in this field, two of which appeared as a result of interest inspired by the Alabama Award: the Institute de Droit International, a selective body which includes most of the great international lawyers of the world; and the International Law Association, as it is now called, which has branches in various countries. A sidelight to the increase in the literature of the law of nations has been provided by the American and English writers. Traditionally much less interested in abstract theory and much more in practical questions, they have stressed material which was not easily available to many other jurists, producing a great number of "casebooks." (Cf. Arthur Nussbaum, *A Concise History of the Law of Nations,* New York, 1947, p. 276-278, 233-237.)

222. The need for rules to regulate increasingly intricate international relations has since the 19th century produced international legislation by means of lawmaking conferences and treaties. Perhaps the first recognition of a need for a consciously constructive process in building the law of nations was the declaration by the Congress of Paris, in 1814, in favor of freedom of navigation on international rivers. This declaration was not very effective, but it was important in showing that the international community had obtained in the conference itself, a sort of rudimentary legislative organ. After the Conference of Paris, in 1856, at which a famous declaration dealing with the laws of maritime warfare was agreed to, in-

It is international legislation that has made it possible for the law of nations to play a role in the unification of national laws,[223] as witnessed by achievements in the field of maritime law[224] and a series of labor conventions.[225]

The establishment of international judicial systems is an important measure for implementing the law of nations. It began with a primary form of arbitration,[226] and has gradually[227] developed into a world court.[228]

---

ternational legislation by conference became fairly frequent. And since 1864, treaties of a legislative kind have grown very rapidly. The number listed by Professor Hudson from 1864 to 1914 is 275, and from 1919 to 1945, 670. "They deal with a variety of interests which were not only not protected by the customary law but which were wholly unforeseen when their foundations were being laid." (Manley O. Hudson, *International Legislation,* Washington, 1931-1950, Vol. I, p. xviii)

223. This has been done by obtaining agreement among nations through international legislation whereby each nation will enact laws within its own jurisdiction, applicable to the individuals therein, in harmony with similar actions within other nations. The result is to put individuals in different nations upon practically the same legal footing. It is an important step towards world legal unity. (Cf. Manley O. Hudson, "The Prospect for International Law in the Twentieth Century," *Cornell Law Quarterly,* Vol. X, 1925, p. 419f.)

224. Since 1897, the International Maritime Commission has held many meetings of its own and has organized several diplomatic conferences which have produced international legislation on maritime law. In 1913, its Secretary claimed that "more than three quarters of the tonnage of the world is now regulated by uniform maritime law elaborated by the international Maritime Commission." (Cf. Quoted in Clyde Eagleton, *International Government,* New York, 1932, p. 311.)

225. *The Conventions and Recommendations Adopted by the International Labour Conference, 1919-1966,* published by the International Labor Office, Geneva, 1966, contains "the authentic texts of the Conventions and Recommendations adopted by the International Labour Conference in the course of the 50 sessions which have been held from 1919 to 1966. During this period 126 Conventions and 127 Recommendations have been adopted by the Conference. On 1 July 1966, 106 Conventions had received the number of ratifications necessary to bring them into force and a total of 3,175 ratifications had been registered." (Preface)

226. An international arbitration system was inaugurated by the Jay Treaty of 1794 by which England and the United States agreed to dispose of certain unsettled issues of the Anglo-American Peace of 1783. This Arbitration Commission worked from 1799 to 1804, rendering 536 awards. For a long period, the United States remained the foremost sponsor of arbitration, and caused arbitration clauses for standing mixed commissions on the Jay model to be incorporated in treaties with various countries. The United States-Mexican Mixed Commission of 1868 was the most significant; between 1871 and 1876, it settled more than 2,000 claims. (Cf. Arthur Nussbaum, *A Concise History of the Law of Nations,* New York, 1947, p. 213.)

227. The favorable attitude of other countries toward the American mode of arbitration led to the establishment of the Permanent Court of Arbitration, in 1900, by the terms of the Hague Conventions. Each nation designated four

The most significant development in the law of nations in recent decades has been the fresh inquiries made into its fundamentals. These inquiries have led to a strong demand for limitations on national sovereignty,[229] and a wide claim for a direct position for the in-

---

members to a panel of arbitrators, to which nations could turn when they desired to submit disputes to arbitration. An Administrative Council of the Court, on which all parties to the Hague Conventions were represented, met annually to consider over-all policy matters. An International Bureau headed by a Secretary-General completed the structure of the court. The Hague Conventions also included provisions for the systematic use of good offices, mediation, and inquiry by governments involved in disputes. The Permanent Court of Arbitration has assisted in some 23 arbitrations, 17 of which took place before World War I. (Cf. *British and Foreign State Papers,* Vol. 91, p. 970; and *U.S. Treaties and Conventions,* Vol. 2, p. 2016, 2220.)

228. After the first World War a new milestone was set in the development of a world judicial system when the Permanent Court of International Justice was created in 1921. The Statute of the Court embodied an "optional clause" under which a government might accept the Court's compulsory jurisdiction toward every other government making the same declaration. Fifty governments accepted this clause, though often with broad reservations. Jurisdiction was also conferred upon the Permanent Court exclusively, or alternatively with other tribunals, by hundreds of international agreements. During the 22 years of its existence, the Permanent Court of International Justice considered 65 cases and handed down 27 advisory opinions and 32 judgments. With the establishment of the United Nations, the Permanent Court of International Justice has been replaced by the International Court of Justice, commonly known as the World Court. The Statute of the new Court is very similar to that of the old. (Cf. Arthur Nussbaum, *A Concise History of the Law of Nations,* New York, 1947, p. 268; Manly O. Hudson, *The Permanent Court of International Justice,* 1920-1942, New York, 1943, Chap. XX, p. 435; Oliver Lissitzyn, *The International Court of Justice,* New York, 1951; and Chapter XIV of the Charter of the United Nations.)

229. These inquiries have been focused on the notion of sovereignty and the position of individuals in the law of nations. Having witnessed the aftermath of the extension of the doctrine of absolute national sovereignty into the international community, many writers began to doubt and even attack the notion of sovereignty at its very roots. More particularly, attempts were made to discover the original source of the law of nations, as well as of national law. Some writers returned to the doctrine of natural law, while others asserted that the law of nations comes into existence when people from different nations, under the impact of external events, widen their sense of right to include international relations. The conclusion of the natural law school and the individual will school are the same; that is, the law of nations must be above the nations, and national sovereignty must be subordinate to the law of nations. (Cf. Arthur Nussbaum, *A Concise History of the Law of Nations,* New York, 1947, p. 281-287; also J.W. Garner, "Limitation on National Sovereignty in International Relations," *Political Science Review,* XIX, 1925, p. 1-24; and Arthur Larson, C. Wilfred Janks and Others, *Sovereignty within Law,* New York, 1965, p. 3-28.)

dividual in the law of nations.[230] In practice, some international judicial agencies have for a long time had the power to deal directly with the individual.[231] There have also been some widely accepted precedents and rules recognizing the direct duties and rights of the individual in the law of nations.[232]

---

230. The doctrine of individual will also led to a direct relationship between international law and individuals; indeed, a large number of international lawyers have claimed a position for the individual in international law. "Looking upon the individual as the real object of all law, it proclaims the necessity of rendering international law democratic by placing individuals in the first rank of its subjects. It is gradually gaining force and ground in all countries. It is followed by an ever-increasing number of jurists, of which the most prominent are: Schucking and Wehbery in Germany, Kelsen and Verdross in Austria, Saldana in Spain, Basdevant, Duguit, de Lapradelle and Scelle, in France, Krabbe in Holland, Mandelstam in Russia, and Alvarez, Garner and Ralston, in America." (N. Politis, *The New Aspects of International Law,* Carnegie Endowment for International Peace, Pamphlet No. 49, 1928, p. 23, quoted by Quincy Wright, *Research in International Law Since the War,* Carnegie Endowment, Division of International Law, Pamphlet No. 51, p. 32. Wright adds to this list the names of Westlake, W. Kaufmann, Diena, Cavaglieri, Osawa, and Eagleton, and could have included himself. See also Philip C. Jessup, "The Subjects of a Modern Law of Nations," *Michigan Law Review,* Vol. 45, 1947, p. 383.)

According to Sir Hersh Lauterpacht, "the law of nations in itself conceivable only as being above the legal order of sovereign States, is not only a law governing their mutual relation but is also upon final analysis, the universal law of humanity in which the individual human being as the ultimate unit of all law rises sovereign over the limited province of the State." (*International Law and Human Rights,* New York, 1950, p. 120)

231. The Danube and Rhine Commissions, for example, are bodies which make regulations affecting individuals, and which can, through their own courts, enforce them directly upon individuals belonging to riparian nations. In a number of cases, the individual has been permitted to appear before an international court. A Central American Court functioned for a number of years with authority to hear complaints of individuals against nations, and several such cases were heard. A series of mixed arbitration tribunals was created to try the claims of individuals arising under Article 297 of the Treaty of Versailles. The burden of these tribunals was formidable. For instance, more than 20,000 claims were submitted to the Franco-German Tribunal, about 10,000 to the Anglo-German Tribunal, and about 13,500 to the American-German Commission. (Cf. Pitman B. Potter, *An Introduction to the Study of International Organization,* 3rd ed., New York, 1928, p. 176-177; Clyde Eagleton, *International Government,* New York, 1948, p. 120-124; and Arthur Nussbaum, *A Concise History of the Law of Nations,* New York, 1947, p. 273-274.)

232. The Nuremburg Tribunal, for instance, clearly accepted the individual as a subject of international law: "That international law imposes duties and liabilities upon individuals as well as upon states has long been recognized.... Crimes against international law are committed by men, not by abstract entities,

The law of nations is evidently transforming into a world law, and its subject of jurisdiction is shifting from the nation to the individual.

As regards international organizations there are, generally speaking, two kinds: official and non-governmental.[233]

Modern international non-governmental organizations did not come into existence until the middle of the last century.[234] Since then, except when effected by the great wars,[235] they have steadily increas-

---

and only by punishing individuals who commit such crimes can the provisions of international law be enforced.'' The General Assembly of the United Nations unanimously approved this opinion and recommended that it be stated and adopted as law. If the emphasis in this trial was upon the duties of individuals, their rights have been equally and more solemnly recognized by the Universal Declaration of Human Rights, proclaimed by the General Assembly of the United Nations on December 10, 1948. (Cf. *American Journal of International Law,* Vol. 41, 1947, p. 220-221; *Resolutions of the General Assembly,* No. 95 (1), p. 188; and Hersh Lauterpacht, *International Law and Human Rights,* New York, 1950, Chap. 17.)

233. "International non-governmental organization" is an all-inclusive term, defined by the Economic and Social Council of the United Nations to mean any international organization which is not established by an agreement among governments. (See United Nations document E/INF/23, April 30, 1948, "Arrangements of the Economic and Social Council of the United Nations for Consultation with Non-Governmental Organizations, Guide for Consultants," p. 16.) This definition was reaffirmed by the Council's Resolution 288 of February 27, 1950, and was amplified by its Resolution 1298 of June 25, 1968, "including organizations which accept members designated by government authorities, provided that such membership does not interfere with the free expression of views of the organizations." An official international organization is established by agreement of national governments. It is also called an intergovernmental organization.

234. Decades, and even centuries, before nations were willing to join in any extensive formal cooperation, private persons were ready and eager to associate their activities across national frontiers. In a formal sense, however, international non-governmental organizations have made their appearance in the world more recently and more slowly. Not until the later nineteenth century did these organizations begin to multiply in the form in which we now find them. The World Alliance of YMCAs, founded in 1855, was probably the first true international non-governmental organization to be established in modern times. (Cf. Lyman C. White, *International Non-Governmental Organizations,* New Brunswick, N.J., 1951, p. 4.)

235. During World War I, nearly all international non-governmental organizations ceased their activities, with the exception of bodies like the Red Cross. However, recognizing the catastrophe of war on a global scale, some international non-governmental organizations were created to prevent its recurrence. Among these was the Women's International League for Peace and Freedom, founded under the leadership of Jane Addams, in 1915. At the end of the war, international non-governmental organizations developed rapidly, such as the extension of the International Chamber of Commerce, representing over three million

ed in number[236] as well as in frequency of meetings,[237] and have greatly outnumbered the official international organizations.[238] Their functions cover every field, every nook and corner of human endeavor,[239] and they have been inclined to develop a distinctly cosmopolitan outlook.[240]

---

firms; the International Cooperative Alliance, with seventy-one million members; and the International Federation of Trade Unions, with twenty million members. A great many new organizations were created. The rise of fascism in Germany led to the withdrawal of its important national groups from certain international non-governmental organizations. Japanese and Italian groups took a somewhat similar attitude. On the other hand, the growth of fascism stimulated many groups to redouble their efforts. This was especially true of those concerned with peace, religion, and labor. (Cf. Lyman C. White, *International Non-Governmental Organizations,* New Brunswick, N.J., 1951, p. 5-7.)

236. A study made by Mr. White of 546 organizations in 1938 shows that 9 were founded in the twenty-year period from 1846 to 1865; 29 from 1866 to 1885; 96 from 1886 to 1905; 289 from 1906 to 1925; and 123 in the six years from 1926 to 1931. The League of Nations *Handbook* shows that 163 international non-governmental organizations were established in the seven years from 1932 to 1938. And this, according to Mr. White, was not a complete list. (Cf. Lyman C. White, *International Non-Governmental Organizations,* New Brunswick, N.J., 1951, p. 279, note 5.)

237. Statistics gathered by Mr. Potter show that from 1840 to 1849 there were 10 meetings held by international non-governmental organizations: from 1850 to 1859, 18; from 1860 to 1869, 64; from 1870 to 1879, 139; from 1880 to 1889, 272; from 1890 to 1899, 475; from 1900 to 1909, 985; and from 1910 to 1914, 458. Statistics are lacking for the period 1919-1939. It can be reliably estimated, according to Mr. Potter, that such meetings occurred in the early 1930s at the rate of 200-250 per year. (Cf. Pitman B. Potter, *An Introduction to the Study of International Organization,* 5th ed., New York, 1948, p. 36, note 3.)

238. According to Professor Waldo Chamberlin of Dartmouth College, the number of official international organizations in existence in 1966 was 199, as opposed to 1935 international non-governmental organizations. (Cf. "International Organization," in *Americana,* 1973 ed., Vol. 15, p. 312.)

239. The *Yearbook of International Organizations, 1964-65,* published by the Union of International Associations, Brussels, records 1470 international non-governmental organizations, excluding those in the European Community, divided according to the following classifications:

Bibliography, Documentation, Press	54
Religion, Ethics	87
Social Sciences, Humanistic Studies	67
International Relations	106
Politics	14
Law, Administration	45
Social Welfare	70
Professions, Employers, Trade Unions	137
Economics, Finance	33
Commerce, Industry	168

Since World War I, there has been a noteworthy advance in regard to cooperation among the international non-governmental organizations.[241] Their associations with the official international organizations have also increased, especially since their importance was formally recognized by the United Nations in arrangements to use them for consultation.[242]

Agriculture 64
Transport, Travel 63
Technology 70
Science 118
Health 150
Education, Youth 83
Arts, Radio, Cinema 65
Sport, Recreation 76

The yearbook did not include all the existing international non-governmental organizations. Its record, however, gives an adequate picture of the functions that international non-governmental organizations have exercised.

240. International non-governmental organizations usually serve as agents of international understanding, as molders of public opinion, and as pressure groups. Frequently, they are pioneers—the first to recognize an international need and the first to do something about it, either in study and research or in a program of action. They do not have a great deal of patience with the national government system. They are more concerned with association on the basis of international interest, and are inclined "to develop a distinctly cosmopolitan outlook, which is a decisive turn in the evolution of the world society." (Cf. Lyman C. White, *International Non-Governmental Organizations,* New Brunswick, N.J., 1951, p. 41.)

241. Sometimes two or more organizations maintain one office and secretariat or divide a field of work in order to avoid overlapping and conflict. It has been, moreover, a common practice for one organization to invite others to participate in its conferences, and sometimes special congresses are held which bring together the representatives of a large number of organizations. In 1928, for example, the International Federation of League of Nations Societies held a conference in Prague on economic problems, in which 33 international non-governmental organizations participated. (Cf. Lyman C. White, *International Non-Governmental Organizations,* New Brunswick, N.J., 1951, p. 15.)

242. Article 71 of the Charter of the United Nations provides that "the Economic and Social Council may make suitable arrangements for consultation with non-governmental organizations which are concerned with matters within its competence." It was on the 21st of June, 1946, that the Economic and Social Council, in accordance with this Article, put into effect arrangements for consultation with non-governmental organizations. These arrangements, as since modified, went further in extending to non-governmental organizations opportunities for the presentation of their views than had ever been granted to such groups by any national government. According to these arrangements, there are three categories of non-governmental organizations in consultative relationship with the United Nations. These have the right to send their authorized representatives to attend meetings of the Economic and Social Council and its Commissions, and they may

The primary form of official international organizations is the consular service and diplomatic system. In modern times, the consular service has undergone a great change both in function[243] and in scale,[244] and has been woven into an elaborate web of international relations.[245] The diplomatic system has developed even more

---

send written statements on matters before the General Assembly, the Security Council, and other agencies. The organizations in categories A and B may submit written statements which are distributed as official documents to all members of the United Nations and to the specialized agencies. The organizations in categories A have additional privileges. There are also special prerogatives, such as attending some of the United Nations meetings as "observers," securing documents, and using the library, for organizations without consultative status as well as for the consultative organizations. (Cf. Economic and Social Council of the United Nations, "Arrangements for Consultation with Non-Governmental Organizations, Guide for Consultants," Document E/INF/23, April 30, 1948, p. 10-12; and "Non-Governmental Organizations Consultative Methods Revised," *United Nations Bulletin,* April 15, 1950.)

243. The consular service is the original and fundamental form of official intercourse between the states. In view of the earlier theory that aliens were subject to the law of their own state, rather than to that of the state of their residence, the first need of agents between the states was to take care of citizens engaged in commerce abroad. Such agents were to be found in ancient Greece and Rome. With the growth of trade in modern times, the office has become more important. But the doctrine that the alien carries with him his own law has been dropped, and has been supplanted by the rule of subjection to the jurisdiction of the state of residence. Naturally, the judicial functions of the consul have been eroded in this process. Meanwhile, with the rise of the diplomatic service, his representative functions have also been diminishing. As a result, the consular service today has become increasingly informational and ministerial in character. (Cf. "Legal Position and Functions of Consuls," by the League of Nations' Committee of Experts for the Progressive Codification of International Law, in the *American Journal of International Law,* Vol. 22, Special Supplement, January 1928, p. 105-110.)

244. The consular system has been universally adopted, and most of the great nations have extended their consular service to the important commercial centers of the world. In the year 1931, for instance, there appeared to be 17,442 consular officers sent by 60 nations and distributed among 850 cities and towns in the territory of 74 states. Great Britain alone sent 1,075 to 744 cities and towns, grouped into 256 consular districts. (Cf. *American Journal of International Law,* Vol. 26, 1932, Supplement, p. 376-378.)

245. The result of the development of the modern consular service is, as Professor Potter pointed out, "an enormous and elaborate web of official bonds connecting the various members of the international community, and that web is growing in complexity and in toughness with each year." (Cf. Pitman B. Potter, *An Introduction to the Study of International Organization,* 5th ed., New York, 1948, p. 75.)

246. Diplomacy, in the modern sense of the word, began to take form in the intercourse between the politically active Italian city-states around the 15th cen-

notably, and is today the most important avenue of international intercourse.[246]

Accompanying the development of the consular service and diplomatic system has been the growth of international conferences and treaties. Since the Congress of Westphalia, the number of international conferences has increased at an accelerated pace,[247] involv-

---

tury. They had so many dealings with each other that it was convenient to have permanent representatives always on watch. Other states found the practice worthy of imitation and helped to develop this system. But it was not until the Vienna Congress of 1815 and Aix-la-Chapelle Congress of 1818 that the status and rules of this system were established by formal international agreement. Nowadays, the result of the practice of international exchange of diplomatic representatives is to cover the world with a web of bilateral bonds running among the capitals of all nations. These bonds are less numerous than in the case of the consular service, but are of great significance. (Cf. League of Nations' Committee of Experts for the Progressive Codification of International Law, "Report of Subcommittee on Diplomatic Privileges and Immunities," in *American Journal of International Law,* Vol. 20, 1926, Supplement, p. 151F; and Elmer Plischke, *Conduct of American Diplomacy,* New York, 1950, p. 14-15.)

247. International conferences grow out of joint consideration and discussion, by the representatives of at least two nations, of matters of interest common to both. The Congress of Westphalia, in 1648, was widely regarded as the first modern conference to serve as an instrument of world affairs. From that date through the centuries, the nations of the world have displayed an increasing tendency to go into council on matters of common interest. Professor Baldwin compiled a list of conferences occurring between 1826 and 1907, (*American Journal of International Law,* Vol. 1, 1907, Appendix, p. 808-829) showing a steady numerical increase, especially after 1850. From 1850 to 1860, a total of 6 conferences were held; between 1860 and 1870, 19; and from 1900 to 1907, 26. A more limited list of conferences of unusual importance, compiled by Sir Satow to cover the century preceding the outbreak of the first World War, shows a similar tendency. (E. Satow, *International Congresses and Conferences,* British Peace Handbook, No. 151, p. 6-7) After the first World War, conferences became more efficient and more numerous, and many have been held regularly under the auspices of the established institutions. Between March 1, 1920, and September 1, 1925, for instance, there were 92 important official conferences, besides the regular meetings of the Council and Assembly of the League of Nations. (Norman L. Hill, *The Public International Conference,* London, 1929, p. 15-16, and Appendix B) After the second World War, this development became even more notable. From July 1, 1946, to June 30, 1947, for instance, the important official conferences and meetings in which the United States participated were 179. (*Participation of the United States Government in International Conferences,* July 1, 1946–June 30, 1947, *Department of State Bulletin* 3031, released June 1948)

M.A. Lafontaine, President of the Union of International Associations at Brussels, said in *The League of Nations Starts,* 1920, Chap. xiii, that from 1843, the number of international conferences regularly doubled from decade to decade

ing more and more nations and more and more subjects of common life.[248] So have been the increases in international treaties[249] and the changes in their character.[250]

(9, 20, 77, 169, 510, 1070), and between 1910 and 1914, it reached a total of 494. It is not clear, however, what criterion was used in defining the term "international conference."

248. In earlier days, conferences were rarely held by more than two nations. Later, conferences of several nations occurred as international interests became further and further interwoven. Now we have conferences in which tens of nations, even the nations of the whole world, participate. Meanwhile, conferences on legal, administrative, social, economic, or technical problems have tended to increase in number as international life has become more and more expanded. The result is that when we reach the later nineteenth century, and the period of multipartite international conferences proper, we find that the meetings which deal with purely political or diplomatic problems are relatively few. (Cf. Norman L. Hill, *The Public International Conference,* London, 1929, p. 9-13, 20-22.)

249. Not until modern times were treaties concluded between nations numerous. Since the 19th century, however, most of the nations have come to be bound by an impressively intertwined network of treaties. It was estimated that some 8,000 treaties were in force throughout the world, in 1914. (Cf. Lassa F. Oppenheim, *International Law,* 4th ed., London, 1928, Vol. I, p. 701, note I.) According to a learned Austrian historian, about 16,000 treaties were concluded between the Congress of Vienna Act and 1924; and an American estimate of 1917 gives the number of treaties then in existence as approximately 10,000. (Cf. Arthur Nussbaum, *A Concise History of the Law of Nations,* New York, 1947, p. 191-192.) During the two and one-half decades between World War I and the end of World War II, 4,822 international engagements were negotiated and registered with the League of Nations. (*League of Nations, Treaty Series*) A typical increase in the number of treaties is to be seen in American diplomatic practice. There were 1981 treaties concluded by the United States with other states from 1789 to 1939. Between 1789 and 1839, there were 87; between 1839 and 1889, 453; and between 1889 and 1939, 1441. (Cf. Elmer Plischke, *Conduct of American Diplomacy,* New York, 1950, p. 307, table 5.)

250. The change in the character of treaties is demonstrated by their subject matter. A collection of treaties issued in 1700 by Jacques Bernard bears the title "collection of treaties of alliance, of peace, of truce." In modern times there have been fewer such political treaties, or treaties dealing with formal and personal diplomatic questions such as marriage and the privileges of rulers and princes, and more treaties dealing with legal, administrative, social, economic, or technical affairs. Meanwhile, treaties signed by more than two nations have enormously increased. This is attributable to the fact that it is natural for several nations to combine in law-making treaties, while it was not natural to expect them to continue to combine in treaties of the older type, creating special and exclusive privileges, or establishing special ties of marriage or alliance between friendly royal houses against hostile dynasties. The more recent international agreements are of a broadly cooperative character in contrast to the narrow competitive agreements of an earlier age. (Cf. Arthur Nussbaum, *A Concise History of the Law of Nations,* New York, 1947, p. 191-210.)

As an extension of international conferences and a means of implementing international treaties, official international organizations come into play. The Confederation of Europe and Concert of Europe were the forerunners, but were too loose in character.[251] The Rhine River Commission was notably the first real modern pioneer,[252] setting an example for a number of active international river administrations.[253] The international sanitary councils set up in 1839 and 1840 were other old-timers.[254]

Since the middle of the 19th century, official international organizations have increased notably in number as well as in scale. In addition to the Universal Postal Union, International Bureau of Weights

---

251. It has been said that the buildup of modern official international organizations began with the post-Napoleonic "Confederation of Europe" and the "Concert of Europe." These were significant not only for the role they played in European settlements for almost a century, but for the pattern they established, which has been continued in the general international organization of the League of Nations and the United Nations. They were too loose in character, however. (Cf. Walter A. Phillips, *The Confederation of Europe: A Study of the European Alliance 1813-1823, as an Experiment in the International Organization of Peace,* London, 1920; Robert B. Mowat, *The Concert of Europe,* London, 1930; and James T. Watkin, IV, and J. William Robinson, *General International Organization,* A Source Book, New York, 1956, p. 3-10.)

252. The Rhine River Commission was created in 1804 to deal with navigation on that river. Prior to that time, the regulation of the river by the separate coastal states had resulted in much inconvenience and expense to commerce. By the treaty of 1804, a group of uniform regulations and tolls were adopted and a commission with a Director-General of the tolls was established to assist in the execution of the document. (Cf. Norman L. Hill, *International Administration,* New York, 1931, p. 10.)

253. The success of the Rhine Commission in the regulation of traffic for the advantage of all led in 1856 to the creation of the European Danube Commission, whose broad powers included the collection of tolls, and dredging and improving the river. (Cf. *The Regime of the International Rivers: Danube and Rhine,* Studies in History, Economics, and Public Law, Columbia University Press, 1923.) So effective were these commissions that their use has been extended to other rivers by more recent agreements. The Congo was provided with an international commission by the General Act of Berlin of February 26, 1885 (*British and Foreign State Papers,* Vol. 74, p. 4); and the Treaty of Versailles created administrative organs for the Elbe and Oder Rivers (*Treaty of Versailles,* Part XII, Sec. II, Chap. 3).

254. About two decades after the Congress of Vienna, the necessity for taking concerted action to prevent the spread of epidemics, which had particularly ravaged the districts of trade, became evident. As a result, international sanitary councils were set up at Constantinople in 1838 and at Tangier in 1840. The agencies were empowered to supervise quarantine and, in other ways, to prevent the spread of infectious diseases. (Cf. Norman L. Hill, *International Administration,* New York, 1931, p. 10.)

and Measures, and international courts already mentioned earlier,[255] there have appeared many others of importance. The International Telegraphic Bureau, for example, was founded in 1867;[256] the International Meteorological Organization in 1878;[257] the International Bureau for the Protection of Industrial Property in 1883;[258] the International Institute of Agriculture in 1905;[259] and the International Office of Public Health in 1907.[260]

---

255. Cf. II: 74, 146 and 226-228.

256. The International Telegraph Bureau was founded in 1868, and in 1906, it was given duties relating to wireless communication. Prior to 1868, the international regulation of telegraphic correspondence was attempted by bilateral treaties, but the results were not regarded as satisfactory. The functions of this organization are indeed essential to the daily lives of people throughout the world, and it has worked so smoothly that few people realize it exists. It was superseded by the International Telecommunication Union in 1932 to include the International Telegraph Union, and was restructured in 1947 as a specialized agency of the United Nations. (Cf. George A. Codding, Jr., *The International Telecommunication Union, An Experiment in International Cooperation,* Leiden, 1952, p. 449-461.)

257. International coordination, and the setting of international standards, procedures, and practices for the operation of meteorological stations, were the responsibilities of the International Meteorological Organization, established in 1878. It was developed into the World Meteorological Organization, in 1950, to be a specialized agency of the United Nations. At present, tens of thousands of meteorological stations are scattered over the face of the earth, both on land and sea. (Cf. Gerard J. Mangone, *A Short History of International Organization,* New York, 1954, p. 220; and "Convention of the World Meteorological Organizaion," Hearing before a Subcommittee of the Committee on Foreign Relations, United States Senate, 81st Congress, first session, March 30, 1949, p. 15-25.)

258. Under the International Convention for the protection of industrial property, the bureau was formed at Berne, Switzerland, in 1883, and by the Convention of 1891, the duties of the bureau were extended to the registration of trademarks. (Cf. Gerard J. Mangone, *A Short History of International Organization,* New York, 1954, p. 84-86.)

259. Inspired by David Lubin, a bold Sacramento merchant, on May 25, 1905, forty nations met in Rome to discuss the formation of the International Institute of Agriculture. After some cautious discussions, the Institute was established with thirty-eight nations ratifying its charter. The Institute was entrusted with the collection and dissemination of worldwide information on agricultural production, rural wages, and plant diseases, while it was urged to study questions of cooperatives, insurance, and agricultural credit. The Institute was superseded by the Food and Agriculture Organization of the United Nations, formed on October 16, 1945. (Cf. Gerard J. Mangone, *A Short History of International Organization,* New York, 1954, p. 88-89.)

260. In 1903, at Paris, eighteen nations agreed to create an International Office of Health according to the principles which guided the formation and the function of the International Bureau of Weights and Measures. Receiving all available information on the status of infectious diseases within the contracting

Immediately after World War I, a unique International Labor Organization was created,[261] and World War II brought in its wake important newcomers such as the International Bank for Reconstitution and Development,[262] the International Monetary Fund,[263] the

---

states, the Office was charged with making regular public reports to all the members. In this work, its expenses were shared by the parties to the Convention. After some delay, the Office finally came into existence, in 1907. It was developed into the International Health Organization of the League of Nations, in 1920, and the World Health Organization, in 1948. It exists as a specialized agency of the United Nations, with headquarters in Geneva, and regional centers covering each of the main geographical regions of the globe. (Cf. Robert Berkov, *The World Health Organization, A Study in Decentralized International Organization,* Geneva, 1957, p. 25, 35-47.)

261. Uniquely, among international agencies, operations of the ILO are governed by tripartite bodies consisting of representatives of government, employers, and workers, each body speaking independently. Well over 100 countries are members of the ILO, which has its headquarters in Geneva, Switzerland. (Cf. Part XIII of the *Versailles Treaty;* David A. Morse, *The Origin and Evolution of the I.L.O. and Its Role in the World Community,* New York, 1969, p. 3-10.)

262. The International Bank for Reconstruction and Development, or simply the World Bank, was created in 1944, and has its headquarters in Washington, D.C. It began operations in 1946, granting loans at "conventional" financial terms to member governments or, under government guarantees, to government agencies, development banks, or private undertakings. It has two offspring: the International Finance Corporation, founded in 1956 to provide funds without government guarantees for private projects in underdeveloped countries; and the International Development Association, founded in 1960 to provide loans on "soft" financial terms. The main task of the World Bank is to provide finance for productive purposes out of its own capital, funds borrowed in capital markets, and retained earnings. Of the initial authorized capital, equivalent to $10 billion, 2% was paid in gold or U.S. dollars and may be used freely by the World Bank in any of its operations. Eighteen percent was paid in the national currencies of subscribing members, but is available for lending only insofar as members deem it advisable to export capital and give their consent. The remaining 80%, not available for lending, is subject to call only when required to meet the World Bank's obligations for funds it has itself borrowed or guaranteed. The authorized capital was raised gradually to the equivalent of $27 billion, in 1971. Cash payments were required only from new members. The voting power of the members is in proportion to their capital subscriptions. (Cf. Arthur Smithies, "The International Bank for Reconstruction and Development," *American Economic Review,* Vol. XXXIV (Dec. 1944), p. 784-797; George N. Halm, *International Monetary Cooperation,* Chapel Hill, N.C., 1945, Chap XIII and Appendix V; and the annual reports of the International Bank for Reconstruction and Development.)

263. The International Monetary Fund, created at the Bretton Woods Conference, in 1944, and headquartered in Washington, D.C., has become an essential segment of international banking. The fund has almost 120 members. Under its charter, member governments have for the first time in history agreed on broad

United Nations Educational, Scientific and Cultural Organization,[264] the International Civil Aviation Organization,[265] the Inter-governmental Maritime Consultative Organization,[266] and the International Atomic Energy Agency.[267]

---

lines of international monetary policy. They aim particularly at the establishment and maintenance of currency convertibility and the avoidance of competitive exchange depreciation. At the same time, they have provided the fund with a substantial pool of resources to help stabilize exchange rates by assisting countries over difficulties in their balances of payments. Each member is assigned a quota for the pool of resources, determined by the size of its economy, foreign trade, and other factors. These quotas, following general increases in 1959, 1966, and 1970, totaled the equivalent of $29 billion in the early 1970s. Each member pays a subscription to the fund equivalent to its quota, normally 25% in gold and 75% in its own currency. Voting power and eligibility to draw on the fund are linked to the size of the quota. (Cf. George N. Halm, *International Monetary Cooperation,* Chapel Hill, N.C., 1945, Chap. VI, and Appendices III and IV; and annual reports of the International Monetary Fund.)

264. UNESCO was organized immediately aftr World War II. Although it submits reports on activities to the United Nations and receives appropriations from it for technical assistance activities, it is an independent body with its own organs, membership, and budget. All members of the UN are eligible for membership. It parallels the UN structure, and is provided with a General Conference, an Executive Board, and Secretariat. As stated in its constitution, the organization's purpose is to "contribute to peace and security by promoting collaboration among the nations through education, science and culture in order to further universal respect for justice, for the rule of law, and for the human rights and fundamental freedoms" of all. (Cf. Julian Huxley, *UNESCO, Its Purpose and Its Philosophy,* Washington, 1947, p. 5-21; and Walter H.C. Laves and Charles A. Thomson, *UNESCO, Purpose, Progress, Prospects,* Bloomington, Ind., 1957, p. 415-431.)

265. The International Civil Aviation Organization, established in 1947 and headquartered in Montreal, administers a convention on conditions of civil aviation and serves as a clearing-house for information. It develops the principles and techniques of international air navigation and fosters the planning and development of international air transport. The ICAO helps to insure the safe and orderly growth of international civil aviation throughout the world; encourage the development of airways, airports, and air navigation facilities for international civil aviation; meet the needs of the peoples of the world for safe, regular, efficient, and economical air transport; prevent economic waste caused by unreasonable competition; and insure that the rights of contracting nations are fully respected and that every contracting nation has a fair opportunity to operate international airlines. (Cf. Lord McNair, *The Law of the Air,* 3rd ed., ed. by Michael R. E. Kerr and Anthony H.M. Evans, London, 1964, p. 9-14.)

266. The Inter-Governmental Maritime Consultative Organization facilitates co-operation among governments in the area of international shipping, and promotes maritime safety and efficient navigation. It was created by the UN Maritime Conference in Geneva, Switzerland, in 1948, but did not come into operation until 1959. By the late 1960s, it had 65 members, including the United States, Soviet

There are about two hundred major official international organizations in existence at the present time,[268] forming a network which runs a great variety of world affairs. They share a common privilege for being official; on the other hand, they suffer a common weakness, which is that they have no ultimate power. They are remotely controlled, as all their important decisions and actions are subject to the consent of the member nations.[269]

Union, Britain, and France. Its headquarters are in London. (Cf. United Nations Maritime Conference, held at Geneva, Switzerland, from February 19 to March 6, 1948, *Final Act and Related Documents,* New York, 1948.)

267. The International Atomic Energy Agency was created to promote the peaceful uses of atomic energy. It came into existence in 1957 after a decade of attempts to establish an international control system for atomic weapons. It has its headquarters in Vienna, Austria. All nations are eligible for membership and, as of 1968, there were 99 members. (Cf. D.A.V. Fischer, "Historical Summary," in *Nuclear Law for a Developing World,* lectures given at the Training Courses of the Legal Aspects of Peaceful Use of Atomic Energy held by the International Atomic Energy Agency in Vienna, April 16-26, 1968, Vienna, 1969, p. 3-15.)

268. (Cf. the latest issue of the *Yearbook of International Organizations,* ed. and published by the Union of International Associations, Brussels.)

269. "In the final analysis, governmental leaders of member states impose their conceptions of international relations upon international organizations and determine the ends toward which and the means by which international agencies operate. While international institutions tend to some limited degree to develop corporate viewpoints and purposes, usually through professional staff members who identify themselves with the organizations which they serve, these institutions are essentially instruments of their member states.... Such agencies are created and maintained by governments for instrumental purposes, and their usefulness depends upon the disposition of statesmen to resort to them for the promotion of values deemed compatible with national interests." (Inis L. Claude, Jr., Part I of "International Organization," in the *International Encyclopedia of Social Sciences,* New York, 1968, Vol. 8, p. 35)

"The weaknesses of existing international institutions—while discouraging to those who see an even greater role for them in the years ahead—should not simply be attributed to shortcomings within the organizations. To a considerable extent, the weaknesses reflect basic political problems, for which no amount of institutional reorganization or reinvigoration could compensate. It may be a truism that international organizations are only as good as their member states are willing to let them be.... while most nations pay lip service to the notion of growing international interdependence, they remain unwilling to allow international organizations to play active roles in fostering international collaborative policies. Before international organizations can become more responsive to the exigencies created by developments in science and technology, these attitudes, and not merely the organizations themselves, will have to undergo some very fundamental changes." (*Science and Technology in an Era of Interdependence,* by UNA-USA National Policy Panel, New York, 1974, p. 46-47)

"Developing nations—having passed through the decolonization process—

h.
General
International Organization

THE DEVELOPMENT OF OFFICIAL INTERNATIONAL OR-
ganizations culminated with the creation of that general international organization,[270] the League of Nations, after World War I, and the
United Nations after World War II.

The League of Nations was born in 1920 and died in 1946. For
most of the time of its existence, most of the important nations of the
world were members.[271] It had two principal bodies: the Assembly
and the Council, with a permanent secretariat.

---

tend to be suspicious of organizations which they do not 'control' . . . It is not only
the smaller, less developed countries which are reserved about developing new and
more effective international institutions. Many larger nations tend to prefer
bilateral dealings over which they believe they can exercise more control. Long-
established governments may be as sensitive as new nations about what seem to be
explicit limitations on sovereignty through the strengthening of multilateral institutions." (*Science and Technology in an Era of Interdependence,* by UNA-USA
National Policy Panel, New York, 1975, p. 21-22)

There are three common methods of remote control: First is that important
decisions in international meetings are usually made upon instructions from the
government of the member nations through their representatives, who do the talking only. Secondly, policies made in international organizations have to be implemented or enforced by their member nations, as the international organizations
themselves usually have no means to follow through directly. And third, treaties,
agreements and even some decisions made in international organizations often require the ratification of the member nations individually. (Cf. Inis L. Claude, Jr.,
"International Organization: Process and Institutions," in the *International Encyclopedia of the Social Sciences,* New York, 1968, Vol. 8.)

270. The term "general international organization" means, taking the
League of Nations as an example, "an international institution more far-reaching
in its composition than any previous entente, except the technical unions, and
more general in its competence than they were. It is more fully supplied with
special institutions but less solidly built than most of the confederations of history.
Its aims are more numerous and ambitious and its functions more varied than
those of the traditional alliances, but it involves fewer restrictions on the freedom
of action of its members." (William E. Rappard, "What is the League of
Nations?" in *The World Crisis,* by the Professors of the Graduate Institute of International Studies, London, 1938, p. 59)

271. The Covenant of the League of Nations was adopted by the Paris peace
conference on April 28, 1919, and included in the peace treaties made by the Allies

All members of the League were represented in the Assembly, each member having one vote. There was at least one session a year, and debates generally covered all phases of the League's activities.[272]

The Council was to have consisted of a small number of great powers with permanent seats, and several non-permanent members elected by the Assembly. It met regularly several times a year and in special session when necessary.[273]

The Secretariat was headed by the Secretary General, who was appointed by the Council with the approval of the Assembly. The staff members of the Secretariat were appointed by the Secretary General with the approval of the Council.[274]

One of the important functions of the Secretariat was to coordinate the activities of the agencies established by the League in the social and economic fields in cooperation with other international organizations.[275] The achievement of the League in this respect was somewhat more than originally envisaged.[276]

---

with Germany, Austria, Hungary, and Bulgaria. The Covenant went into force on January 10, 1920, with 42 Members. Eventually, 63 governments joined the League, although total membership at any one time never exceeded 58, a high reached in 1934. The United States never joined the League. Germany became a member in 1926, and the Soviet Union in 1934. Before the League came to an end, in 1946, Japan, Italy, Germany, and 14 other states, mostly Latin American, had withdrawn, and in 1939, the Soviet Union was expelled. (Cf. Leland M. Goodrich, *The United Nations,* New York, 1959, p. 10-11.)

272. (Cf. Article 3 of the Covenant of the League of Nations; and Margaret E. Burton, *The Assembly of the League of Nations,* Chicago, 1941, p. 94-134.)

273. The Council was originally designed to consist of 5 great powers with permanent seats—the United States, Britain, France, Italy, and Japan—and 4 non-permanent Members, elected by the Assembly. The United States never took its seat, but when Germany and the Soviet Union were admitted to the League, as great powers they had permanent seats on the Council. The number of nonpermanent Members was eventually increased to 11. (Cf. Article 4 of the Covenant of the League of Nations, and Leland M. Goodrich, *The United Nations,* New York, 1959, p. 11-13.)

274. (Cf. Article 6 of the Covenant of the League of Nations, and Egon Ranshofen-Wertheimer, *The International Secretariat,* New York, 1945.)

275. Articles 23 to 25 of the Covenant of the League of Nations made it possible for the League to develop an integrated apparatus for the consideration of social and economic problems. Article 24 of the Covenant envisaged control of about 27 existing intergovernmental organizations, and Article 25 opened the way for cooperation with about 350 private international bodies with interests in social and economic problems. Article 23 of the Covenant specifically mentioned such problems as: eradication of disease and drug addiction; traffic in women and children; and restrictions on communications and transit. The structure to carry out these purposes included five organizations—Health, Economic, Financial, In-

The great impetus to the creation of the League was the cataclysm of World War I, and one of its main objectives was to maintain security and peace. Of the 26 Articles in its Covenant, over half were devoted to methods of achieving this objective.[277] But, in spite of all the provisions, security was often threatened and peace was broken again and again,[278] finally culminating in World War II.[279]

The United Nations was established with a Charter of 111 articles adopted in 1945 by an international conference held in San Francis-

---

tellectual Cooperation, and Communications and Transit—and three bodies to deal with narcotic drugs. (Cf. Pitman B. Potter, "The League of Nations and other International Organizations," in *Geneva Studies,* Geneva Research Center, Geneva, Vol. V., No. 6.)

276. "The League of Nations.... served to co-ordinate the work of the many ad hoc organizations which had sprung up around the turn of the century to deal with new scientific and technological advances.... While the League failed to prevent the outbreak of a major war in 1939, its efforts in the fields of health, international labour legislation, refugee settlement and international administration (in such areas as the Saar and Danzig) were invaluable, and pointed the way forward to the intensification of such international co-operation." (Ruth B. Henig, *The League of Nations,* New York, 1973, p. 153. Cf. A. LeRoy Bennett, *International Organizations: Principles and Issues,* Englewood Cliffs, N.J., 1977, p. 31-32.)

277. Articles 8 and 9 dealt with disarmament; 10 and 11, with aggression and the threat of war; 12 to 14, judicial settlement of disputes; 15, political settlement of disputes; 16, sanction against aggression and hostility; 17, disputes involving non-members of the League; 18 to 20, registration of treaties; 21, other engagements for maintenance of peace; and 22, territorial trusteeship.

278. The very serious cases were the Japanese invasion of Manchuria in 1931 and the Italian attack on Ethiopia in 1935. The Lytton Commission, which was sent by the League to investigate the Manchurian dispute, named Japan as the aggressor, but the League took no action beyond recommending that Members refuse to recognize the Japanese puppet state of Manchukuo. In 1938, it merely urged Members to apply individual sanctions against Japan for the bombing of Chinese cities. The League applied limited sanctions against Italy, but failed to save Ethiopia from conquest. (Cf. James T. Shotwell, *Lessons on Security and Disarmament from the History of the League of Nations,* New York, 1944, p. 45-109.)

279. "In quick succession, League failure to check Japanese aggression in Manchuria was followed by: the rise of Hitler to power in Germany and German rearmament; the collapse of League disarmament discussions; the failure of League sanctions against Italy following Mussolini's attack on Ethiopia in October, 1935; and German remilitarization of the Rhineland in March, 1936, in clear violation of the Treaty of Versailles and the Locarno pact.... why did the League fail? It must be conceded that the League did fail in its principal purpose, namely the maintenance of international peace and security. The outbreak of the Second World War was tragic testimony to this fact." (Leland M. Goodrich, *The United Nations,* New York, 1959, p. 14-15)

co.[280] In structure, it resembled the League, but with many more members.[281]

The General Assembly of the United Nations is, in composition, the League Assembly all over again, the forum in which all member nations are represented with equal rights of speech and vote. It holds sessions every year, and the debates always range widely. It elects its president and other officers, and appoints standing committees to do preparatory work.[282]

---

280. The final charter drafting conference, formally known as the United Nations Conference on International Organization, opened in the Opera House in San Francisco, California, April 25, 1945, chaired by Stettinius, the United States Secretary of State. In all, 50 countries participated. Decisions were taken by vote, a two-thirds majority being required, and the Charter of the United Nations and the proposed amendments were voted on clause by clause. On June 26, 1945, the charter was signed. On July 28, the United States Senate approved it by 89 votes to 2. Other nations quickly followed suit. By October 24, on what has subsequently been celebrated as United Nations Day, the necessary total of ratifications had been attained, and the charter went into force. (Cf. A. LeRoy Bennett, *International Organizations: Principles and Issues,* Englewood Cliffs, N.J., 1977, p. 33-45.)

281. Fifty-one nations signed the Charter of the United Nations as original members. From 1946 to 1950, only nine new nations were admitted, largely owing to the refusal of either East or West to increase the other's voting strength. In 1955, the deadlock was broken to admit 16 nations. In 1960, there was another burst of 17 admissions, all from Africa, with the exception of Cyprus. This marked virtual acceptance of the principle that every nation attaining independence is ipso facto entitled to membership irrespective of its size or viability. Only nations in dispute between East and West remained excluded from membership by reason of votes in the Security Council. In 1967, Secretary-General U Thant requested that a limit be set on full membership of "microstates" because their increased number would only weaken the UN. No action was taken because membership is a sensitive issue among the new nations, mostly Asian and African. In 1971, the permanent member of the Republic of China was replaced by the People's Republic of China. As of 1977, the United Nations had had 149 members. (Cf. A. LeRoy Bennett, *International Organizations: Principles and Issues,* Englewood Cliffs, N.J., 1977, p. 65-69.)

282. The General Assembly holds regular sessions every year, commencing on the third Tuesday in September. Each member nation is entitled to a delegation of five, with five deputies. The Assembly elects its own president to hold office for 12 months. In addition, there are 17 vice presidents and chairmen of the Assembly's seven standing committees. These unite under the president to form the General Committee, which is a kind of steering committee for each session. The Assembly is a forum in which the opinions of all governments can find expression through the spokesmen for member nations. A general debate usually opens each session in which each member nation in turn will proclaim its views on world affairs. Decisions are made by majority vote; in the case of "important decisions," by a two-thirds majority. The seven standing committees of the Assembly are: the Special Political Committee; First (Political and Security) Committee; Second (Economic and Financial) Committee; Third (Social,

The Security Council replaced the Council of the League as the main repository of power in the United Nations for maintaining security and peace. It consists of five great powers as permanent members and ten non-permanent members elected by the General Assembly. Although it only meets when there is business to attend to, it was conceived as a body in continuous session, able to be immediately responsive to any emergency. The presidency rotates monthly among its members.[283]

In its Secretariat, the United Nations Charter built on League experience, but gave more power to the Secretary-General.[284] The structure of the Secretariat has been enlarged, with a great increase in personnel.[285]

Humanitarian, and Cultural) Committee; Fourth (Trusteeship and Non-Self-Governing Territories) Committee; Fifth (Administrative and Budgetary) Committee; Sixth (Legal) Committee. Every member nation is represented on each committee. (Cf. Chapter IV of the Charter of the United Nations; and Sydney D. Bailey, *The General Assembly of the United Nations, A Study of Procedure and Practice,* rev. ed., New York, 1964.)

283. The 5 permanent members are the United States, USSR, United Kingdom, France, and China. The addition of nonpermanent members—originally 6, which increased to 10 in 1965—elected for two-year terms by the General Assembly, was a concession to the demands of the smaller nations and rested on the precedent of the League Council. It was stipulated that these elected members should be those who make a contribution to the maintenance of peace and security, though in practice this stipulation has been largely ignored and these seats have been filled by nations representing the main voting blocs in the General Assembly. (Cf. Chapter V of the Charter of the United Nations; and Leland M. Goodrich, "The UN Security Council," in *The United Nations, Past, Present, and Future,)* ed. by James Barros, New York, 1972, p. 16-63.)

284. The Secretary-General is appointed by the General assembly upon the recommendation of the Security Council. He is not only the chief administrative officer of the organization, he is also endowed by Article 99 with a specifically political role and in this capacity has both a power and an obligation to bring to the notice of the Security Council any matter which threatens international peace security. His reports to the General Assembly on the work of the organization have also often served as guidelines for United Nations action. (Cf. Chapter XV of the Charter of the United Nations; and Leon Gordenker, "The Secretary-General," in *The United Nations, Past, Present, and Future,* ed. by James Barros, New York, 1972, p. 104-142.)

285. The Secretary-General is assisted by a number of undersecretaries. The main departments of the Secretariat are those which deal with Security Council affairs, Economic and Social Affairs, Trusteeship, Public Information, Conference Services and Technical Assistance. The enlargement of structure and the extension of functions have naturally brought about a great increase of personnel. Permanent positions had grown to 2,909 by April, 1950, about four times the maximum of the League Secretariat. (Cf. U.N. Press Release, SA/57/Rev. I, April 10, 1950;

The League's Mandates Commission, which took care of the trust territories, was converted into the Trusteeship Council as a principal organ of the United Nations. The membership of the Council is evenly divided between the nations which administer the trust territories and those which do not.[286]

In view of the large number of activities in the economic and social fields sponsored under the League,[287] an Economic and Social Council was created in the United Nations as a principal organ, with members elected by the General Assembly.[288] It has a number of functional subordinate bodies[289] and has established a series of regional agencies.[290]

---

and Leland M. Goodrich, "The Secretariat of United Nations," in the *UN Administration of Economic and Social Programs,* ed. by Gerard J. Mangone, New York, 1966, p. 1-36.)

286. The original membership of the Council consisted of an even balance of administering and nonadministering nations together with any permanent members of the Security Council not otherwise represented. The places allotted to nonadministering nations were filled by election in the General Assembly for three-year terms. The Council met twice a year in New York City. However, as the number of trust territories shrank as they were converted into independent nations, the membership of the Council declined and its meetings were reduced in 1962 to one a year. (Cf. Chapter XIII of the Charter of the United Nations; and Inis L. Claude, Jr. *Swords into Plowshares, The Problems and Progress of International Organization,* New York, 1964, p. 322-342.)

287. The 1939 Bruce Report had already foreshadowed ways in which the League's social and economic activities could be expanded, and it became the blueprint for United Nations organization in these fields. (Cf. The Bruce Report on the "Development of International Cooperation in Economic and Social Affairs," August 22, 1939. Excerpts of the Report may be found in *General International Organization, A Source Book,* by James T. Watkins IV and J. William Robinson, New York, 1956, p. 84-87.)

288. The Economic and Social Council consisted originally of 18 members (the number later increased to 27), all elected by the General Assembly for three-year terms, one third of the membership coming up for renewal each year. The Council meets twice a year, usually in New York City, in April, and in Geneva, Switzerland, in July. A bare majority of those present and voting suffices for all decisions. The Council is charged with a multiplicity of functions, but basically serves as a forum for debate and a clearinghouse of information in the economic and social fields. (Cf. Chapter X of the Charter of the United Nations; and Walter R. Sharp, "Program Coordination and the Economic Social Council," in *UN Administration of Economic and Social Programs,* ed. by Gerard J. Mangone, New York, 1966, p. 102-157.)

289. The most important of these subordinate bodies are the Committee for Program and Coordination, which is charged with the review and coordination of United Nations assistance programs; the Commission on Narcotic Drugs, which continues the work done by the League's Advisory Committee on Opium and Dan-

In order to promote and coordinate the activities of the official international organizations in the economic and social fields, the Economic and Social Council is empowered to enter into relationships with the most important ones[291] and recognize them as specialized agencies of the United Nations.[292]

---

gerous Drugs; the Commission on Human Rights, which drafted the Declaration on Human Rights and has since been working on conventions to implement it. In 1966, two treaties further defining and implementing the basic rights outlined in the Declaration were completed. Another body responsible to the Council is the United Nations Children's Fund, created in 1946 as a postwar relief measure, but now charged with both long and short-term welfare programs for children. (Cf. Alf Ross, *The United Nations, Peace and Progress,* Totowa, N.J., 1966, p. 132-138.)

290. The first of these regional agencies was the Economic Commission for Europe, set up in 1947 with 28 members, which has its headquarters at Geneva. This served as a model for three other such bodies: the Economic Committee for Asia and the Far East established in 1947 at Bangkok, Thailand; the Economic Committee for Latin America established in 1948 at Santiago, Chile; and finally, the Economic Committee for Africa established in 1958 at Addis Ababa, Ethiopia. (Cf. Robert W. Gregg, "Program Decentralization through the Regional Economic Commissions," in *The UN Administration of Economic and Social Programs,* ed. by Gerard J. Mangone, New York, 1966, p. 231-284.)

291. Agreements with the following specialized agencies came into force on the dates indicated: International Labour Organization (ILO): Dec. 14, 1946; Food and Agriculture Organization of the United Nations (FAO): Dec. 14, 1946; United Nations Educational, Scientific and Cultural Organization (UNESCO): Dec. 14, 1964; International Civil Aviation Organization (ICAO): May 13, 1947; International Bank for Reconstruction and Development (WORLD BANK): Nov. 15, 1947; International Development Association (IDA): Mar. 27, 1961; International Finance Corporation (IFC): Feb. 20, 1957; International Monetary Fund (FUND): Nov. 15, 1947; World Health Organization (WHO): July 10, 1948; Universal Postal Union (UPU): July 1, 1948; International Tele-communication Union (ITU): Jan. 1, 1949; World Meteorological Organization (WMO): Dec. 20, 1951; Inter-Governmental Maritime Consultative Organization (IMCO): Jan. 13, 1959. Although the International Atomic Energy Agency is not a specialized agency, it was established under the aegis of the UN, and its relationship agreement with the UN was approved by the General Assembly on Nov. 14, 1957. (Cf. Articles 57, 63, 64 of the Charter of the United Nations; and Herbert G. Nicholas, *The United Nations as a Political Institution,* 4ed., London, 1971, p. 151-157.)

292. The specialized agencies are autonomous to varying degrees. Their establishment as separate entities is partly due to the particular circumstances surrounding the creation of each, but also to a concept of "functional internationalism," according to which international cooperation in certain fields is more effective if removed from politics, while successful collaboration in technical areas may itself contribute to the relaxation of international tensions. Certain features are common to all the specialized agencies—a permanent secretariat of international officials, a deliberative body or assembly which represents the full membership, and a smaller executive council or board. Decisions are generally reached by

The Economic and Social Council is also empowered to make arrangements for consultation with international and even national non-governmental organizations on matters within their fields of competence.[293]

With such an enlargement of structure and extension of functions, the United Nations should be able to make great contributions to economic and social developments in the world. Most of its important works in this respect, however, have been limited to the level of statistics, debate and recommendations.[294]

In peace and security, it has been apparent that the United Nations, like the League, could not achieve very much.[295] In the last

---

a majority vote. (Cf. Inis L. Claude, Jr., *Swords into Plowshares, The Problems and Progress of International Organization,* New York, 1964, p. 344-367.)

293. (Cf. II, 242.)

294. The United Nations "are so beset with controls exercised for the benefit of individual nations or groups of nations that it is very difficult for them to deal with world threats. Each nation tends to break down all problems into what is good for 'us,' at whatever cost to anyone else, the traditional survival group attitude, ignoring the fact that the survival group has now become the human race itself." (Brock Chisholm, "The Problem of New Problem," in *The Population Crisis and the Use of World Resources,* ed. by Stuart Mudd, Bloomington, Ind. 1964, p. 343. Cf. A. LeRoy Bennett, *International Organizations, Principles and Issues,* Englewood Cliffs, N.J., 1977, p. 204-261; Leon Gordenker, "The United Nations and Economic and Social Change," in *The United Nations and International Politics,* ed. by Leon Gordenker, Princeton, N.J., 1971, p. 151-183; Shirley Hazzard, *Defeat of an Ideal, A Study of the Self-Destruction of the United Nations,* Boston, 1973, p. 217-249; and Robert Jackson, *A Study of the Capacity of the United Nations Development System,* Vols. I and II Combined, UN document DP/5, Geneva, 1969.)

295. The Covenant of the League of Nations provided for peaceful settlement of disputes by the collective action of members, but action could be taken only by the unanimous vote of all members. The same restrictions applied to possible enforcement measures. (Cf. The Covenant of the League, Article 5; and 6 and 7 of Article 15.) This is why the League could not achieve very much in security and peace. The United Nations was given authority to enforce peaceful settlement if, in the 15-member Security Council, a majority of 9, including the 5 great powers of permanent members, could agree. (Cf. The Charter of the United Nations, Article 27.) The requirement of the unanimous vote of the 5 great powers makes it as difficult as in the League to take action for security and peace. There is hardly a dispute without one or more of the great powers directly or indirectly involved.

296. Among the hot wars are: the Middle East War, first in Palestine in 1948; then in the Suez in 1956; followed by the "Six Day War" in 1967; another conflict in 1973; the Cyprus War between Turkey and Greece in 1963-1964; wars between India and Pakistan for Kashmir in 1948, and for Bangladesh in 1971; the Congo War and various other African Wars; the Korean War, 1950-1953, in which more than 20 nations were directly involved; and the Indochina War or Vietnam War,

thirty years, there have been hot wars,[296] cold war,[297] and the threat of atomic and nuclear war.[298]

It is true that the League and the United Nations are the greatest experiments we have had in history in the building of one world. But they could not adequately address the most important problems, especially those concerning their principal goals,[299] which were

---

1946-1975, the longest war in recent centuries. (Cf. Andrew Boyd, *Fifteen Men on a Powder Keg,* New York, 1971, p. 114-221; and Quincy Wright, *A Study of War,* 2nd ed., Chicago, 1965, p. 1544-1547, Appendix C, "Hostilities, 1945-1964.")

"With a broad definition of war including large-scale guerilla wars, Istvan Kende lists 119 wars between 1945 and 1975. The total duration of these conflicts exceeded 350 years. The territory of 69 countries and the armed forces of 81 states were involved. Since September 1945 there was not one day in which one or several wars were not being fought somewhere in the world. On an average day 12 wars were fought. Since 1945, war casualties number tens of millions." (*Disarmament and World Development,* ed. by Richard Jolly, Oxford, 1978, p. 13. Cf. Istvan Kende, *Local Wars in Asia, Africa and Latin America 1945-1969,* Hungarian Academy of Science, Center for Afro-Asian Research, p. 11.)

297. This refers to the conflict between the Communist nations led by the Soviet Union, and the Western nations led by the United States, fought by all means—ideological, economic and political—but falling short of all-out military action. Its main cause has been that the Soviet Union tries to pursue a world revolution while the United States is committed to the maintenance of existing governments. It has been fought during most of the period since the close of World War II, with varying degrees of intensity. (Cf. Walter Lipmann, *The Cold War: A Study in U.S. Foreign Policy,* New York, 1972, p. 5-52; and Hugh Higgins, *The Cold War,* New York, 1974.)

298. Such a great war would have to be fought between the great powers, of course. But "it was recognized that no world organization could effectively keep the peace between the Great Powers. Consequently the Security Council was not an organ to police the Big Five. It was an instrument by which the permanent members defined as the United States, the USSR, the United Kingdom, France, and China, would together keep the peace among the other powers." "Their unity was to be the cornerstone of which the whole United Nations structure would be built. No great thought was given to what would happen if they did not agree. To plan for disagreement was thought to be a contradiction in terms." For the above reasons, the occurrence of a great war has continued to be a threat. (Herbert G. Nicholas, "United Nations," in *Americana,* 1973 ed., Vol. 27, p. 443. Cf. his book *The United Nations as a Political Institution,* 4 ed., London, 1971, p. 72-80.)

299. The Covenant of the League of Nations set this goal in its preamble: "In order to promote international cooperation and to achieve international peace and security, by the acceptance of obligations not to resort to war," and the Charter of the United Nations begins with the expression of determination "to save succeeding generations from the scourge of war, which twice in our lifetime has brought untold sorrow to mankind" and "to unite our strength to maintain international peace and security."

security and peace. Why? What made them ineffective in these areas?

First of all, it is necessary to point out that they were established as associations of nations,[300] with the weakness common to all official international organizations:[301] the domination by their member

---

300. The League of Nations was developed from the last of his famous Fourteen Points, the war aims set forth by U.S. President Woodrow Wilson in a speech delivered on January 8, 1918: "A general association of nations must be formed under specific covenants for the purpose of affording mutual guarantees of political independence and territorial integrity to great and small states alike." (Cf. James T. Watkins IV and J. William Robinson, *General International Organization, A Source Book,* New York, 1956, p. 55-56.)

"The principle on which the League was founded was simple and consistent. It was an association of independent but co-operating states, and its institutions were intended as means for making it as easy as possible for these states to work together. The members retained their sovereignty, but they had all agreed to do and not to do certain things in the exercise of their sovereign rights. Thus the Covenant did not contain even the beginnings of a system of international government in the strict sense of that word. 'The League' was hardly more than a name for describing the members collectively; it was not an organic union, and there was hardly anything that it could do in a corporate capacity." (James L. Brierly, *The Law of Nations; An Introduction to the International Law of Peace,* 4th ed., Oxford, 1949, p. 97)

"The League of Nations is in fact an instrument of cooperation. It is a standing agency facilitating common action by states animated by the cooperative spirit." (Alfred E. Zimmern, *The League of Nations and the Rule of Law 1918-1935,* London, 1936, p. 283)

"The United Nations is an inter-governmental organization. The persons making up its General Assembly and Councils are either Cabinet Ministers or special emissaries of their Cabinets. What they do in the UN is simply to carry out the policies of their governments. In a nutshell, therefore, the United Nations is governments; governments meeting under a pledge and having certain machinery at their disposal." (John Maclaurin, *The United Nations and Power Politics,* New York, 1951, p. 2)

As Pope Paul remarked in his address to the United Nations: "You are an association. You are a bridge between peoples. You are a network of relations between states." (*The Washington Evening Star,* Oct. 5, 1965, p. A-4)

301. "In keeping with this emphasis upon the national values of member states, international organizations have generally functioned as loose associations, heavily dependent upon the voluntary acceptance by states of the obligations of membership, upon the development of consensus among governments as to programs and policies, and upon techniques of persuasion and political influence rather than command and coercion. In limited areas, international agencies have been endowed with legislative authority and enforcement procedures, but their capacity to function is based essentially upon processes of political accommodation. Usefulness to states, not power over states, is the secret of such strength as an international institution may acquire or possess." (Inis L. Claude, Jr., Part I of

nations as the real masters.[302] Furthermore, both the Covenant of the League and the Charter of the United Nations not only did nothing to remedy such weakness, but went so far as to legalize and strengthen the dominant position of the member nations in many ways, such as:

Emphasizing "sovereign equality"[303] and "equal right and self-determination";[304]

"International Organization," in the *International Encyclopedia of Social Sciences,* New York, 1968, Vol. 8, p. 35-36)

302. "In this situation what will be the role of the chief international organization, the United Nations? At the outset it should be pointed out that this world body is composed of member governments, each of which is recognized in international law as possessing sovereign status. Consequently, the United Nations is primarily the agent of its sovereign masters, who in turn have been responsible in the last analysis for the successes and failures alike of this world body since its inception in 1945." (T. Walter Wallbank, Alastair M. Taylor, Nels M. Bailkey, and Mark S. Mancall, *Civilization Past and Present,* 6th ed., Glenview, Ill., 1970, Book I, p. 508)

"The present system of international organizational machinery cannot adequately deal with the types of problems discussed. . . . More fundamental shortcomings, however, reflect the reluctance of national governments to allow international organizations to develop increased responsibility; inadequate decision-making structures that either allow destructive voting blocs or restrict wide participation; limited technological competence on the part of governments and international organizations; and a rigid organizational structure that is not well matched to new global issues." (*Science and Technology in an Era of Interdependence,* by UNA-USA National Policy Panel, New York, 1975, p. 44)

303. Part 1 of Article 2 of the Charter of the United Nations: "The Organization is based on the principle of the sovereign equality of all its members." The preamble of the Charter: "to reaffirm faith . . . in the equal rights . . . of nations large and small." (Cf. Alf Ross, *The United Nations, Peace and Progress,* Totowa, N.J., 1966, p. 77-80; and Robert A. Klein, *Sovereign Equality Among States; the History of an Idea,* Toronto, 1974, p. 143-168.)

This principle has produced, among other problems, peculiar imbalances in the organization, such as the weight of the voting power of Tonga, with a territory of 270 sq. miles and a population of 90,000 being equal to that of India, with a territory of 1,261,810 sq. miles and a population of 550,000,000, in the early 1970s. "A recent study by the U.N. Association points out that it is now possible for 85 members with only a tenth of the world's population and paying 5 per cent of the budget, to pass 'important question' resolutions in the assembly by a two-thirds majority." (William L. Ryan, AP Special Correspondent, "Uncertainty Ahead for United Nations," *South Bend Tribune,* Nov. 11, 1971, p. 2)

"The UN is not a 'parliament of man'; it is an assembly of absolute sovereignties. A group of nations with combined populations equal to about a tenth of the world's total can outvote another group of countries representing two-thirds of mankind. Can such a body really register world opinion or the moral judgment of humanity? . . . The UN's one-nation one-vote rule in the Assembly is

Stressing "territorial integrity and political independence";[305]
Sanctifying "domestic jurisdiction";[306]

---

as fantastically unworkable and indefensible as is the veto right of five powers in the Security Council. The national governments which appoint and instruct delegations in the UN avoid decisions of consequence if at all possible. Majorities when obtained are usually gotten by watering down meaningful resolutions into meaningless compromises." (*The Worried Woman's Guide to Peace through World Law,* ed. by Lucile Green and Esther Yudell, Piedmont, Calif., 1965, p. 85)

304. From the Charter of the United Nations, part 2 of Article I: "To develop friendly relations among nations based on respect for the principle of equal rights and self-determination of peoples...." and Article 55: "With a view to the creation of conditions of stability and well-being which are necessary for peaceful and friendly relations among nations based on respect for the principle of equal rights and self-determination of peoples...."

Herbert G. Wells was skeptical of national-self determination as a program for peace. He castigated Wilson for "his obsession by the idea of the sovereignty of nationalities" and "he thought only of nations struggling to be free. He never thought of man struggling to be free of nationality." (Cf. his works: *The Way the World Is Going,* Garden City, N.Y., 1929, p. 82; and *The Common Sense of World Peace,* London, 1929, p. 32.)

305. According to Article 10 of the Covenant of the League of Nations: "The Members of the League undertake to respect and preserve as against external aggression the territorial integrity and existing political independence of all Members of the League," and part 4 of Article 2 of the Charter of the United Nations: "All Members shall refrain in their international relations from the threat or use of force against the territorial integrity or political independence of any state...."

"The essential idea of nineteenth-century nationalism was the 'legitimate claim' of every nation to complete sovereignty, the claim of every nation to manage all its affairs within its own territory, regardless of any other nation." But, since "the affairs and interests of every modern community extend to the uttermost parts of the earth" it follows that "a world of independent sovereign states means a world of perpetual injuries, a world of states constantly preparing for or waging war." (Herbert G. Wells, *The Outline of History,* New York, 1920, Vol. II, p. 435)

306. According to part 8 of Article 15 of the Covenant of the League of Nations: "If the dispute between the parties is claimed by one of them, and is found by the Council, to arise out of a matter which by international law is solely within the domestic jurisdiction of that party, the Council shall so report, and shall make no recommendation as to its settlement," and part 7 of Article 2 of the Charter of the United Nations: "Nothing contained in the present Charter shall authorize the United Nations to intervene in matters which are essentially within the domestic jurisdiction of any state or shall require the Members to submit such matters to settlement under the present Charter...." (Cf. Inis L. Claude, Jr., *Swords into Plowshares, The Problems and Progress of International Organization,* New York, 1964, p. 164-172; and Alf Ross, *The United Nations, Peace and Progress,* Totowa, N.J., 1966, p. 63-77.)

Extending "self-defense" from individual nation to collective and regional arrangements.[307]

Causing rigidity with the unanimous voting rule[308] and by giving

---

307. Article 21 of the Covenant of the League of Nations states: "Nothing in this Covenant shall be deemed to affect the validity of international engagements, such as treaties of arbitration or regional understanding like the Monroe Doctrine for securing ... peace." Article 51 of the Charter of the United Nations states: "Nothing in the present Charter shall impair the inherent right of individual or collective self-defense if an armed attack occurs against a Member of the United Nations until the Security Council has taken the measures necessary to maintain international peace and security....," and according to part 1 of Article 52 of the charter: "Nothing in the present Charter precludes the existence of regional arrangements or agencies for dealing with such matters relating to the maintenance of international peace and security as are appropriate for regional action, provided that such arrangements or agencies and their activities are consistent with the Purposes and Principles of the United Nations." The first regional arrangement was the Organization of American States, originally founded as the International Union of American Republics, in 1890. After World War II, a series of such organizations were created: the League of Arab States, formed in 1945; the North Atlantic Treaty Organization, 1949; the Southeast Asia Treaty Organization, 1954; the Warsaw Treaty Organization, 1955; and the lately developed Organization of African Unity. (Cf. Alf Ross, *The United Nations, Peace and Progress,* Totowa, N.J., 1966, p. 216-226.)

Regional understanding and arrangements have easily developed into military alliances, such as the North Atlantic Treaty Organization, the Warsaw Treaty Organization, and the Southeast Asia Treaty Organization. As regards the claim of "self-defense," since there is often no clear demarcation to be made between aggression and defense, and since the circumstances required for a nation to resort to war in self-defense are determined by each nation itself, it is not surprising that war is often carried on under its pretence. (Cf. IV, 45 and 46.)

308. Part 1 of Article 5 of the Covenant of the League of Nations states: "Except where otherwise expressly provided in this Covenant or by the terms of the present Treaty, decisions at any meeting of the Assembly or of the Council, shall require the agreement of all the Members of the League represented at the meeting." This was the so-called "rule of unanimity." There are certain exceptions to this rule, especially one providing that when the Council was reporting on a dispute and making recommendations for its settlement, and votes of parties to the dispute were not to be counted. Nevertheless, this rule made it almost impossible for the League to deal with any really important problem, except by talking about it. (Cf. James L. Brierly, *The Law of Nations; An Introduction to the International Law of Peace,* 4th ed., Oxford, 1949, p. 98.)

309. According to part 1 of Article 4 of the Covenant of the League of Nations: "The Council shall consist of Representatives of the Principal Allied and Associated Powers, together with Representatives of four other Members of the League. These four Members of the League shall be selected by the Assembly from time to time in its discretion." (The permanent members of the Principal Allied and Associated Powers were: the United States, Britain, France, Italy, and Japan.

a few great powers permanent seats[309] in the Security Council with a power to veto any important decision.[310]

As a result, the weakness of the general international organization has turned out to be a serious disease, which led to the death of

---

The United States never took its seat, and Germany and the Soviet Union later had permanent seats. The number of non-permanent members was eventually increased to 11). Part 1 of Article 23 of the Charter of the United Nations declares: "The Security Council shall consist of fifteen members of the United Nations. The Republic of China, France, the Union of Soviet Socialist Republics, the United Kingdom of Great Britain and Northern Ireland, and the United States of America shall be permanent members of the Security Council. The General Assembly shall elect ten other Members of the United Nations to be non-permanent members of the Security Council." (The number of non-permanent members was originally 6, and the Republic of China was later replaced as a permanent member by the People's Republic of China.) (Cf. Alf Ross, *The United Nations, Peace and Progress,* Totowa, N.J., 1966, p. 162-172.)

310. According to parts 2 and 3 of Article 27 of the Charter of the United Nations, as amended in 1965: "Decisions of the Security on procedural matters shall be made by an affirmative vote of nine members. Decisions of the Security Council on all other matters shall be made by an affirmative vote of nine members including the concurring votes of the permanent members." This is the so-called veto rule. It has given rise to another possibility of deadlock in the general international organization, and has downgraded the Security Council, which holds a key position in the whole system to a useless debating forum. The veto has been used by the Soviet Union frequently. In 1962, the total number of Soviet Union vetoes passed 100. (Cf. Inis L. Claude, Jr., *Sword into Plowshares, the Problems and Progress of International Organization,* New York, 1964, p. 133-145; and John G. Stoessinger, *The United Nations and the Superpowers,* New York, 1965, p. 3-20.)

"There are two exceptions to this rule of voting, but both are largely illusory: they are that decisions on matters of procedure may be made by the votes of any seven members, and that when a member is a party to a dispute which the Security Council is investigating that member must abstain from voting. But procedural matters are naturally the less important matters, and moreover the question whether a particular matter is or is not procedural is not itself a question of procedure, and apparently a permanent member can use its veto on that preliminary question. Then again there can naturally only be a "party to dispute" if a "dispute" exists, and the question whether there is or is not a dispute is one on which the veto can be used. There is also a distinction in the Charter between a "dispute" and "a situation which might lead to international friction and give rise to a dispute," and when the Security Council is investigating a "situation" there is nothing to prevent a permanent member, however deeply it may be involved, from using the veto." (James L. Brierly, *The Law of Nations Introduction to the International Law of Peace,* 4th ed., Oxford, 1949, p. 104)

"Most of the important decisions are taken by the Security Council, the action agency. Although it has 15 members, only the five permanent ones, the big powers, have vetoes. Thus the big powers, and especially the superpowers, decide what is and what is not done. The small nations present a plausible claim that they are shut out of decision-making. A vote in the assembly is little consolation."

the League[311] and has made the United Nations unable to handle the great issues.[312]

i.
Socialist International Movement

AS A DYNAMIC AND SPECTACULAR PHENOMENON IN modern international developments, the socialist international

---

(William L. Ryan, AP reporter, "U.N. Faces Money Crisis," in *South Bend Tribune,* Nov. 10, 1971, p. 17)

311. The League of Nations was "a complete recognition of the unalienable sovereignty of states," which permitted the continuance of all the "nonsense" of foreign offices and embassies. Since the League was "a repudiation of the idea of an over-riding commonweal of mankind, it was worse than no league at all; hence the best thing about the Covenant was the fact that it was unworkable." (Herbert G. Wells, *The Outline of History,* New York, 1920, Vol. II, p. 558-559)

"By the time of World War II, the League was dead, though it was not given a decent burial until 1946 when it finally dissolved itself. It had been killed by the 'national interest' germ. When a powerful nation's interests were involved in any given situation, those of the world community were ignored." (William L. Ryan, AP reporter, "Will U.N. Follow League?" *South Bend Tribune,* Nov. 9, 1971, p. 2)

312. "To unite humanity in peace . . . to banish war forever . . . Even its most ardent supporters agree it has fallen far short of its goals. Today, after 117 vetoes, after crises, walkouts and paralyzing debates, the organization is at best, in the view of Secretary-General U Thant, 'a hesitant, almost reluctant instrument of nations for world peace and unity.' At worst, in the eyes of American detractors, it is not worth the effort and should be boycotted. . . . A major U.N. ailment is that the organization can be only as strong as the superpowers are willing to make it. 'With some notable exceptions,' Thant has said, 'member governments have been more preoccupied with using the U.N. as an instrument to promote their own national policies than as a new kind of organization in which the nations in co-operation could forge the solution to world problems'. . . ." (William L. Ryan, AP Special Correspondent, "Will U.N. Follow League?" *South Bend Tribune,* Nov. 9, 1971, p. 2. Cf. also, Shirley Hazzard, *Defeat of an Ideal; A Study of the Self-Destruction of the United Nations,* Boston, 1973.)

"Instead of a system that ensures 'prompt and effective action' we have one that can be jammed by the opposition of a single Great Power. We have discarded the system of the Covenant which, though not certainly, might possibly have worked, and we have substituted for it one which hardly even professes to be workable, and instead of limiting the sovereignty of states we have extended the ef-

movement has been a special force in building One World. It began with a booklet called "The Workers' Union," written by Flora Tristan as early as 1843, in France.[313]

Four years later, Karl Marx and Friedrich Engels organized the Communist League in London and issued a declaration, urging that "workers of all lands, unite!"[314] The declaration was later elaborated into the famous Communist Manifesto.[315] As far as world

---

fective sovereignty of the Great Powers." (James L. Brierly, *The Law of Nations, An Introduction to the International Law of Peace,* 4th ed., Oxford, 1949, p. 283)

"Far from undermining the position of national states as the primary actors on the international scene international organization since World War II has in fact served to strengthen their position by enhancing their viability and effectiveness. States newly formed from colonial empires have been particularly reliant upon membership in the United Nations to provide symbolic confirmation of their emergence to independent status and to give them a political base for promoting the causes which they deem most essential to the consolidation of their position. . . . By providing postindependence assistance of various kinds, a diplomatic training ground, and the institutional context within which new states may individually and collectively bring their influence to bear upon international affairs, the United Nations and its specialized agencies have contributed to the working of the multistate system in the difficult period of the drastic alteration of its dimensions and the intensification of its heterogeneity." (Inis L. Claude, Jr., "International Organization: Process and Institutions," in the *International Encyclopedia of the Social Sciences,* New York, 1968, Vol. 8, p. 37)

313. Flora Tristan, the author of the booklet, urged the workers of France to form themselves into a class and to organize with the workers of the other countries, in order to obtain a share in political and economic power. (Cf. Lewis L. Lorwin, *Labor and Internationalism,* New York, 1929, p. 23.)

314. In this declaration Marx and Engels claimed that the struggle of the workers was international in essence. National differences, they pointed out, were being wiped out by the development of free trade, by the growth of a world market, and by the increasing uniformity of industrial and social conditions. The workers in particular were being denationalized by modern industry, and had no fatherland. Thus they urged: "Workers of all Lands, Unite!" (Cf. Julius Braunthal, *History of International,* trans. by Henry Collins and Kenneth Mitchell, New York, 1967, Vol. I., p. 51-59; and Gunther Nollau, *International Communism and World Revolution, History and Methods,* New York, 1961, p. 9-12.)

315. According to John Somerville, author of *The Philosophy of Marxism,* in the *Encyclopedia Americana,* 1973, ed., Vol. 7, p. 439, under "Communist Manifesto," the first two editions of the Manifesto, both published in London in 1848, appeared in German. Translations into French, Polish, Danish, and Swedish followed rapidly. The first English translation appeared in London in 1850, and the first one in Russian in 1869. The first three American editions were published in 1871. Thereafter, editions and translations multiplied. By 1964, more than 1,000 editions had appeared in more than 100 languages with total printings in excess of 14 million copies.

unity is concerned, Marx and Engels were the pioneers who expounded that modern industry had furnished a real foundation for a world unity,[316] and declared not only that "the working men have no country," but also that "the Communists are further reproached with desiring to abolish countries and nationalities."[317] They were also the leaders who tried for the first time in history to organize an international political party for a world revolution.[318]

In 1864, the International Working Men's Association, later

---

316. "The need of a constantly expanding market for its products chases the bourgeoisie over the whole surface of the globe. It must nestle everywhere, settle everywhere, establish connections everywhere. The bourgeoisie has through its exploitation of the world market given a cosmopolitan character to production and consumption in every country.... All old-established national industries have been destroyed or are daily being destroyed. They are dislodged by new industries, whose introduction becomes a life and death question for all civilized nations, by industries that no longer work up indigenous raw material, but raw material drawn from the remotest zones; industries whose products are consumed, not only at home, but in every quarter of the globe. In place of the old wants, satisfied by the productions of the country, we find new wants, requiring for their satisfaction the products of distant lands and climes. In place of the old local and national seclusion and self-sufficiency, we have intercourse in every direction, universal interdependence of nations. And as in material, so also in intellectual production. The intellectual creations of individual nations become property. National one sidedness and narrow-mindedness became more and more impossible, and from the numerous national and local literature there arises a world-literature." (From Section I of the Communist Manifesto) "National differences, and antagonisms between peoples, are daily more and more vanishing, owing to the world-market, to the development of the bourgeoisie, to freedom of commerce, to uniformity in the mode of production and in the conditions of life corresponding thereto." (From section II of the Communist Manifesto)

317. Quoted from section II of the Communist Manifesto. What is the means by which the Communist are going to abolish countries and nationalities? Marx and Engels gave no positive elaboration, but indicated that: "The supremacy of the proletariat will cause them [national differences and antagonisms] to vanish still faster. United action, of the leading civilized countries at least, is one of the first conditions for the emancipation of the proletariat ... In proportion as the exploitation of one individual by another is put an end to, the exploitation of one nation by another will also be put an end to. In proportion as the antagonism between the classes within the nation vanishes, the hostility of one nation to another will come to an end." (From section II of *The Communist Manifesto)*

318. "The Communists are distinguished from the other working class parties by this only: 1. In the national struggles of the proletarians of the different countries, they point out and bring to the front the common interests of the entire proletariat independently of all nationality. 2. In the various stages of development which the struggle of the working class against the bourgeoisie has to pass through, they always and everywhere represent the interests of the movement as a whole." (From section II of *The Communist Manifesto)*

known as the First International, was inaugurated with an "Address to the Working Classes" delivered by Marx in a moderate tone. Marx also wrote the rules of this organization.[319] Membership grew fast,[320] but the importance of the new organization lay less in its numbers than in the opportunity it provided for awakening the idea of an international socialist unity. However, different opinions were soon expressed in the International Congresses,[321] first by the followers of Proudhon,[322] then from the anarchist leader Bakunin.[323] As a result, the First International broke up and disbanded.[324]

---

319. The Rules defined the purpose of this organization as that of a central medium of communication and cooperation between workers' societies in different countries having the same aims, namely, mutual help, progress, and the complete emancipation of the working classes. Membership was open to local or national workers' societies, known as sections. Each section was allowed to organize in its own way and to elect a delegate to the annual congress, which was to elect a General Council. The functions of the General Council were to carry on all the administrative work necessary to achieve their common ends. (Cf. *Address and Provisional Rules of the International Working Men's Association, London, September 26th, 1864,* published by the Labour and Socialist International for the Celebration of the 60th Anniversary, 1924; and A.M. Stekloff, *History of the First International,* trans. by Eden and Cedar Paul, New York, 1928, p. 34-50.)

320. The membership of the First International grew during the first years. In England, a trade union congress held in Sheffield recommended that all unions join the International, and some 20 trade unions complied. In France, a number of new unions were formed which adhered to the International. There was also an increase in the membership in Belgium and Switzerland, and even the American Labor Union established certain connections with the International. From the summer of 1868 to the middle of 1870, the International took a sudden leap forward by gaining rapidly in membership and spreading widely to new countries. By 1869, for instance, French membership in the International was estimated at 200,000. In Germany, Italy, Spain, Portugal, and some other countries, the workers' societies also began to join the International. (Cf. Lewis Lorwin, *Labor and Internationalism,* New York, 1929, p. 43-49.)

321. These Congresses were held at Geneva in 1866; Lausanne in 1867; Brussels in 1868; Basle in 1869; and the Hague in 1872. (Cf. John Price, *The International Labor Movement,* 2d ed., London, 1947, p. 9; and R. Palme Dutt, *The Internationale,* London, 1964, p. 59-71.)

322. The followers of Pierre Joseph Proudhon distrusted Marx's insistence on the necessity for political action and disagreed with his support of the Polish national movement as a means of weakening Russian despotism, but they were outvoted at the Geneva congress. (Cf. Julius Braunthal, *History of the International,* trans. by Henry Collins and Kenneth Mitchell, New York, 1967, Vol. I., p. 121-218.)

323. A more serious challenge to the Marxists was provided by the anarchist supporters of Mikhail Bakunin, who lived in Italy from 1864 to 1878, and then in Switzerland until his death in 1876. Bakunin joined the International in 1868, when he already had a considerable revolutionary following in Italy and Switzerland, as well as in his native Russia. Although an admirer of Marx's

In addition to deep differences of personal opinion in the short-lived First International, the threat of nationalism against class solidarity[325] appeared temporarily when some German workers decided

---

theoretical work, he differed with Marx on particular points of doctrine, especially on organization. Marx believed in a centrally controlled political organization of the working class. Bakunin believed that the International Alliance of Social Democrats, which he had founded, could serve to produce an elite of revolutionaries within the International who could take the lead in direct revolutionary action without having recourse to political organization. He also believed in decentralized organization for the international revolutionary movement. Although Bakunin was willing to dissolve his own organization, the personal, doctrinal, and organizational differences between him and Marx proved insuperable and split the International at the Hague congress (1872), when Bakunin's followers were expelled. (Cf. Julius Braunthal, *History of the International,* trans. by Henry Collins and Kenneth Mitchell, New York, 1967, Vol. I., p. 175-179.)

324. Differences of opinion between Marx and Bakunin proving too great to work together, the International broke up. Marx transferred the seat of the International to New York, and in 1876, at a meeting attended mainly by American members, the International was formally dissolved. The Anarchists continued to hold congresses in the name of the International until the last meeting in 1881, in London. (Cf. John Price, *The International Labor Movement,* 2d. ed., London, 1947, p. 7-10; R. Palme Dutt, *The Internationale,* London, 1964, p. 71-81; and G.M. Stekloff, *History of the First International,* trans. by Eden and Cedar Paul, New York, 1928, p. 248-254, 268-328.)

325. The fundamental reason for nationalism to be a threat and later even a deadly disease to the Communist movement, may be attributed to Marxists' emphasis on class struggle and their ignorance of the fact that a group struggles—between early single families, primitive communities, clans, tribes, and nations—have had a history hundreds of times longer than the class struggles, beginning with the Roman patricians and slaves, which Marx described. The intensity of fighting and killing in group struggles has been much greater than that of class struggles against oppression and exploitation. The class struggles, moreover, have been more or less a part of the group struggles; most of the slaves of ancient times, for instance, were of foreign origins. (Cf. Thomas R. Glover, *The Ancient World,* New York, 1937, p. 131-134), and many of them were captured in wars with foreign countries (Cf. IIa, note 23.) In India, the origin of the caste system was segregation between conquerors and conquered people (Cf. IIa note 22.) In modern Negro slavery, it is obviously impossible to separate the class struggle from the group struggle. The primary reason for such emphasis and ignorance is that the long history previous to recorded history was unknown to Marx and Engels as Engels admitted in a note in regard to the famous sentence that all history is a history of class in Section I of the *Manifesto of the Communist Party.* "That is, all written history. In 1847, the pre-history of society, the social organization existing previous to recorded history, was all but unknown." Engels made this note to the 1888 English edition of the *Manifesto.* (Cf. Karl Marx and Friedrich Engels, *Selected Works,* Moscow, 1955, Vol. 1, p. 34.) The Marxists' emphasis on class struggle and their ignorance of group struggle have induced them to take for granted that a solution to the class struggle would lead to a solution to all prob-

to defend their nation in the Franco-German War of 1870. It did not do much damage to the socialist international movement only because the war ended quickly with a German victory.[326]

In the decades after the dissolution of the First International, the number and strength of labor and socialist parties grew in many countries.[327] Contacts among them led to the founding of the Second International, in 1889.[328] A series of Congresses were held thereafter[329] and an International Socialist Bureau and Secretariat were

---

lems, including the group struggle. Consequently, their efforts in seeking a solution to problems concerning nations have been always far from adequate, and have always met with difficulties.

326. Just before Napoleon III declared war on Prussia, the Paris Federation, on behalf of the International, denounced the threatened war as a crime perpetrated by the ruling dynasty. Some German workers replied, "We earnestly agree with your protest." But some said, "We find ourselves compelled to wage a defensive war as a necessary evil," "So long as French soldiers are so ill advised as to let themselves be dragged in the wake of a Napoleon so that our German lands are threatened with war and devastation," and "We are determined to play our full part in the defence of the inviolability of German soil against Napoleonic or any other despotism." Even Karl Marx himself addressed the International, saying that, "on the German side, the war is a war of defence." (Cf. Julius Braunthal, *History of the International,* trans. by Henry Collins and Kenneth Mitchell, New York, 1967, Vol. I, p. 142-155, 320-325.)

327. In addition to the powerful French and German Social Democratic parties, the Spanish Socialist Party was founded in 1879, the Belgian Labor Party in 1885, the Austrian Social-Democratic Labor Party and the Swiss Socialist Party in 1888, and the Swedish Social Democratic Labor party in 1889. Other labor parties followed in Armenia and the Ukraine in 1890; Argentina, Italy, and Poland in 1892; Bulgaria in 1893; Holland and Hungary in 1894; Lithuania in 1896; Russia in 1898; and Finland and Georgia in 1899. In Britain, the Labor Party was constituted in 1900, though for some years previously political action had been undertaken by the trade unions. (Cf. John Price, *The International Labor Movement,* Ed. ed., London, 1947, p. 10-11; and Julius Braunthal, *History of International,* trans. by Henry Collins and Kenneth Mitchell, New York, 1967, Vol. I, p. 195-242.)

328. By 1889, a number of international contacts between socialists or trade unionists had been reestablished, especially between Britain and France, and these led to proposals for an international socialist congress to be held in Paris in July, 1889. The French socialist movement was divided into several groups, and both the Marxists and the "possibilists," who believed in immediate piecemeal reforms rather than revolutionary change of the entire society, issued invitations to rival congresses. Eventually, however, it was the congress summoned by Jules Guesde and the other French Marxists that emerged as the founding congress of the Second International. (Cf. R. Palme Dutt, *The Internationale,* London, 1964, p. 85-87; and Gunther Nollau, *International Communism and World Revolution—History and Methods,* New York, 1961, p. 21-23.)

329. During the period of the Second International, congresses were held in Brussels in 1891, Zurich in 1893, London in 1896, Paris in 1900, Amsterdam in

established in 1900 to carry on the work during the intervals between Congresses.[330]

Like its predecessor, the Second International had difficulties in working out common tactics for common actions.[331] Above all, it became tangled in the problem of how to join together against war. The issue was discussed at every Congress and no conclusion ever reached, except a compromise made at Stuttgart.[332] Complicating this issue was the danger which nationalism posed against class solidarity, a problem which became more serious as the international situation worsened. At last, the Second International was split wide open along national lines by the outbreak of World War I, and many

---

1904, Stuttgart in 1907, Copenhagen in 1910, and Basle in 1912. The congresses were attended by hundreds of outstanding delegates, representing more than 20 nationalities. (Cf. Lewis L. Lorwin, *Labor and Internationalism,* New York, 1929, p. 86-87; and Julius Braunthal, *History of International,* trans. by Henry Collins and Kenneth Mitchell, New York, 1967, p. 364.)

330. To coordinate and organize the work of the Second International, a Secretariat was established in 1900 in Brussels, together with an International Socialist Bureau. The Bureau was composed of two delegates from each national section and one delegate from each parliamentary group, and it was to meet at least once a year. (Cf. Julius Braunthal, *History of International,* trans. by Henry Collins and Kenneth Mitchell, New York, 1967, Vol. I, p. 243-245; and Lewis L. Lorwin, *Labor and Internationalism,* New York, 1929, p. 84-87.)

331. At the early congresses of the Second International, it was agreed that the anarchists be excluded and membership be limited to those parties that accepted the necessity of political action rather than the direct revolutionary and industrial methods advocated by the anarchists and syndicalists. In 1899, however, Eduard Bernstein, a leading German socialist intellectual, published *Die Voraussetzangen des Sozialismus* (Eng. tr., *Evolutionary Socialism, 1901),* in which he questioned some of Marx's views, especially the belief that the proletariat was doomed to increasing impoverishment under capitalism. Bernstein suggested that Marxism needed revising to allow for the possibility of socialist action to achieve immediate reforms within the framework of existing society. His theoretical discussion caused deep divisions in the German Social Democratic party and effected labor parties elsewhere. (Cf. R. Palme Dutt, *The Internationale,* London, 1964, p. 88-92, 103-105.)

332. A resolution accepted at Stuttgart, in 1907, and subsequently reaffirmed was a compromise between the various views within the Second International: because wars were inherent in capitalist society, only a successful revolution could abolish them; in the meantime, however, socialists should work for such measures as the abolition of standing armies, disarmament, and international arbitration. A final paragraph, reflecting the views of the left wing, led by V.I. Lenin and Rosa Luxemburg, called on socialists to use the crises caused by the outbreak of war "to rouse the people and thereby to hasten the end of capitalist class rule." (Cf. Julius Braunthal, *History of International,* trans. by Henry Collins and Kenneth Mitchell, New York, Vol. I, 1967, p. 325-338, 361-363.)

workers went to fight against each other in the battlefield.[333] Attempts to save the crippled Second International proved to be futile.[334]

In 1919, the Third International, also known as the Communist
International, or Comintern, was established in Moscow on the initiative of the Russian Communist Party and inspired by the Russian
Revolution. It claimed to be the general staff of world revolution,[335]
and the true heir of Marxism through the previous Internationals.[336]

---

333. In 1914, hopes that the Second International might prevent war were
soon gone. In almost every case, the appeal of patriotism proved stronger than the
appeal to international working class solidarity. In Germany, the Social
Democrats, largely from fear of czarist Russia, voted in favor of war appropriations. In France, socialist leaders joined the government in the face of German invasion, and the reaction was similar in almost all the beligerent countries. (Cf.
Lewis L. Lorwin, *Labor and Internationalism,* New York, 1929, p. 89-92; and
Julius Braunthal, *History of International,* Vol. 2, trans. by John Clark, London,
1967, p. 1-35.)

"The war crisis of 1914-1918 was accompanied by the disgraceful collapse of
the Social Democratic Second International. Acting in complete violation of the
thesis of the Communist Manifesto written by Marx and Engels that the proletariat
has no fatherland under capitalism, and in complete violation of the anti-war
resolutions passed by the Stuttgart and Basle Congresses, the leaders of the Social-
Democratic parties in the various countries, with a few exceptions, voted for the
war credits, came out definitely in defense of the imperialist "fatherland" (i.e., the
state organizations of the imperialist bourgeoisie) and instead of combatting the
imperialist war, became its loyal soldiers, bards and propagandists (social-
patriotism, which grew into social-imperialism)." (*Program of the Communist International Together with Its Constitution,* adopted by the 6th World Congress of
Communist International, 1928, chapter two, section 2)

334. After the outbreak of World War I, the Bureau of the International was
forced to move from Brussels to Amsterdam, but the activities of the International
were at a standstill. In 1915, however, some opposition to the war began to be expressed by a minority of socialists. Some of them, from France, Germany, Italy, and
the neutral countries, succeeded in meeting in Switzerland, where Lenin and other
Russian socialists were already living. The participants at this conference at Zimmer-
wald, September, 1915, were divided between a majority, who were primarily concerned with stopping the war at all costs, and a minority, led by Lenin, who called for
the transformation of the war into revolutionary civil war and for the immediate
creation of a Third International. A further meeting was held at Kienthal,
Switzerland, in April, 1916. After the war, congresses were held at Lausanne,
August, 1919 and Geneva, July, 1920. The Geneva congress was the last congress of
the Second International. By this time the splits between socialists and Communists
were becoming too deep to heal and the challenge of the Third International was too
strong to allow for the restoration of the Second. (Cf. Julius Braunthal, *History of
International,* Vol. 2, trans. by John Clark, London, 1967, p. 36-64, 149-161; and R.
Palme Dutt, *The Internationale,* London, 1964, p. 129-132.)

335. The ideas which were to guide the new organization were formulated in a
"Manifesto to the Proletariat of all Countries." According to this Manifesto, the

The nature of the Third International, however, differed from its predecessors. Whereas the previous two Internationals were more or less associations, the Third International was actually a disciplined unitary world Communist Party, subdivided into national sections, with a strongly centralized machinery.[337]

The supreme organ of the Third International was the World Congress, but its real power resided in the Executive Committee elected by the World Congress,[338] the Presidium elected by the Exec-

---

Imperialist War which had pitted nation against nation was passing in all countries into a civil war which lined up class against class. A world revolution was taking place everywhere. The new International would be the general staff of the world revolution, and the source of active support to revolutionary elements or efforts in any country. (Cf. Lewis L. Lorwin, *Labor and Internationalism,* New York, 1929, p. 171-173; and Julius Braunthal, *History of International,* Vol. 2, trans. by John Clark, London, 1967, p. 162-181.)

336. Looking at it historically, the founders of the Third International declared that they were the fulfillers of the program announced 72 years before by Marx in his Communist Manifesto. According to their perspective, the First International had been "the prophet of the future," and the Second International "the organizer of millions." The task of the Third International was to become the "International of Action." (Cf. Lewis L. Lorwin, *Labor and Internationalism,* New York, 1929, p. 173; and V.I. Lenin, *The Foundation of the Communist International,* New York, 1934, p. 26-28.)

337. "The Communist International is aware that for the purpose of a speedy achievement of victory the International Association of workers which is struggling for the abolition of capitalism and the establishment of Communism should possess a firm and centralized organization. To all intents and purposes the Communist International should represent a universal Communist party, of which the parties operating in every country form individual sections. The apparatus of the Communist International is organized to secure to the toilers of every country the possibility at any given moment to obtain the maximum of aid from the organized workers of the other countries." (The last paragraph of the Preamble of the Statutes of the Communist International adopted at the Second World Congress, 1920) "The Communist International—the International Workers Association—is a union of Communist Parties in various countries: it is the world Communist Party." (The first sentence of Article 1 of the Constitution of the Communist International adopted at the Sixth World Congress, 1928)

338. "The supreme body of the Communist International is the World Congress of representatives of all Parties (Sections) and organizations affiliated to the Communist International." It "discusses and decides the programmatic, tactical and organizational questions." It "shall be convened once every two years. The date of the Congress and the number of representatives from the various Sections to the Congress to be determined by the Executive Committee," and the "number of decisive votes to be allocated to each Section at the World Congress shall be determined by the special decision of the Congress itself, in accordance with the membership of the respective Party and the political importance of the respective country." (Article 8 of the Constitution of the Communist International adopted at the

utive Committee, and the Political Secretariat elected by the Presidium.[339]

The Communist Parties of the several countries were merely national divisions of the Third International. They were organized closely after the pattern of the Russian Communist Party, and were strictly controlled by the Executive Committee, Control Commission, permanent bureaus, and special representatives of the Third International.[340]

Sixth World Congress, 1928. Cf. also Article 4 of the Statutes of the Communist International adopted at the Second World Congress, 1920; and Gunther Nollau, *International Communism and World Revolution: History and Methods,* New York, 1961, p. 125-128.)

339. "The World Congrss elects the Executive Committee of the Communist International (E.C.C.I.), and the International Control Commission." "The leading body of the Communist International in the period between Congresses is the Executive Committee, which gives instructions to all the Sections of the Communist International and controls their activity." "The E.C.C.I. elects a Presidium responsible to the E.C.C.I., which acts as the permanent body carrying out all the business of the E.C.C.I in the interval between the meetings of the latter." "The Presidium elects the Political Secretariat, which is empowered to make decisions, and which also draws up proposals for the meetings of the E.C.C.I. and of its Presidium, and acts as their executive body." (Articles 10, 12, 19, and 25 of the Constitution of the Communist International adopted at the Sixth World Congress, 1928. Cf. also Article 9 of the Statutes of the Communist International adopted at the Second World Congress, 1920; and Gunther Nollau, *International Communism and World Revolution: History and Methods,* New York, 1961, p. 156-161.)

340. "The decisions of the E.C.C.I. (Executive Committee of the Communist International) are obligatory for all the Sections of the Communist International and must be promptly carried out." "The E.C.C.I. has the right to expel from the Communist International, entire Sections, groups and individual members." "The Central Committees of the various Sections of the Communist International are responsible to their respective Party Congresses and to the E.C.C.I. The latter has the right to annul or amend decisions of Party Congresses and of Central Committees of Parties." "The programs of the various Sections of the Communist International must be endorsed by the E.C.C.I." "The E.C.C.I. and its Presidium have the right to establish permanent bureaus (Western European, South American, Eastern and other Bureaus of the E.C.C.I.), for the purpose of establishing closer contact with the various Sections." "The E.C.C.I. and its Presidium have the right to send their representatives to the various Sections . . . to supervise the carrying out of the decisions of the World Congresses and of the Executive Committee." They "also have the right to send instructors to the various Sections." "The International Control Commission investigates matters affecting the unity of the Sections . . . and also matters connected with the Communist conduct of individual members of the various Sections." The Sections "must regularly pay affiliation dues to the E.C.C.I.," and "Congresses of the various Sections, ordinary and special, can be convened only with the consent of the E.C.C.I." (Articles 13-16, 20-22, 28, 33-34 of the Constitution of the Com-

The Third International also promoted activities through its youth section, fractions and sympathetic organizations.[341]

As a world political party with the aim of establishing a world government,[342] the Third International was indeed a great adventure. Under its leadership, World Communist membership increased steadily before World War II.[343] Along with the growing threat of war, however, nationalism was creeping into the very heart of the Communist movement: the Soviet Union.[344] On the international front in general, the policy of utilizing the national liberation move-

---

munist International adopted at the Sixth World Congress, 1928. Cf. Gunther Nollau, *International Communism and World Revolution: History and Methods,* New York, 1961, p. 133-142, 159-161, 165.)

341. "The Communist fractions are subordinated to the competent Party bodies." "Communist fractions in international organizations (Red International of Labor Unions, International Labor Defense, Workers International Relief, etc.), are subordinate to the Executive Committee of the Communist International." "The E.C.C.I. has the right to accept affiliation to the Communist International of organizations and Parties sympathetic to Communism, such organizations to have a consultative voice." And "the International League of Communist Youth (Communist Youth International) is a Section of the Communist international with full rights and is subordinate to the E.C.C.I." (Articles 7, 18, and 35 of the Constitution of the Communist International adopted at the Sixth World Congress, 1928. Cf. also Articles 10, 11, 14-16 of the Statutes of the Communist International adopted at the Second World Congress, 1920; and Gunther Nollau, *International Communism and World Revolution: History and Methods,* New York, 1961, p. 146-155.)

342. The world government was called the "International Soviet Republic" in Article 1 of the Statutes of the Third International adopted at the second World Congress, 1920, and the "World Union of Socialist Soviet Republics" in Article 1 of the Constitution of the Third International adopted at the Sixth World Congress, 1928.

343. "The world system of Communist parties grew from 7 national parties with 400,000 members in 1917, to 56 national parties with 4.2 million members in 1939." (George Modelski, "Communism: The International System," in the *International Encyclopedia of the Social Sciences,* New York, 1968, Vol. 3, p. 128. Cf. *The Communist International,* Vol. 3, 1929-1943, ed. by Jane Degras, London, 1965, p. 435.)

344. A peculiar type of nationalism emerged in the Soviet Union in the 1930s. Although Marxism taught that the proletariat had no fatherland, Article 133 of the 1936 Constitution of the USSR pointed in the opposite direction: "to defend the country is the sacred duty of every citizen of the USSR. Treason to the fatherland ... is punishable with all the severity of the law as the most heinous of crimes." (Cf. Samuel N. Harper and Ronald Thompson, *The Government of the Soviet Union,* 2nd ed., New York, 1949, p. 267-277.)

"Proletarians have no Motherland" was the philosophy of the Bolshevik revolutionary in Russia. Patriotism was "a bourgeois prejudice, a capitalistic

ment against imperialism had shifted to that of supporting "complete national independence and national unification" for the colonial and semi-colonial countries.[345] In the Soviet Union particularly, the acknowledgment of "the co-existence of two worlds" led to the announcement of "socialism in one country," which, in turn, gave rise to the policies of "peaceful coexistence" and "collective security" with the capitalist nations, and later to alliances with Fascist Japan and Germany.[346] Reasons can be found to justify all these measures, of course, such as their use as temporary expedients. The fact that a nationalist tendency was getting the upper hand in the Communist movement is nevertheless irrefutable. This tendency once produced in the United States during the war the slogan "Communism is 20th Century Americanism,"[347] and it finally buried the Communist International itself in May, 1943.[348]

---

anachronism." But a volte-face came in 1934, when Communists were urged to be ready to die for the Motherland. The war against Germany became known as the "Holy War," and the "Great War of the Motherland." In December, 1943, the Internationale, the rallying song of communism, composed in French by Eugene Pottier in 1871, and set to music by Adolphe Degeyter, was abandoned in Soviet Russia. No longer was the strain heard: "Arise ye wretched of the earth!" In its stead came a fiery new patriotic anthem beginning with the following lines:

> Unbreakable Union of freeborn Republics,
> Great Russia has welded forever to stand;
> Created in struggle by will of the peoples;
> United and mighty, our Soviet Land!
>
> Sing to our Motherland, glory undying,
> Bulwark of peoples in brotherhood strong!
> Flag of the Soviets, peoples' flag flying,
> Lead us from victory to victory on!

(According to Anatole G. Mazour, *Russia: Past and Present,* New York, 1955, p. 643. Cf. Frederick C. Barghoorn, *Soviet Russian Nationalism,* New York, 1956.)

345. The policy of utilizing the national and colonial liberation movement against imperialism was elaborated in the "Theses on the National and Colonial Questions" adopted by the Second World Congress, 1920, in Moscow. (An English translation may be found in the *Blueprint for World Conquest,* Washington, 1946, p. 118-131.) "Complete national independence and national unification" was one of the important tasks enumerated in article 9 of Chapter four of the "Program of the Communist International," adopted by the Sixth World Congress, 1928, Moscow, New York, 1936, p. 57.

346. (Cf. Samuel N. Harper and Ronald Thompson, *The Government of the Soviet Union,* 2nd ed., New York, 1949, p. 270-280.)

347. (Cf. Dayton D. McKean, *Party and Pressure Politics,* Boston, 1949, p. 418.)

348. In May, 1943, the Third International was formally dissolved by its Execu-

Needless to say, the dissolution of the Communist International could be justified as having been required by special circumstances. But its formal announcement clearly acknowledged a surrender to nationalist forces,[349] and put all emphasis on the differences between the countries,[350] in strong contrast to earlier Communist literature which always focused on the common interests and united action of the world working class.

In October, 1947, a Communist Information Bureau was established with a limited objective and smaller organization, as announced in a Communique[351] which also emphasized the defense of national independence, sovereignty, and self-determination as the fundamental aims of the Communist parties.[352] The Bureau was composed

---

tive Committee in Moscow under the circumstances of the "war of liberation of freedom-loving peoples against the Hitlerite tyranny," and in favor of allowing "great flexibility and independence of its sections in deciding the problems confronting them." (Cf. Martin Ebon, *World Communism Today,* New York, 1948, p. 495-497; the announcement of the Presidium of the Executive Committee of the Communist International on the dissolution of the Communist International, as published in Moscow on May 15, 1943; and Gunther Nollau, *International Communism and World Revolution: History and Methods,* New York, 1961, p. 201-210.)

349. The announcement explained that the reasons for the dissolution of the Third International were the fulfillment of "its historical task of laying the foundations for the development of working class parties in the countries of Europe and America, and, as a result of the matured situation creating mass national working class parties." It took "into account the growth and the political maturity of Communist parties and their leading cadres in separate countries," and recognized that the international organ "has even become a drag on the further strengthening of the national working class parties."

350. The announcement emphasized the differences between the countries in the following tone: "Deep differences of the historic paths of development of various countries, differences in their character and even contradictions in their social orders, differences in the level and the tempo of their economic and political development, differences finally in the degree of consciousness and organization of workers, conditioned different problems affecting the working class of the various countries."

351. The Communique was issued on October 5, 1947, in Poland. (An English translation may be found in *The New York Times,* October 6, 1947.) It stated that its task was to "organize and exchange experience and, in case of necessity, coordinate the activity of Communist parties on foundations of mutual agreement"; and its organization was to "have in its representatives of the Central Committee—two from each Central Committee."

352. The Communique emphasized "the fundamental aims of the Communist parties" as follows: "They must grasp in their hands the banner of national independence and sovereignty in their own countries. If the Communist parties stand fast on their outposts, if they refuse to be intimidated and blackmailed, if they courageously guard over the democracy, national sovereignty, independence,

of representatives of only nine European Communist parties and was soon terminated after having been rebuked by Tito, the Communist leader of Yugoslavia.[353]

Meanwhile, the Chinese Communists came up to challenge the Soviet leadership,[354] and their challenge set in motion forces which led to a greater rift in the Communist world.[355]

---

and self determination of their countries, if they know how to fight against attempts at the economic and political subjugation of their countries and place themselves at the head of all the forces ready to defend the cause of national honor and independence, then and only then no plans to subjugate the countries of Europe and Asia can succeed."

353. The Information Bureau of the Communist and Workers parties, also known as the Cominform, exclusively comprising the major European Communist parties of the Soviet Union, Bulgaria, Rumania, Hungary, Poland, Czechoslovakia, Yugoslavia, France, and Italy, was designed to strengthen Soviet control over the newly created, ruling Communist parties. It ran afoul of Tito's resistance to Stalin's attempt to dominate the Yugoslav Communist party. It expelled the Yugoslav party, but served no further function except to publish a journal, *For a Lasting Peace, For a People's Democracy!* which expired in 1956 when the Cominform was dissolved in the wake of the Soviet-Yugoslav rapprochement. (Cf. Marton Ebon, *World Communism Today,* New York, 1948, p. 497; *World Communism,* a handbook, 1918-1965, ed. by Witold S. Sworakowski, Stanford, Calif., 1973, p. 76-78; Gunther Nollau, *International Communism and World Revolution: History and Methods,* New York, 1961, p. 211-256; and Vladimir Dedijer, *Tito Speaks,* London, 1953, p. 346-347.)

354. "So far as Communists are concerned Marxism today is Marxism-Leninism: Marx as amended by Lenin, and there are two brands of it. Those preaching one brand call the other 'Mao-Tse-Tungism' and say it's not Marxism-Leninism at all. Those practicing the other call the rival ideology 'Khrushevism' and say it's not Marxism-Leninism at all. . . . Mourned Soviet party chief Leonid I. Brezhnev at Budapest: 'Much in the policy of those leaders who shape the present course of the Chinese Communist Party evokes profound regret and inflicts great damage to our common cause.' On the other hand, the Chinese expressed the conviction that 'a world-wide struggle against imperialism, modern revisionism and reactionaries of all countries is surging forward with the irresistible force of a thunderstorm'. . . . Soviet leaders should be overthrown, said Peking, because they 'collaborate with the United States for world domination and are accomplices of American imperialism.' Peking says Soviet leaders are a 'group of renegades who like all freaks and monsters,' should be trampled into the dust of history." (William L. Ryan, AP Special Correspondent, "Karl Marx Would Never Recognize Communist World of Today," *South Bend Tribune,* Jan. 2, 1967, p. 46. Cf. also *Marxist Ideology in the Contemporary World—Its Appeals and Paradoxes,* ed. by Milord M. Drachkovitch, New York, 1966, p. 1-36, 60-112; *Soviet and Chinese Communist, Similarities and Differences,* ed. by Donald W. Treadgold, Seattle, 1967; and the Chinese view: statement of the Central Committee of the Communist Party of China, June 14, 1963, and Soviet view: statement of

Subsequently, international Communism has been plunged into national communism,[356] and international communists have been transformed into red nationalists. They boast of patriotism,[357] stick-

---

the Soviet Government, Sept. 21, 1963, both in the *World in Crisis,* ed. by Frederick H. Hartmann, 3d ed., New York, 1967, p. 373-390.)

355. "The weakening of Soviet authority among communist parties and states contributed to the eruption of the Sino-Soviet dispute, which in turn weakened Soviet prestige even more. The dispute bared the conflicting content of national interests, as interpreted by various communist elites, and it undermined confidence in the wisdom and leadership of both China and the Soviet Union. In over thirty countries communist parties split and rival organizations emerged many of which turned against Soviet leadership and some against the Chinese as well. The Sino-Soviet rift dramatized the evanescence of the single universal communist party 'national.' It provided opportunities for other states either to defy Soviet leadership and survive even when expelled from the fold, as in the case of Albania, or to tacitly and gradually pursue policies sharply at variance with those of other communist states without formal rupture or rebuke, as in the case of Rumania." (Alexander Dallin, "National Communism," in the *International Encyclopedia of the Social Sciences,* New York, 1968, Vol. 3, p. 114. Cf. also Richard Lowenthal, *World Communism, the Disintegration of a Secular Faith,* New York, 1964, p. 99-231; and Helmut Sonnenfeldt, "International Consequences of Sino-Soviet Dispute," in *International Communism after Khrushev,* ed. by Leopold Labedz, Cambridge, Mass., 1965, p. 205-216. The annual report, *World Strength of the Communist Party Organization,* by the U.S. Department of State, has listed both Pro-China and Pro-Soviet Communists in the various countries separately since late 1960s.)

356. "Historically, the primary content of national communism has been the effort to shake or reduce Soviet control or hegemony over other communist parties and states. With the increasing fragmentation of world communism, its various national units are bound to reflect the growing diversity of communism—as a political movement, as an ideology and as a mode of political practice." "... among the greater range of diverse communist types which have emerged, even in eastern Europe, since 1956, some may be considered not merely national in form but also nationalist in content." (Alexander Dallin, "National Communism," in the *International Encyclopedia of the Social Sciences,* New York, 1968, Vol. 3, p. 112, 115. Cf. Gunther Nollau, *International Communism and World Revolution: History and Methods,* New York, 1961, p. 289.)

357. Josip Broz Tito, for instance, the Communist leader of Yugoslavia, proudly and forcefully announced his patriotism when he wrote the Soviet leaders that no matter how much communists of other countries loved the Soviet Union, the land of socialism, they could in no case love their own country less. (Cf. *The Soviet-Yugoslav Dispute: Text of the Published Correspondence,* 1948, London, Royal Institute of International Affairs, p. 19.)

358. For instance, the speech by French delegate Gaston Plissonier, a French Politburo member standing in for French Communist Party Chief George Marchais, at the end of the first week of the 25th Soviet Party Congress, emphasized a widening Soviet rift with comrades in France, Italy and Britain and said that com-

ing to particularities,[358] stressing autonomy,[359] emphasizing sovereignty,[360] reviving traditional enmities and territorial disputes,[361] and fighting against each other, as in the war which has been going on between Vietnam and Cambodia since 1977,[362] and that between Vietnam and China in early 1979.[363]

---

munism in France "will be invested with the specific traits of our country, a socialism under French colors." (Cf. *South Bend Tribune,* Feb. 29, 1976, p. 2.)

359. In his statement to the Soviet leadership, in 1964, Palmiro Togliatti, the Italian Communist leader, reiterated what Tito had stated earlier: "The national sentiment remains a permanent factor in the working class and socialist movement for a long period; also, after the conquest of power, economic progress does not dispel this; it nurtures it. Thus in the socialist camp, too, one needs perhaps ... to be on one's guard against the forced exterior uniformity and one must consider that the unity one seeks to establish and maintain must be in the diversity and full autonomy of the individual countries." (Palmiro Togliatti, 1964 Memorandum, Partito Comunista Italiano, *Foreign Bulletin of the Italian Communist Party,* 1964, no. 5, p. 80)

360. For instance, the Central Committee of the Rumanian Communist Party resolved in 1964 that the sovereignty of the socialist state requires that it effectively and fully hold in its hands all the levers of economic and social life; that transmitting such levers to the competence of a superstate or extra-state bodies would make of sovereignty an idea without content; that there are not and cannot be unique patterns and recipes; and that no one can decide what is and what is not correct for other countries or parties. (Cf. John M. Montias, "Background and Origins of the Rumanian Dispute with Comecon," in *Soviet Studies 16,* p. 125-151.)

361. Notable cases have been the revival of historical hostilities and border conflicts between Yugoslavia and Albania, between Soviet Russia and Communist China, and between Vietnam and Cambodia. Lately, there have also been serious conflicts between Communist China and Vietnam, over the issue of ethnic Chinese. Peking has claimed that more than 160,000 Chinese have fled Vietnam because they were being persecuted by Vietnamese authorities. Peking has ceased all aid to Vietnam and has recalled all Chinese technicians working there because Hanoi has "stepped up its anti-China activities and ostracism of Chinese residents in Vietnam." (Quoted by AP news in *South Bend Tribune,* July 3, 1978, p. 10.)

362. "Vietnam and Cambodia have escalated a border conflict into full-scale battles involving warplanes and artillery, resulting in heavy casualties. The Vietnamese invasion of Cambodia has again shattered the myth of a worldwide communist monolith, bound together by brotherly love based on common economic and political beliefs. Vietnam and Cambodia—onetime 'fraternal comrades and brothers-at-arms'—are ignoring ideology and fighting each other over frontier borders, for national self-interest and because of traditional hatreds just as savagely as nations of diverse creeds and aspirations have done. It seems to be another example of old-fashioned self-interest over Karl Marx, already amply demonstrated by such phenomenon as communist mavericks Yugoslavia and Romania thumbing their noses at the Kremlin, the increasing independence of communist parties in Western Europe, and, of course, the Sino-Soviet clash." (Denis D. Gray, AP reporter, "War Shatters Communist Myth," in *South Bend Tribune,* Jan. 10, 1979, p. 4.)

The Communist Party of the Soviet Union finally retreated from international Communism with a "new Communist Manifesto" recognizing different roads to socialism for all sovereign peoples.[364] Lately, a Summit Conference of European Communist Parties further reaffirmed the principles of equality and sovereign independence for each party, and noninterference in internal affairs.[365]

It is evident that the socialist international movement has been badly disintegrated by nationalism everywhere.

---

363. "Chinese forces backed by tanks, fighter planes and artillery launched a 'large-scale invasion' of Vietnam today, Radio Hanoi reported. China confirmed its frontier troops had attacked Vietnamese forces along the border, but said it was a 'counterattack' designed to 'defend the country's borders.' . . . Tass claimed this afternoon that Chinese troops attacked Vietnam from 14 directions and drove four miles across the border. It reported 'fierce fighting' on all fronts, with hundreds of Chinese troops killed. . . . According to Kyodo, a Chinese Communist Party bulletin issued today said China had decided to battle Vietnam to punish the Vietnamese for violence against Chinese border residents." (First report on the China-Vietnam war by Kay Tateishi, AP reporter, *South Bend Tribune*, Feb. 17, 1979)

364. The "new communist manifesto" was incorporated into the program approved by the 22nd Congress of the Communist Party of the Soviet Union in October, 1961. War between capitalist and communist states was officially proclaimed to be avoidable. Different roads to socialism were validated. Communist parties were to be allowed their own choice of tactics. The "world socialist system" was defined in the program as "a social, economic and political community of free sovereign peoples pursuing the Socialist and Communist path, united by common interests and goals, and the close bonds of international Socialist solidarity." (Cf. Otto V. Kuusinen, *Fundamentals of Marxism-Leninism,* Moscow, 1961, Chap. 25.)

365. (Cf. the record of the Summit Conference of European Communist and Workers Parties, held in East Berlin, June 29-30, 1976, in *World Marxist Review—Information Bulletin,* Vol. 14, No. 12, p. 5-44.) A decision made by this conference is as follows: Communist parties "will develop their internationalist, comradely and voluntary cooperation and solidarity on the basis of the great ideas of Marx, Engels and Lenin, strictly adhering to the principles of equality and sovereign independence for each party, non-interference in internal affairs, and respect for their free choice of different roads in the struggle for social change of a progressive nature and for socialism."

III

Anatomy
of the Nation

AS THE LAST CHAPTER REVEALS, THE PROCESS OF building One World through various contributions has led to the establishment of two general international organizations: the League of Nations and the United Nations. It has also given rise to a special adventure—the socialist international movement. Unfortunately, both the general international and the special adventure have been seriously thwarted by nationalist forces, originated from the independence of the nation, signified with national sovereignty, and enhanced by nationalism. Their core is the nation, of course; hence an examination of the nation is in order.

a.
The Nation
in Space and Time[1]

TERRITORIALLY, A NATION IS A SMALL PART OF THE surface of the earth.[2]

---

1. "The world and history cannot be as they appear to the different nations, unless we disavow objectivity, reason and scientific methods of research." (Emery Reves, *The Anatomy of Peace,* New York, 1946, p. 22)

2. The total surface area of the earth is 196,950,769 square miles, of which 57,469,928 square miles—29% of the total area—is land. The rest of the earth is covered by oceans or seas to an average depth of nearly 3 miles. At the present time, the largest country, the Soviet Union, has a territory of 8,649,489 square miles, about 15% of the land or 4.4% of the total surface. The smallest country,

The earth is a round ball[3] on which no one place is a center for other nations.[4]

Nor is the earth the center of the universe.[5] It is just a small planet of the solar family with the sun as the center.[6]

Maldives, has a territory of 115 square miles, only about 0.0002% of the land, or 0.00006% of the total surface. The average territory of the 135 nations in the United Nations in the early 1970s was approximately 300,000 square miles, about 0.52% of the land, or 0.16% of the total surface. (Cf. *Reader's Digest, Great World Atlas,* Pleasantville, N.Y., 1963, p. 152; and *The Time's Atlas of the World,* Comprehensive ed., New York, 1975, p. xi-xv.)

3. The earth is spherical in shape, with an average diameter of about 7,910 miles, except for a slight flattening at the poles due to the centrifugal force of its daily rotation. Its equatorial circumference is 24,902 miles, and polar circumference is 24,860 miles. (Cf. *Reader's Digest, Great World Atlas,* Pleasantville, N.Y., 1963, p. 152; also Jean Taille, *The Earth and the Moon,* trans. from French by Rhys Matthews, New York, 1963, p. 41-47.)

4. Before modern times when our knowledge of the world was greatly limited, certain places were regarded to be the center of countries, nations, and the earth. For instance, "Paradise is somewhere in the Far East, Jerusalem is the center of all nations, and the world itself is a flat disk surrounded by vast oceans. So the monks, mapmakers of the Middle Ages, saw the world they lived in." (Preface of the *Reader's Digest, Great World Atlas,* Pleasantville, N.Y., 1963) The ancient Chinese thought their homeland—the area of the Up Yellow River— to be the center of the world, and called it the "Central Land," 中原. For that very reason, they named their country the "Central Country," 中國, and their nation the "Central Nation," 中華.

5. The earliest known image that men had of the earth was that it was a flat, rigid platform at the center of the universe. The sun, the moon, the stars, and the planets all seemed to revolve around this platform. As early as the 6th century B.C., however, some Greek thinkers such as Pythagoras had progressed far enough beyond this simple image to realize that the earth might be a sphere. Another Greek, Aristarchus, proposed in the 3rd century, B.C. that the earth is only one of a family of planets revolving around the sun. The concept of a spherical earth and the heliocentric view were not widely accepted until the 17th century, following the work of Nicolaus Copernicus, Johannes Kepler, and Galileo Galilei. (Cf. Milton K. Munitz, ed. *Theories of the Universe,* Glencoe, Ill., 1957, p. 116, 149-201; Howard Robertson, "The Universe," in *The Universe,* A Scientific American Book, New York, 1957, p. 3-13; and Karl Stumpff, *Planet Earth,* Ann Arbor, Michigan, 1959, p. 9-22.)

6. The solar family includes the sun; nine major planets: Mercury, Venus, Earth, Mars, Jupiter, Saturn, Uranus, Neptune, and Pluto; 31 moons (satellites of the planets); 12 belonging to Jupiter, 9 to Saturn, 5 to Uranus, 2 each to Neptune and Mars, and 1 to Earth; about 50,000 known minor planets, or asteroids; and comets. The sun dominates and dwarfs its planets. Its mass is about 333,000 times the earth's mass, and about 1000 times the combined mass of all the planets, asteroids, comets, and other material in the family. Under the gravitational influence of the sun, the solar system is moving with and among the stars and in-

In the solar family, the sun is larger than the earth by hundreds of thousands of times,[7] yet the sun is just a minor star at the edge of the Milky Way.[8]

As a vast rotating system of billions of stars, the Milky Way is

---

terstellar material in the large orbit around the center of the Milky Way. (Cf. Evry Schatzman, *The Origin and Evolution of the Universe,* trans. from the French by Bernard and Annabel Pagel, New York, 1965, p. 15-20; and Zdenek Kopal, *The Solar System,* London, 1973, p. 6-115.)

7. Sizes of the sun and its planets:

		Diameter (miles)	Volume (earth = 1)	Mass (earth = 1)
Sun	Equatorial	865,400	1,306,000.00	333,420.00
Mercury	Equatorial	3,030	0.05	0.05
Venus	Equatorial	7,550	0.90	0.82
Earth	Equatorial	7,927	1.00	1.00
	Polar	7,900		
Mars	Equatorial	4,200	0.15	0.107
Jupiter	Equatorial	88,700	1,350.00	317.45
	Polar	82,800		
Saturn	Equatorial	75,000	800.00	95.2
	Polar	67,000		
Uranus	Equatorial	29,000	63.00	14.54
Neptune	Equatorial	28,000	44.00	17.6
Pluto	Equatorial	3,600?	0.09?	0.03?

(Cf. "Solar System," *Encyclopedia Americana,* New York, 1973 ed., Vol. 25, p. 192.)

8. The Milky Way is a nebulous band of faint stars, extending entirely around the celestial sphere. This band of luminosity is the result of an edge-on view from the earth through a disk-shaped aggregation of stars in which the earth and sun occupy a position well out from the center. The greater number of stars seen looking outward through the flat portion of the disk accounts for the diffuse belt of luminosity in this plane. Since the Milky Way is inclined 62° to the celestial equator, its appearance is variable with the seasons, the time of night, and the observer's latitude. Its brightest portions are in Cygnus, Aquila, Scorpius, and Sagittarius, where many bright star clouds exist. The apparent width of the Milky Way is irregular and its length is interrupted by rifts and superimposed dark nebulae, such as the northern and southern Coal Sacks. The Milky Way, an agglomeration of over 200 billion stars, is about a billion times larger in volume than the space occupied by the solar family. (Cf. William Bonnor, *The Mystery of the Expanding Universe,* New York, 1964, p. 15-17; and Bart J. Bok and Priscilla F. Bok, *The Milky Way,* 3d. ed., Cambridge, Mass., 1957, p. 1-29.)

9. In contemporary cosmology, the universe is identified with the population of galaxies. (The terms "extragalactic nebulae" and "nebulae" are also used by some writers.) The preliminary survey of the population of galaxies was achieved shortly after World War I with the aid of the 100-inch telescope at Mount Wilson.

itself just one among billions of other galaxies[9] in the universe covering distances which exceed billions of light-years.[10]

Thus, the nation in the universe is just like a speck on a particle of sand.

The history of the nation has not been long either.

Crowded as the world is with nations today, it may be hard to imagine that as late as four hundred years ago, only about one-fifth of the land surface of the earth was occupied by nations, and all the rest[11] was scattered with smaller groups: tribes, clans, primitive communities and early single families. It took a long time to explore the vast land areas and to merge the various groups into nations. That is why most of the present nations are under two hundred years old,[12] and some have had only a few birthdays.[13]

It was this instrument that enabled Edwin P. Hubble in 1924 to establish conclusively that there are systems of stars lying beyond the confines of our own galaxy—the Milky Way. The galactic structures in the universe range from single galaxies to mammoth clusters containing as many as 500 galaxies. (Cf. William Bonnor, *The Mystery of the Expanding Universe,* New York, 1964, p. 15-19; and Evry Schatzman, *The Origin and Evolution of the Universe,* trans. from the French by Bernard and Annabel Pagel, New York, 1965, p. 21-78.)

10. The light-year is the distance of six million million miles traveled by light in one year at 186,300 miles a second. For instance, the distance from the earth to Proxima Centauri, the nearest star outside the solar family, is four and one third light-years; to the bright star Altair is about 16 light-years; and to Deneb, 1500 light-years. The distance across the galaxy of the Milky Way is more than 100,000 light-years, and the Hydra of the remote cluster of galaxies is 1.1 billion light-years away. (Cf. Allan Broms, *Our Emerging Universe,* New York, 1961, p. 6-8; and William Bonnor, *The Mystery of the Expanding Universe,* New York, 1964, p. 10-11.)

11. The total land surface of the earth is 57,469,928 square miles. Three hundred years ago, the areas which were not clearly occupied by nations included all of Australia (3,201,100 sq.mi.), North America (9,420,000 sq.mi.), South America (6,860,000 sq.mi.), and Antarctica (5,100,000 sq.mi.); and about one half of Asia's 18,685,000 sq.mi., five sixths of Africa's 11,699,000 sq.mi., and one fifth of Europe's 2,085,000 sq.mi. (Cf. *Reader's Digest, Great World Atlas,* Pleasantville, N.Y., 1963, p. 152; and *Muir's Historical Atlas, Medieval and Modern,* 9th ed., New York, 1962, Maps 35, 40A, and 42.)

12. "There are 131 sovereign nations which make up the world community. This number represents all countries that are recognized by the United States Government as being fully independent. Of the 131 nations, nearly one half have come into existence only since the outbreak of World War II. A list of the 61 new nations accounts for 47 percent of the total number of all nations. The new nations cover an area of nearly 12.4 million square miles, amounting to 24 percent of the total land surface of the world except Antarctica. Altogether, the new nations have a population of more than 1.1 billion, as compared to 2.2 billion living in the older established nations.... More than a century ago 12 colonies in Latin America gained their independence within 20 years, from 1821 to 1840.... More recently,

There are indeed some senior nations, but their actual age is always subject to guessing, because of the difficulty of demarcating them from their various origins, and also because of their practice of counting a long period of pre-nation history as a part of their national age.[14]

---

the events of World War I brought 11 new countries into being during a period of less than 20 years." (G. Etzel Pearcy & Elvyn A. Stoneman, *A Handbook of New Nations,* New York, 1968, p. xiii. Cf. p. 302-303 for the name and year of independence of the 61 new nations.) In addition to the 84 nations counted in the above quotation, there are more than 20 others whose age is also under 200 years. These include Canada (official birth year, 1867), Mexico (1810), Argentina (1816), Chile (1818), Paraguay (1811), Panama (1903), Cuba (1899), Haiti (1804), Albania (1912), Bulgaria (1908), Greece (1827), Italy (1830?), Romania (1881), Switzerland (1815), Australia (1901), New Zealand (1907), Liberia (1847), and South Africa (1910). Adding the nations born in the last ten years, as listed in the following note, the number of nations under 200 years old in 1978 amounts to close to 120, about five sixths of the total number of nations in existence.

Boyd C. Shafer in his *Faces of Nationalism, New Realities and Old Myths,* New York, 1972, p. 146-147, 270-272, lists 11 western nations which became independent before 1783, 39 which became independent between 1783 and 1921; and 10 non-western nations which became independent before 1783, 10 which became independent between 1783 and 1945, and 54 which became independent between 1946 and 1968.

13. The latter include Fiji (officially established in 1970), Tonga (1970), Qatar (1971), United Arab Emirates (1971), Bangladesh (1972), Surinam (1973), Grenada (1974), Malta (1974), Cape Verde (1974), Guinea-Bissau (1974), Seychelles (1974), Papua New Guinea (1975), Angola (1975), Mozambique (1975), Sao Tome and Princope (1975), Comoro (1975) and Djibouti (1977). (Cf. *The Europa Year Book, 1978,* London, 1978, Vol. I, p. 2-3.)

14. China, for instance, did not start to be a nation until 221 B.C. when the first emperor of the Chin Dynasty eliminated all the remaining tribal states. But the Chinese used to claim that their nation was up to five thousand years old, and that their oldest calendar—the Calendar of Emperor Huang—commenced in the year 2698 B.C. Actually, the 2,477 years between 2698 and 221 B.C. belonged to their pre-nation history. (Cf. I,b, 54-60.)

As another example, "Kemal Ataturk offered a theory that the Turks were a white, Aryan people, originating in Central Asia, and that they migrated to various parts of Asia carrying civilization with them. Chinese, Indian, and Middle Eastern civilization had been founded in this way, the pioneers in the last named being the Sumerians and Hittites, who were both Turkic peoples. Anatolia had thus been a Turkish land since antiquity. This mixture of truth, half-truth, and error was proclaimed as official doctrine, and teams of researchers set to work to 'prove' its various propositions. Ataturk also solved the dilemma posed by the need to adopt foreign words so that Turkish would have the necessary technical vocabulary and the countervailing need to extol all things Turkish. His method was to advance the theory that Turkish was in fact the mother of all languages, so

Actually, all ancient history is pre-nation history, and all the famous ancient groups were clannish or tribal kingdoms,[15] cities,[16] or empires.[17] They distinguished themselves with cultural achievement, economic strength, political superiority, or military power, but they did not attain nationhood,[18] mainly because the physical conditions

---

any foreign term, properly "re-Turkified," was merely returning to its own." (Roger Hilsman, *The Crouching Future,* New York, 1975, p. 237)

15. Among these were the Old Kingdom (2664-2180 B.C.), Middle Kingdom (2052-1786 B.C.), and New Kingdom (1554-1075 B.C.) of the ancient Egypt. Except for once, when the New Kingdom extended its power as far as Palestine and Syria to become an Empire, these Kingdoms were generally confined to a narrow area with a small population. "To the Egyptians, their country was the 'Black Land' a name that refers only to the narrow strip of fertile land, the valley and delta of the Nile, separating two deserts.... Estimates of the population of ancient Egypt vary, but during the great periods of Egyptian civilization there may have been about 2 million inhabitants." (Professor Leonard H. Lesko, "Ancient Egypt, 3, Economic Life," in the *Encyclopedia Americana,* 1973 ed., Vol. 10, p. 37)

16. Take Athens and Sparta as examples: "To appreciate the intensity of Greek urban civilization, one must always remember the smallness, both in territory and in population, of the city-states. Sparta (3,360 square miles) and Athens (1,060 square miles) were the largest ... Athens, with 43,000 adult male citizens at its peak in the 5th century B.C., had the largest population and was in a class by itself. The majority of cities, including Sparta, had less than 5,000 citizens." (Professor Norman O. Brown, "History of Greece to 330 A.D.," in the *Encyclopedia Americana,* 1973 ed., Vol. 13, p. 392-393)

17. There were many clannish or tribal empires in history, such as the Empires of Sumer, Babylonia, Assyria, Egypt, Mycenae, Phoenicia, Crete, Macedonia and Rome in the ancient Western world, the Inca Empire in South America before the Spanish conquest, and the dynasties of Shang and Chou in ancient China. The center of these empires was a strong clan or tribe which extended its military and political power over other clans or tribes, but did not make them into a nation.

18. "Nations, thus understood, are something quite new in history. Antiquity was not acquainted with them. Egypt, China and ancient Chaldea were in no degree nations. They were herds led by a son of heaven or of the sun ... Classic antiquity had municipal republics and kingdoms, confederations of local republics and empires: it hardly had a nation as we understand the word. Athens, Sparta, Tyre and Sidon were little centres of an admirable patriotism, but they were cities with a relatively small territory. Gaul, Spain and Italy, before they were absorbed by the Roman empire, were collections of tribal groups which were often leagued together, but without central institutions and without dynasties. Nor were the Assyrian and the Persian empires, or the empire of Alexander, fatherlands. There were never Assyrian patriots; the Persian empire was a vast feudalism. Not one nation can trace its origin to the colossal fortune of Alexander, ..." (*Cyclopedia of Political Science, Political Economy and of the Political History of the United States,* ed. by John J. Lalor, New York, 1904, Vol. 2, p. 924)

"Thus conceiving of the nation, we see that it is a modern growth, and that it

necessary for the growth of the nation did not exist until later in the Iron Age, as discussed earlier.[19]

There were also special phenomena in various regions which hindered the growth of the nation, such as religious domination and feudalism in the Medieval World,[20] and the caste system in the Indian subcontinent.[21]

---

must be, because it takes time and implies high civilization and widespread liberty to develop a nation. Antiquity knew no nations. Egypt, China, Assyria, did not develop nations. They consisted of a people, or various peoples, ruled over by a monarch, Greece had cities or states, but developed no nation. There was liberty, but no widespread union. The Roman Empire was not a nation, it had unity but its various constituent parts did not have liberty or a common will. The Middle Ages saw no nations though nationality was growing. England may be said to have developed as a nation almost before the close of the Middle Ages, and France and Italy and Germany were not far behind, yet Italy and Germany were hindered in the development of national unity by division into rival states." (*The New Encyclopedia of Social Reform,* ed. by William D.P. Bliss, new ed., New York, 1908, p. 806)

19. (Cf. Id-g, and references.)

20. "Still more instructive is the absence of nationalistic feeling during the Middle Ages. In its place we find devotion to feudal lords and ruling dynasties. French battled against French, Italians against Italians according to their allegiance. While feudalism broke up the unity of what we should call nowadays a nationality, the unity of Christianity against Mohammedanism overstepped by far the limits of people of one speech. Both of these aspects of medieval life made impossible the feeling for a nationality as a uniting bond. The National State in our sense was nonexistent." (Franz Boas, *Anthropology and Modern Life,* Rev., New York, 1932, p. 95-96. Cf. Friedrich O. Hertz, *Nationality in History and Politics,* New York, 1944, p. 31-32.)

21. The caste system was probably introduced into India by the Aryan peoples who came down into the area from the north and northwest in a series of invasions between approximately 2400 and 1500 B.C. These Aryans made two principal divisions in the community; one which included themselves, was called the "twice born"; the other, composed of the pre-Aryan inhabitants of India whom they had conquered, was called the "once born." The two principal divisions were again divided into subdivisions, each constituting a rigid caste. The members of a caste are further bound by a common occupation, and by common customs relating particularly to marriage, food, and the questions of pollution by members of lower castes. Thus, within a caste, food and drink are restricted, and only members of the same caste may eat together. The caste is, further, a collection of families or groups bearing a common name and quite often claiming common descent from a mythical ancestor, human or divine. Castes are almost invariably endogamous in the sense that a member of the large circle denoted by the common name may not marry outside that circle. Within the circle, however, there are usually a number of smaller circles, each of which is also endogamous. According to some estimates, there were more than 3,000 castes on the Indian subcontinent, early in this century. Obviously, they were a formidable force which must have hampered the growth of the nation in this great area for hundreds of years. (Cf.

It is clear, therefore, that the nation is not something long in existence, deeply rooted, or a permanent fixture in civilization.[22]

b.
Elements
of the Nation

LANGUAGE, RELIGION, CONSANGUINITY, HISTORY AND territoriality have been generally regarded as the important objective elements of the nation. Historically, they are not elements of the nation alone. They have been elements common to all groups in the series of our group expansion from the early single family, through the primitive community, clan and tribe, to the nation. Their main function has been to form and hold each of these groups together until a new expansion occurs. Such a function has made them known as the "group tie." The importance and significance of the role each of them has played in holding groups together vary in different times, however.

Among the elements mentioned, language has played the role as a group tie most consistently for all early groups through the tribe. For the nation, its importance has still been emphasized in some ways[23]

Emile C.M. Senart, *Caste in India, the Facts and the System,* trans. by E. Denison Ross, London, 1930; and Friedrich O. Hertz, *Nationality in History and Politics,* New York, 1944, p. 136-139.)

22. "Nationalities are groups of very recent origin and therefore are of the utmost complexity. They defy exact definition. Nationality is an historical and a political concept, and the words "nation" and "nationality" have undergone many changes in meaning. It is only in recent history that man has begun to regard nationality as the center of his political and cultural activity and life. Nationality is therefore nothing absolute, and it is a great mistake, responsible for most of the extremities of today, to make it an absolute, an objective a priori, the source of all political and cultural life." (Hans Kohn, *The Idea of Nationalism, A Study in Its Origins and Background,* New York, 1948, p. 13)

23. It is said, for instance, that "The factor of national language is of the utmost importance; it can be considered the major distinguishing mark of nationality. People speaking the same language obviously can understand one another, and this fact alone contributes to a sense of belonging, a sentiment of solidarity. Most men really feel at home only in their own tongue." (Professor John. B. Whitton,

and its significance still noted,[24] but in general, it no longer functions as an essential tie. Some nations have emerged with diversity of languages and dialects,[25] others have broken away from the same language,[26] and still others have maintained several languages not only for traditional, but also for official, use.[27] If the linguistic map

---

"Nationalism and Internationalism," in the *Encyclopedia Americana,* 1973 ed., Vol. 19, p. 749)

24. "When we glance at the national aspirations that have characterized a large part of the nineteenth century, community of language might seem to be the background of national life. It touches the most sympathetic chords in our hearts. Italians worked for the overthrow of the small local and great foreign interests that were opposed to the national unity of all Italian-speaking people. German patriots strove and will strive for the federation of the German-speaking people in one empire. The struggles in the Balkans are largely due to a desire for national independence according to the limits of speech. The Poles have for more than a century longed for a re-establishment of their state which is to embrace all those of Polish tongue." (Frank Boas, *Anthropology and Modern Life,* rev. ed., New York, 1932, p. 90-91)

25. "The national language made its appearance only in recent centuries. At the beginning of modern times, there was still a considerable diversity of languages and dialects in any of the nascent nations. In England, for example, this diversity was so marked that in the 14th century, men of the North were unintelligible to men of the South in oral speech, and books written in one of these tongues had to be translated in order to be understood in other parts." (George H. McKnight, *Modern English in the Making,* New York, 1928, p. 7) "In Germany, Luther's Bible, though written in middle language, was translated into Low-German; and in France, Italy, and some other countries conditions were similar." (Friedrich O. Hertz, *Nationality in History and Politics,* New York, 1944, p. 82) "There were still several hundred languages spoken in India before World War II." (James S. Meston, *Nationhood for India,* London, 1931, p. 45) In China, classical script has indeed made a great contribution to Chinese unity through her long history, but only a small part of the people could understand the extraordinarily difficult script. Spoken Chinese was quite different from the old script and the diversity of Chinese dialects was marked by every small geographical or historical district until recent decades when Mandarin, a language used by the Chinese central administration for some centuries, has spread over most of China.

26. The United States, for instance, broke away from England; Canada, Australia, New Zealand and other English-speaking dominions did the same later; and the nations of Spanish America broke with Spain.

27. Belgium, for example, uses Dutch and French as official languages; Canada, English and French; South Africa, English and Afrikaans; and in Switzerland both French and German are the official languages of the cantons of Froiburg, Valais and Berne; German, Italian and Romansch are official in the Canton of Graubunden; in fourteen cantons, German alone is official; in three, French alone; and in one, Italian alone. (For the complicated language situation in Switzerland, cf. Henry D. Lloyd, *A Sovereign People,* New York, 1907, p. 4.)

of the world were compared with national boundaries today, it would turn out that the two coincide only in a very small number of countries.[28]

In early times, when magic, myth and superstition were common in daily life,[29] totems[30] and various deities[31] were worshipped, com-

---

28. "In many other parts of the world, language areas are either too small (tropical Africa) or too large (Latin America, the Arab Middle East) to provide a suitable setting for modern nation-states. If the linguistic map of the world were compared with political boundaries of the 1960s, it would turn out that the two coincide even roughly in only two dozen countries. The majority of them in Europe. In nearly half the countries of the world less than 70 per cent of the population speak the same language, and in one out of four there is no linguistic majority. Throughout most of the world if present states are to become nations, either linguistic identity will have to be consciously fostered or else some different basis of nationality must be found." (Dankwart A. Rustow, "Nation," *International Encyclopedia of the Social Sciences,* ed. by David L. Sills, New York, New York, 1968, Vol. 11, p. 11)

29. Among primitive peoples, terror of the unknown in the physical world leads to belief in mysterious powers and spirits, and magic, myth and superstition are necessarily involved in their common life all the time. (Cf. Edmund D. Soper, *The Religions of Mankind,* New York, 1921, p. 50-52; Daniel A. Brinton, *Religions of Primitive Peoples,* New York, 1898, p. 88-171; and Bronislaw Malinowski, *Sex, Culture, and Myth,* New York, 1962, p. 268-332.)

30. A totem is an animal, plant, or inanimate object with which a social or religious group feels a special affinity, and which is often considered to be the mythical ancestor of the group. Totemism is based on a religious principle that divides mankind and nature into classes and categories and links a particular cultural group with a specific being or thing, which is the totem. The totem is worshiped or esteemed by members of the group bearing its name. An appropriate myth may explain the role of the totem in the origin of the group. A totemic animal may not be killed or harmed by those who consider themselves to be its descendants, except on certain ritual occasions when it might be eaten sacramentally. (Cf. Emile Durkheim, *The Elementary Forms of the Religious Life,* trans. by J.W. Swain, London, 1915, p. 154-155, 295.)

31. Among the various deities, specialized gods are recognized in more complex societies where there is a conscious division of labor. Specialized deities are the patrons of certain human activities and are often of decisive influence in success or failure. In the Masai tribe of eastern Africa, for instance, there is a chief god, the sky, and, in addition, many other deities who have responsibility for checking disease, establishing honesty in the market place, winning victories in war, protecting life and property from the sea, and correctly channeling sensual desire. Investigation shows a wide variety of specialized deities, but with no general rule determining what activities will be under special divine guidance and what human concerns will be left to natural control and given a natural foundation. Perhaps the most constant of the specialized deities are those who have power over the world which man enters after death. Some of these "death gods" have no relationship of any kind to life; their power begins only when the body is destroyed.

mon rites were a privilege as well as obligation for membership in a community,[32] taboo was obeyed much more seriously than law,[33] and religious leaders were usually political chiefs,[34] it was only natural that religion was a powerful group tie.

Often, however, the gods of the dead invade life because they must determine, by the kind of life a person lived while on earth, whether or not his soul is to be given glory or suffering after death. Whenever the gods of the afterlife have this power of judgment, they tend to be imperialistic and to dictate the way in which the whole of life should be conducted. (Cf. Helmer Ringgren and Ake V. Strom, *Religions of Mankind, Today and Yesterday,* trans. by Niels L. Jensen, London, 1967, p. 7-104, 213-219, 239-243, 304-310, 345-349.)

32. Common religious rites and common burial places appear in all three lists of important rights, privileges and obligations of the members of the Iroquois gens, Grecian gens, and Roman gens. (Cf. Lewis H. Morgan, *Ancient Society,* New York, 1877, p. 71, 222-223, 285.)

33. A taboo is a prohibition applying to something that is forbidden or set apart because it is sacred, consecrated, or unclean and therefore considered dangerous. A person, place, object, or act can be taboo. A taboo is enforced by supernatural sanctions. That is, those who believe in the taboo expect that anyone who breaks it will automatically suffer death, illness, or some other misfortune. The taboo may also be enforced by social sanctions. In 19th century Hawaii, for example, a man who broke a taboo could be put to death by his fellows. (Cf. Franz Steiner, *Taboo,* New York, 1956, especially p. 20-22.)

34. "This introduces an aspect of the chieftainship which has not been accorded proper attention, namely, that it is not infrequently a religious office. Cases occur where there seems to be an original companion-agency alongside the chief in the person of the medicine-man. Again, the chief himself is the head fetishman. In some parts of the world there are two chiefs, one secular and one sacerdotal. There is usually, however, nothing to keep the two offices separate; temporal and spiritual power, on the contrary, tend to coalesce." "It might as well be realized at once that there was no separation of church and state in the early days, and that temporal and spiritual power, like ecclesiastical and secular law, were inseparably intertwined." (William G. Sumner and Albert G. Keller, *The Science of Society,* New Haven, 1927, Vol. I, p. 478, 461. Cf. Chi-Chao Liang, *History of Pre-Chin Political Thoughts* (in Chinese) 6th ed. Taipei, 1972, p. 19-29.)

In ancient times, the Egyptians regarded their king as a god. In Babylon, the ruler was a priest-king, earthly representative of the gods. "Concentration of power probably began among those peoples who developed the totemic system. At first the concentration of authority was religious in nature and consisted in regarding the totem itself as the source and center of all power. Later the clan chief or the tribal chief was regarded as the representative and the embodiment of the totem, and hence was considered to rule by a sort of divine right." (William M. McGovern, "The Growth of Institutions," in *Making Mankind,* New York, 1929, p. 98-99.)

35. The one God is a universal deity who has power over all that is in heaven, earth, and sometimes hell. Most often, monotheistic traditions recognize their single deity as the creator of the world, the source of all good, the regulator of all ceremonial and ethical conduct, the judge who will consign a soul to heaven or

By the time of the nation, however, religion had largely changed from polytheism to monotheism, and a monotheistic religion is hardly apt to act as a national tie, because the concept of one god is essentially universal in character.[35]

Judaism, Christianity and Islam are the major monotheistic religions. Their intellectualization has also made them fundamentally inappropriate as national ties. The core of their belief systems is an ethical universalism: all peoples, as children of God, are brothers and sisters. This belief was sublimated by Judaism,[36] reached its climax in Christianity,[37] and was transplanted into Islam.[38]

---

hell, and the true God who must be worshipped by all men. The one God is never localized, nor is he given temporal existence, although, as in Christianity, he may become incarnate in a historic individual. His essential character is always universal and supernatural. (Cf. Helmer Ringgren and Ake V. Strom, *Religions of Mankind, Today and Yesterday,* trans. by Niels L. Jensen, London, 1967, p. 124-125, 138-144, 184-186; also William F. Albright, *From the Stone Age to Christianity: Monotheism and the Historical Process,* Baltimore, 1957, p. 200-399.)

The monotheistic religion, with an almighty God, has a precedent in Egypt when the Egyptian King Amenophis IV, in about 1400 B.C., promoted Aten, the God of the Sun, to the rank of chief god. He called himself Akhenaten—"he who pleases Aten," and his capital, Akhetaten—"the horizon of Aten." The king's intentions seem to have been to offer to the Egyptians' adoration a deity who was no longer merely local, peculiar to one town, nor exclusively national in character, but who incarnated the essential force of Nature and thus might exact universal worship. To this end the king chose the sun, one of the primitive elemental deities of mankind, whose power, beneficent to some, terrible to others, seems nowhere more absolute than in the lands of the East. This god was no longer presented to men in the form of a falcon, but as a radiant disc, a pictographic sign, a hieroglyph, which all men, Egyptians or strangers, could read and understand at a glance. Aten, who personifies movement and warmth, is the beneficent, life-giving father of all that exists: earth, water, plants, animals, the people of Egypt and of foreign countries. (Cf. Emery Reves, *The Anatomy of Peace,* New York, 1946, p. 77-79.)

36. Judaism shows different trends during different phases. At first, it aimed at restoring Jewish independence and making the Jews a great people. But this idea was more and more sublimated to ethical universalism. God was the father of mankind, which formed one great family. The whole of mankind would enjoy the blessings of peace, brotherhood, righteousness, and love. (Cf. Norman Bentwich, *The Religious Foundations of Internationalism,* 2nd. ed., New York, 1959, p. 59-82.)

37. The tendency towards ethical universalism which had appeared in Judaism reached its climax in Christianity. All mankind were to Jesus children of God and brothers and sisters. The Kingdom of God which he was preaching was neither a Jewish state nor any other political organization. No form of government and no social system can claim to be the basis of Christian society. It is the spirit of the individual that matters, the spirit of love, truthfulness, humble service and prudence, not any external machinery working by compulsion, passion and deceit. Christians regarded themselves as the people of God and rejected the idea of loyal-

In the Far East, Buddhism is also not apt to be a national tie, mainly because it is a philosophy of escape with no interest in temporal strife.[39]

In contrast to Buddhism, Confucianism is a kind of pragmatic teaching. As a religion, it does not serve as a national tie either, because the principle of its philosophy is humanity, and its ultimate objective is a society of "Great Harmony."[40]

---

ty to a specific fatherland. This tradition can be traced through the whole history of Christianity. At the end of the second century, the Letter of Diognetus, ascribed to Justinus, says that the Christians are like strangers in their own country and regard every foreign country as their fatherland. Their real home is heaven. More than a thousand years later, Vincent of Beauvais, quoting Hugo of St. Victor, wrote: "Who is fettered by the fatherland is still weak; strong is he who regards every country as his fatherland; perfect is he to whom the whole world is a place of exile." This was also Thomas More's conviction. In regard to nationality, the biblical story of the Tower of Babel indicates that the diversity of languages and regional individuality was a divine punishment. It is difficult to combine the idea of ethical monotheism and a universal moral law valid for every people with the fact that the different peoples had very different moral standards. Thus nationality had no value, or was even an evil, from the viewpoint of Christianity. (Cf. Friedrich O. Hertz, *Nationality in History and Politics,* New York, 1944, p. 103-108; Norman Bentwich, *The Religious Foundations of Internationalism,* 2nd ed., New York, 1959, p. 83-110. Cf. also Cecil J. Cadoux, *The Early Church and the World, History of the Christian Attitude to Pagan Society and the State Down to the Time of Constantinus,* Edinburgh, 1925.)

38. Mohammed received his religious and ethical inspiration largely from Judaism and Christianity. Islam, therefore, shows an extraordinary number of parallels with medieval Christian thought and practice. All believers in the true faith were to be regarded as brothers and many precepts of Islam admirably served the purpose of welding all Moslems into a great fraternity. (Cf. David S. Margoliouth, *The Early Development of Mohammedanism,* London, 1914, especially p. 230-258.) These teachings formed a creed for enthusiastic warriors, and gave rise to an Arab Empire. Soon, however, fierce enmity revived among the Arabian tribes and brought the empire to an end. The binding force of religion proved insufficient to form a durable unity. On the other hand, the Mohammedan conquerors were often welcomed by sections of the Christians, for example in Spain, Sicily, Naples, and southern France, or were even called in by them in order to obtain help against other Christians. (Cf. Friedrich O. Hertz, *Nationality in History and Politics,* New York, 1944, p. 141-142.) This fact reveals that hostilities between different groups within a religion were sometimes more furious than those between different religions.

39. Buddhism was founded in northern India by Gautama Siddhartha in the sixth century B.C., and spread to southeast Asia and through China to Japan. But there is in this vast region no great country whose nationality has been molded or fostered to a considerable extent by its force, though it has played certain important roles in some areas, such as Tibet, Ceylon, Burma, Siam, and Japan. (Cf. Joseph M. Kitagawa, *Religions of the East,* enlarged ed. Philadelphia, 1968, p. 155-221.)

The foundation of Hinduism is the caste system, which divides people into various classes and groups. Because it divides rather than unites people, it is not suitable to be a national tie.[41]

These six principal religions have spread over most of the world, and have crossed most of the national frontiers.[42] For this reason also they are unfit as national ties.[43]

---

40. The principle of Confucianism is 仁 (Jen), comprehensively equivalent to humanity, and its ultimate objective is 大同 (Ta Tung), which may be interpreted in many ways, and roughly means a great society including all people under the heaven. 天下 means to live in great harmony. (Cf. V. 298; and Chi-Chao Liang, *History of Pre-Chin Political Thoughts,* (in Chinese), 6th ed., Taipei, 1972, p. 67-73.)

41. Hinduism has no founder and is hard to define, there being no common creed, nor one doctrine to bind Hindus together. Intellectually there is complete freedom of belief, and one can be a monotheist, polytheist, or atheist. What matters is the social system: a Hindu is born into a caste. This system strictly divides people into various classes and groups, and has thus not only made Hinduism unsuitable to be a national tie, but may also have hampered national growth in the Indian subcontinent for some hundred years. It should be remarked that during the 19th century there was a Hindu leader named Ramakrishna Paramahamsa who tried to make Hinduism a harmony and unity of all creeds and all beings by overcoming the barriers of caste, passion, Mohammedanism and Christianity. (Cf. Joseph M. Kitagawa, *Religions of the East,* enlarged ed., Philadelphia, 1968, p. 99-154; Horace L. Friess and Herbert W. Schneider, *Religions in Various Cultures,* New York, 1960, p. 118; and III, 21.)

42. Estimated membership of the six principal religions of the world (based on the *Britannica Book of the Year, 1975,* p. 604):

Religion	North America	South America	Europe
Total Christian	225,504,750	161,583,500	352,597,100
Roman Catholic	128,884,000	151,600,000	171,748,500
Eastern Orthodox	4,115,000	54,000	65,534,600
Protestant	92,505,750	9,929,500	115,814,000
Jewish	6,316,525	678,700	3,960,700
Muslim	235,000	191,200	8,730,000
Confucian	96,000	83,000	30,000
Buddhist	148,000	180,300	220,000
Hindu	70,000	502,000	350,000

In modern times, the role of religion as a national tie has been further weakened by the separation of Church and State[44] and the growth of religious liberty.[45]

Religion	Asia	Africa	Oceania	World
Total Christian	86,811,000	100,465,100	17,104,000	944,045,450
Roman Catholic	45,122,000	32,039,500	3,188,000	532,582,000
Eastern Orthodox	1,835,000	17,410,000	363,000	89,301,600
Protestant	39,854,000	51,015,600	13,563,000	327,181,850
Jewish	3,026,150	299,465	75,000	14,893,540
Muslim	422,208,000	97,678,500	66,000	529,108,700
Confucian	205,725,700	500	41,500	206,976,700
Buddhist	247,951,500	2,000	15,000	248,516,800
Hindu	512,118,000	463,400	629,000	514,432,400

(Cf. *Encyclopedia Britannica,* 1974 ed., Vol. 15, p. 630-631, Religious map: "Geographical Distribution of the Religions of the World"; and David E. Sopher, *Geography of Religions,* Englewood Cliff, N.J., 1967, p. 79-115.)

43. A few special cases, under special circumstances, are exceptions, such as Judaism in Israel and Roman Catholicism in Ireland.

44. The question of the proper relationship between Church and State has at one time or another agitated the internal politics of almost every country in western Europe. Historically, a particular religious sect, originally the Roman Catholic, but after the Reformation frequently Protestant, has usually occupied a favored position. This position has varied from that of a state church with the exclusive right to hold all the religious services within the country to that of an institution merely supported at public expense. As early as the 16th century, however, there arose out of the tangled skein of the Reformation a movement for the political separation of church and state which, although it did not gather force immediately, has in the course of the centuries swept the larger portion of the world. After its independence in 1776, the United States repealed most of the legislation supporting one or another religion. The first clause of the 1st Amendment, proposed by James Madison to Congress in 1789, and adopted in 1791, set the tone for the American attitude toward separation of church and state thereafter: "Congress shall make no law respecting an establishment of religion, or prohibiting the free exercise thereof...." The principle of separation, consistently adhered to in the United States, appears in the constitutions of a number of nations that have adopted written fundamental laws since 1945, such as Japan, India, and Italy. (Cf. Luigi Sturgo, *Church and State,* trans. by Barbara B. Carter, New York, 1939, p. 6-9, and parts II and III; William A. Brown, *Church and State in Contemporary America,* New York, 1936, p. 51-81; John VanTil, *Liberty of Conscience, The History of a Puritan Idea,* Nutley, N.J., 1972, p. 168-181; and A.F. Carrillo de Albornoz, *Religious Liberty in the World; a General Review of the World Situation in 1965,* Geneva, 1966.)

45. Religious liberty means the individual's opportunity to accept and practice a religious faith according to his conscience, and for a church or other religious group to worship, preach, and teach according to its own principles. Such liberty includes freedom from the imposition of any one religion, as well as freedom from

The element of consanguinity was the strongest tie for the early single family, because it was constituted by sexual and direct blood relationships.[46] It later developed into a wide kinship in which the blood connection was generally indirect and mixed or nonexistent.[47] Blood relationship was still a very strong tie for the primitive community, as well as for the clan, however.[48] The tribe has generally

---

coercion against any one or all religions. Religious liberty was the focus of open struggle and achievement in European society and has become a general tendency everywhere. Significant expression of this general tendency, in terms officially accepted on every continent, is to be found in several general clauses of the Charter of the United Nations, and more specifically in Article 18 of the Universal Declaration of Human Rights; "Everyone has the right to freedom of thought, conscience and religion; this right includes freedom to change his religion or belief, and freedom, either alone or in community with others and in public or private, to manifest religion or belief in teaching, practice, worship and observance." (Cf. A.F. Carrillo de Albornoz, *Religious Liberty,* trans. by John Frury, New York, 1967, p. 3-24, 189-192; and John C. Murray, "The Declaration on Religious Freedom—A Moment in Its Legislative History," in *Religious Liberty—An End and a Beginning,* ed. by John C. Murray, New York, 1966, p. 15-44.)

46. "The separate little hordes of Bushmen consist always of a single family. Sex feelings and instinctive love for children, or the habit of familiarity between relatives, are the sole bonds which hold them together at all." (William G. Sumner and Albert G. Keller, *The Science of Society,* New Haven, 1927, Vol. I, p. 420)

47. "In general, when men come first into the range of history and ethnography, they appear in societies which make a great deal of the blood-tie, as they understand it. Many of them assert that they have derived their blood from a common ancestral source; even in cases where this seems to be a mere assumption or where it is evidently untrue, or where community of blood has to be established artificially they adhere tenaciously to the doctrine of bloodkinship." (William G. Sumner and Albert G. Keller, *The Science of Society,* New Haven, 1927, Vol. I, p. 419)

"... in Australia, ... 'the recognition and classification of relationships is usually extended without any limit to embrace the whole society.' A man applies kinship terms to almost everybody with whom he is genealogically connected by descent or marriage, and sometimes, as among the Nguni, he also uses them for people of his own and certain other clans, even if no genealogical tie is known to exist." (Isaac Schapera, *Government and Politics in Tribal Societies,* London, 1956, p. 18-19)

48. "The most recent researches into the primitive history of society point to the conclusion that the earliest tie which knitted men together in communities was Consanguinity or Kinship." (Henry S. Maine, "Kinship as the Basis of Society," in his *Lectures on the Early History of Institutions,* New York, 1888, p. 64)

"The organization of all primitive peoples is upon what may be called a popular as opposed to a territorial basis. A man is governed by the fact that he is a member of a family, a gens, ... Even the Greeks and Romans in the historical period had great difficulty in organizing a government with territorial sub-

been too large for kinship to operate[49] and has often contained people of many different ethnic stocks.[50] This is even truer and more
conspicuous for the nation, in which kinship is invariably replaced by
local contiguity as a political unit, such as a township.[51]

Some people have tried to substitute race for kinship to provide a
blood tie for the nation. They are obviously ignorant of the distinction between the nation and race, and their attempt is repudiated by

---

divisions as opposed to a government sub-divided into a number of gens and clans
irrespective of where they dwelt. In the end the Romans succeeded in establishing a
purely territorial type of government, but when the Germanic invaders overthrew
the Roman Empire the latter kept their 'popular' type of government for some
time. Theodorie, e.g., was not King of Italy, but King of the Ostrogoths, ...
though the Ostrogoths controlled Italy....'' (William M. McGovern, ''The
Growth of Institutions,'' in *Making Mankind,* New York, 1929, p. 99-100)

49. ''When one advances from these lesser kinship-organizations to the tribe,
he is passing, in reality, from the blood-tie to a wider, political bond. Association
can develop only to a certain limited degree under the kinship-group, however relationship is reckoned. When men are brought into local contact and held there, the
situation demands an organization of greater potency and comprehensiveness. By
whatever means disintegrated, the kin-group system loses its efficacy as an adjustment and merges gradually into a system better suitable to altered conditions, living on within it to discharge such services as it is capable of performing. The family
remains vigorous within the larger political aggregation; but the effective life of the
constituent kin-groups is about over.'' (William G. Sumner and Albert G. Keller,
The Science of Society, New Haven, 1927, Vol. I, p. 438-440)

50. Speaking of the African tribes, ''but even the smallest tribe nowadays
contains families of alien origin, and in the larger tribes the royal descent group
may constitute only a small proportion of the whole. Thus, in Bechuanaland,
about half the Tlokwa (pop. 2,300) are kinsmen of the chief, the others between
them representing nine different alien stocks; at the other extreme, less than one
percent of the Tawana (pop. 39,000) trace agnatic descent from the founder of the
tribe. Similarly the people of Basutoland, who now form a single tribe, are derived
not only from what were formerly many different Sotho tribes, but partly also
from Cape and Natal Nguni of varied origins, who constitute about 15 percent of
the total; among the Lobedu, a Transvaal Sotho tribe (pop. 33,000), over 90 percent of the people differ in origin from the ruling stock.'' (Isaac Schapera,
Government and Politics in Tribal Societies, London, 1956, p. 18)

51. ''If we compare 'primitive' and 'civilized' groups of men as we find them
in the world to-day, almost the first point of difference that will strike the observer
is that, among the former, the individual identifies himself by particularising his
blood-relationships, whereas, in the latter, the individual defines his status in
terms of relation to a given territory.'' (Frederick J. Teggart, *The Processes of
History,* New Haven, 1918, p. 80)

''Local contiguity ... The idea that a number of persons should exercise
political rights in common simply because they happened to live within the same
topographical limits was utterly strange and monstrous to primitive antiquity.''
(Henry J.S. Maine, *Ancient Law,* Pollock's ed., London, 1930, p. 145)

the fact that there is no major nation in the world which is not composed of many different racial elements,[52] and no major race in the
world which has not penetrated into many nations.[53]

History was closely linked to religion and consanguinity in early
times. This is illustrated by the fact that almost all primitive groups
regarded themselves as having proceeded from a mysterious origin.[54]

---

52. For instance, the United States of America is well known to have a people
comprised of almost all ethnic origins. (For major groups cf. I,88.) The USSR has
more than a hundred different ethnic stocks. (For major groups cf. I, 84.) China
has Manchu, Mongol, Uigur, Tibetan, Thai, Lolo, and many other minority
ethnic groups, in addition to the great majority Han-Chinese. (Cf. George Mosely,
"China's Fresh Approach to the National Minority Groups," in *China Quarterly,*
London, no. 24, 1965.) The Federation of South Africa has two major white and
nine major black ethnic groups. (Cf. I, 71-72.) Nigeria has three major ethnic
groups—Ibo, Yoruba and Hausa. (Cf. I, 76-78.) Almost all nations in Central and
South America have a people with European origins, predominantly Spanish, Indian, Negro and Mestizo. (Cf. Victor Alba, *The Latin Americans,* New York,
1969, p. 17-47.) And in western Europe, racial types "are on the whole distributed
in strata that follow one another from north to south, —in the north the blond, in
the center a darker, short-headed type, in the south the slightly built Mediterranean. National boundaries . . . on the other hand, run north and south: and so we
find many individuals in northern France, Belgium, Holland, Germany and northwestern Russia similar in type and descent; many of the central French, South Germans, Swiss, North Italians, Austrians, Servians and central Russians, belonging
to similar varieties of man; and also persons in southern France, closely related to
the types of the eastern and western Mediterranean area." (Franz Boas, *Anthropology and Modern Life,* rev. ed., New York, 1932, p. 85-86)

53. An example is ". . . the Germans in Germany, Austria, France, Poland,
Czecho-Slovakia, Italy and the Baltic States." "This is proved by the distribution
of bodily forms. Even if it is true that the blond type is found at present pre-
eminently among Teutonic people, it is not confined to them alone. Among the
Finns, Poles, French, North Italians, not to speak of the North African Berbers
and the Kurds of western Asia, there are individuals of this type. The heavy-set,
darker East European type is common to many of the Slavic peoples of eastern
Europe, to the Germans of Austria and southern Germany, to the North Italians,
and to the French of the Alps and of central France. The Mediterranean type is
spread widely over Spain, Italy, Greece, and the coast of Asia Minor, without
regard to national boundaries." (Frank Boas, *Anthropology and Modern Life,*
rev. ed. New York, 1932, p. 82, 85)

54. "All ancient societies regarded themselves as having proceeded from one
original stock, and even laboured under an incapacity for comprehending any
reason except this for their holding together in political union. The history of
political ideas begins, in fact, with the assumption that kinship in the blood is the
sole possible ground of community in political functions. . . ." (Henry J.S. Maine,
Ancient Law, Pollock's ed., London, 1930, p. 144)

"One of the most frequent, almost certainly the most frequent, form of the
clan is one on which all its members believe in their relationship to a species of ob-

The Genesis of the *Old Testament* is a well-known example of history interwoven with religious belief and blood relationship.[55] Religion and consanguinity were both strong ties for early groups. This is why history played a similarly important role in that period.

As the era of the nation approached, however, religion and consanguinity began to weaken as rallying points, and ceased to be strong ties. As a result, history was left alone as a point of attachment. Many means have been employed to manipulate history for use as a national tie. A notorious one is to eliminate all divergent accounts.[56] Another more commonly applied method is to select and record from all events, past and present, what suits the particular

---

jects, animal, plant, or inanimate, called totems, of which animal totems are by far the most frequent." (William H.R. Rivers, *Social Organization,* New York, 1924, p. 21-22)

55. "The First Book of Moses, called Genesis," in *The Old Testament,* consists of a "Book of Human Origins" (1:1 to 11:26) and a "Book of the Fathers," or patriarchal history (11:27 to 50:26). The "Book of Origins" may be divided as follows: the creation of the world and of man (1:1 to 2:4a); the creation of man and woman and their fall (2:4b to 3:24); Cain and Abel (4:1-16); the origins of the Cainites (4:17-24); the origins of the Sethites and their genealogy (4:25 to 5:32); the sons of God and the daughters of men (6:1-4); the Flood epic and the covenant with Noah (6:5 to 9:17); the account of Noah's sons (9:18-29); the table of the origins of the families (10:1-32); the tower of Babel (11:1-9); and the genealogy of the Shemites (11:10-26). The patriarchal history comprises cycles of stories relating to three major figures of the pre-Israelite past, namely Abraham, Isaac, and Jacob, together with supplementary traditions about other ancestors who were of secondary interest. After an introductory genealogy (11:27-32), there appears first the story of Abraham and Isaac (12:1 to 25:18). Included is a fragmentary history, possibly of Moabite origin, of Lot, the ancestor of the Moabites and Ammonites, who were related to the Israelites. There is also the history of Ishmael, who is regarded as the ancestor of the Arab peoples. The second major cycle (25:19 to 36:43) is that of Isaac and Jacob. This cycle also contains supplementary material, some of Edomite origin, relating to Esau, ancestor of the Edomites. Finally, there is the extensive and distinctive story of Joseph (37:1 to 50:26), which is interrupted by a variant history of Judah in chapter 38, and the "blessings" of the Israelite tribes in chapter 49.

56. The First Emperor of the Chin Dynasty of China, for example, at the instigation of his prime minister Lee Ssu, decreed in the 34th year (209 B.C.) of his reign that all historical records except Chin's own be burned, along with various other works (especially political writings such as Confucian works that lauded ancient history and the ancient system), except those dealing with medicine, pharmacy, divination, and agriculture. (According to "The Account of the First Emperor of the Chin Dynasty," in the *Book of History,* by the great historian Ssu Ma Chien, 司馬遷 , who died in c. 87 B.C.) 史記秦始皇帝本紀載，三十四年，丞相李斯冒死言曰：〝今皇帝并有天下，別黑白而定一尊……臣請史官非秦紀

purpose of the nation, and disregard all the rest.[57] But there has been no way to make history as strong as before when it was genuinely allied with religion and consanguinity.

Territory was not an important element for the early single family, simply because there were no limits ascribed to it in their food gathering life.[58] It emerged as a tie for the primitive community when the community started to identify with some exclusive area for hunting and fishing.[59] It became a stronger tie for the clan, as well as for

---

皆燒之。非博士官所職，天下敢有藏詩書百家語者，悉詣守尉雜燒之……所不去者，醫藥卜筮種植之書。若欲有學法令者，以吏為師。"制曰："可"

57. "History is no less equivocal. In Europe there are few areas that have not changed political control many times over the centuries and to which three or four historic claims could not be readily contrived. In any case, nationalist attitudes to history should not be taken at face value. History often serves as a reservoir of symbols from which nationalists instinctively select what suits their particular purpose. For all their historical romanticism, they are usually straining for a break with their society's immediate past of dynastic fragmentation or foreign subjection. Hence the glories of a remote past (real or mythical) become their allies against the recent past in the struggle for a better future." (Dankwart A. Rustow, "Nation," *International Encyclopedia of the Social Sciences,* New York, 1968, Vol. 11, p. 10)

58. "To what degree does the feeling that such natural resources constitute property persist among folk who are essentially food-gatherers rather than hunters? The data bearing on this point may be taken from western and central North America, since it is from this region that some of the fullest studies of land tenure among food-gathering folk are available. In this area some tribes are found which have no sense of real property at all as, for instance, the Klamath. Klamath families do return to permanent winter encampments, but the summer residences, even though they may be reoccupied from year to year, are not held with any sense of vested right. Furthermore, no individual ownership of fishing places or dams exists, nor are proprietary rights recognized to hunting territories, berry or seed patches. A chief neither owns nor controls the use of fishing places, nor do those who live near the dams have any special claim to them. Those living near a dam may be asked to fish for one coming from elsewhere, but this is only because they know best how to use the site." (Melville J. Herskovits, *The Economic Life of Primitive Peoples,* New York, 1952, p. 299)

59. "The Australian aborigines, for example, live in small autonomous bands, each with exclusive and jealously guarded rights to a well-defined tract of land." (Isaac Schapera, *Government and Politics in Tribal Societies,* London, 1956, p. 4)

"The initial challenge to the doctrine of communal ownership of land among hunting and food-gathering peoples was the research of Speck among the Timiskaming Indians ... Among the Timiskaming the social units were families which comprised a given band 'consisting of individuals related by descent and blood together with other women married to men of the family.' They were not only held together by membership in a common socially recognized group, but, more importantly, welded into a unit by control over a common hunting territory, which

the tribe, as they settled down in a definite place and the land became valuable for hoe-cultivation and animal raising.[60]

For the nation, territory has replaced kinship as a basic tie.[61] But it is not only much weaker than kinship, which was personal and

---

was 'the main bond of union and interest.'..." (Melville J. Herskovits, *The Economic Life of Primitive Peoples,* New York, 1952, p. 294. Cf. p. 294-299.)

"The Murngin clan is an exogamic patrilineal group averaging forty or fifty individuals who possess a common territory which averages 360 square miles. This group possesses one or more sacred totemic water holes, formed by a creator totem, in which the whole of the tribal life is focused; all members of the clan are born from this water hole, and all go back to it at death; in it the totem's spirits live with the mythological ancestor, the souls of the dead, and the unborn children. The male members of the clan who can be the permanent occupants of the group's land possess totemic emblems in common." (William L. Warner, *A Black Civilization; A Social Study of an Australian Tribe,* New York, 1937, p. 16)

60. "We have found that among all South African peoples the political community has a definite territory of its own." (Isaac Schapera, *Government and Politics in Tribal Societies,* London, 1956, p. 11)

"The large number of (Indian) independent tribes ... Each tribe was individualized by a name, by a separate dialect, by a supreme government, and by the possession of a territory which it occupied and defended as its own." (Clark Wissler, *An Introduction to Social Anthropology,* New York, 1929, p. 115)

(Cf. I 127-128, 130-131 and 133-134.)

61. "The experience of mankind, as elsewhere remarked, has developed but two plans of government, using the word plan in its scientific sense. Both were definite and systematic organizations of society. The first and most ancient was a social organization, founded upon gentes, phraties and tribes. The second and latest in time was a political organization, founded upon territory and upon property. Under the first a gentile society was created, in which the government dealt with persons through their relations to a gens and tribe. These relations were purely personal. Under the second a political society was instituted, in which the government dealt with persons through their relations to territory, e.g.—the township, the county and the state. These relations were purely territorial. The two plans were fundamentally different. One belongs to ancient society, and the other to modern." (Lewis H. Morgan, *Ancient Society,* New York, 1877, p. 62)

In China, the kinship system was completely superseded by a territorial organization during the Chin Dynasty (221-206 B.C.) when Shih Huang Ti (the First Emperor of the Chin Dynasty) conquered the feudal states and organized their vast territory into prefectures and counties, governed by officials sent out by the central government and responsible to it. Former feudal leaders were forced to migrate to the new capital of the Chin Dynasty, eliminating their power, mostly derived from the kinship system, and enabling the central government to keep a watchful eye on them. These drastic measures were responsible for the destruction of the feudal system and the establishment of a prefecture and county organization (廢封建爲郡縣。).

"These communities have been defined mainly by kinship and territory. The horde, the clan, the tribe, and the nation have each, in theory, if not in fact, been united by descent from a common ancestor. In settled agriculture, however, the

more natural, but it is not even as strong as it was for the primitive community, clan and tribe, because the territory of these smaller groups was usually felt as closer and more intimately connected to the people.[62]

It should also be noted that the home country is different from the national territory, the former usually being just a certain small portion of the latter. Love for the home country is always deeply rooted,[63] while affection for the national territory is more or less ar-

---

basic communities have tended to be distinguished less by blood relationship than by territory. In the modern nation-states both concepts have been recognized. Legal nationality has ordinarily been determined both by the place of birth (jus soli) and by parentage (jus sanguinis)." (Quincy Wright, *A Study of War,* 2nd ed., Chicago, 1965, p. 1014)

62. Among the Timiskaming Indians, for instance, "these hunting 'lots' or territories comprised well-recognized stretches of land, with natural boundary marks such as rivers, lakes, swamps, or clumps of cedars and pines. The test of trespass applies here, since it was forbidden to hunt outside one's own territory; trespassing was either punished with death, or revenged by the use of sorcery. Permission might be given to hunt in the territory of another band, especially if reciprocity for an earlier similar permission was involved, but the privilege was never permanently extended, and was intended only to aid friends to provide themselves with food when game was scarce in their own hunting grounds. Permission was also asked if, when travelling, the land of another family had to be crossed; where animals were killed for food by the traveler, the pelts had to be brought or sent to the owners of the land, while the reciprocal right of passage was in this case automatic. The yield of a tract was not only safeguarded by trespass rules, but care was taken within the family to see that no more of each type of game animal was killed during a given season than was consonant with maintaining the supply.... The limits of the hunting lands of each band were so well recognized that it is still possible to map the hunting territories claimed by each family group, whose land has long since been lost to the dominant white population." (Melville J. Herskovits, *The Economic Life of Primitive Peoples,* New York, 1952, p. 294)

"A typical Australian tribe was so intimately bound up by sentimental and religious bonds with the ancestral tract of land that no victorious group ever dreamt of dispossessing the vanquished of their territory." (Robert H. Lowie, *The Origin of the State,* New York, 1962, p. 15)

"It seems entirely natural that a human being would develop an affection for his immediate surroundings, the village and locality where he was born and grew up, whose people, hills, valleys, streams, fields, and woods he knows well. But even with modern methods of transportation, most citizens of a country will never get to know very much of the terrain of the whole country so intimately, much less the people." (Roger Hilsman, *The Crouching Future,* New York, 1975, p. 238)

63. The home country is the place where we have been born or which is nearest to our heart through long residence and many cherished memories. This narrow land has a psychological significance quite other than that of the national territory. It suggests the remembrance of childhood and youth, of family life, relatives, and early friends. Its woods and meadows, its valleys and rivers, its

tificial.[64] Ignorance of this distinction may lead to a miscalculation of the strength of the territory as a national tie.

The idea that the natural frontier is important to the territory as a national tie often leads to misconceptions also. It is often a polemic device rather than a scientific concept.[65] Furthermore, all national frontiers, natural and artificial, have greatly declined in importance today,[66] and together with the widely advocated concept of "territorial integrity," have been nullified by modern transportation and communication.

Thus, as the above review reveals, all the important elements: language, religion, consanguinity, history and territory are much

---

villages and historic monuments are much more familiar to us than those of other parts of the national territory, many of which we have seen only as passing visitors, if at all. Our youthful hopes and dreams, the decisive phases of our development, the image of our forefathers, are intimately connected with the natal soil. The fact that a certain, rather small area of land is so bound up with the development of our personality explains why the barrenness and bleakness of a home country does not usually diminish our affection for it, nor are people necessarily more home-loving if they have been born in a fertile or beautiful tract of land. Our love for the home country is the product of many intimate personal experiences during an important epoch of our lives. It has, therefore, more the nature of an organic growth. (Cf. Boyd C. Shafer, *Nationalism, Myth and Reality,* New York, 1955, p. 33.)

64. Affection for the national territory is implanted by a common history, by the force of public opinion, by education, by means of literature, the press, national songs, monuments, and in many other ways. It is much more artificial than the love for the home country, though there are some connections between them. (Cf. Hans Kohn, *The Idea of Nationalism; A Study in its Origins and Background,* New York, 1948, p. 8.)

65. "The 'natural frontier' clearly is a polemic rather than a scientific concept. The Pyrenees have long divided Frenchmen from Spaniards, but the Alps have helped make the Swiss into a nation; portions of the Rhine Valley have at times marked off Frenchmen from Germans, but the Nile is the basis of Egypt's unity; and whereas insularity has helped preserve Japan's distinctiveness it did not protect Britons from Anglo-Saxon, Danish, and Norman invasions—each of which made its contribution to British nationality. It is not mountains, valleys, or islands that constitute nations, it is their human inhabitants." (Dankwart A. Rustow, "Nation," in the *International Encyclopedia of the Social Sciences,* New York, 1968, Vol. II, p. 10. Cf. Boyd C. Shafer, *Nationalism, Myth and Reality,* New York, 1955, p. 32-33.)

66. "We have learned, indeed, that through international organization we can transcend the narrow limits of geographical boundaries. We can unify interests which, like those of the wage-earners of the world, were hampered and frustrated by frontiers. . . . We have realised, in brief, that the territory between states which seemed to the last generation a permanently uncharted hinterland is, in fact, not less susceptible of organised government than that which has already been mapped and surveyed." (Harold J. Laski, *A Grammar of Politics,* London, 1925, p. 661)

weaker as ties for the nation than they were for previous groups from the early single family through the primitive community, clan and tribe. Furthermore, the nation is generally larger than the previous groups and is, therefore, more difficult for the much weaker ties to hold it together.

All the smaller groups which had very strong ties have now broken up and gone into oblivion. Can the larger group—the nation—with much weaker ties, hold up and last long?

c.

National Character and Sentiment

IN ADDITION TO THE OBJECTIVE ELEMENTS DISCUSSED above, there are some things intangible which are often described as subjective elements of the nation. Most emphasized among them are national character and sentiment.[67]

People who emphasize the national character always fail to say what it really is.[68] Generally they mean a certain mentality and the traditions, habits and traits of a nation.

Many attempts have been made to trace the origins of national character. In early times, natural influences were considered the main causes.[69] Since the 19th century, however, with the increase of

---

67. National character and sentiment and their contents are regarded by some authors as subjective elements or internal facts of the nation, while language, religion, consanguinity, history and territory are seen as the nation's objective elements or external facts. (Cf. Friedrich O. Hertz, *Nationality in History and Politics,* New York, 1944, p. 9.)

68. Before discussing some concepts of national character, H.C.J. Duijker and N.H. Frijda in their *National Character and National Stereotypes,* Amsterdam, 1960, p. 12, note: "In this chapter we shall present a survey of existing opinions on the meaning of the term 'national character.' Now there are nearly as many opinions as publications on the subject, and these run into the hundreds. Not only has nearly every author his own definition, but most authors show the habit of revising their definitions continually. On account of this we shall only be able to give a sample of current definitions; we hope to have succeeded in making this sample representative at least of the main schools of thought."

69. Many books have been written about the peculiar characteristics of a na-

knowledge in geography and history, it has become clear that national character is made and modified[70] by numerous factors. Among them, the dynamics of history constitute the main force, and the natural environment is only a relative condition.[71] Since the dynamics of history are characterized by restless motion, it is obvious that national character is by no means unchangeable.[72]

---

tion, describing them and attempting to trace their origin and causes. In early times they were chiefly explained by the influence of natural forces, such as the stars or the soil, on the blood, the inner secretions, and the temperament of men. Montesquieu brought together a wealth of important observations and stimulating ideas, and exerted a great influence on all succeeding thought on the subject. He exaggerated, however, the influence of climate. (Cf. Charles Louis de Secondat Montesquieu's *The Spirit of the Laws,* Book XIV.) Hume was among the first who deprecated the idea that climate was all powerful. (Cf. David Hume, *Essays, No. 21, Of National Characters.*)

70. "But I shall assume that the character of a nation belongs mainly, if not entirely, to the sphere of nurture," "which we may call, in the widest sense of the word, the process of education." "That it is therefore made, and is also modifiable, by the creative mind of man." "It follows that there is no such thing as a given and ineluctable national character, which stamps and makes the members of a nation, and is their individual and collective destiny. Character is not a destiny to each nation.... Not only is national character made; it continues to be made and re-made. It is not made once and for all: it always remains, in its measure, modifiable." (Ernest Barker, *National Character and the factors in its Formation,* New York, 1927, p. 6-8)

71. "It was further more and more realized that the peculiar traits of peoples were moulded by the dynamics of history such as wars, migrations, traffic, social differentiation, discoveries, inventions, revolutions, cultural contact, and so on, and that these determined the physiognomy of a civilization. These historical movements were, of course, partly conditioned by nature. But it became clear that nature was on the whole a relative factor. The influence of a specific natural environment was not the same on all peoples and in all circumstances, but its effect depended on the constellation of numerous factors." (Friedrich O. Hertz, *Nationality in History and Politics,* New York, 1944, p. 38. Cf. Boyd C. Shafer, *Nationalism, Myth and Reality,* New York, 1955, p. 31-33.)

72. "A nation may alter its character in the course of its history to suit new conditions or to fit new purposes. The change may be gradual, like that from 'the English people of merry England, full of mirth and game,' in the fourteenth century, to the stern, struggling Samson of Milton's day; or it may be sudden, and almost of the nature of a conversion, like the change in Scottish national character under the influence of Calvinism. Writers of different periods will give you very different pictures of a nation's character. Pope Eugenius III, about 1140, said that 'the English nation was fit to be set to anything it would handle, and one to be preferred to others, were it not for the impediment of levity.' Wycliffe, in the time of Richard II, wrote that 'the English have properly the moon for their planet, by reason of their inconstancy'; and Torcy, about the time of Charles II, could still celebrate their fickle nature. A writer of the Napoleonic period, or of the days of the Great War, would

As far as the national mentality is concerned, it is well-known that many nations have undergone drastic changes in the modern age.[73]

It is also well-known that some specific national traditions were established by a ruling class, and preserved their vitality mainly through their connection with the interests and ideas of this class, and that they faded away when this class lost its position of domination.[74]

---

more naturally speak of fixed ideas and bulldog tenacity. (Ernest Barker, *National Character and the Factors in its Formation,* New York, 1927, p. 8)

"We may accept the position of Sir Francis Galton that 'different aspects of the multifarious character of man respond to different calls from without, so that the same individual, and much more the same race, may behave very differently at different epochs!" (Hans Kohn, *The Idea of Nationalism, a Study in its Origins and Background,* New York, 1948, p. 10)

73. "In the beginning of the eighteenth century, when the English were considered a nation most inclined to revolution and to change, while the French seemed a most stable and stolid nation, Voltaire wrote: 'The French are of the opinion, that the government of this island is more tempestuous than the sea which surrounds it, which indeed is true.' One hundred years later, just the opposite opinion about the English and the French was generally held. The English were then, and are today, considered—by themselves and others—as a stolid nation, proud in their disinclination to violent revolution, while the French were considered a people easily given to and delighting in revolutionary upheavals.... The Mongols under Genghis Khan were warriors famous for their belligerence, and brought all Asia and half of Europe under their yoke. In the sixteenth century, through the adoption of Lamaist Buddhism, their old spirit was completly broken and they were turned into peaceful and pious men. Under the influence of the Soviet government and its revolutionary propaganda the wild instincts of the race have been reawakened, and a new and different consciousness has started to animate the Mongol people and to break their religious inhibitions." (Hans Kohn, *The Idea of Nationalism, a Study in its Origins and Background,* New York, 1948, p. 9-10)

74. "Traditions preserve their vitality mainly through their connexion with the interests and ideals of those classes which form the so-called 'national will' and set the standard for the nation. Now these classes are subject to constant change, and new classes rise and obtain a share in political and social power. Such changes seem to be the main causes of the decay of traditions and the development of new ones. For instance, since World War II, the tradition of the German warrior and English 'gentleman' have been fading away noticeably. "The difference in the national ethos of Germany and England is largely due to the fact that the German nobility to a great extent preserved the character of a warrior caste and that their example was largely followed by other classes, while in England the nobility adopted the mentality of wealthy landowners and capitalists and created a style of life which was widely imitated by other classes. It is significant for the relations between classes in England that the word 'gentleman' which originally designated a social status has come to describe a pattern of behaviour for all classes." (Friedrich

Of the natural factors which preserved specific national habits, the most important was geographical isolation. Since modern transportation and communication have largely eliminated this isolation, most of the specific national habits are gradually diminishing.[75]

According to the comparative study of national character, there is no trait which is exclusively found in one nation or entirely lacking in another during the same phase of social evolution.[76]

It is interesting to note that in some nations, traits which other people mistakenly attributed to them have come to be widely believed even by themselves.[77]

In the last fifty years, increased efforts have been made to explore the nature of national character anthropologically, sociologically and psychologically.[78] Some authors have tried to identify national

---

O. Hertz, *Nationality in History and Politics,* New York, 1944, p. 43, 44-45. Cf. for more examples, Robert Michels, *Der Patriotismus,* 1921, p. 74.)

75. The English, for example, no longer deride the French as "frog eaters" and despise them for wearing wooden shoes, while being proud of the "roast beef of Old England" as in former times. (Cf. Friedrich O. Hertz, *Nationality in History and Politics,* New York, 1944, p. 43. For changing habits in eating, housing, clothing and daily life worldwide in recent centuries, cf. Harry E. Barnes, *An Economic History of the Western World,* New York, 1937, p. 230-232; and Hornell N. Hart, *The Technique of Social Progress,* New York, 1931, p. 681.)

76. "The comparative study of nations in the same phase of social evolution leads to the conclusion that no trait whatever is exclusively to be found in one nation or entirely lacking in the mind of any nation. Differences are only those of time, degree and combination. A certain feature may emerge earlier, or may be more frequent or more pronounced in one nation than in others, or it may be combined with other traits in a way peculiar to one nation." (Friedrich O. Hertz, *Nationality in History and Politics,* New York, 1944, p. 40)

77. For instance, "French naughtiness is largely an invention of the English (and later the Americans) who failed to see the rigid, shrewd and practical morality beneath the surface of French social life. American bluff was created by the French, who simply were incredulous about the stories told, and chalked them up to psychopathic delusions of grandeur." (Sydney Harris, "Nations' Character Sometimes Contrived," in the *South Bend Tribune,* Sept. 22, 1976, p. 10)

78. (Comprehensive reviews of national character studies, from five somewhat different perspectives, can be found in Margaret Mead, "National Character," in *Anthropology Today: an Encyclopedic Inventory,* Chicago, 1953, p. 642-667; Margaret Mead and Rhoda Metraux, *The Study of Culture at a Distance,* Chicago, 1953; Otto Klineberg, "A Science of National Character," in the *Bulletin* of the Society for the Psychological Study of Social Issues, 1944, No. 19, p. 147-162; Alex Inkeles and Daniel J. Levinson, "National Character: the Study of Modal Personality and Sociocultural Systems," in the *Handbook of Social Psychology,* Cambridge, Mass., 1954, Vol. 2, p. 977-1020; and H.C.J. Dui-

character with a model personality,[79] a basic personality,[80] or a social personality,[81] while others have sought to differentiate national patterns among the elite and common people,[82] and in the rural and urban life.[83] Their approaches vary greatly, but all lead to the conclusion that national character is by no means permanent, since all the personalities and patterns they have identified and emphasized are subject to change as a result of radical changes in social conditions.

It is indeed evident that national character is changeable under various situations, and this changeable nature itself is certainly a cogent refutation of all those views which insist that the character of a nation has persisted throughout its whole history, acting as a

---

jker and N.H. Frijda, *National Character and National Stereotypes,* Amsterdam, 1960. The latter is a trend report prepared for the International Union of Scientific Psychology. Cf. also Erich Fromm, *Escape from Freedom,* New York, 1941.)

79. "National character refers to relatively enduring personality characteristics and patterns that are modal among adult members of a society." (Cf. Ralph Linton, *The Cultural Background of Personality,* London, 1952, p. 102; and Alex Inkeles and Daniel J. Levinson, "National Character: The Study of Modal Personality and Sociocultural Systems," in *Handbook of Social Psychology,* ed. by G. Lindzey, Cambridge, Mass., 1954, Vol. 2, p. 977-1020.)

80. Closely related to the concept of modal personality is that of Basic Personality Structure. As a matter of fact, the originators of the latter seem sometimes to consider them as identical. The emphasis, however, is slightly different. Modal personality refers to (the modal class in) a society, basic personality structure to a culture. (Cf. Abram Kardiner, "The Conception of Basic Personality Structure as an Operational Tool in the Social Sciences," in *The Science of Man in the World Crisis,* ed. by Ralph Linton, New York, 1947, p. 107-122; and Ralph Linton, "The Personality of Peoples," *Scientific America,* No. 181, 1949.)

81. "Social personality" may be defined as "the more or less conscious idea systems: beliefs, attitudes, values, sentiments. Some authors believe that social personality is the region where intra-national similarities and international differences are located." (Cf. Alex Inkeles, "Some Sociological Observations on Culture and Personality Studies," in *Personality in Nature, Society and Culture,* ed. by Clyde Kluckhohn, 2d ed., New York, 1953, p. 577-592; and H.C.J. Duijker and N.H. Frijda, *National Character and National Stereotypes,* Amsterdam, 1960, p. 20-21.)

82. (Cf. Raymond A. Bauer, "The Psychology of the Soviet Middle Elite: Two Case Histories," in *Personality in Nature, Society, and Culture,* ed. by Clyde Kluckhohn, 3d ed., New York, 1953, p. 633-650; and Geoffrey Gorer and John Rickman, *The People of Great Russia: a Psychological Study,* New York, 1962.)

83. (Cf. George A. DeVos, "The Relation of Guilt Toward Parents to Achievement and Arranged Marriage Among the Japanese," in *Psychiatry,* 1960, no. 23, p. 287-301; and Everett E. Hagen, *On the Theory of Social Change,* Homewood, Ill. 1962.)

84. "The belief that every people has a specific character which persists through all time, and can be traced through its whole history, and in all branches

spiritual force for every period, and capable of being rejuvenated at any time.[84]

Certainly, too, the changeable nature of national character is a green light for mankind to proceed toward a greater and greater homogeneity of civilization through increasing cultural contacts among peoples, on the basis of common human traits,[85] and with the deposit of general humanity in the various national characters.[86]

In respect to national sentiment, it was John Stuart Mill who first considered mutual sympathy the essence of a nation.[87] His view cor-

---

of its civilization ... forms a powerful element in every national ideology, and commonly implies the glorification of one's own national character and the denigration of that of the national enemy." It has inspired many writers to "interpret the history of civilization of their nation in the light of their idea of the national character. They tried to show the whole history of their nation was actuated by the same spiritual forces." "While the writers of the eighteenth century often overstated the influence of natural forces, the Romanticists stressed organic, historical growth, and often indulged in the construction of a mystical national spirit, alleged to be traceable throughout the whole history of a people. Many historians, especially in Germany and France, tried to show that the whole history of their own nation proved the continuity of its national character, and frequently they interpreted its achievements as an outcome of the national genius, while the failures were ascribed to foreign influence. This view, however, has proved untenable, and has been abandoned by serious students." And such a "concept of the national character has been discredited by these romantic phantasies." (Friedrich O. Hertz, *Nationality in History and Politics,* New York, 1944, p. 11, 37, 39. Cf. Louis L. Snyder, *The Meaning of Nationalism,* New Brunswick, N.J., 1954, p. 162-263.)

85. "The fundamental traits of human nature, of course, have always and everywhere been the same." (Friedrich O. Hertz, *Nationality in History and Politics,* New York, 1944, p. 33)

In a penetrating article, "Men Are More Alike," published in *The American Historical Review,* 1952, Vol. LVII, in p. 596-597, 606-607, 611, Boyd C. Shafer pointed out that our present knowledge does not reveal the extent of differences between men. "Men are physiologically, racially, nationally at least as much alike as they are different." In Shafer's view, scholars who stress such differences to the exclusion of the known similarities do so at the expense of truth and to their own and mankind's great peril.

86. "Each national character is a microcosm of humanity at large, presented from a particular angle; each national tradition is a deposit containing not only indigenous stuff, but also the contributions of general humanity. We are what we are in our country not only because of what happened in London and Edinburgh, but also because of what happened in Jerusalem and Athens and Rome." (Ernest Barker, *National Character and the Factors in its Formation,* New York, 1927, p. 9-10)

87. John Stuart Mill saw the essence of nationality in the mutual sympathy of its adherents and in their desire to be united under a government of their own, produced through a community of history and politics and through feelings of pride

responded to the striving of liberals for freedom and the concept of democracy by majority rule, and exerted a great influence on the thinking which followed in this direction. True, mutual sympathy does play a certain role in national life, but it is the national life that fosters mutual sympathy, not vice versa. Generally speaking, nations result from the merging of a number of tribes, often through wars, conquests and annexations. No nation in history was formed and held together exclusively by mutual sympathy,[88] and there has been no modern national movement for unification based purely on mutual sympathy.[89]

The concept of mutual sympathy became the concept of popular will in the political philosophy of Ernest Renan, who held that the wish of the people was the decisive factor for a nation, a plebiscite was considered the best way of ascertaining that wish, and the existence of a nation resembled a plebiscite repeated every day.[90]

---

and shame, joy and grief connected with experiences of the past. (Cf. his *Considerations on Representative Government,* New York, 1958, originally 1861, Chapter 16.)

88. For instance, "the prussianizing school of historiography tended to give the impression that there was hardly a German nationality before the Hohenzollerns created National Unity through their military power-state, and Bismarck imposed it upon the whole of Germany. Frederick 'the Great' and many other princes who did their best to destroy the unity and strength of the old Empire, and who allowed large sections of the German people to fall under foreign domination in order to obtain foreign support for their own aggrandizement, appear in these histories as national heroes." (Friedrich O. Hertz, *Nationality in History and Politics,* New York, 1944, p. 10)

89. For instance, "the arch-nationalist of our days, Adolf Hitler, in his book *My Struggle* does not conceal his profound contempt for the masses of his own people. His seizure of power was followed by the introduction of a system of the most ruthless terrorism and intimidation against all those Germans who were not in agreement with Nazi policy, and who at that time certainly formed the majority of the German people. It may be that nationalists aim at uniting the whole people in fraternal love, but surely their methods are often such as those described in a German couplet: Und willst Du nicht mein Bruder sein, so schlag ich Dir den Schaedel ein (If my brother you will not be, your skull shall soon be smashed by me). Modern nations, however, have to a large extent really been brought together by this method." (Friedrich O. Hertz, *Nationality in History and Politics,* New York, 1944, p. 13)

90. It is not race, religion, language, State, civilization or economic interests, Ernest Renan said, that make a nation. The national idea is founded on a heroic past, great men, true glory. Common experiences lead to the formation of a community of will. More than anything else it is common grief that binds a nation together, more than triumphs. A nation, therefore, is a great solidarity founded on the consciousness of sacrifices made in the past and on a willingness to make fur-

Popular will has been widely used to support the principle of self-determination, especially among the controversial territories. "On the surface it seemed reasonable: let the people decide. It was in fact ridiculous because the people cannot decide until somebody decides who are the people."[91]

Another view in regard to national sentiment stresses the consciousness of a nation. According to this view, which is generally based on social psychology,[92] national consciousness is a specific kind of group consciousness which binds the members together. It is not necessary to express it in the ways in which the popular will is expressed, nor to affect one another mutually, as with sympathy. National consciousness is sometimes clear and sometimes latent, and is not the same or equally strong in the individual. Obviously, therefore, it is something too fluid and too elusive to be used collectively or individually as a reliable standard of national character.[93]

No less fluid and elusive is the national spirit emphasized by some great historians. Leopold Von Ranke, for example, regarded it as a spiritual air permeating everything, which could be felt but not understood.[94] Arnold J. Toynbee's concept of national spirit is of a similar mysterious nature.[95] Historians have even puzzled about when the national spirit was born in a particular country.[96]

---

ther ones in the future. (Cf. his famous lecture *Qu'est-ce qu'une nation?* 1882, in Modern *Political Doctrines,* ed. by Alfred Zimmern, London, 1939, p. 186-205.)

91. This is a statement by Ivor W. Jennings in his *The Approach to Self-Government,* Cambridge, 1956, p. 56. Jennings' remark is not only meaningful for the controversial territories where the conditions for a plebiscite, its enforcement, etc. to have to be decided by pre-existing neighboring states or else by a majority agreement of outside powers; it is also applicable, as far as the popular will is concerned, to the nations in which voting, if permitted, is not direct, equal and universal; or where the ruling class is the only "people."

92. (Cf. especially William MacDougall, *The Group Mind,* New York, 1920; Morris Ginsberg, *Psychology of Society;* London, 1933; and Wilfred Trotter, *Instincts of the Herd in Peace and War,* 3rd ed., London, 1947.)

93. "National consciousness ... is an exceedingly elusive thing. Its manifestations can be studied in political literature, public speeches or national institutions, but the interpretation of such documents or objects in regard to the underlying national spirit is always more or less insecure.... But political nationality is a very complicated matter as it depends on a sufficient degree of national consciousness which cannot be observed and measured by exact methods." (Friedrich O. Hertz, *Nationality in History and Politics,* New York, 1944, p. 9)

94. "Leopold von Ranke, one of the greatest and most impartial historians of all times, came to the conclusion that the national spirit could only be felt but not understood; it was a 'spiritual air,' permeating everything." (Friedrich O. Hertz, *Nationality in History and Politics,* New York, 1944, p. 37)

95. It is "a spirit which makes people feel and act and think about a part of

A peculiar aspect of national sentiment is a nation's prejudices, which are so widespread that probably few people are quite free from them. The common symptom of national prejudice is that it tends to pride itself even on the faults of one's own nation and discredit other peoples.[97] But sometimes it expresses itself in a different way, such as: things "imported" are better.[98] Some people have felt that prejudice was an important national force.[99] These opinions, however, have changed in the course of time, since the recent increase in intellectual exchanges between peoples has gradually broken up the mental seclusion which harbors national prejudice.[100]

---

any given society as though it were the whole of that society." (Arnold J. Toynbee, *A Study of History,* London, 1934-1961, Vol. IV, p. 407)

96. For instance, "While August Thierry believed that the French national spirit was already awakening in the ninth century, Longnon attributed this process to the early twelfth, and Ranke to the thirteenth. Guizot, Michelet and many others stressed the importance of the Hundred Years War in the fourteenth and fifteenth centuries, the time of Jeanne d'Arc. Many historians assume that the achievement of political unification, great military triumphs and cultural splendour render the sixteenth and seventeenth centuries the decisive epoch. Lavisse and Aulard, however, think that it was the great revolution of the eighteenth century which awakened French patriotism and nationalism." (Friedrich O. Hertz, *Nationality in History and Politics,* New York, 1944, p. 31)

97. Claude A. Helvetius tells in his work *De l'esprit* (English translation, London, 1810) an Indian fable of a humpbacked people where a foreigner whose growth is normal is derided as a monster, and he adds: "Every nation admires its own faults and despises the opposite qualities. In order to have success in a country one must bear the hump of the nation." (Cf. Friedrich O. Hertz, *Nationality in History and Politics,* New York, 1944, p. 45.)

98. "Most people seem to have a split personality about foreign manners, matters and materials. One part of them laughs or sneers at things foreign, while another part imitates and respects them. I thought of this while I happened to examine a tie on the counter of a men's store. The label read: "Imported Polyester." What could be more ridiculous, since polyester is a synthetic, and its country of manufacture is wholly irrelevant? But the word "imported" gets us—or a part of us, every time. The rise in the popularity of Scotch whiskies (when earlier Americans would drink only bourbon) is at least as much a matter of social cachet as it is of taste. And vodka is vodka wherever it is made, but we willingly pay a premium for a Russian label on the bottle. We are not alone in this, of course. Authentic Levis, I am told, are currently selling on the Russian black market for more than $100 a pair. The Russian cognoscenti prefer Polish vodka to their own; while Germans who fancy themselves to be beer experts import a Czechoslovakian brand." (Sydney Harris, "Mixed Attitudes Exist Toward Foreign Things," in the *South Bend Tribune,* June 13, 1977, p. 14)

99. Walter B. Pillsbury says, for instance, that in the U.S.A. national prejudice is one of the strongest forces compelling the foreigner to assimilate. (Cf. his *Psychology of Nationality and Internationalism,* New York, 1919, p. 140.)

Closely connected with national sentiment are the national anthem and flag, which can foster an emotional attachment to the national life.[101] The use of a characteristic figure,[102] and animal,[103] or a plant,[104] as a national image can also arouse national feeling. Of course, these kinds of symbols are not new in history; they resemble the totem of the primitive society, but with a less mysterious power.

Finally, there are some people who have considered national sentiment to be an instinct. To a certain extent their assumption may be right.[105] However, if the definition of instinct excludes certain behaviors, such as impulse modified by customs,[106] the imitation of the ac-

---

100. The following general criticism is very applicable to national prejudices: "Caucasian peoples have been all too guilty of assuming that their particular cultural patterns and activities must be superior to the cultures which they associate with Asian and African peoples. To hold such arrogant, and demonstrably fallacious views was more understandable, if not pardonable, in the era of western colonialism. In today's world, however, to retain such sterotyped concepts of non-western peoples can be dangerously explosive." (T. Walter Wallbank, Alastair M. Taylor, Nels M. Bailkey and Mark Mancall, *Civilization Past and Present,* 6th ed., Glenview, Ill., 1970, Book I, p. 7)

101. "The ideals and symbols of nationalism, like the notion of 'motherland,' 'flag,' 'national anthem,' are typical taboos, which today in the highly civilized countries it is more dangerous to touch than the taboos of the savage cannibals of the South Seas. No man, no party dares to touch these relics; no one dares to criticize them. Nevertheless, it must be said that their exalted cult is one of the central roots of the evils of our time." (Emery Reves, *A Democratic Manifesto,* New York, 1942, p. 41-42)

102. Such figures include the British John Bull, the German Michel, the French Marianne, and the American Uncle Sam.

103. Such animals include the Russian bear, the British lion, the French cock, the Chinese dragon, and the German and American eagles.

104. These include the German oak, the Slav lime tree, the Irish shamrock, the Welsh leek, the Japanese cherry, the Chinese plum, and the Korean Rose of Sharon.

105. This is based on the view that animal gregariousness is an instinct, and that the human being possesses that instinct like any other animal. Gregariousness consists not only in associating with others, but also in excluding outsiders, and this tendency often leads to conflicts without any other motive than positive group feeling. (Cf. Friedrich Alverdes, *Social Life in the Animal World,* London, 1927, p. 107.) This view may be true for a small group or a crowd. How far can it be applied to a group as large as a nation with its people as higher animals, widely spread out? It seems nobody can say exactly and the only answer is "to a certain extent."

106. A portion of the national sentiment is related to primitive customs, such as blood-drinking, cannibalism, human sacrifice, and hatred of strangers. These have a symbolic rather than a practical value. And the strongest emotions must have been evoked in their origin. They are not instincts, although they are maintained by impulses that resemble instincts in certain respects. Each "is not a product of reasoning by the individual; it comes from the past; it may give rise to fren-

tions of a multitude, and response to public expectations, encourage-ments and pressures,[107] its contribution to national sentiment would be insignificant, if any. It is more precise to say that national senti-ment, to a great extent, is the product of education in the broad sense, received through school, the family, society, and especially the mass media.[108]

d.
Artifice
of Nationalism

ACTUALLY, IT IS TRUER TO SAY THAT NATIONAL SENTI-ment is a product of nationalism,[109] because it is nationalism which

---

zied conduct as great as or even more than that produced by recognized instincts."
(Ernest H. Hankins, *Nationalism and the Communal Mind,* London, 1937, p.4)

107. Such behaviors have been explored in mass psychology, of which the well-known exponent was Gustave Le Bon in his *Psychologie des foules,* 1892 (English trans., *The Psychology of Peoples,* New York, 1898) For criticism, cf. Morris Ginsberg, *Psychology of Society,* London, 1933, p. 128-136; and Walter B. Pills-bury, *Psychology of Nationality and Internationalism,* New York, 1919, p. 164-185.

108. All nations have always considered it very important to make the na-tional sentiment of their people as great, and maintain it as high, as possible. For this purpose, they have utilized ceremony, pageantry, festivals, rewards, criminal legislation, vigorous military and foreign policies, and propaganda through press, radio and television. They have glorified national heroes and erected national monuments. They have given a national significance to local phenomena such as old customs, popular ballads, and folk dances. They have given a national flavor to literature, art and music; and above all, they have used schools and other educa-tional institutes to carry out effective civic training for citizens. (For such training in the United States and some other nations, cf. Charles E. Merriam, *The Making of Citizens, a Comparative Study of Methods of Civic Training,* Chicago, 1931, and *Nationalism,* a report by a study group of members of the Royal Institute of International Affairs, London, 1939, p. 200-206.)

109. "Nationalism in its broader meaning refers to the attitude which ascribes to national individuality a high place in the hierarchy of values. In this sense it is a natural and indispensable condition and accompanying phenomenon of all national movements.... On the other hand, the term nationalism also con-notes a tendency to place a particularly excessive, exaggerated and exclusive em-phasis on the value of the nation at the expense of other values, which leads to a vain and importunate overestimation of one's own nation and thus to a detraction

has made use of education in various ways to boost national senti-ment.[110]

It is nationalism, too, which has endeavored by all means to pre-serve and stress national characteristics against their changeable nature.[111]

Furthermore, it is nationalism which has strived desperately to strengthen the increasingly weakened elements of the nation: lan-guage, religion, consanguinity, history and territory.

Nationalists assert that language proceeds from a racial disposi-tion and that a people is mentally crippled if it loses its original tongue. Hence, they strive to maintain, restore, or develop an inde-pendent language as a symbol of national honor, and esteem its ex-clusive domination in their nation more highly than its practical ad-vantage. They are obviously ignorant of the fact that, as linguistic studies have proven, language has little to do with racial disposi-tion[112] and contact between languages is an historical necessity in-evitably leading to mutual influences and modifications.[113]

---

of others." (Max H. Boehm, "Nationalism," in the *Encyclopedia of the Social Sciences,* New York, 1933, Vol. II, p. 231. Cf. Carlton J.H. Hays, *Essays on Na-tionalism,* New York, 1926, p. 1-29; and Louis L. Snyder, *The Dynamics of Na-tionalism,* New York, 1964, p. 371-372.)

110. The most volcanic degrees of nationalism have been consciously and in-sidiously contrived through deliberate education and fanatical propaganda using the "brain washing" technique. The effort is begun among the youngest children, and includes attempts to enlist the active support of family and school. Teaching materials, especially history books, are one-sided and biased, thus seeding a deep anti-foreign sentiment which will last over the course of the youth's lifetime. For the adult, nationalist organizations take the form of clubs, societies, or parties, and all cooperate to glorify their nation, to exaggerate its accomplishments, to declare that "My country is always right," to establish a conviction that the fatherland is in imminent danger of attack and, over it all, to obliterate all sense of measure and any vestige of objectivity in considering and judging the international problems facing their nations. (Cf. Carlton J.H. Hays, *Nationalism: a Religion,* New York, 1960, p. 164-172; Louis L. Snyder, *The Dynamics of Nationalism,* New York, 1964, p. 167-171, with some excerpts from Nazi textbooks as samples; and Jost and Braeunig, "The Three Instructors of the Aisne" quoted in Jonathan F. Scott, *Patriots in the Making,* New York, 1916, p. 76-79.)

111. "Nationalism does not wish to achieve the union of humanity on the basis of 95 percent of its common characteristics, but to divide it on the basis of 5 percent of its differentiation. It is the spiritual conception in absolute contradic-tion to all the conquests realized in the course of the last century." (Emery Reves, *A Democratic Manifesto,* New York, 1942, p. 51)

112. The view that language is an outcome of racial disposition and that a people is mentally crippled if it loses its original tongue and adopts another one has been completely refuted by countless historical experiences and linguistic research

In recent centuries, nationalism has gradually not only subverted all great monotheistic religions,[114] but also established itself as a kind of religion.[115] Various religious rites are adopted for national cere-

---

studies. A Negro may speak English or French as well as any Englishman or Frenchman, provided he has had the same education and access to the same social circles. (Cf. Friedrich O. Hertz, *Race and Civilization,* trans. by A.S. Levetus and W. Entz, London, 1928, p. 93.)

113. Linguistic study has proved that the ideal of a language's uninterrupted, continuous development, sheltered from every outside influence, is scarcely ever realized. On the contrary, the mutual influence of neighboring languages often plays a very important role in linguistic development. Contact between languages is an historical necessity, and this inevitably leads to mutual influence. By virtue of this truth, certain philologists have even gone so far as to say that there is no language which is not in certain respects a mixed language. (Cf. Joseph Vendryes, *Language, a Linguistic Introduction to History,* London, 1925, p. 80-81.)

A great authority once said: "We cannot reasonably deny that English has been immeasurably improved by the incorporation of alien elements." (Henry Bradley, *The Making of English,* London, 1904, p. 110)

"For English is a hybrid language—fewer than half our words are native, and the rest borrowed from foreign tongues, mostly Latin ... English is primarily a 'loan language.' If you want to know how much, read any of the books by Otto Jespersen, the great Danish philologist, and you may be surprised at the enormous debt we owe not only to Latin and Greek but also to the Scandinavian languages, to French and even to the Germanic influences upon Old English." (Sydney Harris, "English Borrows Greatly from Foreign Languages," *South Bend Tribune,* Sept. 29, 1978, p. 8)

114. For example, "Nationalism soon became identified with Christianity and in every country nationalist policy was recognized as Christian policy.... In thousands of churches today, Catholic priests and Protestant preachers of all denominations are praying for the glory of their own nationals and for the downfall of others, even if they belong to the same church. This is indeed in violent contradiction to the highest religious ideal mankind ever produced—universal Christianity." (Emery Reves, *The Anatomy of Peace,* New York, 1946, p. 80-81; and in his *A Democratic Manifesto,* New York, 1942, p. 43): "All these nations hide their pagan instincts under the cloak of Christianity. In all countries nationalism is regarded as a 'Christian policy.' Everywhere the pagan spirit is cultivated under the moral shield of Christianity falsely interpreted. On all the battlefields where wars rage, Christian priests march before the troops, carrying the symbol of the Son of God—this Son of God who sought peace and love—and it is with the same formula that they bless the two opposing camps that are ready to unleash the fury of their national-pagan passions."

115. "To sum up, man's religious sense is exemplified not only in great surviving religions such as Christianity, Hinduism, Buddhism, and Islam, and in the animism and pagan cults of primitive peoples, but in contemporary communism and especially in modern nationalism. Let me stress, however, that there are variant kinds and degrees of nationalism. Some can be reconciled or allied with historical supernatural religion. Others can be utilized to give quasi-religious sanction to an intrinsically materialist and atheistic movement like communism. Still

monies and observances.[116] The public is often rallied into a religious fervor with national mysteries;[117] and certain national heroes are revered as saints.[118] But nationalism, as a new religion, differs greatly from the original monotheistic religions: it praises the nation, not the

---

others can be religions in themselves, mutually jealous and exclusive." (Carlton J.H. Hays, *Nationalism: a Religion,* New York, 1960, p. 18. Cf. p. 164-172.)

116. "The ritual of modern nationalism is already fairly well developed. Its chief symbol and central object of worship is the national flag. Strictly speaking, there was no such thing on the European Continent prior to the French Revolution of the late eighteenth century, and the stars and stripes of the United States are not much older. Now every nation in the world has a flag ... There are universal liturgical forms for 'saluting' the flag, for 'dipping' the flag, for 'lowering' the flag, and for 'hoisting' the flag. Men bare their heads when the flag passes by; and in praise of the flag poets write odes, and to it children sing hymns and pledge allegiance. In all solemn feasts and fasts of nationalism, the flag is in evidence...." (Carlton J.H. Hays, *Nationalism: a Religion,* New York, 1960, p. 166-167. Cf. p. 166-168; and George L. Mosse, "Mass Politics and the Political Liturgy of Nationalism," in *Nationalism, the Nature and Evolution of an Idea,* ed. by Eugene Kamenka, New York, 1976, p. 38-54.)

117. "Nationalism, like any religion, calls into play not simply the will, but the intellect, the imagination, and the emotions. The intellect constructs a speculative theology or mythology of nationalism. The imagination builds an unseen world around the eternal past and the everlasting future of one's nationality. The emotions arouse a joy and ecstasy in the contemplation of the national god who is all-good and all-protecting, a longing for his favors, a thankfulness for his benefits, a fear of offending him, and feelings of awe and reverence at the immensity of his power and wisdom; they express themselves naturally in worship...." (Carlton J.H. Hays, *Nationalism: a Religion,* New York, 1960, p. 164. Cf. p. 168-172.)

118. Take the canonization of Joan of Arc of France as an example. Joan was born in 1412 after France had been invaded by the English and most of it was occupied by the conquerors. In 1429, armed and placed at the head of 10,000 men, she raised the siege of Orleans, defeated Lord John Talbot, and the reinforcements, and electrified the men-at-arms and their commanders, raising their spirits from black despair to wild enthusiasm. But she failed in the attempt to liberate Paris. On May 24, 1430, she was taken prisoner under the walls of Compiègne. Accused of sorcery, she was delivered to an inquisitorial tribunal presided over by Bishop Pierre Cauchon. She was condemned and burned alive at Rouen. A quarter of a century after her death, legal proceedings were undertaken to clear her name; these were successful and her condemnation was annulled. The question of her canonization was first discussed in Rome, in 1875. In 1902, she was pronounced "venerable," and in 1909, she was beatified. She was canonized by Pope Benedict XV on May 9, 1920. The French government declared Joan of Arc's feastday (May 30) a national holiday. (Cf. Hilaire Belloc, *Joan of Arc,* London, 1929.) It suits modern France to evoke Joan of Arc as a French patriot, but the truth, as Charles Seignobos, a leading French historian, testifies, is that Joan was loyal not to France, but to the king of the Armagnac party, which was at war with the Burgundian party, allies of the English. (Cf. Charles Seignobos, *The Evolution of the French People,* trans. by Catherine A. Phillips, New York, 1932, p. 153.)

god, as the Almighty; prays for the material advantage of the nation, not for the spiritual redemption of the individual; and preaches national egoism rather than universal benevolence.[119]

In respect to the element of consanguinity, there appeared a dogma of racial purity and superiority in nationalism at some point. The dogma was widely refuted by reputable anthropologists[120] when it was utilized by Hitler for external aggression and internal oppression.[121] Originally it was the belief of many primitive peoples,[122] and has been proved to be completely fallacious, as there is no race in the

---

119. "The state of affairs that prevails at the present moment in the world would be justly characterized, from the religious point of view, by the term 'polytheism.' The modern religion of nationalism 'devotes not to the universal God,' but the goddess—'Nation.' These gods faithfully resemble the pagan gods of the pre-Christian era. They insist upon war and victory, and they claim vengeance if, instead of victory, it is defeat which comes. England has her god, like France, like the United States, like Germany and Italy; the Russians and the Czechs have theirs, as do the Poles, the Argentines and the Japanese. No matter how small a nation is, it has its own national god." (Emery Reves, *A Democratic Manifesto,* New York, 1942, p. 42-43)

120. The judgement of science in regard to racial doctrines is well expressed in the resolution adopted by the American Anthropological Association: "The American Anthropological Association repudiates unscientific racialism and adheres to the following statement of facts: 1. Race involves the inheritance of similar physical variations by large groups of mankind, but its psychological and cultural connotations, if they exist, have not been ascertained by science. 2. The terms Aryan and Semitic have no racial significance whatsoever. They simply denote linguistic families. 3. Anthropology provides no scientific basis for discrimination against any people on the ground of racial inferiority, religious affiliation or linguistic heritage." (Quoted by Franz Boas in the introduction to the *Race Against Man,* by Herbert J. Seligmann, New York, 1939, p. v)

121. "The prevalent myth of the German fascists is the myth of the Nordic or Aryan Race. In origin this long antedated fascism, since it was popularized by the Germanized Englishman Houston Stewart Chamberlain about the turn of the century and was derived by him largely from the Frenchman, Gobineau, who wrote in the 1850s. The academic center of dispersion for the myth is now Jena, where Hans Gunther has been made Professor of Social Anthropology; its most elaborate philosophical statement is in Alfred Rosenberg's *Der Mythus des 20, Jahrhunderts* (1930). What the myth envisages is the reinterpretation of religion, morals, and art, indeed all branches of culture, and the rewriting of history, from the point of view of race. 'Soul is race seen from within.' The object is, of course, to produce an historical myth serviceable to consolidating the German nation and to strengthening its will to expand.... From a scientific point of view this racial myth is beneath contempt: there never was an Aryan race; all European peoples are biologically mixed; and persons having the superficial characteristics called Nordic are a small minority of the German population. No reliable anthropologist would commit himself to the proposition that there is any clear criterion of racial

world which is pure. Some isolated peoples may be less mixed, but in this they are certainly not superior to others.[123] Even differences in "genetic inheritance" have proved to be relative.[124]

---

superiority or any certain correlation of mental faculty with racial physical traits." (George H. Sabine, *a History of Political Theory,* New York, 1938, p. 761-763)

"There is no Teutonic race, and there never has been.... This nonsense about Keltic and Teutonic is no more science than Lombroso's extraordinary assertions about criminals, or palmistry, or the development of religion from a solar myth." (Herbert G. Wells, *Anticipations,* 1901, p. 237-38. Cf. also Chap. x of *A Modern Utopia,* 1905, an exceedingly effective answer to the aberrations of theories of racial and nationalistic "superiority" prevalent in modern times.)

122. It is doubtful whether there ever was a people which did not claim a particularly noble origin, at least at a certain epoch of its evolution. Many primitive peoples harbored this belief, for they often designated themselves alone as "men" and other peoples with a derogatory name, or they traced their origin to gods or semi-divine eponymous heroes. The Eskimos, for example, are said to entertain the belief that God made a failure of his first attempt to create a man. He therefore rejected it and called it a white man. The next day he tried again and succeeded in making the perfect man—an Eskimo. (Cf. Edvard A. Westermarck, *The Origin and Development of the Moral Ideas,* London, 1906-1908, Vol. II, p. 171)

"The Indian is extremely patriotic. He believes himself to be the result of a special creation by a partial deity, and holds that his is the one favored race. The names by which the different tribes distinguish themselves indicate their belief that as their race is the one favored race, so each tribe of the race is a little ahead of all the others. 'Men of men' is the literal meaning of one name; 'the only men' of another. A Canadian Mohawk offers as the etymology of the term Iroquois, 'I am the real man.' The Plains Indians have 'the conscious feeling of the tribe as a unit or body'; the Mojave feel 'that all members of the tribe are inherently and psychically different from all persons of other tribes.' There is also 'a sense of racial rather than of tribal separateness.' " (William G. Sumner and Albert G. Keller, *The Science of Society,* New Haven, 1927, Vol. I, p. 358)

123. "Quite the contrary happens to be true, as every student of the subject knows. There is not in Europe today, for instance, any such thing as a pure race. The Germans, the French, the Russians, the Italians are all mixtures of various sorts.... The purest races in existence, as Bertrand Russell once pointed out ironically, are the Pygmies, the Hottentots and the Australian Bushmen, none of whom has made exactly a distinguished contribution to human welfare. And the Tasmanians, who were probably the purest of all, are now extinct." (Sydney Harris, "Purest Family Strains Are the Most Decadent," in *South Bend Tribune,* Sept. 23, 1976, p. 12. Cf. Boyd C. Shafer, *Nationalism, Myth and Reality,* New York, 1955, p. 36-39.)

124. "What is a genetic inheritance, anyway? To take one of the simplest and oldest examples in the world, it has always been thought that certain races and peoples have been shorter than others because of some inborn component, like the Asiatics' inferiority of stature compared to us. Now we have learned that improved nutrition greatly affects the growth of the muscles and skeleton—so much so that it has put a full six inches onto the average stature of the Japanese in a generation.... The new breed of Israelis are a dramatic case in point. Visitors to that

Among the means by which history is exploited to foster nationalism, the most notorious are the claimed perfection of some persons as national heroes[125] and the perversion of events for the claims of national success, victory and glory. As Renan once declared: "To forget and—I will venture to say—to get one's history wrong, are essential factors in the making of a nation."[126]

As regards the influence of territory on nationalism, emphasis has ranged from the original settlement to the mystical effect of the dead,[127] and from the border regions to the nerve center of the capi-

---

country have uniformly noted that the Israeli soldier bears little, if any resemblance to the familiar stereotype of the European Jew. He is, on the whole, tall and broad and even far more likely to be blond than would be commonly supposed. He looks more like a Swedish skier than a rabbinical student—and often acts like it. . . . Genetics does not function blindly or dictatorially, but in a symbiosis with the environment and living organism itself. Traits and tendencies are shaped in mutual accommodation, as an ecosystem, and not by implacably determined genetic programing." (Sydney Harris, "New Findings Upsetting the World of Genetics," *South Bend Tribune,* Oct. 8, 1979, p. 12)

125. "In Germany, for example, King Frederick II of Prussia, was by means of intense propaganda elevated to the unique position of Frederick the Great. To the non-Prussians he was represented as the pioneer of German nationality, to the Protestants as the champion of Protestantism, to Catholics and free-thinkers as the herald of toleration, to the intellectuals as the philosopher-king, to the soldiers as the ideal warrior, to the people as the friend of the common man." (Friedrich O. Hertz, *Nationality in History and Politics,* New York, 1944, p. 19)

126. (Ernest Renan in his famous lecture, "What Is a Nation?" (French original "Qu'est-ce qu'une nation?" 1882), pages 186-205, in *Modern Political Doctrines,* ed. by Alfred Zimmern, London, 1939)

Boyd C. Shafer pointed out that for most contemporary European peoples a common group history is almost wholly fictional if it is pressed back much beyond the nineteenth century. "The belief is real," he writes, "the actuality never existed." (*Nationalism: Myth and Reality,* New York, 1955, p. 54)

127. The idea of the land as mother as well as nurse, and the belief in absolute autochthony and original or at least earlier, settlement within a given territory played an enormous role in the struggles between nationalities. Such arguments were brought forward in justification of the revolutionary agrarian measures taken in eastern central Europe. The mystical element in the association of the earth with the cult of the dead has been particularly strongly emphasized in French nationalism as represented by Maurice Barrès. (Cf. Boyd C. Shafer, *Nationalism, Myth and Reality,* New York, 1955, p. 29-31; and Maurice Barrès, *Scènes et doctrines du nationalisme,* Paris, 1902, in *The Dynamics of Nationalism,* ed. by Louis L. Snyder, New York, 1964, p. 125-126, including): "Nothing is more valuable in forming a people's soul than the voice of our ancestors. Our soil gives us a discipline, for we are only the continuation of the dead . . . the dead! What would a man mean to himself if he represented only himself alone? When we look backward, we see an endless train of mysteries. Their recent embodiment we call

tal.[128] The establishment of territorial symbols, such as national monuments, and the encouragement of pilgrimages to the historic sites of national events, such as battlefields, the birthplaces of heroes, and ruins, are primarily intended to promote the patriotic consciousness aspect of nationalism.[129]

The national territory has sometimes been argued to be a body or organism which cannot be mutilated without the risk of destroying the whole nation.[130] This argument represents a theory which identifies the nation as an organism and its citizens as cells. This is indeed an absurd identification, as the nation is not a body born of nature, but a product of history. And the individuals that inhabit it are not merely cells; they can think independently and act separately. The theory of the nation as an organism serves no purpose except to enable nationalism to be more aggressive,[131] more conservative,[132] and more oppressive.[133]

France. We are the products of that collective being which speaks in us. Let the influence of our ancestors be enduring. Let the sons be vigorous and honest. Let the nation be one.''

128. The national frontier, or border region, is the symbol of the territorial contiguity of nations and thus a particularly vital factor in modern nationalism. A threat to the safety of the border region is looked upon as a menace to the whole nation. The capital is necessarily the rallying point of nationalism, because it serves as a barometer of national prestige. (Cf. Louis L. Snyder, *The Meaning of Nationalism,* New Brunswick, N.J., 1954, p. 24-27; and Carlton J. H. Hays, *Nationalism: a Religion,* New York, 1960, p. 167-168.)

129. The scenic attraction of territorial symbols and sites for territorial pilgrimages is usually a secondary and relatively insignificant accompanying phenomenon. For instance, it is not the most beautiful section of the Alps which possesses the greatest symbolic meaning for German nationalism but rather the south Tyrol, which is historically and ethnographically most significant for the German national consciousness. (Cf. Max H. Boehm, "Nationalism—Theoretical Aspects," in the *Encyclopedia of the Social Sciences,* New York, 1933, Vol. II, p. 234; Carlton J.H. Hays, *Nationalism: a Religion,* New York, 1960, p. 167-168; and George L. Mosse, "Mass Politics and Political Liturgy of Nationalism," *Nationalism, the Nature and Evolution of an Idea,* ed. by Eugene Kamenka, New York, 1976, p. 40-41.)

130. When France was forced to cede Alsace-Lorraine to Germany in 1871 both Michelet and Renan put forward this argument. (Cf. Jules Michelet, *La France devant l'Europe,* 1871, p. 113; Ernest Renan, "Qu'est ce qu'une nation?" 1882, in *Modern Political Doctrines,* ed. by Alfred Zimmern, London, 1939, p. 186-205.)

131. Nationalists like to defend their striving for expansion by conquest with the argument that every youthful organism is bound to grow; and they compare those nations which they want to annex or rob to senile, decaying organisms. Their arguments are often based on Darwin's theory of natural selection through the struggle for survival, though Darwin himself did not encourage such views as

In addition, national ideologies have often been employed to enhance nationalism. The prototype of a national ideology is the belief in a divine mission entrusted to a chosen people for a promised land. This was the backbone of the history of the Israelites as told in the Bible.[134] It is doubtful whether there was ever a people without such an ideology at certain times, although such an ideology is obviously a mere myth and has no scientific foundation at all. Yet, such beliefs have frequently been held forth by modern nationalists in a way which influences the national mentality and threatens international stability.[135]

---

theirs. (Cf. Boyd C. Shafer, *Nationalism, Myth and Reality,* New York, 1955, p. 45-47; and Ludwig Von Mises, *Omnipotent Government, the Rise of the Total State and Total War,* New Haven, 1944, p. 120-123.)

132. For example, restrictions on immigration and other measures against foreigners have often been defended on the ground that they form an inorganic element which the national organism is unable to assimilate. (Cf. Donald R. Taft, *Human Migration, a Study of International Movements,* New York, 1936, p. 140-142, 153, 167-169.)

133. According to the theory of the national organism, individuals are completely dependent on the nation. They must therefore be willing to do everything for the nation and to sacrifice everything to the nation. These are the grounds on which most of the anti-liberal and anti-democratic policies have been built up. Curiously enough, Herbert Spencer, an extreme individualist, was one of the writers who elaborated the analogy between organism and society. (Cf. Thomas D. Weldon, *States and Morals,* London, 1947, p. 35-44; and Robert H. Murray, *Studies in the English Social and Political Thinkers of the Nineteenth,* Cambridge, 1929, Vol. 2, p. 25-27.)

134. "Now the Lord had said unto Abram, Get thee out of thy country, and from thy kindred, and from thy father's house, unto a land that I will shew thee:" "And I will make of thee a great nation, and I will bless thee, and make thy name great; and thou shalt be a blessing:" "And I will bless them that bless thee, and curse him that curseth thee: and in thee shall all families of the earth be blessed." "And the Lord appeared unto Abram, and said, Unto thy seed will I give this land: and there builded he an altar unto the Lord, who appeared unto him." (*Bible,* Genesis 12:1-3, 7) "And he said, Thy name shall be called no more Jacob, but Israel: for as a prince has thou power with God and with men, and has prevailed." (Genesis 32:38) "And God appeared unto Jacob again, when he came out of Padanaram, and blessed him." "And God said unto him, Thy name is Jacob: thy name shall not be called any more Jacob, but Israel shall be thy name: and he called his name Israel." "And God said unto him, I am God Almighty: be fruitful and multiply; a nation and a company of nations shall be of thee, and kings shall come out of thy loins:" "And the land which I gave Abraham and Isaac, to thee I will give it, and to thy seed after thee will I give the land." (Genesis 35:9-12) (Cf. Barbara Ward, *Nationalism and Ideology,* New York, 1966, p. 42-43.)

135. "The national ideology may be compared to a pair of coloured or distorting spectacles which only very few persons in the nation concerned are able to

The most forceful appeal of nationalism is its pleading for the highest interest—the power, honor and prestige of the nation.[136] This appeal, however, nearly always implies the subordination of other interests, such as political liberty, social welfare, cultural quality and spiritual treasures, to the nation's "highest interest" on the one hand, and disguises the ambitions of national leaders for their own personal power and prestige on the other.[137]

The most common appeal of nationalism is its urging of patriotic devotion. This appeal easily leads to a confusion between nationalism and patriotism. Yet, there is a basic difference between them: "Patriotism is wanting what is best for your country. Nationalism is thinking your country is the best, no matter what it does."[138]

---

take off." "In fact, any pact or co-operation between nations of vastly different national ideology will always be of doubtful stability. The efficacy of every pact depends on its interpretation, and this depends on ideology." (Friedrich O. Hertz, *Nationality in History and Politics,* New York, 1944, p. 46, 49)

136. To nationalists, all material and spiritual things are seen chiefly as instruments for increasing the power, honor and prestige of the nation. Of course, even nationalists cannot live on power, honor and prestige alone, nor could they hope to win a large following among the people if they neglected all their other interests. Economic, social and cultural aims also form part of their program. The typical nationalist attitude, however, is to assume that national power, honor and prestige are the keys to the treasures of the world, and that a strong nation can solve its social problems and secure the best possible conditions for the development of the national civilization. (Cf. Carlton J. H. Hays, *Nationalism: a Religion,* New York, 1960, p. 90-93, 136-142.)

"Honor is the most dishonored word in our language. No man ever touched another man's honor; no nation ever dishonored another nation; all honor's wounds are self-inflicted." (Address of Andrew Carnegie, President of the Peace Congress in New York, 1907, quoted in the Carnegie Endowment for International Peace, *Year Book for 1912,* p. 1)

137. In fact, a nation's vanity is always fed by the political and military leaders who make use of it to secure their own honor, power, and prestige. Among such leaders, Napoleon, Mussolini and Hitler were the most notorious. (Cf. Don L. Sturzo, *Nationalism and Internationalism,* New York, 1946, p. 239-242.)

138. (Sydney Harris, "Wide Chasm Separates Patriotism, Nationalism," in the *South Bend Tribune,* Sept. 20, 1977, p. 14) He elaborates further: "Patriotism means asking your country to conform to the highest laws of man's nature, to the eternal standards of justice and equality. Nationalism means supporting your country even when it violates these eternal standards. Patriotism means going underground if you have to—as the anti-Nazis in Germany did—and working for the overthrow of your government when it becomes evil and inhuman and incapable of reform. Nationalism means going along with a Hitler or a Stalin or any other tyrant who waves the flag, mouths obscene devotion to the fatherland and meanwhile tramples the rights of people. Patriotism is a form of faith. Nationalism is a form of superstition, of fanatacism, of idolatry. Patriotism would like every coun-

With all the artifices, as described above, at its disposal, nationalism has developed a magic power over simple minds, and can mislead
even its opponents into fatal mistakes.[139]

e.
The Development
of Nationalism

THOUGH NATIONALISM HAS BEEN A GREAT FORCE FOR
almost three centuries, it was not a permanent factor of history and

---

try to become like ours, in its best aspects. Nationalism despises other countries as
incapable of becoming like ours." (Cf. Louis L. Snyder, *The Meaning of Nationalism,* New Brunswick, N.J., 1954, p. 147-152.)

Albert Einstein denounced both patriotism and nationalism, regarding the
latter as a child of the former. He wrote: ". . . Heroism on command, senseless
violence, and all the loathsome nonsense that goes by the name of
patriotism—how passionately I hate them! How vile and despicable seems war to
me! I would rather be hacked to pieces than take part in such an abominable
business. . . ." "Nationalism is an infantile disease. It is the measles of Mankind."
(Quoted by Barnard Collier in his "Einstein's Theory of Free Men," in *South
Bend Tribune's Parade,* July 1, 1979, p. 4.)

139. "Conservatives were often inclined to welcome nationalism as an ally
against democracy and were convinced that they would always be able to control
it. Too late they became aware that this was an illusion and that nationalism contained elements of an entirely anti-conservative, revolutionary character. Liberals
frequently hailed national movements as a striving for freedom, and they were
convinced that a free people would be peaceful, just and well-disposed towards
other peoples. When these nations after their liberation often showed themselves
intolerant and aggressive against minorities in their own territory, or aggressive
against neighbours, this was ascribed by Liberals to their lack of political education and to the machinations of governments and the privileged classes. When at
last the fanatical anti-liberalism of nationalism could no longer be ignored, many
Liberals still consoled themselves with the delusion that all this was only transitory,
or a product of economic distress and would disappear with the improvement of
business and employment. Socialists usually were convinced that nationalism was
a smoke-screen for capitalist interests, or a means for diverting the people from the
struggle for social liberation. They believed, at any rate, that the working classes
were immune against national slogans, and that the ideology of nationalism hardly
required refutation. The orthodox Marxists thought that a vigorous class-war was
the best remedy. The Bolsheviks, however, have also tried to make use of nationalism, especially among Asiatic peoples, by arguing that their capitalist op-

had very little medieval root in its native land of Europe.[140] Its first manifestation occurred in England during the Puritan revolution of the 17th century,[141] followed by the American and French Revolutions of the late 18th century.[142] Since then, it has spread over the whole world.[143]

---

pressors were also their national enemies." (Friedrich O. Hertz, *Nationality in History and Politics,* New York, 1944, p. 4-5)

140. In the Middle Ages, "the basic unit of political organization, the feudal domain, did not lend itself to the development of group solidarity, nor permit the growth of any national sentiment. Mankind in general lived in groups too isolated, too poor and small, too provincial, to feel any sense of attachment to a national or cultural entity. Medieval towns, in general were so separated from one another and so dominated by a spirit of localism that they could not serve as the basis for any larger group loyalty." (John B. Whitton, "Nationalism and Internationalism," in the *Encyclopedia Americana,* 1973 ed., New York, v. 9, p. 752)

141. The first manifestation of modern nationalism occurred in 17th century England, in the course of the Puritan revolution. That century saw England the leading nation in scientific spirit, in commercial enterprise, in political thought and activity. Swelled by an immense confidence in the new age and in the boundless possibilities opening up, the English people felt upon their shoulders the mission of history, and a new sense that they were builders of destiny, at a great turning point from which a true reformation and a new liberty would begin. (Cf. Hans Kohn, "The Genesis of English Nationalism," in the *Journal of the History of Idea,* Vol. 1, No. 1, Jan. 1940.)

142. English nationalism was much nearer to its religious matrix than the later nationalism, which rose in the 18th and 19th centuries after the process of secularization had made much greater progress. The rise of English nationalism coincided with the rise of the English trading middle classes; and found its final expression in Locke's political philosophy. It was in that form that English nationalism influenced American and French nationalism in the following century. American nationalism found its first political realization in the Declaration of Independence and in the birth of the American nation. In France, nationalism, the soil for whose growth had been prepared by Rousseau, was first expressed in the great French Revolution, a noteworthy landmark both in the history of individualist democracy and in the evolution of nationalism. The French Revolution created a true nation, in which distinctions of class and locality were abolished, the church was secularized, and all political as well as ecclesiastical institutions were put on a national basis and made to serve national ends. It also enunciated the doctrine of national self-determination. (Cf. *Nationalism,* a report by a study group of members of the Royal Institute of International Affairs, London, 1939, p. 23-34; and Herbert A. Gibbon, *Nationalism and Internationalism,* New York, 1930, p. 1-30.)

143. From western Europe nationalism spread at the beginning of the 19th century to central Europe, and from there, towards the middle of the century, to eastern and southeastern Europe, until, at the beginning of the 20th century, it put its stamp on the ancient lands of Asia and Africa, after having penetrated the new countries of Latin America. Thus, nationalism has become at present a force

Literature on the origin of nationalism and conditions for its growth have been numerous. Some writers see in nationalism a survival of primeval barbarism,[144] compare it with tribalism,[145] or char-

---

which dominates everywhere on earth. (Cf. Hans Kohn, *Nationalism, Its Meaning and History,* Princeton, N.Y., 1955, p. 16-90.)

"In Asia, Japan saw the beginnings of nationalism in the Meiji restoration in 1868, which was motivated in part as a deliberate defense against the encroachment of the West. In China its beginnings were in Sun Yat-sen's revolution of 1911. Everywhere else in Asia, nationalism found its beginnings in the anticolonial movements starting mainly in the 1920s and 1930s and achieving independence in the wake of World War II, even though nationalism had not yet fully developed in some Asian countries and has not yet done so. And in Africa, as mentioned earlier, even the beginnings did not come until a decade after the war had ended." (Roger Hilsman, *The Crouching Future,* New York, 1975, p. 242)

"All men are by nature partisans and patriots, but the natural tribalism of men in the nineteenth century was unnaturally exaggerated, it was fretted and overstimulated and inflamed and forced into the nationalist mould.... Men were brought to feel that they were as improper without a nationality as without their clothes in a crowded assembly. Oriental peoples who had never heard of nationality before, took to it as they took to the cigarettes and bowler hats of the west. India, a galaxy of contrasted races, religions, and cultures ... became a 'nation.'" (Herbert G. Wells, *The Outline of History,* New York, 1920, Vol. II, p. 433)

144. A typical representative of the survival school is E.H. Hankins, who in a scholarly book defines nationalism as the self-assertion of that redoubtable being, "the cave-man within us." In his view, the mentality of nationalism has developed in response to the conditions of an earlier time and has been preserved in the "communal mind," which exists "independently of the individual mind," and "outside the nervous system and body of the individual." The author attempts to substantiate this thesis by parallels taken from the customs and habits of primitive societies and the behavior of animals. There are many parallels, indeed, between nationalism and the behavior of primitive societies, such as the strength of irrational forces, emotions and traditions; and the belief in mysticism and collectivism. Many primitives consider their names or their shadows as sacred and believe they suffer damage if somebody treads upon their shadow or maliciously pronounces their name. Primitives intensify communal feelings and bonds with ceremonies, dances, and the use of narcotics, producing a high grade of nervous excitement and intoxication. This resembles the technique used in nationalism of arousing the passions of the masses, and whipping them up into ecstasy with symbols, uniforms, music, dances, drumming, the constant repetition of slogans, and mass marching. In many primitive groups, secret societies play a great role. They are often composed of young men who perform mystical dances, exercise themselves in cruel acts, in the shedding of blood and enduring of pain, terrorize and plunder those who are weaker, and try to secure for themselves a privileged position. They show many likenesses to modern nationalist youth organizations. (Cf. Ernest H. Hankins, *Nationalism and the Communal Mind,* London, 1937, p. 151, 183, 187, 193.)

145. "In modern times and with continuously waxing strength since the seventeenth century nationalism has reemerged, first in Europe and then in other conti-

acterize it as ethnocentrism versus universalism at the final phase.[146] Others view it as a process of social communication leading toward a world unity,[147] interpret it as a social neurosis caused by the stress and strain of modern life,[148] or regard it as a product of modern society surfeited with intellectualism and disgusted with its results.[149]

---

nents. It is akin to primitive tribalism in that it directs the supreme loyalty of its adherents to a community of language, customs and historic traditions. But it differs from primitive tribalism in noteworthy respects. Instead of being based on a small group of persons, banded together by actual blood relationship and by identity of religious practises and economic interests, it is based on a relatively large group of persons connected very distantly, if at all, by blood, professing almost any religion, or none at all, and having widely divergent economic interests. Modern nationalism, thus depending on larger units and being less substantial than primitive tribalism, is more artificially engendered and propagated; it relies more on conscious purposefulness, on the written and particularly on the printed word and on a special kind of mass education." (Carlton J.H. Hays, "Nationalism—Historical Development," in the *Encyclopedia of the Social Sciences,* New York, 1933, Vol. II, p. 241. Cf. his *Nationalism: a Religion,* New York, 1960, p. 20-21.)

146. "The contestants in this age-old strife, now in its final phase in our own culture, are Ethnocentrism and Universalism. Preliterate man seeks peace and brotherhood through his totem-gods. Literate man pursues the same goals through his various pantheons and through the sacred symbols of the nation-State. In each instance fraternity among neighbors is bought at the cost of shared contempt and hostility toward other human groups across some invisible barrier of power or belief. Nationalism is ethnocentrism writ large. So also is every dedication to a belief-system whose devotees find spiritual solace only through hatred of heretics and infidels." (Frederick L. Schuman, *The Commonwealth of Man; an Inquiry into Power Politics and World Government,* New York, 1952, p. 488)

147. This is a theory expounded by Karl W. Deutsch who started his study with the premise that nationalism is a process of social learning and habit forming, resulting from a marked increase in social communication. Typically, the increase has come from changes in the pattern of life associated with the beginnings of modernization. He developed his thesis on an optimistic note: "Thus far, the age of nationalism has grouped people apart from each other and may for a time continue to do so. But at the same time it is preparing them, and perhaps in part has already prepared them for a more thoroughgoing worldwide unity than has ever been seen in human history. Even the growth of national consciousness may under certain circumstances contribute to this end. It can become a blinding curse to those who have accepted it uncritically. Like all consciousness, however, it draws much of its strength from being an awareness of something which exists. To reveal that is, to show the true state of affairs, for part of the political problems of a part of mankind may serve as a preparation for teaching men to be aware of the whole pattern of their affairs, and of the single problem of mankind on its painful way to unity. As men attain this insight into the essential unity of their fate on this planet, the age of nationalism and of the growth of nations may recede into its proper historical perspective." (Karl W. Deutsch, *Nationalism and Social Communication,* New York, 1953, p. 164-165)

And there continue to be intellectuals who submerge nationalism in irrationalism with romantic approaches[150] and illogical assertions.[151]

---

148. For example, Caroline Playne in several books interprets nationalism as "a social neurosis caused by the stress and strain of modern life." The explanation of the primitive, fanatical tendencies of today as a return to barbarism, an atavistic upheaval, appears to her far too simple. The neurosis from which nationalism and war spring is due to "the wear and tear to men's nervous make-up caused by the increased pressure, complication, and the fullness of life generally." This thesis is elaborated in detail with an analysis of the psychological effects of social changes. (Cf. Caroline E. Playne, *The Neuroses of the Nations, the Neuroses of Germany and France before the War,* New York, 1925; *The Pre-War Mind in Britain,* London, 1928; *Society at War, 1914-1916,* Boston, 1931.)

149. Nationalism contains much of misused intellectualism, and utilizes for its own purposes the results of intellectual progress. The speculations of some great thinkers, and the expansion of knowledge have all been misused for the elaboration of nationalist ideologies. Biological factors, too, seem to have contributed to the advance of nationalism. Young people are generally more easily inflamed by nationalism than older, more sedate ones, owing to the exuberance of the juvenile temperament, lack of experience, and their inclination for simple, forceful methods. Certain currents of thought have also played a role in disposing intellectuals towards nationalism, by shattering their belief in reason, progress, and humanity. Many intellectuals have been disappointed with the fruits of modern civilization and particularly with the result of their own efforts. Even such as have given much time and thought to the search for truth have often felt that they have failed. Reason has seemed to them unable to solve the riddles of the world and to bring about a satisfactory state of society, and has seemed to have succeeded only in destroying all beliefs without offering a substitute. Intellectualism has appeared to result in interminable quarrels and uncertainties, and some intellectuals have ended in moral nihilism and despair. They have often begun to yearn for the return of a primitive way of life and have believed they would find a new religion in the sensation of mass enthusiasm, a new morality in submitting to the iron discipline of a sort of pan-militarism, and a substitute for science in the intoxicating myth of nationalism. (Cf. Friedrich O. Hertz, *Nationality in History and Politics,* New York, 1944, p. 273-274.)

150. Johann Gottfried Herder, for example, emphasized folklore, folk songs and popular traditions as revealing the true creative forces of a nation. He went beyond Rousseau in his appeal to an often primitive past. Glorifying the instinctive and irrational, and turning attention from the universally human and general to national peculiarities. Under Herder's influence, German romantic nationalism later stressed the factors of irrationalism; instinct against reason; historical tradition against rational attempts at progress and a more just order; and the differences between nations based upon the past, as opposed to their common aspirations turned toward the future. (Cf. Robert R. Ergang, *Herder and the Foundations of German Nationalism,* New York, 1931, p. 248-253, 263; and Hans Kohn, "Romanticism and the Rise of German Nationalism," in *The Review of Politics,* Vol. 12, Oct., 1951.)

151. For instance, "The German intellectual classes, especially many professors

As a matter of fact, in almost all national movements the leading role has been played by intellectuals while the common masses have merely been tools in their hands. In spite of the intellectual character of their philosophies, nationalist leaders have always exalted the emotions, appealed to the instincts, and called for impulsive actions.[152]

Finally, there is a kind of realism which has added a lot of fuel to the fire of nationalism.[153]

No mattter what the origins and conditions of the phenomenon, nationalism has grown into a mixture of barbarism, tribalism, ethnocentrism, traditionalism and irrationalism. It even mixes intellectualism with anti-intellectualism, and idealism with realism. Plainly, it "is the soda water that mixes with all other drinks and makes them sparkle."[154]

---

and teachers in higher schools, have become a mainstay of the philosophy of force underlying the German militaristic system. One of the greatest German scholars, Dubois-Reymond, declared in an academic speech with pride that the German professors were 'the scientific crack regiment of the Hohenzollerns'.... Under the Hitler regime even a special sort of German physics and mathematics has been discovered which is alleged not to be accessible to scholars of non-Nordic blood." (Friedrich O. Hertz, *Nationality in History and Politics,* New York, 1944, p. 46-47. Cf. Robert F. Butts, *A Cultural History of Education,* New York, 1947, p. 575.)

152. (Cf. *Nationalist Movement,* ed. by Anthony D. Smith, New York, 1977, p. 21-25.)

153. "There is still another very important element in most recent civilization which must be mentioned—the supplanting of the intellectual and cultural vogue of romanticism by what has conventionally been termed 'realism.' This realism has been the product of a variety of novel factors: absorption in the mechanical and utilitarian aspects of the industrial revolution; admiration for the 'practical man' of big industry and big finance; acceptance of a mechanistic theory of the universe and of a materialist interpretation of human behavior; interest in sociology, with its 'laws of society' and its fact finding inquests; distrust of human reason and trust in pragmatism and human will; adaptation of the biological hypotheses of Darwin to support such conceptions as the inequality of races, the 'struggle for existence' and the 'survival of the fittest'; enthusiasm for Nietzsche's 'red blooded men' and for his 'superman.' The vogue of realism has paralleled not only the intensification of the industrial revolution but the rise of Marxian socialism and revolutionary syndicalism and also an epochal transformation of nationalism." (Carlton J.H. Hays, "Nationalism—Historical Development," in the *Encyclopaedia of the Social Sciences,* New York, 1933, Vol. 11, p. 246. Cf. his *Nationalism: A Religion,* New York, 1960, p. 89-93.)

154. "In this our day and generation, nationalism dominates democracy, socialism, liberalism, Christianity, capitalism, Fascism, politics, religion, economics, monarchies and republics. Nationalism is the soda water that mixes with all the other drinks and makes them sparkle." (Emery Reves, *The Anatomy of Peace,* New York, 1946, p. 186)

With such a complex nature and colorful appeal,[155] it is no surprise that nationalism as a dominating force has often gotten out of hand. This was first manifested during the French Revolution when nationalism reached a peak after the beginning of a low level during the Puritan revolution and increasing during the course of the American Revolution. In France, under the stress of rebellion at home and attack from abroad, nationalism soon ran wild,[156] gave rise to a new despotism,[157] paved the way for the dictatorship of Napoleon, and

---

155. Herbert G. Wells said he "loathed" nationalism for its parochialism, its egocentricity, its intolerance. It "trumpets and waves its flags, obtrudes its tawdry loyalties, exaggerates the splendours of its past, and fights to sustain the ancient hallucinations." It tends to subvert the schools, the press, the pulpit, and other organs of opinion and propaganda, with the result that it becomes difficult, if not impossible, to submit issues (domestic as well as foreign) to rational judgment or settlement. It became an exacerbating factor in politics only in relatively recent times. However, it is atavistic since it raises nations to the status of tribal gods. (Cf. his works: *The World of William Clissold,* New York, 1926, Vol. II, p. 572; *The Way the World Is Going,* Garden City, N.Y., 1929, Chap. 6; and *Anticipations,* New York, 1902, p. 182-183.)

156. Professing in the beginning absolute fidelity to the doctrines of popular sovereignty, individual liberty, social equality and fraternity, the French revolutionaries, under the stress of rebellion at home and attack from abroad, soon allowed the movement to deteriorate. Force and militarism took precedence over humanitarianism and fraternal love, and the movement became fanatical. Soon there began to emerge those remarkable instrumentalities of nationalism which have been so widely employed ever since, notably by totalitarian dictatorships, but which have not been neglected by the most advanced democracies. The concept of the "nation in arms," universal conscription, emotional appeals for flag and country, the composition of a national anthem, the glorification of national heroes, the establishment of a system of public education grounded in the vernacular and dedicated to spreading revolutionary doctrines, invention of a new kind of popular journalism and finally, the organization of impressive rituals in the form of national ceremonies—all were employed as part of a vast scheme to create and intensify a national cult. It was a peculiarly French mission, the French revolutionaries believed, to spread the new gospel, if necessary, by the sword. In December, 1792, the French National Convention decreed: "The French nation ... will treat as enemies every people who, refusing liberty and equality or renouncing them, may wish to maintain, recall, or treat with a prince and the privileged classes; on the other hand, it engages not to subscribe to any treaty and not to lay down its arms until after the establishment of the sovereignty and independence of the people whose territory the troops of the (French) Republic shall have entered and until the people shall have adopted the principles of equality and founded a free and democratic government." (Cf. Carlton J.H. Hays, *The Historical Evolution of Modern Nationalism,* New York, 1931, p. 43-68; and his *Nationalism: a Religion,* New York, 1960, p. 43-58.)

157. Nationalism induces people to follow the masses, or the strongest party. Robespierre made the inevitable application when he said of the Jacobins, "Our will

led to a great war of more than twenty years, engulfing almost all of Europe as well as some of its outposts.[158]

The enormous excesses of the French Revolution adequately illustrate how difficult is the control of nationalism. Actually, as history has shown, nationalism, after having initially scored a certain success in a nation, has always tended to be either too conservative to deal with new situations or too aggressive to be held in bounds.

One of the most notorious results of the conservative tendency has been the submergence of nationalism into political isolationism[159] and economic protectionism.[160]

In regard to aggressive nationalism, its most dangerous aspect has

---

is the general will." "They say that terrorism is the resort of despotic government. Is our government then like despotism? Yes, as the sword that hashes in the hand of the hero of liberty is like that with which the satellites of tyranny are armed. . . . The government of the Revolution is the despotism of liberty against tyranny." (George H. Sabine, *A History of Political Theory,* New York, 1938, p. 591)

158. The doctrines of the French Revolution were professed to be universal—not designed for Frenchmen alone—but before long the Jacobins were thinking in terms of national self-interest. Nationalism, then as always, feeds on war, and they embarked on expansion and conquest. As the sansculottes marched to do battle abroad, they took their doctrines with them, and spread their nationalism much faster than their democracy. This was true even before the rise of Napoleon, but when the Little Corporal assumed power, he greatly intensified the development already underway. Fortified by supreme power and an admirable political organization and system of laws, he made excellent use of all the Jacobin paraphernalia of nationalism, employing it to the limit of his own keen shrewdness. Thus he was able to indoctrinate a whole generation of Frenchmen with concepts of "glory." He sent them to fight everywhere in Europe and as far as Egypt. The war started with the invasion of the Sardinian island of Maddelena in 1793, and ended in 1815 at Waterloo, where Napoleon was finally defeated by the Anglo-Prussian armies under the command of Wellington. (Cf. Carlton J.H. Hays, *The Historical Evolution of Modern Nationalism,* New York, 1931, p. 79-83; and James M. Thompson, *Napoleon Bonaparte, His Rise and Fall, Oxford, 1952.)*

159. Political isolationism may be illustrated by President George Washington's classic *Farewell Address* (1796), drafted by Alexander Hamilton, in which he counseled his fellow countrymen to steer clear of foreign entanglements: "The great rule of conduct for us, in regard to foreign nations, is in extending our commercial relations, to have with them as little political connection as possible. . . . Europe has a set of primary interests, which to us have none, or a very remote relation. Hence she must be engaged in frequent controversies the causes of which are essentially foreign to our concerns. Hence, therefore, it must be unwise in us to implicate ourselves, by artificial ties, in the ordinary vicissitudes of her politics or the ordinary combinations and collisions of her friendships or enmities." A notable case was the rejection by the U.S. Congress of the Treaty of Versailles and the Covenant of the League of Nations after World War I. (Cf. Albert K. Weinberg, "The Historical Meaning of the American Doctrine of Isola-

been the indulgence in modern militarism,[161] including the concept of "the nation in arms," universal conscription, and the arms race.

Closely connected with modern militarism is modern imperialism, a policy according to which a stronger nation extends its domination, hegemony, or influence over other peoples, politically, militarily, economically or ideologically.[162]

---

tionism," *American Political Science Review,* Vol. 34, 1940; and John B. Whitton, *Isolation: An Obsolete Principle of the Monroe Doctrine,* New York, 1933.)

160. Economic protectionism includes various measures, such as high customs on imports, restrictions on immigration, labor policies which deny the right to work or better posts to aliens, and the exclusion of foreign goods in favor of self-sufficiency. Economic protectionism is a most infectious disease. If one trade is protected, the others want similar treatment, and usually get it, though every extension of protection to additional trades must diminish the profits of those already protected, and though universal protection largely cancels out all individual gains. Likewise, if one nation increases its tariffs or other restrictions, others usually follow suit. Even if the economic grounds given for the imitation are not convincing, the psychological urge is overwhelming. Economic protectionism played a decisive part in bringing about the world crisis of 1929, which devastated the world economy for years. The gravest feature of this crisis was mass unemployment on an unprecedented scale, which paved the way for Hitler and for World War II. A most tragic proof of the mental blindness produced by nationalism is that the remedy for the crisis was largely sought in further increases of economic protectionism. (Cf. Josef Grungel, *Economic Protectionism,* London, 1916; Louis L. Snyder, *The Meaning of Nationalism,* New Brunswick, N.J., 1954, p. 133-141; and Ludwig von Mises, *Omnipotent Government, the Rise of Total State and Total War,* New Haven, 1944, p. 66-78.)

161. The historical root of modern militarism was the old warrior-spirit, as embodied in the traditions and ideals of a privileged warrior-caste. This spirit implied a specific code of honor, centered on the prestige of the warrior, the cult of warlike heroism, of noble blood, and of symbols such as the sword, the uniform, and duelling. This spirit has been modified by the development of military technique and political organization. Whereas the old way of fighting consisted of individual combats between knights, the new way became that of disciplined mass-action. It was no longer so much personal courage and strength which were the decisive factors, but tactics and strategy, the technical means of warfare, and the art of swaying public opinion. No matter how great the change of the warrior-spirit has been in the course of time, its aggressive nature has remained in modern militarism, and has been transmitted to nationalism. The close relation between modern militarism and nationalism was demonstrated especially in Spain and France in the early stages of modern times, and later in Germany and Japan. (Cf. Carlton J.H. Hays, *Essays on Nationalism,* New York, 1926, p. 156-195; and Alfred Vogts, *History of Militarism,* rev. ed., New York, 1959.)

162. Imperialism is "the national policy which tends toward the expansion of national domination and national ideas over a geographical area wider than that of national boundaries." This definition, given in the 1956 edition of the *Encyclopedia Americana,* Vol. 14, p. 724, disappeared in later issues. (Cf. Hans

As a policy, imperialism is as old as civilization itself. In modern times, there have been two major types: capitalist and socialist. The former was intensified by the Industrial Revolution[163] and the latter was a by-product of the Communist revolution.[164] But the driving force behind both types of imperialism is the same: nationalism.[165]

It is true that some of the prophets of the national movements

---

Kohn, "Reflections of Colonialism," in *The Idea of Colonialism,* ed. by Robert Strausz-Hupe and Henry Hazard, New York, 1958, p. 2-13.)

163. The development of capitalist imperialism was greatly accelerated by the Industrial Revolution, a term which in general meant the amazing series of mechanical inventions ushered in by the invention of the flying shuttle, in 1733, by John Kay. In modern states, industry and commerce, and eventually society as a whole, were actually transformed by the developments made possible by the work of Thomas Savery, Thomas Newcomen, and James Watt in steam power, Sir Richard Arkwright and Samuel Crompton in textile manufacture, the Abraham Darbys and Henry Cort in coal and iron, Sir Henry Bessemer in steel, and other pioneers. The consequences were incalculable. Mass production was introduced, great factory cities created, and a working class, or proletariat, developed. Also, a new middle class was engendered, and the ranks of the capitalist class greatly augmented. The power of nations to produce and to expand increased immeasurably. Demand for outlets for the investment of capital, and the need for raw materials to feed the hungry new factories led to the search for new possessions in distant regions. This meant a new wave of capitalist imperialism. (Cf. A.P. Thornton, *Doctrines of Imperialism,* New York, 1965, p. 97-153.)

"Imperialism has greatly developed the productive forces of world capitalism. It has completed the preparation of all the material prerequisites for the socialist organization of society. By its wars it has demonstrated that the productive forces of world economy, which have outgrown the restricted boundaries of imperialist states, demand the organization of economy on a world, or international, scale." (Chapter one, section 4 of the *Program of the Communist International,* adopted by its Sixth World Congress, Sept. 1, 1928)

164. Since the end of World War II, for example, the Soviet Union has extended its hegemony or influence not only over Eastern Europe, including Poland, Romania, Hungary, Czechoslovakia, Bulgaria, and East Germany, but also to a number of countries in Africa, Asia, and as far as Cuba in the Western hemisphere. (Cf. Reinhold Niebuhr, *The Structure of Nations and Empires,* New York, 1959, p. 239-255; Ivo Duchacek, "Soviet Imperialism in East Europe," in the *Current History,* Vol. 36, No. 209, Jan. 1959, p. 7-11; and Hugh Seton-Watson, *The Imperialist Revolutionaries, Trend in World Communism in the 1960s and 1970s,* Stanford, Calif., 1978, p. 8-11, 102-116.)

165. "At the very time, from the 1870s to World War I, when nationalism was being intensified by industrialization and was becoming a truly mass movement in Europe and America, there was an extra-ordinary outburst of national imperialism.... Basically, the new imperialism was a nationalistic phenomenon." (Carlton J.H. Hays, *Nationalism: a Religion,* New York, 1960, p. 94, 97. Cf. p. 94-101 for "Outburst of National Imperialism" and "Nationalism: Seed and Product of the New Imperialism.")

had hoped that nationalism would bring about liberty throughout the world,[166] fraternity among all peoples,[167] a common blessing to mankind,[168] and a world commonwealth.[169] How could their cherished nationalism turn out to be the driving force behind imperialism?

To socialists, nationalism is merely an ideological superstructure;[170] imperialism is the highest stage of capitalism, which is the

---

166. During the course of the Puritan revolution, a new optimistic humanism and Calvinist ethics merged; the influence of the Old Testament formed the new nationalism by identifying the English people with ancient Israel. The new message, carried by the new people not only for England, but for all of mankind, was expressed in the writings of Milton, in whose famous vision the idea of liberty was seen spreading from Britain, "celebrated for endless ages as a soil most genial to the growth of liberty to all the corners of the earth." "Surrounded by congregated multitudes, I now imagine that I behold the nations of the earth recovering that liberty which they so long had lost; and that the people of this island are disseminating the blessings of civilization and freedom among cities, kingdoms and nations." (Quoted in the *Encyclopedia Britannica,* 1956, ed. under "Nationalism," p. 150.)

167. The French Revolution was the triumphant expression of a rational faith in common humanity and liberal progress. The famous slogan of "liberty, equality, fraternity" and the Declaration of the Rights of Man and of the Citizen were not only thought valid for the French people, but for all peoples. Individual liberty, human equality, fraternity of all peoples: these were the common cornerstones of all liberal and democratic nationalism. (Cf. Carlton J.H. Hays, *The Historical Evolution of Modern Nationalism,* New York, 1931, p. 33-36.)

168. For example, Giuseppe Mazzini, who had devoted his life to the unification of the Italian nation by democratic means and to the brotherhood of all nations, believed that nationalism was a struggle for the common blessing of all peoples and was "the consciousness of a mission to be fulfilled for the sake of mankind. It does not depend upon race or descent, but upon a common thought and a common goal." (Cf. his *The Duties of Man and Other Essays,* London, 1936.)

169. Dr. Sun Yat-sen, the founder of the Republic of China, emphasized that the purpose of his first principle—nationalism—was to strive for the liberty and equality of China in order to promote a great commonwealth of the world, "以進大同" for the benefit of mankind. (Cf. his *San Min Chu I, the Three Principles of the People,* Taipei, 1962, p. 36-49, 325-329.)

170. The Socialists have explained nationalism as an ideological "superstructure" which grew up on the "foundations" of the need of the merchant-manufacturer class for a nationwide market and a nationwide economy. Nationalism's function, they explained, was to serve as a banner for a crusade to sweep away all medieval localisms which hindered the development of such a national economy. In other words, nationalism was a smokescreen for capitalist interests, or a means for diverting the people from the struggle for social liberation. They believed, at any rate, that the working classes were immune against national slogans, and that the ideology of nationalism hardly required refutation. (Cf. Lenin's *Critical Remarks on the National Question,* 1913, Moscow, 1951, p.

source of all social evils,[171] and they only adopt nationalism for its expedient use as a weapon for counter-attack against imperialism.[172] How then could their chosen weapon drag the Communist movement into the course of imperialism?

To these questions a primary answer is that nationalism is a force so powerful and so wild that it can easily get out of hand, as demonstrated in the French Revolution.

There are many other reasons for nationalism to be the driving force behind imperialism:

Nationalism connotes an utmost esteem of one's own nation, which leads to detraction from and discredit of other nations.[173]

15-19, 34-37; Louis L. Snyder, *The Meaning of Nationalism,* New Brunswick, N.Y., 1954, p. 142-143; and Boyd C. Shafer, *Nationalism, Myth and Reality,* New York, 1955, p. 41-42.)

171. Marxist theoreticians have elaborated the economic aspects of imperialism in great detail. They interpret imperialism as a late stage of capitalism when the national capitalist economy has become monopolistic and is forced to conquer outlets for its overproduction and surplus capital in competition with the monopolistic economies of other capitalist nations. This state heralds the decline of capitalism itself, or a "general crisis" of capitalism, and this general crisis cannot be averted. This is the view held, for instance, by Lenin and N.J. Bukharin to whom capitalism and imperialism are identical. (Cf. V.I. Lenin, *Imperialism, the Highest Stage of Capitalism,* 1916, paperback ed., San Francisco, 1965.)

172. The use of nationalism as a weapon was started by Karl Marx when he supported the struggle of Poles against Russia for national independence. "Among the Poles, the communists support the party which considers an agrarian revolution essential to national liberation—the party which initiated the Cracow insurrection in 1846," in the last part of the *Manifesto of the Communist Party,* by Karl Marx and Friedrich Engels, authorized English trans. ed. and annotated by Friedrich Engels, Chicago, 1947.

173. The esteem for one's own nation above anything else is a positive attitude, usually including a belief in its achievements, its excellence and its superiority. The detractions and discredit of other nations represent a negative attitude, usually including prejudiced opinions concerning their economic backwardness, political ineffectiveness and cultural inferiority. Both positive and negative attitudes can combine into a force readily leading to imperialistic aggression, which, as it is assumed, is part of the natural struggle for survival. According to this view, nature has made men unequal, and those endowed with superior qualities are destined to rule all others. Nations must prove their strength and virility in combat and the subjection of weaker peoples. Like all organisms, nations must pass through a period of growth (i.e., expansion). (Cf. John A.S. Grenville, *National Prejudice and International History,* Leeds, England, 1968; and Louis L. Snyder, *The Imperialism Reader,* New York, 1962, p. 87-125.)

Nationalism commands a paramount loyalty and duty to one's own nation, leading to rivalry and hostility with other nations.[174]

Nationalism wants one's own nation to be militarily stronger, leading to strategical struggles against other nations.[175]

Nationalism asserts one's own national interests emphatically, leading to economic egoism in dealing with other nations.[176]

---

174. In early times, in most places in the world, man's supreme loyalty was centered on his religion. In recent centuries this place has been taken by the nation as a result of the urge of nationalism. As a consequence, the traitor has displaced the heretic as the most despised of antisocial individuals within the nation. This supreme loyalty is not only self-centered and exclusive; it has likewise a curious negative element. It thrives on anti-foreign sentiment, especially when this can be focused on a particular country, the object of special disdain. The anti-foreign sentiment can easily develop into an imperialistic aggression. (Cf. Carlton J.H. Hays, *Essays on Nationalism,* New York, 1926, p. 196-244.)

175. Nationalism urges the acquisition of bases, strategic materials, buffer states, "natural" frontiers, and the control of communication lines for reasons of security or to prevent other nations from obtaining them. Before World War I, for example, Britain acquired Gibraltar, Malta, and Cyprus to control the Mediterranean Sea and, with the later addition of the Suez Canal, held Aden, Socotra, and Perim to protect the Suez route to India and the East. France annexed large portions of West and Equatorial Africa as strategic hinterlands for the protection of coastal possessions and of travel routes to the coast. (Cf. A.P. Thornton, *Doctrines of Imperialism,* New York, 1965, p. 47-96.) "Means of expansion and motives of defense of those old and new aggrandizements always demand greater and greater guarantees." (Don L. Sturzo, *Nationalism and Internationalism,* New York, 1946, p. 235. Cf. p. 233-236.)

Nationalism wants one's nation militarily stronger, often leading to conquests, because to defeat one's neighbor in battle, occupy his lands, incorporate his subjects, thereby raising one's own power and widening one's own sphere of influence is always regarded as an efficient way to obtain security against attack. But there must be conquest after conquest. The reason for this is simple. No border is completely safe, and no strategical base is without threat. (Cf. Bertrand de Jouvenel's *On Power,* trans. by J.F. Huntington, New York, 1949, p. 140.)

176. "This is the new economic nationalism, which, assuming significant proportions in Germany and the United States early in the 1880s, has been seized upon and pursued with generally augmenting intensity by every civilized nation. Everywhere it has transformed economic interests of the masses as well as of the classes into national interests and has provided substantial foundation for the almost universal and contemporary habit of referring to 'national wealth,' 'national resources,' 'national production,' 'national labor supply.'...." (Carlton J.H. Hays, "Nationalism," in the *Encyclopaedia of the Social Sciences,* New York, 1933, Vol. II, p. 246.) Economic activity is usually regarded as a means of providing the people by peaceful work and cooperation with the greatest possible amount of goods in demand, while economic nationalism looks at it primarily as a means of increasing power. Economic nationalism tends not only to protectionism, but sometimes even harks back to the doctrine of mercantilism where one

In addition, national pride, honor, glory and the particular ideologies stressed, sought, exalted and fostered by nationalism are also sources which give rise to imperialism.[177]

Thus, where there exists a strong nationalism, there is a driving force for imperialism; and armed with this force, it is possible for any nation, given sufficient resources, to engage in imperialistic activities.[178] Yet we are faced with the ridiculous historical phenomenon

---

nation can grow rich only at the expense of another, and what one nation wins, another must lose. The growth of state-industries and rigid state-regulation of industries in this century has added a new factor to economic nationalism. The state-trade arouses more national jealousy and is not unusually mixed with political motive and sinister intention. (Cf. *Nationalism,* a Report by a Study Group of Members of the Royal Institute of International Affairs, London, 1939, p. 217-248; Louis L. Snyder, *The Meaning of Nationalism,* New Brunswick, N.J., 1954, p. 133-145; Charles A. Conant, "The Economic Basis of Imperialism," in the *North American Review,* Sept. 1898, p. 326-340. Ferdinando Martini presented the Italian Case for "Imperialism of the Have-Nots," 1897, excerpt in the *Imperialism Reader,* ed. by Louis L. Snyder, New York, 1962, p. 126-128.)

177. The white man's burden of the English, the civilizing action of the French, the manifest destiny of the Americans, the greater east Asia co-prosperity sphere of the Japanese, the Pan-Slavism of the Russians and the Pan-Germanism of the Germans, and the Communist Liberation movements in recent decades belong in this category. "Pegging out claims for posterity" are the words of Lord Rosebery, the famous English statesman and author. "Seeking a place in the sun" was the arrogant image of the German Emperor Wilhelm II; and Benito Mussolini's reason for the Italian invasion of Ethiopia was "for manhood among nations." The moral appeals of nationalism have often found support from a great number of the population willing to fight for no other gain than the psychological satisfaction. The "devil theory" of imperialism, that only ruthless profiteers have engineered imperialism, is not completely borne out by the fact of history. (Cf. Parker T. Moon, *Imperialism and World Politics,* New York, 1933, p. 25-74; Rienhold Niebuhr, *The Structure of Nations and Empires,* New York, 1959, p. 201-255; A.P. Thornton, *Doctrines of Imperialism,* New York, 1965, p. 154-200; J.A. Cramb, "Britain's World Mission," in the *Daily News* Special Number, Dec. 31, 1900; the excerpt of Rudyard Kipling's "White Man's Burden" in *The Imperialism Reader,* ed. by Louis L. Snyder, New York, 1962, p. 87-88, and other excerpts in the same book, p. 89-125.)

178. Even those who have just fought against imperialistic aggression tend to become imperialistic aggressors themselves. Consider, for example, since World War II, Indian policy toward its Himalayan states and neighbors, Australian policy in New Guinea and Papua, Chinese interest in Southeast Asia, Malaysia's stance on Borneo, Indonesia's activities in West Irian, Cuba's troops in Africa and Vietnam's influence over Cambodia and Laos. (Cf. Robin W. Winks, "Imperialism" in the *Encyclopedia Americana,* 1973 ed., Vol. 14, p. 822; and Amry Vandenbosch, "Chinese Thrust in Southeast Asia," in *Current History,* Vol. 37, no. 220, Dec. 1959.)

that the remedy for imperialism has often been sought in the intensification of nationalism.[179]

Actually, there is no way to get rid of imperialism without eliminating its driving force. That is to say, the first step toward uprooting imperialism has to be the eradication of nationalism.[180]

From the historical point of view, nationalism was a retrogressive element in its native land of Europe, where, for almost two thousand years, universal humanity had generally been stressed along with common Christian traditions.[181] Nationalism became a strong move-

---

179. In order to reduce threats of imperialism, for example, the League of Nations was established on the idea of the U.S. President Woodrow Wilson that "a general association of nations must be formed under specific covenants for the purpose of affording mutual guarantees of political independence and territorial integrity to great and small states alike." (Cf. James T. Watkins IV and J. William Robinson, *General International Organization, A Source Book,* New York, 1956, p. 55-56); and the United Nations "is composed of member governments, each of which is recognized in international law as possessing sovereign status. Consequently the United Nations is primarily the agent of its sovereign masters." (T. Walter Wallbank, Alastair M. Taylor, Nels M. Bailkey, and Mark Mancall, *Civilization Past and Present,* 6th ed., Glenview, Ill., 1970, Book I, p. 508) This is to say, both the League of Nations and the United Nations were designed to curb imperialism by intensifying nationalism with emphases on national sovereignty, integrity, self-determination and independence. (Cf. 1, 4, 7 of Article 2 of the Charter of the United Nations, and Article 10 and 8 of Article 15 of the Covenant of the League of Nations.)

180. "Nationalism undoubtedly helped to defend England and to inspire the heroic underground resistance against German conquest in France, Poland, Norway and other Nazi-occupied countries. But these beneficial effects of nationalism are similar to the effect of antitoxin. Because the diphtheria bacillus is necessary to prepare the serum to fight diphtheria, this does not justify calling the virus itself beneficial or useful. At the present stage of bacteriology, the best we can do to cure diphtheria is to use its virus for the preparation of an antitoxin. But it would be much better to destroy and exterminate the causes of diphtheria, even if, at the same time, we destroyed the agent to cure the disease." (Emery Reves, *The Anatomy of Peace,* New York, 1946, p. 233)

181. After the 18th century, nationalism stressed the peculiar and parochial, the national differences and individualities. This tendency became more pronounced as nationalism developed. It was opposed to all the concepts which had dominated thought for more than 2,000 years. During that period man had commonly stressed the general and the universal and seen in unity the desirable goal. In the 17th and 18th centuries, the common standards of western civilization—the regard for the universally human, the faith in reason, one and the same everywhere, and in common sense, the survival of the Christian and Stoic traditions— all these were too strong to allow nationalism to develop its full tendencies, and to disrupt the society of man. Thus nationalism in its beginning was thought to be compatible with cosmopolitan convictions and with the general love of mankind.

ment and extended over the whole world, mainly because it proved to be a useful weapon in speeding up the growth of the nation.[182] Now that almost all peoples of the world have achieved nationhood,[183] the nation has, in general, outlived its time.[184] Hence, the usefulness of nationalism is diminishing, and what remains merely serves as a detriment to the causes of universal humanity and individual freedom.[185]

This was especially true of nationalism in western Europe and North America. (Cf. Friedrich O. Hertz, *Nationality in History and Politics,* New York, 1944, p. 297-336; Halvoan Koht, "The Dawn of Nationalism in Europe," in the *American Historical Review,* Vol. LII, Jan. 1947; Herbert A. Gibbons, *Nationalism and Internationalism,* New York, 1930, p. 1-30.)

182. "Nationalism ... was in its beginning a high ideal of humanity. Its aim was to liberate the peoples from the domination of absolutism, to proclaim their independence, to transfer the symbol of sovereignty from the king to the people, and to achieve a social order resting on the principles of equality, liberty and justice. At the end of the eighteenth century, nationalism, as it was conceived by the first founders of modern democracy, was a tremendous step forward. It meant the broadening of the fundaments of the state from one man or a small group to the entire nation. It was the basis of individual freedom, of the rule of law, of free elections, of representative government." (Emery Reves, *A Democratic Manifesto,* New York, 1942, p. 40-41)

183. (Cf. I, 40 and III, 11-12.)

184. In the process of our group expansion, the nation basically belongs to the Iron Age, which started about 1000 B.C. and reached its culmination about 1900 A.D. (Cf. I, 383.)

"But once established as a basic principle of policy, nationalism had the same fate as all other closed revolutionary ideals, once they ceased to be an ideal and became reality.... And since that time, like all social ideals which become dogmas, it has been the greatest obstacle to further progress. It became the popular fate of the uncultured masses, the expression of the lowest instincts of mass inferiority complex, and its defenders are the most intolerant priests of a dogmatic religion we have ever had on this earth." (Emery Reves, *A Democratic Manifesto,* New York, 1942, p. 41)

185. "An intolerant attitude and behaviour towards one's fellows; a belief in the imperial mission of one's own nationality at the expense of others, particularly at the expense of backward peoples; a habit of carrying a chip on one's national shoulder and defying another nationality to knock it off; a fond dwelling on the memory of past wars and a feverish preparing for future wars, to the neglect of present civil problems; a willingness to be led and guided by self-styled patriots; a diffidence, almost a panic, about thinking or acting differently from one's fellows; a spirit of exclusiveness and narrowness which feeds on gross ignorance of others and on inordinate pride in one's self and one's nationality; these are all too prevalent aspects of contemporary nationalism. If in these respects nationalism is not mitigated it will be an unqualified curse to future generations." (Carlton J.H. Hays, *Essays on Nationalism,* New York, 1926, p. 250. Cf. p. 245-276. "Nationalism—Curse or Blessing?")

Viewed from another angle, nationalism is a force of reaction against the general trend of our civilization, led by the rapid advance of modern science and technology. While the general trend has been to guide all peoples of the world, mainly through fast transportation and communication and an interdependent economy, to live closer and closer together and cooperate more and more for a better life, nationalism has continued to work desperately to keep them separate and independent, and in a constant struggle against each other.[186]

After almost three hundred years as a strong movement, nationalism is now more or less on the wane in its native lands,[187] and is

---

"Nationalism today unleashes forces which deepen antagonisms and hallow them by appeals to an idealized and oversentimentalized past. Thus nationalism has tended to become what it originally had not been, a threat to individual liberty and to the universality of human culture." (Hans Kohn, "A New Look at Nationalism," in the *Virginia Quarterly Review,* Vol. 32, Summer, 1956.)

186. "Modern inventiveness has afforded the technical means to a degree unimaginable a few decades ago for making cultural interdependence and intercourse even easier than economic interdependence. But at the same time peoples newly awakened to nationalism have begun to stress and to overstress their selfhood and independence, their cultural particularities and self-sufficiency. In the age of the awakening or the revolt of the masses, collective passions and utopian expectations have centered around the newly awakened nationalism to such a degree that ever new barriers disrupt the international community." (Hans Kohn, "A New Look at Nationalism," *The Virginia Quarterly Review,* Vol. 32, Summer, 1956, p. 328-329)

"Nationalism has actually reached the beginning of its end. It has destroyed and decomposed all that human mind, all that human work has conceived. The absurdity of nationalism is best characterized by the fact that we possess today the technical means of crossing the Atlantic Ocean in seven hours, but it takes seven months to obtain a visa." (Emery Reves, *A Democratic Manifesto,* New York, 1942, p. 51)

187. "... nationalism is more or less on the wane in the lands of its origin, in the West, where the peoples are seeking ways for supranational political organization and ever closer cultural integration...." (Hans Kohn, "A New Look at Nationalism," in *The Virginia Quarterly Review,* Vol. 32, Summer, 1956, p. 329)

"Political warfare, whose contribution to Hitler's victories in 1940 and 1941 can hardly be denied, is at once a symptom and a cause of the decline of nationalism. It succeeds only by finding rifts in national solidarity; it aims at widening and deepening those rifts. Some plausibility must be accorded to a shrewd comment penned at the peak of German power in Europe that 'Hitler's successes are basically rooted, not in his extreme nationalism, but on the contrary in his shrewd judgment of the decay of nationalism among his neighbours.' (F. Borkenau, *Socialism, National or International?* 1942, p. 165)...." (Edward H. Carr, *Nationalism and After,* London, 1945, p. 34)

under critical reassessment elsewhere.[188] But, it will strive to remain in force as a root of imperialism, a curse to universal humanity and individual freedom, and a reactionary force against the general trend of modern civilization, unless some drastic action is taken to eradicate it completely.

f.
The Nation-State

THERE HAS BEEN A WIDESPREAD PROPENSITY FOR USing the terms nation and state interchangeably or to identify them with each other.[189] The origin of this propensity is probably the misconception that the state is an independent group like those in the

---

188. "Cultural freedom can only exist if intellectual life is guided by an effort at critical and objective thinking. The greatest threat to such thinking, and therefore to cultural freedom, was represented centuries ago by authoritarian and absolutized religion. Today it is represented by nationalism, above all in its over-resentful or semi-totalitarian forms. But everywhere in the free world, outside the confines of Communist rule and perhaps even there under cover, the critical forces which were born in the seventeenth century in northwestern Europe are at work to combat the exclusivism and egocentrism of modern nationalism. None has spoken more strongly against the cult of one's own nation or nationalism than Vladimir Solovyev in Russia or Rabindranath Tagore in India, both men deeply rooted in the spiritual tradition of their community and yet wide open to the critical insights of the West. Everywhere most of us have allowed our thinking to be channeled into widely accepted stereotypes about nationalism and its relation to liberty. In this time of mental and verbal confusion when general political terms have become so emotionally fraught that they cover disparate realities, we have to start rethinking many concepts in their historical context and in their concrete application. One of the chief concepts about which this rethinking has to be done in the interest of human freedom and of the possibility of cultural intercourse and universal rationality is the concept of nationalism." (Hans Kohn, "A New Look at Nationalism," in *The Virginia Quarterly Review,* Vol. 32, Summer, 1956, 331-332)

189. Webster's unabridged dictionary recognizes this tendency to use the words as synonyms in its fourth of seven definitions of nation and in its fourteenth of twenty-three definitions of state. It defines nation as "loosely, the body of inhabitants of a country united under a single government; a state"; and state as "a political body, or body politic; any body of people occupying a definite territory and politically organized under one government, especially one that is a sovereign, or not subject to external control." (Cf. *Webster's New International Dictionary of the English Language,* 2nd ed. unabridged, Springfield, Mass., 1949, p. 1629,

process of our group expansion: the early single family, primitive community, clan, tribe and nation.

Actually, the state is not an independent group in itself. It is but a political machinery of the independent groups.[190]

As a political machinery of the independent groups, the history of the state has existed almost as long as the independent groups themselves.[191] It was simple in its embryo and infancy,[192] advanced

---

2461; and Benjamin Aksin, *State and Nation,* London, 1964, p. 7-10, "The terminological jungle.")

190. In this regard, the Italian philosopher and historian, Benedetto Croce, went as far as to define the state simply, as "nothing other than the government," in his *Elementi di Politica,* Bari, 1925, p. 14. Likewise, Harold Laski noted: "The state is, for the purpose of practical administration, the government." (Quoted by George H. Sabine, under "State," in the *Encyclopedia of the Social Sciences,* New York, 1937, Vol. XIV, p. 329.) He remarked in his *The State in Theory and Practice,* New York, 1935, p. 11-12, however, that there were certain distinctions between the state and government: "The latter is but the agent of the former; it exists to carry out the purpose of the state." Further, he noted that "the distinction between state and government is rather one of theoretical interest than of practical significance. For every act of the state that we encounter is, in truth, a governmental act. The will of the state is in its laws: but it is the government which gives substance and effect to their content."

"The term State means the executive or legislative authority of the Union or of the unit concerned according as the context may require." (Burma's Constitution, 1947, Article 9. The constitution may be found in the *Constitutions of Nations,* ed. by Amos J. Peaslee, Concord, N.H., 1950.)

191. "Modern anthropologists have sometimes denied that government occurs everywhere. For example, MacLeod says of the Yurok in California that they 'exhibit the picture' of a society 'actually existing without the state, that is, in other words, without government or political organization,' Radcliffe Brown that 'there is no organized government' among the Andaman Islanders, Redfield that 'in the most primitive societies of living men ... political institutions are few and simple, or even entirely absent,' and Malinowski that 'political groupings are absent' among such peoples as the Veddas and Australian aborigines." ... But "except for MacLeod, the writers quoted do not intend to imply that the peoples to whom they refer live in a condition of anarchy; they mean merely that such peoples lack institutional organizations, of the kind found in the modern Western state, ... Nor do those writers maintain that personal leadership and authority are nonexistent." (Isaac Schapera, *Government and Politics in Tribal Societies,* London, 1956, p. 38-39)

"As a matter of fact, (Eduard) Meyer considers the state, as he defines it, the equivalent of the herd among lower species; for him, consequently, it is the primeval social unit, older than the human species, whose evolution was only made possible by its means." (Robert H. Lowie, *The Origin of the State,* New York, 1962, p. 44)

192. Of the Andaman Islanders, for instance, according to Professor

gradually through the clan and tribe states, and has developed into a very complex structure[193] with the growth of the nation and the rise of nationalism. At the same time, it has greatly extended its function[194] and enlarged its power.[195]

Radcliffe Brown, "Each of these minor groups embraced on the average from forty to fifty persons of all ages, the mean area being about 16 square miles. A typical encampment might consist of ten families in as many huts, with a few bachelors and unmarried women. There is no organized government, administration being regulated by the old men and women, to whom their juniors show marked respect. In addition to age, skill in hunting or warfare, liberality, and an even temper bestow prestige, and if men combine these desirable traits they come to rank as headmen, their opinion carries weight, and they are voluntarily aided by young henchmen." (Robert H. Lowie, *The Origin of the State,* New York, 1962, p. 4. Cf. William G. Sumner and Albert G. Keller, *The Science of Society,* New Haven, 1927, Vol. I, p. 460-461.)

193. "Now there are means of conducting human affairs in formal offices and institutions of rule with specialized assignments of roles to governors of provinces, judges, soldiers, kings, ministers, police; or by informal assignments of these roles. People on occasion act as judges, ministers, soldiers in simple societies. But differences in population size and complexity, and formality of office, make for radical differences in modes of government; the larger, more complex and formal governmental roles are usually found in states. The state is a complicating factor in the organization of society, a factor that works two ways: on the one hand, its presence is the mark that a complex form has been achieved; on the other, the process of forming the state is a means for achieving the transition to complex society. That is, a more complex society is established by the process of state formation." (Lawrence Krader, *Formation of the State,* Englewood Cliffs, N.J., 1968, p. 3)

194. In primitive times, life was simple and the public affairs usually administered by the state were: ceremonial, marriage, descent, property, religion, revenge and bloodfeud. The functions of the state in the nation stage generally include: war and other military activities, foreign affairs, security, justice, law and order, economic coordination, social welfare, and cultural development. In some nations, almost every aspect of life has been regulated and controlled by the state. (Cf. Isaac Schapera, *Government and Politics in Tribal Societies,* London, 1956, p. 67-93; and Harold J. Laski, *The State in Theory and Practice,* New York, 1935, p. 10.)

195. In primitive times, the power of the state depended mainly on a personal leadership resulting from birth, age, or some special ability, and a direct relationship with the individual. In modern times, it has been legally distinguished as an over-riding authority, above not only all individuals, but also all other organizations, such as the church and trade union. It is associated with the fact that the political association has "a generality of purpose falling to no other group." (Quoted by Paul H. Appleby in the *Encyclopedia Americana,* 1956 ed., Vol. 25, p. 506, under "State"). So, Bronislaw Malinowski said that "Political organization implies a central authority with the power to administer regarding its subjects, that is, to coordinate the activities of the component groups." (Quoted from his *A Scientific Theory of Culture,* Chapel Hill, N.C., 1944, p. 165.)

In Paul Vinogradoff's words (in his *Outlines of Historical Jurisprudence,* London, 1920, Vol. I, p. 93), the state "has assumed the monopoly of political

With the complex structure, extended function and enlarged power, the state has emerged as so important and so prominent in modern times that it has been seen as a Leviathan;[196] claimed as the basis of all national life;[197] praised as "the Divine Idea as it exists on earth" and "the March of God on earth";[198] exalted as the ultimate goal and highest value;[199] and identified with an organism.[200]

---

coordination. It is the State which rules, makes laws and eventually enforces them by coercion. Such a state ... did not exist in ancient times." And A.D. Lindsay defined the state as "the organization of organizations." ("The State in Recent Political Theory," *Political Science Quarterly,* L, 1914, p. 128)

196. Leviathan, in the Bible, is one of the names of the primordial monster vanquished by God in the creation of the world (Psalm 74:14; Isaiah 27:1). It was used by Thomas Hobbes as the title of his famous work on political philosophy. The book appeared in 1651, shortly before the author's return to England from his voluntary exile in France during the English Civil War. In typical 17th century fashion, Hobbes starts his argument with the concept of the state of nature, in which the life of man is described as "solitary, poor, nasty, brutish, and short." The fear of death induces men to give up the state of nature by forming a sovereign government that makes and enforces the Law without challenge from any side. For practical reasons, Hobbes favors monarchy over aristocracy or democracy. Because Hobbes advocates a strong state, he opposes the division of authority between the various branches of the government. Moreover, he advises the sovereign not to allow the growth of groups and institutions that intervene between the state and the individual. While *Leviathan* favors the strong and even authoritarian state, however, it is not an intellectual forerunner of modern totalitarianism. (Cf. Leo Strauss, *The Political Philosophy of Hobbes: Its Basis and Its Genesis,* Chicago, 1952.)

197. "Heinrich von Treitschke, regarded the state as the basis of all national life. The state appears, he said, in the image of a person; history itself is simply a great drama in which the various states are actors. Just as the individual possesses the abstract thing we call character, so do the states have permanent characteristics. It is wrong to think of the state as an organism: it is rather a person with distinct characteristics. The most important possession of a state is power." (Louis L. Snyder, *The Meaning of Nationalism,* New Brunswick, N.J., 1954, p. 19)

198. Georg W.F. Hegel praised, with all the honorific phrases at his disposal, the omnipotent state, besides which the fate and happiness of the individual count for nothing. The state, to Hegel, is mind objectified. It is the Divine Idea as it exists on earth, "The March of God on earth," the idea of spirit in the external manifestations of human will and freedom. The individual mind is only partly free, because it is guided by its own passions, its prejudices, and its impulses; therefore, of necessity, it must subject itself to the state. To Hegel the mere survival of the state was a test of national righteousness. This view was more or less shared by Francis H. Bradley and Bernard Bosanquet. (Cf. Georg W.F. Hegel, *Philosophy of History,* (J. Sibree's translation), New York, 1944, Introduction III, especially p. 48-54; and Samuel W. Dyde, *Hegel's Philosophy of Right,* London, 1896, Third section of third part; also Bernard Bosanquet, *Philosophical Theory of the State,* London, 1930, p. 238-274.)

All these are but metaphysical, idealistic, or romantic views. They have tried to change the nature and position of the state from a servant to a master, from a superstructure to a foundation, from a human invention to a divine creation, from a means to an end, and from a product of historical development to an agent of natural growth. They stand in sharp contrast with the view that the state is but a political machinery of the independent groups,[201] and they always confuse the state with the nation.[202]

---

199. To Fascists, as Benito Mussolini stressed, the state is an end in itself, the purpose of society, the ultimate goal; individuals have to obey the state just because of what it is; the state may control every act and every interest of every individual or group, insofar as the good of the state requires it, and of this the state is itself the sole judge; there can be no individual outside the state, nor any group; and the state is an absolute, before which individuals and groups are relatively insignificant, and individuals and groups exist only insofar as they are within the state. "For Fascists," he said, "everything is in the state, nothing human or spiritual exists, and less anything of value exists outside the state. In this sense, Fascism is totalitarian, and the Fascist state, the synthesis and unity of all values, interprets, develops and lends potency to the whole life of the people." (Cf. Herman Finer, *Mussolini's Italy,* London, 1935, p. 201.)

200. The organic state idea is based on "The Social Organism" of Herbert Spencer who, almost simultaneously with the publication of the *Origin of Species,* by Charles R. Darwin, (November 1859) published in the *Westminster Review* (January 1860) a reverberating article entitled "The Social Organism." There he sets out "the resemblances between human societies and cellular organisms. Both of them, commencing as small aggregations, insensibly augment in mass: some of them eventually reaching ten thousand times what they originally were. While at first so simple in structure as to be considered structureless, both assume, in the course of their growth, a continually increasing complexity of structure. Though in their early, undeveloped states there exists in them scarcely any mutual dependence which becomes at last so great that the activity and life of each part is made possible only by the activity and life of the rest. The life of a society, as of an organism, is independent of the lives of any of its component units, who are severally born, grow, work, reproduce, and die, while the whole body survives, increasing in mass, in completeness of structure, and in functional activity." (Bertrand De Jouvenel, *On Power, Its Nature and the History of Its Growth,* trans. by J.F. Huntington, New York, 1949, p. 53-54)

The fundamental principle of the organic theory is that the state is actually and not metaphorically an individual person; and that, as such, it has the same unqualified control over its subordinate members as is allowed to reside in a biological organism. (Cf. Thomas D. Welden, *States and Morals,* London, 1947, p. 35-44, 68-88.)

201. The machine theory asserts that the state is not a natural growth, but an historical product, a human invention, and a mechanical device designed for doing a certain particular job. It is an instrument, nothing divine, and nothing organic. The identification of the state with a natural body is a fallacy, because it obviously differs from a natural body in many respects, as in lacking a sharp demarcation,

On the other hand, Marxists have not only distinguished the state from the nation,[203] but also denounced the state as merely an instrument of oppression of one class by another.[204] They hold that the state came into existence only after the division of society into

---

fixity, exclusiveness, specific unity and organic creation. As an instrument, the state is a means, not an end or a goal. It has no value in itself. Its value rests in those who use it, and the way it is used. Its existence depends on those who need it and is not eternal. Machine theorists also point out that the state is a superstructure, not a foundation, and not something coextensive with a society, but a special form of organization within it. Its distinguishing mark is simply the exercise of compulsory organizing power by a selected body of individuals. The state, therefore, is rather what we ordinarily call the government in the wide sense of the term. (Cf. Thomas D. Welden, *State and Morals,* London, 1947, p. 45-51; 98-142.)

202. "The state is therefore the living organism of a nation, its means of self-preservation, and the agency for realizing its ideal powers." (Adolf Hitler, *Mein Kampf,* p. 434)

"The Italian nation is an organism having ends, life, and means of action superior to those of the separate individuals or groups of individuals which compose it. It is a moral, political, and economic unity that is integrally realized in the fascist state." (Quoted in George H. Sabine, *A History of Political Theory,* New York, 1938, p. 765.)

"It is true that there is a slight, but not practically important, difference between the Italian and the German theories. Mussolini has said that the state creates the nation, since the right of a nation to independence arises from its will to political power and not its cultural unity, while Hitler and Rosenberg have said that the state is merely the organ or agent of the nation. The difference is perhaps due partly to the fact that Italy had less cultural unity than Germany, partly to the fact that Hitler wrote before he had become 'the state,' but most of all to the fact that Mussolini's policy looks toward a colonial empire while Hitler's looks toward an expanded but continuous German territory on the Continent. In either case the chief practical implications are the same. The state or the nation may in principle control every act and every interest of every individual or group, in so far as the good of the nation requires it, and of this the state is itself the sole judge." (George H. Sabine, *A History of Political Theory,* New York, 1938, p. 764)

203. In Marxist literature the distinction between the terms nation and state is always clear, and on many occasions these two terms are used in contrast with each other. In *The Civil War in France,* for example, Marx wrote: "The unity of the nation was not to be broken, but, on the contrary, to be organized by the Communal Constitution, and to become a reality by the destruction of the State (power) which claimed to be the embodiment of that unity independent of, and superior to, the nation itself, from which it was but a parasitic excrescence." (English translation, by E. Belfort Bax, Chicago, 1920, p. 45)

204. Marxists define the state as "a machine for controlling the oppressed and exploited class," or "an instrument of oppression of one class by another." They identify the state with "ruling class," or "special repressive force." They point out that in early times the state was the means of the slave owners for the purpose of holding the slaves in check, the feudal state was the organ of the nobility

classes[205] and that it will wither away when the proletariat revolution has put an end to class differences.[206]

The conception of the state as a class instrument stems from

---

for the oppression of the dependent farmers and serfs, and the modern representative state is the tool of the capitalist exploiters of wage labor. (Cf. V.I. Lenin, *State and Revolution,* Peking, 1965, p. 13-17, 26-33.)

A sociological writer, Franz Oppenheimer, holds a similar view. To him, the problem of the state is coterminous with that of caste. All the states known to history, he contends, are characterized by the domination of one class by another for the purpose of economic exploitation. (Cf. his *The State,* tr. by John Gitterman, New York, 1975.)

In addition, Marxists always link the state with armed men, bureaucratic officialdom, police, punitive organs, espionage agencies, etc.; and identify it with phrases such as, "public power," "political power," "a power apparently standing above the society," "a power increasingly alienating itself from the society," "an organ of class rule," and "an organ for the oppression of one class by another." (Cf. V.I. Lenin, *State and Revolution,* Peking, 1965, Chapter I; and "Some Questions of Theory," a passage in Stalin's *Report on the Work of the Central Committee to the 18th Congress of the Communist Party of the Soviet Union.)*

V.I. Lenin on a number of occasions identified the state with "bureaucracy and the standing army" and he proclaimed: "Bureaucracy and the standing army constitute a 'parasite'.... a parasite born of the internal antagonisms which tear the society asunder, but essentially a parasite 'clogging every pore' of existence." (Quoted in Emery Reves, *The Anatomy of Peace,* New York, 1946, p. 59.)

205. Marxists hold that the state did not exist from all eternity; there have been societies without it that had no idea of any state. At a certain stage of economic development, which was of necessity accompanied by a division of society into classes, the state became the inevitable result of this division. "It is the confession that this society has become hopelessly divided against itself, has entangled itself in irreconcilable contradictions, these classes with conflicting economic interests may not annihilate themselves and society in a useless struggle, a power becomes necessary that stands apparently above society and has the function of keeping down the conflicts and maintaining order." (Friedrich Engels, *Origin of the Family, Private Property and the State,* (Untermann's translation), Chicago, 1902, p. 206. Cf. V.I. Lenin, *The State and Revolution,* Peking, 1965, p. 5-9; and Thomas D. Welden, *State and Morals,* London, 1947, p. 110-121.)

206. Marxists predicate that after the proletariat revolution, which will eventually put an end to all class differences and class antagonisms, the state will become superfluous. "As soon as there is no longer any class of society to be held in subjection; as soon as, along with class domination and the struggle for individual existence based on the former anarchy of production, the collisions and excesses arising from these have also been abolished, there is nothing more to be repressed, and a special repressive force, a state, is no longer necessary." It then "becomes dormant" and "withers away." (Friedrich Engels, *Anti-Duhring,* English trans. by E. Burns, p. 314-315. Cf. V.I. Lenin, *The State and Revolution,* Peking, 1965, p. 17-25.) Lenin even so strongly indicated: "This proletarian state will begin to wither away immediately after its victory, because the state is un-

Marx's theory that all history is a history of class struggle.[207] Preoccupied with this theory, Marxists ignore completely the fact that the state is basically an instrument of independent groups for administering their public affairs.[208] They also overlook the fact that the state existed in some rudimentary forms long before class differences appeared,[209] and that it could be created under given conditions with-

_____

necessary and cannot exist in a society in which there are no class antagonisms." (*Ibid*, p. 33)

The vision of a Communist stateless society is simply as follows: After the proletarian revolution, the old bourgeois society will be replaced by "an association, in which the free development of each is the condition for the free development of all." (Last sentence of sect. II of the *Manifesto of the Communist Party*) The state will be replaced by a system "that is to reorganize production on the basis of a free and equal association of the producers." (Friedrich Engels, *Anti-Duhring,* English trans. by E. Burns, p. 211) "The government of persons will be replaced by an administration of things and a direction of the process of production." (Friedrich Engels, *op. cit.,* p. 315) "The whole of society will have become one office and one factory, with equal work and equal pay." "From this moment the need for any government begins to disappear. The more complete the democracy, the nearer the moment when it begins to be unnecessary." "The state will be able to wither away completely when society has realized the rule: From each according to his ability; to each according to his needs. i.e., when people have become accustomed to observe the fundamental rules of social life, and their labor is so productive, that they voluntarily work according to their ability." (Lenin, *State and Revolution*) In talking about the role of state power in Communist society, Lenin was to repeat that it "can be reduced to such simple operations of registration, filing and checking that they will be quite within the reach of every literate person, and it will be possible to perform them for 'workingman's wages,' which circumstance can (and must) strip those functions of every shadow of privilege, of every appearance of 'official grandeur.' " (Quoted in Emery Reves, *The Anatomy of Peace,* New York, 1946, p. 60.)

207. This well-known sentence in section 1 of the *Manifesto of the Communist Party,* first issued in 1847, was later modified as "The history of all hitherto existing society is the history of class struggles." It was expounded by Karl Marx in his work *Class Struggle,* first published in 1851. The theory of class struggle has made it necessary for Marx and his fellows to attack the state by all means, because the power of the state has generally been held by the oppressing class.

208. It is known that from very early times mankind has lived in a group life; that no group life, no matter how simple it might be, has been without a certain instrument to take care of its public affairs, especially external conflicts; and that no public instrument could work smoothly without a certain authority. The native Australians live in a Stone Age culture and depend on food-gathering and elementary hunting. Yet, each group has a council of older men which exercises authority over matters of common interests. (Cf. *American Anthropologist,* Vol. 31, 1928, p. 614-631.)

209. Of Indian society, "How Wonderful this gentile constitution is in all its natural simplicity!" Engels admired. He noted, however, "the gens had a council,

out class antagonism.[210] Further, it is undeniable that the state, instead of withering away, has become stronger than ever since the victory of the proletariat revolution in Russia and elsewhere,[211] and formal state relations have been maintained between Communist countries just like those between capitalist countries.[212]

---

the democratic assembly of all male and female gentiles of adult age, all with equal suffrage. This council elected and deposed its sachems and chiefs; likewise the other 'Keepers of the Faith.' It deliberated on gifts of atonement or blood revenge for murdered gentiles and it adopted strangers into the gens. In short, it was the sovereign power in the gens.'' The Indian gentile council, sachems, chiefs and others, no matter how simple or democratic their constitution is, and no matter how much power they possess, have formed a primitive state. Such a primitive state could in no way be regarded as a class machine, because the division of society into classes has not, according to Engels himself, taken place. At that economic stage, the state is a group instrument. (Cf. Friedrich Engels, *Origin of the Family, Private Property, and the State,* Untermann's translation, Chicago, 1902, p. 107, 117.)

210. A modern example is the Plymouth case. Among the poor Pilgrims who had been living self-exiled in Holland for some years, there existed no economic classes; and, therefore, no organ was needed for keeping class conflicts down. Yet they drew up a compact to establish a public power when they were still aboard the *Mayflower* on the way to an uncertain destination. The same was to occur in many other colonies in the first period of American history, and all the public powers set up by the economically classless colonial people in that period were evidently a primitive form of state which gradually developed to its maturity in the later times. (For the Plymouth case, cf. George C. Blaxland, Mayflower *Essays on the Story of the Pilgrim Fathers as Told in Governor Bradford's Ms.,* Freeport, N.Y., 1972.)

211. Lenin once remarked that through all the innumerable revolutions which have taken place in Europe since the end of the feudal system, this bureaucratic and military machine has developed, improved, and strengthened. "All the revolutions which have occurred up to now perfected the state machine, whereas it must be broken, smashed.'' (In his *State and Revolution,* Peking, 1965, p. 33. Cf. p. 31-33.) Unfortunately, he would find, could he return to Leningrad thirty years later, that his revolution has done even more than past ones did in developing the state instead of diminishing it. It is not because his revolution has been betrayed and a class machine is still needed as a special repressive force, but because the nature of the state as an instrument of the nation remains unchanged.

212. They recognize each other as sovereign states. They maintain formal intercourse with each other through foreign offices and diplomatic delegations. They bind mutual obligations with each other by treaties and agreements. They develop trade and credits with each other to link separate economies and finances. They contract alliances with each other to strengthen military and political positions, and these alliances may extend as long as thirty years, as exemplified by the first Russian-Chinese Pact of Friendship, Alliance, and Mutual Assistance. It was signed February 14, 1950, in Moscow, and is a 30-year treaty, renewable automatically at 5-year intervals after the first 30 years, unless renounced by either party. Although this treaty was revoked in 1980, it serves as an example to show

As a political machinery, the state has appeared in various forms under various conditions since early times.[213] However, no matter in what forms and under what conditions, it is necessary for it to have people to man its structure, perform its functions and exercise its power. The number of these people was very small in the beginning,[214] but has increased remarkably through the ages into what is more or less a ruling class. That they have often abused their public authority and exploited it for their private interests[215] is a fact which gives some credence to the conception of state as a class instrument. In spite of this, the state has survived through a long history with the allegiance of a vast multitude, because it has never completely abandoned its major role as an instrument of independent groups.[216]

---

how the Communist countries have tried to maintain their formal relations as state to state, and have not tried in any way to let their states wither away.

213. Paul Radin studied seven early forms of state in his *Social Anthropology,* New York, 1932, p. 30-94: simple democratic community, the Arunta; simple family community, the Vedas; democratic federated community, the Iroquois; organized democratic community, the Winnebago; the caste system, the Maori; monarchical community, the Baganda; and monarchical theocratic community, the Inca. He pointed out that "From the study of these types it will become apparent that the highly delicate task of organizing a state and adjusting the relations of the individual to the group has been fairly successfully solved innumerable times and in innumerable and diverse ways." (p. 29)

214. "We have just seen how the introduction of domesticated animals and agricultural plants must have influenced the communal habits of primitive man in the direction of the establishment of local government. There are reasons to believe that, prior to taking these steps, the most advanced form of human settlement was the tribe or clan consisting of the members of a single family. The unit of this settlement was the single family itself with a man at its head, who was at once provider, protector, and master. As the various members of a family held together in obedience to the gregarious instinct, which man shares with the greater number of animals, it was natural that some one member of the clan should be looked to as the leader of the whole. In the ordinary course of events, such leader would be the oldest man, the founder of the original family; but there must have been a constant tendency for younger men of pronounced ability to aspire to the leadership, and to wrest from the patriarch his right of master." (*The Historians' History of the World,* by the History Association, London, 1907, Vol. 1, p. 49)

215. "For every government is composed of fallible men. They may deliberately exploit the authority they possess for their own selfish purposes. They may, with the best intentions, but quite unreasonably, mistake the private interest of a few for the well-being of the whole community.' (Harold J. Laski, *The State in Theory and Practice,* New York, 1935, p. 12)

216. From the very beginning, the state has been a group instrument, although its power has subsequently been possessed by a small number of people. No doubt, this small number of people always use the state power for their own selfish purposes, and a complete subordination of their particular interest to the

As an instrument of independent groups, the state is not a divine idea, as praised by the Hegelians, nor an evil device, as denounced by the Communists, but a necessary political machinery.[217] It has no independent value and no separate existence. This is exactly a profile of the nation-state of today. In other words, the modern state is a necessary political machinery of the nation, its value rests in the nation, and its existence depends on the nation; and for these reasons, it is not practical to judge its merits separately.

It is necessary to point out, however, that although it is just a necessary political machinery, the nation-state has legitimately been in a position to exercise the sovereign power of the nation and to represent the independence of the nation; and under the compulsion of nationalism, it has frequently developed into a totalitarianism at the expense of individual rights,[218] and has sometimes indeed ap-

---

general interest is nowhere to be found. But a ruling class pursuing its particular interest to the complete exclusion of the general interest is not found in any actual state either. Furthermore, the theory of the state as a class instrument cannot quite rightly explain the striking phenomenon, a matter of history, of a vast multitude giving allegiance to a comparatively small number of people, if the state is only an instrument of oppression of one class by another. (Cf. Thomas D. Welden, *State and Morals,* London, 1947, p. 52-61, 279-286; and H.R.G. Greaves, *The Foundations of Political Theory,* New York, 1967, p. 42-92.)

"Power took shape and root in habits and beliefs, but it developed its apparatus and multiplied its instruments through knowing how to turn the circumstances of the time to its advantage. But it could only so turn them by serving society. Its pursuit of its own authority never ceases, but the road to authority is through the services which it renders." (Bertrand de Jouvenel, *On Power, its Nature and the History of its Growth,* trans. by J.F. Huntington, New York, 1949, p. 105)

217. Harold J. Laski: "That the State is, in some form or another, an inevitable organisation will be apparent to anyone who examines the human nature that we encounter in daily life. But to admit that it is inevitable is not to admit that it is entitled to moral pre-eminence of any kind. For, after all, the State is not itself an end, but merely the means to an end, which is realised only in the enrichment of human lives. It's power and the allegiance it can win depend always upon what it achieves for that enrichment. We are, that is to say, subjects of the State, not for its purpose, but for our own. Realisable good means always some happiness won for the lives of persons, or it means nothing. Power, therefore, must seek the widest possible distribution of such happiness. We are entitled to suspect the State save as we see under its aegis the unfettered growth of human personality. We are entitled to condemn it save as its powers are used deliberately to defeat the forces which stand in the way of that growth." (Quoted in *Harold Laski,* by Granville Eastwood, London, 1977, p. 103)

218. As an instrument of the nation, it is of necessity that the state becomes more important during the time when the conflicts between nations are getting more and more furious. Every nation needs an effective instrument for dealing

peared as a kind of Leviathan. Anarchist attempts to get rid of it have proved to be futile,[219] and evidently it will not wither away until the day when there is no nationalism to compel it, no national sovereignty for it to exercise, and no national independence for it to represent.

g.
National Sovereignty

THE NOTION OF SOVEREIGNTY HAS DEVELOPED FROM very early times[220] to indicate the supreme power exercised by the dei-

---

with others, and improves it, by all means. That is why the rise of nationalism and the prevailing theory of national sovereignty in modern times have resulted in a great development in the power and form of the state. This development is always at the expense of individual rights; the greater this development, the less are individual rights. At last, the state becomes all-important, the people are confronted with a new terrible tyrant, and all become slaves. Nazi Germany, Fascist Italy, Stalin's Russia, Francisco Franco's Spain, Antonio de Oliveria Salazar's Portugal, and Juan Domingo Peron's Argentina are notorious examples of this kind of authoritarian state. (Cf. Carl J. Friedrich and Zbigniew K. Brzezinski, *Totalitarian Dictatorship and Autocracy,* 2nd ed., Cambridge, Mass., 1965, p. 3-30; and Anthony J. Joes, *Fascism in the Contemporary World: Ideology, Evolution, Resurgence,* Boulder, Colorado, 1978.)

219. Anarchists look upon all law and government as invasive, the twin sources of nearly all social evils, and, therefore, advocate the abolition of the state. They believe that everything now done by the state can be done better by voluntary cooperative effort. "Governments are the scourge of God," said Pierre Joseph Proudhon (1809-1865), the Frenchman with whom the philosophy of modern anarchism may be said to have begun. Germs of his doctrine may be traced even to ancient times. Among his modern precursors were William Godwin (1756-1836) in England; Benjamin R. Tucker (1854-1939) in the United States; Moses Hess (1812-1875) in Germany, and Mikhail Bakunin (1814-1876) in Russia. Anarchism in the hands of Bakunin underwent a change from the advocacy of a purely peaceful revolution to the "Propaganda by action." He was prominent in the Paris Revolution of 1848. His principal work is *God and the State,* in which the overthrow of the state is implicated. Incidents attributed to anarchists include the attempted assassination of German Emperor William I in 1878; the attempts on the life of the German princes in 1883; the assassinations of president Sadi Carnot of France in 1894; of the Empress Elizabeth of Austria in 1898; of King Humbert I of Italy in 1900; and of U.S. President McKinley in 1901. In the Haymarket tragedy of 1886 in Chicago, a number of persons lost their lives in a bomb explo-

ty, secular ruler, ruling body, or ruling class. Plato linked it with the law,[221] and Aristotle discussed its place in the state.[222] Its earliest modern exponent was Jean Bodin[223] and it was Thomas Hobbes who started to assume a social contract as its origin.[224]

In order to unite their nation through a strong central authori-

---

sion, and seven anarchists were subsequently sentenced to die on the gallows. (Cf. Paul Eltzbacher, *Anarchism,* rev. ed., New York, 1960; and Louis Adamic, *Dynamite: The Story of Class Violence in America,* rev. ed., New York, 1934.)

220. "Concentration of power probably began among those peoples who developed the totemic system. At first the concentration of authority was religious in nature and consisted in regarding the totem itself as the source and center of all power. Later the clan chief or the tribal chief was regarded as the representative and the embodiment of the totem, and hence was considered to rule by a sort of divine right. It would certainly appear as if this were the origin of the kingly powers in the early Egyptian and Near Eastern Kingdom and also in the Empires of the new World." (William M. McGovern, "The Growth of Institutions," in *Making Mankind,* New York, 1929, p. 98-99)

221. When Plato speaks of the sovereignty of the laws (*Laws,* 4. 715; *Politics,* 4. 4; 3. 15), he remarks: "I see that the State in which the law is above the rulers, and the rulers are the inferiors of the law, has salvation."

222. Aristotle in his *Politics* discusses the question of what is the supreme power in the State (3. 10), which he defines as an aggregate of citizens (3.i.), and he recognizes that it may be lodged in one, a few, or many. In his view the distinctive mark of the State is not so much sovereignty (7. 4) as self-sufficiency; a State is not a mere aggregate of persons; it is a union of them sufficient for the purposes of life (7. 8).

223. Bodin held that the essence of nationality is the unity of its government; that a confusion of uncoordinated independent authorities must be fatal to a nation; and that there must be one final source and not more than one from which its laws proceed. This source he called summa potestas, or sovereignty. The essential manifestation of sovereignty, he thought, is the power to make the laws, and since the sovereign makes the laws, he clearly cannot be bound by the laws that he makes. Although Bodin intended his sovereign to be a supra-legal power, he maintained that it is not a power without any limit; there are some laws that do bind him: the divine law, the law of nature or reason, and the fundamental laws of the nation, which the sovereign does not make and cannot abrogate and which determine in whom the sovereign power itself is to be vested and the limits within which it is to be exercised. (Cf. Jean Bodin, *Six Books of the Commonwealth,* by M.J. Tooley, Oxford, (Original first published in 1576), Book 1, Chap. 8.)

224. Hobbes in his famous work *Leviathan* (1651) held that the original state of man was that of a solitary being existing in a constant state of warfare and anarchy governed by self-interest. In order to secure order, men entered into an agreement with one another that resulted in the creation of the state. In return for the surrender of all individual rights, the state provided security, order and peace and demanded absolute obedience. Thus, the agreement is the origin of the sovereignty. Hobbes' idea of a social contract as the origin of sovereignty was soon developed by John Locke, Jean-Jacques Rousseau, and others in different ways. (Cf. Thomas Hobbes, *Leviathan,* Chaps. 13-14, 18; and Westel W. Willoughby,

ty,[225] both Bodin and Hobbes allocated sovereignty to the monarch. Consequently, their theories merely served as a pretext for the rise of despotism.[226]

Then the theory appeared that the people as a whole were the sovereign, and, therefore, the sovereignty resided in the nation. This was the main theme of the American and French Revolutions.[227] Since the sovereignty belonged to the nation, it was not only unlimit-

---

An Examination of the Nature of State, a Study of Political Philosophy, New York, 1928, p. 64-88.)

225. As late as the 18th century, diverse local forces were widely existent even in Western Europe. In France, for example, the sharp cleavage between social classes and the traditional loyalty of the masses to locality or province militated against national solidarity; and the Bourbon kings continued to address their subjects not as the "French" people, but as the peoples of Languedoc, Gascony, Burgundy, Picardy and other regions which had been acquired by earlier French monarchs. Devotion to dynasty still seemed to outweigh devotion to nationality and *pays* to be more fundamental than *patrie*. In Germany, the intellectuals, equally with the nobles and the peasants, seemed quite content to leave the fatherland parceled out among some three hundred separate and practically independent states. Very few Germans then talked about the desirability, much less the possibility, of unifying the hodgepodge of German kingdoms, duchies, counties and free cities into a compact nation and inculcating in all its inhabitants a new national loyalty which would transcend their traditional local loyalties. (Cf. Friedrich O. Hertz, *Nationality in History and Politics,* New York, 1944, p. 165-170.)

226. It is evident that both Bodin and Hobbes were making an effort to unite their nation by presenting sovereign theory. They did not express, however, the fact that sovereignty resided in the nation. They asserted that sovereignty should reside in a person or monarch. But when the battle for sovereign monarchy had been won, people began to realize that the danger had now reversed itself. The sovereign monarchy had become too powerful. The sovereign had come to be regarded as a separate and distinct entity, having an end of his own—his own well-being, to which everything else in the nation could and should be subordinated. (Cf. F.H. Hinsley, *Sovereignty,* New York, 1966, p. 120-125, 144-157; Paul W. Ward, *Sovereignty—a Study of a Contemporary Political Notion,* London, 1928, p. 21-28; A.H. Johnson, *The Age of the Enlightened Despot, 1660-1789,* 18th ed., London, 1944; and Max Beloff, *The Age of Absolutism, 1660-1815,* New York, 1962.)

227. "Between the Renaissance and the eighteenth century, as a result of the revival of learning and new methods of rational and scientific thinking, a revolutionary social ideal took shape and found fertile soil among the masses suffering under absolutism. This revolutionary ideal was the principle that no individual, no family, no dynasty, could any longer be regarded as sovereign, that the sovereign lawgiving authority was the people and that 'sovereignty resides in the community.' This revolutionary principle led to the great popular uprisings of the eighteenth century, to the establishment of the American and French republics, and to the 'king reigns but does not rule' parliamentary system in England and many other countries." (Emery Reves, *The Anatomy of Peace,* New York, 1946, p. 130)

With the coming of constitutional government, John Locke in his *Two*

ed as Hobbes held,[228] but also inalienable and indivisible as Rousseau asserted.[229] The theory of national sovereignty thus reached its maturity, and was soon adopted in international relations.[230]

Associated with the development of nationalism, the effect of such adoption was enormous. Sovereignty immediately emerged as a symbol of national independence,[231] and changed its nature from an

---

Treatises on Civil Government (1690) and Jean Jacques Rousseau in his *Social Contract* (1762) propounded the theory that the people as a whole were the sovereign, and therefore, the sovereignty resided in the nation. The Declaration of Independence of the United States asserted this theory when it declared that "governments derive their just powers from the consent of the governed." The same principle was advanced by the French Revolution. "Sachez que vous êtes rois et plus des rois," said a revolutionary orator cited in the *Encyclopedia Britannica,* 1956 ed., Vol. 21, p. 100, under "Sovereignty."

228. Thomas Hobbes in his *Leviathan* held that law neither makes the sovereign, nor limits his authority; it is might that makes the sovereign, and law is merely what he commands. Moreover, since the power that is the strongest clearly cannot be limited by anything outside itself, it follows that sovereignty must be absolute and illimitable; "it appeareth plainly that the sovereign power . . . is as great as possibly men can be imagined to make it." (*Leviathan,* chap. 20) He also held that sovereignty is indivisible and set forth the reason with 12 explanations. (*Leviathan,* chap. 18)

229. "The first and most important deduction from the principles we have so far laid down is that the general will alone can direct the State according to the object for which it was instituted, i.e. the common good: for if the clashing of particular interests made the establishment of societies necessary, the agreement of these very interests is what forms the social tie; and were there no point of agreement between them all, no society could exist. It is solely on the basis of this common interest that every society should be governed. I hold then that Sovereignty, being nothing less than the exercise of the general will, can never be alienated. . . . Sovereignty, for the same reason as makes it inalienable, is indivisible. . . ." (Jean Jacques Rousseau, *The Social Contract,* trans. by G.D.H. Cole, Book II, chaps. 1 and 2)

230. It was the historical development of Europe in the 18th century into a system of independent but interlocked nations which had "given rise to the well-known principle of the balance of power, by which is meant an arrangement of affairs so that no nation shall be in a position to have absolute mastery and dominate over others," that set the ground for the reception of the sovereignty of the nation as the basis of international affairs. (Cf. F.H. Hinsley, *Sovereignty,* New York, 1966, p. 195-208.)

231. Among other meanings, sovereignty denotes "the independent legal or moral status of a community" and "in international law and international politics it is used to denote the independence or autonomy of a state in relation to other states." (G. Marshall, "Sovereignty," in *A Dictionary of the Social Sciences,* ed. by Julius Gould and William L. Kolb, New York, 1964, p. 686)

"Sovereignty in the relations between states signifies independence. Independence in regard to a portion of the globe is the right to exercise therein to the exclusion of any other state the functions of a state." (Permanent Court of Ar-

original principle of internal unity and order to a new doctrine of international separation and anarchy.[232] The main reason for this drastic change is that the nation was the broadest imaginable basis of sovereignty in the 18th century, when the stagecoach was the fastest means of transportation, whereas today, when we can fly around the world in a few hours, it has become two narrow.[233]

When the aftermath of the theory of national sovereignty adapted to international relations became obvious to all, many writers began to evade or circumvent it. Georg Jellinek stressed its auto-limitation.[234] Leon Duguit denied its necessity,[235] and the political pluralists criticized its reality.[236]

---

bitration (1928). *Reports of International Arbitral Awards,* vol. 2, p. 829. Cf. Robert Lansing, *Notes on Sovereignty,* Washington, 1921, p. 37-38.)

232. Since the sovereign power is unlimited, inalienable, and indivisible, once it is applied to the relations between nations, every nation then claims the power to judge its own controversies, to enforce its own conception of its rights, to increase its armaments without limit, to treat its own nationals as it sees fit, and to regulate its economic life without regard to the effect of such regulations upon its neighbors. Consequently, nothing could rule international relations but power, and nothing could settle international conflicts but war. In the form in which Jean Bodin, the earliest exponent, propounded the theory of sovereignty, it raised no special problem for international relations. Sovereignty for him was an essential principle of internal political order, and he would certainly have been surprised if he could have forseen that later writers would distort it into a principle of international anarchy, and use it to prove that the nation is above all, and to keep the peoples of the world separate. (Cf. F.H. Hinsley, *Sovereignty,* New York, 1966, p. 208-213; and Harold J. Laski, *Nationalism and the Future of Civilization,* London, 1932, p. 26-29.)

233. "We must not forget the atmosphere, not merely in which the theory of sovereignty was born, but also in which, at the hands of each of its great exponents, it has secured new emphasis. That has been always, from Bodin to Hegel, a period of crisis in which the state seemed likely to perish unless it could secure the unified allegiance of its members." (Harold J. Laski, *A Grammar of Politics,* London, 1925, p. 46. Cf. p. 45-48)

234. Georg Jellinek and some other German writers have elaborately deduced the doctrine of the auto-limitation of sovereignty inherited from Hegel. They maintain that no one can limit sovereignty but itself, and that it can free itself from any existent limitation, although never from all limitation. They attempt to transfer the philosophy of ethical self-obligation to the realm of jurisprudence. Most of these writers admit, however, that a self-imposed limitation is no limitation at all. This doctrine offers little in regard to actual situations, both internal and international, created by unlimited national sovereignty. (Cf. Hymen E. Cohen, *Recent Theories of Sovereignty,* Chicago, 1937, chap. III; Arthur Nussbaum, *A Concise History of the Law of Nations,* New York, 1947, p. 281.)

235. The school of sociological jurisprudence, of which the outstanding representative is Leon Duguit, denies the very necessity of the concept of

Harold J. Laski, the great leader of the political pluralists, furthered his arguments against national sovereignty with common sense[237] and emphasized that it was incompatible with the interest of humanity and allegiance to the world.[238] His view has not only influenced many scholars, it has also been more or less shared by some statesmen[239] and even military leaders;[240] and some nations have in-

---

sovereignty. Writers of this school stress that a legal theory has reality only insofar as it can establish and sanction rules that assure the satisfaction of human needs in a given society at a definite moment in time. Moreover, it is itself the outgrowth of these needs. If it does not spring out of needs, or if it does not guarantee their satisfaction, it is the artificial product of a jurist and is without force or value. (Cf. Paul W. Ward, *Sovereignty, a Study of a Contemporary Political Notion,* London, 1928, p. 126-134.)

236. The pluralists in the political philosophy of constitutional government have always been impatient with severe theory and feel that all rigid and simple doctrines in political science belie the rich complexity of life. They point out that unlimited power is nowhere existent and that there are a thousand varying influences which go to shape the nature of the sovereign will. (Cf. Harold J. Laski, *A Grammar of Politics,* New Haven, 1925, p. 56, and Paul W. Ward, *Sovereignty, a Study of a Contemporary Political Notion,* London, 1928, p. 82-110.)

237. Laski pointed out that it is impossible to allow any nation, in the sphere of international facts, to decide in an absolute fashion upon the way in which it should live. There are problems of which the impact upon humanity is too vital for any nation to be left to determine by itself what solution it will adopt. Once we realize that the well-being of the world is, in all large issues, one and indivisible, the cooperative solution of problems is indispensable. (Cf. Harold J. Laski, *A Grammar of Politics,* New Haven, 1925, p. 44-45, 64-66, 683.)

238. In a creative civilization, Laski asserted what is important is not the historical accident of separate nations, but the scientific fact of world-interdependence. The real unit of allegiance is the world. The real obligation of obedience is to the total interest of humanity. Surely the concept of an absolute and independent national sovereignty, which demands an unqualified allegiance to government from its members, and enforces that allegiance by the power at its command, is incompatible with the interest of humanity and allegiance to the world. (Cf. Harold J. Laski, *A Grammar of Politics,* New Haven, 1925, p. 44-45, 64-66, 683.)

239. For example, in a speech during debate in the British House of Commons on November 22, 1945, Mr. Anthony Eden stated that in connection with the invention of the atomic bomb, he saw no other way of protecting the world than a rejection of the present concept of sovereignty to "remove nationalism's sting." In the Foreign Minister, Mr. Ernest Bevin's, opinion, in his speech for the establishment of a world assembly elected directly by the people of the whole world, international law would disappear, to be replaced by world law; and in place of the sovereignty of the separate nations there would be the sovereignty of mankind as a whole. (Cf. *American Journal of International Law,* Vol. 40, 1946, p. 747.)

240. "Even military leaders, the last people one would expect to encourage federation, have spoken out. General Omar N. Bradley told a Chicago audience in the spring of 1950 that 'national pride and sovereignty are paid for with life and

dicated in their constitutions a consent to the limitation of national sovereignty.[241]

The attitude of the socialists toward the concept of national sovereignty, which is obviously irreconcilable with the professed international character of Marxism, has had ironic consequences. It is the Soviet Union which first set the example of using it as an armor against capitalist encirclement and imperialist encroachment,[242] and the other socialist nations followed suit. But they soon found that it was an armor which could be used not only against the aggression of bourgeois forces, but also against the domination of the Soviet Union. They have used it against each other as well.[243] Consequently,

---

blood' and warned that some sovereignty would have to be yielded to preserve our freedom." (Alfred M. Lilienthal, *Which Way to World Government? Headline Series,* no. 83, New York, 1950, p. 59)

241. For example, Article 24 of the 1949 constitution of the Federal Republic of Germany (West Germany) provides that "The Federation may by legislation transfer its sovereign power to international institutions." The 1946 constitution of the French Republic and the 1948 constitution of the Italian Republic also indicate consent to the limitations of sovereignty necessary for the organization of peace. (Cf. Edward H. Litchfield, *Governing Postwar Germany,* Ithaca, N.Y., 1953, p. 184-203; and Edith Wynner and Georgia Lloyd, *Searchlight on Peace Plans,* New York, 1949, p. 411, 412.)

242. "The Soviet Union is destined to act as the champion of the doctrine of 'classical' sovereignty in so far as its formal seclusion acts as a legal armour protecting it from interference of those factors under the pressure of which the frontiers of contemporary capitalist states are changed and the forms of their law altered. So long as beyond the frontiers of the Soviet Union there is only the ring of bourgeois encirclement, every limitation of sovereignty on behalf of it would be a greater or lesser victory of the capitalist world over the socialist order." (Statement by Mr. Korovin, an outstanding Soviet jurist, quoted in the *American Journal of International Law,* Vol. 43, 1949, p. 31)

Latterly, V.S. Shevtsor defended national sovereignty as a principle of international cooperation of Communism. It is virtually a reversion to the classical view on national sovereignty in respect to international relations. (Cf. his *National Sovereignty and the Soviet State,* Moscow, 1974.)

"Sovereignty, as conceived by Soviets, is a weapon in the struggle of the progressive-democratic forces against the reactionary-imperialistic ones. Under contemporary conditions sovereignty is destined to act as a legal barrier protecting against imperialistic encroachment and securing the existence of the most advanced social and state forms—socialist and those of a people's democracy; it is a guarantee of the liberation of the oppressed peoples in colonies and dependent territories from the imperialistic yoke." (This explicit explanation was made by *Pravda* on May 3, 1947.)

243. For instance, the Central Committee of the Rumanian Communist Party resolved in 1964 that the sovereignty of the socialist state requires that it effectively and fully hold in its hands all the levers of economic and social life; that

national sovereignty has played a great role in breaking up their ideology of class solidarity and tearing their international movement apart.[244]

So, viewing international relations in general and in the socialist international movement particularly, national sovereignty has clearly been an ill omen rather than a noble emblem.[245] Under either guise, it has served mankind badly.

---

transmitting such levers to the competence of a superstate or extra-state bodies would make sovereignty an idea without content; that there is not and cannot be a pattern or recipe applicable to every country's situation, and that no one can decide what is and what is not correct for other countries or parties. (Cf. John M. Montias, "Background and Origins of the Rumanian Dispute with Comecon," in *Soviet Studies 16,* p. 125-151.)

On July 6, 1971, the Communist Party of the Soviet Union and the Communist Party of France issued a joint statement, which said that the Communists believed it to be their duty to respect and consistently observe such principles as independence, sovereignty, equality and non-interference in internal affairs, because these principles, together with solidarity and mutual assistance, are the organic components of proletarian internationalism. (Cf. *Pravda,* July 6, 1971.)

And a decision made by the Summit Conference of European Communist and Workers Parties, held in East Berlin on June 29-30, 1976, asserted the principle of sovereignty as follows: (Communist parties) will develop their internationalist comradely and voluntary cooperation and solidarity on the basis of the great ideas of Marx, Engels and Lenin, strictly adhering to the principles of equality and sovereign independence for each party, non-interference in internal affairs, and respect for their free choice of different roads in the struggle for social change of a progressive nature and for socialism. (Cf. *World Marxist Review—Information Bulletin,* Vol. 14, no. 12, p. 5-44.)

244. "Thus in 1977 the words 'world communist movement' were bound to cover at least three political phenomena: The Soviet state and the communist parties outside Russia that proclaimed their devotion to Soviet policy; the Chinese state and the communist parties outside China that looked to the theory and practice of Mao Tse-tung as their model; and a miscellaneous collection of Trotskyist and other heretical groups professing themselves to be Marxist-Leninists. To these might possibly be added the Vietnamese state and groups outside Vietnam that took it as their model; and conceivably the same might be said of North Korea." (Hugh Seton-Watson, *The Imperialist Revolutionaries, Trends in World Communism in the 1960s and 1970s,* Stanford, Calif., 1978, p. 4. Cf. Richard Lowenthal, "The Prospects for Pluralistic Communism," in *Marxism in the Modern World,* ed. by Milorad M. Drachkovitch, Stanford, Calif., 1965, p. 225-271.)

245. "The evils we have just considered are directly due to the institution of sovereignty, and can only be finally remedied by the creation of a genuine international authority. Whatever may have been its utility in the past, the sovereign State has now become an unmitigated nuisance, wasting our lives and frustrating our hopes. While it continues to exist and make its preposterous claims, mankind has no hope of a peaceful or even a tolerable existence." (William B. Curry, *The Case for Federal Union,* Harmondsworth, Eng., 1939, p. 62)

As a symbol of independence, national sovereignty resembles ancient totemism.[246] But totemism to primitive people was much more powerful than national sovereignty is to modern man, because the totem was something embodied, a deity of religion and an origin of blood relationship,[247] whereas national sovereignty is merely an abstract hypothesis.

Yet, although national sovereignty is merely an abstract hypothesis, it can curse our world to blow up.[248]

---

246. Sir James G. Frazer developed three variant theories of the origin of totemism. One, totems are the repository of external souls that are reincarnated in people. Two, totems have a religious-economic base in magical techniques used to ensure the food supply. Three, totems might be used to explain the origin of human life. In general, totemism expressed ritually man's relation to the world of animals and plants around him. (Cf. his *Totemism and Exogamy,* London, 1910, V. 1; and Emile Durkheim, *Elementary Forms of Religious Life,* trans. by Joseph W. Swain, first paperback, 1965, p. 155-208.)

247. The totem itself is a being, animate or inanimate, most commonly an animal or a plant, from which the group is held to be descended and which serves at once as emblem and collective name. If the totem is a wolf, all the members of the clan believe that they have a wolf for ancestor and consequently they have something of the wolf within them. That is why they apply to themselves this denomination: they are Wolves. (Cf. Emile Durkheim, *Elementary Forms of Religious Life,* trans. by Joseph W. Swain, New York, 1915, first paperback, 1965, Book 2, I, p. 121-149.)

248. "Genius at Work" under the auspices of national sovereignty:

Alexander in the *Philadelphia Bulletin*

Also dangerous is national self-determination, which is the shadow of national sovereignty, and is actually an anachronism.[249]

It is necessary to stress, however, that national sovereignty is just a symbol of the independence of the nation. The independence of the nation is the substance. It is a substance customarily deemed so important that even its echo—national liberation[250]—has a terrific emotional appeal.[251]

Needless to say, all evils inherent either in the symbol and its shadow, or in the echo, are attributable to the substance.

Finally, in connection with the state and sovereignty, a note has to be made about "empire," which has appeared and perished here

---

249. "Self-determination is an anachronism. It asserts the sacred right of every nation to do as it pleases within its own frontiers, no matter how monstrous or how harmful to the rest of the world. It asserts that every aggregation of peoples has a sacred right to split itself into smaller and ever smaller units, each sovereign in its own corner. It assumes that the extension of economic or political influence through ever-larger units along centralized interdependent lines is, in itself, unjust." (Emery Reves, *The Anatomy of Peace,* New York, 1946, p. 192)

250. "National liberation" is generally advocated by the international socialist movement as a strategy against imperialism. But in their literature, they tend to mix this term with "national self-determination." For example: "The recognition of the right of all nations, irrespective of race, to complete self-determination, that is, self-determination inclusive of the right to state separation. The voluntary unification and centralization of the military and economic forces of all nations liberated from capitalism—for the purpose of fighting against imperialism and for building up socialist economy. Wide and determined struggle against the imposition of any kind of limitation and restriction upon any nationality, nation or race. Complete equality for all nations and races. . . . Every assistance to be rendered to the economic, political and cultural growth of the formerly oppressed 'territories,' 'dominions' and 'colonies,' with the object of transferring them to socialist lines, so that a durable basis may be laid for complete national equality." (Chapter four, section 3, F of the *Program of the Communist International,* adopted by its Sixth World Congress, Sept. 1, 1928)

251. "National liberation" has a terrific emotional appeal. It can be used and is being used by more and more politicians, writers, agitators, in slogans calling for the "end of imperialism," the "abolition of the colonial system," "independence" for this and that racial or territorial group. But "the present world chaos did not come upon us because this or that nation had not yet achieved total political independence. It will not be relieved in the slightest by creating more sovereign units or by dismembering interdependent aggregations like the British Empire that have shown a capacity for economic and political advancement. On the contrary, the disease now ravaging our globe would be intensified, since it is in large measure the direct result of the myth of total political independence in a world of total economic and social interdependence." (Emery Reves, *The Anatomy of Peace,* New York, 1946, p. 193)

and there as a giant political machinery since ancient times.[252] The salient feature of "empire" is that it exercises a sovereign power, not only over its own people, like the state, but also over other people.[253] This feature also distinguishes it from imperialism, which extends domination, hegemony or influence over other people, but does not necessarily take over their sovereign power.[254]

Basically, however, the policy of empire, which is to control other people, is not much different from the practice of imperialism; the nature of empire as a group instrument is the same as that of the nation-state; and the sovereign power the empire exercises over other people has an effect similar to that which national sovereignty has over its own people. Therefore, a separate treatment of empire is not needed at this point, since national sovereignty, the nation-state and imperialism have already been appropriately discussed.

h.
Evaluation

IT IS NECESSARY TO NOTE THAT THE IMPORTANCE OF national independence and sovereignty stems from the assumption

---

252. There were clannish or tribal empires, such as the empires of Sumer, Babylonia, Egypt, Mycenae, Phoenicia, Assyria, Persian, Crete, Macedonia and Rome in the ancient Western world; the Inca Empire in South America before the Spanish conquest; and the dynasties of Shang and Chou in ancient China. There were also national empires, such as the French Empire under Napoleon I, the Russian Empire before the revolution of 1917, and the British Empire in the last century. (Cf. Samuel N. Eisenstadt, "Empires," in the *International Encyclopedia of the Social Sciences,* ed. by David L. Sills, New York, 1968, Vol. 5, p. 41-48. Also his *The Political Systems of Empires,* New York, 1963.)

253. Empire is defined by William Ebenstein in the *Encyclopedia Americana,* 1973 ed., Vol. 10, p. 312, as follows: "a form of political organization in which a central authority exercises sovereignty over a vast and diverse territory and often over a multitude of nationalities. The territory itself is also known as an empire."

254. To take over the sovereign power of other people means actual annexation of their territory, because territory is a major factor of sovereignty, signified as territorial sovereignty. (Cf. Ingrid Delupis, *International Law and the Independent State,* New York, 1974, p. 4-6.) But to annex territory, in modern politics, is not always necessary or desirable for imperial expansion. It is not only expensive, but frequently dangerous, because it might provoke a reaction from another power. Another possibility is that it would produce shock waves in the interior of

that the value of the nation is higher than anything else; that nationalism is actuated and the nation-state functions on such an assumption; that the efforts to magnify, glorify, perpetualize and divinize the position, nature, elements, character and sentiment of the nation are based on no other assumption; and so based also is popular allegiance to the nation.[255]

The crucial problem, therefore, is what is the value of the nation?

Basically, the value of any group in the process of group expansion—the early single family, primitive community, clan, tribe and nation lies in its size as a larger basis for performing two major functions: to extend peace wider in area and to promote more happiness for the people.[256] But the size of these groups is generally determined by the physical conditions inherent in the mode of life of an age identified by the prime material used for tools and weapons.[257] When the physical conditions change into a new age with a new mode of life which favors a larger size for better performance, the value of the old smaller group diminishes.[258]

---

an area so that further annexations would be required to calm and control turbulent frontiers. Annexation may also force adminstrators to make on-the-spot decisions to intervene in intertribal, interethnic, or interpolitical affairs that may force an imperial nation more deeply into moral involvement in the annexed territory than its home population would accept. (Cf. Robin W. Winks, "Imperialism," in the *Encyclopedia Americana,* 1973 ed., Vol. 14, p. 822.)

255. Plainly speaking, the all-important trend of our age is to strengthen the nation; and all the peoples in the world are forced to offer more and more energy and time, property and life, for their nation. Why ought we to do so? Because of allegiance? Allegiance is not a blind loyalty. Because of obedience? Obedience is not for the sake of obedience itself. Because of duty? Duty is a job with sound reason. Because of patriotism? Patriotism must have a constructive meaning. In inquiring into these problems, basically we are confronted with the same question: What is the value of the nation? It is a question more vital than wages, prices, taxes, food, or any major issue of immediate interest to the common man everywhere, because in the final analysis, the solution of all the everyday problems of four thousand million human beings depends more or less upon a correct answer to this question.

256. (Cf. I, c.)

257. Thus, roughly, the early single family was able to function with the food-gathering life in the Old Stone Age; the primitive community, with the hunting-fishing life in the Young Stone Age; the clan, with the hoe-cultivation life in the New Stone Age; the tribe, with the animal-raising life in the Copper Age; and the nation, with the agricultural life in the Iron Age. In addition to the mode of life, the developments of transportation, communication, and weapons are very important factors of physical conditions. (Cf. I, d-g.)

258. For example, the clan in the clan period was of highest value, because it was the largest group allowed by the physical conditions in that period. But it became too small a group and lost its value in the tribe period in which the tribe

As regards the nation, its physical conditions have generally been associated with a mode of agricultural life in the Iron Age. Its value has been higher than that of tribe or other kind of local groups, because its size has generally been larger, enabling it to extend more peace and to promote more happiness.[259] Now, however, situations have changed drastically since late in the last century. Our mode of life has been transformed from local agricultural self-sufficiency to worldwide industrial interdependence, and our time has shifted from the Iron Age to the Machine Age. Our world has shrunk into a small kingdom in transportation and communication, and has come under a serious threat of nuclear and other devastating weapons. It is crystal clear that physical conditions are ready for us to achieve a group much larger than the nation—the One World,[260] with the highest value in extending a permanent peace over the earth and promoting a general happiness for mankind;[261] and that the value of the nation has been necessarily diminishing at an accelerating pace.[262]

---

was the largest group allowed by the physical conditions, and therefore, was of higher value.

259. This value is reflected in the preamble of the constitution of the United States of America: "We the people of the United States, in order to form a more perfect Union, establish Justice, insure domestic Tranquility, provide for the common defence, promote the general Welfare, and secure the Blessings of Liberty to ourselves and our Posterity, do ordain and establish this Constitution for the United States of America."

260. (Cf. I, i and j.)

261. In other words, as the physical conditions for a world community have been completed, it is possible for all peoples in the world to avoid the evil of international wars by getting together as one group, to live a better life by extending cooperation throughout the whole world, and to get rid of all their national burdens by living under a single administrative system.

262. "It is the nation which prevents us from enjoying the advantages of worldwide cooperation which progress in modern science and technology has brought to our very door; induces us to develop egotism, to engage in a desparate trade warfare, to erect tariff barriers, and to dump products; and inflicts upon us recurrent inflation, depression, and unemployment." "It is the nation which wastes our property and saps our vitality. Under the constant pressure of international conflicts, we are forced to pour our money, our labor, and our resources into arsenals, and to use our best brains in the diplomatic arena and in the race for armaments. Not only statesmen and generals, but also our educators, artists, scientists, and philosophers are constantly being mobilized to absorb their energy in defense and warfare." "It is the nation which creates modern dictatorship and totalitarianism, makes serfs of all peoples from the cradle to the grave, and concentrates more and more power in the hands of a few rulers. We are forced to relinquish to that power one after another of our liberties won at such a cost since the Renaissance through the overthrow of feudalism and absolutism, to admit more

In other words, the nation, which before this century was the broadest basis for peace and happiness,[263] today is far too small in scope. Its historical mission has been completed[264] and its reality is gone.[265] It has even become an obstacle to the progress of civilization.[266]

---

and more interference in our everyday life, and to be exposed to oppression and violence." "It is the nation which deteriorates our morality, develops prejudice, suspicion, hate and revenge, and fosters inhumanity and antagonism among the peoples; makes every place full of intrigue and traps; permeates the poisons of spies everywhere; and plunges the world into new barbarism." "And it is the nation which drives us to war, to go forth to kill or be killed, to destroy everything we can, and to produce fear, starvation, maimed lives, disease and death. We have been forced to do so from time to time. The great massacres of world wars have twice been inflicted on this generation. And the third one is imminent. It will be an atomic war, will lay waste the great cities and will even bring us to a total destruction." (Quoted twenty years ago from a paper of which the author has not been identified. It is indeed a very truthful and forceful statement in denouncing the nation.)

263. For instance, nationalism grew in Germany from the continuous conflicts of more than three hundred separate and independent states. The theory of sovereignty was first developed by Jean Bodin in France which had been in anguish, travail and strife for a long time, and the nation-state was originated from Thomas Hobbes' *Leviathan* in the age of religious fanaticism and civil war in England. The extending of peace and promoting of happiness were necessarily of paramount value in these countries during those years.

264. "There is no doubt that the idea of nationality has been a creative force, making possible the fuller development of powers by widening the field of individual activity, and by setting definite ideals to large cooperating masses; but we feel with Fichte and Mazzini that the political power of a nation is important only when the national unit is the carrier of ideals that are of value to mankind." (Frank Boas, *Anthropology and Modern Life,* rev. ed., New York, 1932, p. 96)

"The nation was originally instituted and received its power from its people to carry out clearly defined tasks. . . . The moment the established institution fails to keep abreast of conditions in society and is unable to maintain peace, it becomes a source of great danger, and must be reformed if violent social convulsions and wars are to be averted." (Emery Reves, *The Anatomy of Peace,* New York, 1946, p. 141-142)

265. Almost half a century ago, Harold J. Laski signified the vanishing of the reality of the nation in his discussion on national sovereignty: "Sovereignty in the international field was intelligible enough when difficulties of communication made the kind of interdependence we know almost unthinkable. The influence of science and mass-production was then wholly sporadic in character; Detroit and Nanking were as distant as two planets. All that has passed. Is it not, then, essential that we should effect an institutional recognition of its passing? Can a system of government which developed to fit the needs of a civilization hardly touched by scientific discovery really suffice for one which lives in and by its acceptance of what science achieves? Can a London which the aeroplane now makes a day's journey from New York afford to think on a scale inadequate enough, in all cons-

With the value of the nation diminishing rapidly, there has been no way for national independence and sovereignty to maintain their importance.[267] Nationalism has become merely an evil force[268] and

---

cience, when New York was six weeks' voyage if the winds were favourable? Can an England which could not survive unless its food supplies were brought almost hourly from the ends of the earth afford to think in terms suitable to its simple self-sufficiency of the seventeenth or eighteenth century? Can we look at wars which bring whole populations within the direct ambit of their ghastly outcome as though they were still matters which affected no more than a comparative handful of professional soldiery, or a score of men-of-war at sea. We must learn to think internationally or we perish—that, I suggest, is the clear alternative before us." (His *Nationalism and the Future of Civilization,* London, 1932, p. 26-27)

"... and these very same relationships between man and man living in separate sovereign national units are qualitatively different.... But the scientific and technological developments achieved by the industrial revolution in one century have brought about in our political outlook and in our approach to political and social phenomena a change as inevitable and imperative as the Renaissance brought about in our philosophical outlook. The developments creating that need are revolutionary and without parallel in human history. In one century, the population of this earth has been more than trebled. Since the very beginning of recorded history, for ten thousand years, communication was based on animal power. During the American and French revolutions, transportation was scarcely faster than it had been under the Pharaohs, at the time of Buddha or of the Incas. And then, after a static aeon of ten thousand years, transportation changed within a single short century from animal power to the steam and electric railroad, the internal combustion automobile and the six hundred-mile-per-hour jet propulsion plane." (Emery Reves, *The Anatomy of Peace,* New York, 1946, p. 27)

266. "Our endeavor is to demonstrate that it is the political status quo—the exiting system of sovereign nation-states, accepted and upheld today by capitalists and socialists, individualists, all national and religious groups alike—that constitutes the insurmountable obstacle to all progress, to all social and economic efforts, that bars all human progress on any lines." (Emery Reves, *The Anatomy of Peace,* New York, 1946, p. 74)

267. "The ideal of national sovereignty and national independence springs from long eras of monarchy and colonization. At its inception, it was a great forward step and an incentive to human progress. The American Declaration of Independence, the French Revolution, following on the development of representative institutions in England, were an enormous incentive to other peoples to fight for their own sovereignty and independence. The climax of this evolution was reached in the peace treaties of 1919, when more nations than ever before became completely sovereign and independent." But "the political system established in 1919, an apotheosis of eighteenth century ideals, was an anachronism, and in total contradiction to things as they are in the twentieth century." (Emery Reves, *The Anatomy of Peace,* New York, 1946, p. 131)

268. The dominant and enduring passion of Herbert G. Wells was "the desire to have political and social institutions conform to the scientific and technological realities of the modern world. There was a time in the history of Europe when nationalism may have been a progressive, unifying force giving vitality to our civiliza-

the nation-state, a wicked instrument.[269] The efforts to magnify, glorify, perpetualize and divinize the position, nature, elements, character and sentiment of the nation have not meant much more than blowing some air into a broken tire; and popular allegiance to the nation has the appearance of keeping faith with a dead hero.

Needless to say, the moral reason for patriotism is lost if it is just the blind following of the nation wherever it may lead;[270] and for the citizenship, if it contributes no positive judgment to the public good.[271]

So, as the value of the nation diminishes rapidly, the ground for the nation has been deteriorating in every aspect. The days of the nation as an independent group with sovereignty are numbered. It is doomed to give way to a much larger group.[272] This means, under the law of group expansion, that all nations are destined to merge into One World.[273] This merging is an historical progress and a social

---

tion. But latter-day nationalism was separatist, disruptive, centrifugal, dividing mankind at the very time that powerful forces of science and technology were working in the opposite direction." Edward M. Earle, *Nationalism and Internationalism,* New York, 1950, p. 89)

269. "The nation-state is thus a fellowship of men aiming at the enrichment of the common life. . . . It is judged by what it offers to its members in terms of the things they deem to be good. Its roots are laid in their minds and hearts. In the long run, it will win support, not by the theoretic programme it announces, but by the perception of ordinary citizens that allegiance to its will is a necessary condition of their own well-being. It has no moral claim upon their loyalty save in so far as they are offered proof of its realization." (Harold J. Laski, *A Grammar of Politics,* London, 1925, p. 37)

270. "Patriotism in a citizen is not the blind following of his nation-state wherever it may lead." (Harold J. Laski, *A Grammar of Politics,* London, 1925, p. 226)

"Real patriotism, real love of one's own country has no relationship whatsoever to the fetishism of the sovereign nation-states." (Emery Reves, *The Anatomy of Peace,* New York, 1946, p. 233)

271. "Citizenship, that is to say, means the contribution of our instructed judgment to the public good. It may lead us to support a state; but it may lead us also to oppose it. The will of the state is only my will in so far as I freely lend my judgment to its enforcement." (Harold J. Laski, *A Grammar of Politics,* London, 1925, p. 29)

272. This is just like in the ancient time, "the kin-group system loses its efficacy as an adjustment and merges gradually into a system better suitable to altered conditions, living on within it to discharge such services as it is capable of performing. The family remains vigorous within the larger political aggregation; but the effective life of the constituent kin-groups is about over." (William G. Sumner and Albert G. Keller, *The Science of Society,* New Haven, 1927, Vol. 1, p. 440)

273. Indeed, many people are still standing bewildered in the presence of nations. For them to believe that the nations will merge into a world community is

evolution with an irresistible force.[274] It is not exactly a new adventure,[275] and is just one more step forward in the process of our group expansion which started thousands of years ago. But this is the last step to achieve its ultimate goals: permanent peace and general happiness.

---

just as difficult as for our ancestors in earlier times to believe that their groups would merge into a larger group, such as early single families into a primitive community, primitive communities into a clan, clans into a tribe and tribes into a nation. But the merging was proved to be true again and again. History has the power to overcome any obstacle to its process and has the ability to carry through its mission. It is irresistible.

274. For the time being, the existence of the nations, their importance, and the antagonisms between them still look like a fixed phenomenon. But in the long run of history, all these are nothing more than an accident, as signified by Professor Harold J. Laski in his *A Grammar of Politics* (London, 1925, p. 64). The nations are not less mortal than the tribes, clans, primitive communities, or the early single families; nor are they more important than them in their respective times. The antagonism between the nations, just like the feeling of opposition of one earlier group towards another, is solely an expression of existing conditions, and does not by any means indicate any permanence. History has its own solutions to its own problems. It will sweep away anything intolerable to its process.

275. "Those of us who recognize in the realization of national ideals a definite advance that has benefited mankind cannot fail to see that the task before us at the present time is a repetition of the process of nationalization on a larger scale." "The concept of thoroughly integrated nations of the size to which we are now accustomed would have been just as inconceivable in earlier times of the history of mankind as appears now the concept of unity of interests of all the peoples of the world." (Franz Boas, *Anthropology and Modern Life,* rev. ed., New York, 1932, p. 97, 101)

IV

Permanent
Peace

a.

Recent Tendency of War

THE SALIENT FEATURE OF THE TENDENCY OF WAR IN
modern times is that while there has been a decline in the frequency
of war[1] and the length of war,[2] and consequently in the number of
war years per century,[3] the intensity, extensity, magnitude, severity
and cost of war have enormously increased.

The intensity of war is reflected in the duration of battles, their
number in a war and their total in a century. The duration of a battle
has increased from a few hours from early times on to several days in

---

1. "There were over fifty European Wars in the 16th and in the 17th centuries, there were only one-half as many in the 18th and the 19th centuries, and
there have been only eleven in the first forty years of the 20th century." (Quincy
Wright, *A Study of War,* 2nd ed., Chicago, 1965, p. 236)

2. The average length of general wars in the 17th, 18th, 19th, and 20th centuries was 14, 8, 6, and 4 years respectively, and the average time between these
wars was 6, 8, 33, and 20 years. (Cf. Quincy Wright, *A Study of War,* 2nd ed.,
Chicago, 1965, p. 650.)

3. "In the 16th and 17th centuries the major European states were formally at
war about 65 per cent of the time. In the three succeeding centuries the comparable
figures were 38 per cent, 28 per cent, and 18 per cent, respectively." (Cf. Quincy
Wright, *A Study of War,* 2nd ed., Chicago, 1965, p. 235, also Table 46.)

This conclusion may be compared with the statistics made by George
Glockemeier, a German engineer and historian, of the aggregate number of years

353

the 20th century in most cases.[4] The average number of battles in an European war has grown from less than two in the 16th century to over sixty in the first forty years of the 20th century,[5] and in these respective periods the total number of battles fought by the principal European nations has expanded from 87 to 892.[6]

---

spent per century by different European nations in fighting each other. (See *New York Times,* December 14, 1930, p. 4E, Col. 3.) Glockemeier's statistics:

Century		Total Nation-Years of War (per century)
1600-99		653
1700-99		485
1800-99		254
1900-29	(58 in 30 years, or at a rate per century of)	193

4. A battle consists of the operations during a period of time in which hostile forces are uninterruptedly in contact with each other. (Cf. Quincy Wright, *A Study of War,* 2nd ed., Chicago, 1965, p. 223, note 12.) This period has through most of history been limited by the rotation of the earth on its axis and the consequent difficulty of fighting at night. So the duration of a battle has always been for a few hours in the daytime, and warfare at night has not been very common. But this has been less true in recent wars, owing to changes in military technique. While in the 17th century, 96 percent of the battles lasted for a day or less, in the 18th century, the figure was 93 percent, in the 19th century 84 per cent, and in the 20th century, only 40 per cent as shown in the following table, by century, of the period 1618-1905. (From *Ibid,* p. 631)

	Century							
	17th		**18th**		**19th**		**20th**	
Days	**No.**	**%**	**No.**	**%**	**No.**	**%**	**No.**	**%**
0.0-1.0	183	95.8	527	93.3	463	84.2	239	39.8
1.1-2.0	2	1.0	22	3.9	50	9.1	78	13.0
2.1-3.0	4	2.1	6	1.1	19	3.5	44	7.3
3.1-4.0	0	0.0	2	0.4	4	0.7	30	5.0
4.1-5.0	2	1.0	2	0.4	6	1.1	29	4.8
5.1-6.0	0	0.0	3	0.5	1	0.2	23	3.8
6.1 & more	0	0.0	3	0.5	7	1.3	158	26.3
Total	191		565		550		601	

5. In the 16th century, less than two important battles occurred on the average in a European war; in the 17th century, about 4; in the 18th and 19th centuries, about 20; and in the first forty years of the 20th century, over 60. (Cf. Quincy Wright, *A Study of War,* 2nd ed., Chicago, 1965, Table 45, Item 5.)

6. The increase of the total number of battles in a century of modern times has become very notable. There were 87 battles fought by the principal European

The extensity of war may be measured by the number of belligerents in a war and by the area covered by a war. The average number of belligerents in a war has risen from less than three in the early modern times to more than five in the early 20th century.[7] The spread of the war area is demonstrated by the fact that the European nations fought no important battle outside of Europe from 1550 to 1750. But from 1900 to 1940 alone there were 248 extra-European battles.[8]

The size of armed forces, which may fairly manifest the magnitude of war, has grown from the small mercenary armies before the 17th century to a million men under Napoleon[9] to more than sixty million soldiers in World War I.

---

states in the 16th century, and there had already been 892 in the 20th century by 1940. (Cf. Quincy Wright, *A Study of War,* 2nd ed., Chicago, 1965, Table 22, and Figure 35.)

It is interesting to note "that Napoleon fought more battles than Alexander the Great, Hannibal and Julius Caesar combined." (Sydney Harris, *South Bend Tribune,* Jan. 15, 1980, p. 16)

7. Professor Wright counts 126 wars from 1475 to 1940 in which major battles were fought. Of these wars, the 42 which began in the late 15th and in the 16th centuries averaged 2.4 participants each; the 22 which began in the 17th century averaged 3.5 participants each; the 19 which began in the 18th century 4.8 participants each; the 32 which began in the 19th century averaged 3.1 participants each; and the 11 which began in the 20th century averaged 5.6 participants each. Thus, apart from the 19th century, the number of belligerents in a war has increased steadily. This tendency was accelerated by the first World War in which 33 states, half those of the world, were belligerents. (Cf. Quincy Wright, *A Study of War,* 2nd ed., Chicago, 1965, p. 238 and Table 42.)

8. The European states fought no important battle outside of Europe from 1550 to 1750; there were 13 extra-European battles from 1750 to 1800, 11 from 1800 to 1850, 78 from 1850 to 1900; and from 1900 to 1940, 248 such battles have already occurred. Since 1600, the percentages of extra-European battles in succeeding centuries were 0, 2, 13, and 25. The major battles of the first World War were concentrated in Europe, but extended to the Near East, the Far East, and Africa. (Cf. Quincy Wright, *A Study of War,* 2nd ed., Chicago, 1965, Table 45, Item 2.)

9. In the 16th century, the mercenary armies seldom exceeded twenty thousand. In the 17th century, armies often reached fifty or sixty thousand, and about three in a thousand of the European population were under arms. From then on, there has been a steady rise in the size of European standing armies, absolutely and in proportion to the population. In the 18th century, Marlborough, Prince Eugene, and Frederick the Great had armies of eighty or ninety thousand men. Napoleon had as many as two hundred thousand men in certain battles, and at times he may have had a million men or 5 percent of the French population mobilized. (Cf. Quincy Wright, *A Study of War,* 2nd ed., Chicago, 1965, Tables 29, 30, and Figure 41.) Wright also notes that Gaston Bodart calculates the normal size of armies in the Thirty Years' War at 19,000; in the wars of Louis XIV at 40,000; in the war of Frederick the Great at 47,000; in the Napoleonic Wars at

The severity of war has been greatly enhanced by the drastic development of modern military techniques,[11] leading not only to a

---

84,000, in the Franco-Prussian War at 70,000; and in the Russo-Japanese War at 110,000. (p. 233, note 33)

10. There was some diminution in the size of armies after 1815, but in the latter half of the 19th century, the armies of the great powers grew again. Before the outbreak of World War I, there had been about five million men in the armed forces in Europe. During the War, Russia alone assembled 12,000,000 people under arms; Germany, 11,000,000; Great Britain, 8,900,000; France, 8,400,000; Austria-Hungary, 7,800,000; Italy, 5,600,000; and the United States, 4,300,000. The total mobilization reached more than 63,000,000, about 12 percent of the population of the actual belligerent nations, and 36 percent of their active male population. (Cf. Quincy Wright, *A Study of War,* 2nd ed., Chicago, 1965, Tables 56, 58 and 59.)

Francis Hirst in *The Political Economy of War,* London, 1915, p. 81 ff., gives figures for the standing armies of European states in 1858, totaling 2,675,000, and in 1898, totaling 3,562,000, which he compares with the 300,000 of the Roman Empire of the time of Augustus.

It is interesting to note an early record for comparison: Once Tien Tan, a leader of Chi, one of the seven warring states in the late stage of the Warring States Period (403-222 B.C.) in Chinese history, asked General Chao She: "I heard that in early times an empire reigned everywhere with an army of less than thirty thousand soldiers. Now I am puzzled why you have to have one even two hundred thousand men to fight." Replied She: "It is because you don't know the different situations. In the early time, the world within the four seas was divided into ten thousand states with towns of no more than ten blocks and people of no more than three thousand families in a community. This is why an army of less than thirty thousand soldiers could overcome any resistance. Nowadays, all the small states have merged into a few warring states, with towns of more than two hundred blocks and people of more than ten thousand families in a community everywhere. It is obviously difficult to achieve a victory over a long time without an army of great strength." (Quoted in the *Six Essays on the Study of Chinese History* (in Chinese) by Chi-Chao Liang, 3rd ed., Taipei, 1971, p. 40.) 初齊田單賞問趙奢曰：
"單聞帝王用兵不過三萬而天下服，今將軍必負十萬二 十萬之衆乃用之，此單所不服也。"奢曰："君不明時勢也。古者四海之内，分爲萬國，城雖大無過三百丈，人雖衆無過三千家。而以集兵三萬距此何難哉 。今取古之萬國者爲戰國，七千丈之城，萬家之邑相望也。不能具數十萬之衆 ，曠日持久數歲，何以爲戰？"

11. "All belligerent entities—animals, primitive peoples, and the historic civilizations of the past—have, of course, had war techniques—weapons, tactics, and strategic ideas—but in the modern sense war means the use of firearms and chemicals for striking and of steam, gas, and electrical engines for military movement. This utilization of sources of power other than those of man and beast in hostile operations has transformed the character of such operations and made them war in the modern sense. It is true that human power had been converted in form and direction in the past by mechanical devices such as the bow, arquebus, and siege engine, but the force of these instruments was limited by the power of the human arm to bend the spring upon which the device depended. Until recent

total war which implicates the whole society,[12] but even to an absolute war which aims at the destruction of every object.[13]

---

periods man had no reliable methods for releasing power stored by other than human or animal muscle for the purpose of advancing toward or striking an enemy." (Quincy Wright, *A Study of War,* 2nd ed., Chicago, 1965, p. 40)

As foretold by Herbert G. Wells in his books *The War in the Air* (1908) and *The World Set Free* (1914) when every important capital and every industrial city lay at the mercy of bombing planes operating from bases only hours, or even minutes, away from their targets. Air war, he said, was perforce a "universal guerrilla war, a war inextricably involving civilians and homes and all the apparatus of social life." It would be prepared in secret and launched without warning. It would be incalculably destructive; hence it alters "not only the methods of war but the consequences of war." War, with such winged weapons at its disposal, makes a mockery of civilization. (Cf. these two books, especially p. 49-57 of *The War in the Air.* Cf. also Edward M. Earle, "The Influence of Air Power upon History," in the *Yale Review,* XXXV, 1946, p. 577-593.)

"More important, however, is the fact that mechanization in one form or another has completely altered the former conception of time and space. The dynamics and speed of operations were switched from that of the man on foot to that of the motor, with the result that the battlefield constantly increased in extent, whilst concurrently the development of situations became five times more rapid." (F.O. Miksche, *Atomic Weapons and Armies,* New York, 1955, p. 27)

12. Total war has been defined as "armed conflict between sovereign states, sponsored and waged by a society in arms." (Henry W. Spiegel, *The Economics of Total War,* New York, 1942, p. 37)

As modern military techniques develop, at least a dozen people must be engaged in production and transportation services behind the lines to keep one soldier supplied. As a result, almost the entire working population have to take part in direct or indirect war services. (Cf. Quincy Wright, *A Study of War,* 2nd ed., Chicago, 1965, Vol. I, p. 304-305.)

"Undoubtedly the very worst effect of the war of 1914-1918 is, that it has very largely destroyed the distinction between combatants and non-combatants. From now on nations, not armies, will war. In future wars between great powers the whole nation will be mobilized, either on the fighting lines or in the munition factories or the industrial service of the armies and navies. . . . They will insist upon the destruction of munition factories, shipyards, railroad centers, supply industries; in short, they will tend more and more to destroy centers of population and to murder indiscriminately men, women and children." (Oscar Newfang, *The Road to World Peace,* New York, 1924, p. xii)

13. The Germans have combined the total war with absolute war by describing it as aiming at "the utter destruction of the vanquished nation and its final and complete disappearance from the stage of history." (Henry W. Spiegel, *The Economics of Total War,* New York, 1942, p. 37) Such warfare uses every possible means for its success, is fought in every possible locus, and employs every resource and technique for its prosecution. The degree of its violence is unlimited. It is waged against non-combatants as well as against men in arms, against the old and the young and women as well as against soldiers, and aims at the destruction of property, culture, and morals as well as at military power. "To destroy and lay waste

Finally, we have the rapid rise of the cost of war in human casualties, economic costs and social deterioration. Regarding human casualties, the war deaths in Europe have increased from less than 300,000 in the 15th century to more than 24,000,000 in the first quarter of the 20th century alone.[14] In regard to the economic aspect, Napoleon spent less than $3,000 to kill an enemy, and the cost mounted to $21,000 in World War I.[15] The direct costs of World War I were thirty times more than those of the five major European wars,

---

such towns and districts as might be found assailable." "To introduce into the philosophy of war a principle of moderation would be absurd. War is an act of violence pursued to the utmost." (Karl von Clauseqitz, quoted in Basil H. Liddell Hart, *The Revolution in Warfare,* New Haven, 1947, p. 67. Cf. Chap. II of same.)

14. It was estimated that the war deaths in Europe in the 15th century were 285,000; in the 16th century, 863,000; in the 17th century, 3,454,000; in the 18th century, 4,635,000; in the 19th century, 3,845,000; and in the first quarter alone of the 20th century, 24,035,000. The figures of war deaths per 1,000 population for these periods were 10, 15, 37, 33, 15, 54 respectively. In the first World War, the indirect losses were as great as the direct losses in Europe; each was about ten million. Outside of Europe, the indirect losses were much greater because of the ravages of influenza in Asia and America as a result of the war. The total deaths from military action, and war-distributed disease attributable to the first World War, have been estimated as over forty million. It seems that the total of deaths indirectly due to war have been three times as great as direct war death. (Cf. Pitirim A. Sorokin, *Social and Cultural Dynamics,* New York, 1942, Vol. III, Tables 6-19.)

Quincy Wright in *A Study of War,* 2nd ed., Chicago, 1965, estimates that, of 1,000 deaths in the French population in the 17th century, about 11 died in active military service. The corresponding figure for the 18th century is 27; for the 19th, 30; and for the 20th, 63. For England the corresponding figures for these four centuries are 15, 14, 6, and 48. (p. 243, and Table 57). For comparison of direct and indirect human losses in war, cf. L. Hersch, "Demographic Effects of Modern War," in Interparliamentary Union, *What Would Be the Character of a New War?,* London, 1933. The military casualties in World War I estimated by the U.S. War Department may be reviewed in the *Encyclopedia Americana,* 1973 ed., Vol. 23, p. 775.

To quote the following statement for further comparison: "It is manifest from foregoing evidence that primitive warfare was not so destructive of human life as one has often been given to understand. Battle-casualties were frequently insignificant—the loss of five in a fight 'would mean a serious disaster,' and noncombatants were generally spared." (William G. Sumner and Albert G. Keller, *The Science of Society,* New Haven, 1927, Vol. I, p. 397)

15. According to Herbert Hoover ("Hope in a Poorer World," *Rotarian,* Feb., 1941, p. 10): "War has become more terrible every year since the invention of gunpowder. Every half-century has seen more and more men sacrificed on the battlefield. Lowell M. Limpus, in *Twentieth Century Warfare,* says that it cost Julius Caesar about 75 cents to kill a man, that Napoleon almost bankrupted France because it cost a fraction under $3,000 to kill an enemy in his day. The World War ran the cost up to $21,000 per dead soldier, and it is estimated that before the present conflict ends it will have risen to $50,000."

taken together, in the second half of the 19th century.[16] The costs in social deterioration during and after the war are less susceptible to measurement, but are nevertheless considered very serious.[17]

Thus far the review of the recent tendency of war has not included World War II, which exceeded almost all previous wars in intensity, extensity, magnitude, severity and cost.[18] Most striking was the dropping on Hiroshima of an atomic bomb which annihilated the city and extinguished almost one half of its 200,000 population.[19]

---

16. Economic costs have also increased enormously. It was estimated that the expenditures in the second half of the 19th century in Europe of the five major wars—the Crimean War, the War of 1859, the Austro-Prussian War, the Franco-Prussian War, and the Turkey War, were about $6,000,000,000. This aggregate number becomes a dwarf before a giant when compared with the costs of the World Wars. The first World War was estimated to have direct costs of $186,000,000,000, and indirect costs of $152,000,000,000, making a total of $338,000,000,000. (Cf. Jean de Bloch, *The Future of War,* trans. by Robert C. Long, Boston, 1914, p. 128-32; and Ernest L. Bogart, *Direct and Indirect Cost of the Great World War,* New York, 1919, p. 265-68, 299.)

17. In addition to the human and economic costs, but even less susceptible to objective measurement, are the social and cultural costs in connection with war. Wars waged on a large scale have been followed by anti-intellectual movements in art, literature, and philosophy; by waves of crime, sexual license, suicide, venereal disease, delinquent youth; by class, racial, and religious intolerance, persecution, refugees, social and political revolution; by abandonment of orderly processes for settling disputes and changing law; and by a decline in respect for international law and treaties. The measurement of such costs is technically difficult. Nevertheless, the deterioration of standards is widely considered serious. (Cf. Francis W. Hirst, *The Consequence of War to Great Britain,* London, 1934, p. 64, ff; Helmuth C. Engelbrecht, *Revolt Against War,* New York, 1937, chaps. xi-xv; and *Economic and Social History of the World War,* Washington, 1924, edited by James T. Shotwell, which deals with the consequences of the war in all principal countries.)

18. World War II included 161 bilateral wars. It spread almost all over the world with 57 nations as formal belligerents. Only 6 of the world's independent nations managed to maintain a precarious neutrality (Afghanistan, Ireland, Portugal, Spain, Sweden and Switzerland). It mobilized more than 92,000,000 people under arms, with about 62,000,000 on the Allied side and about 30,000,000 on the Axis and Associated Powers side. It brought death to over 22,000,000 directly and caused other casualties of over 34,000,000. It spent about $50,000 to kill a soldier. Its total cost was estimated at $1,154,000,000,000, and total property damage at $230,000,000,000, excluding China. (Cf. Quincy Wright, *A Study of War,* 2nd ed., Chicago, 1965, p. 1539-1543, Appendices A and B; *Encyclopedia Americana,* 1962 ed., Vol. 23, p. 793q-793r, and 1947 ed., Vol. 29, p. 559yy-560. This ed. notes that the total cost and total property damage of the war were estimated by James H. Brady and the American University. (Cf. also *Encyclopedia Americana,* 1956 ed., Vol. 23, p. 973 Q-R.)

19. The first atomic bomb, dropped by an American airplane on August 6, 1945, annihiliated the city of Hiroshima, Japan, and killed almost one half of its

This bomb brought an end to World War II, and meanwhile, signaled the start of a new era in warfare, which will be looked into after a quick examination of the various methods which have been tried for maintaining peace in recent centuries.

b.
Methods to Maintain Peace

WHILE WAR HAS DEFINITELY BEEN GETTING BIGGER and worse,[20] there were early in this century some experts who tended to believe that recent developments in military techniques had increased the probability of a deadlock in war, which would lead to its disappearance.[21] In fact, however, it has been proved not only that

---

200,000 population. (The official statistics: 78,150 people killed, 13,983 missing, 37,425 injured; 62,000 out of the city's 90,000 buildings destroyed, and 6000 other buildings damaged beyond repair.) It was a uranium bomb, cylindrical in shape, 10 feet long with a diameter of 2 feet 4 inches, weighing about 9,000 lbs. Its explosive force was equal to 20,000 tons of TNT. Three days later another baby atomic bomb, this time of plutonium, was dropped over another Japanese city, Nagasaki. (Cf. Edward Teller and Allen Brown, *The Legacy of Hiroshima,* New York, 1962, p. 1-4; and *The Effect of Nuclear Weapons,* ed. by Samuel Glasstone, Rev. ed., Washington, 1964, p. 196-315, 547-626.)

20. This also is confirmed by Pitirim A. Sorokin, who has compared by centuries the number of wars weighted to take account of duration of war, size of fight-force, number of casualties, number of countries involved, and proportion of combatants to total population. His index for the principal European wars for the 15th century is 100; for the 16th, 180; for the 17th, 500; for the 18th, 370; for the 19th, 120; and for the 20th, 3,080. Apart from being exceptionally high in the 17th century and exceptionally low in the 19th century, his index rises notably, and extra-ordinarily in the 20th century. (Cf. Quincy Wright, *A Study of War,* 2nd ed., Chicago, 1965, Table 49, deriving from Pitirim A. Sorokin, *Indices of the Movement of War,* presented to the American Association for Advancement of Science, December, 1933.)

21. They explained that experience with an inflexible technique tends to favor the defensive, and highly mechanized techniques tend to become inflexible. Again, the success of the offensive depends in large measure upon surprise, and, as the varied applications of a given technique become known, the opportunities for surprise necessarily become less. On the other hand, the defensive depends upon knowledge of the best means of dealing with the enemy's offensive, and this knowledge steadily accumulates with experience of a given technique. This development, they held, will result in a deadlock in the battlefield which may make

their belief was wrong,[22] but also that all the methods for maintaining peace have become less and less effective.

Best-known among these methods has been the balance of power,[23] of which success depends on measuring power and keeping it in balance.[24] It played a good role in maintaining order in Europe

---

war impossible in the future, because that deadlock will lead to a stalemate of mutual attrition and destruction. (Cf. Bernard Brodie, "Defense and Technology," *Technological Review,* XLIII, January, 1941; John F.C. Fuller, *The Reformation of War,* New York, 1922, p. 86; John Holland Rose, *The Indecisiveness of Modern War,* London, 1927, p. 34; Jean de Bloch, *The Future of War,* trans. by Robert C. Long, Boston, 1914, p. 352-356; "Conversations with the Author," and the last chapter.

22. The idea that the new development in military techniques would lead to a deadlock in warfare has been repudiated by new offensive weapons, especially the bombing airplanes, and new strategies, such as the Douhet Doctrine. (Giulio Douhet initiated the idea that victory can only be won by attack, which under modern conditions is only possible by air. See his *The Command of the Air,* Dino Ferrari's trans., 1942.)

In fact, the deadlock which resulted from the development of military techniques after World War I was quickly broken by German Blitzkrieg in World War II. This fact has not only buried the idea that such a deadlock might lead to an end of war, but has also given rise to the observation that, as new weapons are invented so rapidly and new strategies change so fast, no deadlock could long exist in modern warfare, and therefore, no lasting peace could be created by any deadlock which might temporarily result from further development of military techniques. (Cf. *International Arms Control, Issues and Agreements,* by the Stanford Arms Control Group, ed. by John H. Barton and Lawrence D. Weiler, Stanford, Calif., 1976, p. 46-65.)

23. The balance of power means such an equilibrium in power among the nations as will prevent any one or group of them from becoming sufficiently strong to change the status quo by force. This term is based on the assumption that the recurrence of war is due mainly to the state of an uncertain and fluctuating power among the nations, and this state is due mainly to the tendency of the governments to increase their power and their desire for self-preservation. Only if this tendency be checked and this desire assured by an equilibrium can peace be maintained continuously among the nations. (Cf. "Balance of Power," in the *Encyclopedia of the Social Sciences,* New York, 1935; Carl J. Friedrich, *Foreign Policy in the Making,* New York, 1938, p. 117 ff; and *The Balance of Power and Nuclear Deterrence,* ed. by Frederick H. Gareau, Boston, 1962, p. 1-19.)

24. The success of the balance of power depends on the measuring of the power and the keeping of its balance. Here power usually includes actual and potential military power. Actual military power includes land, naval, and air armament. This includes personnel, material, organization, and morale of the armed forces. It also includes railroads, motor vehicles, civil aircraft, and other means of communication and conveyance which, though used in normal times for civilian purposes, are immediately available for military purposes. Potential military power consists of available population, raw materials, industrial skill, and in-

in the 19th century,[25] but has had to struggle for existence since the early 20th century, because the decline in the number of great powers,[26] the increase of uncertainty in military power,[27] and the shrinking in strategical distances[28] have made it more and more difficult to measure power and keep it in a stable equilibrium.

---

dustrial plants capable of producing military power. With the wide variety of factors involved, obviously the task of measuring military power is very difficult. Meanwhile, all these factors are subject to dynamic change every minute; strictly speaking, to keep them in a stable balance is impossible. This is a serious intrinsic weakness of the balance of power. Because of the difficulties of measuring the factors of military power, and of keeping them in a stable balance, this system has never been capable of being sufficiently fine-tuned to preserve the peace. (Cf. Frederick H. Gareau, ed., *The Balance of Power and Nuclear Deterrence,* Boston, 1962, p. 26-41, 89-121.)

25. Policies and ideas similar to the balance of power have been found in ancient history. (Cf. Frank M. Russell, *Theories of International Relations,* London, 1936, p. 30, 42, 61, 79; and "The Idea of Balance in Classical Thought," in the *Balance of Power,* ed. by Paul Seabury, San Francisco, 1965, p. 5-28.) The formulation of the balance of power into a system, however, is hardly to be found until modern times. Some writers have considered the 19th century the classic period of this system, and have asserted that European order during the period from the collapse of the Holy Alliance to the outbreak of the first World War was maintained mainly by it. (Cf. *The Balance of Power, op. cit.,* p. 29-65, "The Balance of Power as a System," and p. 96-149, "Justifying and Rejecting the Balance of Power.")

26. As a result of the World Wars, the number of great powers has been reduced, and power has become more and more concentrated in a few states. This situation has basically affected the balance of power system, since its existence is founded on the assumption of a stability resulting from a large number of nations, with somewhat equal power, independently and continually checking each other, so as to prevent any one of them from becoming too strong. "Stability will increase and the probability of war will decrease in proportion as the number of states in the system (of the balance of power) increases. Obviously a tendency to localize relations would be equivalent to reducing the system, in any particular instance, to a small number of states, and so would make against stability. So also the grouping of states in permanent alliances which are committed to act together would tend to reduce the number of independent entities in the system and so would decrease stability." (Quincy Wright, *A Study of War,* 2nd ed., Chicago, 1965, p. 755)

27. The degree of uncertainty in the actual and potential military power of the nations has greatly increased because of the accelerating development in military techniques, especially in new offensive weapons, such as airplanes. This increase has necessarily added many difficulties to keeping an equilibrium in power, which is the chief aim of, and also an important condition for, the system of the balance of power. (Cf. Hans J. Morgenthau, "Uncertainty," in *The Balance of Power and Nuclear Deterrence,* ed. by Frederick H. Gareau, Boston, 1962, p. 26-37.)

28. "Stability will be promoted by a moderate separation of states from one

Another well-known method for maintaining peace has been collective security,[29] of which the vitality has to be provided by the balance of power.[30] It had been tried several times in modern Europe before being adopted by the League of Nations, and again by the United Nations.[31] Its history has repeatedly showed that it is not able to survive serious disturbances of the balance of power.[32]

---

another.... Thus stability under a balance of power is promoted by artificial devices, such as disarmed zones or strong fortifications, which increase the separation of especially vulnerable frontiers. Without a separation of all frontiers sufficient to prevent sudden attack and continuous anxiety, a stable balance of power system is impossible." "A decrease in technological distance tends to decrease strategic distance.... A general decline in strategic distance tends to increase the vulnerability of all states to attack." (Quincy Wright, *A Study of War,* 2nd ed., Chicago, 1965, p. 755-756, 1245)

29. Collective security assumes that nations generally increase their armaments and go to war either because they are in fear of aggression or because they trust that aggression will succeed without too great a risk. If the community of nations could provide its members with security through collective action, the main motive for war would disappear. It implies legal rules and procedures to maintain the security of all. By establishing commitments of law and procedure before aggression occurs, it seeks to make the system preventive and not merely remedial. It assumes that common action will be taken against any member of the group that is found to have committed an act of aggression within the group as defined by the law and procedure that all have accepted. This system differs from a balance of power in that it rests on interpretation of law rather than on calculation of power. (Cf. Joel Larus, ed. *From Collective Security to Preventive Diplomacy,* New York, 1965, p. 273-303.)

30. "Theoretically, the assumption of the collective security is different with that of the balance of power. In fact, however, none of the practices of the collective security did not depend on the balance of power, and none of them succeeded in subordinating the system of the balance of power to their juridical and ideological postulates." "Only when the balance has been so stable that attention has been diverted from it, because emancipation from its operation has been for the moment deemed impossible, has collective security worked." (Quincy Wright, *A Study of War,* 2nd ed., Chicago, 1965, p. 781)

31. The collective security was early envisaged in the diplomacy of Wolsey (cf. Garrett Mattingly, "An Early Non-aggression Pact," *Journal of Modern History,* X, March, 1930) and Henry IV (cf. Edwin D. Mead, *The Great Design of Henry IV,* Boston, 1909), was actually attempted in the "Confederation of Europe" (cf. Walter A. Phillips, *The Confederation of Europe: a Study of the European Alliance 1813-1823, as an Experiment in the International Organization of Peace,* London, 1920), the "Concert of Europe" (cf. Robert B. Mowat, *The Concert of Europe,* London, 1930), and the "Confederation of the Hague Conferences" (cf. Walther M.A. Schucking, *The International Union of the Hague Conferences,* London, 1918), and was tried to provide permanent institutions first in the League of Nations (cf. *Covenant of the League of Nations,* Articles 8-17), and again in the United Nations (cf. *Charter of the United Nations,* Articles 23-54).

Collective security always puts emphasis on the peaceful settlement of international disputes by consent or sanction.[33] While consent may be reached in settling minor disputes, sanction, if not supported by a balance of power, tends to be either an ineffectual procedure, or leads to war itself.[34]

Efforts which have been made to seek the outlawing of war were crowned in the Paris Pact of 1928.[35] Except for certain moral and

---

32. For example, George Canning gave the *coup de grace* to the Confederation of Europe; Otto von Bismark temporarily eliminated the Concert of Europe; the German Kaiser ignored the Hague system; Japan, Adolf Hitler, and Benito Mussolini wrecked the League of Nations. (Cf. Ludwig Dehio, *Precarious Balance, Four Centuries of the European Power Struggle,* New York, 1962; and *Balance of Power,* ed. by Paul Seabury, San Francisco, 1965, p. 66-95.)

33. Cf. Convention for the Pacific Settlement of International Disputes signed at the Hague, 1907; Articles 13-17 of the Covenant of the League of Nations; Chapters VI and VII of the Charter of the United Nations, and the Statute of the International Court of Justice.

34. International disputes which could be settled by consent are, in fact, confined to unimportant cases that are unlikely to lead to war, and cases where the parties have no intention of resorting to force. Sanction, under present conditions, cannot go a little further beyond the collective security, which, in fact, cannot go a little further beyond the system of the balance of power. When the system of the balance of power has collapsed, it is not surprising that sanction becomes either an ineffectual procedure or a war itself, such as the cases of Manchuria and Ethiopia which led to World War II, and the case of the Korean war in the early 1950s. (Cf. Helena M. Swanwick, *Collective Insecurity,* London, 1937, p. 171-192; and her *The Roots of Peace,* London, 1938, p. 19-34.)

35. It is a treaty renouncing war as an instrument of national policy, signed in Paris by delegates of 15 nations, on Aug. 27, 1928. Originally, Aristide Briand, French foreign minister, in a note to the United States on July 20, 1927, suggested a pact of perpetual friendship between France and the United States, to which Frank B. Kellogg, Secretary of State, replied on December 29th, proposing to invite the nations of the world to join in such an agreement. It was decided to ask Great Britain, Germany, Italy, and Japan, and later the British Dominions, Belgium, and Czechoslovakia to join. On Aug. 27, 1928, 15 leading nations signed the pact, later to be joined by 48 others. It was invoked unsuccessfully in 1931 when Japan invaded Manchuria, and in 1935 when Italy invaded Ethiopia, but with some success in disputes between Bolivia and Paraguay, and Columbia and Peru. Both the Kellogg-Briand pact and the Locarno pact, which was of a similar nature, were flouted by Hitler in his efforts at world domination for Germany. (Cf. James T. Gerould, *The Pact of Paris,* New York, 1929, p. 17-19.)

The Kellogg Pact "was contrived by men who either do not realize at all, or who find it advisable at present not to admit that they realize, the possibility of the world being arranged in any way other than as a sort of patchwork quilt of independent sovereign states with their boundaries fixed forever.... We may sign Kellogg pacts and Kelloggesque Pacts in Europe until there is a shortage of parchment and gold

legal influences, however, these efforts have not gone beyond the collective security, which, again, depends on the balance of power.

As a primary method for maintaining peace, the balance of power is indeed important in international relations.[36] But there has never been wholehearted devotion to it among the great powers. Instead, they have tended to wreck it with arms races, giving rise to a tension of war even in peace time.[37]

Necessarily, then, disarmament has been sought as an important method for maintaining peace. Its rudimental form was armament-building holidays[38] and some principles were first laid down in the

---

pens, and we shall have nothing real for the peace of the world." (Herbert G. Wells, *The Common Sense of World Peace,* London, 1929, p. 12, 15, 21)

36. In fact, not only international security, but the whole system of international law depends on the balance of power. Because the international law system would not go so far as to set up a central authority above the sovereign nations, therefore, the only recourse on which it depends to maintain order and enforce law is that the nations, especially the great powers, keep each other in check. "A law of nations can exist only if there be an equilibrium, a balance of power, between the members of the family of nations. If the powers cannot keep one another in check, no rules of law will have any force, since an over-powerful state will naturally try to act according to discretion and disobey the law.... The existence of the League of Nations makes a balance of power not less, but all the more necessary because an omnipotent state could disregard the League of Nations." (Lassa Oppenheim, *International Law,* R.F. Roxburgh ed., 3rd Edition, 1920, Vol. I, Sec. 51. See also Sec. 136.)

37. Each of the great powers considers the balance of power good for the others but not for itself, each tends to augment its relative power, and each tries to get out of this system in order to "hold the balance" and establish a hegemony over the others. Consequently, there has been, among the great powers under the balance of power system, a continuous armament race, which is always a serious cause of war and threatens the very existence of this system itself. "... and we reach, accordingly, a state of affairs in which each state regards the armaments of its neighbours as a menace and its own armaments as a guarantee of peace. Every increase in the armaments of one State brings a corresponding increase in the armaments of the others, and there is brought into being the familiar race of armaments.... It is astonishing that in every large country there should be those who maintain that peace can be preserved by being stronger than all likely adversaries. According to this logic, we shall have peace when every nation is stronger than every other nation." (William B. Curry, *The Case for Federal Union,* Harmondsworth, Eng., 1939, p. 60)

38. Holidays in naval building, army building, or military appropriations were proposed on a number of occasions during the 19th century, at the Hague Conferences of 1899 and 1907, by Great Britain in 1913, and by the League of Nations in 1920 and 1931. (Cf. Denys P. Myers, *World Disarmament,* Boston, 1932, p. 128; and Hans Wehberg, *The Limitation of Armament,* Washington, 1921, p. 5, 11, 38.)

Covenant of the League of Nations, leading to a series of conferences for implementation, but with little success.[39] Disarmament is generally divided into two categories: quantitative and qualitative. The former implies a general reduction of armaments to a special level,[40] and the latter means the elimination of certain types of weapons deemed to be particularly valuable for aggression.[41] Expert commissions have often been set up to work on the technical problems involved. They have gotten nowhere,[42] mainly because each great power has attempted to take a strategical advantage over the others.[43]

---

39. Cf. Article VIII of the Covenant of the League of Nations. Important conferences were the Washington Conference of 1921, the London Conference of 1931, and the Geneva Conference of 1932. But they achieved nothing, except that of Washington which succeeded in setting up some limitations for the great navy powers for ten years. (Cf. John W. Wheeler-Bennett, *The Disarmament Deadlock,* London, 1934; and *International Arms Control, Issues and Agreements,* by the Stanford Arms Control Group, ed. by John H. Barton and Lawrence D. Weiler, Stanford, Calif., 1976, p. 31-45.)

40. Quantitative disarmament inevitably affects the relative size of armaments in different nations, hence agreement on ratios is exceedingly difficult to achieve. Any new ratio would indeed change the relative power. Even if the existing status quo is taken as the basis for the ratios, a reduction of armaments will also mean an actual change in relative power, because it will augment the importance of the nonmilitary resources of the nations: if navies are reduced, the large merchant marine will count for more; if stocks of arms and munitions are reduced, the larger iron and chemical industry will count for more; and if military effectives are reduced, the larger population will count for more. (Cf. Benjamin H. Williams, *The United States and Disarmament,* New York, 1931, p. 226-233; and Henry W. Forbes, *The Strategy of Disarmament,* Washington, 1962, p. 15-33.)

41. The object of qualitative disarmament is to increase the possession of defensive weapons and to decrease the possession of offensive weapons to such an extent that each country will approximate a perfect defense against any probable attack. Invasion will then be physically impossible. Is such universal perfection of defenses possible to achieve? The answer first meets the difficulties of making a valid distinction between defensive and offensive weapons; and secondly depends on the characteristics of the things to be defended, as the defense of territory, the defense of overseas commerce, the defense of nationals abroad, and the defense of expansive foreign policies may require very different equipments. (Cf. Henry W. Forbes, *The Strategy of Disarmament,* Washington, 1962, p. 34-48.)

42. As concluded by Salvadore de Madariaga, *Disarmament,* 1929, p. 92, "It was as foolish to expect a disarmament convention from such a commission, as a declaration for atheism from a commission of clergymen."

43. Different attitudes toward weapons are well indicated by the parable of the disarmament conference of the animals. The lion wanted to eliminate all weapons but claws and jaws, the eagle all but talons and beaks, the bear all but an embracing hug. (Cf. Salvador de Madariaga, *Disarmament,* New York, 1929, p. 16-66.)

The last resort for maintaining peace has been recognition of the right of self-defense against aggression.[44] This recognition not only casts distrust upon other security methods, but also leaves open loopholes through which any kind of war could be carried on, because there is no clear demarcation which can be made between defense and aggression, and whether the circumstances required to enter into a war of self-defense are to be decided on by each nation itself.[46]

So, as demonstrated in modern history, all the conventional methods for maintaining peace have become less and less effective while war has become bigger and worse. It is obvious that the future of mankind is very gloomy and that total destruction is lying ahead if there is no way to halt this tendency.[47] The situation has become

---

44. The Charter of the United Nations makes it clear that nothing shall impair the "inherent right of individual or collective self-defense" (cf. Article 51 of the Charter of the United Nations), and even the Pact of Paris, which solemnly renounces war as an instrument of national policy, was qualified by Briand's statement that each nation would remain the "sole competent authority to decide whether circumstances required it to resort to war in self-defense." (Cf. James T. Gerould, *The Pact of Paris,* New York, 1929, p. 78-79.)

45. This was well pointed out by Jonathan Dymond a hundred years ago when he discussed Christianity and war: "If Christianity allows defensive war, she allows all wars.... The aggressor is difficult of discovery: for he whom we choose to 'fear,' may say that he had previous 'fear' of us, and that his 'fear' prompted the hostile symptoms which made us 'fear' again. The truth is that to attempt to make any distinction upon the subject is vain." (Quoted in Frank M. Russell, *Theories of International Relations,* London, 1936, p. 287.)

"That Napoleon, the arch-aggressor of modern Europe, declared solemnly in his *Memoirs,* written at St. Helena, that all his wars were purely 'defensive' just as Hitler marched for 'peace and unity.' " (Sydney Harris, "The Cry of the Aggressor Has Ever Been 'Peace,' " *South Bend Tribune,* Jan. 23, 1979, p. 12.

46. "I am not aware that any of the nations that fought in the Great War admitted that they were fighting aggressively. It was Great Britain that declared war on Germany, and not vice-versa. How many Englishmen would entertain for a moment the idea that our declaration of war constituted us an aggressor nation? They believe, for the most part with perfect sincerity, that 'circumstances required us to resort to war in self-defense.' Most Germans believe the same thing of their own nation. They believed that they were in danger of encirclement by England, France and Russia, and that 'circumstances required them to resort to war in self-defense.' " (William B. Curry, *The Case for Federal Union,* Harmondsworth, Eng., 1939, p. 38)

47. "Utterly futile are all efforts to restrict, to regulate, to localize, to humanize warfare. As well try to regulate a prairie fire. Once the conflagration has broken out, it will be driven by the gale of human passions until it burns itself out; and with the ever-increasing destructiveness of methods and the space-annihilating inventions of the present day, it will eventually reach the remotest corners of com-

much worse in the new era of warfare commencing with the dropping of the first atomic bomb.

c.
Nuclear Holocaust

THE MOST SIGNIFICANT AND HORRIBLE PHENOMENON in the new era has been the rapid development of nuclear weapons from atomic to hydrogen bombs[48] with explosive power up to many megatons of TNT.[49] These weapons are being produced more and

---

batant nations and will totally destroy the mechanism of civilization." (Oscar Newfang, *The Road to World Peace,* New York, 1924, p. xii-xiii)

48. An atomic bomb's effects differ from those of conventional bombs in three important respects: first, the amount of energy released (blast) is about a million times that of the same weight of high-explosive bombs; second, the atomic explosion is accompanied by the immediate release of penetrating, harmful, and invisible radiation; and third, substances remaining in the area long after the explosion are radioactive and harmful to living organisms. The hydrogen bomb is called a thermonuclear weapon because high heat is required to start its explosive nuclear reaction. Its energy release exceeds that of the atomic bomb by the same ratio as the atomic bomb's blast exceeds the conventional high-explosive bomb but more widespread. The atomic bomb is a fission device, and the hydrogen bomb is a fusion device. There is a third device: fission-fusion-fission, which is the most economic, compact, and also the dirtiest bomb. (Cf. *The Effects of Nuclear Weapons,* ed. by Samuel Glasstone, rev. ed., Washington, 1964, p. 1-27; and Roger Hilsman, *The Crouching Future,* New York, 1975, p. 543-544.)

49. "Fission bombs and shells for atomic cannon have been made as small as one kiloton—that is, having the energy equivalent of 1,000 tons of TNT. The Hiroshima bomb was 20 kilotons. Fusion and fission-fusion-fission bombs and warheads have been tested that range from about one third of a megaton (i.e. one third of 1 million tons of TNT equivalent) up to 57 megatons, which was the size of a test bomb fired by the Soviet Union in 1961. Present-day arsenals include a wide variety of the so-called tactical or battlefield atomic weapons in the kiloton range. Submarines of the Polaris type carried missiles with warheads of about 1 megaton. The American land-based missiles throughout the 1960s carried 1 warhead of about 3 megatons, while some Soviet missiles carried somewhat larger ones. The American B-52 bomber and Soviet manned bombers generally carried bombs in the 10-to-20 megaton range, although much larger ones are possible. (Roger Hilsman, *The Crouching Future,* New York, 1975, p. 544)

The explosive power of a one megaton nuclear weapon is approximately equal to that produced by one million tons of chemical high explosives. This much high

more[50] and possessed by more and more nations.[51] They can be delivered by guided missiles with multiple independently targeted re-entry vehicle,[52] on targets as far as thousands of miles away[53] in minutes of time.[54]

---

explosive would fill more than 10,000 railroad cars. (Cf. John S. Foster, Jr., "Nuclear Weapons," *Encyclopedia Americana,* 1973 ed., Vol. 20, p. 522.)

50. The nuclear arsenals of the United States and the Soviet Union alone totalled well over a million megatons in 1968, according to David Inglis, a senior physicist at the Argonne National Laboratory writing at the time, and soon thereafter may have been "approaching a hundred million megatons." ("The Outlook for Nuclear Explosives," *Unless Peace Comes,* ed. by Nigel Calder, New York, 1968)

51. Four years after the dropping of the first American baby atomic bomb on Hiroshima (on Aug. 6, 1945), the Soviet Union set off an atomic explosion (some time in Sept., 1949). Then the U.S. decided in 1950 to develop a hydrogen bomb with thermonuclear reactions. The first successful detonation was carried out on Eniwetok atoll on Nov. 1, 1952. The Russions used the thermonuclear principle a few months later in one of their nuclear tests. After the American and Russian tests, thermonuclear explosions were produced by the British (1957), the Chinese (1967), the French (1968), and the Indians (1974). (Cf. Lincoln P. Bloomfield, "Nuclear Spread and World Order," in *Arms and Control and Security, Current Issues,* ed. by Wolfram F. Hanrieder, Boulder, Colorado, 1979, p. 293-306; Amitai Etzioni, *The Hard Way to Peace,* New York, 1962, p. 53-56.)

"1. Each addition to the number of nations armed with nuclear weapons drives its neighbors toward acquiring similar arms. 2. As nuclear weapons pass into more hands, the chance increases that a major war will be started by some human error or technical accident. 3. The spread to more nations increases the chance of deliberate initiation of nuclear war. 4. Increase in the number of nuclear powers would further increase the difficulty of achieving disarmament. 5. After it obtains nuclear weapons, a nation becomes a more likely target in any nuclear war." (Quoted from the Oslo Statement issued by 35 physical and biological scientists and 25 social scientists from 15 countries at a conference held in Oslo, Norway, May 2-7, 1961, sponsored by Linus Pauling, Bertrand Russell and 23 other well-known scientists. Cf. Linus Pauling, *No More War,* 25th anniversary edition, New York, 1983, p. 275-282.)

52. The development of MIRV—the acronym for multiple, independently targeted re-entry vehicle—has been well under way. "Instead of one warhead on the tip of a missile, there will be two, three, or more, each of which can be directed at a different target. The consequence of this development is, first, of course, greatly to increase the number of warheads that can be delivered from a given number of launching pads. Perhaps more important, however, is that MIRV greatly complicates the problem of achieving an effective antiballistic missile defense." (Roger Hilsman, *The Crouching Future,* New York, 1975, p. 553. Cf. *International Arms Control, Issues and Agreements,* by the Stanford Arms Control Group, ed. by John H. Barton and Lawrence D. Weiler, Stanford, Calif., 1976, p. 136-140.)

53. In addition to the long range air bombers, such as the American B-52, the U.S. has had missiles Titan II and Minuteman II, each with a range of 7,000 miles,

What would be the result of fighting between nations with such nuclear weapons?

First of all, most, if not all, of the population of the target nations, together with their big cities, would be annihilated by nuclear blasts and heat,[55] leaving the survivors to "envy the dead."[56]

---

and Minuteman III with a range of 7,500 miles; the Soviet Union has had missiles SS-9 Scarp with a range of 7,500 miles, SS-11 Sego and SS-17, each with a range of 6,500 miles, SS-18 and SS-19 Mod 2, each with a range of 6,300 miles and SS-19 Mod 1 with a range of 7,000 miles. These missiles, and others from submarines or moving bases, can carry nuclear warheads to hit any place in the world. (Cf. Lan Smart, *Advanced Strategic Missiles, a Short Guide,* London, 1969, p. 1-31; and International Institute for Strategic Studies, *The Military Balance, 1978-1979,* London, 1978, p. 80-81.)

54. "Both the Soviet and American ICBMs available in 1970 had a range of well over 5,000 miles, which they could travel in about 30 minutes. Warning time at best would be 15 minutes." (Roger Hilsman, *The Crouching Future,* New York, 1975, p. 547. Cf. Edgar M. Bottome, *The Balance of Terror,* Boston, 1971, p. iv.)

55. "Many estimates have been made by scientists of the probable effects of hypothetical nuclear attacks. One estimate, reported in the 1957 hearings before the Special Subcommittee on Radiation of the Joint Committee on Atomic Energy of the Congress of the United States, was for an attack on population and industrial centers and military installations in the United States with 250 bombs totaling 2,500 megatons. The estimate of casualties presented in the testimony, corrected for the increase in population since 1957, is that sixty days after the day on which the attack took place 98,000,000 of the 190,000,000 American people would be dead, and 28,000,000 would be seriously injured but still alive, many of the remaining 70,000,000 survivors would be suffering from minor injuries and radiation effects. This is a small nuclear attack, made with use of about 1 per cent of the existing weapons. A major nuclear war might well see a total of 30,000 megatons, one tenth of the estimated stockpiles, delivered and exploded over the populated regions of the United States, the Soviet Union, and the other major European countries. The studies of Hugh Everett III and George E. Pugh, of the Weapons Systems Evaluation Division, Institute of Defense Analyses, Washington, D.C., reported in the 1959 hearings before the Special Subcommittee on Radiation, permit us to make an estimate of the casualties of such a war. This estimate is that sixty days after the day on which the war was waged 720,000,000 of the 800,000,000 people in these countries would be dead, 60,000,000 would be alive but severely injured, and there would be 20,000,000 other survivors" under very miserable conditions. (*Linus Pauling on Science and Peace,* New York, 1964, p. 11)

56. President John F. Kennedy said in his television speech on June 26, 1963: "Three times in the last 2½ years I have been required to report to you as President that this Nation and the Soviet Union stood on the verge of direct military confrontation—in Laos, in Berlin, and in Cuba. . . . A full scale nuclear exchange, lasting less than 60 minutes, could wipe out more than 300 million Americans, Europeans and Russians, as well as untold numbers elsewhere. And the survivors, as Chairman Khrushchev warned the Communist Chinese, 'would envy the dead.' " (*The Burden and the Glory,* ed. by Allan Nevins, New York, 1964, p. 62.

Next, the radiation produced by nuclear detonations would spread over everywhere and fall onto everything with deadly poisons,[57] and would persist through generations to come to cause cancer and other serious diseases.[58]

It is also known that nuclear detonations would destroy the atmospheric screen, change global temperatures and deprive people of food crops for years.[59] There are still many more aftermaths, legacies and other effects which remain unpredictable.[60]

Cf. Leiba Brown and Ruth Leeds, "What the Bombs Can Do," in *The Hard Way to Peace,* by Amitai Etzioni, New York, 1962, p. 267-280.)

57. "When an atomic bomb explodes it scoops up great chunks of earth so that a huge crater is formed in the ground. Earth and debris are blown high into the air and crushed to smithereens, then it all descends as dust: radiated dust, with Strontium-90 in it; also carbon-14 and other deadly poisons. The dust mingles with the clouds and then falls with rain. It settles on the leaves of trees and other plants. The rain washes it to the ground where it seeps into the soil, into the fish, into birds and animals and into us. Cows eat the radiated grass and we eat the meat and drink the milk and get radiation into our bodies. There is no escape." (*William Winter Comments,* Vol. VI, no. 40, Oct. 2, 1967. Cf. Linus Pauling, *No More War,* 25th anniversary edition, New York, p. 38-148; Albert Schweitzer, "Declaration of Conscience," *The Saturday Review,* May 18, 1957; and the Stockholm International Peace Research Institute, *Weapons of Mass Destruction and the Environment,* London, 1977, p. 2-14.)

58. "When atomic bombs are detonated, radiation is produced. Any amount of radiation affects the genes, so that the effect is carried into future generations. Scientists have said the effects of the radiation already absorbed by mankind from the nuclear tests in past years will not fully be known for several more generations. We know, for instance, that a poison called Strontium-90 does not exist in nature. It is produced by atomic explosion. Strontium-90 has a 'half-life' of 28 years. That means that 28 years after it enters the human body, half of it is still there; and 28 years after that, half of that amount is still there. What is more, it is cumulative so that the amount which enters the body today is added to what was absorbed yesterday and the day before. Strontium-90 has an affinity for calcium. When it enters the body it finds its way into the bones. Once it gets there, it stays. You can't eliminate it. You can't wash it out, rub it out, you can't neutralize it with medicine. It stays there indefinitely and is passed on to future generations. Strontium-90 is known to cause leukemia and bone cancer." (*William Winter Comments,* Vol. VI, no. 40, Oct. 2, 1967. Cf. Linus Pauling, *No More War,* 25th anniversary edition, New York, p. 49-111; and Stockholm International Peace Research Institute, *Weapons of Mass Destruction and the Environment,* London, 1977, p. 2-14.)

59. One finding of the study of the U.S. National Research Council Committee was that "nuclear detonations would destroy a large part of the atmospheric ozone layer that screens earth from harmful doses of ultraviolet radiation. The scientists predicted a reduction of half the ozone which they said would increase the rates of skin cancer 10 percent in mid-latitudes for 40 years. If 70 percent of the ozone were wiped out, which they said was possible, the radiation would be so intense a person would get a severe, blistering sunburn in 10 minutes. The increased

And finally, therefore, "no nation could expect to survive unscathed and thereby inherit the earth."[61] It is even doubtful that our civilization could survive the catastrophe of a great nuclear war.[62]

---

ultraviolet radiation also could drop global temperatures slightly with serious agricultural impact.... And Fred C. Ikle, director of the Arms Control and Disarmament agency, said on the basis of the report there is a possibility that an 'ecological backlash' would affect an aggressor even if that nation were not struck by retaliatory weapons. He said such a backlash, for example, could deprive the Soviet Union of its food crops for several years." (Al Rossiter, Jr., UPI reporter, "Atomic War Results Theorized," *South Bend Tribune,* Oct. 5, 1975, p. 8. Cf. Stockholm International Peace Research Institute, *Weapons of Mass Destruction and the Environment,* London, 1977, p. 15-22.)

60. There are many uncertainties about the effects of a nuclear war. Fred C. Ikle, Director of the Arms Control and Disarmament Agency, said, "the more we learn about large scale nuclear war, the more we don't know." (Quoted by Al Rossiter, Jr., UPI reporter, in "Atomic War Results Theorized," *South Bend Tribune,* Oct. 5, 1975, p. 8. Cf. Stockholm International Peace Research Institute, *Weapons of Mass Destruction and the Environment,* London, 1977, p. 22-30.)

61. Dr. Philip Handler, President of the U.S. National Academy of Sciences, in a letter to Dr. Fred C. Ikle, Director of the U.S. Arms Control and Disarmament Agency, accompanying a report of the National Research Council on a large nuclear war, warned that "let no reader conclude from this report that distant other nations would survive a major nuclear exchange unscathed and, thereby inherit the earth.... The economic, social and political consequences of the resultant worldwide terror are entirely unpredictable." (National Academy of Sciences, *Annual Report,* fiscal year 1975-76, Washington, 1976, p. 43.)

A declaration signed by 52 Nobel laureates at Mainau, Lake Constance, July 15, 1955, points out that "if war broke out among the great powers, who could guarantee that it would not develop into a deadly conflict? A nation that engages in a total war thus signals its own destruction and imperils the whole world" and that "by total military use of weapons feasible today, the earth can be contaminated with radioactivity to such an extent that whole peoples can be annihilated. Neutrals may die thus as well as belligerents." (Cf. Linus Pauling, *No More War,* 25th anniversary edition, New York, p. 252.)

62. "No one knows how widely such lethal radio-active particles might be diffused, but the best authorities are unanimous in saying that a war with H-bombs might quite possibly put an end to the human race. It is feared that if many H-bombs are used there will be universal death—sudden only for a minority, but for the majority a slow torture of disease and disintegration." (The Russell-Einstein Manifesto, July 1955, as appendix 6 in Linus Pauling, *No More War,* 25th anniversary edition, New York, p. 284)

Review some films such as Sidney Lumet's *Fail-Safe,* showing a president sacrificing New York to nuclear destruction in order to avoid a global war; *The War Game,* made by British filmmaker Peter Walkins, harrowing documentary of England under nuclear attack; and later, *The Testament,* about a suburban housewife in Hamlin, California, who watches her family and community die

There is still something else which might emerge into the terrible picture, such as the additional use of chemical weapons,[63] the resort to the "extremely dirty" bomb or "doomsday" machine,[64] and the

---

from the lethal radiation generated by a nuclear strike on San Francisco; and *The Day After,* a made-for-TV movie, chronicled the demise of the town of Lawrence, Kansas, following a nuclear attack on Kansas City, forty miles away. (Cf. Dolores Barclay, "Day After Spawns Films," *South Bend Tribune,* Nov. 25, 1983, p. 34.)

63. "There are other means of attacking our country and us than with atomic weapons. There are such things as poison not related to radiation. There is a poisonous substance so deadly that a tiny drop, small enough to fit on the head of a pin, touching the skin of a human being will produce death in ten agonizing minutes. You can't wash it off, rub it off, or defend against it once it touches your skin. There are other poisons which destroy the brain, which paralyze the nervous system, damage hearing, vision, digestion, make rational thought impossible. There is botulism which can poison an entire community by contaminating its food supply." (*William Winter Comments,* Vol. VI, no. 40, Oct. 2, 1967. Cf. Stockholm International Peace Research Institute, *Weapons of Mass Destruction and the Environment,* London, 1977, p. 31-43.)

The well-known chemical weapons are tabun, sarin and botulin. Their formidable agents are nerve gases which kill rapidly by inhibiting the action of the enzyme cholinesterase, resulting in lack of muscular control and in respiratory paralysis. Biological weapons use viruses, rickettsiae, bacteria, and fungi as their killing agents. (Cf. U.S. House of Representatives, Committee on Science and Astronautics, *Research in CBR* (Chemical, Biological, and Radiological Warfare), 86th Congress, 1st Session, H.R. No. 815, Washington, 1959; and United Nations, Dept. of Political and Security Council Affairs, *Napalm and Other Incendiary Weapons and All Aspects of Their Possible Use,* New York, 1973, p. 5-59.)

A new binary chemical weapon exists which Dr. R.J. Rutman, a University of Pennsylvania biochemist, has called the "escalatory weapon par excellence." He states: "The only effective response to it is a nuclear weapon or something more exotic.... The binary is the first in a long line of new weapons. They are dazzling, unbelievable, and could 'vaporize' an enemy." (*South Bend Tribune,* August 31, 1976, p. 1)

A report in the "Arms Control Impact Statements" sent to the U.S. Congress from the White House in the latter part of 1980, said starting construction of a plant to manufacture so-called "binary poison gas" weapons would help "keep open an option to upgrade U.S. retaliatory capabilities" if the Soviet Union keeps building up its chemical arsenal, according to Barton Reppert, AP reporter, in the *South Bend Tribune,* Feb. 15, 1981, p. 3.

64. "An extremely 'dirty' bomb can be made by putting a cobalt jacket around an H bomb. Either the Northern or Southern hemispheres could be made uninhabitable with such a bomb.... By using cobalt bombs in both hemispheres, it is also possible to make 'doomsday' machines—weapons capable of making the whole planet uninhabitable." (Roger Hilsman, *The Crouching Future,* New York, 1975, p. 552. Cf. Amitai Etzioni, *The Hard Way to Peace,* New York, 1962, p. 55-60; and Neville Shute, *On the Beach,* New York, 1957.)

extension of the battle into outer space.[65] Any such eventualities would make it more difficult for us and our civilization to escape extinction and would render our planet more uninhabitable.

Indeed, there have been various attempts to erect anti-ballistic missile systems against nuclear weapons. But it is very difficult for such systems to be perfected technically[66] without any loopholes,[67]

---

65. "... No nation is ready to fight such a 'Star Wars' battle in space. But the United States and the Soviet Union have been accelerating an arms race in space. As a result, the security of both countries has become increasingly dependent upon orbiting satellites. U.S. and Soviet satellites spy on each other and on other nations with high resolution cameras. Ships, submarines and planes navigate by satellite. Military leaders communicate around the world by satellite. Other satellites hang in space to warn of enemy rocket launches as infra-red sensors detect their heat. This growing reliance on space systems is causing concern at the Pentagon because the Soviets have introduced the first tactical space weapon—a hunter-killer satellite capable of blasting American payloads out of the sky. The United States is developing its own hunter-killer and extensive research is underway to reduce the vulnerability of U.S. satellites.... Some defense experts believe the Soviets may have started a series of tests of satellites designed to carry high energy laser weapons. They could fire destructive beams of light at other satellites hundreds of miles away." (Howard Benedict, "Competing Nations Looking Skyward; Space May Be Next Arena for U.S.-Soviet Arms Race," *South Bend Tribune,* March 19, 1978, p. 14)

"Beyond this, it now seems clear that the laser will have a prominent role. Lasers can be used to provide secure communications between spaceships, for example, or to burn holes in an enemy vehicle, whether spaceship or tank, and it may turn out that they will be suitable as part of an antiballistic missile weapon. It is also conceivable that lasers may form the basis for 'disintegrator' or death-ray weapons." (Roger Hilsman, *The Crouching Future.* New York, 1975, p. 557)

66. The fundamental reason is that all antiballistic missile systems have to depend on radar and computers. The attacker can take a number of steps to confuse or blind or "blackout" the defending radar. No matter how many missiles an anti-ballistic missile system is designed to handle simultaneously, the attacker could always send in enough missiles to throw the computers into confusion. (Cf. Roger Hilsman, *The Crouching Future,* New York, 1975, p. 560-563.)

67. There has never been an ironclad defense against military attack. Let us assume 100 bombs were directed at the United States, that defense efforts destroyed most of them, and that only 18 "terror" bombs managed to penetrate. *U.S. News & World Report* on July 31, 1967, published a "Scenario" by Rep. Craig Hosmer, a member of the Joint Committee on Atomic Energy and Chairman of the House Republican Conference Committee on Nuclear Affairs. In his "Scenario," he describes what might happen if the U.S. were attacked by just 18 of these bombs. The analysis was based on Atomic Energy Commission release D-279 (rev.) of Oct. 31, 1961, and *The Effects of Nuclear Weapons* by Samuel Gladstone, ed. AEC, April 1962. He concludes: "Three of every five Americans were dead and the nation's military-industrial back was broken."

and to hold certain advantages for some time[68] without inducing counter-measures.[69] In other words, no effective defense has been developed which could provide reliable protection against nuclear weapons.[70]

Under these circumstances, therefore, our world has actually been drawn to the "edge of oblivion,"[71] and we have been living under a continuous "hell-condition"[72] as despairing hostages[73] with

---

68. For example, "Secretary of Defense McNamara announced in San Francisco that the United States will build what he called a limited defense system of ABM—Anti-Ballistics-Missiles. . . . The brilliant scientist, Dr. Simon Ramo who was the chief designer of the Air Force missile program says he does not think the $5 billion figure cited by McNamara will be enough, that by the time we finish building installations of this kind they become obsolete, and further that it is possible for the Chinese or any other would-be attacker to bring weapons into this country piecemeal for assembly and detonation inside the U.S., by-passing the defenses entirely." (*William Winter Comments,* Vol. VI, no. 40, Oct. 2, 1967. Cf. *International Arms Control, Issues and Agreements,* by the Stanford Arms Control Group, ed. by John H. Barton and Lawrence D. Weiler, Stanford, Calif., 1976, p. 132-135.)

69. "Considering all the countermeasures available to an attacker, it seems obvious that an antiballistic missile defense system of the kind contemplated here does not change the earlier conclusion. A defense system, combined with a large scale shelter program, might give enough protection to reduce the percentages for a few years, but then the other side would have taken sufficient additional measures to nullify the defense." (Roger Hilsman, *The Crouching Future,* New York, 1975, p. 563.)

70. "A major nuclear conflict between the United States and the Soviet Union would destroy both great powers no matter what kind of defenses they erect, a congressional committee concludes. The Joint Committee on Defense Production declared in a report issued Monday that the much-touted Soviet civil and industrial defenses would not provide the Russian population or industry with any reliable protection against U.S. strategic forces. Nor could the United States satisfactorily protect its economy, as a superpower, even if it spent huge sums of money constructing industrial defenses, the committee said." (AP report in *South Bend Tribune,* May 17, 1977, p. 8)

71. "The World Lives on Edge of Oblivion," an article by Saul Pett, appeared in the *South Bend Tribune,* July 15, 1962, p. 43. "In sunshine we hear thunder; in stillness, we hear the last tempest." This is the situation described by the author. He quoted J. Glenn Gray, a philosophy professor: "Never before has the contrast between man's power and his importance seemed so stark. . . . Spiritual dizziness has become a permanent state. At last the universe appears to be open and at man's disposal, but at the same time bottomless." He also noted a mother saying, "Why should I have more children to bring into this crazy world?" and a student saying, "Why should I spend 12 years becoming a doctor when the world may blow up?"

72. "I respectfully welcome the statement of the ailing Pope that peace through fear is not real peace. It is a continuous hell-condition." (C. Rajagopalachari, *The Voice of the Uninvolved,* New Delhi, 1960, p. 6-7)

a perpetual nightmare.[74] While some people have been depressed enough to run away from these realities,[75] or to submerge themselves in false illusions,[76] others have tryed desperately to prevent nuclear war by old and new methods for maintaining peace.

d.
No Way to Escape

OF THE OLD METHODS, THE COLLECTIVE SECURITY IS the cornerstone for maintaining peace in the design of the United Nations. But its usefulness has been reduced almost to zero in dealing

---

73. "Under the Hague Convention of 1907 the great civilized nations agreed that the right of belligerents to adopt means of injuring the enemy was not unlimited. It was at that time conceived that the laws of war did not permit unarmed civilians to be killed deliberately. However, in the fifty years that followed the Hague Convention, all that has been changed.... Now, in the conception of nuclear war, the armed forces of each side take the civilians of the other side as their targets, and are unable to safeguard the lives of their own people. In 1907 it was declared to be against the laws of war for armed forces to take hostages whose lives would guarantee submission. Now, whole populations are hostages." (E.L.M. Burns, *Megamurder,* New York, 1967, p. 3-5)

"We confronted the known but not well-publicized fact that in a nuclear war, people—not only soldiers—who live in cities or near military targets, are themselves hostages to accident and escalation." (Robert A. Dentler and Phillips Cutright, *Hostage America,* Boston, 1963, p. ix)

74. "The nightmare of the Western world and of the Soviet Union is that any day instantaneous death may come to millions upon millions of their populations, with the simultaneous destruction of the cities, the structures, the machines and the stored knowledge upon which civilization depends." (E.L.M. Burns, *Megamurder,* New York, 1967, p. 4)

75. "We seem unable to sustain our feeling of fear in the presence of a constant, continual danger," says Dr. Jerome Frank, psychiatrist at Johns Hopkins. Thus, he says, some of us find intellectual escape hatches. A tomahawk could leave you just as dead as an H-bomb; therefore, why worry about the bomb? Since the world began, people have been predicting its end and it has never happened; so why think it will now? Poison gas proved so terrible it was never used a second time; for the same reason, atomic weapons will never be used again. (Cf. Saul Pett, "'The World Lives on Edge of Oblivion,'" in the *South Bend Tribune,* July 15, 1962, p. 43.)

76. "The human mind has many ingenious devices for temporary self-insulation. It can, through wishful thinking or helplessness, rationalize real danger

with the great powers who have nuclear weapons in one hand and a veto power in the other.[77]

As noted earlier, the vital condition for the collective security, as well as for other old methods for maintaining peace, is the balance of power, and the vital condition for the balance of power is the existence of a good number of great powers with some stable strength to keep each other in check and with some geographical obstacles to hold each other in bounds. Since World War II, such a condition has not existed. The world has been divided into two camps led by the two superpowers—the United States and Soviet Union. They have confronted directly, each equipped with a delivery system for the fast growing nuclear weapons capable of destroying the other in hours.[78]

---

away.... Dr. Gordon Allport, Harvard social psychologist, calls the process an 'ego defensive apathy—a defensive against facing the worst.' He is reminded of a study made of the German Jews under Hitler which showed that even as the persecution grew, many Jews refused to believe it." (Saul Pett, "The World Lives on Edge of Oblivion," in the *South Bend Tribune,* July 15, 1962, p. 43)

77. In view of the weakness of the collective security system in the League of Nations, the Charter of the United Nations confers responsibility onto the Security Council, on the five permanent members—the United States, Soviet Union, China, Great Britain, and France. But all the five permanent members have a power to veto any measure deemed unsatisfactory, and all of them have nuclear weapons. For these reasons, they are the appointed sheriffs as well as the suspected criminals. Obviously, it is impossible for this system to work well. (Cf. The Charter of the United Nations, Articles 23-54, especially 24 and 27.)

"It is, however, clear that the veto makes it impossible for the Security Council ever to use its powers against a Great Power.... Yet the only event today which can seriously endanger the peace of the world is aggression by a Great Power, and a system which solemnly declares, as the Charter does, that its purpose is 'to take effective collective measures for the prevention and removal of threats to the peace and for the suppression of acts of aggression,' and yet does not propose to deal with the aggression of a Great Power, is little better than a sham." (James L. Brierly, *The Law of Nations; an Introduction to the International Law of Peace,* 4th ed., Oxford, 1949, p. 281)

78. "Stability will increase as the parity in the power of states increases. If there were only two states, there would be great instability unless they were very nearly equal in power or their frontiers were widely separated or difficult to pass. The same would be true if all the states had become polarized in two rival alliances." (Quincy Wright, *A Study of War,* 2nd ed., Chicago, 1965, p. 755)

"Since World War II it has become even more clear that the balance of power system cannot function effectively for either defense or deterrence when power is bipolarized ... in 1964 it seemed extremely doubtful whether any system of mutual deterrence by national retaliatory forces, or by regional arrangements or alliances, could maintain a stable equilibrium of military power in the atomic age." (*Ibid,* p. 1528-1529)

The shifting position of China between them[79] and the role played by the non-aligned nations[80] have constituted no real condition under which the balance of power can be restored to prevent a nuclear war.[81]

---

79. Communist China, after having overthrown the nationalist regime in 1949, kept a policy of "one side" with the Soviet Union, then started to move away in the late 1950s and tried to build a leadership in the Third World. Since the early 1970s, China has made an effort to "normalize" its relation with the United States against the Russian hegemony. As a nation with almost one fourth of the world population the shift of its position is necessarily of great importance, but has not significantly changed the over-all picture of the bipolarized power struggle in the atomic age. (Cf. Robert C. North, *The Foreign Relations of China,* Belmont, Calif., 1969, p. 72-133; Harold C. Hinton, *China's Turbulent Quest,* new ed., Bloomington, Indiana, 1972, p. 306-312; and Yuan-Li Wu, *Communist China and the World Balance of Power,* Washington, 1971, p. 1-6.)

80. Since World War II, the world has been divided into two camps led by two superpowers—the United States and the Soviet Union. They have confronted directly and both have equipped themselves with nuclear weapons capable of destroying each other. Under these circumstances, the other nations, especially the newly grown Afro-Asian nations, have tried to stay away from the confrontation of the two camps and not be aligned with either side. This policy has been confused with traditional neutrality, but at a meeting in Belgrade in September, 1961, sponsored by Prime Minister Nehru of India, President Nasser of Egypt, President Kwame Nkrumah of Ghana, and President Tito of Yugoslavia, the term "nonalignment," rather than "neutralism" was generally used. The number of members of the nonalignment movement increased from a few to as many as 85 in the Colombo Fifth Summit Conference, August 1976. As their members have increased, however, they have found difficulties in lining themselves up in objectives and policies. This was illustrated by a report that Somalia was seeking the expulsion of Cuba from the ranks of the nonaligned. (Cf. G.H. Janse, *Non-alignment and the Afro-Asian States,* New York, 1966, p. 14-17; "The Role and Place of Nonalignment in the World of Today," in *Nonalignment in the World of Today,* ed. by Ljubivoje Acimovic, Beograd, 1969, p. 17-76; Peter Willetts, *The Non-alignment Movement,* London, 1978, p. 1; and Robert A. Mortimer, *The Third World Coalition in International Politics,* New York, 1980, p. 74-130.)

81. The main reason for this is that in the bipolarized power struggle, a nuclear war can occur between the United States and the Soviet Union at any minute, and destroy both in hours. It would be too quick for even allies to help much immediately in such a war, not to mention a third force. Obviously, therefore, no third force could be weighed very heavily in the balance of power. In this connection, a statement made by Edgar M. Bottome is worth quoting. "This incredible increase in the destructive power available to the modern nation-state has substantially changed the 'rules of the game' in the conduct of a nation's foreign policy. For example, the move from the old balance of power concept to a balance of terror means that additional allies no longer immediately add to a nation's security. On the contrary, additional allies may actually decrease a nation's security." (In his *The Balance of Terror,* Boston, 1971, p. xiii)

The superpowers, then, have adopted an old strategy as a new method called deterrence. It means to build a nuclear arms stockpile so strong that the potential enemy would not dare to risk a nuclear attack.[82] It is doubtful that this method can really work;[83] but for cer-

---

82. Deterrence is a military strategy under which one major power uses the threat of instant, overwhelming reprisal to effectively exclude nuclear attack from an adversary power's available alternatives. It is a function of the terrible striking power of nuclear weapons. An essential element of deterrence is the maintenance by the adversaries of a high level of assured destruction capability; i.e. the ability to inflict overwhelming damage upon an aggressor and the will to use it in case of an attack. It is a method not exactly new in warfare, but which means more in the nuclear age. (Cf. Albert Legault and George Lindsey, *The Dynamics of the Nuclear Balance,* Ithaca, N.Y., 1974, p. 140-146; and Andre Beaufre, *Deterrence and Strategy,* trans. by R.H. Barry, New York, 1966, p. 23-25.)

83. The workability of deterrence depends on a number of factors. "It rests on his estimate of the ability of the deterrent force to survive his all-out attack and effectively penetrate his defenses. . . . Furthermore, during peacetime, the offensive and defensive situation changes constantly, these changes are a consequence of research findings, weapons development, and decisions on production and deployment. History has shown that no weapon system possesses for more than a few years the characteristics necessary to assure deterrence. The effectiveness of such a force also depends on the ability of the system to penetrate enemy defenses. The development of a defense against ballistic missiles is extremely difficult and costly. However, if an effective missile defense were achieved by one nation, it could greatly reduce the deterrence offered by the forces of other nations." (John S. Foster, Jr., "Nuclear Weapons," in the *Encyclopedia Americana,* 1973 ed., Vol. 20, p. 527)

"The power potential of these new weapons is not just the tonnage and the number of the weapons. There is another co-efficient in the calculation, the absence of any compunction in the use of it. Twenty cartridges in the hands of a hesitant moralist are no good against an enemy who does not hesitate, although the latter may have only a couple of cartridges in his belt but knows how to hit his mark and do it without waiting. All this is ugly to argue: but it has become necessary in view of the widespread illusion and the specious points raised by some people. The conclusion is that these nuclear weapons definitely do not add to the strength of the truly peaceloving and conscientious party while it greatly adds to the strength of the wicked. The only result of the possession of these weapons by the peaceloving party is that it gives a justification and an incentive to the party that is less conscientious. . . . There is really no quantitative law of potential that is applicable to these new weapons. A race in them has lost meaning after the H-bomb was made. Strength lies much more in the element of unhesitating readiness to use the weapon than in the tonnage held by either party." (C. Rajagopalachari, *The Voice of the Uninvolved,* New Delhi, 1960, p. 9)

"The theory of deterrence is designed to prevent a future thermonuclear war, but it in no way guarantees that such a war will not occur. It is noteworthy that even the most articulate proponents of our deterrence policy are also extremely careful to point up the dangers of war that go hand in hand with their policy."

tain it will stimulate the opponent to enter into a nuclear arms race.[84] Consequently, with bombs piled on bombs and missiles piled on missiles, the superpowers have reached a nuclear dilemma,[85] with a balance of terror,[86] a burden of enormous expenditures[87] and a continuation of cold war.[88]

(Robert A. Dentler and Phillips Cutright, *Hostage America,* Boston, 1963, p. 2. Cf. *The Balance of Power and Nuclear Deterrence,* ed. by Frederick H. Gareau, Boston, 1962, p. 153-210.)

84. "... Nor can safety and honourable peace be found by piling up nuclear armaments and the means to deliver them, while pressing forward research on new kinds of weapons in the hope of making our own nation strong enough to overawe any other. The idea that security can be bought by amassing armaments is not new in the nuclear age. It has been tried before and it has never worked. The result, as is well known, is to stimulate other nations or coalitions of nations to arm themselves in turn. For if one nation builds armed strength thinking thereby to deter attack, other nations will think the first is preparing an aggression against them. When one nation has the power to attack, other nations cannot but fear that that power will be used, and they will arm to defend themselves against it." (E.L.M. Burns, *Megamurder,* New York, 1967, p. 5-6)

"Dr. Frank, like Dr. Gifford, Reisman and many other intellectuals, are disturbed by the government's policy toward nuclear disarmament. They see it in a dangerous drift toward nuclear war as Russia and the United States seek to match each other, test for test, bomb for bomb, muscle for muscle." (Saul Pett, "The World Lives on Edge of Oblivion," in the *South Bend Tribune,* July 15, 1962, p. 43)

85. The nuclear dilemma is caused by an unique situation in which both sides have the weapons in fairly equal proportions, so that even a surprise attack would not be certain to grant immunity to the attacker from retaliatory measures of such destructiveness that the conflict might well make any distinction between victor and vanquished irrelevant. It creates a "balance of terror" as termed by Sir Winston Churchill. (Cf. Reinhold Niebuhr, *The Structure of Nations and Empires,* New York, 1959, p. 267.)

86. "At the outset, a brief word of explanation of the meaning of a balance of terror is needed. In its simplist form, a balance of terror exists when two nations can annihilate each other no matter which side attacks first. In this sense, in the thermonuclear age, power has become absolute in that mutual destruction is assured in the event of war between the superpowers. With over 50,000 megatons (equivalent to 50,000 million tons of TNT, or 15 tons of TNT for every man, woman, and child on this earth) stored and deliverable by diverse means, there is no way that either the United States or the Soviet Union can guarantee the security of the citizens of their countries. The simple fact of the balance of terror is that the modern nation-state is obsolete as a guarantor of the security of its people." (Edgar M. Bottome, *The Balance of Terror,* Boston, 1971, p. xiii. Cf. Pierre Gallois, *The Balance of Terror,* trans. by Richard Howard, Boston, 1961.)

87. "Thus, in a complicated age of complicated machinery, when one rocket can cost $5 million and we shoot off several a week at Cape Canaveral, when a single nuclear powered carrier costs $500 million, when 5,000 different firms and 1,500,000 people are required to build the DEW line radar fence, we spend 80 per

In order to lessen the tremendous pressure of the nuclear dilemma, another new method has been advocated. It is called "detente," a French word for the easing of international tension.[89] It includes cultural exchanges, trade promotion, efforts to avoid conflicts, and arms control, which is the prime issue.

---

cent of our tax dollar paying for past wars and present defense." (Saul Pett, "The World Lives on Edge of Oblivion," in the *South Bend Tribune,* July 15, 1962, p. 43)

"It is a truism to speak of the cost of modern weapons. Everyone knows the amounts that must be spent on the planning of a bomber or the construction of a missile-launching submarine. Asking an American Senate budget committee to authorize the purchase of new planes for the Navy, Admiral R.E. Dixon, head of the Bureau of Naval Aeronautics, announced that each F8U-3 heavy fighter plane cost about ten million dollars. As for the B-52 bomber, already manufactured by the hundreds, it was then being sold to the American air force (with the necessary spare parts) for eight million dollars. The B-70 Valkyrie bomber, which was to replace the B-52, would cost at least three times as much. The manufacturer already estimated that its planning would require at least seventy times the amount of man hours required for the planning of the Boeing B-17 which constituted the American bomber force during the Second World War. When the 60,000 ton aircraft carrier Independence was launched, the Navy announced that its cost was two hundred million dollars. In his State of the Union message of January 1959, President Eisenhower set at thirty-five million dollars the cost of a single Atlas ballistic missile placed in firing position, and at fifty million dollars the cost of one of the atomic submarines now being mass-produced." (Pierre Gallois, *The Balance of Terror,* trans. by Richard Howard, Boston, 1961, p. 202)

"But inflation cannot be overlooked, particularly the vaulting costs of the past seven years. Next year's budget for defense calls for record spending of $142.7 billion. Pentagon budget officers foresee that climbing to nearly $225 billion in 1985. Although the largest share of the defense outlay goes to the conventional land, sea and air forces, the individual strategic weapons systems are the most expensive and have drawn the hottest debate over the years. The new MX mobile missile system carries a price tag from $31.5 billion to $33.8 billion, depending on how it is deployed starting in 1986. A single Trident submarine, bristling with 24 deep-striking missiles, costs well over $1 billion." (Fred Hoffman, AP Military Writer, "Will Balance of Power Tip in '80s?" in *South Bend Tribune,* March 30, 1980, p. 13. The article runs from p. 1, 12, 13 and continues on April 6, p. 20-21.)

88. "The 'cold war' means a perpetual tension between the two blocs of nations, communist and anti-communist, of such unique intensity that one may question the adjective used to describe it. Yet it is regarded as 'cold' rather than 'hot' because there are no overt hostilities on a large scale. These hostilities are prevented by an historical phenomenon as unique as the cold war itself. Both sides have nuclear weapons which have raised military destructiveness to such a degree of suicidal and lethal efficacy that neither side is tempted to initiate the conflict." (Reinhold Niebuhr, *The Structure of Nations and Empires,* New York, 1959, p. 267. Cf. Hugh Higgins, *The Cold War,* New York, 1974.)

89. Perhaps there is no better way to understand the term "detente" than to go directly to its chief architect in the West, Henry Kissinger. He pointed out that the policy of Detente essentially took into consideration the basic realities of the

In the charter of the United Nations, there have been provisions for disarmament.[90] Organizations have been set up and conferences have been held to do the job, but have gotten nowhere.[91] Arms control is not supposed to go as far as disarmament, but to make it easier

---

contemporary age. First, the U.S. has been confronted by another super-power—the Soviet Union, with a different ideology. Second is the possession of enormous nuclear arms by these two countries. Third, a new arms race has been intrinsically wasteful and could cause economic disruption. Finally, there has been a worldwide yearning for peace. In view of these circumstances, Kissinger believed that U.S. Detente objectives should be first, to move beyond the stage of constant confrontation and establish more stable relationships with the Soviet Union. Second, in lessening tensions, the U.S. must nevertheless remain strong and determined in order to prevent the Soviets from translating its military strength into political gains. (Cf. his "We Are Determined to Resist Expansionism," *U.S. News and World Reports,* March 15, 1976). The Soviet Union, faced with the same set of realities, has been equally anxious to seek an accord with the U.S. Its leader, Leonid Brezhnev, thus explained that the basic premise of Soviet foreign policy was the search for Detente for improving relations with the U.S. in the interest of world peace, in the "Twenty-Fifth Congress of the Communist Party of the Soviet Union," *World Marxist Review, Informa-Bulletin,* Special Issue, no. 1, 1976, p. 20-30. (Cf. Timothy W. Stanley, *Detente Diplomacy; United States and European Security in the 1970s,* New York, 1970; and Adam B. Ulam, "Detente under Soviet Eyes," in *Arms and Control and Security: Current Issues,* ed. by Wolfram F. Hanrieder, Boulder, Colo., 1979, p. 87-98.)

90. The Charter gives the General Assembly authority to discuss and make recommendations on "the principles governing disarmament and the regulation of armaments." (Art. 11) Also, "in order to promote the establishment of international peace and security with the least diversion for armaments of the world's human and economic resources" (repeating a provision in the Moscow Declaration), the Security Council was made "responsible for formulating, with the assistance of the Military Staff Committee, plans to be submitted to the Members for the establishment of a system for the regulation of armaments." (Cf. Henry W. Forbes, *The Strategy of Disarmament,* Washington, 1962, p. 73-74.)

91. In the structure of the United Nations, an Atomic Energy Commission and a Commission for Conventional Armaments were established in 1946. The two commissions were combined into a single Disarmament Commission in 1952. Disarmament conferences were held in 1960 and 1962, both in Geneva, but achieved almost nothing. In the earlier stage of negotiations, when the Soviet Union had not reached a strong position in nuclear power, it insisted on the prohibition of the atomic bomb first, and the United States supported a somewhat quantitative disarmament. Obviously, both wanted to hold a favorable position in their own temporarily dominant technique or strategy. Later on, the Soviet Union and the United States agreed in principle on the need for fixing numerical limits to armed forces and armaments, and each sponsored plans for destroying stockpiles of fissionable materials, for terminating their production, and for destroying nuclear delivery vehicles. But these goals could not be implemented since they maintained opposing views on verification. (Cf. Henry W. Forbes, *The Strategy of Disarmament,* Washington, 1962, p. 75-124; and *International Arms Control, Issues and*

to work out something hopefully leading to disarmament.[92] It is an attempt to find a turning on the dread road of arms race.[93]

Under the policy of detente, some scores have been made in the control of nuclear arms. The first one is the test ban treaty of 1963 prohibiting all but underground testing of nuclear weapons. Its effect has, however, been depleted by the refusal of China and France to go along.[94]

Very significant are the Strategic Arms Limitation Talks between the United States and Soviet Union. Two treaties have been conclud-

---

Agreements, by the Stanford Arms Control Group, ed. by John H. Barton and Lawrence D. Weiler, Stanford, Calif., 1976, p. 66-93.)

92. Some people, "hoping to eliminate or greatly reduce the danger which the existence of nuclear arms creates, developed theories of 'arms control.' The basic idea was that the nations having nuclear armaments should limit, by treaty or convention, their numbers and deployment, and even their use in war, but wihout finally abolishing them. It is to be noted that the term 'arms control' in the context of disarmament negotiations is coming to have a more restricted meaning, referring to measures, which while not involving elimination of weapons or reduction of forces, are intended to reduce international tension, and thus facilitate and lead toward disarmament." (E.L.M. Burns, *Megamurder,* New York, 1967; p. 7. Cf. *Arms Control, Issues for the Public,* ed. by Louis Henkin, Englewood Cliffs, N.J., 1961, p. 201-204.)

93. "What can the world—or any nation in it—hope for if no turning is found on this dread road? The worst to be feared and the best to be expected can be simply stated. The worst is atomic war. The best would be this: A life of perpetual fear and tension; a burden of arms draining the wealth and the labor of all peoples; a wasting of strength that defies the American system or the Soviet system or any system to achieve true abundance and happiness for the peoples of this earth." (President D. Eisenhower's speech to a luncheon of the American Society of Newspaper Editors, appearing in the *Evening World-Herald,* Omaha, April 16, 1953, p. 11)

"Those armaments especially those terrible arms, which modern science has given you, long before they produce victims and ruins, nourish bad feelings, create nightmares, distrust and sombre resolutions; they demand enormous expenditures; they obstruct projects of union and useful collaboration; they falsify the psychology of peoples." (Pope Paul's address to the United Nations. Cf. *The Washington Evening Star,* Oct. 5, 1965, p. A-4)

94. The treaty banning nuclear weapons tests in the atmosphere, in outer space, underwater, and in any other environment if the explosion would cause radioactive debris outside of the state conducting the explosion, was negotiated in 1963 between the United States, Great Britain, and the Soviet Union. Within ten years it was signed by all the major powers except China and France. (Cf. Albert Legault and George Lindsey, *The Dynamics of the Nuclear Balance,* Ithaca, N.Y., 1974, p. 214-215; and *International Arms Control, Issues and Agreements,* by the Stanford Arms Control Group, ed. by John H. Barton and Lawrence D. Weiler, Stanford, Calif., 1976, p. 101-115.)

ed, one signed in 1972[95] and the other signed in 1979,[96] after years of strenuous talks[97] and deep perplexity.[98] They are arrangements of

---

95. The SALT I treaty, including the ABM agreement, Interim Offensive agreement and Protocol was signed on May 26, 1972, in Moscow by the U.S. President Nixon and the Soviet leader Brezhnev. In the ABM agreement, the two nations agree not to build an ABM system for the "defense of territory of its country," and not to build a defense for an individual region except for systems at two allowed sites: one around the national capital and one around an ICBM site; and no more than 100 ABM launchers and interceptor missiles at each site. The development or testing of air-based, space-based, or mobile land-based ABM systems is prohibited. The transfer to other countries of ABM systems is prohibited. The Interim agreement prohibits both parties from starting construction of additional fixed, land-based ICBM launchers after July 1, 1972. Thus, the United States can have no more than 1,054 ICBMs operational or under construction, and the Soviet Union can have no more than 1,618. The SLBM tube and modern ballistic submarine limitations are spelled out in the Protocol. The United States is limited to a total of 710 SLBM launchers and 44 modern ballistic missile submarines, and the Soviet Union to 950 launchers and 62 submarines. The Accident Measures Agreement and the Revised Hot Line Agreement signed earlier were entered into force the same day. (Cf. *International Arms Control, Issues and Agreements,* by the Stanford Arms Control Group, ed. by John H. Barton and Lawrence D. Weiler, Stanford, Calif., 1976, p. 197-201.)

96. The SALT II treaty was signed in Vienna, Austria, on June 18, 1979, by U.S. President Carter and Soviet Union President Brezhnev. The 22-page treaty limits each country to the deployment of 2,250 launchers for intercontinental weapons, a reduction from the 2,400 allowed by the SALT I treaty. It also limits to 1,200 the number of ballistic missiles that can be armed with multiple, independently-targeted warheads. The treaty is accompanied by a two-page protocol, expiring at the end of 1981, banning deployment of mobile and cruise missiles and air to surface ballistic missiles and limiting each country to the development of only one new intercontinental missile. The two countries agreed to continue consultation for more arms limitations and reductions in SALT III. (Cf. Frank Cormier, AP reporter, *South Bend Tribune,* June 18, 1979, p. 1, 14.)

97. The Strategic Arms Limitations Talks started in the late 1960s and reached the first agreement after almost five years of on and off negotiations. It took 7 more years of on and off negotiations to reach the conclusion of the SALT II treaty. During these years, the issue challenged three U.S. Presidents: Nixon, Ford and Carter. The Russian policy in the talks also varied from time to time. (Cf. *International Arms Control, Issues and Agreements,* by the Stanford Arms Control Group, ed. by John H. Barton and Lawrence D. Weiler, Stanford, Calif., 1976, p. 179-196, 208-222.)

98. "One problem is that some countries fear that arms control will turn out to be a trick to disarm them and not their enemies. Others fear that arms control will set forces in motion that will eventually destroy their society. This fear has been exacerbated by the invention of MIRV (multiple, independently targeted reentry vehicle), as already suggested, and the fact that MIRV makes on-site inspection mandatory. Until the invention of MIRV, each side could check on the other side through satellite photography. But when any one missile can carry three, five

mutual restrictions in the strategic arms race, temporary in nature and limited in scope.[99] Unmistakably, the race is still on[100] and "the threat of a nuclear holocaust still hangs over us."[101]

---

or more warheads, the only way of finding out just how many missiles the other side has built is periodically to send a man with a screwdriver to look inside each and every missile. For the United States and other countries whose social systems are based on parliamentary democracy, on-site inspection poses political difficulties, since it arouses considerable opposition among military and technical people who fear the loss of national and industrial secrets. But in the Soviet Union and other countries with social systems based on one party or similar arrangements, on-site inspection would pose difficulties for the system itself, creating strains throughout the whole society." (Roger Hilsman, *The Crouching Future,* New York, 1975, p. 565)

99. Both the SALT I and II treaties are arrangements of mutual restrictions in the strategic arms race, temporary in nature and limited in scope. They only partially halt the race, leaving plenty of room and giving more time for scientific research and experiments to improve existing weapons and develop new ones; for the adoption and practice of new military strategies and techniques; and for piling up essential materials, strengthening tactical positions and spying for vital secrets. (Cf. Richard Burt, "The Scope and Limits of SALT," in *Arms and Control and Security: Current Issues,* ed. by Wolfram F. Hanrieder, Boulder, Colo., 1979, p. 67-86; and William R. Kintner and Robert L. Pfaltzgraff, Jr., editors, *SALT: Implications for Arms Control in the 1970s,* London, 1977.)

100. For instance, "according to the latest intelligence information, the Russians lead the United States by 2,350 to 1,710 in strategic land-based and submarine missile launchers. This is the same as a year ago. But the United States still is ahead, 9,200 to 6,000, in nuclear warheads, including those carried on long-range bombers in which the United States outnumbers Russia, 348 to 156. This lead in warheads traces back to a U.S. head start in deploying multiple weapons on its missiles. But that lead is shrinking. In the past two yers, the Russians have added 2,000 warheads while the U.S. total has remained virtually unchanged. That is mostly because the Soviet Union has been installing new SS17, SS18 and SS19 missiles with multiple warheads at a combined rate of about 125 launchers a year in place of older single-shot ICBMs. All these new Soviet missiles are bigger and carry more warheads than the U.S. Minuteman and Titan ICBMs." (Fred Hoffman, AP military writer, "Will Balance of Power Tip in '80s?" in the *South Bend Tribune,* March 30, 1980, p. 13. The article runs from p. 1, 12, 13 and continues on April 6, p. 20-21.)

The latest development in the armament race is the "stealth technology" for an "invisible" plane, as announced by the U.S. Secretary of Defense Harold Brown on August 22, 1980. He said that this technology would enable the U.S. to build manned and unmanned aircraft—bombers, fighters, cruise missiles—that could not be successfully intercepted with existing air defense systems of the Soviet Union, because it makes radar and other sensors unable to detect the attacking aircrafts until too late. It can also be applied to any military vehicle, such as tanks, trucks and ships, that can be attacked by radar-directed fire. Actually, this technology alters nothing in modern warfare except to make offense more formidable, and therefore, to make war more formidable. (Cf. *The Plain Dealer,* Cleveland, Ohio, Aug. 23, 1980, p. 1, 8A.)

   The more widely concerned measure is the nonproliferation treaty limiting the further development of nuclear weapons. The nuclear
safeguard provided by this treaty is, however, "fragile, at best."[102]
First of all, the scientific and engineering knowledge necessary to
make nuclear weapons has become well-known.[103] It can be learned

---

   101. In the signing ceremony of the SALT II treaty, June 28, 1979, in Vienna,
Austria, President Carter termed the treaty a victory to peace but warned that "the
threat of a nuclear holocaust still hangs over us." (Quoted by Frank Cormier, AP
reporter, *South Bend Tribune,* June 28, 1979, p. 1, 14)
   "Both the United States and Soviet Union are building and deploying new
weapons that could disturb the nuclear balance of terror in the 1980s and 1990s, an
administration study says. The study, prepared by the U.S. Arms Control and
Disarmament Agency, was submitted to Congress and released today. It pointed
specifically to two proposed new missiles under development by the Pentagon, the
MX and the Trident II. Both missiles would carry more warheads, with more blast
power and greater accuracy than the Minuteman and Poseidon missiles they would
replace. As a result, they could threaten the Soviet Union with a disabling first
strike that would catch Soviet missiles still in their underground silos, wiping them
out before they could be fired. The Soviets are developing similar capabilities in
their new generation of missiles with multiple warheads, the report said. The
danger is that in a crisis, one side or the other might be so fearful of a first strike by
the other that it would launch its own missiles first, hoping to stave off
retaliation." ("Study Fears New Weapons Could Rock Nuclear Balance," AP
report, *South Bend Tribune,* March 15, 1979, p. 5)
   102. For two decades, the details of how to build an atomic bomb have been
known widely. Control of their spread has come from control of the availability of
nuclear fuels. This is the aim of the Non-Proliferation Treaty and the International
Atomic Energy Agency's system of inspections, inventories of nuclear materials,
tamper-proof seals, and surveillance cameras in 50 countries. Negotiated in 1968,
the Non-Proliferation Treaty has been signed and ratified by 82 countries. They
have pledged not to develop nuclear weapons or, if they already possess them, not
to aid other countries in their acquisition. But 62 countries either have not signed
or have not ratified the treaty. France and China, which both possess nuclear
weapons, including the hydrogen bomb, haven't signed. They may export any
nuclear technology they choose. India, which exploded its first nuclear device in
June, 1974, is not a treaty signatory. It became the sixth nation to possess nuclear
explosives. The others are the United States, Russia, China, France and Britain.
Government sources say about 20 countries, among them Japan, West Germany,
Argentina, Brazil, South Korea and Pakistan—all not parties to the treaty—probably could produce nuclear explosives if they wanted to, according to William
Stockton, AP science writer, in "Nuclear Safeguard Fragile, at Best," *South Bend
Tribune,* Aug. 15, 1974, p. 13. (Cf. Mason Willrich, ed., *International Safeguard
and Nuclear Industry,* Baltimore, 1973.)
   103. ("... that there are already more than 100,000 scientists and engineers
throughout the world possessing the knowhow for assembling a nuclear bomb of
Hiroshima magnitude." (Quoted by Sydney Harris in his "Random Nuggets," in
the *South Bend Tribune,* May 18, 1976, p. 11)

as a hobby, exposed by a common writer,[104] and practiced by a college student[105] in a kitchen.[106] Second, it is not very difficult to obtain the weapon grade nuclear material, such as plutonium, from spent fuel[107] through peaceful reactors as a stepping stone,[108] or even by stealing.[109] Third, the proliferation of nuclear weapons has been

---

104. An article in *Progressive Magazine,* a Madison-based monthly, telling how to build a hydrogen bomb, was the product of a free-lance writer named Howard Morland who toured atomic facilities with government permission and talked to workers. But the government says the article's publication could quicken the speed of the manufacture of atomic weaponry around the world, because it "provides specific and detailed information concerning the design and operation of a hydrogen bomb, and certain technical information necessary to construct such a bomb." Legally related to this case was the *Press Connection* publication of a letter by Charles Hanse, 32, a computer programmer from Mountain View, Calif., who said studying nuclear weaponry was his hobby. The government claims the letter exposes three critical factors of H-bomb construction. (Cf. UPI report, *South Bend Tribune,* March 10, 1979, p. 2; AP reports, *South Bend Tribune,* March 11, 1979, p. 13; and Sept. 18, 1979, p. 1, 7.)

105. A Princeton University physics student, John A. Phillips, 21, of New Haven, Conn., said anyone could produce a nuclear bomb, and he designed one in four months to prove this claim. The model he made, if actually produced, would be about one-third as powerful as the one dropped on Hiroshima in 1945. "Billions of dollars and years of research and experiment are no longer required for the design and construction of a fission bomb," said Phillips. "The point was to show that any undergraduate with a physics background can do it and therefore that it is reasonable to assume that terrorists could do it, too." (UPI report in *South Bend Tribune,* Oct. 9, 1976, p. 1)

106. (Cf. Bob Bale, *How to Make an Atomic Bomb in Your Own Kitchen— Well, Practically,* New York, 1951.)

107. "If a country is determined to obtain weapons-grade nuclear materials, there are many ways they can proceed," said Dr. Fred Ikle, director of the U.S. Arms Control and Disarmament Agency. "There is nothing, absolutely nothing, not even in this country, that gives absolute protection against diversion," Ikle told a congressional committee in July, 1974, according to William Stockton, AP Science Writer, in "Nuclear Safeguard Fragile, at Best," *South Bend Tribune,* Aug. 15, 1974, p. 13.

108. "As nations turn to nuclear power to solve energy problems, the possibility grows that one might use its peaceful power reactor as a stepping stone to nuclear weapons. More than 100 American-type power reactors are operating or being built or planned abroad. Other nuclear nations also are exporting reactors. The total number will rise into the hundreds in coming years. As a result, the volume of nuclear materials available will grow rapidly.... by 1980, reactors throughout the world are expected to produce more than 130,000 pounds a year." (William Stockton, AP Science Writer, in "Nuclear Safeguard Fragile, at Best," *South Bend Tribune,* Aug. 15, 1974, p. 13)

109. Warning that it is not difficult to make an atomic bomb, a Ford Foundation study said Saturday that the growth of the nuclear power industry carries a

greatly facilitated by the dramatic drop in their cost[110] and the rapid improvement in making them smaller and lighter;[111] and finally the temptation of nuclear arms is too strong to resist.[112] For these reasons, it has been estimated that by the 1990s as many as fifty nations might have nuclear weapons.[113]

"substantial risk" of terrorists or others stealing nuclear materials to make illegal weapons. The 252-page report was sponsored by the Ford Foundation's energy policy project and prepared by Theodore B. Taylor, a physicist and former scientist at the AEC's Los Alamos Center, and Mason Willrich, an attorney and authority on nuclear safeguards and arms control. (Cf. Grant Dillman, UP reporter, "A-Bomb Theft Growing Peril," *South Bend Tribune,* April 7, 1974, p. 10.)

"An anti-nuclear group that claimed responsibility for stealing 14 radioactive slabs from a university has mailed one to a newspaper to demonstrate the ease with which nuclear material can be filched. The head of civil defense in Lyon, France's second largest city, confirmed that 14 slabs—five of strontium, five of cesium, two of thallium and two of cobalt—were stolen from the physics department of Lyon University I. The Revolutionary Antinuclear Ecological Cell, which claimed responsibility for the affair, announced its formation a week ago with a threat of 'pseudo-terrorism to alert the public to the ease with which nuclear material can be obtained.' The director of the physics faculty, Jean Delmau, said the slabs were stolen from a laboratory frequented daily by about 700 students." (AP report from Lyon, France, *South Bend Tribune,* May 25, 1979, p. 8)

110. Defense Secretary Robert S. McNamara said there is no question but that "tens of nations" could have nuclear weapons and the means of delivering them in another 10 or 20 years. This grim prospect will result, he said, from an expected dramatic drop in the cost of making warheads and the spread of advanced, simpler nuclear technology throughout the world. McNamara said the cost of nuclear warheads today ranged from $500,000 to $1,000,000 each; but would "fall dramatically" in the years ahead. This would enable other nations to develop and produce weapons. (Cf. UPI report in *South Bend Tribune,* Oct. 6, 1964, p. 2.)

111. Nuclear bombs are getting smaller, said Harvard Professor Thomas Schelling. "It is very frightening to realize that by 1999 a device with the power to blow up a community the size of Cambridge (Mass.), for example, could probably be carried on the back of any strong person," said Schelling, an arms strategist who worked with Secretary of State Henry Kissinger. (UPI report in *South Bend Tribune,* Nov. 2, 1975, p. 4)

112. "The 'near-nuclear' countries feel themselves threatened by those already in possession of the bomb. The pressure to compete will become—is becoming—irresistible. Like a bar fight, if one man has a broken bottle in his hand, the other is going to find a similarly lethal weapon." (Sydney Harris, "Showdown, Nuclear Style, Won't have Winners, Losers," *South Bend Tribune,* Aug. 1, 1977, p. 6)

Leonard Beaton, in his research *Must the Bomb Spread,* Harmondsworth, England, 1966, p. 128, concluded that "As long as there are sovereign states responsible for their own defence, there will be a strong interest in acquiring nuclear weapons. To that extent, the problem of nuclear proliferation is basic and not subject to definite solutions."

As regards conventional arms, there has been no control at all. Instead, the race has grown wilder and wilder,[114] with arms trade mainly managed by governments,[115] even at the time when they for-

---

113. According to the International Atomic Energy Agency, Canada, Czechoslovakia, West Germany, India, Israel, Italy, Japan, the Netherlands, Pakistan, Spain, Sweden, and Switzerland were all operating power reactors in 1970 that produced plutonium as a by-product in sufficient quantities to make at least a warhead a year and as many as 100. And if any one of these nations has a "breeder" pile deliberately designed to produce plutonium, the capacity would be much, much higher.... It has been estimated that by the 1990s, as many as 50 countries might have nuclear weapons." (Roger Hilsman, *The Crouching Future,* New York, 1975, p. 559. Cf. Herman Kahn and Anthony J. Wiener, *The Year 2000: a Framework for Speculation on the Next Thirty-Three Years,* New York, 1967, p. 246; and Lincoln P. Bloomfield, "Nuclear Spread and World Order," in *Arms and Control and Security: Current Issues,* ed. by Wolfram F. Hanrieder, Boulder, Colo., 1979, p. 293-306.)

114. "This arms traffic is increasing in tempo. For instance, from 1945 to 1955, the world's arms markets were dominated by the United States and Great Britain alone. Both gave away or sold military equipment at an average yearly rate of $2 billion and an estimated $400 million, respectively. But then the Soviet Union entered the picture in a big way in 1955, and every year since has scattered an average of $500 million worth of additional arms around the world. Soon thereafter, a revitalized France broke into the market; she is currently selling another $400 million worth of arms each year. Ironically, it was America's economic aid under the Marshall Plan that hastened France's return to the arms sales field." (George Thayer, *The War Business; the International Trade in Armaments,* New York, 1968, p. 38. Cf. Stockholm International Peace Research Institute, *Arms Trade Registers,* Cambridge, Mass., 1975, p. 153; 156, Figure 2A.1; Chart 2A.2.)

"Like military expenditure, the arms trade has grown rapidly, both in volume and in scope, since World War II. The annual value of the global arms trade in 1976 was probably about $10 billion, with new orders running at about $20 billion.... As it is, participation in arms races is almost worldwide. In 1976, a total of 95 countries imported major weapons—tanks, ships, missiles or aircraft. In almost all of these countries there was no other feasible way of obtaining these weapons." (*Disarmament and World Development,* ed. by Richard Jolly, Oxford, 1978, p. 15)

115. "When I was growing up, between the First and Second World Wars, we knew all about the 'merchants of death'—all those shadowy and sinister figures like Krupp and Zaharoff, who made and sold arms to any nation that could afford them. We naively thought at the time that if such men and their companies could be prevented from turning a profit on weapons of mass destruction, it might help the world along the bumpy road toward disarmament and eventual peace. Such men and their companies no longer exercise the power and influence they once had, instead, their place has been taken by the nations of the world themselves. All of us today through our governments on all sides of all curtains, are the Krupps and Zaharoffs of modern conventional warfare." (Sydney Harris, "Government to Blame for Armaments Business," *South Bend Tribune,* Oct. 3, 1978, p. 12. Cf.

mally adopted the resolution for disarmament.[116] It has reached everywhere[117] with all kinds of military supplies.[118]

So, "mankind almost certainly has already lost the struggle to end a worldwide arms race, to halt the spread of nuclear

---

George Thayer, *The War Business; the International Trade in Armaments,* New York, 1968, p. 258-291, 324-357.)

"As might be expected, the four major arms producers—the USA, the USSR, the UK and France—dominate the weapons trade. Over the period 1950 to 1975 these four countries supplied 92 per cent of the major weapons sold to the Third World. The USSR and the USA accounted for about 34 per cent each, and the UK and France for about 12 per cent each. During the 1950s, however, the USA and the UK were the main suppliers, supplying 33 and 24 per cent respectively. The USSR followed with 15 per cent and France with 8 per cent. During the 1970s, the USSR and the USA each supplied about 36 per cent of the major weapons sold to the Third World, and France and the UK each supplied 10 per cent. In the 1950s China was a significant supplier of arms to the rest of the Third World, accounting for about 6 per cent of the total supplied. Although China supplied about the same absolute value of arms in the 1970s, its percentage share had dropped to about 2 per cent." (*Disarmament and World Development,* ed. by Richard Jolly, Oxford, 1978, p. 15. Cf. table on p. 18.)

"The governments of the industrialized countries involve themselves in the military affairs of Third World countries mainly through the supply of weapons and the technicians to operate the weapons or to train nationals to operate them. The reasons for this involvement vary but include a desire for economic or political influence, the acquisition of military bases, or the temptation to sell weapons to offset high research and development costs, to try to alleviate the effects of an economic recession, or to achieve the economies of scale of large scale production. Commercial armament firms, anxious to maximise profits, are powerful lobbies applying continuous pressure on governments to allow them to participate in the arms trade. The dominant reasons of the largest arms suppliers, the USA and the USSR, are probably associated with their desire to extend their political and economic interests world-wide. This policy, however, carries with it grave dangers for world security." (Richard Jolly, *op. cit.,* p. 24)

116. Dean Rusk, then the Secretary of State, put it best in a television interview on January 3, 1965. Said he: "I recall that at the United Nations General Assembly at a time when they were voting unanimously for disarmament, seventy members were at that moment asking (the United States) for military assistance." (Quoted by George Thayer in his *The War Business; the International Trade in Armaments,* New York, 1968, p. 36.)

117. About two-thirds of the current global arms trade is to Third World countries. Major weapons probably account for about one-half of the total trade in weapons and equipment with the Third World. The remaining items traded—spare parts, small arms, ammunition, support equipment, etc.—are very difficult to trace. But it is unlikely that the basic trend in the arms trade would be much affected if these components were included. Over the past few years the arms trade with the Third World has escalated alarmingly (Fig. 2.4). Between 1970 and 1975 alone the value of major weapons supplied to the Third World was, in constant dollars, nearly as much as that of the major weapons supplied over the entire

weapons."[119] Unchecked by impotent methods, both old and new, for maintaining peace, a nuclear war is obviously inevitable[120] like an overinflated balloon about to blow up.

The last straw which brings about the inevitable nuclear war may

---

period between 1950 and 1969 (Table 2.7)." (*Disarmament and World Development,* ed. by Richard Jolly, Oxford, 1978, p. 15. Cf. Tables on p. 16-17, 19)

Recently, both ACDA and SIPRI estimates show military expenditure expanding more rapidly in the group of developing countries than among the developed states, with correspondingly inverse changes in the ratio of military expenditure to GNP. As the 1974 SIPRI yearbook noted glumly, this trend is not an indication of a decline in military power of the great powers but rather of "the magnitude of the increase in militarization elsewhere. The arms race has become a global phenomenon." (Stockholm International Peace Research Institute, *World Armaments and Disarmament, SIPRI Yearbook, 1974,* Cambridge, Mass., 1974, p. 141. Cf. U.S. Arms Control and Disarmament Agency, *World Military Expenditures and Arms Transfers, 1966-1975,* Washington, 1976.)

The arms race is vigorous even in sub-Saharan Africa. A report by the International Institute for Strategic Studies in London shows how military spending is soaring in sub-Saharan Africa, excluding white-ruled South Africa and Rhodesia. It is estimated at $3.7 billion a year currently. Three years ago, it was barely one fourth that amount, according to an editorial, "African Arms Race," in the *South Bend Tribune,* Jan. 10, 1978, p. 10. (Cf. Stockholm International Peace Research Institute, *Arms Registers,* Cambridge, Mass., 1975, p. 152-153, 156, 159, Figure 2A.2.)

118. "The fact that the United States has pumped some $50 billion worth of arms into the world market in the last 24 years is obscured by the sheer size of the figure. Put another way, it means that between the years 1950 and 1966, for instance, the U.S. government either gave away or sold 9,300 jet fighter aircraft, 8,340 other aircraft, 2,496 naval craft of all types, 19,827 tanks, 448,383 other combat vehicles, 1,445,194 carbines, 2,152,793 rifles, 82,496 submachine guns, 71,174 machine guns, 30,668 mortars, 25,106 field guns and howitzers, and 31,360 missiles of all types. One must add to these totals billions of rounds of ammunition and other explosives, thousands of supporting systems such as computers and radio sets, and millions of man-hours of training sessions both in the United States and in the recipient countries." (George Thayer, *The War Business; the International Trade in Armaments,* New York, 1968, p. 38)

119. "Mankind almost certainly has already lost the struggle to end a worldwide arms race, to halt the spread of nuclear weapons. All the forces of human ambition, greed, fear keep driving us away from our intellectual knowledge that this escalation of the arms race is madness and ultimately suicidal." (Carl T. Rowan, "Mankind Already Has Lost Race to Control Arms," *South Bend Tribune,* July 18, 1977, p. 6)

"So long as the danger of war between nation-states exists, some if not all governments will try to prevent international bodies on which potential enemy states are represented, from inspecting and supervising their laboratories and industries. Each great power will always do its utmost to lead in military science. Atom bomb production in remote parts of the American West, in Siberia, in the Sahara, in Patagonia, in underground factories anywhere, can never be effectively controlled,

be just a desperate first strike[121] or an emotional impulse.[122] A certain overconfidence may start the war.[123] So may accidents,[124] such as

---

if, in spite of pledges, the governments of the respective nation-states decide on secrecy." (Emery Reves, *The Anatomy of Peace,* New York, 1946, p. 278)

120. "Not many months ago, the International Peace Research Institute in Stockholm—an independent organization with an international governing body, set up by the Swedish Parliament to commemmorate 150 years of unbroken peace in Sweden—issued a forecast to mark its 10th anniversary of existence. What was striking about the forecast was the Institute's doubt that it might still be around 10 years from now. Within nine years, the forecast said, some 35 countries around the world will be able to make atomic weapons, and nuclear war will become inevitable. Not, conceivable. Not, possible. Not, probable. Inevitable. The Institute has no vested interest in catastrophe or doom. It speaks for no nuclear power, nor for power at all. It addresses itself simply to the question of global stability and human survival." (Sydney Harris, "Showdown, Nuclear Style, Won't Have Winners, Losers," *South Bend Tribune,* Aug. 1, 1977, p. 6)

"Five panelists at a Harvard-MIT Arms Control Seminar said they believed nuclear war in some form will erupt before 1999. But they said it would likely not originate with the United States and the Soviet Union but with relatively smaller nations like Israel and its Arab neighbors, India and Pakistan or African nations." (UPI report in the *South Bend Tribune,* Nov. 2, 1975, p.4)

Speaking of the position of the United States and the Soviet Union in respect to the nuclear war, "One may take for granted that neither side actually intends to begin the dread conflict. But it may come upon them nevertheless by miscalculation or misadventure." (Reinhold Niebuhr, *The Structure of Nations and Empires,* New York, 1959, p. 269)

121. "Supposing a wicked government calculates the dire consequences of a big war and its intelligence is not clouded by anger or hatred, it could easily see that the destructive nature of the new weapon is such that it would be dangerous to wait for the other side to use it first; for once it is used, it would be so used that no chance would be left for the victim to draw on his own reserves of nuclear weapons for retaliation. It is something like the situation in hunting big game. One does not, and cannot, safely use anything but the most deadly and effective weapons. The sportsman must assure himself that there is no chance for the tiger to spring on him after receiving a wound." (C. Rajagopalachari, *The Voice of the Uninvolved,* New Delhi, 1960, p. 8)

122. "America is suffering from a strange illusion. The U.S. Government has succeeded in making most of the people in that country believe that the holding of a heavier quantity of nuclear weapons as compared with that held by the U.S.S.R. has ensured for America and the world a kind of peace, not the best form of it but a good second best, as against the ambitious plots of the U.S.S.R. and her populous allied friend in Asia. The idea is that no nation will go light-heartedly to war against a Power that holds these nuclear weapons in great bulk, seeing the cataclysmal nature of the destruction that will be involved in any large-scale war at the present time. I say definitely that this is but an illusion. No one goes light-heartedly to war in these latter days, nuclear weapons or no nuclear weapons. It has been abundantly shown, and every nation has realised fully, that war does not and cannot advance the interests of either party in the conflict. What leads to war is,

false pre-emption,[125] human error,[126] and mechanical failure.[127] It is also possible for nuclear powers to plunge into the war through limited conflict,[128] bluffmanship,[129] or complication by other nations.[130]

---

however, not cold calculation but the irresistible hatred or anger which seizes nations at aggression or injustice, real or supposed, or fear, which counts no cost.'' (C. Rajagopalachari, *The Voice of the Uninvolved,* New Delhi, 1960, p. 7-8)

123. A recent study by the U.S. Arms Control and Disarmament Agency said the American research into advanced weapons technology involving lasers and beams of energy could lead to instability in the future. It said the new technology might be useful as a shield for destroying incoming missiles, but the report shed no light on how close either side is to achieving that capability. Arms control experts theorize then an effective shield would increase the dangers of war, since one side or the other might be convinced that it could strike first with impunity, according to an AP report under the title "Study Fears New Weapons Could Rock Nuclear Balance," in the *South Bend Tribune,* March 15, 1979, p. 5. A nation "intentionally begins a war with the confident belief that it can win the war without being vitally damaged in return. This might become the accepted position of either the American or the Russian government if a 'weapons breakthrough' occurs.'' (Robert A. Dentler and Phillips Cutright, *Hostage America,* Boston, 1963, p. 7)

124. Fred C. Ikle, Director of the Arms Control Agency, said there is always a possibility of a nuclear exchange starting by accident. (*South Bend Tribune,* Oct. 5, 1975, p. 8. Cf. Amitai Etzioni, *The Hard Way to Peace,* New York, 1962, p. 45-55.)

125. "The first type of accidental start is false pre-emption. In this case, a false warning of an impending enemy attack is received by a peaceful nation, and it sends off its offensive forces to strike against the non-existent aggressor. This type of accidental cause is entirely possible, and becomes more and more probable in the era of supersonic bombers and intercontinental ballistic missiles.'' (Robert A. Dentler and Phillips Cutright, *Hostage America,* Boston, 1963, p. 2-3)

Within only seven months the United States defense forces have been activated by false alarms three times: "Last November, a technician accidentally fed a war game plan into the computer and our fighters scrambled. A defective part was blamed for a June 3 alert and another one three days later.'' (*South Bend Tribune's* editorial, "Soviet Monitors," June 25, 1980, p. 12)

126. "A second type of accidental trigger involves human 'accidents'—men in command of offensive weapons who lose control of themselves and give an unauthorized order to fire. It takes only one base commander or even one Polaris commander to trigger this type of accidental start.'' (Robert A. Dentler and Phillips Cutright, *Hostage America,* Boston, 1963, p. 3-4)

127. "A third type of accidental trigger involves the mechanical failure of missiles, aircraft and atomic stockpiles, as well as such human errors as throwing the green switch instead of the red one, and other mechanical failures in radar, computer tracking systems.'' (Robert A. Dentler and Phillips Cutright, *Hostage America,* Boston, 1963, p. 4-5. Cf. Christopher Morris, *The Day They Lost the H-Bomb,* New York, 1966; and Flora Lewis, *One of Our H-Bombs Is Missing,* New York, 1967.)

128. "A fourth type of accidental thermonuclear war is one that evolves from a war that is already going on—the so-called 'limited war.' When two opponents are engaged in a war using conventional weapons, there is a danger that if one side

No matter how, where, and by whom a nuclear war is triggered, the result would be the same: millions and millions of people killed and thousands and thousands of cities destroyed; a catastrophe from which there is no way to escape and a holocaust under which there is no place to hide.[131] It is not exaggerating to say that we are now only waiting for the last day to come.[132]

---

is being beaten it will resort to nuclear weapons (small artillery to start with, for example) in order to reverse its losses. The other side, no more willing to lose the war, replies with its own nuclear weapons." (Robert A. Dentler and Phillips Cutright, *Hostage America,* Boston, 1963, p. 5-6)

"The world continues to run the risk that conventional war between small and medium-size powers will suck the great powers into its vortex and escalate into nuclear war or that the great powers will themselves take what they believe to be limited actions, only to find that events spiral out of hand and into Armageddon." (Roger Hilsman, *The Crouching Future,* New York, 1975, p. 577)

129. "A fifth type of accidental war results from brinkmanship—or *'bluffmanship'* as it should be re-named. This occurs when one side becomes overcommitted to a 'tough' position which it really doesn't intend to result in a war but which it hopes will force the other side to concede some small advantage in order that a war will certainly be avoided." (Robert A. Dentler and Phillips Cutright, *Hostage America,* Boston, 1963, p. 6)

130. "Actually, Washington and Moscow fully understand the awesome destructive potential of their two arsenals and are better able than any other state to judge the limits beyond which a conflict must not be allowed to escalate. The hot line linking the two capitals is a tangible expression of sophisticated understanding between the superpowers on the war-and-peace equation. The danger of uncontrollable violence exists rather at the other end of the power spectrum, among newly created states which are all too often both politically unstable and economically unviable but share a common infection of nationalistic ambitions. Furthermore, a number of these small nations are linked by agreements with one or other of the superpowers so that, as client-states, they are in a position to force the superpower into taking action which may go beyond the point which the latter's own predilections or global commitments would counsel." (T. Walter Wallbank, Alastair M. Taylor, Nels M. Bailkey and Mark Mancall, *Civilization Past and Present,* 6th ed., Glenview, Ill., 1970, Book 1, p. 507)

"A future general nuclear war between the USA and the USSR is probably most likely to come about through the escalation of a local war in an unstable region. Such a war may begin as a conventional war and escalate to a nuclear war in which the nuclear weapons of one or more of the participants are used. Subsequently the two great powers may come to the assistance of client states threatened with destruction. This great power involvement may well end in a general nuclear war which would have disastrous consequences for all mankind." (*Disarmament and World Development,* ed. by Richard Jolly, Oxford, 1978, p. 24)

"Thermonuclear war between the great powers can also be triggered by a third nation in a position which allows it to take advantage of the mutual distrust between the U.S.S.R. and the U.S.A." (Robert A. Dentler and Phillips Cutright, *Hostage America,* Boston, 1963, p. 8)

e.
Root of War

IS THERE STILL SOMETHING WE CAN DO TO SAVE OUR-
selves before it is too late?

There is only one thing which has not actually been tried: to
abolish war itself.

The idea of the abolition of war is not new.[133] It has encountered
no opposition in theory except some opinions that war is something

---

131. Cf. two books with the same title, *No Place to Hide*—one by David V.
Bradley, Boston, 1948, and the other ed. by Seymour Melman, New York, 1962.

132. "There is no effective defense against modern methods of mass destruction. Therefore no nation is any longer able to adequately protect its citizens merely through an increase in its military strength. As long as the present condition of
international anarchy prevails, all of us will continue to live under the constant
threat of sudden annihilation." (*Einstein on Peace,* edited by Otto Nathan and
Heinz Norden, New York, 1960, p. 414)

"Barring the discovery of some entirely new scientific principle so far
unimaginable—like an antigravity shield—a defense that achieves anything even
close to 100 per cent effectiveness is highly unlikely. And the power of nuclear
weapons is such that anything less than a perfect defense will result in very high
casualty levels. No matter what technology brings, in sum, the world is simply a
different place than it was before the discovery of nuclear weapons and missiles.
Human beings are too frail and the planet is too small." (Roger Hilsman, *The
Crouching Future,* New York, 1975, p. 563. Cf. again: Leiba Brown and Ruth
Leeds, "What the Bombs Can Do," in *The Hard Way to Peace,* by Amitai Etzioni, New York, 1962, p. 267-280.)

"But, with continued existence of nuclear weapons, the end of the world is,
and will continue to be, as near as the next 30 minutes." (Howard Brembeck, *The
Alternative to Nuclear War,* a booklet published by the Alternative World Foundation, Goshen, Inc., 1983.)

133. The words of Isaiah come from the eighth century B.C.: "And they shall
beat their swords into plowshares, and their spears into pruning hooks; nation
shall not lift up sword against nation, neither shall they learn war anymore."
(Quoted in *International Arms Control, Issues and Agreements,* by the Stanford
Arms Control Group, ed. by John H. Barton and Lawrence D. Weiler, Stanford,
Calif., 1976, p. 1.)

Mo Ti, 墨翟, the Chinese philosopher (about 400 B.C.), taught that universal
love and mutual respect would be infinitely superior to war, which he regarded as
the greatest crime of which men could be guilty. He condemned the economic
wastefulness of war since neither the invading country nor the invaded lands profit
by war. He reasoned that the killing of one man was a crime, that the killing of a
hundred men increases the crime a hundred times, and the greatest of all crimes is
the invasion of a country resulting in the killing of hundreds of thousands of

contained in human nature[134] and that war is an effective instrument for evolution.[135] No matter how much truth these opinions may hold, they obviously cannot justify the nuclear war which threatens to annihilate all human beings, along with their nature, and to destroy the whole civilization, including its evolution.

The real problem, therefore, is how to abolish war.

There were some scholars who predicted that an ultimate weapon of mass destruction would make war impossible,[136] or asserted that

---

human beings. He urged that this large scale killing of human beings should not be praised and called right; and he wanted one standard of morality for individuals and states. (Cf.墨子非戰篇; James Legge's translation of *The Chinese Classics,* Oxford, 1895, Vol. II, p. 109; F.M. Russell, *Theories of International Relations,* New York, 1936, p. 25-27; and Chi Fung Lui, "The Ethical Implications of Moh Tih's Philosophy," *International Journal of Ethics,* Vol. XXXV, p. 77.)

134. Some people hold that war is something contained in the nature of mankind, and is an end desirable in itself. "Of all the ideas the idea of war is perhaps the only one which is innate to man"—the conclusion being that war is likely to last forever. This kind of conception is basically deceptive. It is foolish to speak of war as an idea. It is a fact and a practice. The writer quoted seems to be groping about after some "instinct of combativeness." Even assuming that certain evils are part of human nature, in fact and at any rate, men when they go to war do not do so merely for the joy of killing each other. (Cf. Albert G. Keller, *Through War to Peace,* New York, 1921, chaps. III and IV; and William G. Sumner, "Purposes and Consequences," in his *Essays,* New Haven, 1934, Vol. I, p. 11-19.)

"Why did cities once wage wars against each other and why do municipalities no longer fight each other with weapons today? Why, at certain times, have great landowner barons warred with each other and why have they now ceased that practice? Why did the various churches plunge their adherents into armed warfare and why today are they able to worship side by side without shooting each other? Why did Scotland and England, Saxony and Prussia, Parma and Tuscany, at a certain period in their history, go to battle against each other and why have they ceased fighting today? A careful study of human history reveals that the assumption that war is inherent in human nature—and therefore eternal—is shallow and faulty, that it is only a superficial impression." (Emery Reves, *The Anatomy of Peace,* New York, 1946, p. 120)

135. The evolutionist sees in the practical universality of war a clear proof that it once had its usefulness, just as daimonism and slavery and the motherfamily had theirs. Out of the armed conflict emerges a selection whereby old and effete societal forms are eliminated, new forces are set free, and the process of development enters into its next phase. But there is a big trouble with war: it is that while it may cure the disease, it is likely to kill the patient. (Cf. William G. Sumner and Albert G. Keller, *The Science of Society,* New Haven, 1927, Vol. I, p. 407-410; Luther L. Bernard, *War and Its Causes,* New York, 1944, p. 7, 161.)

136. The atomic bomb may be the ultimate weapon Alfred B. Nobel, the inventor of nitroglycerine, dynamite, gelatin, and the smokeless fire powder—ballistite, wanted to invent: "a substance or a machine with such terrible power of mass

nuclear weapons had rendered war obsolete.[137] Their "impossible" and "obsolete" of war are merely theorized, however. They have offered no positive way to abolish war.

There have been two noteworthy opinions about how to abolish war positively. One is by abolishing weapons. It traces the root of war to weapons, because it holds, without weapons war cannot be fought.[138] But, basically, it is weapons that exist for war, not war that

---

destruction that war would thereby be made impossible forever." (Quoted in *Linus Pauling on Science and Peace,* New York, 1964, p. 6.)

"The late great Robert Hutchins was importantly wrong only once in his life, in my opinion. When he supervised the development of the atomic bomb at the University of Chicago in 1942, he called it 'the good news of damnation,' contending that it would frighten people into banding together to avoid world suicide and achieve world peace." (Sydney Harris, "Showdown, Nuclear Style, Won't Have Winners, Losers," *South Bend Tribune,* Aug. 1, 1977, p. 6)

137. (*War Is Obsolete; the Dialectics of Military Technology and Consequences,* Amsterdam, 1972, by Paul K. Crosser) It is argued that in the nuclear stage of weaponry, technology with missiles applied as means of delivery of hydrogen bombs, the speed and firepower of weapons has reached such proportions that any country made subject to an attack by thermonuclear bomb-laden missiles is threatened with annihilation. The change to thermonuclear bombs and missiles as means of delivery thus constitutes a qualitative change in the evolution of weaponry technology, and this change signifies the preclusion of the winning of a war by way of the application of the most up-to-date weaponry technology, as represented by thermonuclear bombs and missiles. A demonstration is undertaken in the second chapter that the army, the navy and air force, as organized institutional entities, can be expected to disintegrate in the course of a nuclear exchange. That disintegration can, in turn, be expected to be accompanied by the disintegration of the entire institutional framework of the country subjected to a nuclear attack. Any attempt to maintain production, distribution and consumption of civilian goods, in terms of physical and chemical processes, in the course of a nuclear saturation exchange, is doomed to failure. Chapter IV undertakes, on the basis of the dialectical turn in military technology, to demonstrate the futility of the attempt to form strategic concepts on the basis of which a nuclear war could be fought. Any strategy conceived for the fighting of a nuclear war can only prove to be self-defeating. The cohesive institutional framework of the national state, the preconditioning factor for the conduct of such a war, will cease to exist in the course of a nuclear exchange. Such strategic concepts as limited war, preventive war, pre-emption, deterrent, first strike and second strike, are subjected to a critical examination in Chapter IV. (Cf. p. 49-134.)

138. This opinion points out that most of the warlike peoples in history were those who possessed better weapons, that the development of warfare always followed the progress of weapons, and that the present situation in which war has been getting bigger and worse results from the invention of new weapons. It is true that weapons are a great stimulus to war, and that their progress always intensifies the development of warfare. But no evidences can prove that weapons was the root of war. On the contrary, history indicates that it is weapons that exist for war, not

exists for weapons. In fact, weapons only present a real threat if possessed by rivals in warfare,[139] and they can be reproduced even if there is a way to eliminate them all at once.[140] So, to elminiate weapons would not necessarily result in abolishing war, as long as there exist rivals in warfare. Furthermore, the elimination of weapons, if carried out thoroughly, would imply a great depletion of our productive power, because almost all weapons in their original or other forms are tools of production.[141]

---

war that exists for weapons. This is well indicated by a conclusion on disarmament: "The solution of the problem of disarmament cannot be found within the problem itself, but outside it. In fact, the problem of disarmament is not the problem of disarmament. It really is the problem of the organization of the World-Community." (Salvador de Madariaga, *Disarmament,* New York, 1929, p. 56)

139. "Nobody in the United States is afraid of atomic bombs or rockets produced within the sovereign nation-state of the United States of America. Nor is any Soviet citizen affraid of atomic bombs or other devastating weapons produced within the sovereign nation-state of the Union of Soviet Socialist Republics. But the people of the United States feel that atomic bombs produced in the Soviet Union represent a potential danger to them, and the Soviet people feel the same way about atomic bombs produced in the United States. What does this mean? It means that no atomic bomb, no weapon that the genius of man can conceive is dangerous in itself. Weapons only become 'dangerous' when they are in the hands of sovereign states other than one's own. It follows that the ultimate source of danger is not atomic energy but the sovereign nation-state. The problem is not technical, it is purely political." (Emery Reves, *The Anatomy of Peace,* New York, 1946, p. 279)

140. The assumption that weapons are the root of war cannot offer any actual way to achieve peace. Its logical conclusion seems to be that peace would eventually come if we eliminated all the weapons. How can we eliminate all the weapons? It is impossible to convince the powers to do so as long as the chance of war exists. The difficulties of disarmament recorded in recent history have been a fair illustration. Even if the powers were so convinced and eliminated all the new and conventional weapons all at once, they could be produced again. In fact, most modern civilian factories can be adapted to produce munitions within a very short time. Consequently, any success, if possible, in the elimination of weapons or in disarmament does not mean much in eliminating the possibility of war.

141. Such as the bow for hunting, gunpowder for explosion in mining, and the atom for various peaceful uses. "Some people wish that we had never succeeded in splitting the atom. But atomic power, like any other force of nature, is not evil in itself. Properly used, it is an instrumentality for human betterment." (Harry S. Truman's speech at the Inauguration of U.S. President Dwight D. Eisenhower, Jan. 20, 1953)

"Nuclear explosives can, however, be of great benefit to mankind throughout the world. One major limitation on the progress of civilization in the past was the nonhuman energy available per person. The enormous reservoir of power provided by nuclear energy, particularly nuclear explosives, has simply removed that limitation in our time." (John S. Foster, Jr., Director of the Lawrence Radiation

The other proposal is to abolish war by abandoning the private property system which, according to this opinion, is the root of war.[142] This opinion can hardly explain why there were wars between ancient communist societies[143] and why it is unlikely there will be no war between modern Communist countries.[144] In fact, the greatest

---

Laboratory, Livermore, Calif., "Nuclear Weapons," in the *Encyclopedia Americana,* 1973 ed., Vol. 20, p. 528)

142. Some socialists, including some anarchists and communists, have held this view. Some communists further blended it with capitalism, stressing that under capitalism there was an inevitable struggle for the control of market and raw materials, that so long as capitalism endured this struggle would continue, and that the only way to get rid of war was, therefore, to get rid of capitalism. (Cf. Henry Noel Brailsford, *War of Steel and Gold,* 8th ed., London, 1917; and *Political Economy: Capitalism,* ed. by G.A. Kozlov, tr. from Russian by Jane Sayer, Moscow, 1977.) Karl Marx prophesied, in the Address of the General Council of the First International, on July 23, 1870, on the occasion of the Franco-German war: "A new society is springing up whose international role will be peace, because its national ruler will be everywhere the same—Labour. The pioneer of that new society is the International Working Men's Association." (Cf. Karl Marx, *The Civil War in France,* New York, 1940, p. 27.) The communist view was refuted by Norman Angell, among others, who shows that war does not win markets but is likely to lead to their forfeiture, and that in most respects the capitalist is adversely served by war. (Cf. Norman Angell, "Is Capitalism a Cause of War?" *Spectator,* Vol. CLII, 1934.)

143. In primitive times when most of the peoples lived a life of Communist economy, war raged between them. They fought for food, shelter, and women. But they captured these ordinarily for their group as a whole, not for private ownership. In regard to the Communist economy in the ancient societies, Friedrich Engels made a note to the English edition of 1888 of the *Manifesto of the Communist Party* (Karl Marx and Friedrich Engels, *Selected Works,* Moscow, 1955, Vol. 1, p. 34.): "That is, all written history. In 1847, the prehistory of society, the social organization existing previous to recorded history, was all but unknown. Since then, Haxthausen discovered common ownership of land in Russia, Maurer proved it to be the social foundation from which all Teutonic races started in history, and by and by village communities were found to be, or to have been the primitive form of society everywhere from India to Ireland. The inner organization of this primitive Communistic society was laid bare, in its typical form, by Morgan's crowning discovery of the true nature of the gens and its relation to the tribe. With the dissolution of these primaeval communities society begins to be differentiated into separate and finally antagonistic classes. I have attempted to retrace this process of dissolution in: 'Der Ursprung der Familie, des Privateigenthums und des Staats' (The Origin of the Family, Private Property and the State). (2nd edition, Stuttgart, 1886)

144. It is true that war has always been motivated by the ruling circle for their private advantage. But they had to hide their real intentions under the pretext of public interest in order to induce their people to die willingly in the battlefield. Now if the system of private property is abolished and national or state ownership

and most important property war has always been fought for is territory.[145] But territory, in general, belongs to the public. It is not private property under any political and economic system. To fight for it means to fight for the public.

After a brief review of these two opinions, one cannot help but ask who are the rivals in warfare and who is the public for which war has always been fought? These questions lead to an inquiry into the common but fundamental problem: war is fought by whom and for whom?

War has generally been defined as an armed conflict between groups.[146] This means that war is usually fought by groups against each other, and also implies that war is primarily fought for the groups themselves. While there are various kinds of groups, only those which are independent normally have the authority and necessity to wage war by and for themselves; and such authority and necessity are generally derived from their independence.[147] Thus, the

---

is substituted for private ownership, the former will take the place of the latter as an element of war in a more direct manner. Many motives of war, such as for a plan of living, for the relief of population pressure, for economic self-sufficiency, for resources, for the security of public property, etc. would become stronger than under the system of private property, and would become more connected with the public interest. It is obvious, therefore, that the abolition of the system of private property would not automatically result in the abolition of war, and war may occur as well between the nations which have abolished the system of private property, such as the Communist countries, in spite of their ideology that "After abolishing private ownership in the means of production and converting them into social property, the world system of communism will replace the elemental forces of the world market, of competition and the blind process of social production, by consciously organized and planned production for the purpose of satisfying rapidly growing social needs. With the abolition of competition and anarchy in production, the devastating crises and still more devastating wars will disappear." (Passage 3 of Chapter 3 of the Program of the Communist International, together with the Constitution, adopted at the Sixth World Congress, Sept. 1, 1928)

145. Plato finds "at the root of all wars" the necessity to enlarge borders. (*Republic, II,* when discussing the luxurious state)

146. "War is a legal condition which equally permits two or more hostile groups to carry on a conflict by armed force." (Quincy Wright, *A Study of War,* 2nd ed., Chicago, 1965, p. 698. Cf. I, 97-100.)

147. "If we try to detect the mechanism visibly in operation, the single cause ever-present at the outbreak of each and every conflict known to human history, if we attempt to reduce the seemingly innumerable causes of war to a common denominator, two clear and unmistakable observations emerge. 1. Wars between groups of men forming social units always take place when these units . . . exercise unrestricted sovereign power. 2. Wars between these social units cease the moment sovereign power is transferred from them to a large or higher unit. From these

definition of war may justifiably be modified as an armed conflict between independent groups, and the independence of the groups may reasonably be ascribed as the root of war. The groups which distinguish themselves with independence are the ones appearing in the process of group expansion: the early single family, the primitive community, clan, tribe, and lately, the nation.

f.
War by
and for the Nation

FOR CENTURIES, INDEED, WAR HAS BEEN FOUGHT BY nations. From 1480 to 1940 there were 244 important wars engaged by the nations of the world;[148] and 2,659 important battles participated in by European nations,[149] most frequently by the stronger ones.[150]

---

observations we can deduce a social law with the characteristics of an axiom that applies to and explains each and every war in the history of all time: War takes place whenever and wherever nonintegrated social units of equal sovereignty come into contact." (Emery Reves, *The Anatomy of Peace,* New York, 1946, p. 121)

148. The important participants of these wars were: Great Britain, 74; France, 63; Spain, 59; Russia, 57; Austria, 51; Turkey, 43; Poland, 28; Sweden, 25; Italy, 25; Netherlands, 22; Germany, 22; Denmark, 20; the United States, 12; China, 9; and Japan, 9. (Quincy Wright, *A Study of War,* 2nd ed., Chicago, 1965, Tables 31-41)

149. Of these battles, France participated in 1,136; Austria, 807; Germany, 616; Great Britain, 558; Russia, 537; Spain, 404; Turkey, 354; the Netherlands, 181; Sweden, 101; Denmark, 33. Almost all of the other European nations took part in some of these battles. (Quincy Wright, *A Study of War,* 2nd ed., Chicago, 1965, Tables 22, 23, 31-41) A few of the battles were fought within a nation.

150. It is interesting to note that, like a fighter, the stronger the nation is, the more frequently it wages war, and correspondingly that the frequency of participation in war increases when the nation is becoming stronger, and decreases when it is weaker. Of the 2,659 important battles listed above, France participated in 47 percent; Austria in 34 percent; Germany in 25 percent; Great Britain and Russia each in about 22 percent; Turkey in 15 percent; Spain in 12 percent; the Netherlands in 8 percent; Sweden in 4 percent; Denmark in 2 percent; and the others in less than 1 percent. These percentages are for the entire period of four hundred and sixty years. When tabulated by fifty-year periods, it appears that the percentage of participation by France, Austria, Great Britain, and Turkey has been relatively constant, that by

War is sometimes waged by religious groups such as the European Church in the Middle Ages. But no religious group has such capacity in modern times. Classes have sometimes been supposed to be able to fight wars. But this assumption has never been real except in certain civil wars. Civil war, if strictly defined as a war between groups belonging to the same nation, has greatly declined in number as well as in importance.[151]

In the age of feudalism, in principle it was only the feudal nobles who had the privilege to fight, and they regarded fighting as a chivalrous sport.[152] In the era of royal absolution, fighting was the occupation of mercenaries recruited from the scum of the society. It has become more and more clear and real that war is fought by the nation as a whole since the 18th century when general conscription was introduced,[153] and later, the militarization of entire population started to be a common practice.[154]

Germany and Russia has remarkedly tended to increase as they grew in power, and that by Spain, the Netherlands, Sweden, and Denmark has decreased in the last three centuries as they became relatively weak. (Cf. Quincy Wright, *A Study of War,* 2nd ed., Chicago, 1965, Table 22, p. 222; Frederick A. Woods and Alexander Baltzly, *Is War Diminishing?,* Boston, 1915, p. 31.)

151. Quincy Wright listed 34 important wars fought between groups belonging to the same nation in recent centuries, of which from 1480 to 1600 there were 11; from 1600 to 1700, 13; from 1700 to 1800, 5; from 1800 to 1900, 4; and from 1900 to 1940, 1. (Cf. his *A Study of War,* 2nd ed., Chicago, 1965, Tables 31-41.)

152. An old French verse says: "The clerk's duty is to pray to God, the noble's duty is to fight, the peasant has to provide the bread." (Quoted in Friedrich O. Hertz, *Nationality in History and Politics,* London, 1944, p. 228.)

153. The general conscription was first adopted by France, then by Germany, and down to the twentieth century by almost all great nations. Some nations even made military services compulsory for women as well as men. (Cf. Hoffman Nickerson, *Can We Limit War,* New York, 1933, p. 111 ff; and William H. McNeill, "The Draft in the Light of History," in *The Draft,* ed. by Sol Tax, Chicago, 1967, p. 117-121.) A United Nations survey shows that Chile, Israel, Pakistan and Turkey have made military service compulsory for women as well as for men. Lately, the United States has also tried this: On Feb. 11, 1980, President Carter asked Congress to provide funds for drafting women for military service, but it was not approved. (Cf. *Congressional Report Weekly,* Vol. 38, no. 26, June 28, 1980, p. 1819.)

154. A more significant indication in recent decades has been the militarization of entire populations. The armed forces have ceased to be a self-contained service apart from the general population. Soldiers and sailors must be recruited from those men whose services can be most readily supplied by women, children, and the aged. Experts in transportation and industrial services must be largely exempted in order that they may continue their important "civilian services" which, under modern conditions, are no less essential to war. Such a gearing-in of the

For centuries, war has been fought not only by the nation, but also for the nation. While to defend the nation or its security is the primary object of war,[155] to fight for the aspirations of the nation is

---

agricultural, industrial, and professional population to the armed forces requires a military organization of the entire population. Since the perfection of such an organization after the outbreak of war has been impossible, it has become necessary to organize the entire population on a military basis in the time of peace. (Cf. Hans Speier, "Class Structure and Total War," *American Sociological Review,* IV, June, 1939; and Robert B. Armeson, *Total Warfare and Compulsory Labor; a Study of Military and Industrial Complex in Germany During World War I,* The Hague, 1964.)

155. For security and defense, the nation may have to have armed forces, to adopt the conscription system, to improve its conventional weapons, to invent new weapons, and therefore, to engage in the armament race. For security and defense, the nation may have to demand natural frontiers or strategical boundaries, as France demanded the control of both banks of the Rhine in the Conference of Versailles after World War I. For security and defense, the nation may have to find and protect strategical bases and routes, as Britain did in respect to some bases and routes in the Mediterranean Sea for some centuries. For security and defense, the nation may have to maintain the balance of power, as British foreign policy did toward the European Continent for a long time. For security and defense, the nation may have to establish hegemony over a region, and claim a sphere of influence as in the American Monroe Doctrine. For security and defense, the nation may have to establish itself on a basis of self-sufficiency and acquire resources and raw materials. (Cf. Lionel C. Robbins, *The Economic Causes of War,* London, 1939; John E. Bakeless, *The Economic Causes of Modern War,* New York, 1921; and Max Handman, "War, Economic Motives, and Economic Symbols," *American Journal of Sociology,* XLIV, March 1939.) And for security and defense, the nation may even have to make conquests, such as Russia's attacks on Poland and Finland in 1939-1940. In short, the desire for the security and defense of the nation is an endless cause of war, because it is an endless desire.

For security and defense, the nation may have to seek alliances, as when "two States, A and B, each feel themselves to be menaced by a third State C, and they therefore patch up their own quarrel and conclude what is called a 'defense alliance.' The third State, C, however, finds it difficult to believe in the purely . . . defensive intentions of its neighbours and becomes apprehensive. It, therefore, seeks to ally itself with a fourth State, D. . . . This process continues until most of the important States are bound in a network of alliances and counter-alliances, each upholding in public the doctrine of the balance of power, while manoeuvring in private to have the balance upset in its own favour. . . . When two States enter into a formal alliance, it is usual to state in the Preamble that the High Contracting Parties have no object save the preservation of peace of the world. In fact, nothing could be more calculated to upset peace than such a system of bribery and power-seeking, and nothing could make war more destructive and widespread when it comes." (William B. Curry, *The Case for Federal Union,* Harmondsworth, Eng., 1939, p. 60-61)

"Security! The term signifies more indeed than the maintenance of a people's

very common and popular in warfare, too.[156] The actual annulment of the distinction between civilian and military and between rear and front by modern military techniques in total and absolute war makes war fought for the nation more real.[157]

It is true that war is often motivated by the ruling circle, certain individuals or organizations, for their various special purposes.[158] But they have to rationalize their motives in term of national interest,

---

homeland, or even of their territories beyond the seas. It also means the maintenance of the world's respect for them, the maintenance of their economic interests, everything, in a word, which goes to make up the grandeur, the life itself, of the nation." (Jules Cambon, *The Permanent Bases of Foreign Policy*, New York, 1931, p. 25)

156. National aspiration may sometimes even be regarded as more serious than national security and defense, such as the fight for national self-determination, for national independence, for national self-government, for national liberation from foreign domination, for recovery of the lost national land, for the solidarity of nationality, for a certain mission as a "chosen people," for national integrity, and for the nation's honor, prestige, pride, etc. (Cf. Friedrich O. Hertz, *Nationality in History and Politics*, London, 1944, p. 21-24.)

157. The militarization of the entire population has been called "the nation in arms." But this term implies the militarization of all the lives in the nation. All lives are required first to meet military needs, to link tightly with the military system, and to be subject to military discipline directly or indirectly. As a result, the principle of military necessity has tended to be interpreted in a way which overrides the traditional rules of war for the protection of civilian life and property. Thus the population, manufacturing, and transport centers have become military targets; and bombing aircraft and starvation blockades have made it possible to reach these targets over the heads of the army and fortifications. The distinction between the front and rear and between military and civilian, then, no longer exists, and civilian defense has had to extend over the whole nation. These developments have made it clearer and more real that war is fought for the nation. (Cf. Hans Speier and Alfred Kohler, *War in Our Time*, New York, 1939, p. 13-14; Henry W. Spiegel, *The Economics of Total War*, New York, 1942; and Basil H. Liddell Hart, *The Revolution in Warfare*, New Haven, 1947, chap. II.)

158. Politically, they have an interest in war as a means of maintaining their position and privilege, augmenting their power and prestige, or seeking honor and glory for themselves as Fascist leaders sometimes explicitly demonstrated. Economically, they attempt to gain an advantage from war through selling munitions and other war supplies, or contributing various services. (Cf. Helmuth C. Engelbrecht and Frank C. Hanighen, *Merchants of Death*, Garden City, N.Y., 1934.) They need war to acquire markets or to protect their investments abroad, and they want war to solve the economic ills inherent in capitalism. And if such ills cannot be solved, they create frustrations from which war might offer an escape. (Cf. Vladimir I. Lenin, *Against Imperialist War, Articles and Speeches*, Moscow, 1966.) And ideologically, they advocate war to develop an idea, belief, or way of life, such as Hitler's "New Order."

to declare war by the name of the nation, and to use the nation to fight.

We have heard some strong voices from prominent writers who, in an effort to avert the war disaster, have tried to appeal to humanitarianism,[159] rationality,[160] and real economic interest.[161] But their

---

159. Humanitarians have demonstrated the brutality and destructiveness of war. (Cf. for example, David S. Jordan, *The Blood of the Nation, War and Waste, The Human Harvest;* H.M. Swanwick, *The Roots of Peace;* Nicholas M. Butler, *Why War?;* William L. Lawrence, *The Hell Bomb;* and Linus Pauling, *No More War.)* They have characterized war as crime. (Cf., for example, Juan B. Alberdi, *El Crimen de la Guerra.)* But their appeals have been woefully ignored, because war fought by and for the nation has been commonly regarded as of the highest morality.

"Seneca, the Roman philosopher, dramatist, and political leader, was born about the same time as Jesus and lived during most of the first century. In one of his Epistles (95, 30), he wrote: 'We are mad, not only individually, but nationally. We check manslaughter and isolated murders; but what of war and the much vaunted crime of slaughtering whole peoples?'.... If war was nationalized madness then, what is it now, when no one is safe, even neutrals? It has become madder and madder over the centuries, as we have exponentially increased our capacity to destroy not just armies, but whole cities, simply by pressing a button." (Sydney Harris, "National Slaughtering Inaffordable Madness," *South Bend Tribune,* Aug. 2, 1978, p. 12)

160. Since the Enlightenment, our prominent philosophers have often appealed to rationality in order to bring an end to the large-scale mutual-murder. They have urged people to consider, in regard to the problem of peace and war as upon other important problems, the long-time values and consequences and to censure uncritical behavior based on mere impulse and irresponsible emotion. For example, Jean Jacques Rousseau was convinced that the application of reason could produce peace ("Extrait du project de paix perpetuelle," in William E. Darby, ed., *International Tribunals,* 1904, p. 104) and Immanuel Kant believed that political improvement was only possible through the application of reason and that reason could only be applied to world politics if statesmen followed the maxim, which to save their dignity they should keep secret, that "the maxims of the philosophers regarding the condition of the possibility of a public peace shall be taken into consideration by the States that are armed for war." (*Eternal Peace,* 1st ed., 1795, Boston, 1914, p. 7, 100) Philosophers have also proved the fallacy and folly of war. (Cf., for example, Egon Eis, *The Forts of Folly,* trans. by A.J. Pomerans, Philadelphia, 1962; and James R. Newman, *The Rule of Folly,* New York, 1962.) But their appeals have been pitifully ignored, because war fought by and for the nation has been commonly regarded as of the greatest reason.

161. In recent decades our outstanding economists have tried to stop wasteful war by appealing to interest. They have testified, with statistics, that war does not pay, but only wastes resources and results in bankruptcy. Their appeals are practical for people who believe that war can bring a tangible advantage to the nation, who regard war as a struggle for the life of the people, and who even justify war as based on the "sacred egoism" of the group. Their appeals were summed up by

appeals have been deplorably ignored, mainly because war fought by and for the nation has been commonly regarded as of the highest morality, greatest reason, and paramount value.

As modern war is fought by and for the nation, and is thus justified and supported, it is obvious that it would be impossible to abolish it as long as the nation had the authority and necessity to wage war by and for itself; and it has such authority and necessity[162] as long as it remains with independence, which, as pointed out before, is the root of war and is generally symbolized with sovereignty.

g.
Abolition of War

THUS, THE PROBLEM OF HOW TO ABOLISH WAR BE-comes the question of how to get rid of the independence of the na-

---

Norman Angell, a Briton who, after some years in the United States, spent most of his life on the Continent, and published in 1910 a book called *The Great Illusion,* which caused a sensation. Angell said bluntly that wars did not pay. Modern economic life, he argued, was a highly complicated affair and depended on mutual confidence between nations and on an elaborate system of international credit, both of which would be destroyed by war. If governments were so foolish as to go to war, they would lose much more than they could gain, and the victors would be ruined as well as the vanquished. Angell's voice was heard widely. And it was a fact that in July, 1914, the strongest opposition to war came from bankers in England and Germany. But such appeals have been generally ignored, because war fought by and for the nations has been commonly regarded as of paramount value.

162. "But until mankind has banished both war and its instruments of destruction, the United States must maintain an effective quantity and quality of nuclear weapons, so deployed and protected as to be capable of surviving any surprise attack and devastating the attacker. Only through such strength can we be certain of deterring a nuclear strike, or an overwhelming ground attack, upon our forces and allies." (President John F. Kennedy in a television address, March 2, 1962. Quoted in *The Burden and the Glory,* ed. by Allan Nevins, New York, 1964, p. 45.)

"In the world today there is no supranational force to compel nations to obey international law or to behave as the provisions of the United Nations Charter would have them do; therefore the nations have to rely on their own power, or the power of allies, to protect their existence and their vital interests. In short, they must rely on force to repel force." (E.L.M. Burns, *Megamurder,* New York, 1967, p. 5)

Speech by Joseph V. Stalin, Feb. 9, 1946: "Actually, the war was the inevitable result of the development of world economic and political forces on the basis of modern monopoly capitalism." "By now I should think everyone will admit, that

tion.[163] Fortunately, an answer to this question has been provided by the last step of the process of group expansion: to merge all nations into One World.

Historically, the merging of smaller groups into larger ones has proved to be effective in reducing the number of wars, as the number of groups diminishes in the process of group expansion.[164] But there has never been a chance for it to abolish war all at once, because as soon as war between smaller groups is eliminated, war between larger groups is underway. When the interclannish war was checked, for example, the intertribal war took place, and when the intertribal war was checked, the international war took place.[165]

Today, however, the chance for abolishing war all at once is coming, because the merging of all nations into One World would get rid of the independence of all nations and thus deprive them of the

---

the war really was not and could not have been an accident in the life of nations, that actually this was because the war of nations was fought for their existence, and that for this reason it could not be a quick lightning affair. As regards our country, for it, this war was the most bitter and arduous of all wars in the history of our Motherland." (*The Strategy and Tactics of World Communism,* by the Committee on Foreign Affairs, 80th Congress of the United States, 1948, p. 168, 170)

163. "I am convinced that the Great Framer of the World will so develop it that it becomes one nation, so that armies and navies are no longer necessary." (President Ulysses S. Grant, quoted by Lawrence Abbot, "World Federalism: What? Why? How?" published by the World Federalists Association and the American Movement for World Government, New York, 1983, p. 28)

"Early man found he improved his security by joining with others in tribes; more of them in a group could better ward off tigers and enemy men than a man could by himself. As time went on, weapons and methods of conflict became more sophisticated, and man enlarged his security-group into towns and cities. There were moats and walls and drawbridges to keep out an enemy. Cities provided security. As even more sophisticated weapons and methods of warfare were devised, cities merged into nations. That was only a few hundred years ago. Men felt they would be more secure as members of nations which could build military forces to ward off enemy nations." (*William Winter Comments,* Vol. VI, no. 40, Oct. 2, 1967)

164. "Political groups have increased in size from the clan, village, and tribe to the kingdom, nation, and federation; and peace has been striven for within these enlarging areas with varying degrees of success." (Quincy Wright, *A Study of War,* 2nd ed., Chicago, 1965, p. 6. Cf. I, 101-103)

165. "War between given social units of equal sovereignty is the permanent symptom of each successive phase of civilization. Wars always ceased when a higher unit established its own sovereignty, absorbing the sovereignties of the conflicting smaller social groups. After such transfers of sovereignty, a period of peace followed, which lasted only until the new social units came into contact. Then a new series of wars began." (Emery Reves, *The Anatomy of Peace,* New York, 1946, p. 121)

authority and necessity of waging war by and for themselves, while all peoples of the whole world would become one independent group, and obviously one independent group cannot engage in war alone.

Indeed, war can be abolished forever entirely by merging all nations into One World. There are, however, some people who think that it is a way which goes too far[166] and is unlikely to be chosen over survival in crisis.[167] Actually, it is not only not going too far, but is the only way out for survival.[168] In the first place, as explained earlier, the physical conditions are ready for One World to come,[169] and the nation has already outlived its time[170] and lost its value.[171] To

---

166. They are asking whether the burning of the whole house is the best way to roast the pig. They ridicule the notion that it is like the proposal for ending the Nazi submarine menace in World War II by boiling the oceans.

167. "If we seek to draw lessons from history to instruct us in our present perplexities it is important to note the radical difference between two problems which communities in past history have faced. In the first case, communities were confronted with a crisis in which they were forced to make a choice between their survival or liberty—and some larger good, or the good of a larger community. In this situation nations chose their own existence, security, or interest rather than the more universal value, such as the peace of Europe or any other region. In such situations of crisis nations and other communities always have responded by protecting their lives and liberties without regard to the more universal value, particularly as the latter was usually too remote or abstract." (Reinhold Niebuhr, *The Structure of Nations and Empires,* New York, 1959, p. 268)

168. "The world has progressed to its present high position . . . by the integration of small political units into ever larger states, and the consequent abolition of the innumerable wars that formerly raged between every neighboring little principality. If mankind is to progress further the nations of the world must be united under a single world government that will abolish international wars between all the nations. If the process of integration and elimination of warfare does not go on, the opposite process of disintegration through increasing and ever more destructive warfare will take its place. Civilization must abolish war or war will abolish civilization." (Oscar Newfang, *The Road to World Peace,* New York, 1924, p. 62)

169. Our mode of life has changed from a local self-sufficiency of agriculture to a world-wide interdependency of industry. The world has shrunk into a small kingdom through transportation and communications, and has come under the threat of nuclear and other devastating weapons. Unmistakably, the physical conditions are ready for group expansion to proceed into a world community. (Cf. I, i and j.)

170. In the process of our group expansion, the nation basically belongs to the Iron Age, which started about 1000 B.C. and reached its culmination about 1900 A.D. (Cf. I, 383.)

171. As the physical conditions for a world community have been completed, it is possible for all peoples in the world to avoid the evil of international wars by getting together as one group, to live a better life by extending cooperation throughout the whole world, and to get rid of all their national burdens by living

merge all nations into One World is but one step further in the process of group expansion, and is not just an expedient measure for abolishing war. It is a necessary consequence of historical development, a consummation of social evolution, and an outcome of the advance of modern science and technology.

Secondly, as also already explained, a great nuclear war is threatening to destroy the whole world and annihilate all of us. In such a war "there would be no winners, only losers,"[172] and no victory, only "mutual suicide"[173] or "double suicide."[174] Hence, there is left no choice for survival other than to abolish war by merging all nations into One World.[175]

---

under a single administrative system. Under these circumstances, clearly, the nation is not only losing its reality and value, but even becoming an obstacle to peace, a hindrance to our welfare, a fetter to our freedom, and the source of many other evils. (Cf. III, 214-266.)

172. President Richard M. Nixon, in a television address from the Kremlin Palace, spoke of having reached with Soviet leaders "a far-reaching set of agreements that can lead to a better life for both of our peoples, and to a better chance for peace in the world." Had the summit negotiators failed to agree on freezing the total number of strategic offensive and defensive nuclear ballistic missiles, Nixon told his multi-continent audience, "there would be no winners, only losers." (Reported by Frank Cormier, AP reporter, *South Bend Tribune,* May 29, 1972, p. 1.)

173. "We still fail to understand the implications of the atomic age. We have not grasped the overriding fact—clear to every scientist who has studied the matter —that war is now qualitatively different from anything known in the past. It is no longer a 'zero-sum' game, where one side 'wins' what the other 'loses.' It is mutual suicide, beyond rational calculation." (Sydney Harris, "Showdown, Nuclear Style, Won't Have Winners, Losers," *South Bend Tribune,* Aug. 1, 1977, p. 6)

174. "Global war has become a Frankenstein's monster to destroy both sides. If you lose, you are annihilated. If you win, you stand only to lose. No longer does it possess even the chance of the winner of a duel. It contains now only the germs of double suicide." (General Douglas MacArthur, quoted by Sydney Harris in "Gen. MacArthur's Words More Significant Now," *South Bend Tribune,* May 9, 1980, p. 10.)

175. "But if these challenges lack the kind of desperate urgency the threat of an enemy poses, the human race now faces the most cruel and devastating enemy it has ever known—the danger of nuclear bombs. If what the world needs for unification is a common enemy, these superbombs certainly provide one. If we understand the process of history, and accelerate instead of hinder it, the historian of the twenty-second century may review with surprise our biggest misconception: the nuclear bombs, he will know, were a major source not of disaster but of consolidation, not of war to the finish but the finish of wars." (Amitai Etzioni, *The Hard Way to Peace,* New York, 1962, p. 201)

"If the terror of the bomb is great, and properly great, the hope for man in the release of nuclear energy is even greater.... We can not now see more than the

Obviously, therefore, to merge all nations into One World is our most urgent job at present.[176] If we fail to carry it through to abolish war right away, war will soon annihilate us.[177] We cannot do it after

---

faint shadow of what such a new force can mean for man. But it is our faith as scientists and our experience as citizens of the 20th century that it will mean much. It will grow and develop. It will lead a life of its own. No influence that we have seen in our times can prevent this. Yet it is the eloquent and unanswerable argument of this book that such a growth will bring death to the society that produced it if we do not adapt ourselves to it. This is the dilemma that the release of nuclear energy has brought to a world torn already by a horrible war. The nations can have atomic energy, and much more. But they cannot have it in a world where war may come." (The Federation of American Scientists in "Survival Is at Stake," in *One World or None,* ed. by Dexter Masters and Katharine Way, New York, 1946)

As early as 1914, Herbert G. Wells in his book *The World Set Free* recounted the story of the bomb long before its development was even thought of in military circles. He discussed atomic problems which are now commonplace: the fission of uranium; the effects of blast, fire, residual radioactivity—each destroyed city "a flaming center of radiant destruction that only time could quench;" the towering column of flame and smoke arising from the first flash; the possibilities of underwater explosions. He foresaw, also, the potentialities of atomic energy for peaceful purposes and the necessity for placing it under controls. In the face of such weapons and such obliteration of life and property, "war manifestly has to stop." If crowns and flags are in the way, "manifestly they must go, too." If outworn political and legal institutions constitute obstacles to a new world order, they must be ignored, reformed, circumvented, or replaced. "Necessities bury rights. And create them." (*The World Set Free,* New York, 1914, p. 152 and 154)

Nuclear war probably will erupt by the end of this century and a world government may be the only way to keep nations from blowing up the world, according to a group of nuclear arms experts. "A very nasty kind of world government may be necessary if we are to survive in the world I see ahead," said George Rathjens, a Massachusetts Institute of Technology professor writing in the November issue of *Harvard Magazine.* (UPI report in the *South Bend Tribune,* Nov. 2, 1975, p. 4)

176. "We know that the developments of science and technology have determined that the peoples of the world are no longer able to live under competing national sovereignties with war as the ultimate arbitrator.... As we approach what may be the last hour before midnight, the challenge is plain before us. What will be our response?" (Statement of the Emergency Committee of Atomic Scientists led by Einstein, quoted in *Which Way to World Government,* by Alfred M. Lilienthal, Headline Series no. 83, New York, 1950, p. 42.)

177. "The old tendencies of human nature, suspicion, jealousy, particularism and belligerency, were incompatible with the monstrous destructive power of the new appliances the inhuman logic of science has produced. The equilibrium could be restored only by civilization destroying itself down to a level at which modern apparatus could no longer be produced, or by human nature adapting itself in its institutions to the new conditions.... Sooner or later this choice would have confronted mankind. The sudden development of atomic science did but precipitate and render rapid and dramatic a clash between the new

our annihilation.[178] Nor can we expect any miracle to rescue us in this unprecedented crisis.[179]

We have gone to war and have also tried to eliminate war since time immemorial. But war has appeared like a many headed hydra which can grow new heads as soon as old ones are chopped off.[180] We have had to live with it, to justify it, and even to glorify it. Now, as we have the chance to abolish it all at once for the first time in history, any ground for it has lost reality and force, and both its moral and practical values have run into bankruptcy.[181] Hence, it is

---

and the customary that had been gathering since ever the first flint was chipped or the first fire built together." (Herbert G. Wells, *The World Set Free*, New York, 1914, p. 192-193) Edward M. Earle remarked: "These words, it must be remembered, were in print before the first shots were fired in 1914 and three decades before the test at Alamogordo!" (*Nationalism and Internationalism*, New York, 1950, p. 118)

"There is a grave risk that modern inventors have created a Frankenstein monster quite capable of destroying modern civilization. There is special danger in the growing efficiency of the engines of destruction utilized in modern war. Indeed, it is highly probable, unless we are able to avert future wars, that modern technology will be little more than an instrument for collective human suicide." (Harry E. Barnes, *An Economic History of the Western World*, New York, 1937, p. 491)

178. It has been suggested that one sure way to establish permanent world peace would be to have a nuclear war, that the very horror of nuclear war would force mankind to take the drastic social and political measures needed to eliminate war forever and entirely.

179. "Sir Martin Ryle, the Nobel laureate in physics, is no doubt a great astronomer (he is Britain's Astronomer Royal). . . . [He] has asked the International Astronomical Union to persuade radio astronomers of the world to refrain from making the presence of our civilization known to other worlds—for fear we might be invaded by hostile creatures seeking colonization or new mineral resources. As I have said many times before, the discovery of an inhabited alien planet somewhere in the universe might be the only means of uniting the human race. Most 'loyalties' throughout history have grown only in the face of a common enemy. . . . What Sir Martin fears is precisely what I hope for: some galactic shock wave that might stun us into a sudden appreciation of our common human heritage." (Sydney Harris, "Possible Alien Threat Seen as Key to Peace," *South Bend Tribune*, Jan. 10, 1977, p. 10)

180. "Hercules, the Greek hero-god, tested his might against the terrible nine-headed Hydra, a water serpent that terrorized anyone unlucky enough to venture near its swampy nest. Clouting its heads with a huge club, Hercules was astonished to see two new heads sprout where one had been before. He conquered this multiplication problem by seizing a burning timber and searing each headstump until he came to the ninth and last head, the immortal one. This he cut off and disposed of by burying it under a rock." (Ralph E. Lapp, *Arms Beyond Doubt, the Tyranny of Weapons Technology*, New York, 1970, p. 17)

181. Since there has never been a chance to abolish war all at once before, war

absolutely necessary for us to change our habit of mind in respect to war.[182] This change is of a revolutionary nature, and has fortunately and clearly been initiated by some outstanding professionals in the field. General Omar Bradley, for instance, warned of destroying ourselves with new weapons;[183] General E. L. M. Burns pointed out that

---

has been a constant phenomena threatening all peoples. All were always getting ready for war, and always trying to maintain and strengthen their own frightening power. For this reason they regarded warfare and efforts to maintain and strengthen their own group as more moral, rational, valuable, and necessary than peace. But now, the situation has completely changed. We have the possibility of achieving a peace which is not temporary and regional, but total and perpetual, and which can guarantee all the peoples in the world the opportunity to live together forever. This kind of peace is of the highest morality, paramount value, and all-important necessity. Any ground for warfare and for efforts to maintain and strengthen the nation would lose their force and reality before this kind of peace. We should without any hesitation give up any effort to maintain and strengthen the nation, in order to achieve this kind of peace.

182. "Since long before the dawn of history man's survival has been by groups in competition to the death with other groups. During some thousands of years certain feeling, thinking and behaviour patterns, associated with survival, have become firmly established. Exclusive loyalty to the survival group, whether family, clan, tribe, city, state, principality, kingdom, empire, or nation, has been a demand of the highest priority affecting almost all human beings.... Under these circumstances of built-in conservatism in the fields of inter-human and inter-societal relationships, adequate adjustment to new circumstances faces strong barriers. When tension arises between survival groups—in recent centuries usually either nations or groups of nations—a highly emotional state of anxiety is produced. In such a state there is a tendency for emotion to take precedence over intellectual function. Conscience, the early-learned system of values to which every person has been exposed in childhood, is mobilised and strong feelings about what is 'right' or 'good' are felt and expressed. Almost all of us have learned in childhood that when we feel threatened the right and good and effective thing to do is to increase our ability to kill to the greatest possible degree and then to threaten any potential enemy into submission. This has been our standard, admirable and effective pattern throughout history; it is sometimes called 'negotiation from strength.' Unfortunately for the continued use of this old pattern, the conditions have changed. As soon as the potentiality for destruction became absolute, or nearly so, any increase in power became meaningless." (Brock Chisholm, "The Problem of New Problems," in *The Population Crisis and the Use of World Resources,* ed. by Stuart Mudd, Bloomington, Indiana, 1964, p. 341-342)

183. "The central problem of our time is how to employ human intelligence for the salvation of mankind. It is a problem we have put upon ourselves. For we have defiled our intellect by the creation of such scientific instruments of destruction that we are now in great danger of destroying ourselves. This irony can probably be compounded a few more years or perhaps even a few decades. Missiles will bring anti-missiles; and anti-missiles will bring anti-antimissiles. But inevitably this whole electronic house of cards will reach a point where it can be constructed no

our enemy is war itself;[184] and General Douglas MacArthur stressed that war could no longer be a medium for the settlement of difficulties,[185] and that its abolition is in accordance with scientific realism.[186] In this regard, MacArthur further emphasized that "We are in a new era. The old methods and solutions no longer suffice. We must have new thoughts, new ideas, new concepts. We must break out of the strait-jacket of the past."[187]

---

higher. If we are going to save ourselves from the instruments of our own intellect, we had better soon get ourselves under control and begin making the world safe for living." (General Omar Bradley, November 1957, quoted in *William Winter Comments,* Vol. VI, no. 40, Oct. 2, 1967)

184. "The military man, soldier, sailor or airman, thinks of himself as the defender of his countrymen and their protector against the nation's enemies.... They should realize that the greatest threat to the survival of democracy is no longer the Russians or the Chinese or any other country professing antidemocratic ideologies, but rather war itself. It is nuclear war against which the military must protect their fellow-citizens." (E.L.M. Burns, *Megamurder,* New York, 1967, p. 8-9)

185. "Our very triumph of scientific annihilation has destroyed the possibility of war being a medium for the practical settlement of difficulties. The enormous destruction to both sides of closely matched opponents makes it impossible for even the winner to translate it into anything but disaster." (General Douglas MacArthur, quoted by Sydney Harris in "Gen. MacArthur's Words More Significant Now," *South Bend Tribune,* May 9, 1980, p. 10)

186. "Although the abolition of war has been the dream of man for centuries, every proposition to that end has been promptly discarded as impossible and fantastic. But that was before the science of the past decades made mass destruction a reality. The argument then was along spiritual and moral headlines, and lost. But now the tremendous evolution of nuclear destruction has ... brought the problem abreast of scientific realism. This is as true of the Soviet side of the world as of the free side. The ordinary people of the world, whether free or slave, are all in agreement on this solution; and this perhaps is the only thing they agree upon, but it is the most vital and determinate of all .... It may take another cataclysm of destruction to prove the bald truth that the further evolution of civilization cannot take place until global war is abolished. But this is the one issue upon which both sides can agree, for it is the one issue upon which both sides will profit equally." (General Douglas MacArthur, quoted by Sydney Harris in "Gen. MacArthur's Words More Significant Now," *South Bend Tribune,* May 9, 1980, p. 10)

187. "The present tensions with their threat of national annihilation are fostered by two great illusions. The one, a complete belief on the part of the Soviet world that capitalistic countries are preparing to attack them.... And the other, a complete belief on the part of the capitalistic countries that the Soviets are preparing to attack us. Both are wrong. Each side, so far as the masses are concerned, is desirous of peace. Both dread war. But the constant acceleration of arms, without specific intent, may ultimately precipitate a kind of spontaneous combustion.... We are in a new era. The old methods and solutions no longer suffice. We must have new thoughts, new ideas, new concepts. We must break out of the strait-jacket of the past." (General Douglas MacArthur, quoted by Sydney Harris in

Practically, the statements of these generals can well be adopted as a preamble for the measures we have to take in order to speed up the abolition of war, along with the merging of all nations into One World. These measures include:

1. Standing firmly against any kind of war.

2. Destroying all nuclear, chemical and conventional arms except those which can be converted immediately for peaceful use, and those used ordinarily for police use.

3. Turning all arms factories into civil production.

4. Halting any manufacturing, testing and developing of any type of weapons; and

5. Stopping any conscription and any training for military personnel, and dismissing all armed forces, except the local police service along with a small world police corps.[188]

All these measures should be taken whenever and wherever possible, collectively or individually. Their completion, along with the merging of all nations into One World, would bring an end to war

---

"Gen. MacArthur's Words More Significant Now," *South Bend Tribune,* May 9, 1980, p. 10)

188. A world police corps is to be established under the direct control of the world government, to maintain social order and individual security, and to promote general welfare. The scope of the world police will be decided by the world government as to what is necessary to carry out their duties.

189. Nuclear war can be prevented only if large numbers of people change the way they think about atomic weapons. Then, people must make their political and military leaders change their basic attitudes toward nuclear weaponry and towards war, four experts agreed Monday at Western Michigan University during a conference entitled, "Can Nuclear War Be Prevented?" There can be little hope of reducing current stockpiles of nuclear bombs and missiles until people overcome what Robert Jay Lifton, professor of psychiatry at Yale University, called "universal psychic numbing." In a nuclear war, said Prof. Lifton, "everything we know can be destroyed." Still, people continue their lives as if the bombs did not exist, he said. Nuclear arms and strategy are maintained not only by political and military leaders, but by a large corps of professionals committed to maintaining present strategic goals, he noted. Lifton said his study of Nazi medical doctors in Auschwitz showed that professionals sometimes collaborate with political leaders even in committing atrocities. Another absurdity in the atomic arms race, he said, is that nations now have the power "to annihilate the whole world—for what?" ("Nuclear Stop Up to People," reported by Joel Thurtell, *South Bend Tribune,* Sept. 21, 1982, p. 1)

forever, and ensure us for the first time in history of a permanent peace on the earth.

Are we going to go for the permanent peace or rather wait for an imminent total destruction?[189]

"Removing the threat of a world war—a nuclear war—is the most acute and urgent task of the present day. Mankind is confronted with a choice: we must halt the arms race and proceed to disarmament or face annihilation." (Final Document, U.N. Special Session on Disarmament, 1978, quoted by Lawrence Abbot, "World Federalism: What? Why? How?" published by World Federalists Association and American Movement for World Government, New York, 1983, p. 44)

V

General Happiness

IT IS IMPORTANT TO NOTE THAT THE PERMANENT peace achieved with the abolition of war may not necessarily assure a freedom from fear, if it is not accompanied by freedom from want. And freedom from want cannot be attained until the general happiness of all the people of the world is secured.

So, the second objective of the One World is to secure a general happiness.

a.
Abolition of War as Condition and Means

HOW IS THIS OBJECTIVE TO BE ACCOMPLISHED? THE first step has been implied in the abolition of war. It is the elimination of all the cost of war from our civilization.

As mentioned earlier, the cost of war in the 19th century had increased tremendously, but it became a dwarf before a giant when compared with the expenditures of the World Wars in the 20th century. World War I was estimated to have had a total cost of $337,846,189,657.[1] The *Scholastic* made an effort to translate this

---

1. Estimated by Ernest L. Bogart. Cf. his *Direct and Indirect Costs of the Great World War*, New York, 1919, especially p. 265-68, 299. The estimate includes direct costs of $186,233,637,097 and indirect costs of $151,612,552,560. The indirect costs include: the capitalized value of human life, $33,551,276,280 for

417

figure into terms we can visualize: it is sufficient to furnish (a) every family in England, France, Belgium, Germany, Russia, the United States, Canada and Australia with a $2500 house on a $500 one-acre lot, with $1,000 worth of furniture; (b) a $5,000,000 library for every community of 200,000 inhabitants in these countries; (c) a $10,000,000 university for every such community; (d) a fund that at 5 percent interest would yield enough to pay indefinitely $1,000 a year to an army of 125,000 teachers and 125,000 nurses, and (e) still leave enough to buy every piece of property and all the wealth in France and Belgium at a fair market price.[2]

More profoundly, a great American educator pointed out that in World War I "there was destroyed a value equal to that of five countries like France plus five countries like Belgium."[3]

The economic loss in World War II was much more appalling. An incomplete estimate has put its direct cost at six times more than that of World War I, and among the indirect costs, property damage alone amounted to $230,000,000,000,[4] with transportation paralyzed,[5] cities destroyed,[6] and vast countrysides laid waste.[7]

Property damage is only one side of the story of the havoc

---

soldiers and the same amount for civilians; property losses on land, $29,960,000,000; shipping and cargo, $6,800,000,000; loss of production, $45,000,000,000; war relief, $1,000,000,000; and loss to neutrals, $1,750,000,000. No account was taken of subsequent costs such as interest on loans, pensions, and the like.

2. (Cf. *Scholastic,* Nov. 10, 1934, p. 13.) The editor remarked that such was what it cost to return Alsace-Lorraine to France, to try to get the Straits for Russia, to help Britain destroy the German navy, merchant machine, and colonial empire, and to punish Serbian plotters.

3. Speaking of the cost of war, "We are pouring out not only the world's earnings, but the world's savings, savings for a thousand years, and those savings are not illimitable. . . . In the last war, there was destroyed a value equal to that of five countries like France plus five countries like Belgium. Should there be another war tomorrow, that destruction might be of the value of five countries like Great Britain, or five countries like the United States of America." (Nicholas M. Butler, *Why War?,* New York, 1940, p. 5-6) Dr. Butler was the President of Columbia University for 45 years (1901-1945) and also played a great role in national and international affairs.

4. The estimate made by James H. Brady and the American University put the direct cost of World War II at as much as $1,154,000,000,000, and the indirect cost of property damage at $230,000,000,000, excluding China. Other indirect costs were not calculated. (Cf. the *Encyclopedia Americana,* 1947 ed., Vol. 29, "World War II," p. 556yy-560.)

5. For example, "France lost 70% of its total merchant marine tonnage, Belgium 60%, the Netherlands 40%, and Norway 50%. By 1945, with internal transport at a standstill, and agricultural, mineral, and industrial production com-

wrought by war. The other side is the absorption of materials into the manufacture of implements of war.[8] This kind of absorption is invariably a net waste of resources.[9]

---

pletely disrupted, the economies of the continental nations of Western Europe were in a state of virtually complete paralysis.'' (*Encyclopedia Britannica,* 1968, ed. Vol. 23, p. 803-804)

6. For example, the destruction of Japanese cities amounted to 42 percent of the urban industrial area of the 68 cities attacked, according to Henry H. Arnold, ''Air Force in the Atomic Age,'' in *One World or None,* ed. by Dexter Masters and Katharine Way, New York, 1946, p. 29.

7. For example, ''In Poland, a report by the 'War Reparations Bureau' assessed the destruction of transport and scientific and industrial equipment at 80 percent, agricultural implements and buildings at 50 percent, whilst nearly 620,000 acres of forest were completely devastated; 10 percent of Warsaw was destroyed in 1939 and 70 percent in 1944. In all, these losses are assessed at 31 percent of the national wealth; in 1945, grain production had dropped to 39 percent of the 1938 figure; there were 1,500,000 cases of tuberculosis.'' (Henri Michel, *The Second World War,* trans. by Douglas Parmee, New York, 1975, p. 787)

8. The waste of metals in modern war is hardly comprehended. For example, in medieval times, a knight and his steed carried as much as 200 pounds of iron and steel. In 1943, for each man in the American fighting force, the industry poured forth some 24,600 pounds. In order to meet the need of the war industry, the United States in 1942 alone mined 126,527,159 tons of iron ore, and from January, 1942, through July, 1945, its steel industry produced approximately 210,058,000 tons of finished steel, of which 60,335,000 tons went to makers of war equipment and supplies. During the second World War, copper was extensively used in the larger pieces of fighting equipment. A Liberator bomber, fully equipped, required 3,025 pounds of copper, an M-4 Sherman tank required 250 pounds, a battleship of the Iowa class required many tons of copper. Copper was also used extensively in the manufacture of ammunition. To produce a half million cartridges, 14,000 pounds of copper were needed. In one month alone during 1944, 2,000,000 pounds of copper were required for field telephone wire. Aluminum production of the United States in 1938 was 300 million pounds. When the wartime expansion program was completed, installed ingot capacity had reached 2.3 billion pounds per year. The percentage of expansion in magnesium was even greater than in aluminum. War also wastes many materials from vegetable sources. For example, a battleship and its equipment requires seventy-five tons of rubber, and a 28-ton medium tank needs an amount of rubber which is the equivalent of that required to manufacture 120 automobile tires. Out of the total cotton crop in the United States in 1943, about one million bales of cotton linter, each weighing about 630 pounds, were earmarked for munition purposes. Cotton is the basic propelling charge used in all battle weapons, ranging from the .30 caliber rifle to the mammoth 16-inch naval gun. One bale of cotton linters provides enough smokeless powder for 20,440 rounds of machine gun ammunition, 100,000 rounds of rifle ammunition, or 85 rounds of heavy tank ammunition. (Cf. John R. Craf, *A Survey of the American Economy, 1940-46,* New York, 1947, p. 90-103.)

9. How many resources were wasted by the United States in the Second World War? The following record may give a general idea: from July 1, 1940,

The cost of war also has serious economic legacies, such as war pensions,[10] war debts,[11] and economic depression.[12] The last one has

---

through June 31, 1945, industry and labor turned out from the assembly lines 86,338 tanks; 297,000 airplanes of 2,481,000,000 pounds airframe weight; 17,400,000 rifles, carbines, and sidearms; 315,000 pieces of field artillery and mortars; 4,200,000 tons of artillery shells; 41,400,000,000 rounds of small arms ammunition; 64,500 landing vessels; 6,500 other navy ships; 5,400 cargoes; and 2,400,000 military trucks and transports. Munitions production in the five years from July 1, 1940, to June 31, 1945, reached the sum of 186,000 million dollars at standard munitions costs. (Cf. John R. Craf, *A Survey of The American Economy, 1940-46,* New York, 1947, p. 61-62.)

10. In the same way that war has been a chronic disease in international relations, war pension has appeared in many countries as a standing expenditure of the government and a permanent burden of the people. The United States, for example, had not completely liquidated the pensions for the veterans of World War I when the Second World War broke out, and in the seven years after World War II it spent more than 42 billion dollars for veterans' services and benefits. It was (in millions) 559 in 1939; 551 in 1940; 564 in 1941; 556 in 1942; 605 in 1943; 744 in 1944; 2,094 in 1945; 4,414 in 1946; 7,370 in 1947; 6,566 in 1948; 6,668 in 1949; 6,627 in 1950; 5,746 in 1951; and 4,911 in 1952. (Cf. *United Nations Statistical Yearbook,* Table 166.)

11. More permanent in character has been the burden to pay the interest on war debts. In modern times almost all the national governments have had a great amount of debt, and most, if not all, of their debt has been raised for war emergency or for the preparation of war, for no nation can just rely on taxes to deal with the tremendous expenditures for war purposes, except the communist countries, where all property is under the direct control of the state. The United States, for example, had only 1,193 million dollars of debt in 1913, and through the years of World War I, this number rose to 22,964 million in 1922. It was 45,890 million in 1939, and in 1946 it had reached 269,898 million. This means that at the end of World War II, every American family had a debt of about $7,200. As the debt speedily grew, its interest increased enormously. Since World War II, the United States has had to pay every year more than five billion dollars for the interest on the public debt. (Cf. Harry E. Barnes, *An Economic History of the Western World,* New York, 1937, p. 681; and the *United Nations Statistical Yearbook,* 1951, Table 166, for the United States public debts and interests before and after World War II. The United States public debts increased to 898,956 million and interests to 57,022 million in 1980 as revealed in the *United Nations Statistical Yearbook,* 1978, Table 201, p. 818.)

12. There have been three severe depressions since the beginning of the 19th century, each following an important war. After the Napoleonic Wars ended in 1815, there was a prolonged period of distress in both the belligerent and neutral countries, punctuated by a series of violent financial crisis. In 1819, 1825, 1836-39 and 1844-47, the paroxysms of industry were serious. After 1860, the Civil War in the United States and the triad of wars waged by Germany were succeeded by a hectic boom which broke into panic in 1874 and ushered in the long train of falling prices that lasted till 1895 and made the intervening cycles of depression longer and more intense. The actual dates of these two depressions varied somewhat from

been labelled as the ultimate cost of war. Its deteriorating elements can penetrate deeply and extensively into every economic life.[13]

As the cost of war in modern times has been so great a burden to us, generation after generation, the abolition of war by merging all nations into One World is obviously a necessary condition for the pursuit of general happiness.

Next in this pursuit is to convert peacetime military expenditures into the uses of general happiness.

The military expenditure is usually covered under a defense budget with some other appropriations.[14] Its increase has been astonish-

---

country to country, and there was not the same universality of depression as we witnessed after the first World War, because interconnections between the nations were not as close and instantaneous as they have since become. But they created much the same sorts of problems as those with which we became very familiar in the last great depression from 1929 to 1939. (Cf. John B. Condliffe, *War and Depression,* Boston, 1935; Leonard P. Ayres, *The Economics of Recovery,* New York, 1933, p. 1-24; and John Sperling, *Great Depressions: 1837-1844, 1893-1898, 1929-1939,* Chicago, 1966, p. 105-158.)

13. The symptoms of post-war depression usually are: disorganized production, breakdown of credit, vanishing world trade, unemployment, social distress, and so on. Whatever the intervening secondary causes might be, the ultimate cause of the great depressions was to be found in the impoverishment and economic dislocation caused by the great wars. So, our economists have pointed out that depression was an ultimate cost of war, that no people, victor, vanquished, or even the neutral, could escape from this cost. After World War II, various efforts were made to prevent depressions on the international level, such as the programs carried out by the United Nations Relief and Rehabilitation Administration, the Marshall Plan and its counterpart, the Council for Mutual Economic Assistance, as well on the national level, such as the Unemployment Act enacted by the United States Congress in 1946, along with other anti-depression measures. As a result, a great post-war depression was avoided, but the effect of smaller ones has been felt everywhere for a long time. (Cf. John B. Condliffe, *War and Depression,* Boston, 1935; and *The Business Cycle in the Post-War World,* ed. by Erik Lundberg, London, 1955.)

14. "The quantity of resources devoted to military use is usually measured by the level of military expenditure. Estimating world military expenditure is, however, very difficult and, for a variety of reasons, the results are inevitably inaccurate. One main reason for inaccuracy is the absence of a generally agreed definition of the term 'military expenditure.' Another is that many countries fail to include in their official military budgets significant categories of military spending. This problem is compounded by the difficulty of estimating realistic exchange rates so that military expenditures can be converted into a common currency (traditionally US dollars) for summation. For example, the difficulty of realistically expressing the Soviet military budget in US dollars is well known. A third reason for the inaccuracy of military expenditure figures is the underestimation of the real value of some of the resources employed by the military—a particularly gross example being the undervaluation of conscripted manpower." (*Disarmament and World Development,* ed. by Richard Jolly, Oxford, 1978, p. 7. Cf. Abraham S.

ing since the 18th century when the standing army was widely established.[15] Among the great powers, it rose between 1870 and 1937 over
25 times,[16] with per capita from $1.70 in 1870 to $25.00 in 1937;[17] and
in proportion to the national income, it rose from less than 3 percent
before World War I to nearly 10 percent in 1937.[18] World military expenditures exceeded $300,000,000,000 in 1976, at least 30 times more
than in 1900 at constant prices.[19]

It is noteworthy that world military expenditures in 1976 were
about 15 times larger than the total of international aid programs[20]

Becker, *Military Expenditure Limitation for Arms Control: Problems and Prospects,* Cambridge, Mass., 1977, p. 11-26.)

15. As early at 1795, Immanuel Kant had predicated that the growth of
defense expenses would render peace even more burdensome than a short war, and
directly lead to hostilities. He spoke of the standing armies, "For being ever ready
for action, they incessantly menace other states, and excite them to increase
without end the number of armed men. This rivalship, a source of inexaustible expense, renders peace even more burdensome than a short war, and frequently
causes hostilities to be commenced with the mere view of being delivered thereby
from so oppressive a load." (His *Perpetual Peace,* English ed. first published in
London in 1796, New York, 1932, p. 4)

16. The total defense appropriation of the great powers, including the British
Empire, France, Russia, Japan, the United States, Germany, Italy, and Austria-
Hungary in 1870 was 551 (million dollars); in 1880, 710; in 1890, 869; in 1900,
1,280; in 1910, 1,794; in 1914, 2,400; in 1921, 2,914; in 1929, 2,874; in 1937, 14,190.
It multiplied by more than five in the eight years from 1929 to 1937. (Cf. Quincy
Wright, *A Study of War,* 2nd ed., Chicago, 1965, p. 670-671; Table 58 and 59.)

17. The per capita cost for defense of the great powers (named in above note) in
1870 was 1.70 (dollars); in 1880, 1.98; in 1890, 2.12; in 1900, 2.75; in 1910, 3.13; in
1914, 4.27; in 1921, 6.16; in 1929, 5.47; and in 1937, 25.00. (*Ibid,* p. 671, Table 59)

18. (Cf. *Ibid,* p. 672, Table 60.) Some of these powers' military expenditures
were much more than 10 percent of their national income in the years before
World War II. In 1937, for instance, Italy spent 14.5 percent; Germany, 23.5; the
Soviet Union, 26.4, and Japan, 28.2.

19. "Throughout this century, world military expenditure has increased
steadily (Fig. 2.1). According to estimates of the Stockholm International Peace
Research Institute (SIPRI), in 1976 it exceeded $300,000 million, at least thirty
times more than it was in 1900 (in constant prices)." (*Disarmament and World
Development,* ed. by Richard Jolly, Oxford, 1978, p. 8)

"World War II levels of forces lasted until 1948. Since 1948, the world has
spent more than $6,000,000 million, in constant 1976 dollars, on military activities.
This sum is equal to about $1,500 per head of today's world population or about
10 years' income for today's average Indian." (*Ibid,* p. 25)

20. The 1975 SIPRI yearbook pointed out that "world military expenditure is
greater than either world expenditure on education or health; it is some 15 times
larger than official aid provided to the underdeveloped countries; and it is
equivalent to the combined gross product of all the countries in Africa, the Middle
East, and South Asia." (Stockholm International Peace Research Institute, *World*

and about 100 times larger than the actual capital of the World Bank[21] in that year. Yet it was one of the years in which the increase of world military expenditures tended to slow down[22] to about 5.5 percent of the world income.[23] It would be a good start for the pur-

---

Armaments and Disarmament, SIPRI Yearbook 1975, Cambridge, Mass., 1975, p. 100) The comparison between world military expenditures and international aid programs in 1976 is about the same as in 1975. (Cf. the *United Nations Statistical Yearbook 1977,* Tables 202 and 206.)

21. The capital of the International Bank for Reconstruction and Development (World Bank) "is derived from members' subscriptions to capital shares, the calculation of which is based on their quotas in the International Monetary Fund (see page 49). On June 30th, 1976, the total subscribed capital of the Bank was $30,861 million. Of this amount, however, only the sum of about $3,086 million had been paid in, partly in gold or dollars and partly in local currency." (*The Europea Year Book, 1977,* by Europa Publications, London, 1977, Vol. 1, p. 36)

22. "Estimates by ACDA show the military expenditures of NATO at constant prices falling by 15 percent between 1968 and 1975 (interrupted by only slight increases in 1972 and 1974), after having risen by 13 percent between 1966 and 1968." (Abraham S. Becker, *Military Expenditure Limitation for Arms Control: Problems and Prospects,* Cambridge, Mass., 1977, p. 4. Cf. U.S. Arms Control and Disarmament Agency, *World Military Expenditures and Arms Transfers, 1966-1975,* Washington, 1976.) Although the Soviet Union and its Warsaw Pact Allies' programs in dollar valuations are estimated to have grown monotonically between 1966 and 1975 (cf. Thad P. Alton and others "Military Expenditures in Eastern Europe: Some Alternative Estimates," in *Reorientation and Commercial Relations of the Economies of Eastern Europe,* U.S. Congress, Joint Economic Committee, Washington, 1974, p. 306-307) the increase of the world military expenditure in general tended to slow down in the mid 1970s amid the discussion of military expenditure limitation for arms control, which was initiated by Foreign Minister Gromyko of the Soviet Union at the 28th General Assembly of the United Nations in Sept., 1973, and was studied in the following years. (Cf. Abraham S. Becker, *op. cit.,* p. 5-7 and Appendixes C-F.)

23. Speaking of the world military expenditure in the 1970s, "In any case, military uses continue to absorb a significant share of aggregate output, estimated at about 5-6 percent of the planetary total." (Abraham S. Becker, *Military Expenditure Limitation for Arms Control: Problems and Prospects,* Cambridge, Mass., 1977, p. 5) "In the Third World as a whole, military expenditure in the 1970s averaged about 4 percent of gross domestic product. For the developed countries this average was about 6 percent." (*Disarmament and World Development,* ed. by Richard Jolly, Oxford, 1978, p. 12. Cf. p. 11, Table 2.4.)

The nations which had military expenditures in 1976 above 5 percent of their GNP are as follows: East Germany, 5.7; the Soviet Union, 11-13; Britain, 5.2; Turkey, 5.5; the United States, 5.4; Yugoslavia, 5.4; Egypt, (22); Iran, 12; Iraq, 9.6; Israel, 36.3; Jordan, 12.9; Saudi Arabia, 17.7; Syria, 16.3; Nigeria, 7.7; Rhodesia, 5.2; China, 10; China (Taiwan) 9.3; North Korea, 11.2; South Korea, 6.2; Pakistan, 5.5; and Singapore, 5.4. (Cf. *The Military Balance, 1978-1979,* by the International Institute for Strategic Studies, London, 1978, p. 88-89.)

suit of general happiness if only this rather low percentage could be converted into full use for the reconstruction and development of the world. With such a percentage alone as an annual premium, the appropriation for general happiness in 50 years would amount to $17,000 billion at 1976 prices.[24]

There is nothing in civilization more reasonable than to convert military expenditures to the use of general happiness. It is a shift from a preparation for killing and destruction to an arrangement for living and reconstruction. It has been proposed in various ways,[25] but

---

24. The total amount of appropriations for the pursuit of general happiness in 50 years is calculated on the base of a 1976 world military expenditure in excess of 300 billion dollars and its percentage of about 5.5 of the 1976 world income. This has been adjusted by adding a 4 percent annual growth of world income as indicated by various statistics, such as the tables in Vol. 11, p. 206 of the *Encyclopedia of the Social Sciences,* New York, 1933; on p. 80 of *Industrial Growth and World Trade,* by Alfred Maizels, Cambridge, Eng., 1963; on p. 59 of the *United Nations Statistical Yearbook, 1961;* on p. 25 of the *United Nations Statistical Yearbook, 1974;* and in Vol. 1, p. 620 of *The Growth of World Industry* by the Statistical Office of the United Nations, Department of Economic and Social Affairs, 1973 ed., New York, 1975.

25. For instance, President D. Eisenhower's speech to a luncheon of the American Society of Newspaper Editors, appearing in the *Evening World-Herald,* Omaha, April 16, 1953, p. 11, indicates such willingness as follows: "This Government is ready to ask its people to join with all nations in devoting a substantial percentage of the savings achieved by disarmament to a fund for world aid and reconstruction. The purposes of this great work would be: to help other peoples to develop the undeveloped areas of the world, to stimulate profitable and fair world trade, to assist all peoples to know the blessings of productive freedom."

At the Twenty-eighth General Assembly in September, 1973, Foreign Minister Gromyko of the Soviet Union proposed that the five permanent members of the Security Council reduce their military budgets by 10 percent from the 1973 level during the following financial year; that 10 percent of the savings be allotted to assistance to developing countries; and that other states, particularly those with a "major economic and military potential," should follow suit. He also proposed the creation of a special committee to supervise the distribution of the new aid funds. (Cf. Abraham S. Becker, *Military Expenditure Limitation for Arms Control: Problems and Prospects,* Cambridge, Mass., 1977, Appendix C.)

"The spending of 220,000 million dollars on arms, more than 80 percent of which are the responsibility of the six main military spenders, while the official development assistance stands at 8,000 million dollars—a tiny and decreasing portion of military expenditures, 4 cents out of each dollar spent on armaments, this is, I would say, an expression of moral bankruptcy on the part of the rich great Powers. This happens while hundreds of thousands of people starve to death, while people everywhere in the under-privileged world lack the resources needed to build their own future. We must tell the big Powers, in all sincerity, that we are deeply dissatisfied and worried. We must ask the big Powers time and time again: As this meaningless waste of resources in a world of scarcities cannot be allowed to

nothing has been done, for the obvious reason that war has not been abolished. As long as war is possible, a real transfer of military expenditures to finance the general happiness is impossible. So the abolition of war by the merging of all nations into One World is not only a necessary condition, but also an indispensable means for the pursuit of the general happiness.

b.
Application of Science and Technology with Manpower

THIRD IN THIS PURSUIT IS TO APPLY SCIENCE AND technology extensively for an effective management of the world economy in manpower, energy, non-fuel minerals, forest products, water, food, population, environment and conservation.

Historically, the development of the world economy was based on the idea that energy and most materials were relatively inexpensive and abundant, while human resources were scarcer and more costly. This idea is not quite true anymore since modern machines have been able to supplant most of the manpower in industry,[26]

---

continue, what are you going to do about it? Because time is short and serious efforts will have to be started soon." (Speech of the Swedish delegate, Inga Thorsson, at the Conference of the Committee on Disarmament on May 7, 1974, quoted by Abraham S. Becker, *op. cit.,* p. 5)

26. It is the power and the associated development of automatic machinery, both dependent upon applied electrophysics, that give the character and significance of this phenomenon. "The largest single modern turbine has a capacity of 300,000 horsepower or three million times the output of a human being on an eight-hour-day basis. But the turbine runs twenty-four hours a day, which man does not do, and hence its total output is 9,000,000 times that of one man. To say it another way—four of these turbines have a greater energy capacity than the entire adult working population of the United States. At the present moment the United States has an installed capacity of one billion horsepower in engines to do work. What are these billion horses good for? Just one thing—to get work done. If these installed engines were operated continuously at capacity it would require fifty times the number of adult workers now living on the earth to equal this output by human labour alone ... From these figures we may draw two conclusions: 1, the importance of man as a power unit in the United States is over; 2, the steady flow of this huge energy output has become so vital to our national existence that if we

transportation[27] and even in labor-consuming agriculture.[28] This tendency, lately with the advance of the computer and the approach of automation, has made it possible for mankind to do minimum work while enjoying maximum leisure.[29] Through a program of ex-

---

attempted to stop it and go back to hand labour we would die ..." (Frank Arkright, *The A B C of Technocracy,* New York, 1933, p. 28-29)

Equally striking has been the application of automatic machinery to such processes as making electric lightbulbs. "The electric-lamp plant at Corning, N.Y., can produce 650,000 lamps per machine per day. This represents an increase per man of 10,000 times that of the method previously employed in the making of electric bulbs." (Harry E. Barnes, *An Economic History of the Western World,* New York, 1937, p. 481)

"In 1850 work animals and human beings accounted for over 94 percent of the energy in the United States.... [In 1950], the work animal has ceased to be a significant source of energy, and human beings account for less than one per cent of the energy used in industry." (*Zimmermann's World Resources and Industries,* 3d ed. by W.N. Peach and James A. Constantin, New York, 1972, p. 334)

27. It is possible for a man to carry up to 100 pounds of materials on his shoulders for about 25 miles a day. At this possible rate, at least 30,000,000 man-days are needed to carry 100,000 tons of freight from New York to San Francisco. "A study has shown that to move 100,000 tons of freight between New York and San Francisco requires 43,416 man-days by highway, 11,158 by water, and 3,220 by rail. During a 24-hour period, a 4-lane, 2-way expressway can carry 19,000 trucks, each hauling 12 tons of freight, for a daily total of 228,000 tons; in the same time a double-track rail line with centralized traffic control (permitting 2-way movement over a single track) can carry 18,000 freight cars, each hauling 43 tons of cargo, for a daily total of 774,000 tons." (Luther Miller and F.N. Houser, "Railroads," in the *Encyclopedia Americana,* 1973 ed., Vol. 23, p. 153)

28. "We have already mentioned that in the United States about 4 percent of the population remain on the farms—feeding the whole population and still having surpluses to be sent abroad." (Roger Hilsman, *The Crouching Future,* New York, 1975, p. 505)

29. "On the credit side, the machine has been able to supplant a large part of human labor in agriculture, industry, transportation, and commerce; it has thus removed the ancient curse of slavery and freed human energy for other activities, giving mankind at large—at least potentially—the leisure and opportunity once monopolized by a restricted minority. The narrow monopoly of knowledge and power imposed by limited productivity has been eliminated." "If the first step in mechanization is an increase in power and productivity, the next step is the advance toward complete automation, which releases all manpower other than the original designers of the process and machinery and the supervisors and controllers of the plant in operation. This is the ideal goal of the whole machine system, long ago foreseen—only to be dismissed—by Aristotle in the 4th century B.C., when he predicted that slavery would end only when the lyre could play and the shuttle weave by itself." (Lewis Mumford, "Machines," in the *Encyclopedia Americana,* 1973 ed., Vol. 18, p. 61, 60. Cf. Leon Bagrit, *The Age of Automation,* New York,

tensive education and training, using the experience of multinational enterprises,[30] and by mobilizing the elite of brains and skills released from military employment as a result of the abolition of war[31] to work for the developing areas, there would be no place in the world where productivity, together with the living standard, could not be raised to a high level.[32] The four-hour workday predicted for some developed countries[33] can be expected to be a common practice everywhere in the future.[34]

1965; and Morris Philipson, ed., *Automation: Implications for the Future,* New York, 1962.)

Lord C.P. Snow, Britain's Minister of Technology, in a lecture at the British Embassy, Washington, D.C., foresees the time when computers will create a system of "non-work." ... "They are going to transform our world ... they are going to change the world more than it was changed by the first industrial revolution." "Of course," he said, "I think it's good that people will not have to work like beasts of burden."

30. "Another factor in the reverse technological gap has been the establishment around the globe of automobile, chemical, machinery, electronics and other plants by U.S. multinational companies, lured by cheap labor and other incentives. This has caused a transfer of considerable American technology abroad." (Howard Benedict, AP Writer, in "U.S. Losing International Technology Lead," *South Bend Tribune,* May 20, 1973, p. 31)

31. Under the present situation, our labor and brain power employed for the military have always been the very good ones as required by modern military science and technique. Our young men are driven to camp and battlefield; our able engineers to devise tank, sub-boat and warplane; and our outstanding scientists to develop atomic bombs. In addition, a great deal of our wisdom and energy is spent for many other international mutual-checking activities. Their gross number is huge in many countries. In the United States, for example, in 1965, the total manpower of the Department of Defense was 3,678,000 in defense-generated employment; in 1967 with more involved in the Vietnam War, the total manpower of the Department of Defense was 4,668,000, including 3,365,000 military and 1,303,000 civilian, in addition to 7,429,000 defense-generated employment. (Cf. Adam Yarmolinsky, *The Military Establishment; Its Impacts on American Society,* New York, 1971, p. 13-17, Tables 2.4 and 2.5.)

32. "It is, of course, possible to industrialize in spite of being poorly endowed with natural resources. Denmark has no resources 'except the sites to put the factories on.' Japan is not much better endowed than Denmark. The fact that both countries were able to develop a highly skilled labor force prevented the burden of having to import raw materials from becoming more of an obstacle to industrialization than it was." (Roger Hilsman, *The Crouching Future,* New York, 1975, p. 314)

33. A four-hour workday; average per capita income in the United States more than $10,000 with a minimum of effort; holidays galore; and only two per cent of the labor force dirtying their hands on production lines. These are scientific predictions based on present trends by Herman Kahn and Anthony J. Wiener in

However, prudent and precautionary measures have to be taken
to prevent over-mechanization[35] in order not only to avoid "techno-

---

their book *The Year 2000,* New York, 1967. They explain that by that time production will be so computerized and mechanized that people will be needed mainly for
punching buttons and maintaining and repairing the hard-working machines.
Wiener further pointed out that the year 2000 may be like the Augustan Period of
30 B.C. when the Roman Empire was at its height and had 76 holidays. He also
noted that a century later, when Nero ruled and the empire was declining, Rome
celebrated 176 holidays. They had thousands of slaves to work for them. We will
have milions of superior machines to do the job. (Cf. his address, "The Future of
People at Work," to a meeting of the National Association of Management Industrial Relations Institute, *South Bend Tribune,* May 9, 1969, p. 21.)

If a trend toward longer vacations continues, an Indiana University professor
said that by "the 21st century the entire work force would be on permanent vacations." Dr. Mitchell S. Novit, I.U. Associate Professor of Personnel and
Organizational Behavior, said a survey of 1977 Indiana labor contracts revealed a
continuing trend of longer paid vacations for less service time. "The trend
becomes more pronounced when the data is looked at for the decade beginning in
1967," Novit said. "Four weeks for 15 years or fewer has doubled during this
10-year period. Five weeks for 25 or fewer service years has gone from 12 percent
to 50 percent." The survey was issued by the Indiana Chamber of Commerce and
the Graduate School of Business of the University of Indiana. (*South Bend
Tribune,* June 27, 1977, p. 36)

34. "How many hours a day will man have to work to produce nourishing
food, a comfortable home, and necessary clothing for his family? This question
has often preoccupied Socialists, and they generally come to the conclusion that
four or five hours a day would suffice, on condition, of course, that all men worked. At the end of the last century, Benjamin Franklin fixed the limit at five hours;
and if the need for comfort is greater now, the power of production has
augmented, too, and far more rapidly." (Peter A. Kropotkin, *The Conquest of
Bread,* ed. by Paul Avrich, New York, 1972, p. 120. Cf. p. 120-133) Kropotkin's
or other similar dreams can be realized only by the automatic and power-driven
machines for mass production.

The Communists have advocated "Reduction of the working day to seven
hours, and to six hours in industries particularly harmful to the health of the
workers. Further reduction of the working day and transition to a five-day week in
countries with developed productive forces. The regulation of the working day to
correspond to the increase of the productivity of labor." (Chapter four, Section 3,
D. of the *Program of the Communist International,* adopted by its Sixth World
Congress, Sept. 1, 1928)

35. "The fact is that humanity is suffering in the grip of forces beyond its
control and of purposes not its own. There is a form of life on earth which is
already giving man the 'darn good lickin' ' he has been inviting. It does not
threaten our physical life, but it does threaten our supremacy, our freedom of will,
and our control of our own destiny. It is driving man, lashing him onward at a
racking pace towards some goal which he cannot even foresee, let alone choose for
himself." (John M. Clark, "The Empire of Machines," *Yale Review,* Oct. 1933,
p. 132. Cf. W.F. Ogburn, *You and Machines,* Chicago, 1936.)

logical tenuousness''[36] and keep "humanity in technology,''[37] but also to save energy, because the more machines are used, the more energy is consumed.[38]

c.
Energy Resources

IS IT SO NECESSARY TO SAVE ENERGY?

This question leads to an inquiry into the situation of energy resources. Some experts have held that our energy resources are

---

36. "A few observers have begun to appraise the negative results of modern man's wholesale commitment to the machine. One of these has been called by the economist Stuart Chase "technological tenuousness'; that is, the delicate interdependence of all the parts of this mechanized environment, so that a break in power lines, perhaps, by a thunderstorm, can not only bring production to a halt, but can stop the cooking of food and ruin vast quantities of provisions in deep-freeze lockers." (Lewis Mumford, "Machines," in the *Encyclopedia Americana,* 1973 ed., Vol. 18, p. 60. Cf. Stuart Chase, *Men and Machines,* New York, 1929.)

"The chief danger in this situation lies in the possibility that mankind will not be able to carry out with sufficient rapidity the social and economic readjustments that are necessary to use successfully the new technical equipment. Modern technology has put at our disposal potential means for increasing human welfare unparalleled in the accomplishments of man. The future alone can determine whether or not humanity can safely be intrusted with this new machinery." (Harry E. Barnes, *An Economic History of the Western World,* New York, 1937, p. 491)

37. There is in the United States a Human Factors Society, an organization of 2,300 social scientists, engineers and others trying to blend humans and machines into a productive and reliable partnership. The goal of such specialists, said Earl Alluisi, Chairman of the Society, is "to keep humanity in technology—to insure that machines remain useful servants rather than tyrannical adversaries." (Cf. *South Bend Tribune,* Dec. 7, 1980, p. 22.)

38. For example, by the mid-1960s, the annual world consumption of fuels was equivalent to about 4.7 billion metric tons of coal (amounting to nearly 1½ metric tons per person), compared to about 900 million metric tons (about a half metric ton per person) in 1900—a rise of 500% in more than 60 years, according to Richard M. Highsmith, Jr., "Conservation," in the *Encyclopedia Americana,* 1973 ed., Vol. 7, p. 620.

"In 1952 the total world power consumption amounted to 10,200 billion or 10.2 trillion kilowatthours. Estimates based on Jordan and Threlkeld's findings are that in 1975 world consumption will be 27 trillion kilowatthours, and in A.D. 2000 this figure will have leaped to 84 trillion." (Hans Rau, *Solar Energy,* trans, by

enough for billions of years,[39] while others concurred rather cau-
tiously.[40] What they have projected for the long future, basically, is

---

Maxim Schur, New York, 1964, p. 7. Cf. Michael Tanzer, *The Race for Resources,
Continuing Struggles over Minerals and Fuels,* New York, 1980, p. 15-29, Tables
1-1 and 1-3.)

The per capita energy consumption of man before the use of fire was
2000-3000 calories per day, just to keep the human body alive and active. About
5000 were added when he burned 50 or so pounds of wood on a chilly day and
cooked with it (at probably 1 percent efficiency). About 4000 were added when he
domesticated the burro for working around 5000 B.C. Around 1000 B.C., more
were added when he began to harness the kinetic energy of the wind to drive ships
and turn windmills; and about the time of Christ, he developed the waterwheel.
Many more were added about 1000 years ago when he started to use the energy that
the sun had left locked up in the fossil fuels. When the steam engine began to turn
the wheels of the Industrial Revolution in the later 19th century, coal provided
much of the 75,000 calories per day per capita consumption of that period. In the
1970s, he consumed in the United States almost a quarter of a million calories per
capita per day. (Cf. John M. Fowler, *Energy and the Environment,* New York,
1975, p. 66-67.)

39. For example, Ali Bulent Cambel, the dean of engineering at Wayne State
University, is an optimist. He points out that the annual energy consumption of
the entire world at the present time is .1 Q—a Q being quintillion British thermal
units, which is the equivalent of 40,000 million tons of coal. Known recoverable
fossil fuel reserves are 22 Q, and it is estimated that the potential reserves amount
to 12,500 Q. He goes on to say that the potential reserves of uranium and thorium
will last 3 billion years even if the annual consumption rises to 15 Q. If controlled
thermonuclear fusion becomes a reality, as he believes it will, another 1½ billion
years' worth of fuel will become available through the use of deuterium in sea
water. "There are other energy resources," he concludes, "that are non depletable
or renewable such as solar, tidal, geothermal, aero, and hydro energy. Clearly,
man need not fear a shortage for billions of years!" (His "Energy for a Restless
World," in *Science and Technology in the World of Future,* ed. by Arthur B.
Bronwell, New York, 1970)

Voyager II's discovery of a doughnut-shaped zone around Saturn containing
gases 100,000 times hotter than the surface of the sun may one day help scientists
develop a revolutionary new source of energy on earth. "We don't even know the
mechanism that's causing the temperatures," said Stamatios Krimigis, head of the
space laboratory at Johns Hopkins University and a principal member of the team
analyzing Voyager data. But he and collaborating scientists "recognized the importance of what we found." (Marna Perry, AP reporter, *South Bend Tribune,*
Oct. 10, 1981)

40. For example, William C. Gough and Bernard J. Eastlund estimate .17 Q
as the current annual world energy consumption level and assume a population of
7 billion consuming energy at a rate 20 per cent higher than the current U.S. rate,
giving a total in the future of 2.8 Q per year. At the 2.8 Q rate, the "renewable"
sources of energy are simply insufficient for the needs. The one possible exception
is solar radiation. The reserves of fossil fuels, together with the reserves of uranium
available at a cost from $5 to $30 per pound, would not last more than 200 years.

the fusion power of nuclear energy. But how to harness this power
for practical use is still a "tenuous dream" with a "big if."[41]

At the present time, most of the available energy is from fossil

---

But if the uranium price is raised to $30 to $500 per pound, 2600 years for the
known reserves and 10,400 for estimated reserves. If breeder reactors become a
practical economic reality (creating plutonium 239 from uranium 238 by neutron
bombardment, and uranium 233 from thorium 232), things become happier still—
536,000 years for known reserves and 1.8 million years for estimated reserves. If
fusion power is ever successfully harnessed, energy will no longer be a problem.
Deuterium from the ocean would give fuel for 2.7 billion years and tritium from
lithium would give 7.6 million additional years. (Cf. their "The Prospects of Fusion Power," *Scientific American,* Feb. 1971.)

41. Thermonuclear fusion drives the stars and the sun; it also powers the
hydrogen bomb. It "could bale us out of any energy predicament for a very long
time; but it will be some time before we can be sure of this, and even longer before
we can begin to build fusion power stations on any scale." (Michael Kenward,
Potential Energy; an Analysis of World Energy Technology, Cambridge, Eng.,
1976, p. 30-31. Cf. p. 26-28, and 128-133.) Donald E. Carr, in his *Energy and the
Earth Machine,* New York, 1976, discusses fusion power with a subtitle, "Nuclear
Fusion—the Tenuous Dream," p. 111-114, and John M. Fowler discusses this
subject in his *Energy and the Environment,* New York, 1975, p. 339-345, with a
subtitle, "the big if."

Administration scientists recently have given priority to research on controlled
thermonuclear reaction, the quest to harness the hydrogen fusion process that accounts for the H-bomb's explosion. If perfected, as now appears probable, reactors using this process could literally generate power forever because the virtually
limitless hydrogen from the world's oceans would be the fuel, according to Dr.
Richard E. Balzhiser, Assistant Director of the White House's Office of Science
and Technology. He said the hope exists that the technical feasibility of at least one
type of fusion reactor can be demonstrated by 1982, but he adds that any significant
commercialization of such devices "is not envisioned before the year 2000." (Cf.
report of Frank Carey, AP Science Writer, *South Bend Tribune,* Oct. 11, 1972, p. 2.)

42. There are widely different estimates of world resources of fossil fuels:
(equivalent tons of bituminous coal):

Source	Billions of Metric Tons	
	Optimistic Estimate	Pessimistic Estimate
Coal	7,300	730
Liquid Petroleum	200	30
Natural Gas	80	12
Oil Shale	200	10
Tar	200	—
Total	7,980	782

(Harrison Brown, *The Challenge of Man's Future,* New York, 1954, p. 159. Cf.
Hans Rau, *Solar Energy,* trans. by Maxim Schur, New York, 1964, p. 7.)

fuels—coal, oil and gas. Unfortunately, the reserves of fossil fuels are limited[42] and together they can last only a few hundred years.[43]

Most critical among them is the situation of oil. This resource is not only unevenly distributed,[44] but also relatively small. It is esti-

---

43. In their article, "The Prospects of Fusion Power," *Scientific American,* Feb. 1971, William C. Gough and Bernard J. Eastlund estimate .17 Q (a Q is 1 quintillion British thermal units, equivalent of 40,000 million tons of coal) as the current annual level of the world consumption of energy. At this level alone, the world known reserves of fossil fuels—coal, oil, and gas—will be exhausted in 132 years; and their estimated reserves, in 2832 years. But if the rate grows to 2.8 Q per year as they assumed to meet the adequate need of a population of 7 billion, the known reserves of fossil fuels—coal, oil, and gas—will be exhausted in 8 years, and their estimated reserves in 173 years. (Cf. Hans Rau, *Solar Energy,* trans. by Maxim Schur, New York, 1964, p. 6-13.)

44. World oil reserves: These are small and unevenly distributed:

	Proved recoverable reserves (megatonnes)	Production (megatonnes/ year)	Reserves production ratio (years)
Africa	12,848	272.4	47
Asia	53,972	1,021	53
Europe	1,394	35.43	39
USSR	8,138	394	21
Canada	1,075	69.41	15
US	5,569	416.15	13
South America	7,599	218.3	35
Oceania	229	15.4	15
Total	91,525	2,493	17

The reserves/production ratio, found by dividing proved reserves by current production shows that oil reserves can be measured in decades rather than centuries. (Michael Kenward, *Potential Energy; an Analysis of World Energy Technology,* Cambridge, Eng., 1976, p. 20. Original source: *Survey of Energy Resources,* 1974, World Energy Conference)

mated to be only about 3 percent of the total reserves of fossil fuels, while its output has recently accounted for about half of the world's energy consumption.[46] The prospects for its potential supplements, such as oil shale, tar sand, and vegetation, do not appear very bright either.[47]

---

45. World reserves of fossil fuel, as estimated in 1958, and their percentage:

	Coal equivalent (thousand megatonnes)	% of total
Coal and lignite	4,400	91.8
Oil	150	3.1
Natural gas		
with oil	90	1.9
in coal measures	45	0.9
Oil in oil shale	45	0.9
Peat	65	1.4
Total	4,795	

(Michael Kenward, *Potential Energy; an Analysis of World Energy Technology,* Cambridge, Eng., 1976, p. 18)

46. "In the past few decades the world's demand for energy has grown tremendously. During the period from 1940 to 1970 more energy was consumed than in all prior history. In 1973, despite embargoes and production cutbacks, the worldwide consumption of oil—which has recently accounted for about half of the world's energy consumption—increased by 7.3 percent, to a record 2.77 billion tons." (*Science and Technology in an Era of Interdependence,* by UNA-USA National Policy Panel, New York, 1975, p. 33. Cf. M.A. Adelman, "The World Oil Market," in *The Energy Question, an International Failure of Policy,* Toronto, 1974, v. 1, p. 5-38; and "The Availability of Oil," in *Oil, the Present Situation and Future Prospects,* by the Organization for Economic Co-operation and Development, Paris, 1973, p. 51-55.)

47. The supplements to oil may come from the extraction of oil shales and tar sands, and the conversions of some woods or agricultural products such as sugar, corn or algae. None of them can be feasible in great quantities nor at low prices, however. Their resources are not renewable, either, except for the plants growing on the land. But the world needs the land to produce food, and materials for clothing and housing much more urgently than to utilize it in yielding gasoline. (Cf. Michael Kenward, *Potential Energy; an Analysis of World Energy Technology,* Cambridge, Eng., 1976, p. 67-72, 78-90; Harrison Brown, *The Challenge of Man's Future,* New York, 1954, p. 185-186.)

Most of the natural gas is a twin sister of the oil, with an even smaller reserve.[48]

The reserve of coal is not so poor.[49] But this stuff is too "dirty" for a clean environment,[50] and it requires new techniques to utilize it in better ways.[51]

---

48. World gas reserves:

	Proved recoverable reserves (cubic km)	Production (cubic km/year)	Reserves/ production ratio (years)
Africa	5,709	38.82	147
Asia	12,241	151.2	81
Europe	4,513	179.5	25
USSR	17,136	212	81
Canada	2,576	73.11	35
US	7,556.5	637.5	12
South America	1,591	70.57	23
Oceania	693.5	3.73	186
Total	52,532	1,389	38

(Michael Kenward, *Potential Energy; an Analysis of World Energy Technology,* Cambridge, Eng., 1976, p. 22. Original source: *Survey of Energy Resources,* 1974, World Energy Conference. Cf. note 42.)

49. Estimates of world coal resources:

	Reserves in Billions of Metric Tons	
Continent	1913 Estimate	1938 Estimate
Europe	800	800
Asia	1,300	2,000
North and South America	5,100	4,300
Oceania and Africa	200	200
Total	7,400	7,300

(Table 4 in *The Challenge of Man's Future,* by Harrison Brown, New York, 1954, p. 157. Cf. Michael Kenward, *Potential Energy; an Analysis of World Energy Technology,* Cambridge, Eng., 1976, p. 19, and Table 2.2.)

50. Coal burning produces oxides of sulfur and solid waste particles, and the mines themselves empty wastes into the atmosphere. In the Appalachian coal-mining area of the United States alone, millions of tons of sulfuric acid pour from active and inactive mines, while wastes from strip mines scar the mountainsides and slide down into valleys and streams. Surface and underground fires inadvertently set in mines also pollute neighboring regions. In addition, the surrounding areas must be reclaimed after the coal is mined out, if such areas are not to become ugly wastelands. Recently, a National Academy of Science study warned that continued

Recently, the newcomer, the fission power of nuclear energy, has attracted wide attention.[52] However, its resource, uranium, is not unlimited[53] and will run out sooner or later.[54]

---

heavy reliance on coal could lead to major irreversible changes in global climate. (Cf. John F. Fowler, *Energy and the Environment,* New York, 1975, p. 193-204; Edward K. DeLong's report in *South Bend Tribune,* Sept. 11, p. 12.)

51. There is enough coal around to keep us going for some time, but the techniques needed to extract and utilize this fuel, such as better and more economic ways for gasification, liquefication and artificial oil, remain to be developed. (Cf. Michael Kenward, *Potential Energy; an Analysis of World Energy Technology,* Cambridge, Eng., 1976, p. 49-72.)

52. "The International Atomic Energy Agency (I.A.E.A.), for example, forecasts that at least 293,000 megawatts, and possibly as much as 437,000 megawatts, of nuclear capacity will exist in the developing world by the year 2000." (Denis Hayes, *Energy for Development: Third World Options,* Washington, 1977, p. 16)

The growth of the installed capacity of nuclear energy in electricity in recent years is as follows, by thousand kw: 1964, 4,160; 1965, 6,440; 1966, 8,480; 1967, 10,810; 1968, 12,214; 1969, 15,397; 1970, 17,253; 1971, 23,355; 1972, 35,029; 1973, 42,790; 1974, 60,992; 1975, 75,125; 1976, 85,708; 1977, 98,145. (*United Nations Statistical Yearbook,* 1974, p. 371; and 1978, p. 402)

53. World uranium resources:

	Reasonably assured resources up to $26/kg uranium (tonnes)	Total uranium resources (tonnes)
US	329,267	2,041,156
Canada	185,799	716,984
Sweden	—	308,381
South Africa	202,000	298,004
Australia	120,949	160,049
France	34,850	85,000
Niger	40,000	80,800
India	—	61,862
Colombia	—	51,000
Argentina	12,665	38,590
Gabon	20,400	30,240
Rest of Europe	21,814	73,863
Rest of world	16,710	78,023
Total	984,474	4,023,948

(Michael Kenward, *Potential Energy; an Analysis of World Energy Technology,* Cambridge, Eng., 1976, p. 23. Original source: *Survey of Energy Resources,* 1974, World Energy Conference. Cf. p. 23-25. Also M. King Hubbert, *Energy Resources,* Washington, 1962, p. 113.)

It is for these reasons that the warning of an energy shortage or crisis has been widely heard.[55] Actually, what we are facing is not an energy shortage or crisis[56] but a great challenge, the challenge of how to exploit other energy resources besides the exhaustible fossil fuels on the one hand, and how to conserve available energy on the other.

Most of the other energy resources are natural forces and are, in general, clean and renewable. Well-known among them is water power. It is widespread, especially in Africa.[57] Surprisingly enough,

---

54. William C. Gough and Bernard J. Eastlund pointed out that at an annual rate of 2.8 Q for the world consumption of energy, which they estimated to adequately meet the needs of a population of 7 billion, the known reserves of uranium available at a cost of from $5 to $30 per pound will last only 4 years. Estimated total reserves would stretch the time to 8 years. If the price is raised to from $30 to $500 per pound, the picture looks better—2,600 years for known reserves and 10,400 years for estimated reserves. (Cf. their article "The Prospects of Fusion Power," *Scientific American,* Feb. 1971.)

55. The situation has become more serious: "after the Arab-Israeli conflict of October 1973, shipments of oil from the Middle East to most industrialized countries were drastically reduced and were completely shut off to the United States, Denmark and the Netherlands. When the embargo was lifted, prices for petroleum products skyrocketed. . . . leading to inflationary trends world-wide." (*Science and Technology in an Era of Interdependence,* by the UNA-USA National Policy Panel, New York, 1975, p. 58) The price of raw oil has increased almost twenty times in the last ten years, from $1.80 a barrel in 1972 to as much as $40.00 a barrel today.

56. "Although there is an energy crisis, there is no lack of energy. If there were, the sun would not shine, the winds would not blow, and the seas would not rise and hurl their waters in waves and tides. The earth's core would be stone cold and the seas would be frozen over. But the center of the earth is hot with life, the oceans and the air teem with movement and the sun shines steadily. There is a magnificent display of abundant energy in, on, and around the earth." (Joseph J. DiCerto, *The Electric Wishing Well; the Solution to the Energy Crisis,* New York, 1976, Preface)

57. Estimated world water-power resources (in millions of horsepower):

Africa	274
Asia	151
Europe	68
North America	84
Oceania	20
South America	67
Total	664

(From Harrison Brown, *The Challenge of Man's Future,* New York, 1954, p. 170. Cf. Table 8 of *Energy Resources,* by M. King Hubbert, Washington, 1962, p. 99.)

however, its total amount is estimated at much less,[58] and its various limitations are probably much more,[59] than commonly supposed.

An extra source of water power is the energy from ocean tides. It has been proved convertible into practical use and can be exploited significantly in some areas.[60] Some fast-moving ocean currents may also be utilized.[61]

Underground water heated by volcanic formations provides geothermal energy. It has proved convertible into practical use and can be exploited in some areas, too.[62]

---

58. "Water power is of considerable interest because there is little likelihood of its being exhausted in the next millenium or so. Surprisingly enough, however, water power accounts for only 1.8 percent of all existing power sources." (Hans Rau, *Solar Energy,* trans. by Maxim Schur, New York, 1964, p. 11)

59. "Among the limitations placed on waterpower are the following: food from river valleys is often more valuable than the power obtained by flooding the valley as a reservoir; in arid lands, where water is worth its weight in farm crops, vast quantities of water are lost from reservoirs by evaporation; and, in time, the mud and silt dropped by dammed rivers can cause serious clogging of the reservoirs already built." (David Evans, "Energy: Needs and Resources," in the *Encyclopedia Americana,* 1973 ed., Vol. 10, p. 142-343)

60. Waterpower created by the rising and falling of ocean tides, has turned the wheels of small water mills since the 12th century. However, it was not until the 1960s that the world's first major tidal-electric plant was placed in operation in France. Such plants undoubtedly can be of great importance in some areas in the future, and they have the advantage of being pollution-free and not using up exhaustible resources. Nevertheless, tidal plants can never provide more than a tiny fraction of the world's energy needs. (Cf. Hans Rau, *Solar Energy,* trans. by Maxim Schur, New York, 1964, p. 11-12.)

61. To ease the energy crunch, just sink a bunch of giant propellers in the Atlantic Ocean and tap free power from fast-moving ocean currents. That's Bill Mouton's idea. He is a professor at Tulane University. He wants to mount two sets of blades inside an aluminum hull 82 percent the size of the Superdome. The hull would be funnel-shaped, forcing water into a unit submerged in a fast moving current. The water will activate the blades which will be mounted close together with a series of wheels between them. The rotating blades would turn the wheels which would power generators. The resulting energy would be sent ashore via submarine cables. "A single unit will produce more power than all the windmills or solar devices in use in the country today." Still, Mouton said a group of 242 units could produce only 10,000 megawatts of electricity—half of what experts predict will be needed to power the entire state of Florida in the year 2000. (Cf. the report by Joseph A. Reaves of UPI, *South Bend Tribune,* June 17, 1979, p. 15.)

62. Geothermal energy is derived from underground water heated by volcanic formations in some areas of the world. Wells can be drilled to tap steam deposits, and the steam used to power steam-electric plants. Such plants have been in operation in California, Iceland, Mexico, New Zealand, and a few other places around the world. As with tidal power, these plants can be of great local impor-

A recent study indicates that the old-fashioned windmill could be developed to supply a good portion of the energy the world needed.[63]

The largest portion, however, has to be supplied directly with the inexhaustible solar energy[64] which is sent by the sun to the earth generously,[65] but is not easy to collect for heavy use at a low cost.[66]

---

tance, but scientists estimate that geothermal energy is not abundant enough to meet more than 1% of the world's future energy needs. (Cf. Richard T. Sheahan, *Fueling the Future, an Environmental and Energy Primer,* New York, 1976, p. 47-48; and *United Nations Statistical Yearbook,* 1978, p. 402.)

A project to exploit geothermal heat as an energy source in Taiwan was started in 1976 under the direction of David Wang, a specialist who had 10 years' experience at a geothermal power plant in California in the United States.... Taiwan is one of the most important links in the island arc system known as "the Pacific Ring of Fire" and since the widespread occurrence of hot springs on the island indicates great potential for geothermal power, every effort will be put in to explore, develop and utilize this indigenous energy resource. "We are confident that a modern geothermal power plant will be set up in Taiwan in the near future." Wang concluded. (Cf. *Sinorama,* Published in Taipei, Taiwan, Vol. 4, no. 3, March 1979, p. 3-7.)

63. Tens of thousands of giant windmills could supply as much as 18 percent of the nation's energy needs by 1995, far more than previously estimated. Spinning silently in huge circles, wing-like blades as long as football fields could drive generators producing a total electrical output equivalent to 2 billion barrels of oil per year, a federally sponsored study said. The Lockheed-California Co. is the prime contractor of the study presented at an energy symposium, according to Richard Saltus, AP Science Writer. (Cf. *South Bend Tribune,* May 20, 1976, p. 1.) This study is confined to the United States, but there seems to be no reason it would not be applicable the world over, since wind power is available everywhere. (Cf. Volta Torrey, *Wind-Catchers; American Windmills of Yesterday and Tomorrow,* Brattleboro, Vermont, 1976.)

64. The sun's clean and inexhaustible power can supply 40 percent of the world's energy needs within 25 years and 75 percent in 50 years if a drive to develop it starts now, a new study says. "Every essential feature of the proposed solar transition has already proven technically viable," says the study by Denis Hayes, researcher for the Worldwatch Institute, a private think-tank concerned with global resource problems. The study was published Saturday. "If the 50-year timetable is not met," Hayes wrote, "the roadblocks will have been political—not technical." (AP report, *South Bend Tribune,* April 3, 1977, p. 11. Cf. Denis Hayes, *Energy: the Solar Prospect,* Washington, 1977.)

Harrison Brown estimated that in the near future, a world of 7 billion persons would require a total of energy equivalent to that derived from 70 billion tons of coal per year, for "per capita consumption of energy equivalent to 10 tons of coal per year would be a conservative assumption." About two thirds of the total energy needed per year may be provided by covering 30 million acres of desert land with giant machines to convert sunlight into heat and pipe it all over the world in the form of electrical energy. (Cf. his *The Challenge of Man's Future,* New York, 1954, p. 184-186.)

In addition, there is a special fuel in abundant supply and of excellent quality. It is hydrogen, a component of water.[67] The idea of using hydrogen as a fuel is not new.[68] The big problem at the present time is its high cost. It is predictable that the day will come when hydrogen becomes feasible economically.[69]

---

65. "The sun fuses millions of tons of hydrogen into helium each second, and it radiates tremendous amounts of energy into space in every direction. In the form of heat and light, the sun delivers 700,000 trillion kilowatt-hours per year to the surface of the earth. Man used about 50 trillion kilowatt-hours to power all of his vehicles, machines, and factories and to heat all of his buildings in 1971. Thus, in a little less than 40 minutes, the sun delivers to the earth's surface an amount of energy equivalent to what man uses in a year." (Stanley W. Angrist, in the *Encyclopedia Americana,* 1973 ed., Vol. 22, p. 495, under Power, Electric—Production and Transmission Research." Cf. M. King Hubbert's influential article on the energy resources of the Earth in *Scientific American,* Sept. 1971.)

66. "Man has been able to harness very little solar energy to operate his machines because the sun does not deliver much energy in a unit time to a unit area. Even on a clear day with the sun directly overhead, the sun delivers no more than 1,000 watts to a square meter." (Stanley W. Angrist, in the *Encyclopedia Americana,* 1973 ed., Vol. 22, p. 495, under "Power, Electric—Production and Transmission Research")

Solar energy—using the heat and light that reaches the earth from the sun to do the jobs now done by burning fuels—may reduce or eliminate many environmental problems and would last as long as the sun itself. But so far it has generally been considered a distant and probably minor source of energy. Denis Hayes, researcher of the Worldwatch Institute challenges that view. Hayes concedes that solar power may never be cheap because it requires costly equipment. But he claims it could meet most or all of society's energy demands, provided those demands are geared to take advantage of it. (AP report, *South Bend Tribune,* April 3, 1977, p. 11. Cf. Denis Hayes, *Energy: the Solar Prospect,* Washington, 1977.)

67. "The greatest source of clean fuel is water. Why? Because water (H_2O) contains hydrogen (H) and oxygen (O)—the two substances that fueled the upper stage of the Apollo spacecraft. Hydrogen, the simplest of all elements, is the ideal and ultimate fuel. It is storable, cheaply transportable, abundant, efficient, burns with no adverse effects on our environment and works in perfect harmony with nature." (Joseph J. DiCerto, *The Electric Wishing Well; the Solution to the Energy Crisis,* New York, 1976, p. 119)

68. The idea of using hydrogen as a fuel is certainly not new. As far back as 1931, Rudolf A. Erren, a German inventor working in England, suggested the large-scale production of hydrogen from extra electricity available during off-peak hours. Erren also did pioneering work on converting the internal combustion engine to operate on hydrogen. During the same period, an Englishman named F.T. Bacon, who did early work in fuel cells, recommended hydrogen as an excellent medium for storing energy. (Cf. Joseph J. DiCerto, *The Electric Wishing Well; the Solution to the Energy Crisis,* New York, 1976, p. 121, 137.)

69. One reason for the high cost of hydrogen is the expense of the electricity used to produce it. Eventually, however, huge power plants of the 30,000 MW size

These are the major energy resources which can be exploited. But no matter how successful the exploitations are, it is always important to save available energy as much as possible by avoiding waste[70] and by using it wisely.[71]

Needless to say, all measures for saving energy, as well as for exploiting its various resources, have to be strong and efficient. Above

---

may produce electricity much more cheaply, which will bring down the cost of producing hydrogen, while the supply of oil and coal is going down and commanding higher and higher prices. Hydrogen, then, will not only be more cost competitive, but also one of the few fuels left to man. (Cf. Joseph J. DiCerto, *The Electric Wishing Well; the Solution to the Energy Crisis,* New York, 1976, p. 120-121; Michael Kenward, *Potential Energy; an Analysis of World Energy Technology,* Cambridge, Eng., 1976, p. 205-207; and John M. Fowler, *Energy and the Environment,* New York, 1975, p. 311-315.)

70. For example, the United States could live just as well as it does now using only half as much energy, said a study by Denis Hayes of the Worldwatch Institute. Massive energy saving would take time, Hayes said, but would require only cosmetic changes in U.S. lifestyles, such as: travel in smaller and more efficient cars and mass transit systems; better insulation and more efficient heating units; shifting freight haulage from less-efficient to more efficient types of transport, such as from trucks to railroads; improvements in food processing and packaging, supplemented by improved diets and home gardens; less wasteful appliances and lighting; more efficient powerplants; and the re-use of heat now cast off as waste. (AP report, *South Bend Tribune,* Feb. 1, 1976, p. 7; Cf. Joseph J. DiCerto, *The Electric Wishing Well; the Solution to the Energy Crisis,* New York, 1976, p. 21-26.)

71. For example, "Studies have shown that reducing commercial airline cruising speeds by 3 percent would add only 12 minutes to a cross-country trip, but would save the United States 200 million gallons of jet fuel per year. Furthermore, we could reduce many of the half-empty flights that lose money for the airlines and waste a lot of fuel; if by reducing flight frequencies we could raise the national aircraft load factor from 52 to 60 percent, we could save approximately 1.3 billion gallons of jet fuel each year." "The automobile, then, is excellent for practicing conservation in a number of ways. One might change from a regular to a compact car, which uses about 33 percent less gasoline. A car should also be kept well tuned; a badly tuned engine can reduce gas mileage considerably. Reducing driving speed can also save energy. A car driven at 75 miles per hour will consume almost 100 percent more fuel than the same car driven at 50 miles per hour." "It is important in terms of conservation that people use mass transit as much as possible. If one-half of the intercity air traffic and one-quarter of the intercity auto traffic could be switched to passenger trains, and if railroads operated at 70 percent instead of 25 percent capacity, the United States could save about 11 billion gallons of gasoline each year." (Joseph J. DiCerto, *The Electric Wishing Well; the Solution to the Energy Crisis,* New York, 1976, p. 22, 25. Cf. Michael Kenward, *Potential Energy; an Analysis of World Energy Technology,* Cambridge, Eng., 1976, p. 182-207; and John M. Fowler, *Energy and the Environment,* New York, 1975, p. 347-380.)

all, it is necessary to act now.[72] "A forester can't afford to wait until the very last tree has been felled before thinking about reforestation."[73]

d.
Non-Fuel Minerals,
Forest, and Water

THIS URGENT APPEAL MAY ALSO BE APPLICABLE TO other things, including non-fuel minerals, forest products, water and food.

Non-fuel minerals are the most important raw materials for industry.[74] Their production and consumption have increased enormously since the Industrial Revolution.[75] Consequently, the rapid

---

72. "The rhetoric that public officials in the world's capitals lavish upon the energy 'crisis' is not being translated into action." "Most energy policy is being framed as though it were addressing a problem that our grandchildren will inherit. But the energy crisis is our crisis. Oil and natural gas are our principal means of bridging today and tomorrow, and we are burning our bridges," said Denis Hayes of the Worldwatch institute, according to Edward K. DeLong, UPI reporter. (Cf. *South Bend Tribune,* Sept. 11, p. 12.)

73. "Even if we take the optimistic view and extend the deadlines on coal and oil by a few more decades, we have still not answered the question ... what do we do for fuel? A forester can't afford to wait until the very last tree has been felled before thinking about reforestation." (Hans Rau, *Solar Energy,* trans. by Maxim Schur, New York, 1964, p. 10-11.)

74. The vital role of nonfuel minerals in the development of civilization is implied in the terms used for the major periods of history, such as Bronze Age and Iron Age. Today, an industrial economy requires more than 70 different nonfuel minerals from which metals and inorganic chemicals are derived. Among them, most common and important is iron, the principal machine material. Others include copper, aluminum, lead, tin, chromite, manganese, bauxite, cobalt, mercury, tungsten, zinc, platinum, nickel, molybdenum, gold and silver, in addition to various nonmetallic minerals such as sulphur, phosphate and potash. (Cf. U.S. Bureau of Mines, *Commodity Data Summaries,* 1976, Washington, 1976; and Donella H. Meadows, and others, *The Limits to Growth,* Washington, 1972, p. 64-67.)

75. During the 370 years from 1500 to 1870, for example, the world's iron output increased from about 50,000 tons to approximately 12,000,000 tons. In the succeeding 70 years, this figure increased to almost 200,000,000 tons. More striking is the disproportionately large increase in mineral production as compared with

depletion of their exhaustible resources has been alarming.[76]
Although we have been able, with the advance of science and tech-

---

the population in some regions. For example, while between 1860 and 1913 the population of the United States increased threefold, pig iron production increased 38 fold, and the production of copper 76 fold. (Cf. Erich W. Zimmermann, *World Resources and Industries,* New York, 1933, p. 441-442; and Charles K. Leith, James W. Furness and Cleona Lewis, *World Minerals and World Peace,* Washington, 1943, p. 211-212.)

"The world's consumption of aluminum now doubles every nine years, iron every 10 to 15 years, and copper every 12 to 15 years. During the period from 1950 to 1970, the world consumed almost half of the zinc which had been produced until that time." (*Science and Technology in an Era of Interdependence,* by the UNA-USA National Policy Panel, New York, 1975, p. 37. Cf. Michael Tanzer, *The Race for Resources; Continuing Struggles over Minerals and Fuels,* New York, 1980, p. 15-19, Tables 1-1 and 1-3; and Vance Packard, *The Waste Makers,* New York, 1960, p. 183-194.)

"Few realize . . . that the world production of several essential minerals has been doubling about every ten years. The last twenty years have seen as much world gold production as the four hundred years following the discovery of America. A single Lake Superior iron mine now produces every two weeks a volume of ore equivalent to the great Pyramid of Egypt, which required the toil of vast hordes for several decades and has been long regarded as one of the most stupendous works of man. In 1929 the United States produced more zinc than all the world did in the first fifty years of the last century. The copper production of the world in 1929 was more than twice as great as the estimated production for all history up to the nineteenth century." (Charles K. Leith, *World Minerals and World Policies,* Port Washington, N.Y., 1931, p. 3-4)

76. There are two views of the depletion problem, one physical, the other economic. The physical view envisages the world literally running out of mineral deposits. The economic view sees the problem not as the physical exhaustion of all deposits but rather in terms of the higher costs of mineral production that society will have to bear as it depletes its best ore bodies and is forced to turn to lower grade, more remote, and more difficult to exploit deposits. Higher costs will force mineral product prices up, at some point choking off most or all demand. This, of course, could be as devastating in terms of dislocation and hardship and changes in lifestyles as physical exhaustion would be. (Cf. John E. Tilton, *The Future of Nonfuel Minerals,* Washington, 1977, chap. 2, especially p. 6-7, Table 2-1, for life expectancies of nonfuel minerals reserves of the world. Cf. also Donella H. Meadows and others, *The Limits to Growth,* Washington, 1972, p. 64-78; and David B. Brooks and P.W. Andrews, "Mineral Resources, Economic Growth, and World Population," *Science,* July 5, 1974, p. 13-19.)

Recent reports of the U.S. Geological Survey and the National Commission on Materials Policy warned that industrialized countries, particularly the United States, must reduce their consumption of certain seriously depleted resources, including asbestos, chromium, fluorine, mercury, silver, manganese, copper, gold, and iron. The commission recommended that no solution would be adequate without zero population growth. (Cf. "Depletion of Natural Resources must Halt,

nology, to discover new deposits[77] and to extract them in better ways,[78] it would be very difficult to match them with the vast demand of industrialization for the growing population.[79] It is necessary, therefore, to save them by all means, such as: using alternatives or substitutes for them as much as possible;[80] extending their life by reuse and recycling;[81] and reserving their related resources.[82]

Commission Warns," in *Population Crisis,* Vol. 9, no. 2 (July-Aug., 1973), p. 4; and Vance Packard, *The Waste Makers,* New York, 1960, p. 195-214.)

77. "Doubts about the existence of unknown or inferred reserves may be moderated by noting that in recent years major new sources of iron ore, for example, have been discovered in Venezuela, Canada, Liberia, Brazil, and Australia, as well as other places." (Joseph L. Fisher and Neal Potter, *World Prospects for Natural Resources,* Washington, 1964, p. 60. Cf. John E. Tilton, *The Future of Nonfuel Minerals,* Washington, 1977, p. 8-10, Figure 2-1 and Table 2-2.)

78. "New ways of extracting minerals from air and ocean water are frequently being found. The nitrates of Chile, for example, became insignificant when a way was found for the fixation of nitrogen from air.... New processes have made possible the extraction of iron from the relatively abundant, but low-grade deposits of taconite rock, and, as a result, have confounded the predictions of an iron shortage in the United States." (Roger Hilsman, *The Crouching Future,* New York, 1975, p. 510-511)

79. Assuming a world population of 7 billion people living at the current level of the United States, Preston Cloud calculates that more than 60 million tons of lead, 700 million tons of zinc, and more than 50 million tons of tin would have to be kept in circulation. This would be somewhere between 200 and 400 times present world annual production. "As it is not possible to increase metal production by anywhere near the suggested amounts by the end of the century, if ever," he writes, "rising expectations among the deprived peoples of the earth that they too may share the affluent life are doomed to bitter disappointment without population control and eventually reduction in population to its present or lower levels." (Preston Cloud, "Resources, Population, and Quality of Life," in a publication of AAAS, 1969, quoted by Roger Hilsman, *The Crouching Future,* New York, 1975, p. 510. Cf. John E. Tilton, *The Future of Nonfuel Minerals,* Washington, 1977, p. 11-13, Table 2-3. Note the life expectancy of the resources base with 5% and 10% growth rates in the fourth column.)

80. Scarce materials can be allocated to their highest or most critical uses, and abundant materials can be substituted for scarce ones, such as plastics to replace a thousand other materials, and synthetic rubber to supplement natural rubber. (Cf. J.H. Westerbrook, "Materials for Tomorrow," in the *Science and Technology in the World of the Future,* ed. by Arthur B. Bronwell, New York, 1970, p. 329-365.)

81. Recycling will undoubtedly ease the problem with many metals and other materials. Scrap metals can be used more extensively and for new uses. For a number of metals, especially aluminum, copper and iron, scrap may provide a very large reserve for the future. Actually, reusing and recycling are processes of "resource recovery." "Resource recovery, through waste reclamation and recycling, is one of the principles laid down in the Recommendation adopted by the OECD Council in September, 1976, on a comprehensive waste management

Forests cover about 30 percent of the land surface of the world.[83] Their products are the primary material for houses, furniture and paper. While in the face of a probable reduction of forest lands, the rate of wood removals has increased remarkably[84] and is expected to increase even faster in the years ahead in view of the tremendous demands for building many millions of new houses for decent settlements over the world.[85] In order to prevent forests from further

policy: i.e. a coherent system of measures concerning the design, manufacture and use of products as well as the reclamation and disposal of waste, and aiming at the most efficient and economic reduction of the nuisance and costs generated by waste." (*Waste Paper Recovery,* by the Organization for Economic Co-operation and Development, Paris, 1979, foreword)

82. For example, "We should reserve our valuable store of hydrocarbon materials for nonenergy uses—as raw materials for plastics, lubricants, medicines, synthetic fibers and thousands of other products necessary to our society. If we did this, they would last for thousands of years instead of the 50 or 60 years now projected." (Joseph J. DiCerto, *The Electric Wishing Well; the Solution to the Energy Crisis,* New York, 1976, p. 16)

83. According to a 1965 estimate of the Food and Agriculture Organization of the United Nations, forest land accounts for about 10 billion acres, (4 billion hectares), or about 30% of the earth's surface. This is an average of about 3 acres (1.2 hectares) per capita; however, the distribution of forest land is uneven, as is shown in the following table:

Area	Total forest acreage	Acres per capita
North America	1,853,000,000	8.5
USSR	2,248,000,000	9.6
Europe	355,000,000	0.8
Asia	1,358,000,000	0.7
Latin America	2,386,000,000	9.5
Africa	1,754,000,000	5.6
Oceania	237,000,000	15.8
World Total	10,191,000,000	3.0

(J. Granville Jensen, "Forest Conservation," in the *Encyclopedia Americana,* 1973 ed., Vol. 7. p. 630)

84. "In contrast to the probable reduction in world forest lands, the removal of wood from forests of the world increased about 50% between 1945 and 1965, and it is estimated that the world demand for wood will increase two or even threefold in the next several decades." (J. Granville Jensen, "Forest Conservation," in the *Encyclopedia Americana,* 1973 ed., Vol. 7, p. 630)

85. A Human Settlements Conference of the United Nations was held in Vancouver, Canada, in May-June 1976. "In the quest for human dignity, shelter ranks with nutrition and health care as an absolute necessity," said Prime Minister Pierre Elliott Trudeau of Canada in outlining goals for the conference. "In the next 30

depleting, saving practices have to be adopted right now through an efficient management.[86]

Perhaps the most common and also the most precious natural resource is water, because it is indispensable to all forms of life. Although its volume is immense,[87] we are supplied only by a relatively small portion in the recycling process of rain and snow,[88] while almost everything needs a lot of it.[89]

---

years, the United Nations says, 3.5 billion people will need places to live, and that's enough to create 3,500 cities of a million residents each. There are fewer than 300 cities of that size now. Another 600 million housing units will be needed in the next 30 years, or more than those existing in the entire world today. Even now, the World Health Organization believes more than a billion people don't have the basics, like safe water to drink." (AP report, *South Bend Tribune,* May 25, 1976, p. 6)

86. Forest management has three broad objectives: (1) Reduce losses in growing timber by protecting forests from destruction by insects, disease, fire and certain weather phenomena. (2) Improve forest stand by such methods as regular harvesting and adequate stocking of forest lands, and (3) reduce losses in utilization, such as eliminating wood left in the harvest areas and better milling practices. (Cf. J. Granville Jensen, "Forest Conservation," in the *Encyclopedia Americana,* 1973 ed., Vol. 7, p. 631.)

Timber Resources for America's Future, U.S. Forest Service, 1959, p. 476, indicated that nearly a four-fold increase in output was possible in the United States through better management alone. (Cf. *Latin American Timber Trends and Prospects,* FAO, 1963, p. 82-86.)

87. "Every human being is a miniature world, in that 71 percent of his substance consists of salty water, just as 71 percent of the earth is covered by ocean." (Quoted by Sydney Harris in his "Random Nuggets," in the *South Bend Tribune,* May 18, 1976, p. 11.) "Some 95 percent of all the fresh water on earth is ground water, and in the U.S. there is about 20 to 30 times as much water underground as in all lakes, streams and rivers combined." (Sydney Harris, *South Bend Tribune,* Jan. 15, 1980, p. 16)

88. "Most of the water we use is supplied by the recycling process of rain and snow. About 875 cubic kilometers are evaporated from the sea each day. Of this, 715 cubic kilometers return to the sea through precipitation, while 100 cubic kilometers are blown over the land and precipitated there. About 100 cubic kilometers of water are evaporated from the land each day and these are also precipitated mainly over the land. Half of the total water precipitated over the land, whether its source is land or sea, runs off into the sea through rivers and streams. Thus the maximum available if the runoff could be fully utilized would be 200 cubic kilometers a day." (Roger Hilsman, *The Crouching Future,* New York, 1975, p. 507-508)

89. For instance, "producing a pound of dry wheat requires 60 gallons of water; a quart of milk, some 1,000 gallons; a pound of meat, between 2,500 and 6,000 gallons; and an automobile, some 100,000 gallons. Each American, directly or indirectly, uses up almost 2,000 gallons each day." (Roger Hilsman, *The Crouching Future,* New York, 1975, p. 508. Cf. Georg Borgstrom, *Too Many; an Ecological Overview of Earth's Limitation,* New York, 1971, p. 131-155.)

Lately, with the population growing, along with the expansion of industry and agriculture, the demand for water has risen fast.[90] As a result, water withdrawal from rivers and lakes has been increasing[91] and ground water has been used noticeably.[92]

Under these circumstances, it is no wonder that cries of water shortages have been heard from arid and semiarid areas, big cities,[93] and even some regions where the water supply is supposed to be plentiful.[94] In order to lessen the pressure, there have been various sug-

---

90. Meanwhile the demand for water is growing everywhere at an accelerating pace not only because of population increase but also because of the needs of industry and agriculture. Not only the quantity but the quality of water must be improved, both in regions of traditional low living standards and in highly industrialized countries which permit the pollution of rivers and lakes. (Cf. C.S. Cristian, "The Use and Abuse of Land and Water," in *The Population Crisis and the Use of World Resources,* ed. by Stuart Mudd, The Hague, 1964, p. 387-390; and Tinco E.A. Van Hylckama, "Water Resources," in *Environment, Resources, Pollution & Society,* ed. by William W. Murdoch, Stamford, Conn., 1972, p. 135-154.)

91. In the East of the United States, for example, withdrawal depletions (the fresh water taken from streams and lakes and not returned) are projected to increase from 14 billion gallons per day in 1960 to 37 billion in 2000; in the more arid West from 60 to 92 billion gallons per day, and in the Pacific Northwest from 11 to 20 billion gallons per day. (Cf. Hans H. Landsberg, Leonard L. Fischman and Joseph L. Fisher, *Resources in America's Future,* Baltimore, 1963, p. 28.)

92. Thus, besides the fresh water from the recycling process of rain and snow, we have had to use much ground water of which the reserve is indeed abundant, but is being depleted all over the world as the drop in water tables shows. In the developed countries, it is falling at rates that are truly alarming. It has been estimated that the people of Europe have been taking out 3 times as much water from the underground reserve as is returned by the water cycle and that Americans are taking out twice as much. (Cf. Paul R. Ehrlich and Anne H. Ehrlich, *Population, Resources, Environment: Issues in Human Ecology,* San Francisco, 1970, p. 65; and Georg Borgstrom, *Too Many, an Ecological Overview of Earth's Limitations,* New York, 1971, p. 156-183.)

93. "The high cost of supplying fresh water severely limits economic development in many arid and semiarid areas. Precipitation is irregular in most countries, both regionally and seasonally, and water is costly to transport, prohibitively so for long distances." (Joseph L. Fisher and Neal Potter, *World Prospects for Natural Resources,* Washington, 1964, p. 62. Cf. Irving K. Fox, "Water Resources of the World," *Federation Proceedings,* Fifth International Congress on Nutrition, Baltimore, Federation of American Societies for Experimental Biology, Vol. 20, No. 1, March 1961, p. 378-80.)

94. In the United States, for example, "The Southwest always has needed irrigation. The past several years the Great Plains have had critical shortages of moisture. The latest region to feel the water pinch is the east coast, as we found on a recent trip. A resident of one coastal city told of a desalinization project to increase his city's water supply. Another community reportedly has worked out

gestions for saving water. It is also possible to convert salt water from the ocean for common use,[96] and to revitalize the vast semiarid regions by tapping the ground water from the huge reservoirs found under the great deserts.[97]

Ironically, floods have been one of our greatest troubles since ancient times[98] and they have occurred as a natural disaster more widely

---

crisis levels where at the most critical stage, water would not be used to fight fires and efforts would be turned toward evacuation of the population." (*South Bend Tribune's* editorial, Feb. 22, 1981, p. 12)

95. These include constructing more storage reservoirs; checking the evaporation and irrigation canal losses; maximizing recycling in industry; substituting salt or brackish water for fresh water in cooling and other uses; stopping pollution on streams, rivers and lakes, so as to keep more high quality water available; and protecting soil from erosion and other ecological dislocations, including deforestation, so as to reserve more water and reduce the flood. (Cf. Joseph L. Fisher and Neal Potter, *World Prospects for Natural Resources,* Washington, 1964, p. 63-64.)

96. A number of advanced countries are presently making massive efforts to find economical methods of desalinizing water. Studies indicate that atomic power plants will be able to reduce the cost to about 25 cents per thousand gallons, a price which would make the process competitive with the amounts now paid in areas where natural water is plentiful. (Cf. Herman Kahn and Anthony J. Wiener, *The Year 2000: A Framework for Speculation on the Next Thirty Years,* New York, 1967, p. 72.)

For human consumption in a few high cost places, demineralized water is already being produced. Some fifty, water-short areas in various parts of the world have been identified recently in which technical and economic studies appear warranted to determine the possibilities for utilization of desalinated water. (Cf. U.N. Dept. of Economic and Social Affairs, Resources and Transport Division, *Water Desalinization in Developing Countries,* New York, 1964.)

97. "In the vast semiarid belt extending across North Africa, the Middle East, and the central Eurasian land mass, ground water offers the principal additional source. The tapping of these underground basins in the Sahara, Gobi, and elsewhere could literally make the desert bloom and alter the living standards of many millions now eking out a precarious marginal existence." (T. Walter Wallbank, Alastair M. Taylor, Nels M. Bailkey and Mark Mancall, *Civilization Past and Present,* 6th ed., Glenview, Ill., 1970, Book 1, p. 504)

98. The earliest flood story was told in the Bible: a great flood once covered the earth and destroyed all living things except Noah, his family, and the forms of life that he saved by constructing a great ship, or "Ark." This tradition, recounted in Genesis 6-9, was generally accepted in the Western world as the great event in prehistory, which divided the preflood period, characterized by giants, from the postflood age, which is our own and in which people are of normal stature. (Cf. Andrew Parrot, *The Flood and Noah's Ark,* tr. by Edwin Hudson, 2d ed., New York, 1956.) There were also Mesopotamian flood stories. (Cf. Edmond Stollberger, *The Babylonian Legend of the Flood,* London, 1962.) China had its first recorded flood of the Huang Ho (Yellow River) in 2297 B.C. (Cf. John R.

and more frequently than any others.[99] This phenomenon does not prove that we have too much water rather than not enough, however. It occurs primarily because the weather distributes the precipitation, in the recycling process of rain and snow, unevenly, and often in the wrong place or at the wrong time. For this very reason, the weather is also responsible for the common disasters of drought in rural areas.[100] Hence, the ultimate approach to the solution of the water problem has to be sought in the control of the weather.

The idea of controlling the weather is nothing new,[101] and there have been various attempts to make rain in the last hundred years.[102]

Freeman, "Flood Problems in China," *Transactions of the American Society of Civil Engineers,* Vol. 85, New York, 1962, p. 1405-1460.)

99. No region is spared from flood damages, not even the deserts, where sporadic floods form fearsome walls of water that rush down normally dry channels and wash out roads and bridges. Flooding destroys crops, causes extensive damage to property, cuts transportation lines, disrupts the life of cities, and takes a toll in lives. Floods in the United States, for example, cause an average annual loss of 80 lives and a total damage of about $1 billion. Damage to rural and agricultural property accounts for about 50% of this total, urban and industrial property about 30%, and transport facilities about 20%, according to Walter B. Langbein, "Flood," in the *Encyclopedia Americana,* 1973 ed., Vol. 11, p. 408.

100. "Drought is clearly the greatest killer of all weather hazards, although it does not strike with sudden, spectacular violence." "Great as the Dust Bowl (created by the drought of the 1930s in the Southwestern United States) was, nearly all of the people survived, but such is not the case when drought strikes a heavily populated region where people are completely dependent for each year's food supply on the crops produced in that year. China and India are especially vulnerable. Seemingly slight deficiencies of rainfall or slight delays in the onset of the summer monsoon rains will diminish the agricultural production to the point of famine. A single drought-produced famine has cost the lives of a million people in India and several million in China," (James E. Miller, "Drought," in the *Encyclopedia Americana,* 1973 ed., Vol. 9, p. 403)

101. "Man's attempts to control or in some way modify weather go back long before recorded history. From the very beginnings of civilization man has had to depend on rainfall for water to quench his thirst and raise his crops. The distribution of rainfall over the earth's surface has designated the geographical areas where man could live, what he could eat and grow, and what kind of a life he could lead—how he could survive. In the beginning, man tried to influence rainfall by hope and faith, magic and ritual. Witch doctors, medicine men and charlatans have all tried their hand at weather control or rain making. Rain dances of the Hopi Indian tribes in Arizona still attract interest. And African rain queens continue to perform mysterious rites to increase rainfall." (*Final Report of the Advisory Committee on Weather Control* (of the U.S. Congress), Washington, 1958, p. 2)

102. In 1841, an American meteorologist, James Pollard Espy, tried to prove the importance of convection in the formation of clouds and precipitation in his *Philosophy of Storms.* In 1871, an American civil engineer named Powers brought

Today, with the assistance of new efficient instruments, such as satellites and computers, and the efforts of international cooperation,[103] weather modification of several types is, or may soon become, technically feasible,[104] and through the advance of weather modification,

---

out a book, *War and Weather.* Later, he was supported by the U.S. government to make a series of experiments in rain-making. In Holland during the summer of 1930, August W. Veraart directed four scientific experiments in cloud seeding. The real groundwork for modern experiments in weather modification was laid in 1933 when the famous Swedish meteorologist, Tor Bergeron, advanced the theory that rain in appreciable amounts could be released principally by the presence of ice crystals formed in or transported through water clouds. Five years later the German physicist, Walter Findeisen, reemphasized that the coexistence of ice crystals and supercooled water droplets in the proper proportion is a necessary condition for precipitation from a cloud and emphasized the importance of the process of sublimation. This theory, known as the Bergeron-Findeisen Theory, forms the basis of present-day techniques of seeding supercooled clouds. It was carried further by Irving Langmuir and Vincent J. Schaefer, and the U.S. government has organized several large projects of experiment since 1947: Project Cirrus, Cloud Physics Project, and Artificial Cloud Nucleation Project. Some hundreds of testings have been performed. An evaluation was made by the Advisory Committee on Weather Control (of the U.S. Congress) in its *Final Report,* Washington, 1958, p. vi-vii; 2-7.

103. "International coordination and the setting of international standards, procedures, and practices for the operation of meteorological stations are a part of the responsibilities of the World Meteorological Organization (WMO), created in 1950 as a special agency of the United Nations. The first such world body was the International Meteorological Organization, established in 1878. At present, tens of thousands of meteorological stations are scattered over the face of the earth, both on land and sea. The resulting observations are exchanged internationally to an extent which surpasses even the exchange of letters between the postal services of the world." (P.D. McTaggart-Cowan, "Meteorological Stations," in the *Encyclopedia Americana,* 1973 ed., Vol. 18, p. 716. Cf. Carl L.S. Godske and others, *Dynamic Meteorology and Weather Forecasting,* Boston, 1957.)

"Another noteworthy undertaking is the Global Atmospheric Research Program. This program, established jointly in 1967 by the World Meteorological Organization (WMO) and the International Council of Scientific Unions (ICSU), is an experiment in international cooperation for the purpose of increasing the accuracy of weather forecasting and better understanding the physical basis of climate. The program is expected to contribute considerably to international research efforts into the relationship between man's activities and certain climate changes." (*Science and Technology in an Era of Interdependence,* by the UNA-USA National Policy Panel, New York, 1975, p. 49)

104. "Over the past decade, scientific understanding of atmospheric processes has proceeded to the point where weather modification of several types is, or may soon become, technically feasible. These types of weather modification will include rain augmentation or redistribution; suppression of hail and lightning; snow pack augmentation; fog dispersal; and modification of severe storms, in-

it will be possible in the future to overcome water shortages, and reduce the floods, droughts, tornados and other natural calamities. On the other hand, there has been some worry about "weather warfare"[105] and some concern over the change in weather patterns which are probably being caused by such things as nuclear explosions, atmospheric pollution and urbanization,[106] and the effect of such changes on agricultural output,[107] especially the important crops whose growth depends heavily on favorable weather.[108]

---

cluding hurricanes and tornadoes. Small-scale cloudseeding experiments are currently being carried out, and successes such as dispersal of cold fog on airport runways have been reported." (*Science and Technology in an Era of Interdependence,* by the UNA-USA National Policy Panel, New York, 1975, p. 41-42)

105. "Weather modification activities that are on a large scale or take place near a national frontier may pose serious questions of international equity and potential conflict. The potential for using 'weather warfare' has already been demonstrated by U.S. rainmaking operations in Southeast Asia. International guidelines are urgently needed to ensure that such activities are not carried out to the detriment of other countries, including use as possible instruments of warfare." (*Science and Technology in an Era of Interdependence,* by the UNA-USA National Policy Panel, New York, 1975, p. 59-61)

106. "Atmospheric pollution has also increased worldwide, and research is being conducted to determine ways in which industrial activities may pose threats to human health and may effect changes in local and global climate ... Also of concern is the fact that increased urbanization, in both developed and developing countries, may have inadvertent effects on weather and climate. In the U.S., where the impact of urbanization on local weather patterns is relatively well documented, studies indicate that some cities experience 25 percent more wind, considerably more fog and up to 10 percent more precipitation than the surrounding countryside. Urban concentrations form heat islands and take longer to cool off than surrounding areas." (*Science and Technology in an Era of Interdependence,* by the UNA-USA National Policy Panel, New York, 1975, p. 40)

107. "Of growing concern is the effect which climatic changes may be having on agricultural output in various regions of the world. Drought conditions have occurred with increasing severity in Southern Asia and in the Sahelian region of Africa. At the same time excessive rainfall has been experienced in equatorial parts of the Pacific Ocean and along the West Coast of South America. One international group of scientists has suggested that the new worldwide pattern of climate that is now emerging will have serious consequences for world food production and may affect the stability of interstate relations." (*Science and Technology in an Era of Interdependence,* by the UNA-USA National Policy Panel, New York, 1975, p. 41. Cf. "Statement by The International Federation of Institutes for Advanced Study," Project Workshop on the Impact on Man of Climate Change, May 10, 1974.)

108. The most important crops are cereals, including rice, wheat, maize, barley, oats and rye. Others, also important, are roots such as potatoes, sugar beets, sugar cane, fodder roots, cassava, and sago-palm; legumes such as beans, peas, lentils and other pulses; and oilseeds such as flax, olive, soybean, peanut,

e.
Food and Land

THUS, WE ARE LED TO DISCUSS THE PROBLEM OF FOOD, which is the most commonly needed commodity, with the most generally limited resources.

How much food does a human being need every day? Nutritional studies once gave the figures as 3000 calories and 70 grams of protein, plus various minerals and vitamins.[109] It was a standard set too far from the actual situation.[110] Experts then tried to lower the level[111]

---

sunflower, rape, sesame, palm, palm kernel and coconut. Among the factors important to their growth, the most essential are rainfall and temperature. (Cf. Norman W. Desrosier, "Composition and Sources of Food," in the *Encyclopedia Americana,* 1973 ed., Vol. 11, p. 511-515; and Frank A. Pearson and Floyd A. Harper, *The World Hunger,* Ithaca, N.Y., 1945, p. 48.)

109. Nutritional studies have indicated that an average not-too-active man requires a daily intake of carbohydrates to supply him with 3,000 calories, 70 grams of protein, 800 milligrams of calcium, 12 milligrams of iron, 5,000 international units of Vitamin A, 1,800 micrograms of thiamin (vitamin B), 75 milligrams of ascorbic acid (vitamin C), 2,700 micrograms of riboflavin, and 18 milligrams of nicotinic acid, as well as varying quantities of other minerals and vitamins. As a general rule, these requirements vary with a person's age and size, as well as with his physical activities. (Cf. Hilda Faust, *A Nutrition Program for Defense,* University of California Agricultural Extension Service circular, 1941.)

110. A survey of the food supply in 70 countries in the prewar period shows, however, that an average of more than 2750 calories per capita daily was available only in areas containing less than a third of the world's population, about one-sixth of whose average was between 2250 and 2750, and more than a half below 2250. (Cf. UN Food and Agriculture Organization, *World Food Survey,* July 5, 1946, p. 6-7, also Figures 1 and 2, and Table 2 of Appendix III. Cf. also Joseph L. Fisher and Neal Potter, *World Prospects for Natural Resources,* Washington, 1964, p. 23, Table 3.)

111. The expert group set up different targets for 18 areas: 3240 calories for North America, 3160 for Oceania, 3100 for South America I (Argentina, Uruguay, Paraguay), 3070 for Scandinavia, 3015 for the United Kingdom and Iris States, 2840 for Central and Western Europe, 2825 for the U.S.S.R., 2755 for Eastern and Southeastern Europe, 2645 for Southern Europe, 2630 for South America II (Brazil, Chile, Colombia, Peru), 2595 for Africa (excluding North Africa), 2959 for North Africa, 2605 for the Middle East, 2590 for Southeast Asia (mainland), 2575 for Eastern Asia, 2640 for Central America and the Caribbean, 2575 for the Major Southeast Asia Islands, and 2570 for the India Peninsula. (Cf. UN Food and Agriculture Organization, *World Food Survey,* July 5, 1946, p. 13, Figure 4.)

and set up different targets for various geographic areas.[112] They also noted that it required more than seven original calories from plants to reproduce one calorie from animal products.[113] If we count animal products in terms of the original plant calories, therefore, the difference in nutritional balance between the big and small consumers would be much larger.[114]

---

112. In order to promote the health of the people of the world in regard to food concerns, early in 1946 the Food and Agriculture Organization of the United Nations convened a group of nutrition experts to consider the problem of nutritional targets. The group agreed that a per capita calorie intake of 2550-2650 should be taken as the minimum level. They also suggested that it was better to obtain 1200-1800 calories from cereals, 100-200 from starchy roots and tubers and starchy fruits, 100-200 from fats, 200-300 from pulses, 100-200 from meat, fish and eggs, 300-400 from milk and milk products, and at least 100 from fruits and vegetables (excluding starchy vegetables and fruits). Calories from sugar were not to exceed 10 to 15 percent of the total calories. (Cf. UN Food and Agriculture Organization, *World Food Survey,* July 5, 1946, p. 11-12; and Willard W. Cochrane, *The World Food Problem: A Guardedly Optimistic View,* New York, 1969, Tables 3.1, 3.2, and 3.3.)

113. Generally speaking, food may be divided into two great categories: plant food and animal products. But, originally, it is one, because the animal products are, to a very great extent, a reproduction of plant food. This reproduction is a great spending process. When crops are fed to animals instead of being eaten directly by human beings, they lose 80 to 90 percent of their calorie value before they reemerge in the form of meat and milk. For convenience, students have adopted the term original calories, which is used for the calories yielded by crops. About seven of these original calories are required to produce one calorie from animal products. (Cf. UN Food and Agriculture Organization, *World Food Survey,* July 4, 1946, p. 19.) It notes that the multiplier varies from one class of livestock to another and also among countries, according to differences in the quality of livestock and in feeding practices. One acre of the midwestern American corn belt, if used to grow maize, will produce three million calories of food. But if it is used to produce milk, it will provide only 700,000 calories, and to raise beef, only 100,000 calories.... Meat, the world over, requires twenty times the land cereals do. (Cf. C.L. Walker, *Man and Food; Headline Series* no. 73, 1949, p. 21.)

114. Comparing the diets of various areas with original calories, we find more notable differences existing between them. The prewar North American diet contained about 2200 calories per capita daily from plant food and about 870 from animal products. If the latter figure is multiplied by seven, the total value of the diet in original calories becomes 6090 + 2200, or 8290. At the other end of the scale, the diet of certain islands in Southeast Asia contained about 1940 calories from plant food and only 100 from animal products, which gives 1940 + 700, or 2640, as the total value in original calories. Thus the value of the North America diet in terms of original calories was about three times that of the diet in Southeast Asia. (Cf. UN Food and Agriculture Organization, *World Food Survey,* July 4, 1946, p. 19.)

"Americans, as meat-eaters, need 2,200 lbs of grain per head per year to feed

In fact, no matter by what nutritional measurements, the world today has a great number of people who are inadequately nourished[115] in various areas.[116] An obvious reason for this is the disproportion in the distribution of population and food supply, because most of the population is living in the developing countries, while most of the food is produced in the developed countries.[117]

Fundamentally and viewed as a whole, however, the big problem stems from the limitation of the land.

According to experts, of the earth's land, only about 11 percent, or 4 billion acres, are very good for food production and almost all of

---

them (140 lbs direct, and all the rest for their cattle), Chinese People use 400 lbs per head per year, 360 lbs direct, and 40 for their cattle. 1,500 Chinese could live off what 270 Americans eat." (Bob Willmot, *Resurgence, Journal of the Fourth World,* Vol. 5, no. 4, Sept.-Oct. 1974)

115. The Food and Agricultural Organization of the United Nations estimates that the minimum number of calories needed by a person doing active work is 2,200 a day. Before World War II, slightly less than half the people of the world ate that many. By 1955, the number of people receiving less than 2,200 calories a day had risen to 66 percent. There is simply no question that today as man as 10 to 20 million people are slowly starving. (Cf. Paul R. Ehrlich and Anne H. Ehrlich, *Population, Resources, Environment: Issues in Human Ecology,* San Francisco, 1970, p. 72; Raymond F. Dasmann, *Environmental Conservation,* New York, 1972, p. 155-159; and Georg Borgstrom, *Too Many,* New York, 1971, p. 316-340.)

116. Daily protein and calorie requirements are not being supplied to most areas of the world. Inequalities of distribution exist not only among regions, but also within regions. According to the UN Food and Agriculture Organizations, the areas of greatest shortage include the "Andean countries, the semi-arid stretches of Africa and the Near East, and some densely populated countries of Asia." (Cf. UN Food and Agriculture Organization, *Provisional Indicative World Plan for Agricultural Development,* Rome, 1970; and Donella H. Meadows and others, *The Limits to Growth,* Washington, 1972, p. 56-60, and Figure 8.)

117. For example: of the 3.3 billion world population in 1965, slightly more than 1 billion, or 31%, were in the developed countries and nearly 2.3 billion, or 69%, lived in the developing countries of Asia, South America, and Africa. As regards food supply, cereals are the predominant food grown in most of the developing countries, but these countries produced only 40% of the world cereal supply while the developed countries produced 60% of all the cereals in 1965. On a nutritional basis, the per capita cereal production in the developing countries averaged less than 0.2 tons this year, equivalent to 1,860 food calories per day, whereas in the developed countries, each person's share was more than 0.5 tons, equivalent to about 5,000 calories per day. (Cf. United Nations' population statistics and its Food and Agriculture Organization's production statistics for 1965. Cf. also Garret Hardin, "The Tragedy of the Commons," *Science,* v. 162, Dec. 13, 1968, p. 1243-1248; and the issue of "Feeding the World," *Science Journal,* v. 4, no. 5, May 1968.)

them have already been put under cultivation.[118] Opinions on how much good land is needed per capita for production of enough food and other uses vary from 2.5 to 1 acre.[119] If 2.5 acres are necessary, all the cultivated good land could support only 1.6 billion people, about the world total just before World War I; and even if one acre is enough, they could not support a population of more than 4 billion, about the world total reached in 1975.[120]

It is true that there still remains some potentially arable land. But how much? Estimates run from very little to some hundred percent of the land presently under cultivation.[121] A moderate opinion states

---

118. The earth's land surface is about 35,700,000,000 acres. It has been estimated that only 2.5 to 3 billion acres, or about 7 percent, have all the essentials necessary for food production and almost all of them are already under cultivation. In addition, drawn from the drier, colder, wetter, more rugged or less fertile lands are some 6 billion acres of pasture, which are generously weighed by some students as having 20 percent of the productivity of the crop land, making a total of about 4 billion acres of cultivated land, or its equivalent. (Cf. Frank A. Pearson and Floyd A. Harper, *The World Hunger,* Ithaca, N.Y., 1945, p. 41-42, 46-60, and Tables 16-18; and Joe R. Whitaker, "World Land Resources for Agriculture," in *The World Population and Future Resources,* ed. by Paul K. Hatt, New York, 1952, p. 76-77.)

119. Opinions in this vary, mainly because they are based on various nutritional standards and various productive powers of cropland, but also on various measurements of other uses of the cultivated land which not only has to produce enough food, but also has to provide clothes, houses, roads, power lines, etc. Dr. Hugh M. Bennett, Chief of the Soil Conservation Service of the U.S. Department of Agriculture, estimated that it takes, world over, an average of 2.5 acres to clothe a person and provide him with a minimum diet. (Cf. Charles L. Walker, *Man and Food,* Headline Series, no. 73, 1949, p. 17.) But some people have assumed that the 1970s' world average of about 1 acre per capita was enough for food and other necessary uses. (Cf. Donella H. Meadows and others, *The Limits to Growth,* Washington, 1972, p. 58-59; also J.H. Fremlin, "How Many People Can the World Support?" in *The World Population; Problems of Growth,* Toronto, 1972, p. 130-135.)

120. "Some day late this year, somewhere in the world, in some crowded city or some distant town, some woman will labor and bring forth a child. And yellow or black, brown or white or red, there will be four billion of us. Mankind has been around two million years or more. When Christ was born there were only 250 million humans on earth. By 1830 we counted our first billion. We doubled that by 1930. And by the end of this year we'll double again. Even trying not to, we will double again in some 35 years." (John Barbour, "Numbers Game: World Population is Doubling Again," *South Bend Tribune,* June 8, 1975, p. 16)

121. For instance, Dr. Hugh M. Bennett, Chief of the Soil Conservation Service of the U.S. Agriculture Department, stated that "there are no undiscovered reserves of productive land of any substantial area." (Quoted in C.L. Walker, *Man and Food,* Headline Series, no. 73, 1949, p. 17.) The FAO *Production Year-*

that it is possible to double the present acreage,[122] but wonders if it is feasible economically.[123] Furthermore, most of the potentially arable land is in tropical America and Africa[124] where particular difficulties

---

book for 1961, Table 1, reports about 350 million hectares (one hectare is equal to 2.2 acres) as "unused but potentially productive." This is about 25 percent of the 1,409 million hectares listed as arable and under crops. Walter H. Pawley, in FAO's *Possibilities of Increasing World Food Production,* Rome, 1963, p. 30-31, cites "reputable geographers" who have estimated the possibilities of increasing cultivated land as ranging from 35 percent to 300 percent.

Some experts believe that most of the potentially arable land, under today's economic and technological conditions, is already under cultivation. The more hopeful believe that between 2½ and 3 billion acres are currently under cultivation and that another 1½ billion acres that are more or less suitable for agriculture remain unused. This land will help in the short run, but it offers little hope for the longer future. (Cf. Paul R. Ehrlich and Anne H. Ehrlich, *Population, Resources, Environment: Issues in Human Ecology,* San Francisco, 1970, p. 91: and Raymond F. Dasmann, *Environmental Conservation,* New York, 1972, p. 131.)

122. "Undoubtedly the world's croplands can be increased somewhat. How much, however, is a moot question. Present surveys are not sufficiently complete or detailed to permit definitive evaluation. Some estimates suggest the possibility of doubling the present acreage. This would, of course, require the full application of modern techniques such as extensive use of fertilizers, drainage, irrigation, deep plowing, and surface shaping, and the use of improved breeds of crops." (Richard M. Highsmith, Jr., "Conservation," in the *Encyclopedia Americana,* 1973 ed., Vol. 7, p. 624)

123. "The primary resource necessary for producing food is land. Recent studies indicate that there are, at most, about 3.2 billion hectares of land (7.86 billion acres) potentially suitable for agriculture on the earth. Approximately half of that land, the richest, most accessible half, is under cultivation today. The remaining land will require immense capital inputs to reach, clear, irrigate, or fertilize before it is ready to produce food. Recent costs of developing new land have ranged from $215 to $5,275 per hectare. Average cost for opening land in unsettled areas has been $1,150 per hectare. According to an FAO report, opening more land to cultivation is not economically feasible, even given the pressing need for food in the world today." (Donella H. Meadows and others, *The Limits to Growth,* Washington, 1972, p. 58. Cf. *The World Food Problem,* by the President's Science Advisory Panel on the World Food Supply, Washington, 1967, Vol. 2, p. 423, 460-469.)

124. "In Southern Asia . . . in some countries in Eastern Asia, in the Near East and North Africa, and in certain parts of Latin America and Africa . . . there is almost no scope for expanding the arable area . . . In the dryer regions it will even be necessary to return to permanent pasture the land which is marginal or submarginal for cultivation. In most of Latin America and Africa south of the Sahara there are still considerable possibilities for expanding cultivated areas, but the costs of development are high and it will be often more economical to intensify utilization of the areas already settled." (UN Food and Agriculture Organization,

in cultivation have been noted.[125] Actually, elsewhere, various efforts have been made to increase cropland recently, but without significant success.[126]

Significant success, however, has been achieved in the increase in yields of the principal crops. In the decade of the 1950s, they rose about 25 percent for the whole world, with higher scores in Europe and Northern America,[127] owing to various new techniques.[128] Since then, more progress has been made by the Green Revolution in some

---

Provisional Indicative World Plan for Agricultural Development, Rome, 1970, Vol. 1, p. 41)

125. Most of the forests and grasslands not now under cultivation are in the tropics, and utilizing them for agriculture presents problems. When the forest is cut in the tropics, the torrential rainfalls wash away the topsoil and leach out the nutrients. What is often left are iron oxides which form a hard layer called laterite. Laterite is so much like stone that the ancient Khmer used it as the principal material for building the temple of Angkor Wat. Food cannot be grown on laterite. "Most of the soils of the tropical foreign country (Africa, the Amazon, etc.)," Dasmann writes, "cannot produce sustained yields of crops even with the best of treatment, since they do not hold or respond well to fertilizer. At best, they are adapted to the shifting cultivation that allows them decades to recover fertility under covers of natural vegetation." (Raymond F. Dasmann, *Environmental Conservation,* New York, 1972, p. 135. Cf. Kai Curry-Lindahl, *Conservation for Survival; an Ecological Strategy,* New York, 1972, p. 307.)

126. ". . . small areas of new cropland are being developed. The drainage of the Zuider Zee in the Netherlands is an example. The total cropland area, however, has not increased significantly, although there have been some efforts in recent years. The Soviet Union, for example, launched a massive program of grainland development in Kazakhstan during the 1950s and in a number of countries irrigation projects have added modest amounts of land to the cropland base. New developments contributing additional cropland acreage have been offset by shifts of land to other uses. And neither of the two countries with the most pressing food needs—India or China—has significant potential for increasing its croplands. The greatest potential for new croplands appears to be in the undeveloped regions of the humid tropics, such as the Amazon River basin." (Richard M. Highsmith, Jr., "Conservation," in the *Encyclopedia Americana,* 1973 ed., Vol. 7, p. 624)

127. The following table (percentage of increase in yields, 1960-61 over 1948-49 to 1952-53) shows the increase in yields for some of the principal crops as estimated by the FAO for the period of the 1950s. The average increase on a world

developing countries,[129] through the adoption of new high-yielding varieties of wheat and rice[130] with the assistance of various specializ-

---

basis was something like 25 percent for the decade, and about 33 percent in Europe and Northern America.

	World	Europe	Northern America
Wheat	22	25	42
Rye	29	20	53
Barley	31	45	11
Oats	19	21	23
Maize	29	80	37
Millet and Sorghum	43	a	107
Rice	24	-4	52
Potatoes	5	13	29
Sweet potatoes and yams	-3	a	53
Cotton	33	a	56

a—very small quantities produced.

(Source: FAO, *Production Yearbook 1961,* Tables 10A and 10B)

128. "It is now technically possible to lift the level of cropland capability and adaptability through such practices as fertilization, timeliness in cultivation, use of improved cultivation practices and equipment, terracing, land leveling, drainage, and irrigation. With such modern practices as selection of proper crops, contour farming, strip-cropping, and cover cropping, soil erosion can be held to acceptable levels. In most advanced countries such practices are now widely used." (Richard M. Highsmith, Jr., "Conservation," in the *Encyclopedia Americana,* 1973 ed., Vol. 7, p. 624)

129. "It is true that agricultural production in critical areas of Asia has recently made great progress. The Philippines have achieved self-sufficiency in rice for the first time in history in 1970 despite a galloping population increase. Malaysia and South Vietnam are predicting the same for 1971 and Indonesia for 1972. Similar trends are reported from Ceylon and Thailand. Pakistan claims it will shortly be self-sufficient in all cereals. West Pakistan is at present a net food grain exporter, and India became self-sufficient in 1971 with a food grain production of nearly 108 million tons. This is the so-called Green Revolution in Asia." (Kai Curry-Lindahl, *Conservation for Survival; an Ecological Strategy,* New York, 1972, p. 304)

130. "The new wheat and rice varieties have already made a profound impact on Indian and Pakistani agriculture. During the crop year of 1967-1968, India's harvest of food grains was 110 million tons, 40% higher than that of 1966-1967 and 13.2 million tons higher than it had ever been before. While most of this remarkable harvest must be credited to greatly improved weather conditions, at least 11 million tons resulted from the use of the new wheat and rice which were planted over millions of acres and heavily fertilized." (Roger Revelle, "The World Food Supply," in the *Encyclopedia Americana,* 1973 ed., Vol. 11, p. 509)

ed agencies.[131] But how far can the recent upward trend in the yields of crops go? This has been seriously questioned by experts.[132] The heavy use of chemical fertilizers and pesticides for the soil and crops[133] has also caused deep concern for the environment.[134] In this

---

131. Also of interest are the international agricultural research institutes. Eight institutes, such as the International Rice Research Institute in the Philippines and the International Maize and Wheat Improvement Center in Mexico, have been established. They have provided support for research, and extension and "outreach" programs in developing countries, and they have trained technical personnel from national institutions and conducted research at their own facilities in various parts of the world. These institutes are generally supported by the Rockefeller and Ford Foundations. (Cf. *Science and Technology in an Era of Interdependence,* by the UNA-USA National Policy Panel, New York, 1975, p. 50-51.)

132. The following statement is an example: "The 1970 Nobel Peace Prize winner, Norman Borlaug, claimed, in 1965, that 'man can feed the world's mushrooming human population for the next 100-200 years.' Four years later Borlaug shortened the time to 'two or three decades.' The biologists' skepticism about the agriculturists' proclamations of 'miracle grains' and their potential for feeding increasing populations of man for centuries or decades ahead seems well founded. The agricultural dream, or rather dogmatism, to eradicate hunger from our world does not seem to take ecological realities into account." (Kai Curry-Lindahl, *Conservation for Survival: an Ecological Strategy,* New York, 1972, p. 305. Cf. William C. Paddock, "Man: His Environment, His Future," a symposium at North Carolina State University, Raleigh, 1970.)

133. Hope ran high, but many experts remained skeptical. Dr. Ehrlich, for example, points out that the "Green Revolution" depends on enormous quantities of fertilizer, on efficient distribution systems, and on an educated farming population. Take fertilizer alone. The Netherlands uses 100 times the fertilizer used by India. If India were to use fertilizer at a comparable rate, it would require half the world's total production. Such use of fertilizer worldwide is not only almost incredibly unlikely, but, as we shall see, would bring staggering problems of pollution. The miracle grains are steps in the right direction, but nowhere near a final solution. (Cf. Paul R. Ehrlich and Anne H. Ehrlich, *Population, Resources, Environment: Issues in Human Ecology,* San Francisco, 1970, p. 96-97; and Georg Borgstrom, *Too Many; an Ecological Overview of Earth's Limitations,* New York, 1971, p. 36-86.)

134. "Biologically and ecologically the Green Revolution endangers man and his environment. It seems to require an enormous use of agricultural chemicals, an increase of 100 percent for fertilizers and of 600 percent for pesticides. It is easy to imagine and foresee the deleterious effect of this gigantic pollution on the environment, including human beings." (Kai Curry-Lindahl, *Conservation for Survival: an Ecological Strategy,* New York, 1972, p. 307)

135. World fertilizer consumption is increasing exponentially, with a doubling time of about 10 years. Total use is now five times greater than it was during World War II. (Cf. UN Department of Economic and Social Affairs, *Statistical Yearbook 1955, Statistical Yearbook 1960,* and *Statistical Yearbook 1970,* New

connection it is noticeable that the world consumption of fertilizers has increased five times since World War II,[135] and that the present pesticides are becoming more and more recognized as dangerous to all organisms in the long run, including human beings.[136]

Along with the increase of crop yields has been an improvement in food of animal products.[137] This has been achieved largely through a long period of experiments in the grades of domesticated animals,[138] with a remarkable increase in production, such as in the egg[139] and dairy industries.[140]

York, 1956, 1961, and 1971; also Donella H. Meadows and others, *The Limits to Growth,* Washington, 1972, p. 34 and Figure 2.)

136. "The use of pesticides in future agricultural development may also present serious problems. Present pesticides are increasingly becoming recognized as dangerous poisons with unpredictable and possibly catastrophic long-term effects on human beings and other organisms. Although new pesticides have been developed, they have not yet been adequately tested and may prove unsatisfactory." (Roger Revelle, "The World Food Supply," in the *Encyclopedia Americana,* 1973 ed., Vol. II, p. 510)

137. Trends in yields of crops, milk and eggs in the United Kingdom. For example:

Item	Pre-war average	3-year average 1960-63	% increase
Wheat	17-8 cwt/acre	31.3	76
Sugar beet	8-2 tons/acre	13.0	63
Potatoes	6-7 tons/acre	8.9	33
Milk	560 gall/cow	777	39
Eggs	149 eggs/hen	191	28

(I. Michael Lerner and H.P. Donald, *Modern Developments in Animal Breeding,* London, 1966, p. 17)

138. Modern experiments started a hundred years ago to improve the grades of domesticated animals. With each generation measurable progress has been achieved in all the developed countries. Through breeding and selection, improved types are secured; animals are brought to maturity earlier, by better utilization of nutrients; and the turnover is increased. In the case of cattle, the frame and flesh are being improved. The same holds for swine; both the lard-type and bacon-type hogs are brought to maturity earlier and the return of nutrients in the form of edible products is increased. A considerable number of the gains have been the result of cutting down the mortality in early life, thus increasing the turnover of the breeding stock. (Cf. Lewis Corey, *Meat and Man,* New York, 1950, p. 95-126; and I. Michael Lerner and H.P. Donald, *Modern Developments in Animal Breeding,* London, 1966, p. 28-40; and John Hammond, "The Pig as a Producer of Food," in the *Four Thousand Million Mouths,* ed. by F. Le Gros Clark and N.W. Pirie, London, 1951, p. 132-144.)

139. For instance, in the United Kingdom "between 1925 and 1940, the an-

It should be noted, however, that the merits owing to improvements in animal product foods are primarily in quality. Quantitatively, they could not alter the whole picture of the food supply very much, because, as noted earlier, animal products are largely a very expensive reproduction of plant food, principally crops, and the production of plant food is ultimately limited by the land.

Surely, there exists a kind of food which is not limited by the land. It is fish from the sea. Some believe that this resource could supply us with more than enough food, since fish is rich in protein[141] and the sea is immense in scope.[142] Actually, it is a resource mostly confined to areas of shallow water.[143] It has not contributed more

---

nual number of eggs per laying hen rose from 112 to 134, an increase of 1.5 eggs per year. By 1960 the number of eggs rose to 209, the rate of increase having speeded up to 3.75 eggs per year." (I. Michael Lerner and H.P. Donald, *Modern Developments in Animal Breeding,* London, 1966, p. 18)

140. It seems reasonable to predicate that the production and consumption of milk may everywhere be expected to increase. The important religions do not oppose the use of milk. With improvement of the herds in pastoral countries, incidental milk production tends to increase. The decline of animal husbandry on public ranges, with an increase in diversified agriculture, represents an expansion in the production of milk. Finally, improvements in the manufacture of butter, butter oil, cheese, condensed milk and dried milk gradually made practicable the utilization of the milk of animals in outlying regions. The importance of this trend of developments is enhanced by the fact that the milk cow is an efficient converter of feeding stuff into foodstuff. (Cf. I. Michael Lerner and H.P. Donald, *Modern Developments in Animal Breeding,* London, 1966, p. 18-19; and H.D. Kay, "Improving the Milk Supply," in the *Four Thousand Million Mouths,* ed. by F. Le Gros Clark and N.W. Pirie, London, 1951, p. 109-131.)

141. All fish, including shellfish, are rich in protein. For example: trout, haddock, smelt, scallops, lobster, and crab have protein contents of 18%. Tuna has a protein content of 25% and smoked herring, because it is partially dried, may have a protein content of nearly 37%. (Cf. Norman W. Desrosier, "Composition and Sources of Food," in the *Encyclopedia Americana,* 1973 ed., Vol. 11, p. 518)

142. The total area of the earth is 196,950,769 sq. miles, of which land surface is 57,469,928 sq. miles and water surface is 139,480,841 sq. miles (71% of the total area). (Cf. *Reader's Digest, Great World Atlas,* New York, 1963, p. 152.)

143. Fish, like man and other animals, live either directly or indirectly on plants. Since sunlight, which is indispensable to marine plants as well as to land plants, penetrates water only to about 600 feet, marine plants grow largely in the shallow waters near land. It is estimated that only about five percent of the oceans contains an abundance of plants. Another estimate shows that the shallow area of the oceans (probably no more than 200 feet deep) is less than 2,000,000,000 acres. This is why there are only a few areas in the oceans populated by large numbers of edible fish, easily caught. Even in the small areas of the oceans which have sufficient fish to make it worthwhile to attempt to catch them, yields are low. For instance, in the English Channel, which is one of the world's rich fishing spots, the

than one percent of the world food supply[144] and its future prospects remain unpromising.[145]

Recently, developments in chemistry have brought forth some new ideas in the hope of helping to find a solution to the food problem. One is to grow crops using the soilless technique of hydroponics.[146] Another is to produce synthetic foods extensively in factories remote from the farms,[147] and the most novel one is to convert petro-

---

catch has been estimated at only about five pounds per acre. Overfishing would result in a drop in both the daily catch and the size of the fish, as evidenced in the North Sea after World War I. (Cf. Frank A. Pearson and Floyd A. Harper, *The World Hunger*, Ithaca, N.Y., 1945, p. 63-65; and J.A. Gulland, "The Ocean Reservoir," *Science Journal*, May 1968, Vol. 4, no. 5.)

144. The world's harvest from the sea increased about 6% from about 1950 to the mid-1960s. In 1968, 60.5 million tons were harvested, less than one percent of total world food production. John H. Ryther of the Woods Hole Oceanographic Institute says that the maximum that can be hoped for is about 100 million tons. Others, however, believe that the total can be raised to 150 million tons. Unfortunately, neither figure offers much hope when the long-term needs are considered. (Cf. John H. Ryther, "Photosynthesis and Fish Production in the Sea," *Science*, Vol. 166, 1969; and UN Food and Agriculture Organization, *Possibilities of Increasing World Food Production*, Rome, 1963, p. 190.)

145. Some people criticize that "we are today harvesting the oceans by hunting, not by cultivation, in contrast to what we are doing on land. Could not mariculture or marine aquaculture, involving mollusks, crustaceans, and fish, be a zoologic parallel to botanic agriculture? Harold H. Webber (1968) has discussed this possibility and come to the conclusion that the immediate return from mariculture will probably contribute very little to relief from hunger for the undernourished peoples of the world. It is even unlikely that the calorie requirements of the hungry peoples can ever be met from the sea." (Kai Curry-Lindahl, *Conservation for Survival: an Ecological Strategy*, New York, 1972, p. 304-305)

146. Hydroponics is the practice of growing plants in liquid nutrient cultures rather than in soil. In hydroponic cultivation, plants may be grown directly in the nutrient solution or in sand or gravel to which the solution has been added. The particular nutrients used are chemical elements known to be essential for plant growth, and they are the same as those found in fertile soils. The yields of plants grown by hydroponics do not differ greatly from those achieved with plants grown in good soils. The nutritional quality of the plants and their requirements for water, air, and temperature are also about the same as for plants grown in soil. (Cf. Harold F. Hollis, *Profitable Growing Without Soil*, London, 1964.)

147. Generally speaking, synthetic foods are made through a process that makes textured foods from protein isolates. In making textured proteins, the protein of defatted soybeans or other protein-rich oilseeds is extracted by aqueous alkali under conditions that yield a solution containing 95% to 98% protein. Next, the concentrated protein solution is extruded through spinnerets into a coagulating bath to form fibers. The protein fibers are then combined with fat, supplementary nutrients, flavorings, coloring agents, and stabilizers, and heat is applied to bind

leum into a pure protein for all people of the world.[148] But thus far none of these ideas has proved to be very practical and really able to break through the limitation of the land.

Historically, the limitation of the land is nothing new. It has been a trouble since the very early time when our ancestors began to rely on the land for living, and has underlain all fightings for territory in history. But it was never as real and as serious a threat to mankind as it is today, not only because we are drawing close to the ultimate limit of the soil, but also, more importantly, because of the rapid drop in the ratio of arable land to people: about four acres per capita in 1800, one acre per capita in 1975, and probably a quarter of an acre per capita in the middle of the next century.[149] This rapid drop is primari-

---

the ingredients together. The finished product may resemble ham, chicken, fish, beef, fruit or other foods. (Cf. Magnus Pyke, "Synthetic Foods," *Science Journal,* May 1968, Vol. 4, no. 5.)

148. The idea comes from British Petroleum experiments that indicate that yeast can be grown on petroleum in the ratio of 2 tons of petroleum producing 1 ton of pure protein. A total of 160 million tons of petroleum would supply 9 billion people with 50 grams of protein a day. (Cf. Nigel Calder, *Eden Was No Garden,* New York, 1967, p. 147.)

149. The teeming billions of insects, animals, and humans who inhabit this globe depend ultimately upon a relatively few inches of soil, itself the highly complex product of geological, climatic, and biological factors. Mankind has to exist on the produce of less than 3 percent of the earth's total surface. In the early 1970s, the amount of arable land totaled one acre per person, a figure that could drop to about a quarter of an acre by the year 2070. This means that the average acre will then have to produce four times as much as it does now. (Cf. C.S. Cristian, "The Use and Abuse of Land and Water," in *The Population Crisis and the Use of World Resources,* ed. by Stuart Mudd, The Hague, 1964, p. 390-406; and Marion Clawson, "Land Resources," in *Environment, Resources, Pollution & Society,* ed. by William W. Murdoch, Stamford, Connecticut, 1972, p. 117-133.)

"In 1800, the world's supply of cropland per person was four times as great as it is today. In 2000, it will be about one-half of what it is today." (*World EQ Index,* Washington, 1972, p.8)

ly a consequence of the fast growth of the world population in
modern times.[150]

150. Estimates of world population, 1650 to 2000: (in millions)

Year	World total	Europe & USSR	Northern America	Oceania	Asia	Latin America	Africa
2000	6,130	880	354	31.9	3,458	638	768
1990	5,188	820	306	27.0	2,951	498	587
1980	4,330	757	262	22.6	2,461	378	449
1970	3,592	700	227	18.7	2,017	283	346
1960	3,008	640	200	16.5	1,685	211	255
1950	2,509	576	267	13.0	1,384	162	207
1940	2,249	573	146	11.3	1,212	131	176
1930	2,015	532	135	10.4	1,072	109	157
1920	1,811	487	117	8.8	966	91	141
1900	1,590	423	81	6	886	63	130
1850	1,131	274	26	2	698	33	98
1800	912	192	6	2	596	21	95
1750	711	144	1	2	456	10	98
1650	508	103	1	2	292	10	100

(Sources: Projections for 1970-2000 from the United Nations, *World Population
Prospects, Population Study* no. 4, 1966; data for 1920-1960 from the United Nations, *Demographic Yearbook,* 1953, Tables 2 and 3; 1961, Table 1. For the
1650-1900 statistics, cf. Warren S. Thompson, *Population Problems,* New York,
1965, p. 405-417. Cf. "The Growth of the World's Population," a brief history by
John D. Durand, projections by Louis B. Young and Robert C. Cook, in the
World's Population, Problems of Growth, ed. by Quentin H. Stanford, Toronto,
1972, p. 14-32.)

"Unless there is a sharp rise in mortality, which mankind will certainly strive
mightily to avoid, we can look forward to a world population of around 7 billion persons in 30 more years. And if we continue to succeed in lowering mortality with no
better success in lowering fertility than we have accomplished in the past, in 60 years
there will be four people in the world for every one person living today." (Donella H.
Meadows and others, *The Limits to Growth,* Washington, 1972, p. 44-45)

f.
Population

THE FAST GROWTH OF WORLD POPULATION IN MOD-
ern times is in sharp contrast to the slow development in the long
past.[151] With its accelerating rate,[152] the pace of this fast growth has

---

151. In 1650—a date that can be used to mark the dawn of the Industrial
Revolution—it is estimated that the world population was about 500 million persons. In the 320 years up to 1970, the world population increased sevenfold, to
nearly 3.6 billion. This phenomenal achievement is in sharp contrast to the situation that must have existed during the many thousands of years of man's existence
before this time. Estimates suggest that there were 200 to 300 million persons on
earth at the beginning of the Christian era, and during the first 16 centuries A.D.,
world population increased by about 250 million persons. This represents only a
doubling in 1,600 years. Back further, from the dawn of civilization at about
15,000—20,000 B.C. to the time of the Roman Empire, the rate of increase in
world population could have averaged at most about 1,000 persons per year. This
is the amount of growth in world population that takes place in approximately
eight minutes in the 1970s. (Cf. Donald J. Bogue, "Population," in the *Encyclopedia Americana,* 1973 ed., Vol. 22, p. 366-367; and M. King Hubbert,
Energy Resources, Washington, 1962, p. 16-18.)

152. What is more, there has been increase in the rate of increase itself. If we
take the figures from the beginning, we find the rise gradual until comparatively
recent times:

Period	Rate of Increase
5500 B.C.—3000 B.C.	0.04%
3000 B.C.— 850 B.C.	0.06
850 B.C.—1650 A.D.	0.07

Since the Renaissance, however, the rise in population has been more marked.
Consider, for example, the following figures, the first five of which come from
Professor Kirtley Mather, the last from the UN Statistical Office.

Period	Rate of Increase
1650-1750	0.29%
1750-1800	0.44
1800-1850	0.51
1850-1900	0.63
1900-1950	0.75
1937-1947	0.82

(Quoted from Julian Huxley, "Population and Human Destiny," *Harper's
Magazine,* Vol. 201, no. 1204, Sept. 1950.)

been described as "super exponential."[153] It may increase the population to four times greater than today by the middle of the next century,[154] and to much, much more later.[155] What a danger!

---

153. "In 1650 the population numbered about 0.5 billion, and it was growing at a rate of approximately 0.3 percent per year. That corresponds to a doubling time of nearly 250 years. In 1970 the population totaled 3.6 billion and the rate of growth was 2.1 percent per year. The doubling time at this growth rate is 33 years. Thus, not only has the population been growing exponentially, but the rate of growth has also been growing. We might say that population growth has been 'super' exponential." (Donella H. Meadows and others, *The Limits to Growth,* Washington, 1972, p. 41. Cf. A.M. Carr-Saunders, *World Population: Past Growth and Present Trends,* Oxford, 1936, p. 42; and the U.S. Agency for International Development, *Population Program Assistance,* Washington, 1970, p. 172.)

154. The most recent projections by UN experts estimate that there will be a world population of 6 to 7 billion persons by the year 2000, and that world population will still be growing at the rate of 1% per year, or faster, by the year 2000. According to these assumptions, the population in the year 2000 would be increasing at the rate of 1.5 billion persons every 10 years. Incredibly large additions may be expected during the 21st century. (Cf. United Nations, *World Population Prospects as Assessed in 1963,* New York, 1966, p. 13-15; Philip Hauser, "The Emergence of the Population Problem," in *Population Crisis,* ed., by Sue Titus Reid, London, 1972, p. 4-9; David M. Kieffer, "Population," *Chemical and Engineering News,* Oct. 7, 1968, p. 118-144; and Nathan Keyfitz, "The Numbers and Distribution of Mankind," in *Environment, Resources, Population, & Society,* ed. by William W. Murdoch, Stamford, Conn., 1972, p. 31-51.)

"The world's human population increases by six million per month. That's one metropolitan Chicago. That's almost four Californias per year. The Population Council has calculated that if zero population growth is achieved in the developed world by 2000 and in the developing world by 2040—an optimistic prediction—then the world's population will finally stabilize in about 2070—*with over four times as many people as live on the earth today.* Yet today that rate of six million per month is accelerating, not slowing." (R. Thomas Tanner, *Ecology, Environment and Education,* Lincoln, Nebr., 1974, p. 9)

155. Dr. Ehrlich believes that people will overcrowd the earth and that this will happen very, very soon. He offers convincing arguments that we will run out of food, that we will run out of space, that we will run out of resources, that we will run out of places to dump our wastes, that our wastes will so pollute the atmosphere, the water, the ocean, and the earth that the planet will soon become unliveable for all forms of life. (Cf. Paul R. Ehrlich and Anne H. Ehrlich, *Population, Resources, Environment: Issues in Human Ecology,* San Francisco, 1970, p. 1.)

If the rate of 35 years' doubling time stayed constant—stayed constant and did not increase at all—in 900 years the population of the earth would be 60 million billion people. Dr. Paul Ehrlich quotes a physicist who has calculated that such a population could be housed in a continuous 2,000 story building covering the entire planet. Air conditioning and other equipment would occupy the top 1,000 stories, and people would occupy the bottom 1,000, leaving 3 to 4 square yards of floor space per person ... The ultimate fantasy is that at the current growth rate it would be only a few thousand years, before the visible universe

Rapid population growth as a danger is nothing new either.[156] It is the basis on which the famous Malthusian theory is founded. This theory was simplified into a formula according to which food increases in an arithmetical ratio, whereas population increases in a geometric ratio.[157] If not taken literally, the tendency expounded by Malthus, viewed in the long run as a whole, is actually no less than a natural law.[158] Indeed, there have been some exceptional periods in

---

would be filled with people, and the mass of humans would be expanding at the speed of light. (Cf. Paul R. Ehrlich, *The Population Bomb,* New York, 1968; and Roger Hilsman, *The Crouching Future,* New York, 1975, p. 503.)

156. In the second edition (1803) of his *Essay on the Principle of Population, As it Affects the Future Improvement of Society* (the second edition of the essay has a subtitle: *A View of its Past and Present Effects on Human Happiness, with an Inquiry into Our Prospects Respecting the Future Removal or Mitigation of the Evils Which it Occasions),* Thomas Malthus noted early: "In the course of this inquiry I found that . . . The poverty and misery arising from a too rapid increase of population had been distinctly seen, and the most violent remedies proposed so long ago as the times of Plato and Aristotle. And of late years the subject has been treated in such a manner by some of the French Economists, occasionally Montesquieu, and, among our own writers, by Dr. Franklin, Sir James Stewart, Mr. Arthur Young, and Mr. Townsend, as to create a natural surprise that it had not excited more of the public attention." (Cf. Charles E. Stangeland, *Pre-Malthusian Doctrine of Population,* New York, 1904.)

157. The substance of Malthus' theory was that man's propensity to increase his numbers would surpass, in the course of successive generations, the world's ability to produce more and more food. He claimed, and of course supplied many facts and figures to back his contention, that population tends to increase at a geometric ratio while the food supply cannot possibly increase at more than an arithmetic ratio. "Isn't it obvious," Malthus asked in effect, "that before long there will be too many people, not enough food, and increasing misery and hardship as a result for the sons of man?" (Thomas Robert Malthus' theory expressed in his *An Essay on the Principle of Population, As it Affects the Future Improvement of Society,* first edition published in 1798. Cf. especially chaps. 1 and 2.)

158. Malthus' formula that food increases in an arithmetic ratio, whereas population increases in a geometric ratio has been seriously questioned, but it is generally admitted that unless a people can make food production keep pace with the natural increase in numbers, the death rate will rise until a balance is reached. This is why in history poverty and misery were the common lot of most of mankind. Some people were hungry all the time, and most people were hungry some of the time. For instance, Cornelius Walford in his "The Famines of the World: Past and Present," *Journal of the Royal Statistical Society,* Vol. 41, 1878, p. 433-526, listed 201 famines which occurred in the British Isles between A.D. 10 and 1846, and 31 in India between 1769 and 1878. Walter H. Mallory in his *China: Land of Famine,* New York, 1926, p. 1, referred to a study made by students at the University of Nanking listing 1,828 famines in China between 108 B.C. and A.D. 1911. "The worst famine in China in the past century appears to have been that which occurred as the result of a great drought in the northwest in the years 1876 to

some regions when the fast growth of the population presented no danger because food production was able to keep pace with it. Perhaps the greatest of such periods in history was the last two centuries, in which the population has almost trebled without notable food shortages. This situation has prompted some contemporaries to scorn Malthus' theory as an intellectual curiosity.[159] Obviously, they have overlooked the fact that the extra food supply in this period

---

1879. The area affected included about 300,000 square miles (about the area of New England, the Middle Atlantic States, Ohio, Indiana, and Illinois). Somewhere between 9 and 13 million people are supposed to have perished from hunger and the disease and violence accompanying prolonged famine. What the population was at this time is not known, but possibly as many as one-fifth of the people died.... The story is much the same for India as for China. Droughts are common, and almost every year some region suffers more or less from the shortage of food. In 1769 to 1779 there was a great famine in Bengal, which is said to have carried off one-third of the total population, or about 10 million people." (Warren S. Thompson and David T. Lewis, *Population Problems,* 5th ed., New York, 1965, p. 390-391) As regards diseases, we may cite only the Black Death (1348-1350 in Europe) as an example. According to J.F.K. Hecker in his *The Epidemics of the Middle Age,* London, 1844, p. 22-24, all Europe was devastated. London is supposed to have lost 100,000; Venice, 100,000; Florence, 60,000; and Paris, 50,000. The populations of these cities at that time are not known, but it is not at all unlikely that nearly one-half or even more of their people perished within a period of several months. For the entire continent, it is quite generally believed that not less than one-fourth of the people and quite possibly one-third perished during this epidemic. The loss may very well have amounted to 25 to 35 million.

Malthus' theory is true for the food-gathering and fishing-hunting lives of the primitive societies, too. A hunting people cannot kill an excess of game without facing starvation. The Eskimo, for example, live on a close margin. As Rasmussen says of them: "Life is thus an almost uninterrupted struggle for bare existence, and periods of dearth and actual starvation are not infrequent. Three years before my visit, eighteen people died of starvation at Simpson Strait. The year before, seven died of hunger north of Cape Britannia. Twenty-five is not a great number perhaps, but out of a total of 259 it makes a terrible percentage for death by starvation alone. And yet this may happen any winter, when there are no caribou to be had." (Knud Rasmussen, *Across Arctic America,* New York, 1927, p. 223)

159. The world population increased from about 550 million in 1700 to about 1,600 million in 1900, but the food supply has not shown a notable shortage. On the contrary, in some regions, people have eaten much better than before, and there have sometimes even appeared food surpluses. For this reason, some writers have concluded that Malthus' theory was sound only in history; it has become an intellectual curiosity in our era. And some of them have even gone so far as to say that Malthus' theory will never be realized in our future. These writers have apparently not examined the whole situation from the viewpoint of the long run, and have been distracted on a temporary and regional development of food and population. (Cf. Warren S. Thomson, *Population Problems,* New York, 1965, p. 28-31.)

resulted from a big unprecedented coincidence: the exploitation of the vast virgin soils after the discovery of the New World and the rapid advance in agricultural techniques along with the Industrial Revolution.[160] Since this coincidence passed away, the Malthusian theory has reemerged even clearer and stronger for today than for the past.

Associated with the Malthusian theory is the formula of Ricardo, according to which, food production is generally limited by the law of diminishing returns by the land on the one hand, and by the level of agricultural techniques on the other.[161] What we are facing now is not just a situation of relatively diminishing returns from the land, but the reality of absolutely not having enough land itself in the very

---

160. Soon after the western Hemisphere and Oceania were opened up, immigrants flowed to these new lands and relieved somewhat the pressure of the population on the food supply of the old world, especially Europe. And soon these immigrants produced increasing amounts of food by exploiting the virgin soils and changing the hunting grounds of the native people into agricultural use. It was a great event in our history, and most significantly, it was accompanied by the invention and improvement of agricultural instruments and methods, such as the reaper, binder, thresher, tractor, gang-plow, reaping and threshing combine, scientific fertilization, and many ways of storing and preserving food. These new instruments and methods of agriculture have played a great role in helping the farmers to exploit the new lands, and in the old world they have also made a certain contribution to the increase of food production. As a result, mankind experienced an exceptional period in which the increase of food supply could keep pace with, and in some case even surpass, the rapid growth of population. But this situation resulted from a great coincidence: the exploitation of the vast virgin soils after the discovery of the New World and the rapid advance in agricultural techniques which were part of the Industrial Revolution. This was a coincidence we never had before. It began to draw to a close about 1900, and will probably never reoccur in the future. (Cf. Warren S. Thompson, *Population Problems,* New York, 1965, p. 402-405.)

Thomas Malthus had "recognized that during the expansion into new lands such as those of the United States, subsistence could increase at a very rapid rate and, like population, could double in about 25 years." (Warren S. Thompson and David T. Lewis, *Population Problems,* 5th ed., New York, 1965, p. 26. Cf. Malthus' first *Essay,* first published in 1798, p. 101-113.)

161. Considering the relation of food resources to population, we face the so-called law of diminishing returns. This proposition came into prominence in the early 19th century and is commonly associated with the names of David Ricardo and Thomas Malthus. Revised by John Stuart Mill, it was later stated by Alfred Marshall as follows: "Whatever may be the future development of the arts of agriculture, a continued increase in the application of capital and labour to land must ultimately result in a diminution of the extra produce which can be obtained by a given extra amount of capital and labour." (Alfred Marshall, *Principles of Economics,* London, 1920, p. 153)

near future.[162] Meanwhile, in spite of the significant contributions made by progress in agricultural techniques over the last decades, food production per capita in many countries is barely holding constant at an inadequate level.[163] Hence, the fast growth of population today is not just a danger, as envisaged by Malthus: it is a crisis.

It is a crisis, the so-called "population crisis,"[164] and its explosion is as horrible as that of nuclear bombs.[165]

---

162. "By now it should be clear that all of these trade-offs arise from one simple fact—the earth is finite. The closer any human activity comes to the limit of the earth's ability to support that activity, the more apparent and unresolvable the trade-offs become. When there is plenty of unused arable land, there can be more people and also more food per person. When all the land is already used, the trade-off between more people or more food per person becomes a choice between absolutes." (Donella H. Meadows and others, *The Limits to Growth,* Washington, 1972, p. 93-94)

163. No one knows exactly how many of the world's people are inadequately nourished today, there is general agreement that the number is large—perhaps 50 to 60 percent of the population of the less industrialized countries, which means one-third of the population of the world. Estimates by the UN Food and Agriculture Organization indicate that in most of the developing countries basic caloric requirements, and particularly protein requirements, are not being supplied. Furthermore, although total world agricultural production is increasingly remarkable, food per capita in the nonindustrialized countries is barely holding constant at an inadequate level. (Cf. UN Food and Agriculture Organization, *Provisional Indicative World Plan for Agricultural Development,* Rome, 1970; and *The State of Food and Agriculture 1970,* Rome, 1970. Cf. also *The World Food Problem,* by the President's Science Advisory Panel on the World Food Supply, Washington, 1967, Vol. 2, p. 5, and John Barbour, "Numbers Game: World Population is Doubling Again," *South Bend Tribune,* June 8, 1975, p. 16.)

164. A number of books or articles are entitled "population crisis," such as *Population Crisis; an Interdisciplinary Perspective,* ed. by Sue Titus Reid and David L. Lyon, London, 1972. In addition, "colorful expressions, such as 'population explosion,' 'population bomb,' and 'demographic doom,' are often used to dramatize the immediacy and seriousness of the population crisis. The gravity of this crisis, as a cause of impending mass misery, as a threat to world peace, and as a major obstacle in the path of worldwide efforts to raise levels of living, has been acknowledged by large and influential national and international organizations.... The United Nations has declared the population crisis to rank equally in importance with the problems of world peace, peaceful control of atomic energy, and human rights." (Donald J. Bogue, "The World Population Crisis," in the *Encyclopedia Americana,* 1973 ed., Vol. 22, p. 365)

165. "A prospect even more horrifying than the hydrogen bomb faces the world today—the prospect that man may continue to reproduce at such a high rate that he will scrape the last crumb of food from the surface of the earth," writes Dr. C.P. Idyll in his recently published book, *The Sea Against Hunger.* (Reported by Howard Benedict, AP correspondent, *South Bend Tribune,* May 9, 1971, p. 14.)

Through a wide observation, Malthus found two kinds of checks to the tendency of population to outrun its food supply. One is positive: war, pestilence and starvation. The other is negative: moral restraint, resulting in a limit set to the birth rate.[166] The positive check always prevails,[167] and in addition to it, there is one more

"Collision Course"; deadly double threats to mankind: (*South Bend Tribune,* Jan. 29, 1966, p. 4)

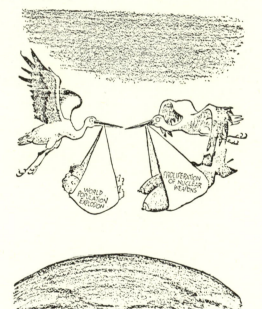

166. In the second edition (1803) of his *Essay on the Principle of Population, As it Affects the Future Improvement of Society,* Thomas Malthus added the idea that besides infant disease, plague, famine, and war—called "positive checks— there were "negative" checks as well. The negative checks consisted of voluntary action such as late marriages, sexual restraint in marriage, and the regulation of further population growth. (Cf. *Everyman's Library,* ed., Vol. 1, p. 315.)

167. Malthus was thinking about England and Europe as well as Asia when he wrote, in 1789, in his *An Essay on the Principle of Population, As it Affects the Future Improvement of Society:* "The power of population is so superior to the power in the earth to produce subsistence for man that premature death must in some shape or other visit the human race.... Sickly seasons, epidemics, pestilence, and the plague advance in terrific array and sweep off their thousands and ten thousands. Should success be still incomplete, gigantic inevitable famine

violent check not specified by Malthus. It is infanticide, which seems to have been a general practice with all peoples in primitive times.

The positive checks have been described as the "death solution" to the population crisis.[169] Actually, they are our enemies. We have fought against them all the time, and the elimination of them has been the primary objective of civilization. Our success in the fighting has been regarded as "progress" and "improvement" and has had a great deal to do with the fast growth of population in modern times, such as the significant reduction of mortality[170] through new medi-

---

stalks in the rear, and with one mighty blow levels the population with the food of the world." (Quoted in "Foods," in the *Encyclopedia Americana,* 1973 ed., Vol. 11, p. 506-507. Cf. Alexander Alland, Jr., "War and Disease: An Anthropological Perspective," in *Population Crisis: An Interdisciplinary Perspective,* ed. by Sue Titus Reid and David L. Lyon, Glenview, Ill., 1972, p. 44-49.)

"When all the world is overcharged with inhabitants, then the last remedy of all is war, which provides for every man, by victory or death." (Thomas Hobbes, *The English Works of Thomas Hobbes of Malmesbury,* ed. by Sir William Molesworth, London, 1839-1845, Vol. 3, p. 335)

168. "Infanticide seems to have been general with all peoples, except a few modern nations. It is, in fact, the method most easily administered by primitive man. Recalling that the primitive woman must carry and nurse the child for several years, the birth of a second within a year or two of the first, would create a difficult situation, the probable result of which would be death to one or more of the trio." (Clark Wissler, *An Introduction to Social Anthropology,* New York, 1929, p. 40. Cf. Mary Douglas, "Population Control in Primitive Groups," in *Population Crisis, an Interdisciplinary Perspective,* ed. by Sue Titus Reid and David L. Lyon, London, 1972, p. 49-55.)

169. "We tend to talk about a life solution or a death solution," says Peter Cott, Executive Director of the Population Institute, which operates with foundation grants. "The death solution will take care of itself, and we'll starve a lot of people to death before we get around to bringing it into balance. We'll probably have enough wars and enough collapsing governments to take care of the death part." ("Enough collapsing governments," John Barbour, "Numbers Game: World Population Is Doubling Again," *South Bend Tribune,* June 8, 1975, p. 16)

"The most important problem facing human beings today is the problem of atomic war or, in biological terms, the problem of extinction. Ironically, the next most important problem is the problem of overpopulation. These two problems are clearly interrelated. Failure to solve the first constitutes a solution for the second. However, this solution is clearly unacceptable." (Clement L. Markert, "Biological Limits on Population Growth," *BioScience,* Vol. 16, no. 12, Dec., 1966, p. 859)

170. "Demographers estimate that in the middle of the 17th century, the average newborn infant could expect an average of only 25 years of life. About 40% of all infants died before their first birthday. By 1970 the life expectancies in most nations of Europe and northern America were nearly three times this

cines and effective health techniques,[171] notable even in some developing countries.[172] Now, if we let the "death solution" take care of the
population crisis, we would have to forsake all the recent "progress"
and "improvement," to abandon the primary objective of civilization, and to surrender to our enemies unconditionally. If not, we

---

figure." (Donald J. Bogue, "The World Population Crisis," in the *Encyclopedia Americana,* 1973 ed., Vol. 22, p. 365)

"Before the industrial revolution both fertility and mortality were comparatively high and irregular. The birth rate generally exceeded the death rate only
slightly, the population grew exponentially, but at a very slow and uneven rate. In
1650, the average lifetime of most populations in the world was only about 30
years. Since then, mankind has developed many practices that have had profound
effects on the population growth system, especially on mortality rates. With the
spread of modern medicine, public health techniques, and new methods of growing and distributing foods, death rates have fallen around the world. World
average life expectancy is currently about 53 years and still rising." (Donella H.
Meadows and others, *The Limits to Growth,* Washington, 1972, p. 44. Cf. *World
Population Data Sheet,* by the Population Reference Bureau, Washington, 1968.)

The Euro-American expectation of life at birth since the 16th century, as thus
approximated, has changed as follows:

Year	Expectation of life in years	Year	Expectation of life in years
1550	21.0	1855	40.0
1650	26.0	1865	40.8
1750	34.0	1875	42.0
1805	36.8	1885	44.4
1815	37.3	1895	47.0
1825	38.3	1905	50.7
1835	39.2	1915	54.5
1845	39.9	1925	55.6

(Hornell N. Hart, *The Technique of Social Progress,* New York, 1931, p. 491)

171. "Louis Pasteur of France developed the germ theory of disease. Joseph
Lister of England carried out pioneering studies of infections and antiseptics.
Robert Koch of Germany made early findings of specific agents causing diseases,
which led in time to the production of immunizing substances. Many others participated in the early stages, and the expansion, of modern scientific medicine.
Subsequent developments have now spread around the world. They include better
obstetrical and child care, the use of vaccines and antitoxins, and the discovery of
insulin, sulfa drugs, penicillin, and other antibiotics. Increased specialization and
the allocation of greater resources to research have made possible an acceleration
of progress in the medical sciences. One area of inquiry and application has been
that of public health, directed mainly toward the prevention of common
diseases." (Y.C. James Yen and others, *Rural Reconstruction and Development,*
Silang, Cavite, Philippines, 1967, p. 8)

have only one way out of the big crisis: from birth control to the population control implied in the Malthusian theory as negative checks.

Birth control is essential to check the population growth. Various methods have been applied to achieve it. The old but not very reliable one is periodic abstinence.[173] Gradually gaining ground are contraceptives.[174] Most effective is sterilization,[175] and abortion has been widely practiced.[176]

---

172. "One among many illustrations that might be cited is that of Ceylon, where international public health programs have almost eradicated malaria and notably reduced deaths from other causes. Deaths per thousand of population dropped from 20 in 1950 to 11 in 1955. Such a drastic decline in the death rate was achieved in Europe only over a period of centuries. With this sharp reduction in deaths, and with no corresponding decline in the birth rate, Ceylon's population increased in ten years from about 7 million to nearly 10 million. By 1980, it may reach 20 million." (Y.C. James Yen and others, *Rural Reconstruction and Development,* Silang, Cavite, Philippines, 1967, p. 8-9)

173. "Periodic abstinence, better known as the rhythm method of contraception, is based on the fact that the human female is fertile only during a period of at most four days during each menstrual cycle. The fertilizable lifespan of the sperm in the female reproductive tract is not more than three days, and the lifespan of the released egg is not more than one day. This four-day fertile period occurs near the middle of the typical 28-day cycle and is linked specifically to the time of ovulation. If the menstrual cycle were of constant and predictable length, the fertile period could be estimated with reasonable accuracy because ovulation occurs about 13 to 15 days before the next expected menses." (Roy O. Greep, "Population Control," in the *Encyclopedia Americana,* 1973 ed., Vol. 22, p. 369e-f)

174. "Since the 1920's, increasing use has been made of the diaphragm and the various spermicidal preparations for vaginal application. In the 1960s, two new contraceptives were introduced—the oral contraceptives (popularly known as "the pill") and the intrauterine devices (IUD). It is estimated that by 1970, 18 million women were using oral contraceptives." (Roy O. Greep, "Population Control," in the *Encyclopedia Americana,* 1973 ed., Vol. 22, p. 369e)

"Some day a woman may be able to obtain at a drug store vaginal suppositories that excite the uterus in early pregnancy, making it convulse somewhat—resulting in expulsion of contents. That's non-surgical abortion," and has been tested with great success by New York University doctors recently, as reported by Patricia McCormack, "Non-surgical Abortion May Take Place in Future," in the *South Bend Tribune,* Nov. 20, 1980, p. 11.

175. "Sterilization as a fertility control measure generally involves only the surgical interruption of the sperm duct (vas deferens) in the man or of the oviduct in the woman. In a man this operation is known as a vasectomy, and in a woman it is called a tubectomy. Vasectomy is a much simpler and faster operation than tubectomy and is practiced on a much larger scale.... It has been practiced as a major population control measure in India, where it is advocated for men who have fathered three or more children." (Roy O. Greep, "Population Control," in the *Encyclopedia Americana,* 1973 ed., Vol. 22, p. 369f)

Population control is a step further in the same direction.[177] It tries to intensify birth control with various measures in order to attain zero population growth as its immediate goal.[178] These measures include family planning,[179] incentive and disincentive programs,[180] and medical and technical assistance.[181]

---

176. "Abortion is undoubtedly the most widely practiced means of birth control. Laws restricting the practice of abortion have already been repealed or liberalized in England, Japan, most of the eastern European nations, and in some parts of the United States. However, these areas represent only a small fraction of the total population. Elsewhere, even in areas where abortions are illegal, they are practiced on a vast scale. The number of abortions performed throughout the world each year is estimated at 30 to 40 million, roughly half the number of live births. In 1947, Japan introduced the first and most noted example of an effective program of easily available abortions as a population control measure. Within 10 years, the birthrate there was cut by nearly 50%. In those countries where abortions can be had upon request, as in Poland and Hungary, the number of abortions approximates and occasionally exceeds the number of live births." (Roy O. Greep, "Population Control," in the *Encyclopedia Americana*, 1973 ed., Vol. 22, p. 369e)

177. "Therefore man cannot escape from his obligation to institute population control. It must be based on a careful population planning—something quite different from family planning. Ecologists, in cooperation with sociologists and economists, must take the leadership in this task. Irrational, short-term solutions are to be avoided. The goal must be a birth rate that does not exceed the death rate." (Kai Curry-Lindahl, *Conservation for Survival: an Ecological Strategy*, New York, 1972, p. 308. Cf. "Population Control," in *The World Population; Problems of Growth*, ed. by Quentin H. Stanford, Toronto, 1972, p. 206-210.)

178. Zero population growth generally means that the number of births equals the number of deaths. But to Robert Avedon, president of the privately funded Population Reference Bureau, and to his research doctor, Leon Bouvier, zero population growth is when the population's fertile age group is in balance with the rest of the population, thereby defusing the population "bomb." (John Barbour, "Numbers Game: World Population Is Doubling Again," *South Bend Tribune*, June 8, 1975, p. 16)

179. Family planning tries to urge and help a family not to have more than two children, born at intervals that will protect the mother's health and make it more possible for each family to provide a healthy upbringing and a good start in life for the child. It is sponsored by the International Planned Parenthood Federation with such slogans as: "Whatever your cause, it is a lost cause if we cannot limit our population." (Quoted by Kai Curry-Lindahl, *Conservation for Survival: an Ecological Strategy*, New York, 1972, p. 308. Cf. Alice Taylor Day, "Parenthood: Its New Responsibilities," in the *Population Crisis, an Interdisciplinary Perspective*, ed. by Sue Titus Reid and David L. Lyon, London, 1972, p. 173-176.)

180. "For example, China's newest weapons in the war on population growth are bonuses to one-child couples and a 'baby tax' on couples producing a third child. The tax on big families consists of wage reductions ranging from 5 percent to 10 percent for the birth of a third child to 20 percent when baby no. 5 shows up, the *International Family Planning Perspectives* magazine said Sunday.

Also favoring population control are certain developments in modern society, such as: the great progress made in reducing infant mortality which has largely eliminated the traditional need for having more children to insure the narrow survival to adulthood; the increase in the need of mobility for jobs and the dependence of income on wages have made the small size family much more desirable; and the advantages in taking care of fewer children well and in educating them better have been recognized by intellectual parents.[182]

Economic rewards and punishments for childbearing are part of the plan by the world's most populous nation to reach zero population growth by the year 2,000. The Chinese now number 960 million. The economic 'incentive and disincentive' system—now in effect in nine of China's provinces—is expected to go country-wide when a gutsy new birth planning law goes into effect at year's end.'' (Reported by Patricia McCormack, UPI Health Editor, *South Bend Tribune,* Nov. 19, 1979, p. 13. Cf. Georges Tapinos and Phyllis T. Piotrow, *Six Billion People; Demographic Dilemmas and World Politics,* New York, 1978, p. 51-58, 112, the Tables.)

181. The United Nations has undertaken to offer assistance in population control. The International Planned Parenthood Federation provides family planning services, and the World Health Organization lends assistance in the biomedical and public health aspects of family planning and the study of reproduction. Many other public organizations, as well as private foundations, contribute substantial support to family planning programs and research in the fields of reproduction and sexual biology. For instance, "In its 10 years, AID has spent about $750 million on population control ... has distributed 345 million monthly cycles of birth control pills, at 15 cents a cycle, almost a billion condoms and over six million IUDs.'' (John Barbour, "Numbers Game: World Population Is Doubling Again,'' *South Bend Tribune,* June 8, 1975, p. 16)

182. It is interesting to note that all these developments are more or less related to industrialization. Although there are some exceptions, in most cases, industrialization has resulted in a great decrease of population growth. This is what has happened in modern urban-industrial civilization, notably in Ireland, France, Sweden, Norway, Denmark, the Netherlands, etc., where the growth of population has not been restricted by subsistence but rather by the desire for leisure, education, advancement, and material goods. (Cf. Robert R. Kuczynski, *The Balance of Births and Deaths,* New York, 1928-1931, Vol. I, p. 1-62; and Alan B. Mountjoy, "Industrialization—The Panacea?'' in *The World Population; Problems of Growth,* ed. by Quentin H. Stanford, Toronto, 1972, p. 242-255.)

"Most couples in the Russian Republic, which makes up 75 per cent of the Soviet Union and has over half of its 246 million citizens, limit themselves to one child. 'My husband wanted to have three children, but I told him he'd have to shoot me first,' Mrs. G. Alexandrova wrote in the latest issue of the weekly newspaper, *Literary Gazette,* ... Russians today are enjoying a material well-being unheard of 20 years ago. They are loath to spend their wages on kids when clothes, washing machines, refrigerators and cars are beginning to appear on the market in modest quantities. N. Koltsov of Leningrad wrote that a one-child fami-

Furthermore, since the 1960s, there has been a remarkable increase in awareness concerning population control among prominent leaders and governments,[183] and a noticeable lessening of resistance, on cultural or religious grounds, to birth control.[184] This tendency is more significant and encouraging if compared with some perverse at-

---

ly means 'the good life at home, good food, fashionable clothes for my wife and vacation trips to the Black Sea.' " (AP report, *South Bend Tribune,* Nov. 19, 1972, p. 8) This is in sharp contrast to the situation of twenty years ago when Russian women were interested in being mother heroines. "Thirty-five thousand Russian women are wearing on their bosoms the jeweled and enameled insignia of 'Mother Heroine of the Soviet Union,' showing that they are the mothers of 11 or more children. More than 3,500,000 wear one or the other of the various classes of the order 'Glory of Motherhood,' awarded in its various degrees to mothers of between five and 11 children." (Reported by the North American Newspaper Alliance, *Evening World Herald,* Omaha, March 18, 1952, p. 3.)

183. This awareness is signified by the various resolutions of the General Assembly of the United Nations, such as: Population Growth and Economic Development of 1962 and of 1966, and World Population Year of 1970; and by the Declaration of the United Nations Conference on the Human Environment of 1972; and the United Nations Declaration of Population Strategy for Development of 1972. (Cf. *The United Nations and Population; Major Resolutions and Instruments,* published in cooperation with the United Nations Fund for Population Activities, by Ocean Publications, Dobbs Ferry, New York, 1974.)

It is that particular awareness—a political awareness—that is changing the fertility scene, many experts believe. "Mexico has done a tremendous turnaround," says the Population Reference Bureau's Robert Avedon. "When the new government of Luis Echeverria came in in 1970, his hue and cry was 'More Mexicans.' But . . . in 1972, the president went on national television and called on the nation to exercise 'responsible family planning.' And somehow he evoked a pastoral letter from 80 Mexican bishops of all Christian faiths saying at least that they did not disagree." (John Barbour, "Numbers Game: World Population Is Doubling Again," *South Bend Tribune,* June 8, 1975, p. 16)

184. "Birth-control efforts have generally lagged in Latin America. This area, with a total population of about 250 million, has the highest rate of population growth in the world, about 2.8% a year (the world average is about 2%). According to the Population Council, Latin America has resisted birth control 'in part because of the predominantly Catholic religion and in part because of the countries' traditional image of themselves as underpopulated, with large areas capable of new settlement.' There are signs this situation may be changing, however. Government-supported family-planning campaigns have been launched in Chile, Honduras, Venezuela, Peru and Jamaica. In Colombia a nongovernmental birth-control drive has started." "In Africa the United Arab Republic, Tunisia and Kenya are pressing birth-control programs." (Alfred L. Malabre Jr., *Wall Street Journal,* Dec. 6, 1966, p. 18)

"Italy is 97 percent Roman Catholic, but the Vatican's influenced apparently doesn't reach inside the polling booth where Italians voted 2-1 to keep a liberal abortion law. . . . The law, in effect the past three years, permits women over 18

titudes[185] and pessimistic opinions[186] on population control in earlier decades.

There is also some good news: the age at first marriage has tended to be up;[187] the number of voluntary sterilizations has been increas-

---

free abortions in state hospitals during the first 90 days of pregnancy." (AP report in the *South Bend Tribune,* May 19, 1981, p. 5)

185. Some nations considered the source of cannon fodder more important than food supply. They regarded the big populations of their neighbors as a serious threat, and set up a policy to increase their own population. They urged their people to prove their patriotism by producing more children, and gave awards and financial assistance to the mothers who successfully raised large families. One of Mussolini's statements of 1927 to the Chamber of Deputies, for example, stated that "I affirm that the fundamental, if not the absolutely essential datum for the political, and therefore the economic and moral power of nations is their ability to increase their population. Let us speak quite clearly. What are 40,000,000 Italians compared to 90,000,000 Germans, and 200,000,000 Slavs? Let us turn toward the west. What are 40,000,000 Italians compared to 46,000,000 Englishmen plus 450,000,000 who live in England's colonies? Gentlemen, if Italy is to amount to anything, it must enter into the second half of this century with a population of at least 60,000,000 inhabitants ... If we decrease in numbers, gentlemen, we will never create an empire but become a colony." (Quoted in Warren S. Thompson, *Danger Spots in World Population,* New York, 1929, p. 228.) Article 122 of the Soviet Union provides state aid to mothers of large families and unmarried mothers. It was reported that Soviet Union subsidies to mothers in 1951 totalled six billion rubles, equivalent to 1,500 million U.S. dollars. Russian mothers of 10 or more children have been granted the honor of "Mother Heroine," and of five or more children, "Glorious Motherhood," etc. (*Evening World Herald,* Omaha, March 3, 1952)

186. The opinion that population stabilization is impossible has been expressed forcefully by Sir Charles Galton Darwin in his stimulating and highly provocative book entitled *The Next Million Years,* New York, 1953. He argues that any nation which limits its population becomes less numerous than nations which do not limit their populations. The former will then sooner or later be crowded out of existence by the latter. Therefore, it would be very difficult to reach any international agreement in establishing limits to the numbers admissible for the various populations, and extremely difficult to enforce such an agreement if it were ever reached. (Cf. Harrison Brown, *The Challenge of Man's Future,* New York, 1954, p. 259-260.)

187. For example, in the United States, "The median age at first marriage in 1960 was 22.8 for males and 20.3 for females. In 1969 the median age for males had risen to 23.2; and for females, 20.8. Thus, within the 1960s the trend toward early marriage has been reversed, and marriage occurred half a year later than it did a decade earlier. Unusually low rates of marriage in the late 1960s indicate that this trend will continue." (Donald J. Bogue, "Population Composition," in the *Encyclopedia Americana,* 1973 ed., Vol. 22, p. 369b) In China, there has been a rule requiring a male to be at least 27 years old and a female to be 23 to qualify for marriage.

ing;[188] some countries have stabilized their population;[189] and finally, the growth rate of the population the world over has been slowing down.[190]

Despite these encouraging signs, however, the population crisis is far from over.[191] The effort required to avert it has just begun. We have to do much more and to work much harder in order to attain as soon as possible the immediate goal of population control, zero

---

188. Voluntary sterilization is the contraceptive phenomenon of the decade, a Worldwatch Institute report said Saturday. It indicated that the number of couples using sterilization to prevent pregnancy now exceeds the number using any other single preventive family-planning measure. The paper, written by Worldwatch member Bruce Stokes, estimated that 75 million couples have used sterilization. In 1950, Stokes said, no more than 4 million couples were sterilized. He predicted the number of voluntary sterilizations will increase fast, because the methods for sterilization have been greatly simplified in recent years. (UPI report, *South Bend Tribune,* May 22, 1977, p. 16)

189. "Three European nations—West Germany, East Germany and Luxembourg—have stabilized their populations. Three others probably will reach that point this year—Austria, Belgium and the United Kingdom," says Lester Brown of the Worldwatch Institute. They only constitute 4 percent of the world's population, but, says Brown, "it's a beginning and it shows countries can do it, if they want to." (John Barbour, "Numbers Game: World Population Is Doubling Again," *South Bend Tribune,* June 8, 1975, p. 16)

190. Most experts are heartened by lowering birthrates in the last five years, a trend they attribute at least in part to family planning programs. One of these is Dr. Reimert Ravenholt, head of the population program for the U.S. Agency for International Development Aid. Ten years ago, he said, the world was growing at the rate of 2 percent per year. For every 14 deaths per thousand people there were 34 births. That meant with a 3.2 billion population, there were 66 million more people per year in 1965. Today (1975), the growth rate has fallen to 1.6 or 1.7 percent. That still means an annual increase of 64 million people. "But the trend is favorable and the annual decrease will be favorable in the years ahead," Ravenhold says. (John Barbour, "Numbers Game: World Population Is Doubling Again," *South Bend Tribune,* June 8, 1975, p. 16. Cf. Georges Tapinos and Phyllis T. Plotrow. *Six Billion People, Demographic Dilemmas and World Politics,* New York, 1978, p. 128, the Table.)

191. "We got some good news in this area a while back. The rate of world population growth is down—from a peak of two percent annually to about 1.7 percent. Instead of having 6.3 billion people on our planet by 2000, as previously estimated, it now appears we'll have only 5.8 to 6 billion. But that doesn't mean we're out of danger.... Not when world population still is increasing by about 74 million a year or one million every 5 days, and every one of those people will need food, water, jobs, shelter, medical care, schools, all of which are in short supply even now. Now when, according to the Population Reference Bureau, there will be 500 million more children under age 15 in 20 years—90 percent of them in poorer countries." (Carl T. Rowan, "Hunger, Overpopulation Still Threaten," *South Bend Tribune,* Feb. 6, 1980, p. 14)

population growth, before starting work on its long-range goal. This is the only way to get rid of the population crisis[192] and is also the most effective way to raise per capita income in the very crowded countries.[193]

The long-range goal of population control is to render a population into an optimum size[194] in relation not only to food, but also to energy and other natural resources, along with social problems.[195] This goal may involve the reduction of population in some areas to a level corresponding to the supporting capacity of all the resources,[196] and may also involve the transfer of farm population from over-

---

192. The National Security Council Ad Hoc Group on Population Policy, representing 17 U.S. government agencies and departments, put the population picture in perspective: "We reject suggestions that the problem is beginning to resolve itself, just as we reject counsels of despair that nothing significant can be done about it. Much is being done, but the situation requires a major and urgent expansion of effort, if the world is to be spared unprecedented deprivation and turmoil." (According to Carl T. Rowan, "Hunger, Overpopulation Still Threaten," *South Bend Tribune,* Feb. 6, 1980, p. 14.)

193. Stephen Enke has estimated that channeling resources into population control might be 100 times more effective in raising per capita incomes than putting them into attempts to increase production. (Cf. his "The Economic Aspects of Slowing Population Growth," in *The Economic Journal,* March, 1966; and "Birth Control for Economic Development," in *Science, May 16, 1969.)*

194. "By optimum population is meant that population level at which the peoples of the earth can live in harmony with the earth indefinitely, maintaining reasonable standards of health and well-being. The latter will include opportunities for satisfying employment and recreation, with a variety of natural and man-altered settings for both." (R. Thomas Tanner, *Ecology, Environment, and Education,* Lincoln, Nebr., 1974, p. 13. Cf. Gordon R. Taylor, "Optimum Populations," in *The World's Population: Problems of Growth,* ed. by Quentin H. Stanford, Toronto, 1972, p. 191-195.)

195. Inflation and unemployment may become permanent problems even for highly developed nations unless world population growth is reduced, says a new United Nations-financed study. In reviewing 22 issues affected by population, the study concluded that "nearly all have one thing in common: They can be expected to get much worse before they get better." Population growth is leading to increased urbanization, overgrazing of forage lands, destruction of forests, crowding and political conflict, and demands on energy, minerals and resources, the study said. The study was prepared by the Worldwatch Institute, a private nonprofit research organization, with funding from the United Nations Fund for Population Activities. (AP report, *South Bend Tribune,* March 22, 1976, p. 2)

196. "Once population stability is achieved, population reduction will be necessary. The means for this must, of course, be humane and preferably voluntary. It follows that massive education programs must be mounted at once, and sustained everywhere." (R. Thomas Tanner, *Ecology, Environment and Education,* Lincoln, Nebr., 1974, p. 13)

crowded areas to areas where more potentially arable lands are available.[197]

In short, the long-range goal of population control is to keep an equilibrium between population and resources.

g.
Environment, Pollution, and Conservation

CLOSELY RELATED IS ANOTHER EQUILIBRIUM WE HAVE to keep, the equilibrium between man and his environment.

Ecologically, man is an integral part of his environment[198] in the biosphere.[199] He cannot live without the environment and his welfare

---

197. "Most of the world's potentially arable but uncultivated land is in Africa and in South and North America, but most of the world's people live in Europe and Asia. In Africa, where only 22% of the potentially arable land is now cultivated, and in South America, where 11% of the potentially arable land is cultivated, much additional land could be brought under plow at the level of subsistence agriculture.... In Asia nearly 85% of the potentially arable land is already cultivated, and the remainder can be developed only through very large expenditures for large-scale irrigation projects." (Roger Revelle, "The World Food Supply," in the *Encyclopedia Americana,* 1973 ed., Vol. 11, p. 509)

198. "In an overall view, the environment can be thought of as a giant ecosystem composed of four groups of constituents: nonliving elements, such as the climate, rocks, and water; the green plants (the producers); animals (the consumers); and bacteria (the decomposers). As a dweller on the earth, dependent upon it for foods, raw materials, and space for activity, man himself is part of this ecosystem." (Richard M. Highsmith, Jr., "Conservation," in the *Encyclopedia Americana,* 1973 ed., Vol. 7, p. 622. Cf. Barry Commoner, *The Closing Circle; Nature, Man, and Technology,* New York, 1972, p. 14-48.)

199. All life on earth exists in the biosphere—that thin layer at the surface of the earth made up of the seas and oceans, the top crust of the land, and a few thousand feet of air. Within the biosphere are innumerable ecosystems by which energy is passed through extremely complicated food chains. The basic energy through which all these processes operate comes from the sun, but other substances are also needed for life—carbon, nitrogen, phosphorus, and others. Each of these is recycled by plants and animals to make the continuation of life possible. (Cf. Roger Hilsman, *The Crouching Future,* New York, 1975, p. 515-519.)

depends on being in harmony with it by minimizing any threat to its health.[200]

Most deplorable among the threats to the health of the environment is the destruction of natural resources. This takes place in various ways deliberately or through ignorance.[201] It is not of recent origin nor limited to a certain region,[202] but is as old as mankind and as widespread as the inhabited portion of the earth. The result of this long and extensive destruction is that the environment has undergone a gradual impoverishment with heavy damage in some areas.[203]

---

200. "The quality of the living landscape around us reflects the environmental health and the future possibilities for survival. To most people the landscape they see is characterized by its vegetation. In reality it consists of much more than that. It is a community of living things—plants, trees, animals, including ourselves. Man is an integral part of this environment—not just a spectator viewing it. His impact on the environment is so great as to constitute a formidable challenge to himself. His welfare depends on using the living landscape in a way that causes a minimum of deterioration, despite growing populations, and expanding exploitation pressures." (Kai Curry-Lindahl, *Conservation for Survival: an Ecological Strategy,* New York, 1972, p. 303. Cf. Barry Commoner, *The Closing Circle; Nature, Man, and Technology,* New York, 1972, p. 112-124.)

201. The most evident way is the deliberate removal of resources in order to use them. All the so-called extractive businesses—hunting, fishing, lumbering, and mining—are included in this category. The other way is to damage resources through use, even though they are left in place. In this case, there is no intent to remove or to destroy the resources, but during their use they are worn out or injured in some way. The effect of farming on the soil is an outstanding example. A more ignored situation is the injury resulting from damage to native vegetation, such as when the destruction of trees hastens the runoff of rain water and thus reduces the amount that soaks into the ground, thereby aggravating erosion and the effects of drought. (Cf. Joe R. Whitaker, "The World Problem of Conservation," in *Global Geography,* ed. by George T. Renner, New York, 1947.)

202. "Primitive man also altered the landscape. The slash-and-burn technique of agriculture still practiced by the mountain tribes of Southeast Asia and elsewhere created the giant Thar Desert in India, which was a jungle only two thousand years ago. A similar desert was created in Burma." (Roger Hilsman, *The Crouching Future,* New York, 1975, p. 518)

203. For example, the great grass and desert land that extends from the Atlantic across northern Africa to the Red Sea and on eastward to the Great Wall of China was early overgrazed. Depletion of the resources of the Mediterranean region also began at an early date. Soil erosion had begun to be serious in southern Italy long before the end of the Roman Empire. The famous cedars of Lebanon, in Syria, have shrunken to a tiny grove; the soil cover of the Judean upland has worn so thin that bedrock is at the surface over wide areas. (Cf. Joe R. Whitaker, "The World Problem of Conservation," in *Global Geography,* ed. by George T. Renner, New York, 1947.)

"Superficially, it is puzzling that the ancient cities of Mesopotamia are

Yet, in early times, when the world was thinly inhabited and tools were rough, the destruction of natural resources was slow and its impact on the environment was rather light.[204] Now, with the fast growth of population and the extensive use of power tools, the destruction of natural resources has been growing at an ever-increasing rate, and consequently, has inflicted more and more injuries on the environment,[205] as exemplified by quickening soil erosion,[206] vast mining extractions,[207] and the serious menace to wildlife.[208]

---

situated in deserts that can now support no more than a few nomads. Some of this may have been caused by climatic changes, but much of it came from cutting the forests at the headwaters of rivers." (Roger Hilsman, *The Crouching Future,* New York, 1975, p. 518)

204. This situation may be reviewed in the small mining industry in early times. Rogers and Tryon cite the following facts to illustrate the difference in the size of ancient and modern mining industries. When Alexander the Great took Susa and Persepolis, he is reported to have seized precious metals valued at $190 million, the accumulation of a thousand years or more. The gold mines of the South African Rand have produced that much in less than a year. It is estimated that modern mines could equal the entire output of the Athenian silver mines in Laurion in less than a year. Modern blast furnaces would take less than one day to produce the world's total output of iron in 1750. (Cf. H.O. Rogers and F.G. Tryon, "Mining," in the *Encyclopedia of the Social Sciences,* New York, 1935.)

205. When the world was thinly inhabited, natural resources were abundant in proportion to man's needs, despite destruction; and even when a place was worn out, he was generally able to move on to fresh fields. Later, however, this movement became a fundamental cause of war. Now, the world has been pretty well filled up, and there is nowhere to go. The destruction of natural resources, which has been growing at an unprecedented speed, has inflicted more and more injuries on the environment. Once Woeikof, a Russian geographer, indicated the 19th century as being disharmonious with nature to a supreme degree. Yet the situation has become much more serious since then. (Cf. Joe R. Whitaker, "The World Problem of Conservation," in *Global Geography,* ed. by George T. Renner, New York, 1947. Woeikof's indictment was cited in page 247.)

206. C.V. Jacks and R.O. Whyte, two conservationists, assert in a study of worldwide soil conditions called *Vanishing Lands,* that man's land mismanagement in recent times has created nearly a million square miles of new deserts. Much greater areas, they add, are fast becoming deserts. On continent after continent the prospect shows little difference. Erosion in Africa is said to be worse than in the United States, and the same goes for Australia. It is reported to be especially bad in Asiatic countries like India, because of overcultivation forced by excessive rises in population.

Another authority, Ward Shepard, in his study, *Food or Famine: the Challenge of Erosion,* sums up the situation without glossing over its seriousness, this way. "Despite the brilliant advances in agricultural science, the productivity of the world's soils in output per unit is slowly diminishing. Mankind is fighting a slow retreat before the gathering forces of famine. An ominously and swiftly increasing process of soil destruction is undermining the foundations of our shaky

A recently developing threat to the health of the environment is pollution.[209] It has penetrated through international boundaries[210] to

---

civilization. Beginning as the sapping of soil fertility, it ends in what can be described as a new, man-made cataclysmic geologic era, in which our food-producing soils are being swept in the rivers and the seas. Armed with machinery and industrialism, modern man is devastating the farms, the grasslands, and the forests of the world. In the long evolutionary chain of life, he is the only creature who has achieved the dubious distinction of being able to destroy nature's harmony and fecundity on a cosmic scale.''

"Perhaps the most serious single threat humanity now faces is the widespread loss of topsoil," Lester Brown, an agricultural specialist, said in a study which is being published as a book titled *Building a Sustainable Society.* "Civilization cannot survive this continuing loss of topsoil. If not arrested, this loss could cause the food problem to unfold during the '80s as the energy problem did during the '70s.'' Brown, now head of the Worldwatch Institute, pointed out that a doubling in world food output since 1950 was achieved at the expense of severe land abuse, and that the productivity of 34 percent of American cropland is declining because of an excessive loss of topsoil each year. The Agriculture Department estimated last year that soil has lost, for example, 14.1 tons an acre in Tennessee, 11.4 tons an acre in Missouri, and 10.9 tons in Mississippi. (AP report, *South Bend Tribune,* Oct. 11, 1968, p.4)

207. For example, six million acres in the United States have been destroyed by strip mining. That's two Connecticuts. The work goes on at the rate of 4,650 acres per week, or one more Connecticut per decade. (Cf. Harry M. Caudill, "Strip Mining: Partnership in Greed,''' in *American Forests,* v. 79, no. 5, May, 1973, p. 16-19.)

208. "Since 1600, 359 species of animal life have become extinct. The rate accelerated in the last century, largely due to man's destruction of suitable habitat. It is estimated that 100 species of mammals have become extinct in the last two thousand years, 75 of these having become extinct in the last two hundred. Thus the rate has accelerated, from one species every 72 years to one every 2⅔ years.'' (R. Thomas Tanner, *Ecology, Environment, and Education,* Lincoln, Nebr., 1974, p. 9-10. Cf. Paul R. Ehrlich and Anne H. Ehrlich, *Extinction: The Causes and Consequences of the Disappearance of Species,* New York, 1981.)

209. "At the present time only the developed nations of the world are seriously concerned about pollution. It is an unfortunate characteristic of many types of pollution, however, that eventually they become widely distributed around the world. Although Greenland is far removed from any source of atmospheric lead pollution, the amount of lead deposited in Greenland ice has increased 300 percent yearly since 1940. DDT has accumulated in the body fat of humans in every part of the globe, from Alaskan eskimos to city-dwellers of New Delhi, as shown in table 5.'' (Donella H. Meadows and others, *The Limits to Growth,* Washington, 1972, p. 92)

210. "In the past decade nations have become increasingly aware of their vulnerability to activities carried out beyond their own national boundaries. Industrial activity in England and the Ruhr Valley is thought to have contributed to increased levels of sulfuric acid in Sweden's rainfall. Deforestation at the foot of the Himalayas in Nepal has led to soil erosion throughout large areas of Pakistan

spread all over the world,[211] and is involved largely with air, heat, water, pesticides, nuclear wastes and noise.

Air pollution contains vast quantities of various pollutants.[212]

---

and India. And each year over one million tons of oil are spilled from tankers and other ships, with potentially serious effects on ocean resources. No nation is exempt from possible disaster, and no nation can maintain that it is not accountable to others for its own actions." (*Science and Technology in an Era of Interdependence,* by the UNA-USA National Policy Panel, New York, 1975, p. 39)

"Acid rain (sulfuric acid mixed in the air) also affects fish. In Norway and Sweden, which receive their pollution from the industrialized countries to the south and west, the rivers are becoming acidic, so much so that fish such as salmon and trout are ceasing to breed. If the acid level continues to rise, many of the fish will die. Nor is North America being spared. Fish kills have been reported in acidified lakes in northern Ontario, Canada, and in some parts of New Hampshire the rain has a very high level of acid." (Joseph J. DiCerto, *The Electric Wishing Well; the Solution to the Energy Crisis,* New York, 1976, p. 17)

211. Researchers at Texas A & M University, after testing the air at a remote Pacific island and finding a toxic chemical, say there is probably no longer any place on earth free of contamination by man-made pollutants. Hexachlorobenzene, known as HCB, which causes cancer in laboratory animals, was detected in the air on Eniwetok Atoll, the first time the chemical has appeared in the isolated region. "The chances are there's now no place on earth you can go without finding HCB. The thing wasn't meant to be dramatic or frightening to people, but it is a scientific fact," said C.S. Giam, head of chemistry at A & M and leader of the Eniwetok expedition. The results of the study have been published in the journal *Science.* HCB is a byproduct of more than a dozen manufacturing processes, including rubber manufacturing, and is also a key ingredient to fungicides. (AP report, *South Bend Tribune,* Feb. 4, 1981, p. 20)

212. Some figures from the United States Public Health Service in the late 1960s are instructive. Heating houses and office buildings released 2 million tons of carbon monoxide, 3 million tons of sulphur oxides, 1 million tons of hydrocarbons, and 1 million tons of particulate matter into the atmosphere. Trash burning alone contributed 1 million tons of carbon monoxide, almost 1 million tons of sulphur oxides and nitrogen oxides, 1 million tons of hydrocarbons, and 1 million tons of particulate matter. Industrial sources, such as paper and pulp mills, iron and steel mills, petroleum refineries, smelters, and chemical plants contributed 2 million tons of carbon monoxide, 9 million tons of sulphur oxides, 3 million tons of nitrogen oxides, about 1 million tons of hydrocarbons, and 3 million tons of particulate matter. The 90 million automobiles and trucks contributed 66 million tons of carbon monoxide, 1 million tons of sulphur oxides, 6 million tons of nitrogen oxides, 12 million tons of hydrocarbons, 1 million tons of particulate matter, and a variety of other harmful substances. (Cf. Roger Hilsman, *The Crouching Future,* New York, 1975, p. 520-523; and Richard J. Hickey, "Air Pollution," in *Environment, Resources, Pollution & Society,* ed. by William W. Murdoch, Stamford, Conn., 1972, p. 189-210.)

At present, about 97 percent of mankind's industrial energy production comes from fossil fuels (coal, oil, and natural gas). When these fuels are burned,

Among them, sulfuric acid is a dangerous chemical spreading as "acid rain"[213] and carbon monoxide is a "merciless killer."[214]

Waste heat is the final product of all uses of energy and the ultimate form of pollution. It affects the weather directly,[215] while its introduction into water for cooling is hazardous to aquatic life.[216]

---

they release, among other substances, carbon dioxide (CO_2) into the atmosphere. Currently about 20 billion tons of CO_2 are being released from them each year. The atmospheric concentration of CO_2 observed since 1958 at Mauna Loa, Hawaii, has increased steadily. At present, the increase averages about 1.5 part per million (ppm) each year. Calculations including the known exchanges of CO_2 between the atmosphere, biosphere, and oceans predict that the CO_2 concentration will reach 380 ppm by the year 2000, an increase of nearly 30 percent of the probable value in 1860. The source of this exponential increase in atmospheric CO_2 is man's increasing combustion of fossil fuels. (Cf. Lester Machta, "The Role of the Oceans and Biosphere in the Carbon Dioxide Cycle," Paper presented at Nobel Symposium 20, "The Changing Chemistry of the Oceans," Gateborg, Sweden, August 1971.)

213. Sulfuric acid is a dangerous chemical and must be handled with extreme care. Even a drop falling on one's skin could cause a very painful burn. Each year upwards of 400 billion pounds (counting water content) of sulfuric acid are dumped upon the surface of the earth, mainly as a result of burning fossil fuels. "Acid rain," as it is called, sinks into the ground, stripping away or leaching precious calcium from the soil. Since tree growth is correlated with the calcium content of the soil, trees suffer. Furthermore, acid rain destroys fish, people, and structures. (Cf. Joseph J. DiCerto, *The Electric Wishing Well; the Solution to the Energy Crisis,* New York, 1976, p. 17-18; and Richard T. Sheahan, *Fueling the Future; an Environmental and Energy Primer,* New York, 1976, p. 80-84.)

214. "Among the more dangerous constituents of air pollution is a colorless, tasteless, odorless gas that is a merciless killer—carbon monoxide (CO). Because of some quirk in nature, carbon monoxide has a greater affinity (200 times greater than oxygen) for the hemoglobin molecules in the red blood cells of our body. When we inhale CO, it crowds out the oxygen molecules that normally attach themselves to the red blood cells in our lungs. Therefore CO starves our body of its important oxygen supply. Significant amounts of inhaled CO can cause serious illness and even death." (Joseph J. DiCerto, *The Electric Wishing Well, the Solution to the Energy Crisis,* New York, 1976, p. 18. Cf. John M. Fowler, *Energy and the Environment,* New York, 1975, p. 147-158.)

215. Waste heat is the final product of all uses of energy and is the ultimate form of pollution. Aside from making us very uncomfortable, heat pollution can create far more serious problems. It has an effect on the weather: frequency and amount of rain, local temperature, air quality, all are influenced by the amount of heat discharged into the environment. Since the difference in temperatures around the earth is a major factor governing weather patterns, any significant change in heat input and heat concentrations will affect weather conditions. Eventually, the introduction of vast quantities of heat into the atmosphere and water systems may create totally new weather patterns, which could be highly destructive. And this is only one aspect of the heat pollution problem. (Cf. Joseph J. DiCerto, *The Elec-*

Water pollution can result not only from the waste heat, but also from the transfer of dangerous elements of air pollution and from the dumping of various wastes[217] into streams, rivers and lakes. It can also come from domestic sewage, oil leaks and coal mining.[218] With such dirty sources, water pollution has even caused some lakes and

---

tric Wishing Well; the Solution to the Energy Crisis, New York, 1976, p. 19; and Gordon J.F. MacDonald, "Pollution, Weather and Climate," in *Environment, Resources, Pollution & Society,* ed by William W. Murdoch, Stamford, Conn., 1972, p. 326-335.)

"Waste heat released over the 4,000 square mile area of the Los Angeles basin currently amounts to about 5 percent of the total solar energy absorbed at the ground. At the present rate of growth, thermal release will reach 18 percent of incoming solar energy by the year 2000. This heat, the result of all energy generation and consumption processes, is already affecting the local climate." (Cf. L. Lees, *Man's Impact on the Global Environment, Report of the Study of Critical Environmental Problems,* Cambridge, Mass., 1970.)

216. A great amount of waste heat is introduced into streams and lakes by the water which is used for cooling purposes. "It takes a lot of water to cool the power plants of the United States. In 1959 over 26 trillion gallons were used for this purpose. By 1970 the figure jumped to 57 trillion gallons. It is predicted that by 1980, 106 trillion gallons of water will have to flow through power plants to keep them cool. To appreciate this alarming situation one need only look at the demands for cooling water predicted for the turn of this century. The amount of water required to cool all the electrical power plants that will exist in the year 2000 will equal all the fresh water runoff (resulting from rain) of the entire continental United States for a full year." The introduction of the wasted heat into water not only wastes huge quantities of energy, but also has an effect on aquatic life. Since heated water holds less oxygen, fish suffer loss of appetite, digestive problems, difficulty in breathing and reduced rates of reproduction. (Cf. Joseph J. DiCerto, *The Electric Wishing Well; the Solution to the Energy Crisis,* New York, 1976, p. 19-20; and John M. Fowler, *Energy and the Environment,* New York, 1975, p. 173-181.)

217. Water pollution can come from agricultural wastes, municipal wastes, and especially industrial wastes. From the start of the industrial age, streams, rivers, and lakes have been used as dumping grounds for industrial wastes. Industrial wastes also put poisons into the water. Mercury is only one example. Over the years, much mercury has found its way into the sea and through the food chain has made its way into the bodies of such predator fish as swordfish. Many are now no longer fit to eat. (Cf. W.T. Edmondson, "Fresh Water Pollution," in *Environment, Resources, Pollution & Society,* ed. by William W. Murdoch, Stamford, Conn., 1972, p. 213-228.)

218. "Adding to this already serious condition is the water pollution resulting from coal mining. Our once beautiful streams and lakes are being degraded on a grand scale. The Department of the Interior estimates that by 1973, 13,000 miles of streams and 145,000 acres of lakes and reservoirs had been adversely affected by acid mine drainage and siltation from coal extraction." (Joseph J. DiCerto, *The Electric Wishing Well; the Solution to the Energy Crisis,* New York, 1976, p. 19. Cf. John M. Fowler, *Energy and the Environment,* New York, 1975, p. 193-204.)

seas to slowly die,[219] which some scholars warn may possibly lead to the death of the whole ocean.[220]

The application of chemical compounds to destroy harmful

---

219. "Lake Erie, for example, receives waste discharge of over ten million people, of which 45% receives primary and secondary sewage treatment, 50% only primary treatment, and 5% no treatment at all. Pollutants from these discharges and others have lead to a reduction in the commercial and sport fishery in the area. For example, in 1925 about 25,000 pounds of cisco were harvested each year, while in the mid 1960's only about 1,000 pounds were harvested.... Lake Michigan is also used as a dumping ground for many wastes. A steel plant has discharged into the lake over 230 million gallons of wastes per day; this includes 13,750 pounds of nitrogen that enhances algae growth and 54,000 pounds of oil that is damaging to the aquatic life and waterfowl." (Verne H. Scott, "Water Pollution," in the *Encyclopedia Americana,* 1973 ed., Vol. 28, p. 441b)

As a result of heavy dumping of municipal, industrial, and agricultural wastes into Lake Ontario, the concentrations of numerous salts have been rising exponentially. The chemical changes in the lake have resulted in severe declines in the catches of most commercially valuable fish. (Cf. A.M. Beeton, *Statement on Pollution and Eutrophication of the Great Lakes,* Milwaukee, Wisc., 1970.)

Deep samples of snow from the Greenland Ice Sheet show increasingly high deposits of lead over time. Concentrations of calcium and sea salt were also measured as a control. The presence of lead reflects increasing world industrial use of the metal, including direct release into the atmosphere from automobile exhausts. (Cf. C.C. Patterson and J.D. Salvia, "Lead in the Modern Environment—How Much Is Natural?" *Scientist and Citizen,* April 1968.)

Increasing accumulation of organic wastes in the Baltic Sea, where water circulation is minimal, has resulted in a steadily decreasing oxygen concentration in the water. In some areas, especially in deeper waters, oxygen concentration is zero and almost no forms of aquatic life can be supported. (Cf. Stig H. Fonselius, "Stagnant Sea," *Environment,* July/August 1970.)

220. The greatest threat to the water in the sea by far, according to Mrs. Elizabeth Borgese in her book, *The Drama of the Oceans,* New York, 1976, p. 20, 207-225, is that of pollution and radioactive wastes, which she fears may eventually destroy the phytoplankton in the upper layers of the sea, which gives us more than half the world's oxygen. The ultimate disaster here would be the cessation of all marine life, global oxygen shortage, and death by asphyxiation in the struggle for the decreased supply of breathable air.

The pollution of the ocean that has attracted most attention is oil spills. The death toll in sea birds, fish, and crustaceans from oil spills is appalling. The damage to beaches and the loss of revenue from tourism are also regrettable. But potentially much more serious pollution of the ocean is also taking place. What is even more disturbing is the possibility that the combined impact of all these different kinds of pollution—oils, plastics, mercury, DDT, and so on—will be a collapse of oxygen-producing plankton. (Cf. Ferren MacIntyre and R.W. Holmes, "Ocean Pollution," in *Environment, Resources, Pollution & Society,* ed. by William W. Murdoch, Stamford, Conn., 1972, p. 230-251.)

There are different views, however: the world's seas and oceans are far from

plants and animals gives rise to pesticide pollution. Generally speaking, pesticides are poisons and are capable of damaging organisms other than the target species.[221] Their residues are dangerous[222] and some persist for years.[223] They can be dispersed by wind and water,[224]

---

dying and have proved much more resilient to the abuses of man than was imagined a decade ago, according to scientists and environmentalists who met in Nairobi, Kenya, during the May 10-18 conference which attracted delegates from about 105 countries, to take stock of the environment in the decade since the world's first major environmental gathering in Stockholm, Sweden, in 1972. "To talk about dying seas is nonsense," said one of them, Stjepan Keckes, a marine biologist who directs 10 regional seas programs around the world for the United Nations Environment Program. Keckes, a Yugoslav of Hungarian extraction, scoffed at what he called "alarmist" warnings in the 1960s and 1970s by such noted figures as French oceanographer Jacques Cousteau and Norwegian explorer Thor Heyerdahl. Lloyd Timberlake, an American from Atlanta, Ga., who is editorial director of the London-based environmental lobby, Earthscan, said in another interview with the Associated Press that he generally agrees with Keckes's optimistic prognosis on the world's oceans. Timberlake said he thought most marine scientists have come around to a more hopeful view than "back in the '70s when Heyerdahl was riding around in reed boats and reporting oil slicks in the middle of the ocean." Erik Eckhold, another American environmentalist, writes in a book on the environment to be published in June that "reports of death at sea are greatly exaggerated." . . . The state of the world's seas was a bright spot amid gloomy predictions about rapid loss of forests, expansion of deserts, the buildup of carbon dioxide in the atmosphere, acid rain and the irreversible loss of animal and plant species. (As reported by James R. Peipert, AP reporter, "Scientists Diagnose Oceans As in Good Health," *South Bend Tribune,* June 6, 1982, p. 14)

221. Pesticides regularly strike at nontarget species as well as the species for which they are intended. Moreover, pesticide applications cannot always be confined to the intended area. Nor does their effectiveness cease after the pest population has been sufficiently reduced, often with unpredicted results. These characteristics of pesticides enlarge the inherent risk associated with using toxic chemicals and give rise to the controversies surrounding their use. (Cf. Kai Curry-Lindahl, *Conservation for Survival: an Ecological Strategy,* New York, 1972, p. 218-231.)

222. Many pesticides cannot be controlled after they have been applied. These residues may cause unintended effects in the places where the compounds were applied. They may also occur at places a considerable distance from the original site. Following their dispersal they may become part of the food chain and accumulate in such a way that those animals near the top of the food chain consume very large quantities of the residues. (Cf. Robert L. Rudd, "Pesticides," in the *Environment, Resources, Pollution & Society,* ed. by William W. Murdoch, Stamford, Conn., 1972, p. 279-300.)

223. The pesticides whose residues persist most are the chlorinated hydrocarbon insecticides, such as DDT, and those compounds containing heavy metals such as lead, mercury, and arsenic. Agricultural use of pesticides is only one source of pollution by these metals, however. Lead emitted from car exhausts creates a serious environmental problem, as does organic mercury from industrial affluents,

thus adding more hazards to air and water pollution everywhere.[225] DDT provides a well-known example of their deep and wide effects.[226]

The use of nuclear power to generate electricity raises the possibility of pollution containing nuclear radiation in waste heat, cooling

---

and the polychlorinated byphenyls (PCB) from the plastics and paint industries. (Cf. Morton W. Miller and George C. Berg, eds., *Chemical Fallout: Current Research on Persistent Pesticides,* Springfield, Ill., 1969.)

"The 'pest control' enterprise places a billion pounds of toxic materials into the environment every year, some of whose consequences may not be known for a decade or more." (Sydney Harris, "Pest Controls Materials Could Sting Us in Future," *South Bend Tribune,* Nov. 11, 1980, p. 16)

224. Transfer of the pesticide residues "occurs through either physical or biological systems. Generally, the movements of air and water are responsible for residue transfers over long distances. Residues may be leached out of the soil by rainfall, they may become absorbed to suspended particles in the air or water, or they may volatilize in the air. The discharge of pesticide residues into San Francisco Bay from the Central Valley of California has been estimated at almost 2 tons a year. Soil particles to which traces of DDT adhered have been found in the air over the Barbados Islands. When the particles were analyzed, the soil type was identified as Moroccan; thus the particles must have been carried across the South Atlantic Ocean on the prevailing northeasterly trade winds." (Robert L. Rudd, "Pesticide," in the *Encyclopedia Americana,* 1973 ed., Vol. 21, p. 653)

225. Pesticide residues have been found everywhere. "In California, 86 different species of wildlife and their physical environments were sampled, and all were found to contain pesticide residues. Even the air over large cities contains traces of residues. One estimate indicates that there may be as much as 2.4 million pounds of DDT and its metabolites in Antarctic snow and ice. Other studies have shown residues in Antarctic penguins, fishes, and seals." (Robert L. Rudd, "Pesticide," in the *Encyclopedia Americana,* 1973 ed., Vol. 21, p. 653)

226. DDT is a man-made organic chemical released into the environment as a pesticide. After its application by spraying, part of it evaporates and is carried long distances in the air before it eventually precipitates back onto the land or into the ocean. In the ocean, some of the DDT is taken up by plankton, some of the plankton are eaten by fish, and some of the fish are finally eaten by man. In this process its negative effect on the ecosystem may not appear until some decades later. This is also true with all long-lived toxic substances, such as mercury, lead, and cadmium, other pesticides, polychlorobiphenyl, and radioactive wastes. (Cf. Donella H. Meadows and others, *The Limits to Growth,* Washington, 1972, p. 89-92.)

"DDT and other persistent pesticides have built up in the marine environment; it is estimated that 25 percent of the total amount of DDT manufactured to date is still present in the world's oceans. Also accumulating are polychlorinated biphenyls, or PCBs. These organic compounds, which are used in the manufacture of plastics, have many of the same characteristics as DDT and can be highly toxic to aquatic life." (*Science and Technology in an Era of Interdependence,* by the UNA-USA National Policy Panel, New York, 1975, p. 40)

water and the atmosphere.[227] Thus far, this possibility has been generally limited by careful controls,[228] and except for some accidents,[229] there has not been much trouble. The greatest danger may be nuclear war, not the threat to the environment; because certain waste can be used to make nuclear weapons.[230] However, this is a political rather than technological problem.

---

227. "Utilizing today's technology, a nuclear power plant generates heat by fission, which is used to turn water into steam, which then is used to drive turbines that generate electricity. Huge amounts of heat are generated, and vast quantities of water are needed as coolants. The plant releases small quantities of radioisotopes in the water and through its smokestacks. There is also some danger of accidents—not explosions, but other kinds that might release a certain amount of radioactive substances into the atmosphere." (Roger Hilsman, *The Crouching Future,* New York, 1975, p. 523)

228. "Insofar as the radiation hazards are concerned, it is worth noting that no other potential pollutant has been so carefully monitored and controlled as the nonmilitary use of radioisotopes. If our control over other pollutants came close to equalling our control over radioactive pollutants, we would have a remarkably clean planet today." (Raymond F. Dasmann, *Environmental Conservation,* New York, 1972, p. 398. Cf. the "Myths and Facts About Nuclear Power," by Alvin Shapiro, professor of nuclear engineering, University of Cincinnati, distributed by the Cincinnati Gas & Electric Co., 1980.)

229. "After the Three Mile Island accident in the United States, there has occurred a case in Tsuruga, Japan. Radioactive waste apparently leaking from a disposal building adjacent to a nuclear power plant here has seriously contaminated soil in the area, the Ministry of International Trade and Industry reported Saturday. A statement said soil samples showed 9,941 pico-curies of cobalt-60 and 1,458 pico-curies of manganese-54 per gram. A pico is one-trillionth of a curie, the unit of measure of radioactivity. The Kyodo News Service quoted officials of Fukui state as saying the amount of cobalt-60 was 5,000 times the previous highest reading and 'the effects on the human body could be serious if the radioactive waste has spread throughout the bay.' " (AP report in the *South Bend Tribune,* April 19, 1981, p. 8)

230. "The inextricable link between commercial nuclear power and the spread of nuclear weapons poses still another obstacle to the use of the 'peaceful atom.' A standard 1,000-megawatt reactor operating at full power will produce about 375 pounds of plutonium each year. A crude atom bomb requires less than 20 pounds of plutonium. Weapons development may proceed whether or not nuclear power is commercialized, but commercialization certainly makes acquiring the equipment fissile isotopes, and trained scientists needed for bomb building easier than it would otherwise be.... The prestigious British Royal Commission report on nuclear power concluded that the spread of nuclear power will inevitably facilitate the spread of the ability to make nuclear weapons and that with respect to the construction of these weapons, there is no reason to trust the stability of any nation of any political persuasion for centuries ahead." (Denis Hayes, *Energy for Development: Third World Options,* Washington, 1977, p. 18-19)

Noise becomes pollution when exceeding certain decibels.[231] It is evident that noise pollution can do more harm than merely to annoy.[232]

The most common dirty pollution comes from solid wastes, which result mainly from the great increase in the production and consumption of goods,[233] and necessarily caused more troubles in the developed countries.[234] Attempts to handle solid wastes have encountered various problems.[235]

---

231. The noise level of a room in which people are conversing quietly is about 50 decibels. At 80 decibels noise becomes annoying. An automobile creates about 70 decibels. Heavy automobile traffic creates about 100. The noise that people often are subjected to in cities—riveting machines or discotheques—is frequently 110 decibels or more. Noise levels as low as 50 decibels may disturb sleep. Ninety-decibel noise levels may also damage the nervous system and be a factor in diseases related to stress, such as ulcers and hypertension. (Cf. Kai Curry-Lindahl, *Conservation for Survival: an Ecological Strategy,* New York, 1972, p. 16.)

232. Sirens whine. Truck rumble and roar. Rock music blares. These and other loud sounds of modern day life are hurting people both physically and mentally. That's the opinion of Dr. T. Walter Carlin, director of the Speech and Hearing Institute at the University of Texas Health Science Center in Houston. "Our society is driving itself nuts with noise," Carlin said in a recent interview. He said noise pollution is not only a cause for the loss of hearing but triggers other physical ailments, stress in marriages, a lack of productivity by workers and "all in all makes our life miserable.... The decibel count in a typical disco is 130. A jet airplane has a decibel of only 120. And remember, sound was used for centuries as a method of torture. Place a bell over a person's head and ring it and eventually the person would go crazy." (Reported by Rob Wood, AP reporter, *South Bend Tribune,* Dec. 29, 1980, p. 1, 9.)

233. Some solid wastes are due to greater affluence—more automobile bodies must now be disposed of than before, more worn-out refrigerators, more worn-out TV sets. The increase in population is also partly responsible. If there are more people, there are more old clothes thrown away, more empty food containers to be thrown away, and so on. But the major responsibility for the stupendous increase in solid wastes lies with the new technologies. Beer now comes in cans rather than in returnable bottles; soda bottles are no longer returnable. The production of nonreturnable soda bottles in the United States since World War II has increased 53,000 per cent. (Cf. Barry Commoner, *The Closing Circle,* New York, 1972, p. 140-145; "Properties of Waste Materials" and "Estimation of Solid Waste Production Rates," in the *Handbook of Solid Waste Management,* ed. by David Gordon Wilson, New York, 1976, p. 10-62, 544-574.)

234. For example, one authority estimates that each year the United States "must dispose of some 55 billion cans, 26 billion bottles and jars, 65 billion metal and plastic bottle caps, and more than half a billion dollars worth of packaging materials. Seven million automobiles are junked each year, and the amount of urban solid wastes (trash and garbage) collected annually is approximately 150 million tons." (Paul R. Ehrlich and Anne H. Ehrlich, *Population, Resources, En-*

Closely associated with pollution in general and with air, noise and solid wastes pollution in particular is another threat to the health of the environment, namely, overcrowding in urban areas.

The phenomena of overcrowding in urban areas is nothing new. In most of history people have tended to flock to cities for safety, jobs and a better life. What is new in modern times is the great speed and scope of urbanization. Of the United States population, for example, urban dwellers increased from 40 percent in 1910 to more than 70 percent in 1970, along with the development of huge urban complexes.[236]

It is not just in the developed countries that urbanization has been growing fast and wide, but also in the developing countries. Their urban population increased 55 percent between 1950 and 1960.[237]

---

vironment: Issues in Human Ecology, San Francisco, 1970, p. 128. Cf. *Use of Waste Materials and By-Products in Road Construction,* a report by the Road Research Group of the Organization for Economic Co-operation and Development, 1977, p. 16, Table I.1.)

235. "What is to be done with all this solid waste? If burned, it greatly contributes to air pollution. Flashlight batteries, for example, contain mercury. Burning trash puts this mercury into the air as vapor; the vapor is transformed into methyl mercury, and one more poison has been added to the atmosphere. If the waste is dumped at sea it pollutes the ocean and creates 'dead seas.' If the trash is put into open dumps, the result is not only unsightly, but it is a breeding ground for rats, flies, and other such disease-carrying pests. Water percolating through the dump also contributes to the pollution of streams and rivers. Using it for fill in the wetlands destroys the nurseries for marine life." (Roger Hilsman, *The Crouching Future,* New York, 1975, p. 526)

236. "In the United States the percentage of the population living in urban areas in 1910 was 46 percent. By the census of 1970, it was 73.5 percent. What has developed in the United States are huge urban complexes—the Boston-New York-Washington complex, the San Francisco-Los Angeles-San Diego complex, and the complex centering around Chicago. In these huge areas one city and town merges into another in one vast urban sprawl." (Roger Hilsman, *The Crouching Future,* New York, 1975, p. 519)

237. "But it is not just in the developed countries that cities are burgeoning. According to the Secretary General of the United Nations, 40 percent of the world's peoples live in urban areas, and the percentage is growing fast. Between 1950 and 1960 the urban population of the developing countries increased by 55 percent. There has been little or no planning for this tremendous expansion, and the result is the growth of shantytowns on every available space, with inadequate water and sewerage, breeding places for disease and misery." (Roger Hilsman, *The Crouching Future,* New York, 1975, p. 519-520)

The total urban population is expected to increase exponentially in the less developed regions of the world, but almost linearly in the more developed regions.

The result of overcrowding in urban areas, as far as the environment is concerned, is a decrease in quality, both in terms of aesthetics and sanitary conditions,[238] and an increase in the disorder of development.[239] This is in addition to augmenting pollution, of which the center is the big cities. Perhaps another result is the inadvertent effect on weather and climate.[240]

Under the heavy threats of the destruction of natural resources, pollution and overcrowding, the health of the environment is deteriorating.[241] It is a situation so serious that not only our welfare, but even our survival is in peril.[242]

The present average doubling time for city populations in the less developed regions is 15 years. (Cf. UN Department of Economic and Social Affairs, *The World Population Situation in 1970,* New York, 1971; also Donella H. Meadows and others, *The Limits to Growth,* Washington, 1972, p. 35, and Figure 3.)

238. This is evident in the current spread of slum areas, clogged streets, cluttered roadsides, mixtures of graceless buildings, park deterioration, garbage dumps, infestations of rodents and pigeons, filth, and the hundred other annoyances that go with overcrowding; not to mention crime in the streets and drug abuse. (Cf. Edward C. Higbee, *The Squeeze: Cities Without Space,* New York, 1960.)

239. "Urban growth more often than not is unplanned. It often follows the pattern of highways or is determined by private real estate developers. Frequently the growth proceeds in leapfrog fashion, and an unorganized sprawl is the consequence. As a result, numerous problems arise, including the increase of service and transportation costs and the neglect of recreation space and the appearance of the landscape. Not the least of the problems is the diversion of prime cropland to urban uses." (Richard H. Highsmith, "Conservation," in the *Encyclopedia Americana,* 1973 ed., Vol. 7, p. 620)

240. "Also of concern is the fact that increased urbanization, in both developed and developing countries, may have inadvertent effects on weather and climate. In the U.S., where the impact of urbanization on local weather patterns is relatively well documented, studies indicate that some cities experience 25 percent more wind, considerably more fog and up to 10 percent more precipitation than the surrounding countryside. Urban concentration form heat islands and take longer to cool off than surrounding areas." (*Science and Technology in an Era of Interdependence,* by the UNA-USA National Policy Panel, New York, 1975, p. 40)

241. "The earth as a life-support system is deteriorating. This the reader must understand clearly, in case he hasn't noticed or has been persuaded otherwise. In some respects our children's world will be better than ours, but on balance it will be uglier, less interesting, and more dangerous. This is not a pleasant fact to face, but denial is not a sufficient response to the problem." (R. Thomas Tanner, *Ecology, Environment and Education,* Lincoln, Nebr., 1974, p. 9)

242. Some conservationists estimated recently that there are 817 bird and mammal varieties that must be considered "endangered species." They should have said 818. They forgot homo sapiens, otherwise known as man, a mammal. The process of extinction appears to have speeded up in recent centuries. For many species, the extinguisher has been man. Now man himself is an endangered species,

To get out of this peril, there is only one way, called conservation, which means not merely saving, but positively developing.[243] It is a rational management, which means keeping an equilibrium between man and his environment in accordance with ecosystems.[244]

---

and in his case, too, the villain is man. A species is deemed to be endangered when its habitat is endangered. Now polluting man is jeopardizing his own habitat, the planet itself. Dr. William D. McElroy, outgoing director of the National Science Foundation, said: "The simple truth today is that man's survival in an acceptable society is by no means assured . . . self-destruction by environmental degradation is a real possibility." (Joseph L. Myler, UP reporter, "Future of Man in Doubt," *South Bend Tribune,* Dec. 11, 1971, p. 7. Cf. Barry Commoner, *The Closing Circle; Nature, Man, and Technology,* New York, 1972, p. 216-249.)

Quoted from a paper issued by the Friends of the Earth, with the title, "The Earth," San Francisco, not dated:

"... we are destroying the means of our existence. Fast.

"One main cause is overpopulation. Our numbers are increasing and we cannot cope with the needs of the people we have.

"We are using up our natural resources as if there were no tomorrow.

"Already vast tracts of the Great Lakes in America are dying. And at least one river is a fire risk.

"The Rhine is called the sewer of Europe.

"The Baltic Sea is poisoned.

"In a mere ten years a clean Atlantic has become a mess of oil globs and plastic.

"And many once common animals, birds, insects and plants are becoming rare.

"Dying. Because of our waste. Our carelessness. Our selfishness . . . .

"We need your help to take action now.

"Because soon (and without being melodramatic) it'll be too late to be sorry."

243. Development is the positive aspect of conservation. Lynton R. Caldwell is right: "The development process itself—whatever its scope or complexity—is inherently ecological. It is a process of purposeful change in the systematic interrelationships of living and inanimate things as they have evolved and continue to evolve in a biosphere dominated by human society." (Quoted in *Science and Technology in an Era of Interdependence,* by the UNA-USA National Policy Panel, New York, 1975, p. 84)

244. In discussion of cropland conservation, related to the fundamental role of land in all ecosystems, Richard M. Highsmith pointed out: "Some alteration of the land through cultivation is a necessary price for the benefits of agriculture, but uncoordinated practices, uncontrolled use of agricultural chemicals, and other factors result in needless damage to natural ecosystems. Man can prevent such damage only if he recognizes that he is part of the earth's ecosystems, and that the understanding of these ecosystems is, in the long run, basic to the rational management and optimum use of the total environment." ("Conservation," in the *Encyclopedia Americana,* 1973 ed., Vol. 7, p. 623-624)

Considering conservation an applied ecology, Kai Curry-Lindahl said: "With

A modest conservation movement started a hundred years ago with George P. Marsh as one of the leaders.[245] But it was not until recent decades, when the threats to the health of the environment have become increasingly alarming, that more people the world over have begun to wake up and respond attentively to urgent appeals for conservation.[246]

The primary work of conservation is to reduce the destruction of natural resources to a minimum by all means,[247] to hold down pollu-

---

ecological awareness, conservation would automatically become an exercise in applied ecology to provide man his environmental present and future needs by maintaining qualitative habitats." (*Conservation for Survival; an Ecological Strategy,* New York, 1972, p. 310. Cf. p. 303.)

245. George P. Marsh, in his book, *Man and Nature or Physical Geography as Modified by Human Action* (1864), sought to "indicate the character and, approximately, the extent of the changes produced by human action in the physical conditions of the globe we inhabit." He pointed to the dangers of large-scale interference with the "spontaneous arrangement of the organic and inorganic world" and suggested the importance of "the restoration of disturbed harmonies" in the preface of the first edition. An 1874 edition with the title, *The Earth As Modified by Human Action,* was reprinted by Arno Press in 1970.

246. "But in the last decade or so the facts of life caught up with the Soviet Union as with all industrialized countries. The leaders are now about to set out to do what a prominent dissident urged four years ago—in an underground pamphlet. The 1968 pamphlet of A.D. Sakharov, a physicist, said the two superpowers, rather than spend their wealth on weapons of mass destruction, might better seek ways to co-operate in saving the world from pollution and avoiding such situations as 'the sadly celebrated problem' of Lake Baikal, which was being poisoned by industrial waste. 'Otherwise,' Sakharov wrote, 'the U.S.S.R. poisons the United States with its wastes while the United States poisons the U.S.S.R. with its.' " (Reported by William L. Ryan, AP reporter, *South Bend Tribune,* May 25, 1972, p. 2.)

Extinction seems to be the fate of species in accordance with the evolutionary law: adapt or perish. The dinosaur, as people are always pointing out, didn't adapt to changes imposed on its world by nature. So it perished some 180 million years or so ago. But in man's case today it is not a question of evolutionary adaptation to the changing moods of nature. Adaptation won't work. There isn't enough time for it. What man must do is to stop fouling his own nest, according to Dr. William D. McElroy, outgoing Director of the U.S. National Science Foundation. Man can lick environmental degradation, if he is willing to do the arduous research which must be done to discover how to go about it and how to develop alternatives. "We can survive," he said, "if we act to preserve a balanced environment, for by so doing we preserve ourselves." (Joseph L. Myler, UP reporter, "Future of Man in Doubt," *South Bend Tribune,* Dec. 11, 1971, p. 7)

247. By all means including: 1. to prevent abuse and misuse; 2. to reduce depletion, erosion and deterioration; 3. to avoid exhaustion and extinction; 4. to restore, reclaim, recover, renew and reuse; 5. to protect growth; 6. to alleviate uneven distribution; and 7. to promote development. (Cf. Richard M. Highsmith,

tion to a harmless level,[248] and to relieve overcrowding with a global pattern of small towns.[249] This work is of such a great magnitude that it is impossible to elaborate anything here except to note some principles.

First, it is necessary to take into account the total environment because its elements are closely interrelated and interdependent.[250]

Second, it is necessary for man to be self-restrained under the natural laws and not to exploit nature at will.[251]

Jr., Granville Jensen and Robert D. Rudd, *Conservation in the United States,* Chicago, 1962, p. 1-6, 16-18.)

248. For example, how best to control pests and at the same time remove environmental hazards? Restrictions on pesticide use and the substitution of other methods of pest control seem to be the solutions. Restriction can mean simply more limited use or total banning of the chemicals. Several countries have already limited or banned the use of DDT. Among these are Sweden, Hungary, and some Canadian provinces. In the Soviet Union, all production of DDT has been stopped. In the United States, the phasing out of DDT began in 1970, and the other major chlorinated hydrocarbon insecticides will likely meet the same fate. (Cf. Gordon R. Conway, "Better Methods of Pest Control," in *Environment, Resources, Pollution & Society,* ed by William W. Murdoch, Stamford, Conn., 1972, p. 302-324.)

249. "A happier alternative—indeed, the only viable alternative—is a global pattern of small cities and towns, separated by countryside.... such a pattern of population distribution would be more compatible with the measures suggested above, would be more satisfying and humane for the human inhabitants, would be more able to support diverse cultures and would be more ecologically sound and attuned to the earth's resources than the present pattern of planless metropolitan growth, which is a global phenomenon." (R. Thomas Tanner, *Ecology, Environment and Education,* Lincoln, Nebr., 1974, p. 13-14)

250. Other troubles may occur if we fail to consider the total environment. For instance, "The Aswan Dam of Egypt was built for irrigation and electric power. But it is also encouraging the multiplication of the snail that carries the crippling disease bilharzia. The reduced flow of the Nile will prevent the deposit of silt that has kept the delta fertile. Salinization of the soil is becoming a problem." (Roger Hilsman, *The Crouching Future,* New York, 1975, p. 519)

251. "Man has achieved a considerable degree of ecological dominance.... Yet he does not hold complete sway over nature—as a part of the ecosystem, he is still subject to the governing laws of nature, and failure to take these laws into account can lead to the destruction of the present and potential resources that are necessary for his survival and welfare." "A third aim of conservation is the protection of plants, animals, and the land itself, on the assumption that nature is important for its own sake and is not simply a storehouse for man's needs, to be exploited at will." (Richard M. Highsmith, Jr., "Conservation," in the *Encyclopedia Americana,* 1973 ed., Vol. 7, p. 618, 622)

Third, it is necessary to consider changes in technology and man's need for different resources in the long future.[252]

Fourth, it is necesary to measure the life of the biosphere in which man and his environment are integrated, not by years or decades, but by at least thousands of years.[253]

And finally, it is necessary to view and treat the world, which is finite and integral, as a whole.[254]

It is notable that the last principle has been primarily recognized by the establishment of the United Nations Environment Programme which works for global information.[255]

---

252. "There is always the danger that the resources most heavily demanded at a given time will gain disproportionate attention to the disadvantage of those that are little used and those that may have only potential value." (Richard M. Highsmith, Jr., "Conservation," in the *Encyclopedia Americana,* 1973 ed., Vol. 7, p. 622)

253. "Many people ... are concluding on the basis of mounting and reasonably objective evidence that the length of life of the biosphere as an inhabitable region for organisms is to be measured in decades rather than in hundreds of millions of years. This is entirely the fault of our own species." (G. Evelyn Hutchinson, "The Biosphere," *Scientific American,* Sept. 1971, p. 53)

254. "Man's dilemma is that the world's natural resources will be wasted away if he fails to comprehend the ecology of the living landscape and act accordingly. This problem is of such magnitude and global importance for the future of mankind that it demands intergovernmental involvement. Conservation principles must be implemented on an international scale." (Kai Curry-Lindahl, *Conservation for Survival: an Ecological Strategy,* New York, 1972, p. 303)

> "... the greatest beauty
> is organic wholeness,
> the wholeness
> of life and things,
> the divine beauty
> of the universe.
> Love that, not
> man apart from that ..."

(By the famous American poet, Robinson Jeffers, quoted by *Not Man Apart,* published by the organization of Friends of the Earth, Vol. 3, no. 7, July 1973)

255. Only in the last few years have nations come to realize that industrial and other activities in one country or region can have adverse effects on the environment of another country—even on opposite sides of the globe. In June, 1972, as a result of the Swedish initiative, a UN conference was held in Stockholm to discuss international actions to alleviate environmental deterioration. Though this was the first global effort by governments to deal with environmental problems, 113 countries participated—a testament to the importance accorded this issue all over the world. One of the most important results of the Stockholm Conference was the establishment of an international environmental organization, known as the

We now come to the conclusion of the long review of the situations and relationships of manpower, energy, non-fuel minerals, forest products, water, food, population, environment and conservation, with a discussion of the principles of a general management for all the works considered in the review.

h.
All Resources to Mankind

GENERALLY SPEAKING, ALL THE WORKS CONCERNED are complex, interwoven in nature, and worldwide in scope.[256] The major function of a general management is to conduct all such works in a spirit of teamwork, performing smoothly and harmoniously. However, there already exists a big obstacle to the functioning of a

---

United Nations Environment Programme (UNEP). Through its "Earthwatch" program and its monitoring component, the Global Environmental Monitoring System (GEMS), UNEP will attempt to anticipate growing environmental dangers, to identify potentially harmful environmental activities, such as the accumulation of toxic substances in living organisms, and to inform the appropriate national governments or international institutions of these dangers. In this enterprise it will rely chiefly on existing national and international monitoring and research mechanisms. (Cf. *Science and Technology in an Era of Interdependence,* by the UNA-USA National Policy Panel, New York, 1975, p. 48-49.)

256. "A review of the international issues which have been raised by developments in science and technology indicates that these problems have become increasingly complex and interrelated, just as the interdependencies among nations have grown. In the ongoing law-of-the-sea negotiations, there are interactions among such diverse issues as management of ocean fisheries, which are an essential component of the world's protein supply, and transit through international waters, a question of strategic interest to the major maritime powers. The worldwide rise in oil prices has meant higher cost for fertilizers and for the crops to which they are applied, as well as higher gasoline prices. And advances in the atmospheric sciences can lead not only to better forecasting but eventually to large-scale weather and climate modification. Such capabilities could in turn serve activities as diverse as air transport and agriculture. Because of their complexity it is difficult to treat these issues as separate problems, or even to categorize them as primarily scientific, economic or political. They are issues which do not respect the standard patterns of international affairs and have already begun to transform relationships among the nations of the world." (*Science and Technology in an Era of Interdependence,* by the UNA-USA National Policy Panel, New York, 1975, p. 23)

general management, the claim and control by the individual nations of the natural resources which are important to all the works. In order to remove the big obstacle, it is necessary, first of all, to make a proposition that all the natural resources of land, ocean and space belong to mankind as a whole,[257] as the precedent established in the open seas.[258]

This proposition is very important not only for the effective management of all the works, but also for the elimination of a permanent cause of international disputes, conflicts and wars. This cause is the rivalry among nations for natural resources, as signified by the struggles for the control of minerals which have led to wars engulfing the world.[259]

---

257. "26. God, who hath given the world to men in common, hath also given them reason to make use of it to the best advantage of life and convenience. The earth and all that is therein is given to men for the support and comfort of their being. And though all the fruits it naturally produces, and beasts it feeds, belong to mankind in common, as they are produced by the spontaneous hand of nature; and nobody has originally a private dominion exclusive of the rest of mankind in any of them as they are thus in their natural state." (John Locke, *Of Civil Government,* second essay, 1690, reprinted, Chicago, 1940, p. 15)

258. At the time when the seas began to come under the control of mankind, most maritime states claimed sovereignty over certain seas; for example, Venice claimed the Adriatic; England the North Sea, the Channels, and large areas of the Atlantic; Sweden and Denmark the Baltic. Under Bulls of Pope Alexander VI of 1493, Spain and Portugal even claimed to divide the New World between themselves; Spain claimed the whole Pacific and the Gulf of Mexico, Portugal the Indian Ocean and most of the Atlantic, and both excluded foreigners from these vast areas. It was these claims that prepared the ground for a reaction against any sovereignty over the seas, and the claim of the Portuguese in 1609 provoked the *Mare Liberum* of Grotius, in which he maintained that the sea could not be made the property of any state. Gradually, the claims of sovereignty over the seas were dropped, and since the end of the first quarter of the nineteenth century the freedom of the open sea has been regarded as established. This precedent has provided a rational basis for the proposition that all natural resources of land, ocean, and space belong to mankind as a whole. (Cf. James L. Brierly, *The Law of Nations; an Introduction to the International Law of Peace,* 4th ed., Oxford, 1949, p. 223-224.)

259. The Industrial Revolution has brought into the essential use of modern industry more and more natural resources which are so unevenly distributed that no nation is fully endowed. Most serious in this situation are the mineral resources in which no nation can claim self-sufficiency. Consequently, the control of mineral resources has become a major subject of international rivalries. Cases in point were the German efforts to secure iron ore in Morocco, the British efforts to secure additional territory in Venezuela, and the dispute between Chile and Peru, before World War I. Much political friction was created in Europe by the redistribution of territories under the Versailles Peace Treaty which deprived some nations of mineral resources. Austria was almost stripped of its mineral deposits,

Certainly there have been attempts to ease this rivalry, such as the famous slogan of "equal access to raw materials."[260] But they have accomplished almost nothing.[261] On the contrary, the situation has become even tenser in recent years with the superpowers contending for the domination of the oil-rich Middle East,[262] the growing worry

---

and Germany lost important mineral districts both in the east and the west. The control of iron ore was an important factor in the German seizure of Lorraine in the war of 1870, and the occupation of Lorraine, Alsace, and the Saar by the French after World War I had among its principal goals the acquisition of mineral resources. The acquiring of mineral resources and some other raw materials was an important motive of Italy's aggression on Abyssinia, Japan's occupation of Manchuria, and Germany's attempt to reclaim the lost lands in the west and in the east. Since World War I demonstrated the vital dependence of military power on minerals and since the blockade of the hostile nations in regard to vital minerals was used as a very important means of fighting, international rivalries for the control of mineral resources became more acute, and these rivalries played a great part in the development of World War II. (Cf. Charles K. Leith, *World Minerals and World Politics,* Port Washington, 1931; and Charles K. Leith, James W. Furness and Cleona Lewis, *World Minerals and World Peace,* Washington, 1943.)

260. The euphonious phrase, "equal access to raw materials," has received wide public attention since it was used by the Germans in the first World War, and has been regarded as a possible way to solve the problems resulting from the unequal distribution of resources. This idea has also been given the highest official status in the Atlantic Charter which was issued by U.S. President Roosevelt and the British Prime Minister Churchill in 1942 and was subsequently endorsed by the United Nations. The related paragraph in the Atlantic Charter reads as follows: Their countries "will endeavor, with due respect for their existing obligations, to further the enjoyment by all states, great or small, victor or vanquished, of access, on equal terms, to the trade and to the raw materials of the world which are needed for their economic prosperity." (Cf. Charles K. Leith, James W. Furness, and Cleona Lewis, *World Minerals and World Peace,* Washington, 1943, chap. V.)

261. The main reason for this is that the primary concern of the nations is their security. No nation will feel secure as long as the resources of its needed raw materials are in the possession of other nations, no matter what guarantee may be arranged for free access to raw materials in a free market. This insecure feeling has grown since the blockade of war materials proved an efficient fighting means, and with the realization that many vital materials are scarce.

262. The involvement of the Soviet Union in the Middle East is complex. Its trade has expanded from being negligible in the early 1950s to a total turnover of $1,500 million in 1970. It supplied in 1954-1970 a total of $3,019 million of economic aid, and more than $4,000 million of military aid, with hundreds of military advisers. It has exercised a predominant influence in Algeria, Iraq, Sudan, Syria, Libya, and South Yemen; has supported the Palestine Liberation Organization; and has greatly increased navy and air power in the Mediterranean and Indian Ocean to challenge the powerful Sixth Fleet and air force of the United States which has tried to maintain its dominant position and protect the vital interest in the oil-rich region for itself and for its allies since the Straits and Azerbaijan crises

about shortages or scarcities of some essential materials,[263] and the spreading of organized boycotts and cartels.[264] Obviously, there is no way to get rid of this rivalry unless the proposition that all natural resources belong to mankind is realized.[265]

The realization of this proposition can also lessen among the peoples the economic inequality which has appeared since the Industrial Revolution[266] with the uneven distribution of natural

---

of 1945-1946. (Cf. Charles Issawi, *Oil, the Middle East and the World,* London, 1972, p. 54-64; and Lincoln Landis, *Politics and Oil: Moscow in the Middle East,* New York, 1973, p. 21-22.)

263. "Recent and projected shortages of such essential materials as food, fuel and fertilizer raise serious questions as to the obligations of nations to constrain their patterns of consumption and to share resources in times of scarcity. These are complex issues, which will not be settled quickly or easily.... Attention must also be given to developing arrangements which will discourage nations from provoking severe economic dislocations by exploiting shortages of essential resources for political purposes." (*Science and Technology in an Era of Interdependence,* by the UNA-USA National Policy Panel, New York, 1975, p. 55)

264. In view of the intensifying competition for resources, the supplier nations have tended to organize cartels or take other measures to raise prices, deny supplies to political adversaries, and thus increase international economic instability. Well-known in this respect has been the Organization of Petroleum Exporting Countries whose members are: Abu Dhabi, Algeria, Ecuador, Gabon, Indonesia, Iran, Iraq, Kuwait, Libya, Nigeria, Qatar, Saudi Arabia, and Venezuela. They account for one-half of world production of petroleum and fully 90 percent of world petroleum exports. Producer groups have been organized for copper and bauxite, and both producer and consumer states participate in the International Tin Council. Morocco, the world's largest phosphate exporter, has tripled its phosphate prices, and Jamaica has almost tripled taxes and royalties on its bauxite production. Other developing supplier states have expressed particular interest in such actions, since they have been hard hit by the rise in oil prices and must pay high prices for finished goods produced from raw materials supplied by them at much lower prices. (Cf. *Science and Technology in an Era of Interdependence,* by the UNA-USA National Policy Panel, New York, 1975, p. 33, 38; and John E. Tilton, *The Future of Nonfuel Minerals,* Washington, 1977, p. 1.)

265. Noting that nations have often gone to war over natural resources, U.S. President Gerald Ford added that "no one can foresee the extent of the damage nor the end of the disastrous consequences if nations refuse to share nature's gifts for the benefit of all mankind." (Quoted in the *South Bend Tribune,* Sept. 23, 1974, p. 1.) If all natural resources belonged to mankind under the management of the world government, the rivalry for them among nations would eventually pass away just as at present there is no serious problem concerning them within a nation.

266. The birth of modern economic inequality was given by the Industrial Revolution. Because before this Revolution our civilization was essentially agricultural: and as the basic prerequisites of an agricultural civilization—soil and water—are widely scattered over the face of the earth, the differences between

resources,[267] and has been deepened recently by the increase of disproportionate burdens to the resource-poor countries as victims of the vicious antagonism between the resource-rich ones.[268]

---

regions were not essential, and therefore, no great inequality existed in the world economy. Modern industry is founded on iron, which is the principal machine metal, and coal, which is the primary provider of power to run the machines. Although these two minerals are widely distributed over the world, their main deposits occur concurrently in a belt which extends from the Mississippi Valley through Central Russia. The combination of these two minerals has prompted this belt to be known as the industrial heart of the world, and has created an inequality in the world economy. Erich W. Zimmerman described this as the "resource hierarchy of modern world economy" in his *World Resources and Industries,* New York, 1933, p. 805-809. (Cf. Charles K. Leith, James W. Furness, and Cleona Lewis, *World Minerals and World Peace,* Washington, 1943, p. 32-33.)

267. For example, "the coal reserves of the world are far from equitably distributed among the world's people. The continent of Asia, for example, has 49.4 percent, or almost exactly half, of the world's coal reserves, nearly all of which are in the U.S.S.R. and China. North America has 34.4 percent, or about one third; Europe has 13.0 percent and the remaining 3.2 percent is divided between the three whole continents of Africa, South America, and Australia. By countries, the United States has approximately one-third, Russia one-fourth and China one-fifth of the world's coal. Of the 13.0 percent in Europe, Germany has about one half, the United Kingdom one-fourth, and Poland one-eighth." (M. King Hubbert, *Energy Resources,* Washington, 1962, p. 37-38. Cf. the table on p. 37.)

"Significant reserves of petroleum are found in only a handful of countries. Thirteen countries, which make up the Organization of Petroleum Exporting Countries, Abu Dhabi, Algeria, Ecuador, Gabon, Indonesia, Iran, Iraq, Kuwait, Libya, Nigeria, Qatar, Saudi Arabia and Venezuela, account for one-half of world production of petroleum, and fully 90 percent of world petroleum exports. At the beginning of 1974, over half of the world's total proven petroleum reserves were located in the Middle East alone. The concentration of such a significant percentage of petroleum resources in this small number of oil producing states has given them extraordinary leverage over worldwide oil price structures. Prices for oil have risen steadily since 1971 and have quadrupled in the last year. It is estimated that in 1974 the developed countries will pay $53 billion more for the same amount of oil products they consumed in 1973. In the non-oil-producing developing countries the bill is expected to increase by $10 billion." (*Science and Technology in an Era of Interdependence,* by the UNA-USA National Policy Panel, New York, 1975, p. 33-34)

268. "Of particular concern should be the economic situation of the non-oil-producing developing countries. As noted, these countries were expected to pay an additional $10 billion in 1974 for their oil imports. Combined with increased costs for other essential imports, such as foodstuffs and fertilizers, their total import bills were expected to rise by $15 billion in 1974." (*Science and Technology in an Era of Interdependence,* by the UNA-USA National Policy Panel, New York, 1975, p. 34)

Concerning the artificial rigging of oil prices by the oil producing countries, U.S. Secretary of State Henry A. Kissinger said, "It cannot be in the interest of any nation to magnify the despair of the least developed who are uniquely

It should be noted, however, that if all the potential natural resources are taken into account,[269] viewed in the long run, not in the short term, and weighed by social value, not by commercial standards, there is no region which is not rich in some of them while poor in others; and it is impossible to compare the uneven distribution region by region and to measure the inequality between them. Therefore, the proposition that all natural resources belong to mankind is not unfair to anyone, but beneficial to everyone.

Furthermore, the real value of natural resources lies not in what they are, but in how they are processed by technology.[270] It depends

---

vulnerable to exorbitant prices and who have no recourse but to pay." (*South Bend Tribune,* Sept. 23, 1974, p. 1)

269. "What are natural resources? The earth's surface provides the stage for human life, and the useful elements of the natural environment—the natural resources—provide the materials necessary for man to survive. At any given time and place, of course, some features of the natural environment may form obstacles calling for modification or circumvention, while others may be more or less neutral; such features would not then be regarded as resources. Potentially, however, almost any feature of the environment may be useful to some human societies at some stage of their technological development, and thus nearly all features of the environment must be regarded as potential natural resources. The technological and social conditions that make environmental features both useful and available, and thus lead to their recognition as resources, vary from place to place and change with the passage of time. Paleolithic hunters and American Indians, for example, were largely dependent upon flint and other rocks for materials to make axes, arrows, and other tools. When bronze and other metals began to be used for this purpose, these rocks lost most of their resource value, while previously valueless ore-bearing rocks became highly prized. The American Indians and even the early European settlers found little or no value in the coal deposits of Appalachia, since they could easily get all the fuel they needed from the forests that surrounded them." (Richard M. Highsmith, Jr., "Conservation," in the *Encyclopedia Americana,* 1973 ed., Vol. 7, p. 618)

In the long run, as far as natural resources are concerned, there is no country in the world which is always rich or poor. Saudi Arabia, for example, was a poor country fifty years ago, and has suddenly become probably the richest country of the present time, owing to its huge quantity of oil output. But how can it maintain such a lucky position when its oil reserve will probably be exhausted in fifty years as estimated by experts?

270. "It is technology which gives value to the stuffs which it processes; and as the useful arts advance the gifts of nature are remade.... With technology on the march, the emphasis of value shifts from the natural to the processed good." (Walton H. Hamilton, "Control of Strategic Materials," *American Economic Review,* June, 1944, p. 262)

"Resources can only be defined in terms of known technology. Half a century ago the air was for breathing and burning; now it is also a natural resource of the chemical industry. Two decades ago Vermont granite was only building and tomb-

not on their static property, but on their dynamic function.[271] Clearly, its mother is knowledge, which is the common heritage of our civilization.[272] The proposition that all natural resources belong to mankind just carries this heritage one step forward.

i.
Cooperation of
Various Systems

NEEDLESS TO SAY, THIS PROPOSITION WOULD MAKE the general management the sole authority to explore and exploit space, the ocean and the uncontrolled portions of the land; but it would not necessarily mean to change or strip the existing private ownership of land resources. Under the administration, regulation,

---

stone material; now it is a potential fuel, each ton of which has a useable energy content (uranium) equal to 150 tons of coal." (Harold J. Barnett and Chandler Morse, *Scarcity and Growth; the Economics of Natural Resource Availability,* Baltimore, 1963, p. 7)

271. "And somebody had the effrontery to call the world 'a bundle of hay'! It is incredible. And others insist to this very day that resources are, that they are static and fixed! One has but to consider some of the most precious resources of our age—electricity, oil, nuclear energy—to see who is right, the exponent of the static school who insists that 'resources are,' or the defender of the dynamic, functional, operational school who insists that 'resources become.' " (*Erich W. Zimmermann's Introduction to World Resources,* ed. by Henry L. Hunker, New York, 1964, p. 14)

272. "Incomparably greatest among human resources is knowledge. It is greatest because it is the mother of other resources. The aboriginal inhabitants of what is now the United States lived in a poverty-stricken environment. For them no coal existed, no petroleum, no metals beyond nuggets of pure copper. Of electrical energy they had no inkling. Their agriculture was so crude that they could use only tiny patches of the soil. Their rudimentary social organization combined with their ineffective production to keep their groups small and mutually hostile. . . . Not only is knowledge the greatest of resources, it is also the resource that we have counted upon to grow richer with every decade. The cumulative expansion of science and of its practical applications has emboldened us to expect that each generation of our descendants will discover new resources and more efficient ways of using old ones." (Wesley C. Mitchell, "Conservation, Liberty, and Economics," in *The Foundations of Conservation Education,* by the National Wildlife Federation, New York, 1941, p. 1-2)

supervision and allocation of the general management in the interest of all peoples, private ownership can go as far as traditions allow. For where no private ownership is allowed, such as in the Communist countries generally, public ownership may be treated in the same way as private ownership, with communes, collective farms, industrial councils, and so on. This treatment illustrates another necessary proposition, that all existing economic systems are entitled to operate, compete, and to adjust by free will under the general management. This proposition is intended to alleviate the differences of the various economic systems, which are also an obstacle to the functioning of the general management.

In theory, there are indeed some wide differences among the various economic systems, especially between the capitalist and Communist systems. In practice, however, even between these two great different systems, the gap is narrowing at a quick pace.[273] In various ways, for example, the United States has taken a number of significant actions for social reforms with some Communist flavor,[274] while the Soviet Union has permitted some small private

---

273. "Nor have Communist value systems remained unaffected by this progressive technological impact upon traditional ideologies and work habits. By the end of the century Soviet society can be expected to continue to have much lower per capita production and consumption than the United States; nevertheless, it will enjoy a living standard possibly twice as high as that prevailing in the 1960s. Such relative prosperity will almost certainly contribute in turn to a further decline of traditional Marxist dogma, which has been manifesting itself in Communist countries in the form of new, critical attitudes. The younger and more sophisticated Russians display little of the militancy of the revolution that took place before their birth. Instead, they insist upon greater freedom of thought and expression for their writers and artists and upon more opportunity for travel and affluence." (T. Walter Wallbank, Alastair M. Taylor, Nels M. Bailkey and Mark Mancall, *Civilization Past and Present,* 6th ed., Glenview, Ill., 1970, Book 1, p. 510)

274. These actions include the No Slavery Proclamation of 1863, the Sherman Antitrust Act of 1890, the Clayton Antitrust Act of 1914, Federal Estate Tax acts to limit inheritance fortunes, the Revenue Act of 1932 with a fair progressive income tax, the Social Security Act of 1935, the Federal Public Contracts Act of 1936, the Fair Labor Standards Act of 1938, the Employment Act of 1946, and the Labor Management Relations Act of 1947. They are signified as social legislation of which the purpose "is the promotion of the social welfare of the people. In accomplishing this the government may forbid acts that are harmful to the community, it may compel things to be done for the good of the community, and it may go even further than this and develop right attitudes by the promotion of preventive legislation in dealing with the underlying causes of social evils and maladjustments to changing conditions." (Mary S. Callcott, *Principles of Social Legislation,* New York, 1932, p. 10. Cf. Robert N. Covington, *Social Legislation,* 2d ed., Washington, 1974.)

enterprises and personal property,[275] and has made some great adjustments to stimulate productivity by capitalist methods.[276] Lately, Mitterrand has been blending the old capitalist France with a Communist program,[277] just as twenty years ago Tito reshaped the new

---

275. In the Constitution of the USSR (1936), Article 7: "... Every household in a collective farm, in addition to its basic income from the common collective farm enterprise, has for its personal use a small plot of household land and, as its personal property, a subsidiary husbandry on the plot, a dwelling house, livestock, poultry and minor agricultural implements—in accordance with the rules of the agricultural artel." Article 9: "Alongside the socialist system of economy, which is the predominant form of economy in the USSR, the law permits the small private economy of individual peasants and handicraftsmen based on their own labor and precluding the exploitation of the labor of others." And Article 10: "The personal property right of citizens in their incomes and savings from work, in their dwelling houses and subsidiary home enterprises, in articles of domestic economy and use and articles of personal use and convenience, as well as the right of citizens to inherit personal property, is protected by law." (Cf. Samuel N. Harper and Ronald Thompson, *The Government of the Soviet Union,* 2nd ed., New York, 1949, p. 328.)

276. "Communist leadership today ordered managers of Soviet industry to revamp their personnel policies to include such capitalistic schemes as incentive pay and employee profit sharing. It was a bold move to boost productivity. Experiments in this new concept have proven successful in about 30 major enterprises in the Soviet Union since 1966. The decree from the Central Committee of the Communist Party cited an experiment in incentive pay and profit sharing at the Shchokino Chemical Plant as the basis for the nationwide reform. According to the announcement, the chemical plant increased its productivity by 87 per cent in the past year while reducing its labor force by 870 persons—the result of incentives of employees. 'The work carried out at the Shchokino Chemical Plant has an important economic significance,' the decree said. 'Wide use of this experience ... opens great prospects for placing into action the existing labor reserves, increasing production output and raising the productivity of labor.' The decree gives plant managers great discretion in production methods and empowers them to fire employees or award incentive raises and shares of the profits." (UPI report, *South Bend Tribune,* Oct. 9, 1969, p. 10)

277. In France, the Socialist Party won a presidential election on May 10, 1981, for Francois Mitterrand, as the first leftist head of state. Its reform programs include raising the minimum wage, increasing social benefits, raising taxes on the rich, creating new public service jobs and lowering the work week to 35 hours. Included also are heavy taxation on corporations and nationalization of the remaining private banks and 10 major industrial groups, ranging from steel to data processing. During his first few weeks in office, President Mitterrand has embarked on part of the programs by creating 54,000 new government jobs (at a cost of $1.2 billion), raising the minimum wage 10 percent, hiking family benefits by 25 percent, increasing pensions over two stages by 50 percent and socking France's 100,000 most wealthy people with higher taxes. (Cf. 1981 AP reports in the *South*

communist Yugoslavia in a capitalist fashion.[278] Yugoslavia's pattern has been followed more or less by the Communist countries in
eastern Europe,[279] and has even had some effect in the recent struggle
for modernization in China.[280]

Bend Tribune, June 20, p. 8, June 21, p. 6. Cf. also Smith Hempstone's comment
on p. 4, June 20, 1981 of the *Tribune,* .)

278. "In the world of communism Yugoslavia today is a thing apart. It is
neither democracy as America knows it, nor communism as Russia knows it.
Yugoslavia is a unique blend of Marxist ideals and capitalistic practice.... The big
breakthrough toward the dynamism now at work began in 1966 when Tito took his
independent form of communism around a drastic new turn toward Western ways.
In a major gamble.... At one stroke he exposed the sluggish economy to open
competition with capitalism and warned, in effect, 'Sink or swim' .... today a
spirit of ferment, experimentation and excitement is abroad in the land, unleashed
by an explosion of opportunities and rising expectations. 'People became suddenly
aware that the more and better they work, the more they could earn,' says a
Belgrade journalist.... With workers getting a share of the income their companies earn, production has skyrocketed, pouring a growing flood of consumer
items onto a market hungry for them.... Small entrepreneurs operating
businesses of their own can hire up to five employees before regulations turn the
business into a 'public enterprise' run by workers' councils. Many bring in relatives—who don't officially count as employees—to work in growing business
operations like restaurants, laundries and hotels." (Gerald Miller, AP Reporter,
"Economy of Yugoslavia, Where Socialism Swings, Is More Market Than Marxist," *South Bend Tribune,* May 9, 1969, p. 9)

279. "East European Communist factory managers and economists have
broken many party shackles hampering industrial independence, and their upris-
ing has swept across the frontier into the Soviet Union.... Independent
Yugoslavia led years ago in loosening the party reins, and now has gone a step farther. Parliament is demanding, and getting, a speed-up. East Germany,
Czechoslovakia and Romania are all moving into the first stages of decentralized
planning. Romania in fact is well along. Result: Romanian industrial production
has increased a steady 13 per cent annually for five years, ahead of any other
Socialist state, including the U.S.S.R. ... What is happening exactly? As described to me by planners in Czechoslovakia, the Soviet Union, Yugoslavia, East Germany and more recently in Romania, the essentials are these: 1. Central planning
of all industry is being cut back to include only general objectives. 2. Individual
plants whose every movement, every design, formerly had to be cleared through
the central planning authority, now make many of their own plans. 3. The plant
managers who do well get higher awards and can pay their employees more. 4. In
the long run—and perhaps not so long—it is likely to have a strong impact on the
position of the party leaders, especially at the grass roots level." (Preston Grover,
AP reporter, "Private Initiative, Newly Found by Communists, Gains Support in
Eastern Europe," *South Bend Tribune,* Jan. 24, 1965, p. 19)

280. In order to pursue the "four modernizations," i.e., agriculture, industry,
defence, and science and technology, Deng Xiaoping, the Chinese Communist
leader, stressed in early 1980 that the fundamental task of economic development

In ideology, the capitalist emphasizes liberty, while the communist stresses equality. But both liberty and equality are empty if not accompanied by a decent living standard; a decent living standard cannot be achieved without high productivity; and high productivity can be obtained only through the progress made by science and technology. Thus, science and technology only can make both liberty and equality really meaningful. They are the joint point for the capitalist and Communist systems, as well as the other economic systems, to enter into a common road.[281]

Furthermore, it is possible for science and technology to introduce the various economic systems, freed from their ideological fetters and national controls, into a common pattern suitable for everywhere, and differentiated only by natural conditions.

---

was first for solving China's problems. Development, not sloganeering or vast social movements, was the "new revolution" the country should pursue for the foreseeable future. "If a revolution," Deng said, "is divorced from the development and modernization of production—on which after all the prosperity of any people depends—then the aim and goals of this revolution are mere empty words." Second, Deng asserted that China would win the economic race only by broadening its contacts—especially economic and technological—with the outside world. "In no country has the process of modernization occurred in isolation. It has always depended on cross-fertilization among different peoples.... The managerial skills of the capitalist countries—particularly various methods of developing science and technology—are part of man's common heritage. There is no reason why these skills cannot be put to good use in a socialist China." (*China Briefing, 1980,* ed. by Robert B. Oxnam and Richard C. Bush, Boulder, Colorado, p. 10)

281. A sign of such joint cooperation has been erected by the Moscow summit conference of 1972: "Here is a capsule summary of agreements already signed at the Moscow summit: —Co-operation to fight environmental pollution. —Joint research in combating cancer and heart disease. —Joint mission in 1975 by a three-man Apollo spacecraft to link with a Soviet Soyuzship. —Co-operation in science and technology including high-energy physics and the exchange of scientists and documents in various fields." (UPI report, *South Bend Tribune,* May 25, 1972, p. 2) The summit conference was held by U.S. President Nixon and the Russian leaders, Leonid Brezhnev and Alexei Kosygin.

Modern Communist advocates have had to hold out hopes to science and technology. "All the new marvels of modern science in the twentieth century, the releasing of nuclear energy or the magic wand of the latest chemicals discovery and techniques, should have belonged to the era of socialism, speeding the path to abundance for all." (R. Palme Dutt, *The Internationale,* London, 1964, p. 399)

j.
Economic Equalization

THE DEVELOPMENT OF A COMMON ECONOMIC PAT-
tern may also be helped by several important measures the general
management will have to take eventually. Among these measures are
the establishment of a central world bank,[282] the issue of a world currency,[283] the collection of a universal income tax[284] and an inheritance tax,[285] the removal of barriers to trade and travel,[286] the

---

282. The central world bank would not quite resemble the present World
Bank, or, by its full title, the International Bank for Reconstruction and Development, created in 1944, not only in scope, but also in function. It would also serve as
the center of all banks, in somewhat the same way as the Federal Reserve Bank of
the United States. (Cf. II, 262; and Paul B. Trescott, "Federal Reserve System,"
in the *Encyclopedia Americana,* 1973 ed., Vol. II, p. 74-76.)

283. "A world government would make possible a single, stable monetary
system throughout the world, in place of the large number of unrelated and
unstable systems which prevail at present. This would greatly facilitate trade
among the various countries of the earth, and as trade in its last analysis is the
transfer of goods from a place where they are less needed to a place where they are
more needed, anything which facilitates world trade is a blessing to mankind."
(Oscar Newfang, *The Road to World Peace,* New York, 1924, p. 68-69)

The world currency would be the official medium of exchange and the common standard of value for goods, services, and related matters, such as credit and
debt, through the whole world. It would also be the sole standard for exchange of
local currencies if their existence is allowed. An economist pointed out: "The fact is
that, just as unified national currency was necessary to facilitate the development
of national economies up to their present level, so a unified world currency is the indispensable condition for further development of world economy from the present
stage. . . . The complicated machinery of world economy, world-wide production,
world-wide use of raw materials, distribution on the world markets, demands a
stable standard of exchange that only a single world currency can provide."

284. The universal income tax would be a direct and progressive one. It is the
appropriate way to channel all the current military expenditures of the world into
use for the pursuit of general happiness. Thus, it means much more than what
Justice Oliver Wendell Holmes, Jr., meant when he said, "taxes are the price we
pay for civilization."

285. An inheritance is imposed on the shares of estates going to the various
beneficiaries and heirs and is payable by them. It may be levied on the value of all
tangible and intangible property left by the decedent after the exclusion of
charitable bequests, the deduction of funeral and administrative expenses,
specified exemptions, and the payment of debts. It has effects on the redistribution
of fortunes and reduction of concentration of wealth. The current rates of the U.S.

stabilization of prices and employment the world over,[287] and the adoption of a social security system for all the people.[288]

It is necessary to note that the project for a universal social security system does not indicate that the general management will perform all works of local welfare. The primary responsibility for local welfare always goes with the local people. Local welfare, like local politics, is autonomous in nature. What the general management is supposed to do concerns matters which are above and beyond local abilities, in principle.

---

federal estates range from 3% on estates over $60,000 to 77% on those exceeding $10 million. (Cf. Carl S. Shoup, *Federal Estate and Gift Taxes,* Washington, 1966, p. 1-11, and 228-236.)

286. "Under a world government commodities would move freely and without restriction by tariffs or otherwise from parts of the world where they are less needed to parts where they are more needed, and the great blessing which this would confer upon the whole human race can hardly be conceived by us at present." "If the reader will consider the vast benefits derived by the citizens of any large modern country from the economic unity which prevails throughout that country, and the intolerable hampering of trade that would result, if tariffs and immigration restrictions were applied at every state, provincial or departmental boundary, he can dimly begin to comprehend what an inestimable blessing to all mankind would result from the real economic unity of the world, which would be the natural consequence of a world government." (Oscar Newfang, *The Road to World Peace,* New York, 1924, p. 100-101, 72)

There will be no customs, no tariff on merchandise, and no restriction to travel, any place. A good example for zero tariff among the members has been set by the European Common Market. Serious physical barriers to trade and travel, such as the lack of transportation means and facilities in some areas, will also be removed by building more railroads and highways, and opening more airlines and waterways, to meet the needs.

287. It is possible to stabilize prices and employment permanently through an effective control of world population and appropriate adjustments of supply and demand in the world market; with a sound monetary system, and after the elimination of international conflicts, which are the main direct or indirect cause of inflation and unemployment. The war debts and indemnities of World War I, for example, led to a world economic turmoil, including the Great Depression in the United States; and the recent oil embargo by the oil-producing countries and grain ban by the grain-producing countries have intensified terribly the current inflation and unemployment throughout the world.

288. The social security system in the United States may be a good example. As embodied in the Social Security Act of 1935 and its amendments, it provides for six broad types of programs: social insurance, public assistance, social services, health insurance for the aged and disabled (Medicare), payment of medical costs for the needy (Medicaid), and health services for maternity and for crippled children. (Cf. Shirley Jenkins, *Social Security in International Perspective,* New York, 1969.)

In this respect, the attention of the general management would be focused first on helping poor areas to raise their living standards. This requires not only the provision of adequate financial assistance, but also the mobilization of skills, equipment and capital from the rich countries for the economic development of the poor areas.[289] What the poor areas have to do first is to control their population to an optimum level by all means, because the basic reason for their increasing plight is that their population in general is too dense and is growing exponentially.

The primary purpose of the general management in such efforts projected for the poor areas is to narrow the economic gap as much as possible between countries as well as between individuals. With the help of modern science and technology, it is possible to achieve this goal by raising the low living standards without reducing the high ones. Nor is it necessary to stress the future promise at the sacrifice of the present reward, or to emphasize the spiritual pursuit at the sacrifice of the material satisfaction.[290] What the rich countries, and the rich individuals as well, have to do is to strive for a life of high quality rather than great quantity by restoring their pride in prudence, avoiding self-indulgence, and maintaining an enduring style of life.[291]

---

289. Even today, when the nations retain separate sovereignty, a serious conscience for this kind of obligation has been clearly revealed by various leaders. For example, "We believe, however, that the United States, with its abundant scientific and natural resources, has a special obligation to adapt its policies to the realities of interdependence. We think that the American people, apprised of the implications of their actions for other countries, will respond positively. And we believe that if the United States affirms its international obligations, other countries will in turn come to recognize their own unique responsibilities and will begin to formulate their policies in this spirit." (*Science and Technology in an Era of Interdependence,* by the UNA-USA National Policy Panel, New York, 1975, p. 81)

290. Appeals for the poor at the expense of the rich, for the future promise at the expense of the present reward, and for the spiritual pursuit at the expense of material satisfaction, have been heard everywhere in the name of reforms, revolutions and religions throughout history. But modern science and technology have made it possible to pursue the general happiness for all peoples of the world through a more rational, practical and realistic approach.

291. This kind of quality has actually been preached by almost all religions and is sometimes called the "Puritan ethic" in America, where, ironically, the current lifestyle is in favor of great quantity—more cars, more highways, more urban centers, more houses, more clothes, and so on; and people have been called the "Waste Makers" (cf. Vance Packard, *The Waste Makers,* New York, 1960), with energy consumption of almost a quarter of a million calories per person per day against only 2000-3000 calories per person per day for our ancestors before the use of fire. (Cf. M. Fowler, *Energy and the Environment,* New York, *1975, p. 67.)*

k.
Life in Harmony

ACTUALLY, THE STRIVING FOR HIGH QUALITY RATHER
than great quantity is a challenge to modern man.[292] By the application of modern science and technology to industrial production, it is
not so difficult to make a great quantity through growth. It is difficult, rather, to achieve a high quality in balance. Yet, growth is encouraged by all means,[293] and balance is generally ignored.[294] In fact,
growth without balance is no better than balance without growth.
Balance is indispensable to quality just as growth is indispensable to
quantity. It is for this reason that the main economic theme for the
general management is growth with balance.

Under this theme, the world economy would be planned so as to

---

292. "... the insane quantitative growth must stop, but innovation must not
stop: it must take an entirely new direction. instead of working blindly towards things
bigger and better, it must work towards improving the quality of life rather than increasing its quantity. Innovation must work towards a new harmony, a new equilibrium; otherwise it will only lead to an explosion. There is much in Arnold Toynbee's
monumental *Study of History* with which I do not agree, but I fully subscribe to his
thesis that a civilization without a challenge must perish. Here is a supreme challenge
for all the creative spirits of the new generation; stop the insane race towards overcrowding; stop the armaments race; stop growth addiction; form the New Man who
can be at peace with himself and with his world." (Denis Gabor, *Innovations: Scientific, Technological and Social,* Oxford, 1970, introduction, p. 3)

293. "Unfortunately all our drive and optimism are bound up with continuous growth: 'growth addiction' is the unwritten and unconfessed religion of
our times. In industry and also for nations, growth has become synonymous with
hope. Undoubtedly, quantitative growth will have to go on for many more years,
but unless we prepare for a turning-point well before the end of the century, it may
by then be too late." (Dennis Gabor, *Innovations: Scientific, Technological and
Social,* Oxford, 1970, introduction, p. 3)

294. "The really odd, and ominous, thing about much technology is that the
better it gets, the more vulnerable we become. In our electronic and mechanized
society, an old-fashioned act of nature like a blizzard is apt to do more damage
than was possible in grandpa's time. We are simply not set up to handle it.... On a
larger scale, we are totally dependent upon the utility companies. If they go out, we
go out. We have sacrificed our former autonomy for a great deal of comfort and
convenience.... This is the part we haven't understood yet—just as, in a grimmer
context, we fail to understand that the growth of nuclear weapons may make us
"stronger" but at the same time far more vulnerable to global extinction."
(Sydney Harris, "Technology Leaves Us Vulnerable to Elements," *South Bend
Tribune,* April 13, 1977, p. 10)

give each area an opportunity to develop its potentialities in a harmonious order for the whole,[295] and would be managed not in a rush of flow,[296] but with adequate supplies to meet decent demands,[297] while machines work for man, and man treats his environment wise-

---

295. "One of the greatest economic benefits of a world government would be, that each country could manufacture, mine or raise the commodities for which it is naturally best adapted and exchange freely with other countries for the commodities in which they excel; in other words, the people of each country could devote their labors to the branch of production in which that labor produces the greatest amount of goods; and with the people of every country likewise directing their labor into the channels most productive in their situations." "The specialization of each country in its best industries is possible only under a world government, which would obviate the necessity for each country to be self-supporting, and which would guarantee freedom of trade throughout the entire world at all times." "This natural flow of trade is beneficial both to the exporting regions and to the importing regions; it finds a market for surplus commodities and satisfies a need where there is a shortage of those commodities. Furthermore, it equalizes supply and demand for the various commodities throughout the world, and in this way gives the greatest possible evenness and stability to agriculture, industry and employment everywhere." (Oscar Newfang, *The Road to World Peace,* New York, 1924, p. 65, 67, 95-96)

"The world-order is built upon an experience compounded of all the interests that are seeking expression of their purpose. It affords an opportunity for integration of resources instead of antagonism of resources. It provides channels of connection for those interests which transcend the boundaries of a single state and are yet limited, by the technique of geographical organization, to adjustments which are wasteful and unreal." (Harold J. Laski, *A Grammar of Politics,* London, 1925, p. 236)

296. "The industrial nations of the world now operate largely on an economy of flow: materials flow from their source (mines, farms, forests) to the consumer and quickly on to disposal sites in a one-way pattern of traffic. Since profits and incentives are directly related to the speed of this flow, people are valuable in large numbers as consumers (in that role they speed the flow) but are not valuable as workers (machines are faster). Thus modern industrial societies, as presently conceived, tend to increase unemployment on the one hand while needing people as consumers on the other, and they tend to use up and disperse both materials and energy (machines require more energy than workers) as rapidly as possible." (R. Thomas Tanner, *Ecology, Environment and Education,* Lincoln, Nebr., 1974, p. 12)

297. "A machine whose pace cannot be altered, whose advancement cannot be halted, whose destination cannot be plotted and directed, is a dangerous instrument, and without a farsighted system of human control the whole system of mechanization may finally wreck itself just for lack of brakes, reverse gears, and steering wheel. Hence the problem posed by the success of the machine is how to restore those human goals that have been abandoned in the pursuit of extra-human powers, without forfeiting the gains that the machine has brought into existence." (Lewis Mumford, "Machines," in the *Encyclopedia Americana,* 1973 ed., Vol. 18, p. 61-62)

ly. It is a situation which was profiled by Harrison Brown a quarter
of a century ago.[298]

---

298. "I can imagine a world within which machines function solely for man's
benefit; turning out those goods which are necessary for his well-being, relieving
him of the necessity for heavy physical labor and dull, routine, meaningless activity. The world I imagine is one in which people are well fed, well clothed, and well
housed. Man, in this world, lives in balance with his environment, nourished by
nature in harmony with the myriads of other like forms that are beneficial to him.
He treats his land wisely, halts erosion and overcropping, and returns all organic
waste matter to the soil from which it sprung. He lives efficiently, yet minimizes ar-
tificiality. It is not an overcrowded world; people can, if they wish, isolate
themselves in the silence of a mountaintop, or they can walk through primeval
forests or across wooded plains." (Harrison Brown, *The Challenge of Man's
Future,* New York, 1954, p. 258)

The Communist idea of world economy may be summarized as follows: "The
most expedient utilization of the forces of nature and of the natural conditions of
production in the various parts of the world; the removal of the antagonism between town and country that under capitalism results from the low technical level
of agriculture and its systematic lagging behind industry; the closest possible
cooperation between science and technics, the utmost encouragement of research
work and the practical application of its results on the widest possible social scale,
planned organization of scientific work; the application of the most perfect
methods of statistical accounting and planned regulation of economy; the rapidly
growing social needs, which is the most powerful internal driving force of the
whole system—all these will secure the maximum productivity of social labor,
which in turn will release human energy for the powerful development of science
and art." (Chapter three, part of passage 6 of the *Program of the Communist International,* adopted by its sixth World Congress, Sept. 1, 1928)

It is interesting to note that more than two thousand years ago, some Chinese
sages had thought about a great society of harmony through a "great way":
"When the Great Way is practiced, the world under the heaven is shared by all
alike. Rulers are selected according to their wisdom and ability. Mutual confidence
is promoted and good neighborliness cultivated. Hence men do not regard as
parents only their own parents, nor do they treat as children only their own
children. Provision is secured for the aged till death, employment for the able-
bodied, and the means of growing up for the young. Helpless widows and
widowers, orphans and the lonely, as well as the sick and the disabled, are well
cared for. Men have their respective occupations and women their homes. They
hate to see goods lying about in waste, yet they do not hoard them for themselves.
They despise indolence, yet they do not use their energies just for their own
benefit. In this way selfish schemings are repressed, and robbers, thieves, and
rebels no longer exist. And there is no need for people to shut their outer doors.
This is called the Great Harmony." 大道之行也，天下為公。選賢與能，講信修
睦。故人不獨親其親，不獨子其子。使老有所終，壯有所用，幼有所長，鰥寡
孤獨疾廢者有所養也。男有分，女有歸。貨惡其棄於地也，不必藏諸己，力惡
其不出於身也，不必為己。是故謀閉而不興，盜竊亂賊而不作。故外戶而不閉。
是謂大同。(From "Li Yun" 禮運篇 of *Li Chi* 禮記, edited by Confucius (551-479

Finally, let us turn to a crucial question: What kind of authority is suitable for the job of the general management?

Since all the works to be managed are complex and interwoven in nature and worldwide in scope, as noted before,[299] it is obviously impossible for any national government or any specialized international agency to do the job.[300] The United Nations is supposed to be able to perform some.[301] Unfortunately its almost four decades of history have clearly proved that it can do very little, if not nothing, because of the fundamental weakness as discussed earlier. Hence, the only logical, necessary and realistic answer to the crucial question is a World Government with an overriding power.

B.C.). For another translation, see Wm. Theodore de Bary, *et al. Sources of Chinese Tradition,* N.Y. 1960, p. 191-192.)

299. In addition to the earlier note 256, here is a reminder: "One important area involves use of the seas and seabeds, with complex military, economic, environmental and scientific interests at stake. Another important area of concern is the use of satellite technology. The development both of direct broadcasting capabilities and of satellites for surveying the earth's resources has political and economic implications not limited by national boundaries." "All of these issues are complex and interwoven, and it will become increasingly difficult to deal with them as distinct unrelated problems. The search for new sources of petroleum and other minerals on the seabeds may have deleterious consequences for the marine environment. Changes in weather patterns could disastrously affect world food supplies. The interrelationships are almost endless, and are only beginning to be appreciated." (*Science and Technology in an Era of Interdependence,* by the UNA-USA National Policy Panel, New York, 1975, p. 42)

300. "Governments exist—or believe they exist—to protect national interests. They recognize, in a theoretical way, the need for solutions which promote the wider interests of all mankind. But they assume that such solutions can only be the end-product of a fight: of bitter and protracted wrangling among many different representatives, each bargaining for their own nation, rather than from a common, disinterested effort among all to devise the system that would best serve the interests and promote the welfare of the world as a whole. They accept the need for mutually acceptable arrangments. But their first aim is to ensure that the arrangements are acceptable to themselves. This is the inevitable effect of a situation in which political power and political parties are still organized on a national rather than an international basis. (Evan Luard, *The Control of the Sea-Bed; a New International Issue,* London, 1974, p. 197)

301. Article 55 of the Charter of the United Nations: "With a view to the creation of conditions of stability and well-being which are necessary for peaceful and friendly relations among nations based on respect for the principle of equal rights and self-determination of peoples, the United Nations shall promote: (a) higher standards of living, full employment, and conditions of economic and social progress and development; (b) solutions of international economic, social, health, and related problems; and international cultural and educational co-operation; ...."

VI.

Structure of the One World

a.
General

ACTUALLY, A WORLD GOVERNMENT IS A LOGICAL AND realistic organ of the One World resulting from the merging of all nations, which is the necessary way to achieve a permanent peace and a general happiness and, fundamentally, is the inevitable consequence of a long process of group expansion as an historical, evolutionary and universal law. All these aspects have been previously expounded. What we have to discuss now is the structure of the One World in general, and of its organ—the World Government—in particular.

The One World cannot be dreamed of as a stateless society. It has to be organized as a world state.[1] In an attempt to connect with certain political ideas and also to avoid certain controversies over the meaning of the "state," different names have been used for it, such as World Republic,[2] World Federation,[3] World Union,[4] and World

---

1. The "world state" is a ready-made and natural term literally. It has been loosely used by writers since early times. Modern literature on it can be found here and there. For instance, Harold J. Laski discussed the "world state" in his *A Grammar of Politics,* London, 1925, p. 66 and other places; and Edward M. Earle described "H.G. Wells, British Patriot in Search of a World State" in his *Nationalism and Internationalism,* New York, 1952, p. 79-121.

2. Jean Baptiste Du Val-de-Grace was probably the man in modern time who first spelled out the "World Republic" ("Une République du Monde," in his language). (Cf. Alfred M. Lilienthal, *Which Way to World Government, Headline Series* no. 83, New York, 1950, p. 3.) Some others have followed. For example: "Alfredo Cardinal Ottaviani, secretary of the Vatican holy office, today received the longest and warmest applause of this session of the Vatican council

Commonwealth.⁵ Generally speaking, however, all these names are superficial. The world is one, and there is no other to compare with it. The World State is a common name, but stands clearly enough for the One World. Therefore, no other distinct or particular name is needed for it anymore.

It is natural that the territory of the World State contains the whole earth, together with its space as far as mankind can control. It may also include colonies possibly established by mankind on other

---

when he proposed that it take the initiative for the creation of a 'world republic' open to all nations." (Reported by the *Chicago Tribune,* Oct. 8, 1965, p. 2—Sect. 1A) However, there is a "confusion between, the terms 'democracy' and 'republic.' Strictly speaking, a republican form of government is one in which the chief titular head of government is not hereditary. A republic can have an undemocratic form of government (for example, Nazi Germany or the Soviet Union) whereas a monarchy can be a democracy (for example, Britain and the Scandinavian countries)." (Sidney Hook, "Democracy," in the *Encyclopedia Americana,* 1973 ed., Vol. 8, p. 685)

3. Since Alfred Tennyson wrote in his memorable *Locksley Hall* of a "parliament of man, the federation of the world" about 140 years ago, the term "World Federation" has often appeared in literature, and many people have joined forces to struggle for it. For example, the organization, called in French "Le Mouvement Universel pour une Fédération Mondiale," which became later "The Association of World Federalists," founded in Montreux in 1947, defines its purpose in Article 1 of the Statutes as follows: "To work for the creation of a world federation, having a constitutional defined sphere of jurisdiction, functioning through a legislature to make world law, a judiciary to interpret it, and an executive with adequate powers to enforce it upon individuals." (Quoted by Max Habicht in *Across Frontiers,* bulletin of the World Constitution & Parliament Association, no. 13, Feb. 1981, Lakewood, Colo., p. 2)

4. ". . . the Communist International strives . . . fights for the establishment of the world dictatorship of the proletariat, for the establishment of a World Union of Socialist Soviet Republics. . . ." (Article 1 of the Constitution of the Communist International, as adopted by the 6th World Congress of the Communist International, 1928)

5. Some writers call the world state a World Commonwealth (for instance, *The Bases of a World Commonwealth,* by Charles B. Fawcett, London, 1941), or the Commonwealth of Man. (For instance, Frederick L. Schuman entitles his work "An Inquiry into Power Politics and World Government," *The Commonwealth of Man,* published in New York, 1952.) The reason may be found in Professor Franz Oppenheimer's opinion: "All states known to history, he contends, are characterized by the domination of one class by another. . . . It is indeed possible that these features may disappear in the future, but the change wrought thereby would be so fundamental as to render the old concept inapplicable and we should have to coin some new designation, such as 'Freiburgerschaft' (free commonwealth) for the resulting type of civic organization." (Robert H. Lowie, *The Origin of the State,* New York, 1962, p. 20)

planets and celestial bodies. Exterior relations can only be recognized and maintained with the different beings who possibly exist outside its territory.

A suitable place will be chosen to be the capital of the World State,[6] as well as several seats to be its regional centers of administration.[7]

It is natural, too, that all peoples of the world are citizens of the World State.[8] Their world citizenship, however, necessarily demands their supreme loyalty to all peoples through humanity forever[9] and

---

6. The site for the headquarters of the League of Nations—Geneva, and that for the United Nations—New York, probably have qualities for prior consideration.

7. It is interesting to note that the draft of the Constitution for the Federation issued by the World Constitution and Parliament Association, Lakewood, Colorado, 1977, suggests that (Article XV); "Five World Capitals shall be established in each of five Continental Divisions of Earth, . . . One of the World Capitals shall be designated by the World Parliament as the Primary World Capital, and the other four shall be designated as Secondary World Capitals. The primary seats of all organs of the World Government shall be located in the Primary World Capital, and other major seats of the several organs of the World Government shall be located in the Secondary World Capitals."

8. In this respect, it is interesting to note "the World Citizenship Movement which started at Oberlin College and, under the leadership of Colonel Thomas Tchou, seeks to bring about a 'practicing of citizenship on a world level' through an educational non-political program. Several London groups in 1948, including the World Unity Movement, World Foundation and Service-Nation Movement were amalgamated into the World Citizenship Movement." (Alfred M. Lilienthal, *Which Way to World Government? Headline Series* no. 83, New York, 1950, p. 40)

It is also interesting to note that there is an International Registry of World Citizens with a world center: 55, rue de Lacepede—Paris—5. It distributes a world citizen identity card which "is not a membership card in a movement. It is valid for life." (See *World Citizen,* New Delhi, Aug. 1968, p. 10.)

"The world we live in is undergoing a transformation which vitally affects all of us. We believe that the time is come when States which otherwise are independent and distinct from each other, must federate into a world government and national citizenship should be transformed into world citizenship. World citizenship as an idea has not been conceived by us; we are only one of the many earnest advocates of the great idea and it is our desire to link ourselves with all those who are already in the field, individuals as well as organizations and who are possibly better equipped than ourselves for the holy march to the happy goal. We are eager to be in line with them and we cordially invite all those who hate war and love peace to associate themselves in this pious purpose. (Alim T. Gidwani, "Men of Goodwill, Let Us Unite," *World Citizen,* New Delhi, Aug. 1968, p. 4)

9. "Externally, surely, the concept of an absolute and independent sovereign State which demands an unqualified allegiance to government from its members, and enforces that allegiance by the power at its command, is incompatible with the interests of humanity. If we are to have a morally adequate theory of political

no longer to any nation through nationalism.[10] It is true that such supreme loyalty is not easy to develop under the present circumstances, but surely it will grow fast when every eye sees the world flag raised and every ear hears the world anthem sung.[11]

Like the world citizenship common to everyone, there must be in the World State a common language for general as well as for official use, in addition to various native tongues.[12] The common language

---

obligation, we must approach the problem from a different angle. In a creative civilisation what is important is not the historical accident of separate States, but the scientific fact of world-interdependence. The real unit of allegiance is the world. The real obligation of obedience is to the total interest of our fellow-men." (Harold J. Laski, *A Grammar of Politics,* London, 1925, p. 64)

10. "In different periods of history, and in different civilizations, we find different groups to which this supreme loyalty is given. The modern period of history, starting with the French Revolution, is characterized by the fact that in this period and in this period alone, the nation demands the supreme loyalty of man, that all men, not only certain individuals or classes, are drawn into this common loyalty, and that all civilizations (which up to this modern period followed their own, and frequently widely different, ways) are now dominated more and more by this one supreme group-consciousness, nationalism." (Hans Kohn, *The Idea of Nationalism; a Study in its Origin and Background,* New York, 1948, p. 12)

11. "We cannot expect loyalty to an institution that does not exist. The institution must be created before we can demand loyalty to it. There is no reason to doubt that once universal institutions are established which bring people security, peace, wealth, which unite them in common ideals and common interests, the loyalty of the peoples, today claimed by the inefficient institution of the nation-state, will infallibly turn to them." (Emery Reves, *The Anatomy of Peace,* New York, 1946, p. 233)

"Discussion of world government has been criticized as being futile and even harmful, because there is no present formula for achieving it. This is putting the cart before the horse. We must change our state of mind and the focus of our allegiance before any formula will work." (Elwyn B. White in his book, *The Wild Flag,* a very interesting writing on the topic of world government, New York, 1946, quoted on the book's jacket.)

12. "A further great advantage which could be derived from a world government would be the gradual development of a single, standard language throughout the world. . . . The benefits that the world would derive from a single universal language, in place of the Babel of tongues now prevailing, would be incalculable. The people of different lands would learn to understand one another far better than they do now. Misunderstandings and friction would be dissipated, and harmony would be greatly promoted. . . . This fruitful source of misunderstanding, hatreds and fightings could be very largely removed by the adoption of a universal, standard language under a single world government." (Oscar Newfang, *The Road to World Peace,* New York, 1924, p. 85-86. Cf. Albert L. Guerard, *A Short History of the International Language Movement,* New York, 1922; and Mario Pei, *One Language for the World,* New York, 1958.)

may be chosen from the newly created languages[13] or from the major existing languages with some modifications.[14]

A common language can facilitate the exchange of ideas just as a world currency can facilitate the exchange of goods and services. The issue of a world currency, together with the establishment of a world

---

13. Such as the well-known ESPERANTO, a constructed or extracted, not an artificial, international language or interlanguage. It is based on the elements of the most important European tongues, reduced to a minimum by strict regularization and an ingenious system of suffixes and prefixes, also taken from the natural languages. Its alphabet has 28 letters and its grammar consists of 16 rules without any exceptions. It was created by Iudovic L. Zamenhof, a Russian or Polish physician. In 1887 his first publication, *Lingvo Internacia,* setting out the basic rules of the new language, appeared under his pen name, Dr. Esperanto (one who hopes)—a name soon attached to the language itself. (Cf. Marjorie Boulton, *Zamenhof,* London, 1960.)

Another newly created language which may be mentioned for consideration is Interlingua. It is the result of 25 years of research by a committee of natural scientists, working under the International Auxiliary Language Association of New York, to perfect a medium in which researchers all over the world could converse. It has a 27,000-word vocabulary, 17,000 of the words being scientific and technical terms. The language is based on French, Italian, English and Spanish words and looks more like Spanish than anything else. (Cf. Alexander Gode and Hugh E. Blair, *Interlingua: A Grammar of the International Language,* New York, 1956.)

14. Major existing languages include the five languages—English, French, Spanish, Russian and Chinese, recognized by the United Nations as its official languages. But none of them is close to perfection. "Language is so complex, so sophisticated and so copious that one of the most surprising things about it is the lack of so many useful words in so many individual languages—French has nothing that accurately corresponds to 'home,' while English has no single word for 'a blind man.'" Meanwhile, every language has thousands upon thousands of words that are useless or archaic or redundant. Of the hundreds of thousands in English at his time, Shakespeare used fewer than 16,000. Today, nobody knows more than one-tenth of the words in an unabridged dictionary. The same is true of other languages, yet neither German nor French nor most European languages have a word for 'pet,' a dog or a cat in the house. And, according to S. Stephenson Smith, it would require 43 French words for a proper translation of the American 'know-how.' Just as it takes nearly a dozen words in English to give the full meaning of the German 'Schadenfreude.' The Romans actually had no words for 'yes' or 'no,' and Chinese still doesn't. Neither Hindu nor Urdu, the most common tongues of India and Pakistan, has a verb meaning 'to have'. . . . What we need to do, obviously, is to abolish a lot of words we have, and to import some from other lands. If we ever achieve a universal tongue, it will be by such synthesis, not by inventing some artificial language never spoken on land or sea." (Sydney Harris, "Many Complex Languages Fall Short on Useful Words," *South Bend Tribune,* April 16, 1980, p. 12)

bank and the collection of universal taxes, have already been spelled out as important measures the general management has to take.[15]

Also for facilitating exchanges, the metric system will be used, which sets standards for measures and weights.[16] Although this system has been widely accepted, more efforts are still required to make it prevail over the whole world.

More efforts are also required to perfect a world calendar[17] for the common good of mankind.[18]

There are some small things which can be developed for the common good, too, such as the adoption of a world zip code[19] and the application of a universal identification code.[20]

---

15. Cf. V, 282-285, and the related text.

16. Cf. II, 143-148, and the related text.

17. Cf. II, 133-138, and the related text.

18. "Calendar change is a vital, far-reaching momentous movement with The World Calendar a true agent encouraging peace. Here is one of man's noblest achievements—The World Calendar—not of man's design but truly and divinely inspired for the common good of mankind—everywhere." "The world calendar is harmonious, ordered, regular, saving and perpetual; wherein everything fits, everything agrees, everything is stable." (Elisabeth Achelis, *The Calendar for the Modern Age,* New York, 1959, p. 142-143)

19. Zip Code is a code system used to speed the sorting and delivery of mail in the United States. The name stands for Zoning Improvement Plan. The ZIP system has five numerals that appear after an address. In the ZIP number 22207, for example, the first numeral—2—designates one of 10 geographical areas. Area 2 consists of the District of Columbia, Maryland, North Carolina, South Carolina, Virginia, and West Virginia. The second two numerals—22—indicate a metropolitan area or sectional center. In this case, the mail is going to the Arlington area of Virginia. The last two numerals—07—represent a small town or delivery unit from which the mail will be delivered. Plans called for expansion of the ZIP code to nine numbers in the early 1980s. The United States Postal Service introduced the ZIP Code in 1963. By that time, the volume of the mail in the United States had increased almost 900 percent since 1900. The ZIP code has since then facilitated the mail process tremendously. (Cf. *The World Book Encyclopedia,* Chicago, 1981 ed., Vol. 21, p. 499.)

20. In order to cope with the rapid progress in computers, it is necessary to apply a particular number for each person in the World State, good for social security, employment, credit, traveling, voting, and so on. The number-assigning may be developed from the current social security system of the United States. (Cf. Douglas F. Parkhill, *The Challenge of the Computer Utility,* Reading, Mass., 1966, p. 157.) Sydney Harris in the *South Bend Tribune,* Jan. 19, 1982, p. 10, mentioned "That with the new Post Office nine-digit Zip Code, every man, woman and child in the U.S., Canada and Mexico could have his own personal code, with enough left over for every dog in North America."

b.
Human Rights
and Obligations

MUCH MORE IMPORTANT FOR THE COMMON GOOD, however, are human rights and fundamental freedoms for all in the World State without any distinction as to race, sex, language or religion.[21] These include:

Right to life, liberty and security of person.[22]
Right to privacy, honor and reputation.[23]
Right to own property individually or collectively.[24]
Right to protection of scientific, literary and artistic work.[25]
Right to free marriage and small family.[26]

---

21. This principle is included in the Preamble and Articles 1, 13, 55, 62, and 76 of the Charter of the United Nations; and Article 2 of the Universal Declaration of Human Rights, which reads: "Everyone is entitled to all the rights and freedoms set forth in this Declaration, without distinction of any kind, such as race, colour, sex, language, political or other opinion, national or social origin, property, birth or other status...."

22. This right is particularly expressed in the Universal Declaration of Human Rights: "Article 3. Everyone has the right to life, liberty and security of person; Article 4. No one shall be held in slavery or servitude; slavery and the slave trade shall be prohibited in all their forms;" and Article 5. "No one shall be subjected to torture or to cruel, inhuman or degrading treatment or punishment."

23. Article 12 of the Universal Declaration of Human Rights: "No one shall be subjected to arbitrary interference with his privacy, family, home or correspondence, nor to attacks upon his honour and reputation. Everyone has the right to the protection of the law against such interference or attacks."

24. Article 17 of the Universal Declaration of Human Rights: "(1) Everyone has the right to own property alone as well as in association with others; (2) No one shall be arbitrarily deprived of his property."

25. Article 27 of the Universal Declaration of Human Rights: "(2) Everyone has the right to the protection of the moral and material interests resulting from any scientific, literary or artistic production of which he is the author."

26. Article 16 of the Universal Declaration of Human Rights: "(1) Men and women of full age, without any limitation due to race, nationality or religion, have the right to marry and to found a family. They are entitled to equal rights as to marriage, during marriage and at its dissolution; (2) Marriage shall be entered into only with the free and full consent of the intending spouses," and "(3) The family is the natural and fundamental group unit of society and is entitled to protection by society and the State."

Right to freedom of movement.[27]
Right to freedom of thought, conscience and religion.[28]
Right to freedom of opinion and expression.[29]
Right to freedom of assembly and association.[30]
Right to work and leisure.[31]
Right to economic and social security.[32]
Right to education on an equal basis for a useful purpose.[33]

---

27. The spirit of freedom of movement is expressed in Article 13 of the Universal Declaration of Human Rights and also in Article 12 of the International Covenant on Civil and Political Rights. It includes free movement for recreation, education, conference, trade, and temporary employment. Movement for permanent employment or residence may be subject to the limitations of plans and measures for reasonable redistribution of population decided and taken by the World Authority.

28. Article 18 of the Universal Declaration of Human Rights: "Everyone has the right to freedom of thought, conscience and religion; this right includes freedom to change his religion or belief, and freedom, either alone or in community with others and in public or private, to manifest his religion or belief in teaching, practice, worship and observance."

29. Article 19 of the Universal Declaration of Human Rights: "Everyone has the right to freedom of opinion and expression; this right includes freedom to hold opinions without interference and to seek, receive and impart information and ideas through any media and regardless of frontiers."

30. Article 20 of the Universal Declaration of Human Rights: "(1) Everyone has the right to freedom of peaceful assembly and association. (2) No one may be compelled to belong to an association." This right includes the right to form and to join trade unions as expressed in Article 23, (4), of the Declaration.

31. The Universal Declaration of Human Rights states: "Article 23. (1) Everyone has the right to work, to free choice of employment, to just and favorable conditions of work and to protection against unemployment; (2) Everyone, without any discrimination, has the right to equal pay for equal work; (3) Everyone who works has the right to just and favourable remuneration...." and, "Article 24. Everyone has the right to rest and leisure, including reasonable limitation of working hours and periodic holidays with pay."

32. Article 25 of the Universal Declaration of Human Rights: "(1) Everyone has the right to a standard of living adequate for the health and well-being of himself and of his family, including food, clothing, housing and medical care and necessary social services, and the right to security in the event of unemployment, sickness, disability, widowhood, old age or other lack of livelihood in circumstances beyond his control." And "(2) Motherhood and childhood are entitled to special care and assistance. All children, whether born in or out of wedlock, shall enjoy the same social protection."

33. The American Declaration of the Rights and Duties of Man, adopted by the Ninth International Conference of American States, Bogota, 1948, published by the Pan American Union, Washington, 1957, states: Article XIII. "Every person has the right to an education, which should be based on the principles of liberty, morality and human solidarity. Likewise every person has the right to an educa-

Right to participation in government in democratic, practical and effective ways.[34]

And right to equal, fair and just protection of the law.[35]

Equally important for the common good are human obligations for all in the World State without any distinction as to race, sex, language, or religion. These include:

Obligation to humanity,[36]

Obligation to peace,[37]

---

tion that will prepare him to attain a decent life, to raise his standard of living, and to be a useful member of society. The right to an education includes the right to equality of opportunity in every case, in accordance with natural talents, merit and the desire to utilize the resources that the state or the community is in a position to provide. Every person has the right to receive, free, at least a primary education.''

34. Article 21 of the Universal Declaration of Human Rights provides such principles as ''Everyone has the right to take part in the government,'' ''Everyone has the right of equal access to public service'' and ''The will of the people shall be the basis of the authority of government; this will shall be expressed in periodic and genuine elections which shall be by universal and equal suffrage and shall be held by secret vote or by equivalent free voting procedures.''

35. The complex of this right is expressed in Articles 6-11 of the Universal Declaration of Human Rights, including: ''Everyone has the right to recognition everywhere as a person before the law''; ''All are equal before the law and are entitled without any discrimination to equal protection of the law''; ''Everyone has the right to an effective remedy''; ''No one shall be subjected to arbitrary arrest, detention or exile''; ''Everyone is entitled in full equality to a fair and public hearing'' for any charge against him; ''Everyone charged with a penal offence has the right to be presumed innocent until proved guilty according to law in a public trial'' and ''No one shall be held guilty of any penal offence on account of any act or omission which did not constitute a penal offence, under national or international law, at the time when it was committed. Nor shall a heavier penalty be imposed than the one that was applicable at the time the penal offence was committed.''

36. Article 29 of the Universal Declaration of Human Rights: ''(1) Everyone has duties to the community in which alone the free and full development of his personality is possible.'' The first passages of the preamble of the American Declaration of the Rights and Duties of Man, adopted by the 9th International Conference of American States,'' Bogota, 1948, published by the Pan American Union, Washington, 1957: ''All men are born free and equal, in dignity and in rights, and, being endowed by nature with reason and conscience, they should conduct themselves as brothers one to another. The fulfillment of duty by each individual is a prerequisite to the rights of all. Rights and duties are inter-related in every social and political activity of man. While rights exalt individual liberty, duties express the dignity of that liberty.''

37. An old teaching of the obligation to peace was ''Thou shalt not kill.'' (This was one of Moses' ten commandments. Cf. Chapter 5, Deuteronomy, *Bible*.) In modern times, there are many ways for everyone to carry out this obligation, such as: rejecting the call of military conscription and refusing to work for the developing and making of weapons of mass destruction.

Obligation to the general happiness,[38]
Obligation to care for the environment,[39]
Obligation to respect the rights and freedoms of others,[40] and
Obligation to obey the law.[41]

---

38. The American Declaration of the Rights and Duties of Man adopted by the 9th International Conference of American States, Bogota, 1948, published by the Pan American Union, Washington, 1957 states: "Article XXXV. It is the duty of every person to cooperate . . . with respect to social security and welfare, in accordance with his ability and with existing circumstances." And "Article XXXVI. It is the duty of every person to pay the taxes established by law for the support of public services."

39. The following is 8, 9 and 10 of Article XIII of the draft of "A Constitution for the Federation of Earth," by the World Constitution and Parliament Association, Lakewood, Colo., U.S.A., on human rights. They are quoted here for consideration as human obligations: "Protection for everyone against the hazards and perils of technological innovations and developments." "Protection of the natural environment which is the common heritage of humanity against pollution, ecological disruption or damage which could imperil life or lower the quality of life." And "Conservation of those natural resources of Earth which are limited so that present and future generations may continue to enjoy life on the planet Earth."

40. The American Declaration of the Rights and Duties of Man adopted by the 9th International Conference of American States, Bogota, 1948, published by the Pan American Union, Washington, 1957, stated: "Article XXVIII. The rights of man are limited by the rights of others, by the security of all, and by the just demands of the general welfare and the advancement of democracy;" and "Article XXIX. It is the duty of the individual so to conduct himself in relation to others that each and everyone may fully form and develop his personality."

41. Article XXXIII of the American Declaration of the Rights and Duties of Man adopted by the 9th International Conference of American States, Bogota, 1948, published by the Pan American Union, Washington, 1957, states: "It is the duty of every person to obey the law and other legitimate commands of the authorities. . . ." and its preamble emphasizes that: "Duties of a juridical nature presuppose others of a moral nature which support them in principle and constitute their basis."

c.
World Law
and Judiciary

IT IS NECESSARY TO POINT OUT THAT THE OBLIGATION to obey the law is the keynote of all human obligations, just as the right to the protection of the law is the keynote of all human rights. Indeed, the law is indispensable to both human rights and human obligations, although it is their last resort. This explains why a World Law is urgently needed for all the people of the world.

The World Law will be a set of standard domestic rules, and any local law, if allowed to exist, will have to conform to them.[42] There is no room for the existence of any international law in the world state.[43]

The function of the World Law is to govern all individuals directly.[44] Hence, its contents and procedures must be clear enough for the common people to understand and follow by themselves, not in normal circumstances through lawyers. More lawyers do not necessarily mean more justice.[45]

---

42. Although there has been a growing similarity in the domestic laws of all countries in modern times (Cf. II, f, 193-209 and their related text), various divergences still exist among them. The World Law would eliminate these divergences by its own standard, and would not allow any of their differences to stand against it.

43. "We are living in an age where the ordinary relationships of nations no longer exist. The forms and rules and laws which have been developing for two hundred or three hundred years and which we thought had established themselves in an elaborate and highly useful code of international law and conduct have all been thrown to the winds, and we are now confronted by pressure politics in the international field of a sort with which we are quite familiar on a much smaller scale in the national field." (Nicholas M. Butler, *Why War?* New York, 1940, p. 4)

44. Article X, Section A of the draft of "A Constitution for the Federation of Earth," by the World Constitution and Parliament Association, Lakewood, Colo., U.S.A., explains: "World law and world legislation shall apply directly to individuals, and individuals shall be held responsible for compliance with world law and world legislation regardless of whether the individuals are acting in their own capacity or as agents or officials of governments at any level or of the institutions of governments, or as agents or officials of corporations, organizations, associations or groups of any kind."

45. U.S. President Jimmy Carter said: "We have the heaviest concentration of lawyers on earth—one for every 500 Americans, three times as many as En-

Justice has to be upheld, however, by a World Judiciary and an enforcement system. The World Judiciary will consist of a World Supreme Court, regional courts, district courts, and certain special courts as deemed necessary. They shall have mandatory jurisdiction in all cases and their decisions shall be binding on all parties.[46]

The enforcement system will consist of an Attorney General and regional and district attorneys, together with a small World Police force armed only with weapons appropriate for the prevention of violence and the apprehension of lawbreakers.[47]

The World Judiciary is an independent branch of the World Government. Its principal judges shall be chosen by the central organ of the World Government—the World Council. The Attorney General shall be chosen by the World Council, too. But he, together with the whole enforcement system, is subordinated to the executive branch of the World Government—the world Administration.

d.
World Administration

THE MAIN JOB OF THE WORLD ADMINISTRATION IS TO carry out the detailed and continuous works in the implementation

---

gland, four times as many as West Germany, 21 times as many as there are in Japan. We have more litigation, but I am not sure we have more justice. Ninety per cent of our lawyers serve 10 per cent of the people. We are overlawyered and underrepresented." Carter's point is that our justice system is clogged with excessive litigation, "legal featherbedding," and cases that serve only to enrich lawyers. Justice delayed is, truly, justice denied; according to Jerald F. Ter Horst, in "Carter's Speech on Lawyers His Best." (*South Bend Tribune,* May 26, 1978, p. 8)

46. Article IX, Section A of the draft of "A Constitution for the Federation of Earth," by the World Constitution and Parliament Association, Lakewood, Colo., U.S.A., has this to say in this respect: "The World Supreme Court, together with such regional and district World Courts as may be established, shall have mandatory jurisdiction in all cases, actions, disputes, conflicts, violations of law, civil suits, guarantees of civil and human rights, constitutional interpretations, and other litigations arising under the provisions of this World Constitution, world legislation, and the body of world law approved by the World Parliament. Decisions of the World Supreme Court shall be binding on all parties involved in all cases, actions and litigations brought before any bench of the World Supreme Court for settlement."

47. "A policeman seeing a fight between two men, does not attempt to deter-

of world laws, legislations and policies as decided by the World Council. It will consist of a Board of Directors under the leadership of a chairman, and a number of departments and agencies each headed by a director. The chairman, together with all the directors, shall be chosen by the World Council, and shall be responsible to it.

The departments and agencies of the World Administration, as far as deemed necessary at present and for the near future, may be listed by subject matters as follows: population, food and agriculture, health and nutrition, energy, water supplies, forest, housing and settlements, environment and ecology, oceans and seabeds, atmosphere and space, weather and natural calamities, education, science and technology, the arts, athletics and recreation, labor and management, commerce and industry, transportation and travel, communications and information, social welfare, and finance, together with the office of the Attorney General for public safety.

Conspicuously omitted in the list is an agency of disarmament and war prevention, which is generally considered indispensable to a World Government. Actually, there is no need for such an agency to have a permanent position in the World Administration, because when all nations have merged into One World, the process of world disarmament should have been completed, and no nation will have the authority and capacity to wage war anymore. If there is any outbreak of violence, the World Police should be able to handle it.

More significant is the omission of two important departments from the tradition of governmental establishment. One is for foreign relations, and the other for military affairs. The reason is simple: there is no foreign world for us to deal with and to fight against unless creatures from other planets appear to compete with mankind for domination.

While the reason for the omission of these two important departments is simple, its meaning is profound, because traditionally they have not only been where most of the money and manpower have

---

mine which of them is in the right and then help him beat up the one he considers in the wrong. His function is to restrain violence by both, to bring them before a judge who has authority to determine the rights of the dispute, and to see that the court's decision is carried out. In carrying out his duties, the policeman must apprehend the suspected individual without jeopardizing either the property or the lives of the community safeguarded against destruction of property and loss of life but the rights of the suspect are also carefully protected by an elaborate network of judicial safeguards." (Edith Wynner, "Policing under World Law," in *The Worried Woman's Guide to Peace Through World Law,* ed. by Lucile Green and Esther Yudell, Piedmont, Calif., 1965, p. 73)

been spent, but also where the dirtiest political tricks have been played[48] and feverish power struggles engaged.[49] Their omission means not only saving enormous expenses, but also cutting two deep, wicked roots of the government; and thus making it possible for the government to emphasize services rather than politics, and for experts rather than politicians to run the government.[50]

e.
Experts, Commons, and World Council

IN THIS RESPECT, IT IS NECESSARY TO POINT OUT THE
tendency that, owing to the rapid advance of modern science and

---

48. "Diplomacy, like military strategy consists of hoodwinking, tricking and outwitting the other party. In every other field of human activity, if someone succeeds in making his opponent believe the exact opposite of his real intentions we call this man a liar, a deceiver, a cheat. In military life he is regarded as an outstanding tactical genius and becomes a general. In diplomacy, he is looked upon as a great statesman and he is called Your Excellency." (Emery Reves, *The Anatomy of Peace,* New York, 1946, p. 152)

"... Most politicos would not care for a world government, as it would leave them stranded without the diplomatic poker game they so love." (E.B. White, in a letter, Oct. 1972. Quoted in the *World Peace News,* Vol. VI, no. 2, Feb. 1975, p. 2)

49. Thomas Hobbes in his *Leviathan* described the relations of states to one another as they appeared to him to be in a famous passage: "Kings and persons of sovereign authority, because of their independency, are in continual jealousies, and in the state and posture of gladiators: their forts, and garrisons, and guns upon the frontiers of their kingdoms, and continual spies upon their neighbours, which is a posture of war." (Chapter 13)

50. "We are employing our best brains and talent—and immense sums of money—to enable people to live better and longer, to enjoy leisure, to take full advantage of our brilliant technological breakthroughs. But whether any of us will survive the next decade still depends upon the ancient (and proved ineffective) devices of power politics. The world's leaders are the same kind of men they always have been; but we can no longer afford that kind of men, any more than a modern corporation can afford to have a caveman as its top executive. The world desperately needs professional managers to integrate and implement the new knowledge of the 20th century, not the same old powerdriven, honor ridden, cliche-mouthing politicians. The disparity between our New World technology and our Stone Age statesmanship would not be tolerated for a moment in any com-

technology, more and more special knowledges are required for public services,[51] and less and less room is left for common politics to work.[52] This fact provides another important reason for having experts rather than politicians run the government.

To run the government means not only to have all services performed by experts, but also to include their participation in lawmaking and policy decisions. It is for this reason that a House of Experts is projected to do the primary works of legislation in the World Council.

The House of Experts will consist of up to 400 members and a chairman they have selected. They will be divided into a number of committees under various subject headings to consider related proposals on law, policy, and assignment of important government jobs. Any proposal, either initiated by the committees themselves, by the World Administration, by the other house of the World Council —The House of Commons, or by other competent agencies, must first be deliberated by the related committee, then debated by the whole house, and finally forwarded to the House of Commons for decision.

The House of Commons will consist of up to 1000 members with a chairman they have selected. They will take up the measures forwarded from the House of Experts for a general review rather than detailed discussions or minor modifications. If the measure is favored by the House of Experts, they can approve it by a simple majority, but cannot reject it without a two-thirds majority. If the measure is not favored, they can reject it by a simple majority, but cannot approve it without a two-thirds majority. If they cannot arrive at the number of votes needed to either approve or reject, some solution may be worked out through consultation with the House of Experts, or decided by a majority of the World Council.

---

pany, or college, or hospital, or any other institution of our time. Only in the field of government—most crucial of all—are we still trying to operate with the crude instruments of a vanished age." (Sydney Harris, "Stone Age Statesmanship Overshadows Technology," *South Bend Tribune,* Sept. 10, 1976, p. 6)

51. "If the system of international organizations is to adapt to the new demands being placed on it by science and technology, and by related economic developments, it will also require a capacity for leadership and direction which it does not presently have." (*Science and Technology in an Era of Interdependence,* by the UNA-USA National Policy Panel, New York, 1975, p. 45)

52. "In the modern world politics is obsolete." (Edward M. Earle summarizing Herbert G. Wells' view on modern politics in *Nationalism and Internationalism,* New York, 1950, p. 115)

The World Council will be composed of all Experts and Commons of the two Houses as its members, each with an equal vote. They will elect a president from the three candidates nominated by the House of Experts. The President of the World Council will also serve as the World President, whose function is primarily in matters of official ceremony and formality.[53]

The term for the World President will be five years. This will also be the term for the Commons. The Experts will serve a term of ten years, but one-half of them will be limited to five years in the first election, so that an election of one-half of them will take place every five years.

Now the essential problem is how to elect the Experts and Commons.

It would be unrealistic to ask the people to elect the Experts directly. They can hardly know even who, how and where are the experts. It would be unrealistic, too, to ask the experts to conduct electoral campaigns everywhere. They are usually either unaccustomed or reluctant to do that. Fortunately, there are many worldwide academic, learned and professional associations whose millions of members are experts themselves and can be well entrusted on behalf of the people to elect outstanding ones among them for public service.[54]

As regards the election of the Commons, it has to be done by the people directly. However, as long as the nations remain essentially as the high level local units, they can be used as basic electoral districts, with a rational allocation of the seats for election.[55] It is important to

---

53. The official ceremonies and formalities are those normally performed by the figurehead of a country in the traditional political system. They include the appointing of the high level officials duly chosen by the proper authorities, the signing of laws and rules duly made by the proper authorities, and the proclaiming of important measures duly decided by the proper authorities.

54. A practical way can be worked out as follows: Let the worldwide academic, learned and professional associations group themselves into, say, 100 units by general subjects, and each unit on behalf of the people elect two Experts every five years for a ten-year term. The unit should also elect several alternatives for substitution in case the Experts are removed for cause or die before the term. Nominations may be made by a conference of the presidents, chairmen, or other leaders of the component associations, and their retired presidents, chairmen, and other prominent leaders should be the primary candidates.

55. The allocation of the seats of the Commons for the electoral districts may be rationalized as follows: One (Common) for 1,000,000 (population) as the minimum; one for every 5,000,000 for the first addition of 50,000,000; one for every 25,000,000 for the second addition of 500,000,000; and one for 125,000,000

note that no matter how many Commons are elected from a district, they are not supposed to represent any particular interest of the district, but the highest good of all the people as a whole.[56] They shall take a pledge of service to humanity.

Since the Commons are not obliged to spend as much time as the Experts on the delicate and detailed primary works of legislation, they can pay more attention to looking over extensively any violations of human rights, laws and ordinances; any neglect of duties and responsibilities by public offices or officials; and the way the policies of government are being carried out, and the well-being of the people is cared for. This kind of function is performed in some political systems by the public defender, control organ[57] or ombudsmus.[58] Actually, there is no one else in a position to do the job more appropriately than the Commons.

---

for any further additions. But no district is allowed to elect more than 35. If a large nation wants to divide into several high level local units, with the approval of the World Government, these units will be applied automatically as separate electoral districts. Neighboring high level local units of less than 1,000,000 population may join in groups to elect Commons.

56. Edmund Burke "rejected the idea of a constituency as a numerical or territorial unit and of representation as implying the possession of the ballot by any considerable portion of the population represented. He denied that individual citizens as such are represented and that numerical majorities have any real significance in forming the mature opinion of the country." (George H. Sabine, *A History of Political Theory,* New York, 1938, p. 610)

Article 38 of the constitution of the Federal Republic of Germany (West Germany) makes clear that the representatives to the Bundestag (lower chamber) "are representatives of the whole people, not bound by orders and institutions, and subject only to their conscience."

57. In China, for example, there was a system of control established as early as the Chin Dynasty (221-206 B.C.) with a supervisory power exercised by a group of officials known as Chien Cha Yu Shih, 監察御史 . It was so useful in the long history of Chinese politics, that Dr. Sun Yat-Sen, the Founder of the Republic of China, tried in his political theory to set a control organ as one of the five important branches of the government, namely, Legislative Yuan, Executive Yuan, Judicial Yuan, Examination Yuan, and Control Yuan. Thus, the 1948 Constitution of the Republic of China defines the Control Yuan as the highest organ of control. It is composed of members elected by the people. It exercises powers including impeachment and censure and proposes corrective measures. (Cf. *China Yearbook,* 1978, by China Publishing Co., Taipei, Taiwan, 1979, p. 116-121.) The International Control Commission of the Communist International was another example, although it was not a proper organ of the government. (Cf. Article 28 of the Constitution of the Communist International, adopted by its sixth World Congress, Sept. 1, 1928.)

f.
Four Essences and World Presidium

IN PERFORMING THE FUNCTION INDIVIDUALLY OR COL-
lectively as public defenders, the Commons render their opinions to
the right authorities for action, but do not try to interfere with their
proper jurisdiction. The role of the Commons either as legislators or
as public defenders is to reflect the general view of the people by
voice and voting. They are the authorized bearers of general
opinion.[59] Hence, opinion is the essence of the function of the Commons, just as knowledge is for the Experts, service for the World Administration, and justice for the World Judiciary.

It is the four essences of opinion, knowledge, service and justice
that constitute a division of labor in the government,[60] and with such
a division, the World Government will work not only effectively, but
harmoniously.

In order to make the functions more harmonious, a World Presidium will be established to serve symbolically as the head office of
the World Government. It will consist of the World President, the
Chairmen of the Board of Directors of the World Administration, of
the House of Experts and the House of Commons, and the Chief

---

58. Article XI of the draft of "A Constitution for the Federation of Earth,"
by the World Constitution and Parliament Association, Lakewood, Colo.,
U.S.A., suggests a World Ombudsmus with some details.

59. Plato eloquently points out that it is not the cobbler who knows best what
a good pair of shoes is, but the wearer. This leads to the homely maxim that he who
wears the shoes knows best where they pinch. (Cf. Sidney Hook, "Democracy,"
in the *Encyclopedia Americana,* 1973 ed., Vol. 8, p. 690.)

60. It is worth noting that in political theory as well as in practice, while the
separation of power into three branches of the government—legislature, executive
and judiciary—is still emphasized in some countries, the separation of function
between the two chambers of the legislative branch is rather negligent. For example, in the U.S. Congress, the Senate and the House of Representatives do almost
identical work with identical procedures, while on the contrary, in British Parliament, the House of Commons can do almost everything, and the House of Lords
can do almost nothing. In order to increase the efficiency of the government, it is
necessary to separate the function of the two chambers of the legislative branch on
a logical and workable basis, so as to create a reasonable division of labor in
government.

Justice of the World Supreme Court. Meetings may be called and presided over by the World President for nothing more than consultation, coordination and reconciliation.

Within the scheme of the World Presidium, there will be a World Statistical Bureau, a World Auditing Office, a World Civil Service Commission, and a Secretary-General who will act as a medium of consultation, coordination and reconciliation for governmental technical, procedural and other minor matters, in addition to his regular duty of assisting the World Presidium to take care of official ceremonies and formalities.[61]

Thus, an outline of the World Government is drawn up. Obviously, there are in it deviations from traditional thinking as well as practice in the governmental establishment. The reason is simple: the World Government thus outlined is a government of tomorrow, not of yesterday.[62]

g.
Positive Democracy

SINCE EARLY MODERN TIMES, VARIOUS METHODS have been developed to implement the generally accepted democratic

---

61. The subordinate agencies in the scheme of the World Presidium are normally of a technical nature, are generally concerned with almost every office of the government, and play certain integrative roles among them. Thus, the draft of "A Constitution for the Federation of Earth," by the World Constitution and Parliament Association, Lakewood, Colo., U.S.A., includes this kind of organ in its novel "Integrative Complex" of which the definition is "Certain administrative, research, planning and facilitative agencies of the World Government which are particularly essential for the satisfactory functioning of all or most aspects of the World Government." It deals with the complex in its Article VIII with as many as 6 pages.

62. "Those who can visualize the realities of tomorrow only in things and beliefs already existing today will never be able to solve our problem, will never be capable of searching for principles nor of shaping the future according to the principles of tomorrow." (Emery Reves, *The Anatomy of Peace,* New York, 1946, p. 252)

"If the hypotheses we have laid down are dismissed as Utopian, that does not mean that they are unnecessary or impractical. For we are so often the prisoners of our old traditions that we do not recognize our presence in a new world." (Harold J. Laski, *A Grammar of Politics,* London, 1925, p. 661)

conception of government: "for the people, by the people and of the people." They include the well-known popular voting, majority rule, representative system and separation of powers. Their application, however, has been rather in a negative way aimed at eliminating despotism and dictatorship, and preventing them from rising again. This is not good enough for meeting the needs of a government of tomorrow for all the peoples of the world. For such a government, it is necessary to apply them in a positive way, in order to make the three principles of the democratic conception of government work more effectively.

Most important is the principle "for the people," of course. With the elimination of military and foreign affairs, and with the experts in a position to run the government, there is no doubt that this principle can be carried out positively to a point where no government which has ever existed could reach.

Obviously, the principle "by the people" cannot be applied to the World Government directly through popular meetings or by popular voting, for the business of the World Government is too wide in scope and too complex in nature;[63] it is necessary to apply it

---

63. As compared with modern states, the ancient city-state was exceedingly small both in area and population. There were several hundred city-states in the small Greek world. For instance, Plato in *The Law* fixed the number of citizens at 5040, and the famous investigation of the constitutional history of the city-state conducted by Aristotle with his students included as many as 158 Greek cities. Modern states are "so large, so remote, so impersonal, that they cannot fill the place in modern life that the city filled in the life of a Greek." (George H. Sabine, *A History of Political Theory,* New York, 1938, p. 13. Cf. p. 3-7, 80 and 89.)

Commenting on Jean Jacques Rousseau's theory of general will, "The practical uses to which that theory might be put were various, and Rousseau had neither the knowledge nor the patience to explore them. His belief that a small community like the city-state is the best example of the general will made it impossible for him to discuss contemporary politics with much point." (George H. Sabine, *A History of Political Theory,* New York, 1938, p. 587. Cf. Rousseau's *Du Contrat social,* livre 111, chap. XV.) The principle "by the people," as it was practiced in a New England town meeting in the very early colonial stage, is certainly only an historic epic. (Cf. James T. Adams, *The Epic of America,* Boston, 1933, p. 36-41.)

Edmund Burke wrote, in his addresses to his constituents at Bristol, the classic defense of a member's independence of judgment and action. Once elected he is responsible for the whole interest of the nation and the empire, and he owes to his constituents his best judgment freely exercised, whether it agrees with theirs or not. As Burke said, a member does not go to school to his constituents to learn the principles of law and government." (George H. Sabine, *A History of Political Theory,* New York, 1938, p. 610. Cf. also Charles E. Merriam, *A History of American Political Theory,* New York, 1920.)

indirectly through some entrusting and delegation.[64] The combination of electing the Commons by rational allocation to reflect the general opinion, entrusting the expert groups to select the Experts to contribute their special knowledge, and delegating the power of choosing the high level officers to the Commons and Experts together, is actually a positive way to serve the purpose of the principle "by the people," and is more realistic than any other ways in search of ideal government leaders, such as the "Philosopher King,"[65] the "perfect ruler,"[66] the "Conscious Part,"[67] and the "Elite."[68] It can also reduce some of the weaknesses of modern

---

64. "Sovereignty cannot be represented.... Therefore the deputies of the people are not and cannot be its representatives.... The English think they are free but they are quite wrong; they are only free when Parliamentary elections come round; once the members have been elected, they are slaves and things of naught." (Jean Jacques Rousseau, *Du contract social,* Book III, chap. xv., p. 111-115. Cf. *The Federalist,* nos. 4 and 70.)

65. Plato's conception of philosopher-ruler or philosopher-king is based on his theory of division of labor and specialization. To him, the philosopher is talented and trained to know the good, or to have exclusively a knowledge of the good. This knowledge is at once his right and his duty to rule. (Cf. George H. Sabine, *A History of Political Theory,* New York, 1938, p. 50, 102-103.)

66. "Every co-operative enterprise requires direction, and hence every community must have a ruler. In this way Dante proved that the whole race forms one community under a single ruler. The government of this ruler he compared to the government of God over nature. As the latter is perfect because of its unity, so the former to be perfect must embrace all men under a single authority. That which has the most reality has the greatest unity, and that which has the greatest unity is best." (George H. Sabine, *A History of Political Theory,* New York, 1938, p. 258-259)

67. The "conscious part" is the conception of Georg W. Hegel: "It is now, in short, a question of inducing in the body social a new efflorescence, the vision of which is possessed by its conscious members only. These latter form 'the universal class' in distinction to all the rest, who remain the prisoners of their own particularisms. It is, then, the business of the conscious part to do for the whole the necessary willing. That, for Hegel, does not mean that the part is free to choose for the whole whatever future it pleases. So far from that, it would be truer to say that its recognition of what the whole should be both now and in the future is what makes it the conscious part... The vision of what should be, thus envisaged in a group, casts this group for a leading part. In Marx's scientific socialism there is no doubt as to what the proletariat should be. Therefore the proletariat, being the conscious part, may speak and will in the name of the whole; its duty is to give the inert mass consciousness of the building of a proletarian whole." (Bertrand de Jouvenel, *On Power; its Nature and the History of its Growth,* trans. by J.F. Huntington, New York, 1949, p. 50-51)

68. The "elite" idea was particularly emphasized by Fascism: "Fascism insists that the government be entrusted to men capable of rising above their own private interests and of realizing the aspirations of the social collectivity, con-

voting practices, such as popularity over competence,[69] and party control.[70]

As for the application of the principle "of the people," the positive way is to assert that all peoples are the common master as well as the common owner of the world. Thus they, as a whole, are endowed with a supreme authority which is vested in the World Government.[71]

---

sidered in its unity and in its relation to the past and future. Fascism therefore not only rejects the dogma of popular sovereignty and substitutes for it that of state sovereignty, but it also proclaims that the great mass of citizens is not a suitable advocate of social interests for the reason that the capacity to ignore individual private interests in favor of the higher demands of society and of history is a very rare gift and the privilege of the chosen few. Natural intelligence and cultural preparation are of great service in all such tasks. Still more valuable perhaps is the intuitiveness of rare great minds, their traditionalism and their inherited qualities." (Rocco, "The Political Doctrine of Fascism," quoted by George H. Sabine, in *A History of Political Theory,* New York, 1938, p. 13. Cf. p. 768.)

69. "It was the late Adlai Stevenson who made the wry observation that by the time a candidate gets nominated for the presidency of the United States, he is no longer worthy to hold the office.... What a sad commentary on life that personal character and professional competence bear so small an influence on popularity, as though the election of our president were a beauty contest.... Rather, it is a rebuke to the general electorate for basing its vote on shadow and symbol rather than on substance. It is equally true that superior men will continue to shun the political arena, leaving the field open for the hacks, the hams, and the hollow men." (Sydney Harris, "Competence Counts Little in Candidate's Popularity," *South Bend Tribune,* Dec. 17, 1979, p. 16)

70. Under the modern political party system, "anxious to strengthen itself, the group makes its presence felt in the electoral body, from which it asks that it choose a man who stands in the name of the group in preference to a man with distinguished personal qualifications.... The first result of this is a degradation of the assembly, which no longer draws its recruits from the best men. A man must now be ready to rely on the support of the controller of his group's votes and to let his name be boosted for election by his whip. He must be ready to become a mere numerical, and not a qualitative, addition to the assembly." (Bertrand de Jouvenel, *On Power: its Nature and the History of its Growth,* trans. by J.F. Huntington, New York, 1949, p. 268-269)

71. "The political evolution of the international community must pass through the phase of the idea of sovereignty, just as that of the national community did. This means that the formation of an international state also requires a center of power through which the subjection of mankind, divided among the states, can alone be brought about. The production of an international law and the organization of a world court cannot alone break the national consciousness of power which continually finds new nourishment in the increasing preparations for war. To accomplish this it is necessary to establish a sovereign which, as of old, will enforce the law by means of an instrument of power subject to its orders, and which from the outside will imbue the consciousness of peoples and their leaders

Consistent with this positive application, an important economic proposition has been made for mankind as a whole to own all the natural resources of land, ocean and space.

There has also been in this connection an indication that the World Government has an overriding power to manage the general business in pursuit of the happiness of all peoples.

And in jurisdiction, an interpretation has been made earlier that the World Law is a set of standard domestic rules, any local law has to conform with them, and there is no room for any international law to exist in the World State.

h.
Nations as Local Units

YES, THERE IS NO ROOM FOR THE EXISTENCE OF ANY INternational law anymore. Since all nations have merged into One World, they have been transformed into high level local units, and are governed by domestic rules like other local units. They are no longer independent, and therefore, have no sovereignty anymore.[72]

---

with the domination of an ethical power.... But however the concentration may be accomplished, it is necessary in any event that the international sovereign should possess independence. Only thus can the binding force of law be made independent of states which must be brought and kept under subjection to the law." (Hugo Krabbe, *The Modern Idea of the State,* New York, 1930, p. 271-273)

To quote Mr. Ernest Bevin, then British Foreign Minister, again: "International law would disappear, to be replaced by world law, and in place of the sovereignty of the separate nations there would be the sovereignty of mankind as a whole." (*American Journal of International Law,* Vol. 40, 1946, p. 747)

"The inescapable economic and technical realities of our age make it imperative to re-examine and reinterpret the notion of sovereignty and to create sovereign institutions based on the community, according to the original democratic conception. Sovereignty of the people must stand above the nations so that under it each nation may be equal, just as each individual is equal under the law in a civilized state.... The creation of institutions with universal sovereign power is merely another phase of the same process in the development of human history—the extension of law and order into another field of human association which heretofore has remained unregulated and in anarchy." (Emery Reves, *The Anatomy of Peace,* New York, 1946, p. 137)

72. Harold J. Laski: "The fact that in the great society actions ramify until Tokyo and Paris become cities of a single community implies the organization of

This is a logical consequence, and also a necessity for the World Government to draw loyalty and support directly from the people,[73] in order to fulfill its ends.[74]

---

statehood for that community. In a world-state, however it be built, and whatever the measure of decentralisation that obtains, there is no room for separate sovereignties. Those functions which influence the life of the great society must be subject to the common and concerted decision of men." (*A Grammar of Politics,* London, 1925, p. 66) Again, "that is to say that the world-community and the sovereign-state are incompatible terms. We must choose between the one and the other; we cannot have both." (*Nationalism and the Future of Civilization,* London, 1932, p. 43)

"Today, sovereignty has far too narrow a basis; it no longer has the power it should and was meant to have. The word is the same. The conception it expresses is the same. But the surroundings have changed. The conditions of the world have changed. And this changed situation calls for corresponding changes in the interpretation of this basic principle, if we desire to preserve this, the only foundation of democratic society yet discovered. The great change brought about by the technical and industrial achievements of the nineteenth century is that the nation, which in the eighteenth century was the broadest imaginable basis of sovereignty, today is far too narrow a basis." (Emery Reves, *The Anatomy of Peace,* New York, 1946, p. 133)

"Science has made unrestricted national sovereignty incompatible with human survival. The only possibilities are now world government or death." (Bertrand Russell, quoted by Lawrence Abbot, "World Federalism: What? Why? How?" published by the World Federalists Association and the American Movement for World Government, New York, 1983, p. 49)

73. "As a transition stage to this, however, it is necessary that there be a precedent condition, similar to that which developed at the beginning of modern history, when a self-constituted sovereign, standing above the patch-work of legal communities and superior to an unorganized judiciary, was able by means of an instrument of power dependent upon itself alone to imbue the entire people with the idea of authority. In this way alone it was possible for this idea to gain a firm basis in the ethical and impersonal power of the law. In this way alone it is possible at the present time for the same idea to gain a similar basis for the international community." (Hugo Krabbe, *The Modern Idea of the State,* New York, 1930, p. 274)

Speaking of the League of Nations, "because of the League's care to preserve the sovereignty of states and the principle that the loyalty of individuals is owed primarily to the state, it was not able to rely upon a sufficient public opinion to give effect to its own policies when in conflict with the policies of particular states." (Quincy Wright, *A Study of War,* 2nd ed., Chicago, 1965)

74. Harold J. Laski pointed out that "the lawyer is witnessing, in fact, the transformation of the sovereign nation into a unity of local importance in a greater society of which it is a part. That greater society will, as it grows into the common consciousness of men, take to itself the power and authority that it needs to fulfill its end." (*A Grammar of Politics,* London, 1925, p. 663. Cf. his *Nationalism and the Future of Civilization,* London, 1932, p. 42.)

"The men, who oppose a strong and energetic government, are in my opinion

Consequently, all nations, as local units, will have no authority to engage in diplomatic business, enter into military alliances, wage war, make military conscriptions, maintain armed forces except for some strictly limited local police units, produce and store arms, impose tariffs, block transportation and communications, and so on. All these and other harmful activities will be positively prohibited by the World Law, of course.[75]

There will also be no right for any nation, as a local unit, to claim secession,[76] nor to reject any necessary adjustment in territory, population, or other systems, made by the World Government in the interest of the permanent peace and general happiness of mankind.

In principle, however, all nations are regarded as autonomous areas and as self-ruled people. Their culture, economy and government are respected as much as possible. They can even have a king, queen, national flower and other symbols if they like. They are en-

---

narrow-minded politicians, or are under the influence of local views. The apprehension expressed by them, that the people will not accede to the form proposed, is the ostensible, not the real cause of opposition. But, admitting that the present sentiment is as they prognosticate, the proper question ought nevertheless to be, Is it, or is it not, the best form that such a country as this can adopt? If it be the best, recommend it, and it will assuredly obtain maugre opposition." (George Washington to Alexander Hamilton, quoted in Kenneth B. Umbreit's *Founding Fathers,* New York, 1941, p. 318)

75. The United States Constitution, for example, prohibits the states to enter into any treaty, alliance, or confederation; to grant letters of marque and reprisal, to keep troops, or ships of war in time of peace; to enter into any agreement or compact with another state, or with a foreign power; or engage in war, except under certain special conditions. (See Section 10 of Article I of the Constitution of the United States.)

76. A lesson from the history of the United States: According to the states' rights interpretation of the U.S. Constitution, the individual states, in forming the Union, had merely delegated certain limited powers to the federal government, retaining full sovereignty. Any state, therefore, was legally entitled to withdraw from the partnership if it decided that its rights were being violated. This theory was opposed by early nationalists—such as Chief Justice John Marshall and Daniel Webster—who argued that the federal government was fully sovereign within the spheres assigned to it, and that it derived its powers directly from the people and was not merely a league of states. Hence, under no circumstances was there any right of secession. This issue led to, and could not be settled without, the Civil War. (Cf. Henry B. Parkes, *The American Experience,* 2nd ed., New York, 1955; and Gerald M. Capers, "Sectional Conflict and Preservation of the Union, 1815-1877," in the *Encyclopedia Americana,* 1973 ed., Vol. 27, p. 561-579.)

"The League of Nations has experienced these difficulties.... It witnessed the secession of Brazil, Japan, Germany, and Italy, as well as of several smaller states, during its history." (Quincy Wright, *A Study of War,* 2nd ed., Chicago, 1965, p. 984)

couraged to do whatever is deemed appropriate for social welfare and other local business with which the World Government is not supposed to interfere. But they are not allowed to do anything against any law, policy or measure of the World Government. Instead, they are obliged to carry them on by all means.

The above is a general description of the relationship between the World Government and the nations as its high level local units. Details remain to be worked out especially if a federal form is adopted for the world organization.

i.
Problem of Federation

IT IS INDEED THAT THE IDEA OF A WORLD FEDERAL government has gained wide interest since World War I, as demonstrated by the numerous literature[77] and organized activities.[78] But

---

77. Among them from 1915 to 1948 in English alone are the following: A.O. Crozier, *A Nation of Nations,* 1915; T. Harris, *A Proposed Constitution for the United Nations of the World,* 1918; Swiss Committee for the Preparation of the League of Nations, *Draft of the Constitution of a Universal League of Nations,* 1918; R.C. Minor, *A Republic of Nations,* 1918; I.M. Lloyd and R. Schwimmer, *Chaos, War, or a New World Order,* 1924; H.J. Paintin, *The League of Nations at the Bar of Public Opinion, and the Federation of Man,* 1926; Women's Organization for World Order, *Protocol: A New Declaration of Human Rights,* 1935; S.J. Cantor, *The Constitution of a Commonwealth of Nations,* 1939; W.L. Walton, *Workable World Peace,* 1939; W.C. Brewer, *Permanent Peace,* 1940; H. Heymann, *Plan for Permanent Peace,* 1941; O. Newfang, *World Government,* 1942; R.B. Owen, *Look Forward, Warrior,* 1942; I.B. Bain, *Chaos or Peace,* 1943; P. Bordwell, *A Constitution for the United Nations,* 1943; E.J. Byng, *A Five Year Peace Plan,* 1943; J.B. Corliss, Jr., *The Greatest Project of All Time,* 1943; E. Griffin, *Clinching the Victory,* 1943; M. Habicht, *Is an Enduring Peace Possible?* 1943; R.B. Johnson, *Armistice Terms, Emergency World Legislative Assembly, Universal Bill of Rights, a World Constitution,* 1943; A. Rogow, *A Plan for Immediate and Lasting Peace,* 1943; J.H. Rossner, *A Constitution for the Post-War World,* 1943; W.C. Speers, *Coorder Nations,* 1943; J.M. Turner, *Proposed Constitution of the United Nations,* 1943; M.Young, *The World Settlement from the Trial of Adolf Hitler,* 1944; H.O. Eaton, *Federation,* 1944; and J.E. Johnsen, *Federal World Government,* 1948. To the above list I would like to add my own doctoral thesis, *Conditions for Federation,* at the University of Nebraska, Lincoln, Nebr., 1956.

how to apply this idea to the reality of the modern world has not yet been fully explored.

According to classic federalism,[79] the federal government and its components exist side by side, each possessing certain powers;[80] and all its components are equal, with a partial, if not complete, sovereignty.[81] This is designed to maintain a balance of power as an

---

78. For instance, the United World Federalists was founded in February, 1947, as the successor to several organizations, notably Americans United for World government and World Federalists. Its fundamental thesis is the strengthening of the United Nations by giving it the powers of government, "the power to make, interpret and enforce world law concerning world affairs." The transformation of the UN into a federal world government is to be accomplished under the amending procedure of the UN Charter followed by member-nation ratification. To achieve this goal the organization is working with federalists in other countries through the World Movement for World Federal Government. *World Government News,* is the UWF's lively monthly pamphlet-magazine setting forth all developments in the federation field. The publication has a wide circulation and makes annual awards for outstanding contributions to the movement. (Cf. Alfred M. Lilienthal, *Which Way to World Government, Headline Series* no. 83, New York, 1950, p. 12-18.) The title of the UWF was changed later to the Association of World Federalists.

79. "Federalism is the principle according to which two levels of government, general and regional, exist side by side in the state, each possessing certain assigned powers and functions. Each level of government is limited to its own sphere and within that sphere is autonomous and independent; neither may arrogate to itself powers assigned to the other; each operates directly upon the people and neither is dependent on the other for its legislation, taxes, or administration. Federal government is to be distinguished from a confederacy, in which the general government is dependent on the regional governments, and from a unitary system, in which the regional governments are dependent on the general government." (William S. Livingston, in the *Encyclopedia Americana,* 1973 ed., Vol. 11, p. 77. Cf. his *Federalism and Constitutional Change,* Oxford, 1956.)

80. "The essential element of federalism is the distribution of powers between the general government and the component states. This can take several forms. The powers of the general government may be enumerated and the rest left to the states, as is true in Switzerland, Australia, and the United States. The powers of the states may be enumerated and the rest left to the general government, as in Canada. Or the powers of both governments may be listed, as is done in India and elsewhere. If both are enumerated, it is usually provided that the conflicts between the two shall be resolved in favor of the general government." (William S. Livingston, in the *Encyclopedia Americana,* 1973 ed., Vol. 11, p. 77)

81. The tenth Amendment of the United States Constitution stipulates that the "powers not delegated to the United States by the Constitution, nor prohibited by it to the States are reserved to the States respectively, or to the people." This Amendment reflects Thomas Jefferson's insistence on limited powers for the central government. Based on this, some theoretical exponents of the states' rights, such as John Taylor and John Calhoun, insisted that the states had a complete

interior order. It is a delicate scheme, often with difficulties in working very well[82] and enduring very long.[83]

A hundred years ago, John S. Mill stated as a condition for classic federalism that "there be not a very marked inequality of strength among the several contracting states."[84] Obviously, no such condition exists among the nations today.[85] Without it there will also be more practical difficulties in arranging the relative position of the

---

sovereignty, good for secession and nullification. Calhoun held a states' compact theory, and reasoned that the states possessed indivisible sovereignty and had created the central government as their agent. His views are expressed in the posthumous publications, *Disquisition on Government* and *Discourse on the Constitution and Government of the United States.*

82. "To look for a continuation of harmony between a number of independent, unconnected sovereignties, situated in the same neighborhood, would be to disregard the uniform course of human events, and to set at defiance the accumulated experience of ages." (Alexander Hamilton, in the *Federalist,* No. 6)

83. "National federations have experienced difficulties. They have tended to break up or to form unitary states. The Netherlands and Germany passed through the transitional stage of federation and became unitary states. Switzerland and the United States remain at the stage of federation, although each has steadily increased the power of the central government. The historian Freeman entitled his book written during the American Civil War *History of Federation Government from the Foundation of the Achaian League to the Disruption of the United States,* and supported the thesis that federations are inherently unstable. Confederations have usually succumbed if unable to develop into true federations. Twice, in 1787 and again in 1865, the United States avoided disruption only by drastic steps toward centralization." (Quincy Wright, *A Study of War,* 2nd ed., Chicago, 1965, p. 982)

84. See his *On Liberty and Considerations on Representative Government,* originally published in 1854 (*On Liberty*) and 1861 (*Considerations on Representative Government*), edited by Ronald B. McCallum, Oxford, 1947, p. 299.

85. Members of any federation cannot, indeed, be exactly equal in all respects, and in any federation there will be a gradation of strength among the members: some will be larger in population, or area, or wealth, or some other respect, than others. The essential thing is that most of them should belong to a middle-sized class, and that this class can form a dominant force to keep an equilibrium in the federation. When we try to apply this requirement to a world federation, however, we arrive at a very disappointing situation. We have a few nations which are outstandingly large, and a great mass of nations which are small. What we are lacking is a class of nations in the middle, between the few at the top and the many at the bottom, which can provide a dominant force to keep an equilibrium in a world federation. Among the approximately 170 nations, China, India, the Soviet Union, and the United States have a population of about half of the world's total; the Soviet Union, China, Canada, Brazil, the United States, and Australia have a territory of about half of the world's total. This well-known fact alone illustrates how unequal the strength of the nation is today.

components to be represented in the federal government,[86] to apply their voting power,[87] and to maintain their financial capacity[88] for a successful world federation.

In contrast to classic federalism, there is a type of federation framed under the leadership of one of its components, which is much larger in all important respects than all the others, such as Prussia in the German Empire and Russia in the Soviet Union.[89] The rank and

---

86. In arranging the relative position of the components to be represented in the federal government, there are some ways to make a compromise between the principle of equality and the numerical strength of the components which are found in the federal system. The common way is to set up a bicameral congress: one chamber representing relative numerical strength, composed of representatives elected according to the number of population of the members, and the other chamber marking the principle of equality by being composed of an equal number of representatives sent from each member. The United States Congress is an outstanding example. This is possible only in a federation in which most of the members belong to a middle class, and the weights at both extreme sides are not very heavy. Our world, as we pointed out above, furnishes no foundation for such a federation. (In the United States, the House of Representatives represents the numerical strength while the Senate marks the principle of equality. See Sections 2 and 3 of Article I of the Constitution of the United States of America)

87. A compromise between strength and equality is made in the United Nations Charter by giving a veto power to the five big powers in the Security Council and an equal vote to every member in the General Assembly. It is ridiculous that one member can veto a decision which may be favored by all the rest of the Security Council. It is ridiculous, too, that in the General Assembly the resolution of an "important question" may be passed by two-thirds of the members with only a tenth of the world's population, who pay 5 percent of the United Nation's budget. But how to find a better compromise, if it is necessary for the voting power to represent the relative position of the nations in a world federation, is still a hard question to answer. (Cf. Fremont Rider, *The Great Dilemma of World Organization,* New York, 1946.)

88. In respect to the financial capacity and to a certain extent human resources, the components have to support both the federal government and their own governments. It is not enough that the federal government should be able to finance itself, it is essential also that their own governments should be able to do likewise. If some components are too small and/or too poor, they will be unable to perform their functions so as to keep pace with the others, or they will be able to do so only at the price of financial dependence upon the federal fund drawn from the others, which will seriously affect the healthy development of the federal system. The Union of South Africa, Australia, and some of the Latin American republics have been confronted with this problem in their federal system. In a world federation in which the member nations so greatly vary in size and financial resources, this problem would be much more serious. (Cf. Kenneth C. Wheare, *Federal Government,* London, 1947, p. 53-54.)

89. For the German Empire, cf. the Constitution of the German Empire (1871) in Edith Wynner and Georgia Lloyd's *Searchlight on Peace Plans,* New

rights of its components are not necessarily equal either.[90] This type of federation furnishes no model for a world federation however, not only because there is no nation at the present time which is large enough to provide such a leadership;[91] but also because there is in the Soviet Union a special factor[92] which makes this type of federation work, and meanwhile makes it virtually no different with a unitary system.[93]

In fact, it is not only the Soviet Union which has a unitary practice under a federal form. The United States and almost all the other federal countries have been going in the same direction by extending the power of their federal governments in various ways.[94] This is

---

York, 1949, p. 416-420. Speaking of Russia, its territory is about 72 percent, and its population is about 58 percent of the whole Union. (See *Soviet Union in Maps,* edited by George Goodall, London, 1949, p. 32.)

90. The Soviet Union classifies its components into: a. Union Republics; b. autonomous republics; c. autonomous regions; and d. national areas. Its congress, the Supreme Soviet, is divided into two houses, the Soviet of the Union representing the numerical strength, and the Soviet of Nationalities characterizing the federal system. In the Soviet of Nationalities, the Union republics are assigned 25 delegates each, the autonomous republics 11, the autonomous regions 5, and the national areas one. (See Articles 22-29, and 33-5, of the Constitution of the USSR of 1936.)

91. The Soviet Union, which is the largest nation in area in the world, has only about one sixth of the world's land. China, which is the largest nation in population in the world, has less than one fourth of the world's population. And the United States, which for the time being is the largest nation in national income in the world, has only about one fourth of the world's income, according to recent statistics of the United Nations.

92. In the Soviet Union, the special factor is the Communist Party, which is a unitary and monopolistic organization, which completely controls the whole Union, and which can with certainty carry any measure it considers necessary through the whole Union. (Cf. Samuel N. Harper and Ronald Thompson, *The Government of the Soviet Union,* 2nd ed., New York, 1949, p. 74-81.)

93. "The Soviet Union with a high degree of centralization assured through the dominant control of the Communist party, has made modifications of this type. It should perhaps be regarded as a unitary state rather than as a federation, though it has permitted considerable cultural autonomy to the member states and the autonomous regions." (Quincy Wright, *A Study of War,* 2nd ed., Chicago, 1965, p. 983-984) Early John S. Mill questioned this type of federation as a true federation system (cf. his *On Liberty and Consideration on Representative Government,* edited by Ronald B. McCallum, Oxford, 1947, p. 298-299), and most of the federal theorists have taken the same position.

94. In recent decades, as an illustration, Switzerland has conferred new areas of jurisdiction upon the general government to a considerable extent; Australia and Canada have also made some important changes in this direction; and in the United States there have been three constitutional amendments—XIV, XVI and XVIII, which notably increased the powers of the general government. Judicial in-

because they increasingly need a stronger federal government to handle their growing overall business.[95] But the real driving force is the rapid advance of modern science and technology which makes their people more and more interdependent economically, and keeps them closer and closer through convenient transportation and communications. It is the very force which is driving the whole world into one and is rendering it impossible for any people to live separately anymore. Clearly, therefore, the theoretical ground for a world federation is being lost even as regards an evolutionary sequence,[96] or a transitional step towards a complete union,[97] and the distinction between the federal and unitary forms of government is no longer important.

What is important is the fundamental, which may be summarized as follows:

The world has shrunk into a small place, and mankind is not allowed to live in isolated groups anymore. In the small world there is only one supreme authority, which belongs to mankind and is vested

---

terpretation of the constitution in most of the modern federations has tended to enlarge the powers of the general government. And still many other ways lead in the same direction. (For some details in general, see Kenneth C. Wheare, *Federal Government,* London, 1947, parts 4 and 5; and in particular about the United States, cf. Carrol H. Wooddy, *The Growth of the Federal Government,* New York, 1934; and Ezra C. Buehler, *Increasing the Power of the Federal Government,* New York, 1940.)

95. "In the 20th century the general trend in all federations has been to enlarge the sphere of the national government.... The basic reason for the shift in emphasis lies in the rise of problems that can be solved only by the national government. The growth of a complex and interdependent industrial economy has required national action on a large scale. The 'welfare state' requires national support since only the national government has the necessary financial resources. Wars and threats of wars have required national governments to increase defense spending and defense establishments." (William S. Livingston, in the *Encyclopedia Americana,* 1973 ed., Vol. 11, p. 78. Cf. his *Federalism and Constitutional Change,* Oxford, 1956; and Geoffrey Sawer, *Modern Federalism,* London, 1969.)

96. "It may be said that there seems to be a general law of evolution of federal states in accordance with which independent states associate themselves first in looser forms of union, such as confederations, which then develop naturally into the higher form of a federal union. Examples of the operation of such an apparent law of evolution are afforded by virtually all of the outstanding federations of the world.... But to this law Brazil constitutes an exception." (Hla G. James, *The Constitutional System of Brazil,* Washington, 1923, p. 1)

97. "Federation is a transitional form towards the complete union of the workers of all countries ... (for this reason) we must strive for ever closer federative connections." (Sections 7 and 8 of the "Theses on the National and Colonial Questions" adopted by the Second Congress of the Communist (Third) International, 1920)

in the World Government; the World Government is run by experts to serve, not to rule, the people, and is responsible for managing the general happiness of all peoples; while the nations are respected as autonomous units with self-ruling governments to take good care of their local business.

With this fundamental, the world can be organized to operate well regardless of the form.

With this fundamental, a World Constitution will be drafted for adoption. Other drafts, such as those worked out by the Committee to Frame a World Constitution[98] and by the World Constitution and Parliament Association[99] will be duly consulted. Various proposals

---

98. In March, 1948, after more than two years of drafting, 13 meetings and 146 preparatory documents, a tentative blueprint of global government was put forward in the form of a complete constitution, by the Committee to Frame a World Constitution, headed by Chancellor Robert M. Hutchins of Chicago University. The constitution provides for a world president, stronger than the President of the United States, assisted by a chancellor, like the British Prime Minister, a one-chamber legislature of 99 members, world courts, an international armed force and a federal convention or electoral college. Delegates to the federal convention who would choose the 99 members of the unicameral legislature would be elected on the basis of one delegate for each one million of population. Among the proposed powers of the world government are the maintenance of peace; the organization and disposal of federal armed forces; control and limitation of weapons; establishment of agencies for the global development of natural resources and advancement of physical and intellectual standards; the laying and collection of taxes and establishment of a budget for federal expenditure; the administration of a world bank; and the regulation of commerce and the movement of peoples. (Cf. Alfred M. Lilienthal, *Which Way to World Government, Headline Series* no. 83, New York, 1950, p. 31-35.)

99. "Work upon the draft was begun in 1968 by a commission that included twenty-two men and women from eleven countries. The commission met as part of the first sessions of the Peoples World Parliament and World Constitutional Convention, at Interlaken, Switzerland, and Wolfach, Germany. Behind the 1968 sessions were ten years of work that began when four persons undertook to find an international group willing to convene a world constitutional convention. Following 1968, the drafting commission held a long working session during January and February of 1972; and the draft was finally completed and printed in November, 1974, titled 'A Constitution for the Federation of Earth.' " (Philip Isely, the editor and architect of the draft, "Nineteen Seventy-Seven," in *The Humanist*, July/August, 1975) It was adopted by a World Constituent Assembly meeting from June 16 to 29, 1977, at Innsbruck, Austria, with participants from 25 countries of all continents. A universal call for its ratification and a model resolution for provisional ratification, were issued by the World Constitution and Parliament Association, Lakewood, Colorado, U.S.A.

and related documents[100] will be extensively studied, and new suggestions will be highly appreciated. Our goal is a perfect world.

j.
First Step

NEEDLESS TO SAY, THIS GOAL IS FAR AWAY FROM THE first step yet to be taken. Right now, the problem is from what point and how to take the first step.

There are scholars who have sought to renovate the United Nations as the first step.[101] Some are adherents of the specialized-func-

---

100. There is a considerable and ever-growing supply of unofficial plans for world organization. From time to time anthologies of such proposals have been published. (See *Searchlight on Peace Plans: Choose Your Road to World Government,* by Edith Wynner and Georgia Lloyd, New York, 1949; *Documentation on a World Authority,* by Beatrice Albrekisen and Gerd-Liv Valla, done for the Nordic Working Group for a World Constitution, Oslo, Norway; *Documentary Textbook on the United Nations: Humanity's March Toward Peace,* by John E. Harley, Los Angeles, 1947; and *World Government Proposals Before Congress,* by Percy E. Corbett, New Haven, 1950.) No less important are special problem studies, such as those projecting possible formulas for weighted voting, peacekeeping, and policing techniques. Certainly, any serious effort to put more muscle into world organization requires a familiarity with this literature, for however foolish a particular plan may be, it could harbor at least one useful idea.

101. For example, the proposals by Cord Meyer, Jr. (*Peace or Anarchy,* Boston, 1947), Werner Levi (*World Organization,* Minneapolis, 1950), and Grenville Clark and Louis N. Sohn (*World Peace Through World Law,* Cambridge, Mass., 1958) have much in common. They all favor a world government having the essential features of a national government: an executive, a legislature, and a judicial authority. As a "practical" measure, they all suggest renovating the existing structure of the United Nations rather than starting from scratch. The most elaborate is the proposal of Clark and Sohn, and it will serve to indicate the general nature of these proposals. Their New United Nations will legislate and enforce a world law under which all countries will disarm; it will have the necessary agencies to insure that disarmament is observed. To safeguard the new world order, all weapns will be destroyed or transferred to the hands of the world state. No nation will be allowed to remain armed, just as at present no group of citizens is allowed to maintain a private army in the nation state. The world government will not interfere in the internal economic and social affairs of any nation, not even in their immigration policy or matters concerning international trade. In hundreds of pages, Clark and Sohn provide for multitudinous legal, technical, and institutional

tion approach.[102] Others are "maximalist,"[103] and between them are those who try to patch up critical spots.[104]

Actually, the weakness of the United Nations cannot be attributed just to something wrong in its structure and procedure. It lies in

---

details, from the number of representatives allowed each country to the size of the world police force.

102. "Most numerous now are adherents of the specialized-function approach to world problems. A host of issues, highly publicized in recent years, such as environmental pollution, control of multinational corporations, overpopulation, food scarcity, shortages and maldistribution of energy and other depletable resources, and exploitation of the seabed have led to growing clamor for separate world authorities to cope with these intractable subjects. The tendency of these single-problem specialists is to go their isolated ways . . . their proposals must go to as many as one hundred thirty-eight governments and must wait months, years, or sometimes forever for ratifications. For enforcement they must rely on the various governments whose performances may vary from good to bad to none at all. . . . Advocates of increasing use of this approach may succeed in getting a little something—to be touted as a mighty triumph—but the overall situation will continue to deteriorate. This piecemeal granting of would-be authority over each separate world problem, commended as the easier approach, has proved a failure. Even a village would find it next to impossible to function if it had first to establish a separate administration over every local concern. Proponents of this method are advocating procedures at the world level they would never tolerate in their own locality." (Edith Wynner, "Noah, the Flood, and World Government," in *The Humanist,* July/August, 1975, p. 25)

103. "The most radical supporters of more-effective world organization tend to question whether the major conversion from present confederation to future federation can ever be attained through amendment or review of the Charter. They stress the two major transformations involved: the first is the alteration of the United Nations from an organization based on national governments to a federation based on its member peoples . . . Second is the transfer of real legislative, judicial, administrative and enforcement authority over world problems to such a federalized United Nations Government. . . . These are 'maximalist' views and their proponents claim that to settle for less, to accept some minor patching in procedure, voting, or funding, would be extremely dangerous. They insist that the problem of applying the right dose has become even more important in world organization than in medicine. Too little now is really going to be too late." (Edith Wynner, "Noah, the Flood, and World Government," in *The Humanist,* July/August, 1975, p. 25-26. Cf. her *World Government, Why? What? How? In Maximum Terms, Proposals for United Nations Charter Revision,* Afton, N.Y., 1954.)

104. "Some of the more conservative scholars and federalists favor a number of highly useful changes in the Charter touching on peaceful settlement of disputes, expansion of the use of the International Court of Justice, first-rate proposals on peacekeeping, certain modifications in the use of the veto, and others. . . . Today, however, even the best of these suggestions appear meager alongside the multidimensional pandemic of problems that must be dealt with. They are much too modest and undemanding. . . . If all one seeks are a few slices,

the principles on which it was constructed as merely an agency of the masters—the member nations. These principles include "sovereign equality," "territorial integrity and political independence," "equal right and self-determination," "domestic jurisdiction," the veto power and self-defense.[105] They have grown out of the independence of the nation, national sovereignty, and nationalism. These three are the original evils. If the original evils are not eliminated to allow the abandonment of the principles on which the United Nations was constructed, any magnificent plan to renovate it would turn out to be futile[106] if not completely thwarted by the provision for the revision of its Charter.[107]

So, if the renovation of the United Nations is the first step toward organizing a better world, this step has to begin with the elimination of the original evils.

There are also some leaders who have advocated a popular convention to work out a world constitution as the first step in organizing a better world.[108] They disavow the monopoly on law-making by

---

one ends up with crumbs." (Edith Wynner, "Noah, the Flood, and World Government," in *The Humanist,* July/August, 1975, p. 25. Cf. the World Association of World Federalists, *Proposals for United Nations Reform,* July 1, 1974.)

105. (Cf. the Charter of the United Nations: 2 of Article 1; 1, 4, and 7 of Article 2; 3 of Article 27; Articles 51, 55, 108 and 109. Also cf. II, 303-310 and the related texts.)

106. "These severe limitations on the effectiveness of the United Nations are chiefly due to the lack of a sociopolitical basis for world government, and not to the organization's structure; hence, restructuring it will be of little value. The big power veto, for instance, is simply an instrument used to prevent decisions that a major bloc finds objectionable. If a different procedure were established, one to which a bloc took major exception, the objecting bloc would either ignore United Nations decisions or simply walk out of the organization—and this would be the end of its limited usefulness. After all, even now more United Nation resolutions are ignored than vetoed." (Amitai Etzioni, *The Hard Way to Peace,* New York, 1962, p. 199)

"When a nation disagreed with peacekeeping efforts, such as those in the Middle East, Cyprus and the Congo, it refused to pay a share of the costs. The Soviet Union and its allies have done this; so has France. All this has helped to develop acute financial trouble for the United Nations." (William L. Ryan, AP reporter, "Will U.N. Follow League?" *South Bend Tribune,* Nov. 9, 1971, p. 2)

107. Revision of the UN Charter calls for a two-thirds vote in the Assembly and ratification by two-thirds of all member governments, by their own constitutional processes, including all five permanent members of the Security Council. In short, Charter revision is subject to great-power veto. (US, USSR, England, France and China). (Cf. U.N. Charter, Articles 108 and 109.)

108. The earliest pioneers of these broad approaches to world government, Rosika Schwimmer and Lola Maverick Lloyd, feminists and pacifists preoccupied as early as 1924 with improving the League of Nations, were already thinking in

the government and want the people to act directly.[109] Their attempts have met with various practical problems.[110] When the government, good or bad, is still in a position to represent the independence of the

---

terms of parallel action, pressuring governments to call a "world congress of elected delegates to formulate a plan for a new world order" at the same time that they proposed preparations for an "unofficial international congress" that was also to formulate "an alternative constitution for an unofficial world parliament." During the Second World War, their thinking telescoped into "the immediate creation of a self-constituted Provisional World Government to draw up a World Constitution." In 1945, in connection with the San Francisco Conference, which was to adopt the United Nations Charter, Rosika Schwimmer proposed the holding of a parallel "United Peoples' Conference" to "function as a yardstick and pace-setter" and to revise the draft proposals considered at the official conference "into an effective instrument of federalized world government." This parallel assembly was also to "represent those not invited to the United Nations Conference. (Cf. *World Government, Why? What? How? in Maximum Terms,* by Edith Wynner, Afton, N.Y., 1954, p. 73-78. Cf. also Lola Maverick Lloyd and Rosika Schwimmer, *Chaos, War, or a New World Order. What We Must Do to Establish the All-Inclusive, Non-Military, Democratic Federation of Nations, Campaign for World Government,* Chicago, 1942; and Rosika Schwimmer and Lola Maverick Lloyd, *How to Achieve World Peace. Outline of a Plan,* Winnetka, Ill., 1924.)

109. In a discussion on the ratification and adoption of the Constitution for the Federation of Earth, Dr. Max Habicht of Switzerland, an international lawyer and a professor of International law, remarked that "lawmaking is the monopoly of governments. Therefore, no real progress can be obtained without the cooperation of governments." His opinion was argued by Dr. Terence P. Amerasinghe of India and Mr. Philip Isley of the U.S.A. Dr. Amerasinghe asked, "When Manu made his laws, where was the Government? When Moses brought down the Ten Commandments from Sinai, where was the government? When Solon became law giver, where again was the government?" He further states that "peoples movements have toppled many monstrous regimes in Asia, Africa and Latin America in recent years. 'We the Citizens of the World' should be in the preamble of any Constitution for a Federal World Government and should remain so not in words only but physically as well." (Cf. "World Federalist Papers" no. 1 [*Across Frontiers,* no. 13, Feb. 1981], by the World Constitution & Parliament Association, Lakewood, Colo., U.S.A., p. 1-4.)

110. For example, in Britain more than 100 members of the House of Commons had banded together in a non-partisan parliamentary committee to advance what they called the Crusade for World Government. Henry C. Usborne was the driving force of this group, which included such leaders as Lord Boyd Orr, former Director-General of the UN's Food and Agriculture Organization and Nobel Peace Prize winner in 1949; Lord Beveridge, noted Liberal leader; and philosopher Bertrand Russell. Their plans called for a convening of a people's world convention, or world constituent assembly, in Geneva, in the fall of 1950. One delegate for each million of population was to be chosen by the respective countries of the world, selected by such means as may be decided within the respective countries.

nation adhered to by the people, the national sovereignty rallied to by people, and the nationalism followed by the people, it is obviously difficult to ask the people to take action bypassing their government.[111]

Also, if a popular constituent convention is the first step to organize a better world, this step has to begin with the elimination of the original evils.

Practically, there is no way leading to a better world that can start without the elimination of the independence of the nation, the national sovereignty, and nationalism, as the original evils.

With the elimination of the original evils as its primary mission to approach a perfect world, we are launching the One World Movement.

Unfortunately, the Geneva convention did not have many delegates from the people. The United States had only three from Tennessee. In test voting in Chelmsford, England, Usborne's own country, only 11 percent of the electorate turned out to favor world government. As a result, the convention did not get very far. (Cf. Alfred M. Lilienthal, *Which Way to World Government, Headline Series* no. 83, New York, 1950, p. 19-23; and Henry C. Usborne, *Towards World Government; the Role of Britain,* London, 1946.)

111. "Long years of deception and bitterness have shown that most sovereign governments and those who direct their policies are no closer to yielding their sovereignty to an international body than at any previous time. Most world government groups as well as peace groups have failed in their mission. Nationalism, or modern tribalism, remains the dominant value by which governments and the majority of their citizens view the world and upon which they act. There is little hope of attaining world peace and international law until the blinding barrier of nationalism is broken and a sense of world unity established." (Douglas Mattern in the *World Citizen,* New Delhi, Aug. 1968, p. 8)

VII.
The One
World Movement

a.
Principles

WE HAVE LEARNED:

—that mankind has continued to expand his group life in a social evolution for thousands of years by merging smaller groups into larger ones, from the early single family, through the primitive community, clan, and tribe to the nation; and now a last step is being taken to merge all nations into one world. This step is a consequence of the long process of group expansion which prevails everywhere as a law. It is an historical necessity and an evolutionary consummation, not only desirable but logical, and not only anticipated but also inevitable.[1]

—That the great utility of group expansion is to achieve peace and to pursue happiness. Success has been made in this respect step

---

1. "Thus the history of mankind shows us the spectacle of the grouping of man in more or less firmly knit units, of ever-increasing size that live together in peace, and that are ready to go to war only with other groups outside of their own limits. Notwithstanding all temporary revolutions and the shattering of larger units for the time being, the progress in the direction of recognition of common interests in larger groups, and consequent political federation has been so regular and so marked that we must needs conclude that the tendencies which have swayed this development in the past will govern our history in the future. The concept of thoroughly integrated nations of the size to which we are now accustomed would have been just as inconceivable in earlier times of the history of mankind as appears now the concept of unity of interests of all the peoples of the world ..." (Franz Boas, *Anthropology and Modern Life*, rev. ed., New York, 1932, p. 101. Cf. I, a.)

555

by step.[2] Now it is quite possible for it to attain its ultimate goals: a permanent peace on earth and a general happiness for mankind, through the merging of all nations into one world as the last step.[3]

—That the crucial conditions for group expansion are primarily provided by science and technology with tools and energies which change the mode of life and improve transportation and communications, as well as weapons.[4] The rapid advance of modern science and technology has now made all crucial conditions ready for the merging of all nations into One World: the mode of life of locally independent agriculture has been replaced by that of a worldwide interdependent industry; the vast world has been shrunk into a small kingdom and all national border lines have been completely swept away by the fast transportation and communications; and finally, there is on earth no place which deadly weapons cannot reach within minutes and no place to which the people can escape.[5]

—That, along with the rapid advance of modern science and technology, the One World has actually been in the making through the contributions of geographical exploration, migration, travel, intellectual dissemination, agricultural dispersal, uniformity and standardization, social progress, and developments in international relations and organizations, together with the socialist international movement. Any single one of these contributions in a short period of time may be of little importance, but as a whole and in the long run, they have laid down a broad foundation for the One World.[6]

It is based on these known facts that we have a firm confidence in the future of mankind with One World, and that we have a deep conviction for the future of mankind with One World, and it is based on such confidence and conviction that we commit ourselves to work for the merging of all nations into One World.

This work is very urgent for us, because mankind and his civiliza-

---

2. (Cf. I, c.)

3. (Cf. IV, 164-175; V, 257-298, and the related texts.)

4. (Cf. I, d-g.)

5. "Never before have the 'dreamers' had so compelling an ally, for never have science and nature cooperated to such an extent. The jet-propelled plane, capable of whisking a human in twenty odd minutes from New York to Washington, and the atomic bomb make one world a physical reality.... It may not be now or never, but by their actions today's proponents of world government can decide the outcome of this historic opportunity." (Alfred M. Lilienthal, *Which Way to World Government, Headline Series* no. 83, New York, 1950, p. 59. Cf. I, i and j.)

6. (Cf. II.)

tion are in danger of total destruction by a nuclear war which may occur at any minute,[7] and by an array of other serious crises, including
the fast growth of the population, the quick depletion of resources,
the steady increase of pollution, and the gradual deterioration of the
environment.[8] We have to head off the danger by working hard and
acting quickly, and we have to get the job done before it is too late.
Time is a factor more important than ever before and it is running
out fast.

b.
Primary Mission

SINCE THE MERGING OF ALL NATIONS INTO ONE WORLD
is an historical development and a social evolution, the best we can
do is to release it from the interference of nationalist forces, which
have raged since late last century in reaction to the general trend of
civilization led by the rapid advance of science and technology. The
nationalist force stems from the three original evils: the independence of the nation, national sovereignty, and nationalism. These
have not only slowed down, but have even tried to hold back the historical development and social evolution in various ways.

The independence of the nation is standing against a world in
which all peoples are interdependent and geographical isolation no
longer exists; and is standing for the nation, which has no big place in
the universe and no deep root in history, and whose time is gone and
whose value is lost. In short, the independence of the nation is stand-

---

7. (Cf. IV, 48-74, 119-132 and the related texts.)

8. "The world is threatened with a rapidly increasing population on a planet
with a limited and declining amount of natural resources. Coal, oil, and perhaps
the supply of drinking water will be exhausted before the year 2062. Food scarcity
will mount as population continues to 'explode.' New sources of energy and
calories must be found; oceans must be desalted; nuclear energy must be harnessed
for peaceful use; the bottoms of the seas, heart of the earth, and outer reaches of
space must be combed for new resources, if the children of our grandchildren are
not to go hungry. This requires the shifting of an ever increasing amount of funds
and talent now wasted on arms and duplication (or multiplicity) of national efforts
to shared worldwide endeavors to solve these problems." (Amitai Etzioni, *The
Hard Way to Peace,* New York, 1962, p. 200-201. Cf. V, e-g.)

ing against a real world and for an outmoded political body.[9] And finally, it is the root of war between nations.[10]

National sovereignty is a completely man-made hypothesis, just as totemism was in ancient times. It was originally designed to curb the subversive influence of local rivalries by strengthening a national government. It has done an enormous disservice to mankind since its change from a principle of internal unity and order to a symbol of international separation and anarchy.[11]

Like national sovereignty, nationalism has changed from a force of internal unity to a factor of international separation. It magnifies local characters which are by no means unchangeable. It exploits public sentiment, which is always fluid and elusive. It manipulates history and distorts facts as a standard tactic. It creates prejudice and hatred by artificial measures. It subordinates political liberty, social welfare, and cultural treasures to dictatorship. It nourishes militarism for war, and it is a return to tribalism and barbarism.[12]

---

9. "There are problems of which the impact upon humanity is too vital for any state to be left to determine by itself what solution it will adopt. . . . In such an aspect the the notion of an independent sovereign state is, on the international side, fatal to the well-being of humanity." (Harold J. Laski, *A Grammar of Politics,* London, 1925, p. 65)

"The truth is that the passion for national independence is a leftover from a dead past. This passion has destroyed the freedom of many nations." "The institution of the sovereign nation-state has been dead now for several decades. We cannot revive it by refusing to bury the corpse." (Emery Reves, *The Anatomy of Peace,* New York, 1946, p. 193, 251)

10. "What we do know is that war is the result of contact between nonintegrated sovereign units, whether such units be families, tribes, . . . We also know that today, the conflict is between the scattered units of nation-states. During the past hundred years, all major wars have been waged between nations. This division among men is the only condition which, in our age, can create—and undoubtedly will create—other wars." (Emery Reves, *The Anatomy of Peace,* New York, 1946, p. 125. Cf. IV, f.)

11. "National sovereignty has been as important in the life of the modern world as has been the cow in the life of pastoral peoples. It is not surprising that the cow should have become sacred in India or that the leviathan should have become sacred in the modern world. It it not, however, inevitable that people should insist on feeding and caring for 'sacred cows' beyond a point where their costs exceed their value, as they do in some Indian villages and in the community of nations. Both cows and states should be servants, not masters of men." (Quincy Wright, *A Study of War,* 2nd ed., Chicago, 1965, p. 1044. Cf. III, g.)

12. "The earthlings who have achieved television, atomic fission, and stratospheric flight are still 'barbarians' devoted to the ways of the clan and the gods of the tribe. The new cults of nationalism among the Asiatic and African peoples are but twisted reflections in a broken mirror of the older Atlantic worship

The independence of the nation, national sovereignty, and nationalism are the main stumbling blocks on the way to the merging of all nations into One World. This is why we are determined to uproot them as our primary mission. Their elimination would be followed automatically by other obstacles which originate from them, such as the "national liberation" which is an echo of the independence of the nation, the "national self-determination" which is a shadow of the national sovereignty, and the notorious imperialism which is an outgrowth of nationalism.[13]

c.
Objective 1:
Permanent Peace

IT IS ONLY THROUGH THE SUCCESS OF OUR PRIMARY mission that the merging of all nations into One World can be accomplished right away, and only through the accomplishment of the merging of all nations into One World that our objectives can be achieved at once. Our objectives are the ultimate goals of group expansion: a permanent peace on earth and a general happiness for mankind.

While war has been getting bigger and worse in recent centuries,[14] the methods for maintaining peace have become less and less effective: the conventional ones, such as the balance of power, collective security, and disarmament have been able to do very little[15] and the new ones, such as deterrence, detente, non-proliferation and SALTs do not make much sense either.[16] Consequently, war has been threat-

---

of jealous local deities. Human-kind, even in its most sophisticated societies, has moved but a short step from the mysticism and blood-sacrifices of savagery. Everywhere in our world, even as in ancient days, those most highly honored as 'heroes' are still those who have killed or been killed in the service of tribal creeds." (Frederick L. Schuman, *The Commonwealth of Man: An Inquiry into Power Politics and World Government*, New York, 1952, p. 482. Cf. III, d and e.)

13. (Cf. III, 249-254 and the related text.)
14. (Cf. IV, 4-19, 47-74, 131-132 and the related texts.)
15. (Cf. IV, 23-46, 77-81, 90-93, 114-118 and the related texts.)
16. (Cf. IV, 82-89, 95-113, 119-130 and the related texts.)

ening mankind with total destruction at any minute. There is no way to escape the catastrophe unless war is completely abolished,[17] and there is no way to abolish war completely until the nation no longer remains in independence which is the root of war and is signified with sovereignty.[18] This is why the merging of all nations into One World is the only effective way to achieve a permanent peace over the whole world.

Since we are under the threat of total destruction by an imminent war, urgent measures have to be taken right away to prevent the catastrophe before the completion of the merging process. These measures include:

1. Standing firmly against any kind of war;

2. Dismissing all armed forces except the police, and stopping military conscription and training; and

3. Stopping the making and development of any weapons, and destroying all already made and stockpiled; or converting them to peaceful use.

d.
Objective 2:
General Happiness

IN RESPECT TO THE OBJECTIVE OF GENERAL HAPPI-ness, there is a necessary condition, which is the elimination of all

---

17. (Cf. IV, 133-145 and the related texts.)

"The problem of preventing an atomic war is the problem of preventing War, no more, no less. Once war breaks out and nations are fighting for their existence, they will use every conceivable weapon to achieve victory." (Emery Reves, *The Anatomy of Peace,* New York, 1946, p. 279)

"If we are to have security from the atom bomb and other man-made weapons, we must find a way to prevent war. Unless we are able to do that, you can be sure that, despite all the promises they may make, nations will, in the event of war, employ every means of destruction at their disposal. . . . War must be abolished at all costs." (*Einstein on Peace,* edited by Otto Nathan and Heinz Norden, New York, 1960, p. 394)

18. "Logical thinking and historical empiricism agree that there is a way to solve this problem and prevent wars between the nations once and for all. But with equal clarity they also reveal that there is one way and one way alone to achieve this

war costs forever,[19] and an indispensable means, which is the transfer of all military expenditures to finance the general happiness.[20] The prerequisite for both the condition and the means is the abolition of war through the merging of all nations into One World. Thus, the merging of all nations into One World is also crucial for the pursuit of general happiness for all peoples.

The program for pursuing the general happiness includes two propositions, two themes, two priorities and six important measures. The two propositions are:

1. All natural resources of land, ocean, and space belong to mankind as a whole,[21] and

2. All existing economic systems are entitled to operate, compete and adjust by free will.[22]

The two themes are:

1. Advance through science and technology with humanity and the ecosystem;[23] and

2. Growth with balance.[24]

The two priorities are:

1. Raising of the living standard in the poorer areas through the improvement and development of agriculture, industry, transportation and education,[25] and

---

end: The integration of the scattered conflicting national sovereignties into one unified, higher sovereignty, capable of creating a legal order within which all peoples may enjoy equal security, equal obligations and equal rights under law.'' (Emery Reves, *The Anatomy of Peace,* New York, 1946, p. 125. Cf. IV, 146-187.)

"As long as there are sovereign nations possessing great power, war is inevitable." (Albert Einstein, quoted by Lawrence Abbot, "World Federalism: What? Why? How?" published by World Federalists Association and the American Movement for World Government, New York, 1983, p. 6)

19. (Cf. V, 1-13 and the related text.)

20. (Cf. V, 14-25 and the related text.)

"Every gun that is made, every warship launched, every rocket fired signifies, in the final sense, a theft from those who hunger and are not fed, those who are cold and are not clothed. This world in arms is not spending money alone. It is spending the sweat of its laborers, the genius of its scientists, the hope of its children." (President Dwight D. Eisenhower, quoted by Lawrence Abbot, "World Federalism: What? Why? How?" published by World Federalists Association and the American Movement for World Government, New York, 1983, p.5)

21. (Cf. V 257-272 and the related text.)

22. (Cf. V 273-281 and the related text.)

23. (Cf. V 26-38, 243-254 and the related texts.)

24. (Cf. V, 292-298 and the related text.)

25. (Cf. V, 30-34, 289-291 and the related texts.)

2. Control of the population into an optimum size in relation to food and other natural resources.[26]

The six important measures are:

1. Saving and developing energies;[27]

2. Saving and developing non-fuel minerals, forest products, and water;[28]

3. Improving and increasing food production;[29]

4. Preventing and reducing natural calamities;[30]

5. Protecting the environment with conservation by minimizing the destruction of natural resources, holding down pollution, and relieving urban overcrowding with a pattern of small towns;[31] and

6. Unifying and equalizing the economy with a central world bank and world monetary system, universal income and inheritance taxes, and social security for all; by removing any barrier to trade and travel; and by stabilizing price and employment.[32]

e.
Sketch of
World Government

IN ORDER TO DO ALL THESE WORKS, IT IS OBVIOUS THAT the establishment of an effective World Government is urgently needed.[33]

---

26. (Cf. V, 150-197 and the related text.)

27. (Cf. V, 38-73 and the related text.)

28. (Cf. V, 74-97 and the related text.)

29. (Cf. V, 109-149 and the related text.)

30. Cf. V, 101-107 and the related text.)

31. (Cf. V, 198-255 and the related text.)

32. (Cf. V, 282-288 and the related text.)

33. There were various criticisms on Herbert G. Wells' opinions concerning the necessity, the urgency, and the inevitability of a world state. He was impatient with all those who said it was impracticable. He asserted, on the contrary, that it was the only practicable and "the only sane objective for a reasonable man, it towers high over the times, challenging indeed but rationally accessible; the way is indicated and the urgency to take that way gathers force." (Cf. his works *Experiences in Autobiography,* New York, 1934, p. 642-43; *The Common Sense of World Peace,* London, 1929, p. 22-24.) "My reply to anyone who charges me with

Vested in the World Government is a supreme authority derived from all peoples as a whole, and subordinated to the World Government are the nations as autonomous local units.[34]

Under the World Government human rights and obligations will be well respected without any distinction as to race, sex, language or religion.[35]

The World Government will consist of a World Judiciary, a World Administration and a World Council. The World Council will be the central organ of the World Government, and will be composed of a House of Commons and a House of Experts. Its President, elected by itself, will serve as the World President in formality and ceremony.[36]

---

visionary Utopianism in my demand for the world federation of the common interests of mankind is that it is he who dreams. He is sleeping in a cramped position called patriotism which can produce nothing for him but a series of ... nightmares." (Quoted by Edward M. Earle, *Nationalism and Internationalism,* New York, 1950, p. 118.)

"It is of utmost importance to look at these things in their proper perspective. We must reject the exhortations of reactionaries who say: 'Of course, world government is the ultimate goal. But we can't get it now. We must proceed slowly, step by step.' World government is not an 'ultimate goal' but an immediate necessity. In fact, it has been overdue since 1914. The convulsions of the past decades are the clear symptoms of a dead and decaying political system. The ultimate goal of our efforts must be the solution of our economic and social problems. What two thousand million men and women really want on this wretched earth is enough food, better housing, clothing, medical care and education, more enjoyment of culture and a little leisure. These are the real goals of human society, the aspirations of ordinary men and women everywhere. All of us could have these things. But we cannot have any of them if every ten or twenty years we allow ourselves to be driven by our institutions to slaughter each other and to destroy each other's wealth. A world-wide system of government is merely the primary condition to achieving these practical and essential social and economic aims. It is in no way a remote goal." (Emery Reves, *The Anatomy of Peace,* New York, 1946, p. 283-284)

"There is no salvation for civilization, or even the human race, other than the creation of a world government." (Albert Einstein, quoted by Lawrence Abbot, "World Federalism: What? Why? How?" published by World Federalists Association and the American Movement for World Government, New York, 1983, p. 20)

"Is there a doubt whether a common government can embrace so large a sphere? Let experience solve it. . . . It is well worth a fair and full experiment." (George Washington, *Ibid.,* p. 17)

34. (Cf. VI, 71-75 and the related text.)
35. (Cf. VI, 21-41 and the related text.)
36. (Cf. VI, 46-59 and the related text.)

There are four essences contained in the World Government: justice, service, opinion and knowledge. Justice will be upheld by the World Judiciary, service performed by the World Administration, opinion expressed by the House of Commons, and knowledge furnished by the House of Experts. To coordinate the functions of the four essences there will be a World Presidium with an integrative complex.[37]

Accompanying the four essences are two features projected for the World Government. One is to run the government by experts rather than by politicians, and to serve rather than rule the people. The other is to apply the democratic conception of "for the people, by the people and of the people" in a positive way.[38]

Finally, it is necessary to note the importance of the World Law, which is superior to any local law, and governs the individuals directly, leaving no room for the existence of either the national sovereignty or international law.[39]

Of the World Law, most important is a World Constitution, of course. Based on the fundamentals thus projected for the World Government along with the world structure, a practical World Constitution will be drafted for adoption.

f.
Expedient Setup
of the Movement

STARTING WITH A PRACTICAL WORLD CONSTITUTION, there will be a perfect world in the future. This is an unshakeable

---

37. (Cf. VI, 61-62 and the related text.)
38. (Cf. VI, 50-52, 54, 62-70 and the related texts.)
39. (Cf. VI, 42-47, 71-74 and the related texts.)
 "We have to think of the world-community, the civitas maxima, as the starting point of the social adventure. No part of this community can have the right of the power to act as its own will deems best warranted, without regard to the will of other parts. That body of law which represents the needs of the whole must bind the will of each of its constituent members. Differences between their wills, adjustments of their relationships, can not be a matter of the independent volition of any state. We need institutions which prevent the state from hindering the needs of

belief of the One World Movement (Abbreviated as OWM hereafter).

The OWM is a common endeavor of the people[40] who want to work consciously, voluntarily and actively for the merging of all nations into One World with the principles, the primary mission, the objectives, and the scheme of government, as summarized above. It is an endeavor for all people of the world. Thus, everyone everywhere is urged to join in the cause.

First of all, we want to have our membership extend as fast as possible. Membership requires a pledge of loyalty to humanity,[41] of

---

the world-community and the sovereign-state are incompatible terms. We must choose between the one and the other; we cannot have both." (Harold J. Laski, *Nationalism and the Future of Civilization,* London, 1932, p. 42-43)

40. Government may impede, but it cannot frustrate, the formation of a single world community, since "a really functional social body of engineering, managing men, scientifically trained and having common ideals and interests, is likely to segregate and disentangle itself from our present confusion of aimless and ill-directed lives." These were the elite, the Samurai—composed of technicians, creative-minded industrialists and financiers, scientists, journalists and other writers, a specially educated group of intellectuals, and the like—who would bypass the national state and bring the world state into being without regard to political obstacles. These were the groups who would engage in an Open Conspiracy—"a sort of outspoken secret society ... an informal and open freemasonry"—a revolutionary force designed not "to overthrow existing governments but to supersede them by disregard." (Herbert G. Wells, *Anticipations,* New York, 1902, p. 267. Cf. his *A Modern Utopia,* 1905, Chap. IX; *The New Machiavelli,* 1946 ed., p. 243-245; *The New World Order,* 1939, Chaps. III and X; and *The Open Conspiracy,* 1928.)

"Who do they think they are? (Where do they get their authority?) They're parents who are sick to death of the deplorable conditions of the world which the generations of men have been leaving to their children. They're people who want to live in peace. They get their authority from themselves, from their hopes, from me and from you, if you'll give it. They are citizens of a new world of love, faith and hope:—they are members of the great fraternity of mankind—the human family." (*World Citizen,* New Delhi, Aug. 1968, p. 3)

41. "Everyone gives his loyalty to something larger than himself. But who is loyal to humanity? Humanity has no flag, no song, no colors, no troups, no salutes, no rituals, no face nor body. It is a word like 'justice' or 'peace'—cold, perfect and dead." "Almost every other species of animal is loyal to its own kind, and not merely to its own pack or flock or den. Only man and the shark mortally attack their own kind, and represent their own worst enemy. The other species are loyal by instinct; and we must learn to be loyal by intellect. But the time is running out for us to learn that it is not enough to be a good parent, a good communicant, a good citizen. It is time to be a good man. This means that no loyalty must override the survival of mankind, that in any conflict of interest between this and lesser loyalties, the lesser loyalties must be curtailed or surrendered." (Sydney Harris,

allegience to mankind, and of devotion to One World with peace and happiness for all. A small sum for annual membership dues is also required.[42]

The warmest welcome is extended to those who would like to become members consciously, to recruit voluntarily good men and women to be members, and to organize our members of an area into local units, and members of a country into a political party,[43] while at the same time serving as a chapter or a section of a chapter of the OWM. As a chapter or a section, the group is obliged to carry out all assignments of the OWM and is responsible to it; and being a political party of the country, it is appropriate and convenient to exercise political influences, to sway public opinion, and to campaign for power in order to lead the country into One World.

Meanwhile, we would like to invite all groups who strive for one world, world government, peace, humanity, and the like to unite with us into one movement.[44] There are in existence hundreds of

---

"Humanity Has No Flag, No Song, No Face or Body," *South Bend Tribune,* Sept. 14, 1976, p. 10)

42. The annual membership dues is regarded as a token but serious obligation of the member of the OWM. Its exact amount may be decided by the organization of each country, according to its economic condition and currency situation in proportion to the amount paid by the members in Northern America, which is suggested to be $2.00. Of the membership dues collected by the local unit, one third is kept for the local unit, one third goes to the organization of the country, and one third goes to the central organization of the OWM through the organization of the country.

43. It bears the name of the One World Movement of the given country (its complete official title is not to be used if possible). There have been some political parties which may be regarded as examples, such as the Progressive Party for World Government in the Netherlands and the World Citizens Party in West Germany. The latter "has incorporated in its program the full content of the Constitution for the Federation of Earth, regarding it as an integral part of its policy and strategy." (*Across Frontiers,* by the World Constitution and Parliament Association, Lakewood, Colo., No. 11, March 1978, p. 9. Cf. Alfred M. Lilienthal, *Which Way to World Government, Headline Series* no. 83, New York, 1950, p. 58.)

44. It is interesting to note, as a pioneer, the birth of the first international association of national world government groups which took place in Luxembourg in October, 1946. Thirty-seven organizations from 14 countries formed the World Movement for World Federal Government, with headquarters in Geneva, and Lord Boyd Orr, Monica Wingate and Elizabeth Mann Borgese, as leaders. Later, it was joined by more organizations from more countries. It has tried to embrace all ideas and approaches to world government and to advocate parallel lines of action, calling both for the exertion of pressure on national governments to transform the United Nations into the world government and also for the conven-

these kinds of groups with millions of members in the world.[45] We believe that our goal is the same and that the OWM can represent all of us as a whole. If we remain separate to stress certain differences, no one can accomplish much,[46] but if we stand together as one movement, nobody can stop us. The time requires us to unite together more urgently than ever before.[47] Let us put the One World ahead of

---

ing of a people's convention. (Cf. Alfred M. Lilienthal, *Which Way to World Government, Headline Series* no. 83, New York, 1950, p. 24-28.)

45. Of peace groups alone, for example, there were in 1963 a great number in the U.S.A. Total membership "was said to number around 85,000." "One of the chief American peace organizations, Turn Toward Peace, reported an active year of training specialists in community relations and opening peace information centres in several areas. Its national budget ran over $100,000 for 1963, and it ended the year with a large conference in Washington, D.C., on 'Voluntary Organizations and a World Without War.' " Elsewhere, "a World Conference on Peace Through Law in Athens, Greece; a massive petition campaign by the Swiss Campaign Against Nuclear Arms to prohibit Swiss manufacture of such weaponry; pressure from the Australian and New Zealand Campaigns for Nuclear Disarmament against testing in the southern hemisphere and for extending the Antarctic nuclear-free zone to the whole of the hemisphere; British C.N.D. demonstrations at all three party conferences; and efforts by the Continuing Committee of the Accra (Ghana) Assembly (a 1962 international peace conference) to establish a UN Peace and Disarmament Research institute in a neutral country." (*Encyclopedia Britannica, Book of the Year,* 1964, p. 646. Cf. *Directory of Organizations and Institutions Working for World Government and Unity of Mankind,* published by World Citizen Publications, Feroze Gandhi Rd., New Delhi, 24, India.)

There are in 1982 two government-approved Soviet groups: the Soviet Committee for Peace and the Committee of Soviet Women. There is also a group called "Group for Establishing Trust Between the U.S.S.R. and the U.S.A." "The independent Moscow peace group, unlike government-run Soviet peace groups, has called on both the United States and the Soviet Union to take steps to end the arms race and to improve trust between the two countries." (Marc Rosenwasser, AP reporter, *South Bend Tribune,* July 18, 1982, p. 3)

46. "This experience points up certain suggestions that might be considered by the world government movement: 1) All the existing little side-shows might be brought under one tent into an effective working organization with adequate financing ... 2) A popular leader who commands universal respect might be found. If ever a Moses was needed to lead a bewildered people to the promised land, the world government movement requires such a one today.... As there are too many organizations and too little organization, there are too many generals and no one commander-in-chief." (Alfred M. Lilienthal, *Which Way to World Government, Headline Series* no. 83, New York, 1950, p. 57-58)

47. "To further complicate the situation, the comparatively small number of persons who seem to be aware of the danger are much divided about what to do. 34 years ago, after the second world war, the need for world government was seen clearly by many as the only way to achieve disarmament and solve world problems peacefully. In fact, public opinion polls in the late 1940s indicated that a majority

anything else. Let us unite now. To unite ourselves is an initial step toward uniting the world.

Along with the development of our organization, we have to establish an effective information system in every important area over the whole world, with necessary instruments such as newspapers, magazines, radio and television networks. We cannot carry on mass educational campaigns to rouse the world public without an effective information system. We cannot make our voice and the rumblings of the people against evil forces heard without the necessary instruments.

Needless to say, the most urgent work before us at the moment is to prevent and abolish war. We have to have a task force to handle this extremely important job. Since the early days of this century, war has been developed by modern science and technology to a point where its real meaning and actual effects can be understood by nobody else better than the scientists themselves. This is why Kapitsa[48] and Sakharov[49] conciously refused to participate in it any longer

---

agreed on the need for world government. The questions remaining were: How? When? and What Kind? But today, when the need for world government is greater than ever, the movement for world government is weak and divided." (Philip Isely, "Escape Route," in *Across Frontiers,* bulletin of the World Constitution and Parliament Association, no. 12, June 1980, Lakewood, Colo., p. 1)

48. In 1949, after the Soviet Union exploded its first atomic bomb, there was speculation in the Western press that famed Nuclear Scientist Pyotr Kapitsa had played a crucial role in the bomb's development. But Kapitsa, according to Khrushchev, refused to get involved in military research. Here is Krushchev's version of their relationship. I asked him, "Comrade Kapitsa, why won't you work on something of military significance? We badly need you to work on our defense program." ... "Not I, I refuse to have anything to do with military matters." ("Khrushchev's Last Testament: Power and Peace," *Time,* May 6, 1974, p. 42)

49. Khrushchev further wrote: "I would like to compare Kapitsa with another of our most brilliant nuclear physicists, Academician Andreil Sakharov. He, too, had misgivings about military research. I used to meet frequently with Sakharov, and I considered him an extremely talented man. Literally a day or two before the resumption of our (hydrogen) bomb testing program, I got a telephone call from Sakharov. He addressed me in my capacity as the Chairman of the Council of Ministers and said he had a petition to present. The petition called on our government to cancel the scheduled explosion and not to engage in any further testing, at least not of the hydrogen bomb. 'As a scientist and as the designer of the hydrogen bomb, I know what harm these explosions can bring down on the head of mankind.' ... I wanted to be absolutely frank with him: 'Comrade Sakharov, believe me, I deeply sympathize with your point of view. But as the man responsible for the security of our country, I have no right to do what you're asking. For me to cancel the tests would be a crime against our state. Can't you understand that?' My arguments didn't change his mind, and his didn't change mine; but that

and Linus Pauling has worked vigorously against it for years.[50] We urge brilliant scientists to provide us with a strong leadership for the task force.[51]

A team of experts is also needed to work out practical and detailed plans on every important subject for pursuing the general happiness of mankind. The draft of a World Constitution and other important laws, and bylaws for the OWM is their responsibility, too.

Finally, we need a group of business leaders to raise money for a One World Fund and guide its use in the best interest of peace and humanity. It is obviously impossible for us to carry out extensive programs without a huge fund.

---

was to be expected.'' (''Krushchev's Last Testament: Power and Peace,' *Time,* May 6, 1974, p. 42) Sakharov's account of this conversation appears in his book *Sakharov Speaks,* published by Alfred A. Knopf, May, 1974.

50. Dr. Linus Pauling won his first Nobel Prize, for chemistry, in 1954, and the second one, the 1962 Nobel Prize for a technical paper, ''I Like People,'' printed in 1959 in the *American Journal of Orthopsychiatry.* He also won an award as ''humanist of the year'' in 1961 from the American Humanist Association. He was a thorough-going pacifist. He went on lecturing about the dangers to future humans from the radioactive fallout of nuclear bombs whenever the opportunity arose. On January 15, 1958, he presented a petition to the United Nations urging that ''an international agreement to stop the testing of nuclear bombs be made now'' signed by 9235 scientists of 49 countries, including 37 Nobel Laureates. (Cf. his *No More War,* 25th anniversary edition, New York, p. 180-201. Cf. also p. i-vi, ''About the Author,'' by Robert J. Paradowski.)

51. There have been some initial actions. For example, fifty-five scientists attended the conference on nuclear warfare at the Pontifical Academy of Sciences in Vatican City, Sept. 23 and 24, 1982. Twenty were presidents of national academies of sciences or engineering. Fourteen were from Eastern or Western Europe, five from South America, seven from Asia and three from Africa. One-fourth of the group was from Soviet Bloc countries. They issued a statement that includes a prescription to ''nuclear powers'' which urges them never to use weapons first. ''The current arms race increases the risk of nuclear war. The race must be stopped, the development of new more destructive weapons must be curbed, and nuclear forces must be reduced, with the ultimate goal of complete nuclear disarmament. The sole purpose of nuclear weapons, as long as they exist, must be to deter nuclear war.'' It also warns that countries which do not yet have nuclear weapons must be stopped. ''Proliferation of nuclear weapons to additional countries seriously increases the risk of nuclear war and could lead to nuclear terrorism.'' The presentation of the statement by the scientists represents the hope of Father Hesburgh and other organizers that religious and scientific leaders will ignite a grass roots protest against nuclear weapons. Father Hesburgh, by his own description, became knowledgeable about the threat of nuclear war only last fall. Once informed, he almost immediately joined forces with Franz Cardinal König of Vienna, Austria, to organize scientists and religious leaders. (Reported by Gail Hinchion, *South Bend Tribune,* Oct. 1, 1982, p. 26)

We plead all foundations to channel, all governments to appropriate,[52] and all rich people and groups to contribute as much as possible to help us.[53] No money is needed more urgently than for our effort to save the world from total destruction, and no money could be used more meaningfully than by our seeking for a bright future for mankind. We believe no one else can serve the purpose better than we can for foundations such as the Carnegie Foundation for International Peace[54] and the Foundation for World Government;[55] and we believe we are the best place for great philanthropists to realize noble dreams.[56]

Further, it is important to note that in the long history of civiliza-

---

52. Precedents have been made in supporting the World Federal Authority by some national governments: "Financial support has been received through several years from the Government of Norway and from the Government of the Federal Republic of Germany, and for one year from the Government of Denmark and from the Government of Mexico. Contacts have also been established on the governmental level with Yugoslavia, and approaches with applications have been made to the governments of India and of Japan." ("Draft Agenda" for the meeting of the World Federal Authority Committee and its International Institute on the 19th, 20th and 21st of April, 1979, published in Oslo, March 5, 1979)

53. If only all foundations would channel one thousandth of their interests, all governments would appropriate one thousandth of their military expenditures, and all rich people and groups would contribute one thousandth of their incomes, to finance the OWM, we are sure we could achieve a permanent peace on the earth and pave the way for pursuing a general happiness of mankind through the merging of all nations into One World before the year 2000.

54. Mr. Carnegie's letter to the trustees read at their first meeting December 14, 1910: "Gentlemen: I have transferred to you as Trustees of the Carnegie Peace Fund, Ten Million Dollars of Five Per Cent First Mortgage Bonds, the revenue of which is to be administered by you to hasten the abolition of international war, the foulest blot upon our civilization." The "abolition of international war" is the purpose of the fund clearly set by Andrew Carnegie himself. The letter appears in the Carnegie Endowment for International Peace, *Year Book for 1912*, p. 1.

55. It is paradoxical to find the name of McCormick, a symbol of arch isolationism, as the "angel" of world government. Anita McCormick Blaine established a million-dollar Foundation for World Government in 1948. Stringfellow Barr, former president of St. John's College in Maryland was appointed president. (Cf. Alfred M. Lilienthal, *Which Way to World Government, Headline Series* no. 83, New York, 1950, p. 35-36.)

56. As Dr. Armand Hammer, a successful business leader, expressed in Geneva, April 27, 1981, quoted in the 1981 annual report of the Occidental Petroleum Corporation, inside of the cover page: "My greatest dream, for which I have been working throughout my life and to which today I give my highest priority—a secure and lasting world peace—remains to be realized. In this decade, I plan to continue my efforts and those of my organization ... to see that all peoples are fed, and to work to achieve a secure peace on earth for all men."

tion there has never been a cause which is as great as One World. The opportunity to support the greatest cause is unique. It has not appeared before, and may disappear very soon. Please take this unique opportunity to support the greatest cause by making generous donations right now.

Thus far, we have projected five working groups: organization, information, peace, planning and finance. Each group will have a standing committee headed by a chairman. In order to guide and coordinate the works of the various groups, there will be an executive council, composed of the chairmen of the standing committees, together with a president, one or more vice presidents, and a secretary-general to run the general business. In addition, there will be a world university as the center of activities.

g.
One World University

THERE HAVE BEEN SOME UNIVERSITIES UNDER THE title of world, and there are also many plans for new ones, with the emphasis on intercultural understanding.[57] Actually, that is not a good enough reason to create a world university, because such an emphasis has to be common for all universities.

The university in our plan will not offer regular academic courses, which other universities can do well. It will concentrate on

---

57. The project of a U.N. university, an academic world center of merging cultures, has long been talked about but hasn't progressed much beyond the idea stage. Now it has received considerable impetus at the current General Assembly session from Secretary General Thant. "Working and living together in an international atmosphere," he said of the university project in his annual report on U.N. activities, "these students from various parts of the world would be better able to understand one another. Even in their formative years, they would be able to break down the barriers between nations and cultures which create only misunderstandings and distrust." As the site of the university, some officials have mentioned Switzerland or India as possibilities. UNESCO officials say that some 60 blueprints for a world university, submitted over the years by private organizations from various nations, are locked away in the files of its Paris headquarters. (Reported by R.M. Sorge of UPI, *South Bend Tribune,* Oct. 19, 1969, p. 18.)

developing a solid nucleus of trained personnel, and analytical subtlety with firm principles, to do the job of eliminating the independence of the nation, national sovereignty, and nationalism for the permanent peace and general happiness of mankind, through the merging of all nations into One World.

Students will be recruited from all countries. They must have good academic qualifications and a high interest in working for mankind. They will be sent back to staff the chapters or local forces of the OWM, after graduation.

Most of the faculty members are the leading staff members of the OWM in organization, information, peace, planning and finance. They will study and discuss theories, problems, policies and strategies with the students, thus making the university a workshop of the OWM.

The faculty members will also work together as the general staff of the OWM to provide guidance and coordination for all its activities throughout the world, and will always be ready to help with the establishment of a provisonal world government.

With the World University as the center of activities, the setup of the OWM so sketched is indeed of an expedient nature. As soon as our membership is growing significantly, our local units and chapters are developing close to maturity, and other friend groups are uniting with us into one movement, a world congress will be convened to adopt bylaws and to adjust our structure accordingly. Until then, owing to the extreme urgency and necessity for peace and humanity, we must in the name of mankind start and continue to work with the expedient setup to the best of our ability, and carry out our strategies as far as possible.

h.
Strategies

OUR STRATEGIES CALL FIRST FOR A CAMPAIGN FOR LIBeration: to get rid of the independence of the nation which keeps mankind in separated prisons;[58] to discard national sovereignty,

---

58. "The modern Bastille is the nation, no matter whether the jailers are conservative, liberal or socialist. That symbol of our enslavement must be destroyed if

which is merely a dead duck;[59] and to uproot nationalism, which is a revival of tribalism.[60]

The campaign for liberation necessarily includes the release of mankind from the heavy burden of nationalized histories,[61] from the serious bondage of nationalized traditions,[62] and from the deep

---

we ever want to be free again. The great revolution for the liberation of man has to be fought all over again." (Emery Reves, *The Anatomy of Peace,* New York, 1946, p. 270)

59. Sovereignty, Mr. Elwyn B. White points out, is a dead duck. "The world, being now afraid of its own shadow, is ripe for something bigger than it seems likely to get, broader than it believes itself capable of achieving. If ever people needed to see clearly that their special national interests are identical with their special national decline, it is in these nervous times . . . The pattern of life is plain enough. The world shrinks. It will eventually be unified. What remains to be seen (through eyes that now bug out with mortal terror) is whether the last chapter will be written in blood or in Quink." (His *The Wild Flag,* New York, 1946, quoted on the book's jacket.)

"These indisputable facts prove that our present conception of national sovereignty is obsolete and pregnant with deadly danger to us all." (Emery Reves, *The Anatomy of Peace,* New York, 1946, p. 137. Cf. W.C. Sickesz, *Sovereignty, the Right of the Nations to Commit Suicide Unhindered,* Amsterdam, 1948. First part.)

60. "Nationalism is a herd instinct. It is one of many manifestations of that tribal instinct which is one of the deepest and most constant characteristics of man as a social creature. It is a collective inferiority complex, that gives comforting reactions to individual fear, loneliness, weakness, inability, insecurity, helplessness, seeking refuge in exaggerated consciousness and pride of belonging to a certain group of people." (Emery Reves, *The Anatomy of Peace,* New York, 1946, p. 186. Cf. III, e and f.)

"Nationalism is an infantile disease. It is the measles of mankind." (Albert Einstein in the speech when he received the Nobel Prize in 1921, quoted by Sydney Harris in a speech given before the Chicago Region of the World Federalists Association, May 20, 1979.)

61. "Men and women tried to recall the narrow history teaching of their brief schooldays and found an uninspiring and partially forgotten list of national kings or presidents. They tried to read about these matters, and found an endless wilderness of books. They had been taught history, they found, in nationalist blinkers, ignoring every country but their own, and now they were turned out into a blaze. It was extraordinarily difficult for them to determine the relative values of the matters under discussion. Multitudes of people, all the intelligent people in the world, indeed—who were not already specially instructed—were seeking more or less consciously to 'get the hang' of world affairs as a whole. They were, in fact, improvising "Outlines of History" in their minds for their own use." (Herbert G. Wells, *The Outline of History,* 1949 ed., New York, Vol. 1, p. 2)

"I am trying to use our knowledge of history as a telescope-lens for taking a look at the universe as a whole." (Arnold J. Toynbee, *Journal of the History of Ideas,* Vol. 16, 1955, p. 421)

62. For a long time we have been accustomed to think and act around the nation which has virtually been a center of our daily life. Our habits, behaviors and

penetration of nationalized education.[63] In other words, we have to get out of a small fabricated world[64] and not regard our own nation as the center of the universe anymore;[65] and we must no longer linger over yesterday's flower[66] or hesitate to cut down any evil fruit tree.[67]

---

the like have been nationalized; and often we have fallen deep into a national myth, ideology and emotion. One important aspect of this pattern is a tendency to cherish historical traditions, notably by purposeful commemoration of historical events such as national independence and great military victories. Beloved national heroes of both peace and war are glorified and their praises sung. Pilgrimages to battlefields and the birthplaces of great men of the past are fostered. All these have become our traditional bondages. (Cf. Friedrich O. Hertz, *Nationality in History and Politics,* New York, 1944, p. 18-19.)

63. "However, in our educational systems cultural nationalism is hardly mentioned, political nationalism is stressed. Devotion to the political interests of the nation, to political power, is taught as the paramount duty and is instilled into the minds of the young in such a form that with it grows up and is perpetuated the feelings of rivalry and of hostility against all other nations." (Franz Boas, *Anthropology and Modern Life,* rev. ed., New York, 1932, p. 104)

"From the end of the 18th century on, the nationalization of education and national life went hand in hand with the nationalization of states and political loyalties. In many cases poets and scholars emphasized cultural nationalism first, reformed the national language, elevated it to the rank of a literary language, delved deep into the national past, so as to prepare the foundations for the political claims for national statehood soon to be raised by a people in which the spirit of nationalism had been kindled by writers and educators." (Hans Kohn, "Nationalism," in the *Encyclopedia Britannica,* 1952 ed., Vol. 16, p. 149-150)

64. "In the day to day demands we tend to have fabricated a world of our own. With walls of isolation to secure our meager existence ... It is a fabricated world because it is apart from history. It is apart from the ongoing humanization of man. It denies the sharing that is so essential to life. In short, it traps us to become unaware of the historicity of man and the necessity of a world community to qualify it." (Quoted from a pamphlet of One Earth Week, April 14-19, 1975)

65. "Nothing can distort the true picture of conditions and events in this world more than to regard one's own country as the center of the universe, and to view all things solely in their relationship to this fixed point. It is inevitable that such a method of observation should create an entirely false perspective. Yet this is the only method admitted and used by the national governments of the world ... Within such a contorted system of assumed fixed points it is easy to demonstrate that the view taken from each point corresponds to reality. If we admit and apply this method, the viewpoint of every single nation appears indisputably correct and wholly justified. But we arrive at a hopelessly confused and grotesque over-all picture of the world." (Emery Reves, *The Anatomy of Peace,* New York, 1946, p. 1)

66. Some people, even highly intellectual, like to look back for the "good old days." For instance, Plato (427?-347? B.C.) in his work, gives an abstract account of a form of life that the Age of Pericles (461-429 B.C.) lived concretely. Aristotle's lifetime (384-322 B.C.) coincided with the period in which the Greek cities lost their independence because the Battle of Chaeronea (338 B.C.) resulted in the

Going along with the campaign for liberation is a campaign for promotion: to raise humanity,[68] to build up an ultimate allegiance and a supreme loyalty to mankind,[69] and to develop a world patriotism[70] to replace the old, narrow and blind patriotic taboo.[71]

---

complete subjection of Greece to Macedonia. But he wrote the political philosophy of the city-state as though it were eternal, instead of being a phenomenon peculiar to an age which had already passed. In spite of his close connection with the kings of Macedon, he showed no awareness of the importance of the revolution which they had brought about. (Cf. George H. Sabine, *A History of Political Theory*, New York, 1937, p. 123-138, 631-632.)

67. It is the ill-informed mind which is the servant of the past, and it is the sound judgment in which lies our future. "It is important for our generation and for that which follows us that we should judge all living, growing trees by their fruit, and that if to our taste any tree brings forth evil fruit, we should attempt to cut down or at least engraft good fruit upon that tree." (Carlton J.H. Hays, *Essays on Nationalism*, New York, 1926, p. 247)

68. "The caution is perhaps needed that we must not form too loose a conception of the kinship which once stood in the place of the multiform influences which are now the cement of human societies. It was regarded as an actual bond of union, and in no respect as a sentimental one. The notion of what, for want of a better phrase, I must call a moral brotherhood in the whole human race has been steadily gaining ground during the whole course of history, and we have now a large abstract term answering to this notion—Humanity." (Henry S. Maine, *Lecture on the Early History of Institutions*, New York, 1888, p. 64-65)

"Watching the U.N. proceedings early this summer, I thought of how fluently and ardently the partisans of each nation spoke up for their sides. But nobody spoke up for everybody, for that faceless, stateless man called 'humanity.'... Yet all the crises of our time can be rolled up into one crisis—that nobody speaks for mankind, even though mankind today is threatened with annihilation as a whole species." "... Space and time have shrunk with terrifying compression in our age. Ancient boundaries are meaningless, except for political purposes: old divisions of clan and tribe are sentimental remnants of the pre-atomic age; neither creed nor color nor place of origin is relevant to the realities of modern power to utterly seek and destroy. Yet we walk around as if nothing had changed, mouthing the same old platitudes, waving the same frayed flags, imagining somehow that we are invulnerable to the tremors that are shaking the whole of the earth. It is hard, almost impossible, to cherish mankind beyond all else. But nothing less, in our century, will suffice. This crisis in loyalty may well be the watershed of the human race, leading to survival or extinction.... If no one speaks for humanity alive, what is there to prevent humanity's death?" (Sydney Harris, "Humanity Has No Flag, No Song, No Face or Body," *South Bend Tribune*, Sept. 14, 1976, p. 10)

We stand for the "Abolition of man created barriers, divisions, discriminations, prides, prejudices and all that which obstructs the path of equality and progress towards one humanity and one world." (*World Citizen*, New Delhi, Aug. 1968, p. 2)

69. "In fact, so great is the temptation for every nation to erect about itself high walls of race prejudice and exclusivism, that one of the first steps toward the creation of an effective international organization would have to be to break

A third campaign is for survival, the prerequisite to liberation, promotion and anything else. This campaign includes various anti-war activities; refusal of military conscription; protest against the manufacture, development and sale of weapons, whether nuclear, chemical or conventional, with further actions to destroy them or convert them into peaceful uses; and the disbanding of the armed forces.

The three campaigns will amount to a real world revolution, for they will be carried everywhere with a determination to bring forth a fundamental change in the social, political and economic systems of the whole world.[72] But they differ from conventional revolutions in

---

through these walls and work to promote a higher form of loyalty, namely, loyalty to the whole human race." (John B. Whitton, "Nationalism and Internationalism," in the *Encyclopedia Americana,* 1973 ed., Vol. 19, p. 750)

"Restriction of loyalty to within national boundaries is obsolete, and loyalty to the whole of mankind is now a necessity. Individuals must bear personal responsibility for acts contrary to the interests of mankind." (Oslo Statement issued by 35 physical and biological scientists and 25 social scientists from 15 countries at a conference held in Oslo, Norway, May 2-7, 1961, sponsored by Linus Pauling, Bertrand Russell and 23 other well-known scientists. (Cf. Linus Pauling, *No More War,* 25th anniversary edition, New York, 1983, p. 275-282.)

70. Love of country, to Gotthold E. Lessing (1729-1781), the great leader of the Enlightenment, was "at best but an heroic vice." Patriotism which obscured one's duties to humanity was not something to cultivate. "To be praised as a zealous patriot is the last thing I desire—a patriot, that is, who would teach me to forget that I must be a citizen of the world." (George P. Gooch, *Nationalism,* New York, 1920, p. 12. Cf. Henry E. Allison, *Lessing and the Enlightenment,* Ann Arbor, Mich., 1966.)

71. "Real patriotism can have but one single purpose: to protect one's own country, one's own people, from the devastation of war. As war is the direct result of the nation-state structure, and as modern aerial and mechanized warfare indiscriminately destroys women, children, cities and farms, the nation-state is Enemy No. 1 of patriotism.... As soon as people realize that in fact the nation-state institution destroys their countries, devastates their provinces and murders their kinsmen, true patriots will revolt against that institution, a threat to everything they love. Nothing is more incompatible with true patriotism than the present nation-state structure of the world and its inevitable consequences." (Emery Reves, *The Anatomy of Peace,* New York, 1946, p. 234)

"In teaching, one soon discovers that an attack on nationalism draws yawns from students, but the same content addressed as patriotism brings them to their feet. Clearly, our society tends to put a taboo on the subject of patriotism." (G.J. Ringer, "Patriotism a Taboo," in a letter to the *War/Peace Report,* Jan., 1966, issue)

72. What revolution means generally? "When people speak of ideas that revolutionize society, they do but express the fact, that within the old society, the elements of a new one have been created, and that the dissolution of the old ideas

one important aspect: they do not rely upon violence. This is not only a necessary demonstration of our sincere efforts for peace, but also a logical application of our deep belief that reason and conscience are essential aspects of humanity.[73] Non-violence is our principle, and we observe it strictly, even in the strikes which we may have to call for under certain circumstances. We also adopt a practice of non-violent resistance[74] as our tactic.

Admittedly, there are in human nature some viruses[75] which make violence a part of human behavior as it is in other animals. But this is just what we have to purge away rather than to live with, in order to perfect our spiritual civilization.[76]

---

keep even pace with the dissolution of the old conditions of existence." (Karl Marx, *Manifesto of the Communist Party*). "Revolution means the clear recognition of the roots of the evils of society at any given moment, the concentration of all forces to exterminate these roots, and to replace a sick society by a new social order that no longer produces the causes of the evils of the previous regime." (Emery Reves, *The Anatomy of Peace*, New York, 1946, p. 270)

73. Article 1 of the Universal Declaration of Human Rights: "All human beings are born free and equal in dignity and rights. They are endowed with reason and conscience and should act towards one another in a spirit of brotherhood."

"Dante assigned the highest place among communities to the universal empire. Since the special character of man is reason, the end or function of the race is to realize a rational life, and this is possible only if there is universal peace, which is the best of things for human happiness and a necessary means to the ultimate end of man." (George H. Sabine, *A History of Political Theory*, New York, 1938, p. 258. Cf. Alexander P. D'Entreves, *Dante As a Political Thinker*, New York, 1952.)

74. "The term Satyagraha . . . means hold on to truth. Hence truth-force. I have also called it Love-force. . . . Carried out to its utmost limit, this force is independent . . . Its universal applicability is a demonstration of its permanence and invincibility. It can be used alike by men, women, and children. It is totally untrue to say that it is a force to be used only by the weak so long as they are not capable of meeting violence by violence. It is impossible for those who consider themselves to be weak to apply this force. Only those who realise that there is something in man which is superior to the brute nature in him, and that the latter always yields to it, can effectively be Satyagrahis. This force is to violence, and therefore to all tyranny, all injustice, what light is to darkness." (Mahatma Gandhi's Call for Non-Violent Resistance, 1914, quoted in *The Imperialism Reader*, ed. by Louis L. Snyder, New York, 1962, p. 417)

75. "But humans are commonly self-defeated by their atavistic values, and by non-rational patterns of response as old as protoplasm, and by the dark, irrational forces of the mind as ancient as the psyche." (Frederick L. Schuman, *The Commonwealth of Man; an Inquiry into Power Politics and World Government*, New York, 1952, p. 482)

76. "Assuming or even admitting that certain evils are part of 'human nature,' this does not mean that we should sit passively and refuse to investigate the conditions which cause the evils to become deadly and the possibility of

In the intensity of violence, terrorism ranks only next to war. Although not a new phenomenon in the political arena,[77] terrorism has been more active in recent years, and has endangered more innocent people as in the skyjackings.[78] Consequently, the image of terrorists has turned from bad to worse in the public mind. Yet they are dedicated and smart people.[79] We believe, if only they knew that what they do debases their goal,[80] they would give up their violent way at once; and that if they decide to join us, they will be able to make a contribution to the cause of One World which is much greater and more urgent than any causes which have raised their enthusiasm and devotion.

---

avoiding their devastating effects. Since man began to think about life and himself, it has been generally accepted that appendicitis and gallstones were in the nature of man. Indeed, they are. But after thousands of years, during which men died from these fatal evils of 'human nature,' some people had the courage to take a knife and cut open the diseased part to see what was happening. Appendicitis and gallstones continue to be 'in the nature of man.' But now man does not necessarily die from them." (Emery Reves, *The Anatomy of Peace,* New York, 1946, p. 117)

77. "Political assassination has been a staple of political life since Brutus stabbed Caesar. In the Middle Ages, kings and princes were often kidnapped and held for ransom. Bombing was used by 19th Century Russian nihilists and European and American anarchists." (Dave Goldberg, "World Pays Bloody Price for Terrorism," in *South Bend Tribune,* Aug. 24, 1980, p. 1)

In the Roman Empire, for example, in the 50 years between A.D. 235 and 285, there were 26 emperors. Only one of them died a natural death, all the rest died by intrigue or counter-intrigue. (Cf. R. Freeman Batts, *A Cultural History of Education,* New York, 1947, p. 85.)

78. "After more than a decade of skyjackings, kidnappings, hostage seizures, shootouts and bombings aimed at advancing often obscure political causes, law enforcement officials and other experts on terrorism fear the worst bloodshed may be yet to come. For the last five years there has been an average of more than one incident of international terrorism each day, making it so routine as to bump all but the most spectacular incidents from the front pages and the evening newscasts." (Dave Goldberg, "World Pays Bloody Price for Terrorism," in *South Bend Tribune,* Aug. 24, 1980, p. 1)

79. U.S. Brig. Gen. James L. Dozier today called his Red Brigades kidnappers "dedicated people" who are intelligent and sincere about what they are doing. "They are a bunch of dedicated people. They are smart. They believe in what they are doing, and they are very serious about it," Dozier told reporters, according to an AP report from Verona, Italy, where he was kidnapped for 42 days. (*South Bend Tribune,* Jan. 30, 1982, p. 1)

80. "What the terrorists don't know, or refuse to admit, is that what you do to achieve your goal can debase and corrupt that goal so much that by the time you achieve it you are not fit to govern. Terrorism begets terrorism; it can no more beget a society worth living in than an ape can give birth to an angel." (Sydney Harris, *South Bend Tribune,* Oct. 31, 1979, p. 12)

Under the principle of non-violence, our campaigns may not be so sensational and so exciting as to induce an impulsive public response. But what we seek is public judgment rather than public impulse. We believe that mankind has grown mature enough to see what and where his real interest is and to know how to act appropriately, if only we can fully present to the public all the undeniable facts and truths.

For this very reason, we will campaign openly with open minds and open policies toward an open world, and we will campaign with common sense and straight actions. We have nothing to hide, we do not pretend mystery, and we tolerate no superstititions.[81]

It would be an unforgivable mistake to figure that our peaceful, open and plain campaigns are an easy and broad way to the success of world revolution. On the contrary, it is the most difficult approach, especially during the early stages in which we have not obtained sufficient instruments and developed them to do the job efficiently, and while we have excluded the use of the old methods of revolution, such as bloodshed, myth and intrigue.

The instruments we need include television, radio, newspapers, magazines, movies, art, song, dance, sports, and so on. They are nothing new. But we have to have them in sufficient quantities to carry out our campaigns everywhere and to develop their effectiveness to the highest degree possible for our service. Meanwhile, we want to enlist the service as much as possible of all such instruments under any private or public direction the world over. If only half of them come to help us positively, the world revolution may succeed suddenly at any moment. We believe that no single one of them is not interested in peace and humanity. We urge all of them to do their best for the cause of One World, not to stay away at the critical time, and at least not to spread any nationalist curses under any circumstances.

With all the instruments available, we will bring our campaigns directly to all people, to have them spread and discussed in homes, farms, factories, universities, and other schools. We want to have a chain reaction set forth by the people[82] and to get the initiatives and

81. "Nothing can destroy the nationalist fetishes, prejudices and superstitions except the explosive power of common sense and rational thinking. Only a struggle in our minds can prevent further struggles on the battlefields." (Emery Reves, *The Anatomy of Peace,* New York, 1946, p. 235)

82. "We have to get to work at once. Every citizen ... must persuade ten other citizens of the same belief, and urge each to persuade, on his behalf, ten more. The nuclear physicists have explained that atomic energy is released by what

demands of the people reflected throughout villages and town-ships,[83] to county, province and state levels,[84] and finally up to their national governments. The major object of our campaigns is to con-vince all national governments to give up their independent status and join in a world government, through persuasion and pressure, but mainly by voice and voting of their people.

---

is called a chain reaction. One atom is split. The released particles split other atoms and so on. The force of ideas always explodes in the form of such a chain reaction." (Emery Reves, *The Anatomy of Peace,* New York, 1946, p. 290)

83. An example may be seen in the ratification of the Constitution for the Federation of Earth by the first two Town Councils of the neighboring towns of Wolfach and Oberwolfach, Federal Republic of Germany. October 25, 1977, the first action of the ratification by the Town Council of Wolfach in an official but non-public meeting of the Council. 16 members of the Town Council signed the ratification resolution on this day. Two members were absent on November 9, 1977, the other two council members signed, together with Mayor Arthur Martin, making the ratification unanimous. On December 21, 1977, a letter sent by Mayor Willi Rauber of Oberwolfach confirmed that the Town Council of Oberwolfach had also ratified the Constitution for the Federation of Earth at a meeting on December 14th. All 12 members of the Council signed the ratification resolution, together with Mayor Rauber. (Cf. *Across Frontiers,* by the World Constitution and Parliament Association, Lakewood, Colo., No. 11, March, 1978, p. 1 and 9.)

84. In the United States, for example, four years after World War II, the United World Federalists urged the state legislatures "to pass resolutions calling on Congress to summon a convention for consideration of such constitutional amend-ments as will 'expedite and insure the participation of the United States in a world federal government.' ... The insertion of proper clauses in the Constitution, it is argued, would permit the United States to take the lead in negotiating with other nations for the creation of federation. Without this amendment other nations might hesitate to rely on mere transitory policy, even if a chief executive of the United States were to take the risk of initiating negotiations without a prior public mandate. Maine, California, New Jersey, North Carolina, Florida and Connec-ticut have passed the world government amendment to the Constitution, and some twenty additional states are targets for action." (Cf. Alfred M. Lilienthal, *Which Way to World Government, Headline Series* no. 83, New York, 1950, p. 18.)

i.
Provisional World Government

NATURALLY, THE IDEAL SOLUTION WOULD BE IF ALL nations were convinced simultaneously. But such a development can hardly be counted on; and the process of merging the nations must start at the earliest possible moment, even with a minimum of two nations. For this reason, our strategies call for the formation of a provisional world government as the second step of the world revolution. The start of this step may be very arduous, but some breakthrough will be no surprise once it sets foot on the ground and gets going.

The main job of the provisional world government includes: 1. to have all works of world disarmament completed; 2. to have a World Constitution worked out and ratified by a World Constituent Assembly or through some other process;[85] 3. to establish a permanent world government in accordance with the World Constitution; and 4. to have important projects prepared for the pursuit of general happiness, and to start some actual works on an emergency basis.

Since the operation of the provisional world government has to be concentrated in a few activities for a transitional period which is supposed to be very short, it is not necessary to organize it with a full structure of government. The sketches projected earlier for the World Government and the OWM may serve as guidance, and expedient plans and personnel assistance will be provided by the OWM to meet any exigency.

There are three ways possible to form a provisional world government: by converting the United Nations, by the experiment of the OWM with support initiated by any nation or a group of countries, and by direct action of the people with the assistance of the OWM.

If most of the members, including the permanent members of the United Nations, were convinced to give up their position as its

---

85. The organization of the World Council and the methods to select its Members of both Experts and Commons, as projected earlier for the World Government, may be adopted for the formation of the World Constituent Assembly, and also as an experiment of the World Council itself. (Cf. VI, 54-56 and the related texts.)

masters by dropping national sovereignty and other related principles from the Charter, there would be little difficulty in converting
the world organization into a provisional world government. This is
a practical approach and deserves to be tried by all means.

Meanwhile, the OWM should try to form a provisional world
government as soon as possible, because the conversion of the
United Nations may not proceed fast enough to cope with urgency.
Of course, the OWM will not maintain a separate government if the
conversion succeeds on time.

The support which the OWM needs from every nation to form a
provisional world government includes: 1. moral and financial assistance; 2. pledges of allegiance to mankind for permanent peace and
the general happiness, and not to press for capitalism or communism; 3. denouncement of the independence of the nation, national
sovereignty and nationalism; and 4. preparation for destroying its
own weapons and dismissing its own armed forces. These are also
common requirements for all nations to pursue the great cause of
One World. In addition, a suitable area and adequate facilities for
the operation of the provisional world government is sought as a
special support.

The crucial problem now is which nation would start the support.
There is no doubt that if any nation, especially a great nation or a
group of countries, at the most critical moment in history, took the
initiative, many others would follow suit immediately. The initiative
is indeed a great challenge for response.

The American people enjoy an excellent position for meeting the
challenge. They are highly advanced in science and technology, are
richly composed of all kinds of racial origins and cultural varieties,[86]
and are often respected as traditionally generous.[87] They know that

---

86. "The height of our civilization, it seems to me, has been reached not by
our assembly lines, our inventions, or any of our great factitious development, but
by the ability of peoples of varying beliefs and of different racial extractions to live
side by side here in the U.S. with common understanding, respect, and
helpfulness.... Our way of living together in America is a strong but delicate
fabric. It is made up of many threads. It has been woven over many centuries by
the patience and sacrifice of countless liberty-loving men and women. It serves as a
cloak for the protection of poor and rich, of black and white, of Jew and gentile,
of foreign and native-born." (Wendell L. Willkie, *One World,* New York, 1943,
p. 194, 195. Cf. John F. Kennedy, *A Nation of Immigrants,* rev. ed., New York,
1964, p. 1-4, 64-68, and 84-88.)

87. "Americans, this Canadian thinks it's time to speak up for the
Americans, the most generous and probably the least-appreciated people in all the

the world is one and they cannot withdraw their responsibility away from it as clearly expressed forty years ago by Wendell Willkie,[88] one of their many openminded and far-seeing leaders.[89]

The Russians are also in an excellent position to meet the challenge. We have faith in them,[90] and we believe that they are interested in the "creation of secure peace and tranquility for all mankind"

---

earth." "As long as 60 years ago, when I first started to read newspapers, I read of floods in the Yalu River. Who rushed in the men and the money to help? The Americans did." ... "I can name you 5,000 times when the Americans raced to the help of other people in trouble. Can you name me even one time when someone else raced to the Americans in trouble? I don't think there was outside help even during the San Francisco earthquake." (A 3-minute recording written in early 1973 as an editorial by Gordon Sinclair, 73, owner of radio station CFRB in Toronto. Reprinted in newspapers throughout the year, it was read on Dec. 2 on station CKLW that beams across the border from Canada into Detroit, by Byron MacGregor, 25, also a Canadian.)

88. "A withdrawal from the problems and responsibilities of the world after this war would be sheer disaster. Even our relative geographical isolation no longer exists. At the end of the last war, not a single plane had flown across the Atlantic. today that ocean is a mere ribbon, with airplanes making regular scheduled flights. The Pacific is only a slightly wider ribbon in the ocean of the air, and Europe and Asia are at our very doorstep." (Wendell L. Willkie, *One World,* New York, 1943, p. 202) "When you fly around the world," he says in another passage, "you learn that the world has become small not only on the map, but also in the minds of men. All around the world, there are some ideas which millions and millions of men hold in common, almost as much as if they lived in the same town." (*Ibid,* p. 157)

89. For example, Senator Glen Taylor (D. Ida.) introduced a resolution into the upper chamber in 1945 placing the United States squarely in favor of the establishment of a World Republic. (Cf. Alfred M. Lilienthal, *Which Way to World Government, Headline Series* no. 83, New York, 1950, p. 48.) As another example, Adlai E. Stevenson, the U.S. Democratic Party's presidential nominee in the elections of 1952 and 1956, urged the U.S. to press for world unity. He said: "If the United States does not press on" in support of world policing and world law, "the world, I believe without rhetoric or exaggeration, is lost." He noted that Americans were still divided on the question of nationalism versus world government, despite the fact that "the rationale of separate, disparate sovereignty has all but vanished." This is the main point of his speech in the 96th charter anniversary ceremonies at the University of California, April 2, 1964.

90. A new act of faith on the part of the Western world in the ultimate humanity and sobriety of its Soviet Communist adversaries has been urged by a noted authority on Russia, George F. Kennan, former U.S. Ambassador to the Soviet Union and to Yugoslavia, who addressed the same act-of-faith plea to the Communist bloc: "For in the predication of only the worst motives on the adversary's part there lies, today, no hope at all: only a continued exacerbation of mutual tensions and the indefinite proliferation of nuclear weaponry." (Reported by H.D. Quigg, UPI, *South Bend Tribune,* Feb. 19, 1965, p. 3.)

with "full readiness for common effort," as their scientists have expressed.[91]

China can meet the challenge with one quarter of the world's voices.[92] India can do it with strong voices, too.[93]

As a pioneer of the World State, H.G. Wells started to urge not only the British people, but all peoples of the world to take action eighty years ago.[94] Harold J. Laski made a similar effort in the years over the two world wars.[95] And in the late 1940s, more than 100 members of British Parliament banded together to advance a Crusade for World Government.[96] With such a great background,

---

91. "We Soviet scientists express our full readiness for common effort with scientists of any other country, to discuss any proposals directed toward the prevention of atomic war and the creation of secure peace and tranquility for all mankind." (Quoted from a statement signed by 198 members of the Academy of Sciences and other Soviet academies, in Linus Pauling's *No More War,* 25th anniversary edition, New York, p. 179-180)

92. "How to put the world in order? By (uniting into) ONE only." Mencius (372-289 B.C.) 孟子： "天下烏乎定？定於一。"

93. "If we work hard enough, we can achieve world peace. But I have long believed that the only way it can finally be achieved is through world government." (Jawaharlal Nehru, quoted in the *World Citizen,* New Delhi, Aug. 1968, p. 3)

94. H(erbert) G(eorge) Wells' works in search of a world state include *Anticipations* (1901), *Mankind in the Making* (1903), *A Modern Utopia* (1905), the best selling *Outline of History* (1920), the *Open Conspiracy* (1928) calling scientists, technicians and other intellectuals to start a revolution for a world state, and *The Work, Wealth and Happiness of Mankind* (1932) explaining the idea that a world state might bypass political methods and build its foundations on international economic activities. "Wells cared desperately about the World State. It was an obsession with him. He regarded it as imperatively, critically urgent that the World State be brought about now, before our civilization had wrought its own destruction." (Edward M. Earle in his "H.G. Wells, British Patriot in Search of a World State," *Nationalism and Internationalism,* New York, 1950, p. 116) He also said, "If mankind does after all achieve an ordered world society" Wells "must for ever be high in the list of its prophets and pioneers." (*Ibid,* p. 119)

95. "What there is of purpose in the world, what soul of goodness also, is there by the deliberate effort of men. That, after all, is the groundwork of hope. Amid passion and differences, amid, also, the passion of differences, we are able dimly and yet securely to discern interests of mankind that make them one and indivisible. For the interests of men are less and less set by the geographical frontiers of the nation-state. Social organization has transcended those limited boundaries." (Harold J. Laski, *A Grammar of Politics,* London, 1925, p. 664)

96. In the late 1940s in Britain, more than 100 members of the House of Commons banded together in a non-partisan parliamentary committee to advance what they called the Crusade for World Government. Henry Charles Usborne was the driving force of this group, which included such leaders as Lord Boyd Orr, former

we cannot see how the British people will not stand up to meet the challenge today.

Rejuvenated after the terrible disaster of World War II, the Germans and Japanese can meet the challenge with much bitter memory and new vigor.

There are countries which historically or geographically are in an important position to meet the challenge, such as France, Australia, Mexico, Pakistan and Nigeria.

Undoubtedly more ready to meet the challenge are the countries which a humanitarian spirit has traditionally permeated, such as Canada, Switzerland, Sweden, and the other Scandinavian countries.

The Scandinavians would be in a stronger position if they met the challenge together as a group.[97]

The European Community has indeed established a strong position to meet the challenge.[98] Also in a strong position to meet the

---

Director-General of the UN's Food and Agriculture Organization and Nobel Peace Prize winner in 1949; Lord Beveridge, noted Liberal leader; and philosopher Bertrand Russell. Their plans called for the convening of a people's world convention, or world constituent assembly. (Cf. Alfred M. Lilienthal, *Which Way to World Government? Headline Series* no. 83, New York, 1950, p. 2-23.)

97. In this respect it is interesting to note that "A carefully controlled group of 300 Scandinavian peace demonstrators, the first Western protesters permitted to tour the Soviet Union, received an official welcome Saturday as they entered the country from Finland.... Participants in 'Peace March '82' were greeted by Mayor Alexei Roslyakov as they arrived by train in Vyborg, the official news agency Tass reported. Later, the vice chairman of a local, government-sponsored peace organization welcomed them upon arrival in Leningrad. The group—from Denmark, Sweden, Norway and Finland—began their journey Tuesday in Stockholm. They will hold rallies in Leningrad before traveling to Moscow, Minsk, Kalinin and Smolensk later in the week.... 'The joint action of the public of East and West demonstrates the cohesion and unity of the anti-war movement in countries with different socio-political systems,' Mayor Roslyakov said in his welcoming statement. The slogans for the demonstrators are 'stop the arms race; avert a thermonuclear catastrophe; ensure universal disarmament and peace.' ... Two government approved Soviet groups, the Soviet Committee for Peace and the Committee of Soviet Women, are co-sponsors of the tour and will designate about 60 Soviet representatives to join it." (Marc Rosenwasser, AP reporter, *South Bend Tribune,* July 18, 1982, p. 3)

98. The European Coal and Steel Community was created by a treaty signed in Paris on April 18th, 1951 (effective from July 25th, 1952), to pool the coal and steel production of the six original members. It was seen as a first step towards a united Europe. The European Economic Community and European Atomic Energy Community were established by separate treaties signed in Rome on March 25th, 1957 (effective from January 1st, 1958), the former to create a Common

challenge are groups such as the Pan American Union,[99] the League of Arab States[100] and the Organization of African Unity.[101]

The strongest position for meeting the challenge is held by the

---

Market and to approximate economic policies, the latter to promote growth in nuclear industries. The common institutions of the three Communities were established by a treaty signed in Brussels on April 8th, 1965 (effective from July 1st, 1967). Political union is regarded as the ultimate aim of the Communities. Increasingly, the three institutions are being regarded as a single entity, the European Community. Members are: Belgium, Denmark, France, Greece, Ireland, Italy, Luxembourg, the Netherlands, West Germany, the United Kingdom. (Cf. *Europa Yearbook,* 1981, Vol. 1, p. 179.)

99. The Pan American Union, the general secretariat or headquarters of the Organization of American States (OAS), is located in Washington, D.C. The OAS is the official international agency of the 21 sovereign republics of the Western Hemisphere: Argentina, Bolivia, Brazil, Chile, Colombia, Costa Rica, Cuba, the Dominican Republic, Ecuador, El Salvador, Guatamala, Haiti, Honduras, Mexico, Nicaragua, Panama, Paraguay, Peru, the United States, Uruguay, and Venezuela. They occupy a total area of more than 12,000,000 square miles and had a combined population of 330,000,000 in the early 1970s. (Cf. Edith Wynner and Georgia Lloyd, *Searchlight on Peace Plans,* New York, 1949, p. 574-577.)

100. The League of Arab States is a voluntary association of Arab states designed to strengthen the close ties linking them and to coordinate their policies and activities and direct them towards the common good of all the Arab countries. It was founded in March 1945. Members are: Algeria, Bahrain, Djibouti, Egypt, Iraq, Jordan, Kuwait, Lebanon, Libya, Mauritania, Morocco, Oman, Palestine, Qatar, Saudi Arabia, Somalia, Sudan, Syria, Tunisia, the United Arab Emirates, North Yemen, South Yemen. The status of Palestine as a full member of the League was confirmed at a meeting of the Arab League Council in September, 1976. In March, 1979, Egypt's membership in the Arab League was suspended, and it was decided to make Tunis the temporary headquarters of the League, its Secretariat and its permanent committees. (Cf. *Europa Yearbook,* 1981, Vol. 1, p. 124.)

101. The Charter of the Organization of African Unity was signed on May 25th, 1963, in Addis Ababa, Ethiopia. It superseded the Charter for the "Union of African States" adopted in January, 1961, at a conference in Casablanca, Morocco, which provided for a degree of political union, and the association formed at a conference in Monrovia, Liberia, which approved basic principles later incorporated into the OAU Charter, but did not imply political integration. All but two of the then 32 independent black African nations signed the Charter. The remaining two, Morocco and Togo, signed later and since that time all African states have joined the OAU upon gaining independence. Members are Algeria, Angola, Benin, Botswana, Burundi, Cameroon, Cape Verde, Central African Republic, Chad, Comoros, Congo, Djibouti, Egypt, Equatorial Guinea, Ethiopia, Gabon, Gambia, Ghana, Guinea, Guinea-Bissau, Ivory Coast, Kenya, Lesotho, Liberia, Libya, Madagascar, Malawi, Mali, Mauritania, Mauritius, Morocco, Mozambique, Niger, Nigeria, Rwanda, Sao Tome and Principe, Senegal, Seychelles, Sierra Leone, Somalia, Sudan, Swaziland, Tanzania, Togo, Tunisia, Uganda, Upper Volta, Zaire, Zambia, Zimbabwe. (Cf. *Europa Yearbook,* 1981, Vol. 1, p. 246.)

Third World as a group.[102] This is a unique opportunity for it to lead the divided world into an integrated one.

Finally, we want to emphasize that to meet this challenge is a privilege belonging to every nation and every group of countries, not just to the ones listed above; that to pursue the great cause of One World is an obligation to all nations and all groups of countries, not just to any one that takes the initiative; and that this great cause is something for which everyone has to do the best right away, and is not something in regard to which anyone can wait and see how the others act and react.[103]

When people are convinced to apply persuasion and pressure on their governments by voice and voting, but their governments are still stubbornly controlled by die-hard reactionaries and refuse to join in the great cause, it is time for the people to take direct action either to support the provisional world government formed or to be formed by the OWM, or to form one through a world convention by their representatives. If the latter is the case, the OWM will do as much as possible in helping them to achieve their goal, but refrains at the moment from prescribing what action they should take. They have the right and wisdom to do what they deem necessary.[104]

---

102. "The Third World has the votes and therefore could work successfully to declare the establishment of some kind of world government." This is the first sentence of *World Peace,* Vol. VI, no. 2, Feb. 1975. Can the Third World live up to such an expectation? We are anxiously waiting for their action to prove it.

103. Regarding Russia's attitude toward a world government, Henry Charles Usborne has stated: "We cannot answer that yet. What the Russians will do very largely depends on what we ourselves do in our own countries. When we have solved the question of what the United States will do, what Britain will do, and so on, then and not before will be the moment to ask whether the U.S.S.R. will be willing to make an equal surrender of sovereignty." (Quoted in Alfred M. Lilienthal, *Which Way to World Government? Headline Series* no. 83, New York, 1950, p. 21)

"If we ourselves sincerely want a world-wide legal order and wholeheartedly begin work on the problem of creating governmental institutions . . . we have no reason to assume that Russia will stubbornly refuse to participate. If, under any conditions, she does not want to join, then let this be her decision. But let us not make our own actions dependent upon the hypothetical behavior of someone else. With such lack of faith, with such lack of courage, no progress is possible." (Emery Reves, *The Anatomy of Peace,* New York, 1946, p. 291)

104. "The chief problem before the progressive revolutionary (working for the world state) . . . is to bend, break, evade, minimize, get around or over or through the political institutions of the present time." Above all, he must circumvent the national state, since "each sovereignty is an implicit repudiation of his purpose." The legal, political way is "a way of highly improbable issue." (Herbert

The formation of a provisional world government is only a step, not a goal, of the world revolution. The goal of the world revolution is the establishment of a permanent world government. Until this goal is achieved, no success can be claimed for the world revolution.

j.
Urgent Appeals

THE ROAD OF THE WORLD REVOLUTION FROM ITS starting point to success is unequivocally rough and precipitous. But we are marching on it courageously without any hesitation[105] and regardless of sacrifice.[106] We are sure we can overcome all difficulties encountered when more and more people join in the march and more and more support comes from those to whom we are appealing urgently:

To begin with the common people among them, there exist the

G. Wells, quoted by Edward M. Earle, *Nationalism and Internationalism,* New York, 1950, p. 115)

"If the governments of the world have not the wisdom to unite for the good of man, then we, the people, must unite! We must arm ourselves to the hilt with every bit of wisdom, understanding and love we can find in ourselves . . . and the victory we will win will not mean the defeat of one man by another. It will be a victory for all men." ("A Call from Denver" for the World Constitutional Convention, Interlaken, Switzerland, and Wolfach, Germany, Aug. 27 to Sept. 12, 1968; quoted in the *World Citizen,* New Delhi, Aug. 1968, p. 3)

105. "We are as small as our fear and despair, as great as our courage and hope." (*World Citizen,* New Delhi, Aug., 1968, p. 3)

106. As the example set by our first modern pioneer: "On a frosty December morning in 1793 in the small village of Chaillot, just outside Paris, a proud French aristocrat was led from his prison cell. A few minutes later Madame Guillotine claimed the life of Jean Baptiste Du Val-de-Grace, the Baron de Clootz, whose crime had not been that he was an aristocrat nor even a Dantonist nor a Maratist of the counterrevolution—but simply that of evolving a plan for Une République du Monde, a World Republic. Paris was to be the capital, an elected legislative assembly was to govern under a bill of human rights, and, above all, independent nations and boundaries were to be abolished. De Grace presented this proposal, startling in its suggested infringement on the rights of nation states, to the revolutionary French National Assembly, but that body voted it down—overwhelmingly. Shortly afterwards De Grace was charged with treason and convicted. So died one of the earlier advocates of world government." (Alfred M. Lilienthal, *Which Way to World Government? Headline Series* no. 83, New York, 1950, p. 3)

moral virtues in the greatest purity.[107] We urge you not to remain as a "silent majority" anymore. Speak out loudly against, and never vote for, those who do not work truly for humanity and peace.

Leading the common people are those who work hard on farms and in factories. We urge you not to provide for military establishments or activities with your products, and to refuse to make or transport weapons.

"As one-half of the human race, women must take on their share of helping to improve it world wide."[108] You, the peaceful half of the human race, can contribute even more to solving the problems that spell life or death for all families.[109] We urge you particularly to persuade your husbands and sons not to take part in killing and in getting killed.

A key position is held by the younger generations of today for a better world of tomorrow which belongs to them. Start to do whatever you can for your future right now. Reject to any call for, and get rid of, military services; and work vigorously for the cause of One World, in the tradition of examples set thirty years ago by young Carry Davis,[110] the World Student Federalists,[111] and the students who started to form a World Republic.[112]

---

107. Jean Jacques Rousseau supposed that the moral virtues exist in the greatest purity among the common people. As he said in *Emile:* "It is the common people who compose the human race; what is not the people is hardly worth taking into account. Man is the same in all ranks; that being so, the ranks which are most numerous deserve most respect." (Quoted by John Morley, *Rousseau,* 1886, Vol. II, p. 226)

108. As one-half of the human race, more or less, women must take on their share of helping to improve it worldwide, says Pearl Buck, the winner of both the Nobel and Pulitzer prizes for her writings. "Most of today's women I meet have nothing to complain about, nothing to fight about in their own lives," said Miss Buck. "Now, they must accept more responsibility in the area of world problems. There is nothing women can't do if they want. We need the minds especially of the brilliant women. Nature does not dole brains out by sex. ("The world's problems are too stupendous for only one half of the population to shoulder them," UPI report, *South Bend Tribune,* March 28, 1965, p. 84)

109. "It is my own view of some of the ways in which war affects women differently from men and it expresses my conviction that, if women all the world over learnt to think as women, from the depths of women's experience of life, and if such authentic and free-minded women took their due place as one-half of humanity in the world's counsels, the attitude of humanity in relation to war would be completely changed." (Helena M. Swanwick, *The Roots of Peace,* London, 1938, p. 177)

110. Carry Davis, the son of an American band leader, was young when he started to campaign for a world government. By employing theatrical techniques,

Naturally, one of the most important problems which concerns young people is the choice of study and subsequently profession. If the chance presents itself, it is suggested to study science, which is the foundation of civilization, and to become one of the scientists from whose activities flow the currents of real history.[113]

The value of science, as the foundation of civilization, lies not only in its usefulness, but also in its nature, which is independent of national boundaries, races and creeds.[114] The contributions of scien-

---

Davis hit the front pages of the world press. His picture slumbering on the steps of the entrance to the UN brought him the sympathy and support of many, including leading French literary and artistic figures. The interest in Davis increased when he was thrown out as he attempted to interrupt an Assembly session with an appeal for world government. (Cf. Alfred M. Lilienthal, *Which Way to World Government, Headline Series,* no. 83, New York, 1950, p. 37.)

111. Formed and operated under the World Movement for World Federal Government, the World Student Federalists met at Hastings, England, in 1948, in Amsterdam, Holland, in 1949 and in Kent, England, in 1950. They have undertaken to bring federation ideas to young people in lands where little is known about the Movement: in Malta, Sicily, Turkey, Lebanon and Egypt. These students have been led by Norman Hart of Britain and Joseph Wheeler of the United States, both of whom have interrupted their studies to follow their cause. (Cf. Alfred M. Lilienthal, *Which Way to World Government? Headline Series* no. 83, New York, 1950, p. 25-26.)

112. The World Republic was started by a group of Students for World Government led by 25-year-old Jack Whiteside, with an office in a one-car garage in Chicago. Its credo declares: "There can be no peace in any community without justice, no justice without law and no law without government to make, interpret and enforce that law. In the world community, as it strives to be a world brotherhood of man under God, we need a federal world government of the people, by the people, for the people." Its board of directors contains representatives of practically all of the other federalist movements, and as an organization, it has tried to coordinate the programs of the respective groups but has pursued the people's convention approach exclusively. (Cf. Alfred M. Lilienthal, *Which Way to World Government? Headline Series* no. 83, New York, 1950, p. 40-41.)

113. "The currents that flowed from the activities of scientists were the real history. Compared to the scientists and the inventors, the politicians were merely what H.G. Wells says the ancient kings and dynasties were—bubbles that bobbed along upon the surface, merely 'showing the swirl of the forces underneath.' " (Mark Sullivan in *Our Times)*

114. A resolution adopted by the American Association for the Advancement of Science: "Science is wholly independent of national boundaries and races and creeds and can flourish only when there is peace and intellectual freedom." (Quoted by Franz Boas in an introduction to *Race Against Man,* by Herbert J. Seligmann, New York, 1939)

"Who invented the steam-engine? Most us would say 'Watt'—but before him there had to be Rivault, Porta, de Caus, Worcester, Savery, Desaguliers, Blakely, Papin and Huygens. Did Benjamin Franklin discover the identity of lightning and

tists, as the origin of real history, include not only their discovery of the laws of nature, but also the increase in their interest in humanity.[115] In this respect, modern examples, in addition to those referred to earlier, such as Linus Pauling, Andrei Sakharov and Pyotr Kapitsa, may be found in Bertrand Russell,[116] Albert Einstein,[117] Alfred Kastler[118] and many other Nobel Laureates.[119]

---

electricity in June of 1752? So did the French scientist, D'Abolard, in a similar experiment—a month earlier. Did Joseph Henry lay claim to the electric motor? Simultaneously, the electric motor appeared in America, England, France, Germany and Italy. There were six 'inventors' of the thermometer, and nine of the telescope—all in different countries. It is good and necessary to remember—as National Brotherhood Week draws to a close—that this 'scientific progress' we are so proud of in this country is the result of collaboration among many men of many nations, creeds and cultures.... The fact that this scientific brotherhood has worked practically across the centuries indicates (more than all the idealistic sermons) that human beings are capable of advancing themselves only through active sharing, not by envy, hate and hostility." (Sydney Harris, "Scientific Breakthroughs Know No National Bounds," *South Bend Tribune,* Feb. 25, 1977, p. 6)

115. "Scientists have long considered themselves a brotherhood working in the service of common human ideals ... In the great task lying ahead, which places on our generation the greatest responsibility toward posterity, scientists all over the world may offer most valuable services. Not only do the bonds created through scientific intercourse form some of the firmest ties between individuals from different nations, but the whole scientific community will surely join in a vigorous effort to induce in wider circles an adequate appreciation of what is at stake and to appeal to humanity at large to heed the warning that has been sounded." (Niels Bohr, "Science and Civilization," in *One World or None,* ed. by Dexter Masters and Katharine Way, New York, 1946)

116. "That Bertrand Russell, the philosopher, heir to an earldom, was so profoundly shocked at the contrast between general squalor and privileged extravagance in England in the early years of this century that he gave away all of his inherited wealth and reduced himself to poverty." (Sydney Harris, *South Bend Tribune,* Jan. 15, 1980, p. 16)

117. "Mankind's desire for peace can be realized only by the creation of a world government." (Albert Einstein, quoted by the Campaign for a World Constitution, in a paper issued in 1968, in New York.)

118. Professor Alfred Kastler, Nobel Prize winner in Physics in 1966, issued a Call for World Citizenship: "... As a man, I feel solidarity with all men. I believe that they shall unite and build, beyond the differences of race and ideology, the community of mankind, our ultimate goal and vow." Professor Kastler's Call was circulated by J. Hasle of Régistre International des Citoyens du Monde Centre International, and quoted in the March *Newsletter* of the U.S. Campaign for a World Constitution, Vol. 11, no. 2.

119. (Cf. the "Mainau Declaration" signed by 52 Nobel Laureates, July 15, 1955; and the "Declaration of the Pugwash Movement and 97 Nobel Laureates" on the occasion of the XXVth Pugwash Anniversary Conference in Warsaw, August 26-31, 1982.) The latter appeals "to our colleagues of the world's scientific

At the present time, however, the increase in their interest in humanity has not been generated into a force strong enough to head off the threat of a total destruction of mankind by nuclear war. In spite of their efforts in warning the public and their governments,[120] this threat is growing greater and greater. It is a deadly challenge to civilization itself.[121] For an effective response, all scientists are urged to work actively[122] for the cause of One World as pioneered by the

community: accept responsibility and become directly involved in actions to avert nuclear war." It also appeals "to all peoples: support measures to remove the nuclear menace that threatens the survival of mankind." (The two declarations are reprinted in Linus Pauling's, *No More War,* 25th anniversary edition, New York, p. 252-254, 288-293.)

120. "It must be laid to the credit of the scientists that they perceive the results of using the weapons and modes of war that they have created, and that this has touched the conscience of a majority of them. Even so, for all their thinking and good intent, they have not been able to devise a sure way to safeguard humanity from the monsters of their invention. They have furnished a range of possible answers. Since 1960 they have been publishing many books and writing many articles, much study of which is a weariness of the flesh. But they are more convincing in warning us about the catastrophe to be expected than in devising practical policies to avoid it." (E.L.M. Burns, *Megamurder,* New York, 1967, p. 7. Cf. Alice K. Smith, *A Peril and a Hope; the Scientists' Movement in America, 1945-1947,* Chicago, 1965.)

121. "While the increasing mastery of the forces of nature has contributed so prolifically to human welfare and holds out even greater promises, it is evident that the atomic power of destruction that has come within reach of man may become a mortal menace unless human society can adjust itself to the exigencies of the situation. Civilization is presented with a challenge more serious perhaps than ever before, and the fate of humanity will depend on its ability to unite in averting common dangers and jointly to reap the benefit from the immense opportunities which the progress of science offers.... Certainly the handling of the precarious situation will demand the good will of all nations, but it must be recognized that we are dealing with what is potentially a deadly challenge to civilization itself." (Niels Bohr, "Science and Civilization," in *One World or None,* ed. by Dexter Masters and Katharine Way, New York, 1946)

122. "Another dilemma, or paradox, is the close relationship between science and war. It has become increasingly obvious that only a hair's-breadth divides the constructive from the destructive capacities of science. Atomic energy is as easily used for war as it is for peace. Is man really capable of controlling himself and his society to the extent that he can reap the benefits of science without suffering destruction at its hands? After World War II many physicists, like the great Leo Szilard, realized that the optimistic concept of a 'value-free' science was no longer valid. No longer is it possible for the scientist to pursue the 'truth' in his laboratory unencumbered by the social and moral implications of his work. Henceforth, scientists will have to confront ethical considerations in determining the course of their work in the same way that policy makers must confront them in the determination of political, social, and economic change." (T. Walter

Emergency Committee of Atomic Scientists,[123] and to at least not take part in developing and making nuclear weapons and other armaments or in planning military strategies and tactics.[124]

Science in its proper sense includes both the natural and social

---

Wallbank, Alastair M. Taylor, Nels M. Bailkey and Mark Mancall, *Civilization Past and Present,* 6th ed., Glenview, Ill., 1970, Book 1, p. 514)

"We have in common with our fellow men a deep concern for the welfare of all human beings. As scientists we have knowledge of the dangers involved and therefore a special responsibility to make those dangers known." ("The Scientists' Petition to the United Nations," presented by Linus Pauling, January 15, 1958, with the signatures of 9235 scientists from 49 countries. Linus Pauling, *No More War,* 25th anniversary edition, New York, 1983, p. 181)

123. The Emergency Committee of Atomic Scientists made public in November, 1946, a six-point statement on the awesome facts of atomic-age life. In 1947, this statement was reiterated, following a meeting at Chairman Einstein's home, with one significant addition: the scientists unequivocally advocated world government. "The American people," the statement declared, "should understand that there is no easy path ... that, in the long run, the creation of a supra-national government with powers adequate to the responsibility of maintaining peace is necessary ... We believe that nothing less is realistic. We know that the developments of science and technology have determined that the peoples of the world are no longer able to live under competing national sovereignties with war as the ultimate arbitrator ... As we approach what may be the last hour before midnight, the challenge is plain before us. What will be our response?" (Cf. Alfred M. Lilienthal, *Which Way to World Government? Headline Series* no. 83, New York, 1950, p. 42.)

124. "In this age of nuclear plenty, another profession shares responsibility with the military for theorizing about and even planning the strategy of possible wars. Since World War II the development of atomic and nuclear weapons and other 'sophisticated' armaments has constantly been changing the conditions of warfare, with a result that the services of scientists have become essential to the government and the nation in the preparation for war. It is they who must imagine and design the weapons, and they have acquired an increasingly great influence in determining how those weapons ought to be used." (E.L.M. Burns, *Megamurder,* New York, 1967, p. 6)

"Pope John Paul II called today on the scientists of the world to abandon their 'laboratories and factories of death' and replace them with 'laboratories of life.' He urged scientists to insure that 'the discoveries of science are not placed at the service of war, tyranny and terror,' and he strongly implied that military research should be abandoned. The Pope delivered his remarks today to members and guests of the Pontifical Academy of Sciences, the officially designated 'scientific senate' of the Vatican. It consists of 71 scientists from 29 nations, selected on the basis of their scientific ability and moral character without regard to religion or race. Most are not Catholics. He reminded scientists they enjoyed 'freedom of thought' and urged them to heed the 'unarmed prophets' of peace, such as Isaiah, who advised all men to change 'their swords into plowshares and their spears into pruning hooks.' " (Reported by Philip M. Boffey, *The New York Times,* Nov. 13, 1983, p. 1 and 12. For excerpts from the Pope's talk, cf. p. 12.)

sciences together with their technologies. Needless to say, the responsibility of the social scientists is as important as that of the natural scientists.[125] In addition, social scientists are urged to serve the cause of One World by giving due regard to the uniformity of cultures,[126] and by not exaggerating indulgently the differences in ideology.[127]

Equally important is the responsibility of philosophers, educators, writers, artists, actors, musicians, athletes, and other profes-

---

125. "Modeled on the natural sciences and pursuing their own 'truths' with the same avidity, the social sciences face a similar crisis in confronting tomorrow. Indeed, the responsibility of the social sciences is no less than that of the natural sciences, for theirs is the task of enabling man to understand himself and his society so that he can, at the very least, avoid the total destruction that science has now made possible." (T. Walter Wallbank, Alastair M. Taylor, Nels M. Bailkey and Mark Mancall, *Civilization Past and Present,* 6th ed., Glenview, Ill., 1970, Book 1, p. 514)

126. In economies, for instance, "So far as can be observed, the main elements of human behavior are the same throughout and community life itself seems to follow a general pattern. In the study of group life, social anthropologists necessarily emphasize the observed differences between communities and ignore their similarities, but social science, in general, must give due regard to the uniformities in society. We have seen how similar are the feeding methods of mankind, that hunting takes a similar form wherever found, and that the securing of vegetable foods also shows considerable sameness throughout. Also, the division of responsibility between the sexes is strikingly similar." (Clark Wissler, *An Introduction to Social Anthropology,* New York, 1929, p. 79)

W.H.R. Rivers in his *History of Melanesian Society,* Cambridge, 1914, v. 2, p. 595, asserted the contribution of contact in promoting culture as follows: "The assumption which underlies the whole construction of this book is the importance of the contact of peoples in the history of human culture. It has been the main task of this volume to show how all the chief social institutions of Melanesia, its dual organization, its secret societies, its totemism, its cult of the dead, and many of its less essential customs, such as its use of money, its decorative art, its practice of incision and its square houses, have been the direct outcome of the interaction between different and sometimes conflicting cultures ... The Oceanic evidence points unmistakably to degradation and even to disappearance as the result of isolation, and suggests that the mixture of peoples will have to be taken much more into account by the historians of human culture than it has been in the past. Indeed, the study of this part of the world suggests that the contact and interaction of peoples have furnished the starting points of all the great movements in human history which we are accustomed to regard as Progress."

127. "Is a 'value-free' social science really possible, or are all social sciences ultimately ideological? Is a true 'science of man' possible when the social sciences are fragmented into a variety of competing methods and disciplines? For instance, is man as studied by the sociologist the same as man as studied by the psychologist? If a value-free 'empirical' social science is impossible, can mankind ever break out of the cycle of conflicts engendered by ideological disagreements?" (T. Walter Wallbank, Alastair M. Taylor, Nels M. Bailkey and Mark Mancall, *Civilization Past and Present,* 6th ed., Glenview, Ill., 1970, Book 1, p. 514-515)

sionals. All of you are urged, each in your own position and in your own way, to do your best for the cause of One World in the pursuit of humanity and peace, as Emery Reves did with his famous work *Anatomy of Peace.*[128]

Originally, the pursuit of humanity and peace for one world was a common objective of the major religions, especially the monotheistic creeds including Judaism, Christianity and Islam.[129] It is tragic that this objective has been largely subordinated to nationalism in the individual countries.[130] In order to save civilization, of which religion

---

128. "More active converts have been won by one book than by any other influence except the bomb and the threat of Russia. That book, assailed by isolationists as the 'bible of the one world absolutists,' is Emery Reves' *The Anatomy of Peace.* While he failed to open up a market in Russia, Reves can point to 30 different editions in 24 countries and 20 different languages." (Alfred M. Lilienthal, *Which Way to World Government, Headline Series* no. 83, New York, 1950, p. 16)

129. Judaism, Christianity and Islam are the major monotheistic religions. Their single god is for a single world in essence, and accordingly the core of their intellectualization is an ethical universalism: all peoples are children of God, they themselves are brothers and sister, and they should live together in peace by "beating their swords into plowshares and their spears into pruning hooks." These beliefs were sublimated by Judaism, reached their climax in Christianity, and were transplanted into Islam. (Cf. III, 35-39.)

130. Speaking of Christianity, for example, "in any case, outside the Society of Friends, a small body of mystic cults, the two thousand years of Christian history suggest that religious creeds are subdued to nationalisms, and even to political opinions, rather than that they possess the power to transcend them. And this is a factor quite apart from the philosophic and historical objections to which all organized forms of the Christian faith give rise." (Harold J. Laski, *Faith, Reason, and Civilization,* New York, 1944, p. 34)

"The same development can be observed in the second great monotheistic creed, in Islam. The great unity which had been maintained by the Koran for so many centuries among peoples of different stock, from the Atlas to the Himalaya Mountains, has been visibly splitting up into nationalist groups within which allegiance to the new nationalist ideal is more powerful than loyalty to the old universal teachings of Mohammed." "Not only Christianity and Islam . . . are being completely absorbed and dominated by neopagan nationalism. Even the originators of monotheism, even the Jews have forgotten the fundamental teaching of their religion: universalism. They seem no longer to remember that the One and Almighty God first revealed Himself to them because He chose them for a special mission, to spread the doctrine of the oneness of the Supreme Lawgiver, the universal validity of monotheism among the people of the world. They too, just like the followers of other monotheistic creeds, have become abject idolaters of the new polytheism—nationalism." (Emery Reves, *The Anatomy of Peace,* New York, 1946, p. 81, 82)

Some good signs have been seen, however. For example, Christian and Moslem leaders representing millions of faithful around the world joined lately in

is an important factor, all the leaders of the major religions are urged to preach their holy objectives rather than to pray to nationalist fetishes.

Blessed by nationalist fetishes are the military and political leaders portrayed as the "third type of man" who cares only for power,[131] and as the very small number of men who hold the policies of the world in their hands.[132] But they are human beings, too.[133]

---

calling for a ban on nuclear arms. In a statement issued at the end of a three-day meeting, the 11 clergymen urged their fellow religious leaders to work for disarmament, saying nothing could "morally justify" atomic warfare. "This was an important meeting," said one of the organizers, Rev. Theodore Hesburgh, President of Indiana's Notre Dame University. "For the first time we have had sessions among church leaders of many different faiths from all over the world." "We must stop an arms race that produces ever more sophisticated agents of annihilation at enormous costs, diverting resources that could be used to feed, clothe, house and cure millions of people," the conference statement said. (Reported by AP reporter Kenneth Jautz, *South Bend Tribune,* Jan. 16, 1983, p. 1)

131. "What is now called innovation still has an element in it of the instinct that drove primitive man to produce such wonderful inventions as the bow and arrow, or to devise such complicated social arrangements as totemism. Mechanical inventions and social innovations have remained indispensable but uneasy partners from prehistory to modern times. They were devised by two different kinds of human minds, and both were suppressed for long periods by the third type of man, who cared neither for technology, nor for social progress, but only for power. Regrettably, history records mostly the deeds and misdeeds of this third type of man." (Dennis Gabor, *Innovations: Scientific, Technological and Social,* Oxford, 1970, Introduction, p. 1)

132. "One of the outstanding statesmen of Europe said to me in private conversation a few months ago that the appalling thing was that all this trouble in the world is being caused by not to exceed twelve hundred or fifteen hundred men. He insisted that the peoples everywhere in these democracies, in these totalitarian states, in Asia and South America, want peace and prosperity, but that some twelve or fifteen hundred human beings in positions of great responsibility and authority, that authority being largely based on emotional grounds, held the policies of the world today in their hands." (Nicholas M. Butler, *Why War?* New York, 1940, p. 4)

133. Even in a person as stubborn as Nikita Khrushchev, we find humanity in his consciousness. He wrote about Andreil Sakharov, "the scientist in him saw his patriotic duty and performed it well, while the pacifist in him made him hesitate. I have nothing against pacifists—or at least I won't have anything against them if and when we create conditions which make war impossible. But as long as we live in a world in which we have to keep both eyes open lest the imperialists gobble us up, then pacifism is a dangerous sentiment." About the intelligentsia as a whole, he wrote: "A more difficult and slippery problem is posed by the creative intelligentsia. Our creative intelligentsia suffer more than any other category of people in our society. Materially, they're better off than other categories, but spiritually,

And as human beings, you leaders are urged to change your outmoded concepts and methods in steering your ships,[134] and to work for a permanent peace and general happiness instead of leading your people to the slaughterhouse and pushing your countries into hell. Your leadership would enable you to make extraordinary contributions to the cause of One World. The opportunity is unique for each of you to be a hero to all the peoples of the world.

---

members of the creative intelligentsia are troubled. Creative work, especially by writers, has a tendency to interfere in the political sphere. Writers are forever delving into questions of philosophy and ideology—questions on which any ruling party, including the Communist Party, would like to have a monopoly." ("Khrushchev's Last Testament: Power and Peace," *Time,* May 6, 1974, p. 42)

134. No wonder you are far behind!

Justus in the Minneapolis Star

k.
Common Destination

FINALLY, IT IS NECESSARY TO EMPHASIZE THAT NO ONE
is without responsibility for taking the necessary actions at the time
of greatest crisis in history.

The most serious symptom of this crisis is the threat of the total
destruction of mankind and his civilization by a nuclear war. In
origin, however, it stems out of two great gaps: science and technology
have advanced much faster than social adjustment,[135] and material
developments have left spiritual traditions far behind.[136]

---

135. "Some parts of a culture pattern change more rapidly than others, so
that one institution sometimes becomes outmoded in relation to others in a society.
When different parts of a society fail to mesh harmoniously, the condition is
often called a culture lag ... culture lag has assumed its most dangerous form in
the apparently widening gap in communications and outlook between science and
the accelerating technological sector on the one hand and our traditional
humanistic culture and values system on the other. These two major segments of
our culture pattern appear to be advancing and changing, at the speeds of a supersonic
jet and of a horse and buggy respectively." (T. Walter Wallbank, Alastair
M. Taylor, Nels M. Bailkey and Mark Mancall, *Civilization Past and Present,* 6th
ed., Glenview, Ill., 1970, Book 1, p. 7-8)

"We delude ourselves if we suppose that our major problems are physical or
technical, when they are really social and moral—as they have always been. The
human animal throughout history has been an absolute genius at solving the
former kinds of problems, and a near-idiot at solving the latter.... Our power to
control and direct nature is only just beginning, even though it has already increased
a thousand fold since ancient times. What has remained almost static is our
ability to subdue our own nature, to work with each other and with the earth in the
obtainment of a harmonious social order and a high moral sense." (Sydney Harris,
"Man Can Conquer Nature, But Fails to Rule Himself," in the *South Bend
Tribune,* Nov. 12, 1979, p. 6)

136. "Yet it has become commonplace to point out that Homo sapiens in this
century, by virtue of his obsession with technology and warfare, has devised
modes of collective murder that are wholly disproportionate to his 'progress' in
morals—i.e., in the discovery and enjoyment of truth, beauty, and goodness and
in the gentle skills of living together as brethren." (Frederick L. Schuman, *The
Commonwealth of Man; an Inquiry into Power Politics and World Government,*
New York, 1952, p. 481)

"Our material surroundings have changed in the past century and a half with
a rapidity out of all proportion to the very slight alteration of our social point of
view. We have vastly increased human control over nature, without increasing correspondingly
man's control over his own selfish passions. Our social ideals are still

Obviously, there is no sure way to close the two gaps except to speed up social adjustments and revitalize spiritual traditions;[137] and there is no one who can do these speeding up and revitalizing jobs except man himself. Man is his own salvation.

It is true that the merging of all nations into One World is a fast means of speeding up social adjustments and the pursuit of permanent peace and general happiness is an effective method of revitalizing spiritual traditions; and that the goals of both the merging and the pursuit will eventually be achieved. But we cannot afford to wait for eventualities when our survival is at stake. We have to push them through by all means before it is too late. Here again, man is his own salvation.

To be our own salvation, we have first to resort to reason[138] and the natural law[139] for readjusting ourselves as rational beings to face

---

based on pecuniary standards, our conduct is founded on selfishness and exploitation rather than cooperation and service." (Harry E. Barnes, *An Economic History of the Western World,* New York, 1937, p. 491)

137. "Broadly speaking. While we have been daring and imaginative in technology, we are evasive and over-conservative on our thought and conduct. Such is the present challenge of our social order. The chief need of the world today is for innovators such as Jeremy Bentham in the 19th century, who can apply in the social and institutional realms the imagination and the capacity that have been repeatedly demonstrated by our inventors in the field of technology, and a chief part of this new inventiveness must be an avenue of approach to the hearts and minds of men, persuasive of the urgent necessity of accepting a rational solution of social problems. Whatever secures and sustains these new social objectives will be the religion of the future." (Harry E. Barnes, *An Economic History of the Western World,* New York, 1937, p. 492)

138. "After a disastrous half a century of antirationalism, guided by mysticism, transcendental emotions and so-called intuition, we must return to the lost road of rationalism, if we want to prevent complete destruction of our civilization. The task is by no means easy. The deceptions caused by rationalism are real and understandable. Yet, to try to escape the complexities of life revealed to us by reason by seeking refuge in irrationalism and to let our actions be determined by superstitions, dogmas and intuition, is sheer suicide. We must resign ourselves to the fact that there is no other fate for us than to climb the long, hard, steep and stony road guided by the only thing that makes us different from animals: reason." (Emery Reves, *The Anatomy of Peace,* New York, 1946, p. 274)

139. The natural law (jus naturale) which was "developed by the Stoics in Greece and borrowed from them by the Romans, meant, in effect, the sum of those principles which ought to control human conduct, because founded in the very nature of man as a rational and social being." (James L. Brierly, *The Law of Nations: an Introduction to the International Law of Peace,* 4th ed., Oxford, 1949, p. 18)

the great changes of the world.[140] In other words, we have to rely on intellect which is like light,[141] and which illuminated ancient Greece and Asia Minor,[142] early China,[143] and lately, the Renaissance.[144]

---

140. Edward C. Tolman, in a penetrating little book, *Drives Toward War,* suggests that our society needs a new social value, a new ideal personality to be held as a model, which is labeled as the "Psychologically Adjusted Man." According to his suggestion, society should idealize, and citizens should be encouraged to aim for, the goal of psychological adjustment or emotional maturity. To the end of this sentence, we add: from the myth of nationalism to a faith in humanity. (Cf. Ross Stagner, *Psychology of Personality,* New York, 1948, p. 442-443. Cf. also, Roderick Seidenberg, *Post-Historic Man,* Chapel Hill, N.C., 1950.)

"A new type of thinking is essential if mankind is to survive and move to higher levels," and "Science has brought forth this danger, but the real problem is in the minds and hearts of men. We will not change the hearts of other men by mechanism, but by changing our hearts and speaking bravely." (Albert Einstein, "Only Then Shall We Find Courage," in the *New York Times Magazine,* June 23, 1946)

141. "It is the conquest of knowledge that is the real source of our hopes, its conquest and its extension to the common man. For the real root of conflict is ignorance. It is the ill-informed mind and the narrow mind which are the servants of national hate. It is they which are exploited by the evil forces of an age. What is wanted, if we are to break down the barriers between knowledge and ignorance, is education. We can only surmount our problems by enlisting the service of every citizen in that task; and we can only make men citizens by training their minds to grasp the world about them. When the masses can understand they will have the courage to act upon their understanding. For intellect, as Carlyle said, is like light; from a chaos it makes a world." (Harold J. Laski, *A Grammar of Politics,* London, 1925, p. 240)

142. An intellectual revolution occurred in the 8th and 7th centuries B.C. in Greece and Asia Minor. The vigor and independence of mind of the people who at this period abandoned their roving life for more settled commercial activities brought forth this great event. It brought ancient Greek civilization to its zenith, and also advanced the tribal life of both Greece and Asia Minor to a climax. (Cf. Lynn Thorndike, *A Short History of Civilization,* New York, 1937, p. 102-129.)

143. In the 6th and 5th centuries, B.C., an intellectual revolution occurred in China. Taking advantage of the growth of commerce and the radical competition of politics among the tribe-states, Chinese people expanded their freedom of thought and action, produced a Golden Age of ancient Chinese civilization, and brought forth a rudimentary Chinese nation in the Yellow River and Yangtze areas. (Cf. Lynn Thorndike, *A Short History of Civilization,* New York, 1937, p. 244-265.)

144. Renaissance is a collective term used to include all the intellectual changes which were in evidence at the close of the Middle Ages and at the beginning of modern times. It was stimulated by the Crusades and explorations, and was manifested in an interest in the past and a desire for an understanding of the present. Perhaps its greatest attribute was the development of the inquisitiveness which is necessary to intellectual progress. At the close of the Middle Ages, the decline of feudalism, of the influence of the nobility, of the importance of the guild system, and of the prestige of the church enabled people to think and act more freely. A

Now let it illuminate our time with new sources of scientific knowl-edge.[145]

And second, we have to have faith in ourselves and our future along the lines started by the Enlightenment Movement.[146] While we have been sailing in a great stream of historical forces, the rudder of the ship has been held in our own hands. We have always responded to great challenges with an unprecedented effort.[147] We have never given up our struggle for survival and the betterment of life,[148] and

---

further step in the same direction was the Reformation which might conceivably be considered as a part of the early period of the Renaissance. (Cf. Lynn Thorndike, "Renaissance," in the *Encyclopedia Britannica,* 1973 ed., Vol. 19; also James Thompson and others, *The Civilization of the Renaissance,* New York, 1959.)

145. From a "Manifesto on Freedom of Science" signed by 1300 American scientists: "The man of science must educate the people against the acceptance of all false unscientific doctrines which appear before them in the guise of science, regardless of their origin." (Quoted by Franz Boas in an introduction to *Race Against Man,* by Herbert J. Seligmann, New York, 1939)

Mankind also inherits, from an earlier ancestry, the powers of blood and glands and viscera driving him to meet challenges in ways that are often the nega-tion of rational judgment. Even the most civilized of men and women live the larger segment of their lives by magic and myth, superstition and stereotype, con-ditioned reflex and nonlogical inference." (Frederick L. Schuman, *The Com-monwealth of Man; an Inquiry into Power Politics and World Government,* New York, 1952, p. 483)

146. The Renaissance was followed by the Enlightenment Movement in which mankind made a fundamental change in his attitude towards himself and the world in which he lived. This point of view is commonly called humanism. It focused attention on the things of this world, on the exaltation of human nature. The natural, the human, and the sensual were given precedence over the ascetical, the supernatural, and the theological. Above all, it dignified the position of the in-dividual and converted our faith towards the future. (Cf. Peter Gay, *The Enlightenment; a Comprehensive Anthology,* New York, 1973, p. 13-25.)

147. According to Arnold J. Toynbee: "challenge and response" explain the rise and fall of civilizations. Man achieves civilization "as a response to a challenge in a situation of special difficulty which rouses him to make a hitherto un-precedented effort." (Referred to in T. Walter Wallbank, Alastair M. Taylor, Nels M. Bailkey and Mark Mancall, *Civilization Past and Present,* 6th ed., Glen-view, Ill., 1970, Book 1, p. 5)

148. "To many, it seems almost hopeless to try to rectify a world which, in Hamlet's phrase, seems so 'out of joint.' The authors disagree heartily with these prophets of doom. A study of history quickly proves that the 'good old days' were actually not that good and that every age has had to bear its full burden of dire forebodings. Moreover, history teaches us that man has never yet given up his struggle for survival and the betterment of life." (T. Walter Wallbank, Alastair M. Taylor, Nels M. Bailkey and Mark Mancall, *Civilization Past and Present,* 6th ed., Glenview, Ill., 1970, Book 1, p. 8)

have proved to be one of the toughest, most tenacious, and most adaptable creatures.[149] There is nothing which is absolutely impossible for us to achieve. We have made the old dream of flying come true and have even flown to the moon. There is no reason why we cannot make another old dream of One World come true.[150] We have been able to control nature very well, and there is no reason why we should not be able to readjust ourselves to be our own salvation.[151]

Further, it is necessary to emphasize that if we fail to be our own salvation, it means not only the destruction of ourselves, but also the destruction of the history of thousands of generations in the past and of the future of millions of generations to come; and it means the destruction of a civilization which we are proud to be the only one as far as we know in the infinite universe, which has been built for millions of years by the hard work of our ancestors,[152] and which can

---

149. "Others claim man will destroy himself, which is of course a political prediction. This seems to me a fate as unlikely as committing suicide by holding your breath. Man, for all his frailties, is now one of the toughest, most tenacious, most adaptable animals in the kingdom ... and I am sure that he is here to stay." (William W. Howell's *Mankind So Far,* New York, 1952, p. 312)

150. Herbert G. Wells pointed out that for two thousand years or more men dreamed of flying and sought to fly. "But for a wearisome sequence of centuries they got nowhere ... the general wisdom remained quite sure that flying was forever denied to man. There is a long list of names of solitary men, who announced that they were discovering or had discovered flying. They achieved nothing; they left nothing to their successors but broken bodies, broken wings and discouragement. Only when a convergence of tendencies stimulated the general imagination to believe in the possibility of flying was there a sufficient and interlocking continuity and multitudinousness of effort for a real advance. Then in scarcely a dozen years the problem of flying was solved. By whom? You do not know, for the simple reason that it was done by a multitude of men working in correlation." Is it too much, asked Wells, to hope that similar miracles can be worked out in the field of politics? (His book *The Anatomy of Frustration,* New York, 1936, p. 116)

151. "Assuredly, since a generation that has achieved the means of self-destruction has also thereby achieved, if the will to live is still alive, the means of self-preservation and of a more abundant life for most of humanity than any of our ancestors ever knew. Are we free to choose? Undoubtedly, if we cease to cling fearfully to the ways of darkness and raise our eyes to the sunlit heights where we can finally banish savagery and unreason and live, if we will, as men like gods. As to whether we shall choose wisely and in time, each must answer for himself." (Frederick L. Schuman, *The Commonwealth of Man; an Inquiry into Power Politics and World Government,* New York, 1952, p. 493-494)

152. "To get the matter clearly before one, let us imagine, as the writer has suggested elsewhere, that 500,000 years of developing culture were compressed into 50 years. On this scale mankind would have required 49 years to learn enough to desert

soon be advanced to a much higher degree for the benefit of ourselves and our posterity.

When we realize how important the responsibility is and how
heavy the duty is for us, as our own salvation, to carry on, we see
clearly that there is no way for us to retreat at all. We have to seek for
nothing less than a full triumph and we have to accomplish nothing
short of a complete success.

For a full triumph and complete success, we have to march
together[153] with fearless courage, the utmost determination and
above all, an unshakable faith;[154] and also, we have to work hard and
act quickly. We can no longer afford to depend on any inevitability,
nor to wait for any miracle.[155] Time is running out very fast.

Let us march together, work hard and act quickly to merge all nations into One World for a permanent peace on earth and a general
happiness of mankind; to establish a World Government to serve all

---

here and there his inveterate hunting habits and settle down in villages. Half through
the 50th year writing was discovered and practised within a very limited area, thus
supplying one of the chief means of perpetuating and spreading culture. The
achievements of the Greeks would be but three months back, the prevailing of
Christianity, two; the printing press would be a fortnight old and man would have
been using steam for hardly a week. The peculiar conditions under which we live did
not come about until Dec. 31 of the 50th year." (David G. Mandelbaum," "Civilization and Culture," in the *Encyclopedia Britannica,* 1973 ed., Vol. 5, p. 827)

153. "To move on toward one earth is not hard to imagine. To move on
toward one community is hard. It takes action. At this point in history, the earth
can no longer stand as an abandoned garden. There is no more room for weeds and
the season of flowers is just around the corner. The step is to move on together and
not to take the walk alone. The thought to keep in mind is: 'If one earth, why not
one people?' " (Quoted from a pamphlet of One Earth Week, April 14-19, 1975)

154. "The immortal glory of all the apostles of the unity of mankind,
whatever the results of their own works, is their faith in man's potentiality for
brotherhood, in his ultimate rationality, and in his talents for finding ways to
realize his fairest dreams." (Frederick L. Schuman, *The Commonwealth of Man;
an Inquiry into Power Politics and World Government,* New York, 1952, p. 485)

155. "Undoubtedly, if the inhabitants of Mars or another planet suddenly
descended upon the earth and threatened to conquer us, all the nations of our
small world would immediately get together. We would forget all our ridiculous
inter-national quarrels and would willingly and gladly place ourselves under one
rule of law for sheer survival. Are we certain that the unleashing and national use
of atomic energy, the apocalypse of an atomic world war, is not an equal threat to
our civilization and to mankind, imperatively requiring us to rise above our outdated inter-national conflicts and to organize human society politically so that an
atomic world war could be checked?" (Emery Reves, *The Anatomy of Peace,* New
York, 1946, p. 289)

the people, and to advance our civilization to shine the whole universe, for billions of years to come.[156]

Let us march together, work hard and act quickly to achieve the greatest mission of all times for our glorious common destination.[157]

---

156. "The remote future may be considered in the same spirit of speculation as the early universe. In some 10^{10} years, the Sun will have evolved into a luminous red giant and have a radius much greater than at present, perhaps reaching the orbit of Mercury. The oceans will have disappeared and the Earth lost much of its present atmosphere, and life as it is now known will have become impossible if only because of the intense heat. The gas and dust in the Galaxy must slowly disappear as it forms into new stars, and in 10^{10} years most stars will be old and only a very few will be young. Inevitably, in the course of time, the Milky Way will become faint and dark and the Galaxy a graveyard of stars that have reached the end point of stellar evolution, and similarly with other galaxies. Man, if he has survived, in a form beyond the wildest dreams of the 20th century, will have embarked on his last and perhaps greatest adventure." (Ernest R. Hilgard, "Universe," in the *Encyclopedia Britannica,* 1947 ed., Vol. 18, p. 1011)

157. Let us conclude here with Walt Whitman's "Old Age Echoes" (Quoted by Hans Kohn, *The Age of Nationalism; the First Era of Global History,* New York, 1962, p. 127):

"One thought ever at the fore—
That in the Divine Ship, the World
    breasting Time and Space,
All Peoples of the globe together sail,
    sail the same voyage, are bound to
    the same destination."

Index to Text

605

Author
Index to
References

Reminder for Action

The One World Movement (OWM) is a common endeavor of the people who want to work consciously, voluntarily and actively for the merging of all nations into One World for permanent peace and general happiness. It is a world revolutionary organization with open policies and open activities, and relies on no violence, myth or intrigue. You and your organization are cordially invited to join it and take part in the world revolution it launches.

The world revolution calls for a campaign for liberation to get rid of the independence of the nation, national sovereignty and nationalism; a campaign for promotion to raise humanity, loyalty to mankind, and world patriotism; and a campaign for survival, including anti-war activities, protest against weapons development, and a demand for total disarmament. It will also campaign for the formation of a provisional world government to complete world disarmament and to work out a world constitution through due process, so as to establish a permanent world government to serve all peoples.

In order to accomplish the world revolution, it is necessary for the OWM to set up a worldwide information system including newspaper, radio and television networks, and also to set up a working, training and directing center called the One World University. Obviously, public and private support for a huge One World Fund for the world revolution and the set-ups are most urgently needed.

The OWM is initiated by the manifesto, *ONE WORLD, the Approach to Permanent Peace on Earth and General Happiness of Mankind,* which deals with all important issues relating to humanity, world peace and world government, as the most embracing and penetrating treatise in the vast field based on the development of history on the one hand and the achievements of science and technology on the other. In civilization it keeps old faith while promoting new ideas with a great number of discoveries and innovations on world peace, world government and the general happiness of mankind. It appeals to both the general public and the academic world. Its distribution and translation are a primary step for promoting the OWM.

The time is now for us to march with the OWM, the greatest cause in history. Do the very best for it before it is too late. *(over)*

Action Note Form *(Please type or print)*

Date:_____

Name: _____

Address: _____

_____

1. ____ I would like to be a member of the OWM.

2. ____ I/We will help to form a local unit of the OWM.

3. ____ Our organization will join the OWM. Name and address of our organization: _____

_____

4. ____ I/We will support the One World Fund.

5. ____ Our organization will support the One World Fund.
Name and address of our organization:

_____

_____

6. ____ I/We will help to set up the OWM information
system.

7. ____ I/We will help to establish the One World University.

8. ____ I/We will help to distribute the manifesto, *One
World.*

9. ____ Other ways in which I/We can help the OWM:

_____

_____

(May continue on separate paper)

10. ____ Suggestions and comments: _____

_____

_____

(May continue on separate paper)

Please send your note to *(temporary mailing address):*
One World Movement,
P.O. Box 423, Notre Dame, Indiana, U.S.A. 46556